Lecture Notes in Computer Science   4280

Commenced Publication in 1973
Founding and Former Series Editors:
Gerhard Goos, Juris Hartmanis, and Jan van Leeuwen

Ajoy K. Datta   Maria Gradinariu (Eds.)

Stabilization, Safety, and Security of Distributed Systems

8th International Symposium, SSS 2006
Dallas, TX, USA, November 17-19, 2006
Proceedings

 Springer

Volume Editors

Ajoy K. Datta
School of Computer Science
University of Nevada Las Vegas
Las Vegas, USA
E-mail: datta@cs.unlv.edu

Maria Gradinariu
Universite Paris 6, LIP6
8 rue du Capitaine Scott
75015, Paris, France
E-mail: Maria.Gradinariu@lip6.fr

Library of Congress Control Number: 2006935958

CR Subject Classification (1998): C.2.4, C.2, C.3, F.1, F.2.2, K.6

LNCS Sublibrary: SL 1 – Theoretical Computer Science and General Issues

ISSN   0302-9743
ISBN-10   3-540-49018-3 Springer Berlin Heidelberg New York
ISBN-13   978-3-540-49018-0 Springer Berlin Heidelberg New York

Springer is a part of Springer Science+Business Media

springer.com

© Springer-Verlag Berlin Heidelberg 2006
Printed in Germany

Typesetting: Camera-ready by author, data conversion by Scientific Publishing Services, Chennai, India
Printed on acid-free paper   SPIN: 11924517   06/3142   5 4 3 2 1 0

Preface

This symposium has been the main forum for presentation of research results in the area of self-* for 17 years. It started as The Workshop on Self-Stabilizing Systems (WSS), and met in 1989 in Austin, 1995 in Las Vegas, 1997 in Santa Barbara, 1999 in Austin, and 2001 in Lisbon. It was then renamed The Symposium on Self-Stabilizing Systems (SSS), and has since met in 2003 in San Francisco, and in 2005 in Barcelona, Spain.

This year, we extended the scope of the symposium to cover all safety and security related aspects of self-* systems. The title of the symposium was changed to the International Symposium on Stabilization, Safety, and Security of Distributed Systems (SSS) to reflect this expansion.

The decision by Mohamed Gouda, the General Chair, to expand the scope of the symposium was timely and successful. From 33 papers submitted for SSS 2005, the number of submissions increased to 155. Reviewing this surge of submissions to select the final set of papers for the symposium was a monumental task for the Program Committee. The 61 Program Committee members devoted countless hours reading and evaluating the papers. But even this effort was not enough; we recruited 143 external reviewers, whose work was also very substantial.

This volume contains 36 regular papers and 12 brief announcements that were presented at the symposium. The papers published here were selected by the Program Committee after five days of extensive electronic discussions and phone calls. The call for papers sought only regular papers, but the Program Committee decided to include a few brief announcements which were considered to be of high quality and great importance to the community. Selected papers from the symposium will be published in a special issue of the *ACM Transactions on Autonomous and Adaptive Systems* (TAAS).

Ted Herman and Chen Zhang received the Best Paper Award for their paper, "Stabilizing Clock Synchronization for Wireless Sensor Networks." We had three very interesting and entertaining invited talks this year. The speakers were Shlomi Dolev, Rachid Guerraoui, and Yi-Min Wang. Shlomi's and Rachid's invited papers are included in these proceedings. Unfortunately, Yi-Min's invited paper was not ready for print before the proceedings went to print.

On behalf of the Program Committee, we would like to thank all authors of submitted papers for their support. We also thank the members of the Steering Committee for their advice. We cannot thank the Program Committee members and additional external reviewers enough for their tremendous effort and invaluable time to help us get the job done. We would like to extend special thanks to the Publicity and Web Chair, Florent Claerhout, for his sincerity, diligence, and willingness to do everything we asked. Florent worked very hard for several months, maintaining the webpage and making many changes in the conference management system to fit the needs of SSS.

We are also grateful to Jorge A. Cobb and Ravi Prakash for handling local arrangements. Jorge's efforts enabled us to obtain the conference venue and hotel rooms at very good rates.

November 2006   Ajoy K. Datta
                                                      Maria Gradinariu
                                                     Program Co-chairs

Message from the General Chair

On a warm spring day in 1989, SSS was born almost by accident. At the time, the world had no more than a dozen researchers who were interested in the area of self-stabilization. And six of those researchers happend to be in Austin, Texas at the same time; so they decided to have a workshop to present their work to one another. The six researchers were Anish Arora and Paul Attie (who were working on their PhD dissertations at the University of Texas at Austin), Jim Burns (who was visiting me for a week to kick off our collaboration in the area of self-stabilization), Mike Evangelist (who was working for MCC, Inc.), Shmuel Katz (who was spending a sabatical year at the University of Texas at Austin), and myself. The idea for the workshop came to us shortly before the workshop was to be held, and so we had no time to announce the workshop, to select a Technical Program Committee, to publish a call for papers, or to invite anyone else to attend. Mike Evangelist arranged for the workshop to be held in the facilities of MCC, Inc. And if my recollections are correct, only five papers were presented in the workshop, which lasted just over half a day. No proceedings for the workshop were ever published, but eventually all the papers that were presented in the workshop were published in the journal *Distributed Computing*, thanks to an invitation by its editor Fred Schneider.

I tell this story to show how grateful I am that in 2006, 17 years after the first SSS was held, SSS has matured into a vital yearly symposium with a strong Technical Program Committee, and with a rich and creative program. My gratitude goes to the many individuals who supported SSS over the years, and especially to Ajoy K. Datta and Maria Gradinariu, Program Co-chairs of SSS 2006, who led SSS 2006 to an unprecedented success.

November 2006

Mohamed G. Gouda
General Chair

Organization

General Chair   Mohamed G. Gouda
University of Texas at Austin, USA

Program Co-chairs   Ajoy K. Datta
University of Nevada at Las Vegas, USA
Maria Gradinariu
IRISA, Université Rennes 1, France

Local Arrangements Co-chairs   Jorge A. Cobb
University of Texas at Dallas, USA
Ravi Prakash
University of Texas at Dallas, USA

Publicity and Web Chair   Florent Claerhout
IRISA, Université Rennes 1, France

Steering Committee

Anish Arora	The Ohio State University, USA
Ajoy K. Datta	University of Nevada at Las Vegas, USA
Shlomi Dolev	Ben-Gurion University, Israel
Sukumar Ghosh	University of Iowa, USA (Chair)
Mohamed G. Gouda	University of Texas at Austin, USA
Ted Herman	University of Iowa, USA
Shing-Tsaan Huang	National Central University, Taiwan
Toshimitsu Masuzawa	Osaka University, Japan
Vincent Villain	Université de Picardie, France

Program Committee

Mustaque Ahamad	Georgia Institute of Technology, USA
Anish Arora	Ohio State University, USA
James Aspnes	Yale University, USA
Roberto Baldoni	Università di Roma "La Sapienza," Italy
Farokh Bastani	University of Texas at Dallas, USA
Joffroy Beauquier	LRI, Université de Paris Sud, France
Jorge A. Cobb	University of Texas at Dallas, USA
Sajal K. Das	University of Texas at Arlington, USA
Ajoy K. Datta	University of Nevada, Las Vegas, USA (Co-chair)
Xavier Défago	Japan Advanced Institute of Science and Technology (JAIST), Japan

Program Committee (Continued)

Carole Delporte-Gallet	LIAFA, Université de Paris 7, France
Shlomi Dolev	Ben Gurion University, Israel
Paul Ezhilchelvan	University of Newcastle upon Tyne, UK
Hugues Fauconnier	LIAFA, Université de Paris 7, France
Faith Fich	University of Toronto, Canada
Paola Flocchini	University of Ottawa, Canada
Felix C. Freiling	University of Mannheim, Germany
Laurent Fribourg	LSV, ENS Cachan, Paris, France
Roy Friedman	Technion, Israel
Thomas Fuhrmann	Universität Karlsruhe, Germany
Sukumar Ghosh	University of Iowa, USA
Maria Gradinariu	IRISA, Université Rennes 1, France (Co-chair)
Lisa Higham	University of Calgary, Canada
Jaap-Henk Hoepman	Radbound University Nijmengen, Netherlands
Chin-Tser Huang	University of South Carolina at Columbia, USA
Shing-Tsaan Huang	National Central University, Taiwan
Michel Hurfin	IRISA, INRIA, Rennes, France
Raj Jain	Washington University in St. Louis, USA
Arshad Jhumka	University of Warwick, UK
Mehmet Kaarata	Kuwait University, Kuwait
Anne-Marie Kermarrec	IRISA, INRIA, Rennes, France
Sandeep S. Kulkarni	Michigan State University, USA
Shay Kutten	Technion, Israel
David Lee	Ohio State University, USA
Toshimitsu Masuzawa	Osaka University, Japan
Stéphane Messika	LRI, Université de Paris Sud, France
Mikhail Nesterenko	Kent University, USA
Fernando Pedone	University of Lugano, Switzerland
Franck Petit	LaRIA, Université de Picardie, France
Ravi Prakash	University of Texas at Dallas, USA
Giuseppe Prencipe	Università di Pisa, Italy
Sergio Rajsbaum	Universidad Nacional Autonoma de Mexico, Mexico
Sylvia Ratnasamy	Intel Research Berkeley, USA
Michel Raynal	IRISA, Université Rennes 1, France
Andre Schiper	EPFL, Switzerland
Pierre Sens	LIP6, Université de Paris 6, France
Alex Shvartsman	University of Connecticut, USA
Neeraj Suri	TU Darmstadt, Germany
Oliver Theel	Carl von Ossietzky University of Oldenburg, Germany
Srikanta Tirthapura	Iowa State University, USA

Sébastien Tixeuil   LRI, Université de Paris Sud, France
Philippas Tsigas   Chalmers University, Sweden
Paulo Verissimo   Universidade de Lisboa, Portugal
Vincent Villain   LaRIA, Université de Picardie, France
Antonino Virgillito   Università di Roma, Italy
Cliff Wang   Army Research Office, USA
Yi-Min Wang   Microsoft Research, USA
Roger Wattenhofer   ETH Zurich, Switzerland
Joseph Widder   Technische Universität Wien, Austria
Dong Xuan   Ohio State University, USA
Masafumi Yamashita   Kyushu University, Japan

Additional Reviewers

Alexander Alexandrov
Mahesh Arumugam
Eithan Bachmat
Xiaole Bai
Mahesh Balakrishnan
Somprakash
    Bandyopadhyay
Sandip Bapat
Michael Becher
Doina Bein
Roberto Beraldi
Vincent Bernat
Vijayendra
    Bhamidipati
Martin Biely
Karun Biyani
Erik-Oliver Blass
Borzoo Bonakdarpour
Francois Bonnet
Christian Boulinier
Olivier Bournez
Olga Brukman
Krzysztof Brzezinski
Marcio Bystronski
Lasaro Camargos
Hui Cao
Uday Chakraborty
Subhendu
    Chattopadhyay
Shantnu Chaturvedi

Guillaume Chelius
Sriram Chellappan
Florent Claerhout
Thomas Clouser
Gabor Cselle
Ariel Daliot
Sylvie Delaët
Murat Demirbas
Jerry L. Derby
Abhishek Dhama
Yoann Dieudonné
Dan Dobre
Lucia D. Penso
Matthias Függer
Eric Fleury
Akihiro Fujiwara
Philippe Gauron
Anders Gidenstam
Mohamed G. Gouda
Isabelle Guérin-Lassous
Rachid Guerraoui
Arobinda Gupta
Sandeep Gupta
Thomas Hérault
Phuong Ha
Sammy Haddad
Philipp Hahn
Yinnon Haviv
Naohiro Hayashibara
Ted Herman

Thorsten Holz
Martin Hutle
David Ilcinkas
Taisuke Izumi
Qasim Javed
Jehn-Ruey Jiang
Jinjing Jiang
Colette Johnen
Jason Jue
Eunjing Jung
Hirotsugu Kakugawa
Prasanth Kalakota
Ronen Kat
Yoshiaki Katayama
Dogan Kesdogan
Boris Koldehofe
Marina Kopeetsky
Steve Kremer
Michael Kuhn
Santosh Kumar
Taewoo Kwon
Hamida S. Lagraa
Mikel Larrea
Bill Leal
Pierre Lemarinier
Ron R. Levy
Thomas Locher
Darrell D.E. Long
Stefan Lucks
Fredrik Manne

Additional Reviewers (Continued)

Sebastian Max
Adnan N. Mian
Alessia Milani
Neeraj Mittal
Nathalie Mitton
Aad V. Moorsel
Heinrich Moser
Vinayak Naik
Nicolas Nisse
Regina O'Dell
Fukuhito Ooshita
Yvonne-Anne
   Oswald
Anand Padmanabhan
Jennie Palmer
Olivier Peres
Scott M. Pike
Lexi Pimenidis
Rami Puzis

Vivien Quéma
Leonardo Querzoni
Shrisha Rao
Aina Ravoaja
Jared Saia
Kamil Sarac
Elad M. Schiller
Nicolas Schiper
Stefan Schmid
Ulrich Schmid
Rodrigo Schmidt
Sirio Scipioni
Samia Souissi
Paulo Sousa
Neil Speirs
Mukundan Sridharan
Marija Stamenkovic
Tomoko Suzuki
Sapon Tanachaiwiwat

Mansi Thoppian
Alan Tully
Chi-Hung Tzeng
Marco Voss
Limin Wang
Xun Wang
Timo Warns
Pihui Wei
Bettina Weiss
Marcin Wieloch
Matthias Wiesmann
Bojian Xu
Zhe Xu
Yukiko Yamauchi
Chau-Yuan Yang
Wei Yu
Hongwei Zhang
Qing Zhang
Zhijan Zheng

Table of Contents

Invited Talks

Regular Papers

Brief Announcement

Stabilization Enabling Technology[*]
(Extended Abstract)

Shlomi Dolev and Yinnon Haviv

Department of Computer Science, Ben-Gurion University of the Negev,
Beer-Sheva, 84105, Israel
{dolev, haviv}@cs.bgu.ac.il

Abstract. Hardware and software components are suggested for enabling the creation of a self-stabilizing OS on top of an off-the-shelf, non-self-stabilizing processor. Simple "watchdog" hardware called periodic reset monitor (PRM) provides a basic solution. The solution is extended to a stabilization enabling hardware (SEH) which removes any real time requirement from the OS. A stabilization enabling system that extends the SEH with some software components provides the user (the OS designer) with a self-stabilizing processor abstraction. Adapting the current OS code to be self-stabilizing is supported using a mechanism for enforcing the software configuration.

1 Introduction

Self-stabilization. Self-stabilization is an important fault-tolerance paradigm [2,3]. A system that is designed to be self-stabilizing automatically recovers from an arbitrary state. The paradigm makes no assumption on how the unexpected state is reached, only that the error that caused the unexpected state is transient.

One event that can be modeled as a transient fault is a transient violation of input sequence assumptions. Currently, a significant number of system failures are caused by sequences of inputs which were not addressed during the implementation of the system. In most cases, the unpredicted sequence is defined as illegal in the specifications. Still, the implementation failed to properly verify the consistency of the input sequence, causing the system to fail and reach an illegal state after which the system will not recover. Notice that, even if these erroneous sequences are not frequent, and even if they are handled manually (i.e., by a human operator), the system may suffer from a considerable downtime since identifying the problem may take time. Assuming these errors are rare and not malicious, one can model them as transient faults.

Another example of transient errors are soft-errors (see [4]). Soft-errors are changes in memory values caused by cosmic rays. Decrease in computing features size, decrease in power usage and shorting the micro-cycle period, enhance the influence of soft-errors.

---

[*] Partially supported by Microsoft, IBM, NSF, Intel, Deutsche Telekom, Rita Altura Trust Chair in Computer Sciences, Intel, vaatat and Lynn and William Frankel Center for Computer Sciences.

A.K. Datta and M. Gradinariu (Eds.): SSS 2006, LNCS 4280, pp. 1–15, 2006.

Enforcing stabilization on a blackbox processor. Processor specifications expose the programmer to an abstract presentation of the processor behavior and hide implementation details. Among other benefits, the abstract description eases the programming and allows the processor designer to change the implementation. However, in the context of soft-errors and self-stabilization, the abstract presentation implies the following hazard. The processor state space (in terms of implementation) contains many states which were not supposed to be reached. The behavior from these *erroneous states* does not correspond to the behavior specified when starting from any of the abstract states. When such an erroneous state is reached, the self-stabilizing program may face a permanent illegal behavior of the processor. Notice that under this persistent illegal behavior of the processor, no software can exhibit the desired behavior.

In [4], we showed an implementation of a self-stabilizing processor. Started in any state, the processor converges into a subset of its states in which it performs fetch, decode and execute of machine instructions according to the manufacturer's specifications. In [4], a simple processor was considered (the one in [12]), allowing to prove the self-stabilization property by considering (the micro-code of) the whole implementation.

In contrast, the implementations of current processors are very complex and may contain high coupling between components. Using the above approach will practically require redesigning the processor from scratch. In this paper we suggest the first solution that forces the stabilization property on off-the-shelf commercial processors. The solution uses only a modest additional hardware that is external to the processor. The hardware enforces the consistency and the setup parameters of the processor.

We propose three methods for enforcing stabilization on a blackbox processor. The first method (Section 2) is based on periodically resetting the processor by the OS. An additional hardware is added to the processor which monitors and assists in the reset procedure. The OS may choose the time to perform such a reset, but if the OS fails to request a reset within a predetermined amount of time, the additional hardware enforces this reset. The second method (Section 3) extends the first method by notifying the OS concerning the upcoming (maybe enforced) reset. This addition enables the third method to remove the requirement to request a reset within the predetermined amount of time at the cost of slightly restricting the processor specifications.

In [4], we suggested using a watchdog for detecting that the processor repeatedly executes the fetch, decode and execute cycle. The method suggested in [4] used a signal sent by the processor to decide when to reset the watchdog. The signal indicated that the processor is starting a new cycle (of fetch, decode and execute). The signal sent by the processor actually indicated that a predicate p, over the internal state of the processor holds. The predicate p ensured that the processor is in a legal state and therefore behaves according to the specifications. Moreover, the predicate p is correct infinitely often. The existence of such a predicate is reasonable for basic processors, such as the one in [4][1]. However, the internal state of commercial processors is complex, making the problem of finding such a predicate hard and even practically infeasible. In this paper, on the contrary, the watchdog is used for ensuring that the OS resets the processor infinitely often, enforcing its internal state to a legal one.

Self-stabilizing OSs. Operating systems (OSs) are used for sharing resources and providing hardware abstraction in virtually all computer systems. Therefore, it is crucial that OSs never fail. Designing a system that never fails is impossible in the presence of transient errors. The reason is that a transient error may change the output of the system and by that create a (non-maskable) fault. Fortunately one can ensure that the system will automatically repair itself following such transient error. Started in an arbitrary state, a self-stabilizing OS exhibits a legal behavior following a finite and preferably short stabilization period.

The stabilization property of OSs is crucial for supporting self-stabilizing software ([3]) and self-stabilizing monitoring environment, such as the one presented in [1]. In [6] a self-stabilizing OS is designed. The operating system is designed from scratch and written in machine code. The OS presented in [6] is comparable to the TinyOS [10]. In contrast, current OSs are very complex. Redesigning a fully functional industrial quality kernel from scratch and proving its stabilization may take enormous amount of resources.

Thus, we propose in Section 5 a framework that enables the adaptation of existing OSs code to be self-stabilizing. The framework reduces the amount of required code changes by allowing the designer to focus only on the parts of the state which are dynamic; i.e., parts that may be changed after the system setup and configuration. Moreover, the stabilization enabling system, presented in Section 4 assists the design of the OS by providing a framework for enforcing invariants on the state of the self-stabilizing OS.

2   Periodic Reset Monitor

The first method suggests enforcing the stabilization on the processor by issuing a periodic reset. The OS is required to request a reset every predetermined amount of time. Notice that, the operating system cannot guarantee anything when the processor behavior is not legal and when the OS converges from a transient fault. Therefore, we suggest using additional hardware, the Periodic Reset Monitor (PRM), which ensures that resets are performed periodically.

Figure 1 illustrates the state machine of the PRM. Initially the PRM is set to probe for a reset request (state 10). The watch-dog counter (WDC) is a variable used by the state machine and is initially set to MaxWDC. If a request was made (50), the system continues into a state in which a reset of the processor takes place (state 70). If no request was made (20), the PRM decrements the watch-dog counter (WDC) (state 30). Then, the value of WDC is examined. If the value

---

[1] The predicate p in [4] verifies that the value of the micro-program-counter corresponds to the first micro-code instruction.

0 was not reached and the value of the WDC is less than MaxWDC (i.e., the value is correct, 40) then the PRM continues to probe for a reset request (state 10). Otherwise (the WDC values is incorrect or the time to enforce a reset is reached, 60), the system continues into a state in which a reset of the processor takes place (state 70). After resetting the processor, the PRM continues to state 80, resets the WDC to its initial value, MaxWDC (state 80), and returns to the initial state (state 10).

The value of MaxWDC influences the time the PRM waits for the OS to request a reset. If the OS does not request a reset within this time, the PRM enforces one. Setting the value of MaxWDC too low may have a negative influence on the performance or even lead to a situation in which the OS does not request a reset on time during fault free periods. On the other hand, the stabilization time of the processor is proportional to this value; a high value implies a long stabilization period.

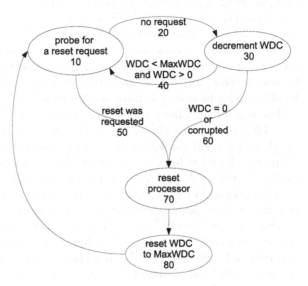

Fig. 1. State machine of the periodic reset monitor (PRM)

When implementing the PRM, one must make sure that any refinement made in the implementation eventually behaves according to the automaton presented in Figure 1. In [5], we introduced the same relation for programs compiled by a stabilization preserving compiler. The top level automaton can be implemented, for example, using EPROM by placing commands that branch into the initial state in all locations that are not used in the implementation. The refinements of steps 30 and 80 can be easily performed by functional blocks (that have no state), ensuring that the automaton in Figure 1 never ceases to advance in these states.

The implementation of the probe (state 10) and reset (state 70) is specific to each embodiment. The implementation is made by a sub-automaton with an initial state and a non empty set of final states. When the top level state (10 / 70) is reached, the sub-automaton is set to its initial state. Then, the top level automaton stops and only the sub-automaton advances. When the sub-automaton reaches one of its final states, the top level automaton continues according to the final state reached. One can imagine the interaction between the top level automaton and the sub-automaton as calling a procedure. The result of the procedure is expressed in the final state of the sub-automaton that was reached.

Making sure that the automaton in Figure 1 never ceases to advance requires that the sub-automaton implementing each of the two external procedures (probe and reset) reaches one of its final states, when started in any of its internal states. The following requirement summarizes the property required from the implementation of the probe and reset procedures.

Requirement 1. *Started in any of their internal state, the probe and the reset procedures eventually terminate.*

Assuming that the implementation satisfies Requirement 1, we can prove that the PRM executes a periodic resets. The following lemma summarizes this behavior.

Lemma 1. *Started in any state, eventually a reset of the processor takes place.*

Proof. The only loop in the state machine presented in Figure 1 which does not reach state 70 is the loop traversing states 10 and 30. After the first iteration in this loop, the watch-dog counter (WDC) must be in the range $\{0,$ MaxWDC$-1\}$. Since each iteration decrements WDC by one and no other changes to WDC are made during the iteration, eventually WDC reaches 0 and a reset is initiated.

Using the PRM. The designer of an OS that uses the PRM is required to request a reset before such a reset is enforced by the PRM. Notice that resetting the processor implies that the registers are set to their initial values as specified in the processor specifications. However, the main memory of the processor is left unchanged.

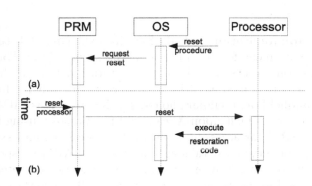

(a)

time

(b)

Fig. 2. The interaction between the OS and the PRM

Therefore, the OS designer must save all the registers which contain information required following the reset. Notice that the designer can avoid saving registers that have a constant value throughout the OS runtime. These registers can be restored into their predetermined initial values. The interface between the PRM and its user includes two points: The first is the *request-reset* method, a method for requesting a reset from the PRM (which is executed by the OS). The second point is the *restoration-code*, executed by the processor following a reset.

Figure 2 illustrates the interaction between the OS, the processor and the PRM. The upper part, (a), illustrates the scenario in which the OS requests a reset from the PRM. The lower part of Figure 2, (b), illustrates the message exchanged between the OS and the SEH when the SEH executes its reset procedure (state 70 of Figure 1).

The designer of the OS must follow some simple steps for using the PRM. First, a program point p, which is reached infinitely often, is picked by the designer. The designer must be able to show that this program point is reached at least every t' time units (for some constant t'). For example, the context switch point between tasks has this property in systems with preemptive scheduling. Then, the designer must write a code that saves the parts of the state which will be needed after the reset. A reset request from the PRM is added at the end of this code (the request-reset procedure), followed by an infinite loop. Next, the designer must add the code for restoring the state (the restoration-code). The restoration-code can use the parts of the state which were saved prior to the reset by the save-code. Next, the designer must establish an upper bound, t, on the time it takes until the system reaches the request-reset, and set MaxWDC to a value that corresponds to t. Notice that the requirement that the system reaches the rest request every t time units can be relaxed to consider only executions that start in a state in which the processor behaves according to the specification and the internal state of the OS is legal.

Following a reset, the processor operates according to its original specifications, with the augmented ability[2] to request a reset from the PRM and with the added requirement to request a reset before the watch-dog timer expires. We denote this behavior of the processor (augmented with the PRM) as LE_{PRM}.

Implementation details for the PRM (using Intel XScale). One possible embodiment for the PRM is in the scope of the *XScale* environment. In this section we describe the implementation details in this embodiment. The XScale core is used in various Intel processors, ranging from network processors to handhelds and cellular phones. The XScale core is ARMv5TE compliant. Specific processors built upon XScale add functionality using the standard mechanisms of ARM for accessing additional coprocessors and system configurations. The implementation details are based on the ARM v5 specifications [11], Intel XScale core specifications [8] and the specifications of Intel's 80200 processor (which is used for network and I/O processors [9]). The three parts of the specifications ([11], [8], [9]) may define the behavior of the processor to some scenarios as "undefined" or "unpredictable". It is assumed that following such scenarios, the processor remains in a legal state; Thus, the processor continues to fetch, decode and execute instructions according to the specifications.

The XScale core allows the programmer to perform "on chip emulation". That is, debugging of programs by executing them on the processor, and using the debugging mechanism, integrated in the processor, for accessing and controlling the debugged program. The programmer uses a debugger, which is executed on a remote host and interfaces with the XScale processor through the "Test Access Port" (TAP) using a protocol defined by the "Joint Test Action Group" (JTAG,

---

[2] Notice that the ability to request a reset overrides some functionality of the processor. When implementing the PRM, one should choose to override redundant functionality of the processor, which is not used by the OS.

IEEE Std 1149.1, see [7]). The JTAG protocol is simple and allows scanning data into and from special "JTAG registers" in the processor.

Our XScale embodiment uses TX, a JTAG register designed for sending data from the processor to the debugger. The TX register is scanned out by the PRM whenever the PRM wishes to probe for a reset request. The OS, on the other hand, writes to the TX register for requesting a reset. The scanning of the TX register is a procedure that is composed of a constant number of steps and therefore can be implemented in the PRM as a strait line automaton. Moreover, the reset of the processor (and the TAP), known as "cold-reset" in XScale terms, is also performed using a constant number of steps. The above mentioned ensures that Requirement 1 holds for this implementation.

3   The Stabilization Enabling Hardware (SEH) — Supporting Enforced Resets

The designer of the OS may wish to remove the requirement to request a reset periodically. In order to support such an OS, we suggest adding a warning message from the PRM to the OS before executing the reset. In terms of the state machine of the PRM (Figure 1), state 70 is split into two states (71 and 72), as illustrated in Figure 3. The first state (71), executes an asynchronous call to the OS, notifying the upcoming reset. Then, the PRM waits for the OS to save the state into the memory and to acknowledge that it is ready for a reset. Upon receiving an acknowledgement or if such an acknowledgement does not arrive within a predetermined amount of time,

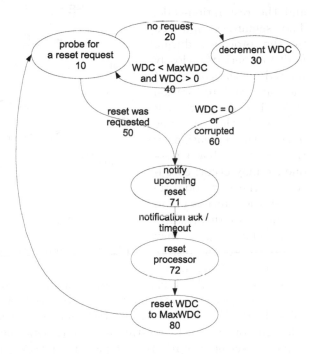

Fig. 3. State machine of the Stabilization Enabling Hardware (SEH)

the PRM advances to state 72, in which the processor is reset. Notice that bounding the time the PRM waits in state 71 for a notification from the OS ensures that the state machine presented in Figure 3 never ceases to advance. We denote this behavior of the processor (augmented with the SEH) as LE_{SEH}.

Using the SEH. The designer of the OS that uses the SEH interacts with the SEH at four different points. The first two points are identical to the PRM; i.e. the request-reset method and the restoration-code. The third interface point is a code that is called by the SEH before executing a reset (at state 71 of Figure 3). We denote this code as the *save-code*. Since the execution of the save-code is initiated by the SEH (as opposed to the OS), the third interface point is implemented as an interrupt handler. The forth interface point is a method executed by the save-code, which acknowledges the SEH notification and signals the SEH that the OS is ready for a reset. The execution of this method while the SEH is in state 71 will cause the SEH state machine to advance to state 72. Figure 4 illustrates the interaction between the OS and the SEH. The upper part, (a), illustrates the scenario in which the OS requests a reset from the SEH. The lower part of Figure 4, (b), illustrates the message exchanged between the OS and the SEH when the SEH executes its reset procedure (states 71 and 72 of Figure 3).

The designer is required to write the save-code and the restoration-code. The semantics obtained by the processor during fault free periods is closely related to the content of the save and restoration code. The designer must be aware that anytime during the execution of the OS, the following sequence may occur: execution of the save-code, reset of the processor and execution of the restore-code. The designer may choose to save and restore any parts of the processor

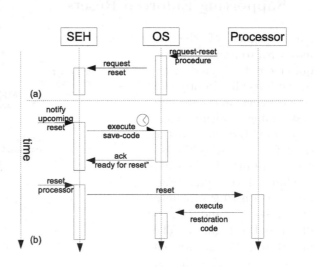

Fig. 4. The interaction between the OS and the SEH

state. Moreover, the designer is free to enforce invariants on the restored state.

The designer may optionally choose to initiate a reset at a timing which best suits the OS. For example, the designer may choose to request a reset during the idle time of the OS. Requesting a reset is performed as in the PRM, using the request-reset procedure. After requesting a reset, the OS must wait by entering an infinite loop. When using this option, the restoration code must check if the restored program counter is inside the infinite loop, and enforce the program counter to point to the instruction following the loop.

As noted in Section 2, one must implement the additional features (notifying the OS on the upcoming reset and probing for an acknowledgement message) so that the state machine of the SEH never ceases to advance. The following requirement summarizes the property required from the implementation of the notification and acknowledgement probing procedures.

Requirement 2. *Started in any of their internal state, the notification and probing for acknowledgement procedures eventually terminate.*

Implementation details for the SEH **(using Intel XScale).** The implementation of the SEH is an extension of the implementation of the PRM. Two components are added. The first component is used for notifying the OS on the upcoming reset by triggering the save-code. We detail the specifics of this component in the sequel. The second component is responsible for probing for a notification acknowledgement and is implemented using the same technique as the component used for probing for a reset-request.

Notifying the OS on the upcoming reset is performed by invoking an external debug break. The invocation of an external debug break causes the highest priority exception to occur. In the XScale debug mechanism, the code that handles the exception is known as the debug handler and is supposed to interact with the remote debugger. We override the debugging mechanism and install the save-code at the debug vector.

Since the save-code is executed as an interrupt, the program counter that needs to be saved is held at the register holding the return address from the interrupt (the `lr` register). Since the implementation of the SEH involves adding code to the OS, the restoration code must avoid restoring a state in which the program counter points to the newly added code. The restoration-code does that by checking that the program counter is not in the predefined range used by the debug handler.

In the following sub-section, we use the functionality obtained by the SEH, in order to establish a system that enables composing a self-stabilizing OS on top of a blackbox (non self-stabilizing) processor.

4 Stabilization Enabling System (SES)

In this section we suggest a system that enables composing a self-stabilizing OS on top of an off-the-shelf non self-stabilizing processor. The system is based upon the stabilization enabling hardware (SEH), presented in Section 3. The SES enables the designer of a self-stabilizing OS to assume that the processor eventually executes the unchanged code according to specifications that are almost identical to the ones presented in the processor specifications.

The stabilization enabling system (SES) is responsible for ensuring that the processor does not stay in an erroneous state forever. Roughly speaking, the SES monitors the fact that the processor repeatedly executes warm-boots and aids in performing these warm-boots. The term warm-boot refers to saving the processor state into the main memory, restarting (only) the processor, leaving the main memory unchanged and then restoring the processor state prior to the restart. The execution of a warm-boot ensures that the internal state of the processor is legal (non-erroneous); i.e., enforces the stabilization of the processor.

Moreover, executing such a warm-boot during a fault free period does not effect the execution of the OS (up to stuttering).

In other words, instead of designing the processor to be self-stabilizing, we create a system that periodically refreshes the state of the processor to exactly the same state when this state is legal, or to some legal state, otherwise. Once the processor is in a legal state, and as long as there are no additional soft/transient errors, the state of the processor remains legal and the processor execution will be identical to the execution of the processor with no SES installed[3].

Processor operational configuration. In [4], the legal behavior of the processor was defined as fetching the instructions from the main memory, decoding and executing them as specified in the vendor manual. Here, we refine this definition to support initial configuration for the processor. We separate the state of the processor into two parts. The first part of the state includes registers which are configured during the system boot and are not changed since. These registers essentially determine the operational configuration of the processor, which we call the *configurational* part of the state. For example, the ARM ([11]) architecture defines the control register (Section 2.4 in [11]) which is used, among others, to configure the MMU. The non configurational part of the state includes the rest of the registers, as described in the specifications. For example, in the $x86$ architecture, the *eax*, *eip*, and *esp* registers are included in the non configurational part of the state. Once such a separation is defined, the processor legal behavior is described for a specific configuration. Here, the state space includes any assignment to the registers of the non configurational part of the state and machine instructions that may change the configuration (the content of registers included in the configurational part) are omitted from the specification.

Warm-boot behavior. Performing a warm-boot in a legal processor state forces the configurational part of the state into its predetermined value and leaves the rest of the state unchanged. Performing a warm-boot in erroneous state results in *any* of the allowed states for which the configurational part of the state is set to its predetermined value. Moreover, the execution of a warm-boot in either a legal or an erroneous state ensures that the code executed by the processor is the code of the OS.

The implementation of the SES uses some features of the processor for interacting with the SEH. The original behavior of these features, as defined in the processor specifications, is therefore overridden by the SES. We refer to the specifications of the processor with the overridden features as the SES-*modified specifications*. An OS that avoids using these features will not be effected by the change in the specifications. In our suggested implementation for the XScale processor, we override the on-chip debug functionality of the processor. The debug mechanism is used only in the development stages of the system and can therefore be safely overridden by the SES.

---

[3] Up to clock speed and minor specification changes resulting in the SES-*modified specifications* described in the sequel.

Performing warm-boots infinitely often ensures that eventually the processor behaves according to the SES-modified specifications with respect to the pre-determined configuration and executes the original program. Notice that, when using the SEH, the programmer is still responsible for the stabilization of the program from an arbitrary state. The following theorem summarizes the behavior of a system that uses the SES.

Theorem 1. *Started in any state, eventually the processor behaves according to the SES-modified specification, up to stuttering, with respect to the predetermined configuration and executes the original code.*

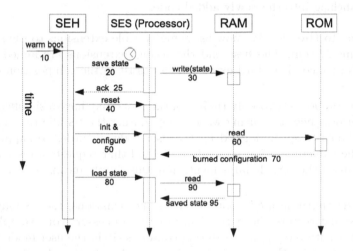

Fig. 5. Sequence diagram of a warm-boot scenario

Implementing a warm-boot. Figure 5 illustrates the sequence of messages exchanged between the SEH and the reset of the SES in the scenario of a warm-boot. The scenario starts with a notification of an upcoming reset, initiated by the SEH (20). The save-code, executed on the processor saves the non-configurational part of the state. This includes the value of any registers used by either user or OS code. For example, the stack pointer. Since the state of the processor may be corrupted at this stage, no assumptions are made on the correct operation of the processor at this stage. In particular, the SEH does not assume that the save-code execution is finished in a finite period of time. Therefore, a simple timeout on the call is applied by the SEH, denoted by the clock icon near the "save state" call (20). When the save-code execution terminates, it sends an acknowledgement message to the SEH, notifying that it is safe to perform a reset (25). Then, a reset of the processor is invoked (40). Notice that the main memory is left unchanged (and in particular, is not erased). From that point on, the processor operates according to the specifications. Next, the SEH invokes the restoration-code.

The first part of the restoration-code is responsible for restoring the processor initial configuration (50). In this processes, the configuration of the processor is loaded from a ROM device (60). This configuration was captured and burned during the design stage of the system. The second part of the restoration-code is responsible for loading the non-configurational part of the state, which was saved by the save-code (80).

Using the SES. The only requirement from the designer of the OS, when using the SES is to adapt the code to the SES-modified specifications. Performing code adaptation must ensure that the OS code: (a) Avoids using mechanisms overridden in the implementation of the SES (in XScale, the debug mechanism), (b) Avoids branching into the newly added code.

Extensions to the SES. We now list some possible extensions to the stabilization enabling system. The first and the second extensions are aimed towards better performance. The third extension can assist in the composition of a self-stabilizing OS.

• Timing warm-boots. Properly timing warm-boots may have a significant influence on performance. Executing warm-boots during the OS idle time can cause the warm-boots to go unnoticed by the user code. In order to support these features, the implementation may add a method that requests a reset from the SEH. In terms of the XScale implementation, this simply means writing into the TX register.

• Supporting "burning-hot"-boots. Under some situations, the OS may choose not to save and restore the entire state of the processor. For example, if the warm-boot is initiated by the OS during context switch, the user mode registers are already saved by the OS and there is no need to save and restore them in the warm-boot processes. After the OS scheduler chooses the next process to execute, it can store this decision in memory and request a "burning-hot"-boot. The save-code and the restoration-code can use settings placed in RAM by the OS in order to decide which parts of the state should be saved and restored. The method used by the OS for requesting a warm-boot is now modified to contain an infinite loop after requesting a reset from the SEH. This enables the OS to wait in place until the SES performs the warm-boot. The loop is broken using a special condition on saved state (in XScale, the `lr` register, containing the return address), in the restoration code. Notice that using this feature requires caution from the OS designer, since the SEH-modified specifications now contains instructions that reset parts of the state.

• Supporting OS invariants. The OS designer may choose to add some functionality to the restoration-code in the form of invariants checks. For example, the OS designer may choose to ensure that if in the current state (the state restored) the processor is in supervisor mode, then the instruction pointer points to OS code (rather than to the user code).

Implementation details for the SES **(using Intel XScale).** The XScale processor is configured by setting the registers of two coprocessors (The *System Control Coprocessor* (CP15) and coprocessor 14). The separation of the processor state into its configurational and non-configurational parts is therefore strait forward. The configuration of the debug mechanism is also performed by writing in these registers. Our implementation ensures that the configuration defined for the debug mechanism will be as required.

In XScale, some of the registers have different copies for different processor modes (such as user-mode, supervisor-mode etc.). The save-code in our implementation saves the main processor registers by traversing the different modes and saving the values held in the different copies of the registers[4]. The registers of all coprocessors (but CP14 and CP15) are also saved to the memory and the dirty data cache pages are written into memory. The last instruction of the save-code is a write instruction to the TX register, signalling the SEH that the system is ready for a reset.

The restoration code enforces immediate (constant) values on the registers of CP14 and CP15 which hold the configurational part of the state. Then, in a process reversed to that of the save code, the restoration code restores the non configurational part of the state from memory.

5   Beyond the Processor — Enforcing Software Configuration

The self-stabilization property of the processor is crucial for creating a self-stabilizing system. The systems presented in Sections 2, 3 and 4 are used for enforcing the stabilization of a processor without using detailed knowledge on its implementation. In fact, the systems presented in previous sections are used for saving the required vast development effort needed for creating self-stabilization processors.

However, the environment on top of which current systems operate is much richer than the processor. In particular, operating systems are used extensively. Developing a self-stabilizing OS with industrial quality from scratch requires an enormous development effort. In this section, we aim towards reducing this effort by introducing a scheme and a design of additional hardware that ease the adaptation of legacy code (of, e.g., an OS) into a self-stabilizing one.

An important assumption when designing self-stabilizing algorithms is that the code running on the processor is not corrupted. We suggest extending this assumption also to the program data that change only during the system boot and configuration. Since most of the variables of computer software remain constant following the boot and configuration stages, it is easier to define the portions of memory in which there are content changes during the system run.

We suggest adding a hardware that supports capturing and "burning" the current state of the portions of memory defined earlier to contain configuration

---

[4] User mode registers are saved from supervisor mode using special instructions.

parameters. Memory read operations from addresses which where marked as containing configuration variables are later simulated in the additional hardware by reading from the burned ROM instead of the main memory.

The presence of the mechanism presented above allows easier modification of legacy code to be self-stabilizing. The designer needs only to identify the portions of memory which change after the boot and setup stages and only to enforce the stabilization of these portions to a consistent value.

Our scheme may require the software to expose the addresses (physical page numbers) that contain the information that should remain constant during runtime. A manual switch, the "configuration enforcement switch" (CES) may be added to the hardware. The switch is turned manually and may be in one of two states: "setup" and "runtime". Initially, the configuration enforcement switch is in the "setup" state. In this state the machine operates with no interference from the additional hardware. Then, when the user decides that the setup stage is over, she flips the switch to the "runtime" state. This flip triggers burning into ROM the content held in the memory addresses which were marked to contain configuration. From that point on, any request to read software configuration from RAM memory is serviced by reading from ROM. Notice that using any of the solutions presented in Sections 2, 3 and 4 ensures that the data cache is eventually consistent and therefore the configuration used by the software is eventually correct.

6   Conclusions

The existence of a self-stabilizing microprocessor is essential for the implementation of self-stabilizing systems. The PRM, SEH and SES enable the enforcement of the stabilization property on commercial processors. The three solutions give the designer of the OS three different starting points.

The PRM provides the most simple and flexible solution but requires some effort from the OS designer. In particular, the designer must make sure that the OS request a reset at least every predetermined amount of time. However, using the PRM, no code is added to the OS.

A designer who wishes to remove the requirement for requesting a reset at least every predetermined amount of time, while preserving some of the flexibility may use the SEH. The SEH allows the designer complete flexibility in choosing the save and restoration-code, which is also the downside of the solution.

Using the SES requires a very small effort from the OS designer in exchange to loosing some of the flexibility. The only requirement when using the SES is that the OS avoids using the mechanisms which were used for implementing the SES. An implementation of the SES may choose redundant mechanisms (such as the debug mechanism in XScale), which are not used in deployed systems. However, the assistance provided by the SES to the OS designer is important, the designer may write invariants on the restored state and choose the preferred times for the OS to perform a warm-boot.

The aim of the solutions in Sections 2, 3 and 4 was to achieve stabilization (of the processor) by only modifying an existing solution instead of redesigning a new one. We believe that the same concept should be used in the creation of a self-stabilizing OS. For example, the solution presented in Section 5 may form necessary technology for applying the same concepts on OSs. Using the solution presented in Section 5, the designer can concentrate on proving the stabilizing of the non-configurational part of the software state.

References

1. Olga Brukman and Shlomi Dolev, "Recovery Oriented Programming", this proceedings, also in Technical Report #2006-06, Department of Computer Science, Ben-Gurion University of the Negev, Israel, 2006.
2. Edsger W. Dijkstra. "Self-stabilizing systems in spite of distributed control". *Commun. ACM*, 17(11):643–644, 1974.
3. Shlomi Dolev, *Self-Stabilization*, MIT Press, 2000.
4. Shlomi Dolev and Yinnon Haviv, "Self-Stabilizing Microprocessor Analyzing and Overcoming Soft-Errors", *IEEE Transactions on Computers* ,vol. 55, no. 4, pp. 385-399, April. 2006, Also in *Proc. of the International Conference on Architecture of Computing Systems, Organic and Pervasive Computing* (ARCS) Lecture Notes in Computer Science 2981, Springer, pp. 31–46, 2004.
5. Shlomi Dolev, Yinnon Haviv, and Mooly Sagiv, "Self-stabilization preserving compiler", *Proc. of the 7th International Symposium on Self-Stabilizing Systems,* Lecture Notes in Computer Science 3764, Springer, pp. 81–95, 2005. Also in Technical Report #2005-06, Department of Computer Science, Ben-Gurion University of the Negev, Israel, 2005.
6. Shlomi Dolev and Reuven Yagel, "Memory management for self-stabilizing operating systems". *Proc. of the 7th International Symposium on Self-Stabilizing Systems,* Lecture Notes in Computer Science 3764, Springer, pp. 113–127, 2005.
7. IEEE, IEEE 1149.1 Standard Test Access Port and Boundary-Scan Architecture, 2001. http://standards.ieee.org
8. Intel, *Intel XScale Core, Developer's Manual*, 2004. http://www.intel.com/design/intelxscale/273473.htm
9. Intel, *Intel 80200 Processor based on Intel XScale Microarchitecture*, 2000. http://www.intel.com/design/iio/manuals/273411.htm
10. Jason Hill et al. "System Architecture Directions for Networked Sensors", Architectural Support for Programming Languages and Operating Systems, pp. 93–104, 2000.
11. David Seal. *ARM Architecture Reference Manual (2nd Edition)*, Addison-Wesley, 2000.
12. Andrew S. Tanenbaum. *Structured computer organization*, Prentice-Hall, 1984.

A General Characterization of Indulgence

R. Guerraoui[1,2] and N. Lynch[2]

[1] School of Computer and Communication Sciences, EPFL
[2] Computer Science and Artificial Intelligence Laboratory, MIT

Abstract. An indulgent algorithm is a distributed algorithm that, besides tolerating process failures, also tolerates arbitrarily long periods of instability, with an unbounded number of timing and scheduling failures. In particular, no process can take any irrevocable action based on the operational status, correct or failed, of other processes. This paper presents an intuitive and general characterization of indulgence. The characterization can be viewed as a simple application of Murphy's law to partial runs of a distributed algorithm, in a computing model that encompasses various communication and resilience schemes. We use our characterization to establish several results about the inherent power and limitations of indulgent algorithms.

1 Introduction

Indulgence

The idea of *indulgence* is motivated by the difficulty for any process in a distributed system to accurately figure out, at any point of its computation, any information about which, and in what order, processes will take steps after that point. For instance, a process can usually not know if other processes have failed and stopped operating or are simply slow to signal their activity and will indeed perform further computational steps. More generally, a process can hardly exclude any future interleaving of the processes.

This uncertainty is at the heart of many impossibilities and lower bounds in distributed computing, e.g., [9], and it has been expressed in various forms and assuming specific computation models,e.g., [7,4,19]. The goal of this work is to capture this uncertainty in an abstract and general way, independently of specific distributed computing and communication models, be they time-based, round-based, message passing or shared memory.

In short, an *indulgent* algorithm is an algorithm that tolerates this uncertainty. In a sense, the algorithm is *indulgent* towards its environment, i.e., the operating system and the network. These can thus be unstable and congested for an arbitrarily long period of time, during which an unbounded number of timing and scheduling failures can occur.

An obvious class of indulgent algorithms are asynchronous ones [9]. These do not make any assumption on communication delays and relative process speeds. As a consequence, no process can for instance ever distinguish a failed process

A.K. Datta and M. Gradinariu (Eds.): SSS 2006, LNCS 4280, pp. 16–34, 2006.
© Springer-Verlag Berlin Heidelberg 2006

from a slow one. However, indulgent algorithms do not need to be asynchronous. In particular, an algorithm that eventually becomes synchronous, after an unknown period of time [7], is also indulgent. Similarly, algorithms that rely on an eventual leader election abstraction, such as Paxos [19], or an eventually accurate failure detector, such as the rotating coordinator algorithm of [4], are also indulgent. Other examples of indulgent algorithms include those that assume a time after which processes execute steps in a certain order [21], or an eventual bound on the ratio between the delay of the fastest and the slowest messages [8], as well as algorithms that tolerate an unbounded number of timing failures [23]. All these non-asynchronous indulgent algorithms have the nice flavor that the assumptions they make about the interleaving of processes can only be used for *liveness*. *Safety* is preserved even if these assumptions do not hold.

All these algorithms are devised in specific models that refer directly to specific failure detector machinery or specific synchrony conditions, typically assuming a message passing model [10,6,24,13,22].

Murphy's Law

The goal of this work is to characterize the notion of indulgence in a general manner, encompassing various distributed computing models, be they round-based or time-based, as well as various communication schemes, be they shared memory or message passing. By doing so, the goal is to determine the inherent power and limitation of indulgent algorithms, independently of specific models.

To seek for a general characterization of indulgence, it is tempting to consider an abstract approach that looks at *runs* of an algorithm as sequences of *events* that occur at the *interface* between the processes executing the algorithm and the *services* [1] used in the algorithm; each event representing a *step* of a process consisting of a process id, a service id, together with the operation invoked by the process on the service with its input and output parameters.

This is in contrast to an approach where we would look into the internals of the individual services involved in the computation and the automata executed on the processes. While appealing for its generality, the abstract approach is not straightforward as we explain in the paper. In particular, it is not easy to devise an abstract characterization without precluding algorithms that assume a threshold of correct (non-faulty) processes. This would be unfortunate for indulgent algorithms typically assume for instance a majority of correct processes [7,19,4].

The main contribution of this paper is to characterize indulgence by applying *Murphy's law* to partial runs of an indulgent algorithm. Basically, we characterize indulgence through the following property: if the interleaving I (sequence of process ids) of a partial run R (sequence of steps) of an algorithm A *could* be extended with steps of certain processes and not others, while still be tolerated by the algorithm, then the partial run R can *itself* be extended in A with such steps. More specifically, we say that an algorithm A is indulgent if, given any partial

---

[1] Shared memory object, broadcast primitive, message passing channel, failure detector, clock, etc.

run R of A and the corresponding interleaving I of processes, if A tolerates an extension I' of I where some subset of processes stop taking steps (resp. take steps) after I, then A does also have an extension of R with interleaving I'. In a sense, partial run R does not provide the processes with enough information to predict the extension of the interleaving I: if some extension of I is tolerated by the algorithm, then this extension can also be associated with an extension of R.

Power and Limitation of Indulgence

We first show in the paper that our characterization of indulgence is *robust* in the sense that it does not depend on the number of failures tolerated by an algorithm. In short, if an algorithm A that tolerates k failures is indulgent, then the restriction of A to runs with $k - 1$ failures is also indulgent.

We then highlight the *safety* aspect of indulgent algorithms. Basically, even if an indulgent algorithm relies on some information about the interleaving of processes to solve some problem, the algorithm can only rely on this information to ensure the *liveness* part of the problem. *Safety* is preserved even if the information is never accurate.

We then proceed to show that any indulgent algorithm A is inherently *uniform*: if A ensures the *correct-restriction* of a safety property P, then A ensures the actual property P. A corollary of this, for instance, is that an indulgent algorithm cannot solve the correct-restriction of consensus, also called *non-uniform* consensus (where a process can decide a different value from a value decided by a failed process) without solving consensus (where no two processes should ever decide different value - uniform agreement). This is not the case with non-indulgent algorithms.

We use our uniformity property to show that certain problems are impossible with indulgent algorithms. In particular, we show that no indulgent algorithm can solve a *failure sensitive* problem, even if only one process can fail and it can do so only initially. In short, a failure sensitive problem is one the specification of which depends on the fact that certain processes takes steps or not after a decision is taken. Failure sensitive problems include some classical ones like *non-blocking atomic commit, terminating reliable broadcast*, (also known as the *Byzantine Generals* problem) as well as *interactive consistency*. There are known algorithms that solve these problems but these are not indulgent.

Our reduction from uniformity to the impossibility of solving failure sensitive problems is, we believe, interesting in its own right. By showing that our impossibility applies only to initial failures, and holds even if the algorithm uses powerful underlying services like consensus itself, we emphasize the fact that this impossibility is fundamentally different from the classical impossibility of consensus in an asynchronous system if a process can fail during the computation [9].

Finally, we prove that, given n the number of processes in the system and assuming $n - \lfloor n/x \rfloor$ processes can fail ($x \le n$), no indulgent algorithm can ensure a $x-divergent$ property using only *timeless* services. In short, a $x-$divergent property is one that can hold for partial runs involving disjoint subset of processes but not in the composition of these runs, whereas a timeless service is one that does not provide any real-time guarantee. We capture here, in a general way, the traditional partitioning argument that is frequently used in distributed computing. Corollaries of our result include the impossibility for an indulgent algorithm using message passing or sequentially consistent objects [18] to (a) implement a safe register [18] if half of the processes can fail, as well as (b) implement k-set agreement [5] if $n - \lfloor n/k \rfloor$ processes can fail.

To conclude the paper, we discuss how, using our notion of indulgence, we indirectly derive the first precise definition of the concept of *unreliable* failure detection [4]. Whereas this notion is now folklore in the distributed computing literature, it has never been precisely defined in a general model of distributed computation.

2   Model

Processes and Services

We consider a set Π of processes each representing a Turing machine. The total number of processes is denoted by n and we assume at least 2 processes in the system, i.e., $n > 1$. Every process has a unique identity. Processes communicate through shared abstractions, called *distributed services* or simply *services*. These might include sequentially consistent or atomic objects [18,15], as well as message passing channels and broadcast primitives [14]. The processes can also consult oracles such as failure detectors [4] about the operational status of other processes, or randomization devices that provide them with arbitrary values from a random set. Each service exports a set of operations through which it is accessed. For instance [20]:

- A message passing channel exports a *send* and a *receive* operations. The *send* takes an input parameter, i.e., a message, and returns simply an *ok* indication that the message was sent. On the other hand, a *receive* does not take any input parameter and returns a message, possibly *nil* (empty message) if there is no message to be received. Message passing channels differ according to the guarantees on message delivery. Some might ensure that a message that is sent is eventually received by every correct process (the notion of *correct* is recalled more precisely below). Others ensure simply that the message is received if both the sender and the receiver are correct.
- An atomic queue exports a *enqueue* and a *dequeue* operations. The *enqueue* takes an input parameter (an element to enqueue) and returns an *ok* indication. On the other hand, a *dequeue* does not take any input parameter and returns an element in the queue (the oldest), if there is any, or simply *nil* if there is no element in the queue.

- A failure detector exports one *query* operation that does not take any input
  parameter and returns a set of processes that are suspected to have failed and
  stopped their execution. In a sense, a failure detector provides information
  about the future interleaving of the processes. More generally, one could also
  imagine oracles that inform a process that certain processes will be scheduled
  before others.

Steps and Schedules

Each process is associated with a set of possible states, some of which are initial
states. A set of n states, each associated with one process of the system, is called
a *configuration*. A configuration composed of initial states is called an *initial
configuration*. A process is also associated with an automata that regulates the
execution of the process according to a given algorithm.

The system starts from an initial configuration, among a set of possible initial
configurations, and evolves to new configurations by having processes execute
steps. A *step* is an atomic unit of computation that takes the system from a
configuration to a new configuration.

Every step is associated with exactly one process. In every step, the associated
process accesses exactly one shared service by invoking one of the operations of
the service and getting back the operation's reply. (We do not assume here any
determinism.) Based on this reply, the process modifies its local state before
moving to the next step.[2] The automaton of the process determines, given a
state of a process and a reply from the invocation of an operation, the new state
of the process and the operation to invoke in the next step of the process.

The visible part of a step, at the interface between a process and a service, is
sometimes called an *event*. It is modeled by a process *id*, a service *id*, the *id* of an
operation, as well as input and output parameters of the operation's invocation.
By language abuse, we also call this a step when there is no ambiguity between
the event and the corresponding step.

An infinite sequence of steps S is called a *schedule* and the corresponding
sequence of process ids is called the *interleaving* of the schedule S and is denoted
by $I(S)$. If the sequence is finite, we talk about a *partial* schedule and a partial
interleaving. Sometimes we even simply say a schedule and an interleaving if
there is no ambiguity. If a process p has its id in an interleaving I then we say
that p *appears* in I.

We say that a (partial) schedule S_2 (resp. an interleaving I_2) is an extension
of a partial schedule S_1 (resp. partial interleaving I_1) if S_1 (resp. I_1) is a prefix
of S_2 (resp. I_2). We write $S_2 \in E(S_1)$ (resp. $I_2 = E(I_1)$).

Runs and Algorithms

A *run* (resp. a partial) R is a pair (S, C) composed of a schedule (resp. a partial
schedule) S and a configuration C, called the initial configuration of the run R.

---

[2] Executing a local computation, with no access to a shared service in a given step, is
simply modeled by an access to an immutable service.

The interleaving of the schedule S, $I(S)$, is also called the interleaving of the run R, and is also denoted by $I(R)$. We say that a (partial) run $R_2 = (S_2, C)$ is an extension of a partial run $R_1 = (S_1, C)$ (we write $R_2 \in E(R_1)$) if S_2 is an extension of S_1. In this case, $I(R_2)$ is also an extension of $I(R_1)$. We denote by $R/p = (S/p, C)$ the restriction of $R = (S, C)$ to the steps involving only process p.

A process p is *correct* in a run R if p appears infinitely often in the interleaving $I(R)$ of that run R, i.e., p performs an infinite number of steps in R. A process p is said to be *faulty* in a run R if p is not correct in R. We say that a process p *initially fails* in a run R if p does not appear in $I(R)$. We denote the set of faulty processes in a run R (resp. interleaving I) by $faulty(R)$ (resp. $faulty(I)$), and the set of processes that do not take any step in R by $faulty^\star(R)$ (resp. $faulty^\star(I)$).

We model an *algorithm* as a set of runs. If R_i is a partial run of a run $R \in A$, we write $R_i \in^\star A$. The interleavings of the runs of an algorithm A are said to be *tolerated* by A and the set of these interleavings is denoted by $I(A)$.[3]

For instance, in *wait-free* computing [15], an algorithm tolerates all possible interleavings: it has at least one run for every possible interleaving.

It is also common to study algorithms that tolerate a threshold of failures, as we precisely define below.

- We say that A is a *k-resilient* algorithm if $I \in A$ if and only if $faulty(I) < n - k$. That is, $I(A)$ contains exactly all interleavings where at least $n - k$ processes appear infinitely often.
- We say that A is a *$k^\star$-resilient* algorithm if $I \in A$ if and only if $faulty^\star(I) = faulty(I) < n - k$. Every process that appears once in any interleaving I of A appears infinitely often in I. (We capture here the assumption of initial failures.)

We assume that the algorithms are *well behaved* in the following senses. (1) Every partial interleaving tolerated by an algorithm A has a *failure-free* extension also tolerated by A. (2) Let A be any algorithm and $R = (C, S)$ any run of A. If C' is an initial configuration similar to C, except for the initial states of the processes in $faulty^\star(R)$, then $R' = (C', S)$ is also a run of A.

3   Indulgence

Overview

Informally, an algorithm is *indulgent* if no process, and any point of its computation, can make any accurate prediction about the future interleaving of the processes. For instance, no process can ever declare another process as being faulty or correct.

---

[3] This conveys the idea that the interleaving is chosen by the operating system and not by the algorithm. In some sense, the operating system acts as an *adversary* that the algorithm needs to face and it is common to talk about the interleaving of the adversary.

As we discuss below, it is not trivial to capture this intuition without precluding algorithms that tolerate certain interleavings and not others. Example of these algorithms are t-(or t^*-) resilient algorithms. In such algorithms, certain interleavings are known to be impossible in advance, i.e., before the processes start any computation. As we will explain, a naive definition of indulgence would preclude such algorithms.

- Consider a first glance approach (*characterization 1*) that would declare an algorithm A indulgent if, for any partial run R of A, for any process q, A has an extension of R with an infinite number of steps by q. This clearly captures the idea that no process can, at any point of its computation (say after any partial run R) declare that some other process q is faulty, for q could still take an infinite number of steps (after R) and thus be correct. Although intuitive, this characterization is fundamentally flawed, as we discuss below.
- With characterization 1, we might consider as indulgent an algorithm that relies on the ability of a process to accurately learn that at least *one out of two* processes have failed, or learn that certain processes will perform steps in a round-robin manner, provided they perform future steps. Indeed, characterization 1 above simply says that *any* process q can still take steps in *some* extension of the partial run R. For some pair of processes q_1 and q_2, there might be no extension of R with both q_1 and q_2 taking an infinite number of steps in any arbitrary order.

  In particular, we would like indulgence to express the very fact that any *subset* of processes can still take steps after any point of the computation, i.e., after any partial run R, and in any possible order. In fact, there is an easy fix to characterization 1 that deals with this issue. It is enough to require (*characterization 2*) that, for any partial run R of A, for any subset of processes Π_i, A has an extension of R with an infinite number of steps by all processes of Π_i, in every order. As we discuss below however, this characterization raises other issues.
- Characterization 2 might unfortunately lead us to consider as indulgent an algorithm that relies on the ability for the processes to learn that some specific process *will* take steps in the future. A naive way to prevent this possibility is to also require (*characterization 3*) that, for any partial run R of an indulgent algorithm A, for any subset of processes Π_i, A has an extension of R where no process in Π_i takes any step after R. Characterization 3 however excludes algorithms that assume a threshold of correct processes. As we pointed out earlier, many indulgent algorithms [3,7,19] assume a correct threshold: in particular, they assume that every partial run has an extension where a majority of processes take an infinite number of steps.

Characterization

Very intuitively, we cope with the issues above by proposing a definition of indulgence inspired by Murphy's law, which we apply to partial runs. Basically, we declare an algorithm A indulgent if, whenever the interleaving $I(R)$ of any partial run R of A could be extended with a certain interleaving, then R also would. In other words, if the interleaving $I(R)$ of a partial run R has an extension $I' \in I(A)$, then A also has an extension R' of R with the interleaving $I(R') = I'$.

Definition (indulgence). An algorithm A is indulgent if, $\forall I_1, I_2 \in I(A)$ s.t. $I_2 \in E(I_1)$, $\forall R_1 \in A$ s.t. $I(R_1) = I_1$, $\exists R_2 \in A$ s.t. $I(R_2) = I_1$ and $I_2 \in E(I_1)$.

In other words, for any pair of interleavings I_1 and I_2 tolerated by A such that I_2 extends I_1, any partial run R_1 of A, such that $I(R_1) = I_1$, has an extension R_2 in A such that $I(R_2) = I_2$.

Basically, our definition says that no partial run R_1 can preclude any extension R_2 with interleaving I_2, provided I_2 is tolerated by A. The definition does not preclude t-resilient algorithms from being indulgent. This would not have been the case for instance with a definition that would only consider as indulgent an algorithm A such that, for any partial run R of A, for any subset of processes $\Pi_i \subset \Pi$, A has an extension R_1 of R where all processes of Π_i are correct, and an extension R_2 of R where no process in Π_i takes any step after R.

Examples

Clearly, an algorithm that makes use of a perfect failure detector [4] is not indulgent. If a process is detected to have failed in some partial run R, then R cannot be extended with an interleaving including steps of p. In fact, even an algorithm relying on an anonymously perfect failure detector is not indulgent [12]. Such a failure detector might signal that *some* process has failed, without indicating which one. When it does so in some partial run R, this indicates that it is impossible to extend R with a run where all processes are correct. Similarly, an algorithm that uses an oracle which declares some process correct, say from the start [11], would not be indulgent if the algorithm tolerates at least one interleaving where that process crashes.

An obvious class of indulgent algorithms are t-resilient asynchronous ones [9]. Such algorithms do not have any partial run providing meaningful information about the future interleaving of the processes. However, and as we explained in the introduction, indulgent algorithms do not need to be asynchronous. Algorithms that rely (only) on eventual properties (i.e., that hold only after an unknown periods of time) about the interleavings of the processes are indulgent. These include eventually synchronous algorithms [7], eventual leader-based algorithms [19], rotating coordinator-based algorithms [4], as well as algorithms that tolerate an unbounded number of timing failures [23], or assume eventual interleaving properties [21], or an eventual bound on the ratio between the delay of the fastest and the slowest communication [8].

In the following, we prove three properties of indulgent algorithms: *robustness*, *safety*, and *uniformity*. Later, we will also prove some inherent limitations of indulgent algorithms.

4 Robustness

In short, the robustness aspect (of our definition) of indulgence conveys the fact that if an algorithm A that tolerates t failures is indulgent, then the restriction of A to runs with $t-1$ failures is also indulgent. Before stating and proving this property, we define notions of extensions of an algorithm.

Let A and A' be any two algorithms.

- A' is an *extension* of A if $A \subset A'$. (Every run of A is a run of A'.) We also say in this case that A is a *restriction* of A'.
- A' is a *strict extension* of A if (a) $A \subset A'$ and (b) $\forall R \in A'$ s.t. $I(R) \in I(A)$, $R \in A$. (Every run of A' with an interleaving tolerated by A is also a run of A.) We also say in this case that A is a *strict restriction* of A'.

Proposition 1. *Every strict restriction of an indulgent algorithm is also indulgent.*

Proof. (Sketch) Consider an algorithm A that is a *strict restriction* of A'. We proceed by contradiction and assume that A' is indulgent whereas A is not.

The fact that A is not indulgent means that (a) there are two interleavings I_1 and $I_2 \in I(A)$ such that $I_2 \in E(I_1)$, (b) a partial run $R \in A$ such that $I(R) = I_1$, and (c) (*) A has no extension of R, R', such that $I(R') = I_2$.

The fact that I_1 and $I_2 \in i(A)$ means that there are two runs R_1 and $R_2 \in A$ such that $I(R_1) = I_1$ and $I(R_2) = I_2$.

Since A' is an extension of A, and R, R_1 and R_2 are (partial) runs of A, then R, R_1 and R_2 are also partial runs of A'.

Since A' is indulgent, then A has an extension R' of R such that $I(R') = I_2$.

Finally, since A' is a strict extension of A, then $R' \in A$: a contradiction with (*).

Consider an algorithm A that is t-resilient. Remember than this means that A tolerates all interleavings where at least $n - t$ processes are correct, i.e., $n - t$ processes take an infinite number of steps. The subset of all runs of A where at least $n - t - 1$ processes take an infinite number of steps is a $t - 1$-resilient algorithm A' that is a strict restriction of A. The proposition above says that if A is indulgent then so is A'. The same reasoning applies to t^*-resilient algorithms. (Note that robustness does not hold for the naive characterization 3 of indulgence discussed earlier in Section 3.)

5 Safety

The safety aspect of indulgence means, roughly speaking, that, even if an indulgent algorithm relies on some information about the interleaving of processes to solve some problem, the algorithm can only rely on this information to ensure the *liveness* part of the problem, and not its *safety*. We first recall the notions of safety and liveness.

Safety and Liveness

The specifications of a distributed computing problem are typically expressed in terms of predicates over runs, also called properties of runs. An algorithm solves a problem if those predicates hold over all runs of the algorithm.

Informally, a safety property states that *nothing bad should happen*, whereas a liveness property states that *something good should eventually happen* [17,1].

Consider a predicate P over runs and a specific run R. We say that P *holds in* R if $P(R) = true$; P does not hold in R if $P(R) = false$.

A safety property P is a predicate that satisfies the two following conditions: any run for which P does not hold has a partial run for which P does not hold; and P does not hold in every extension of a partial run where P does not hold. A liveness property P, on the other hand, is one such that any partial run has an extension for which P holds.

It was shown in [17,1] that any property can be expressed as the intersection of a safety and a liveness properties. Given a property P, possibly a set of properties (i.e., a problem), we denote by $S(P)$ the safety part of P and $L(P)$ the liveness part of P.

We capture in the following the safety aspect of indulgence through the notions of *stretched extension* and *unconscious* algorithms, which we introduce below. Let A and A' be any two algorithms.

- A' is a *stretched extension* of A if (a) A' is an extension of A and (b) $\forall R \in^\star A'$, $R \in^\star A$. (Every partial run of A' is a partial run of A.)

Notice that the notions of strict and stretched extensions are orthogonal. Algorithm A' might be a strict (resp. stretched) extension of A but not a stretched (resp. strict) extension of A.

Safety and Unconsciousness

By the very definition of safety, we immediately get the following:

Proposition 2. *If the stretched extension A' of an algorithm A solves a problem P then A' ensures $S(P)$.*

Proof. (Sketch) Assume by contradiction that A' does not ensure $S(P)$. By definition of safety, there is a partial run $R \in^\star A'$, such that $S(P)$ does not hold in R, nor in any extension of R. Because A' is a stretched extension of A, $R \in^\star A$, which implies that A does not solve P.

This property is interesting because it helps expresses the fact that, if an indulgent algorithm A solves some problem P, while relying on some information about the interleaving of the processes, then A preserves the safety part of P even if the information turns out not to be accurate. The stretched extension of A precisely captures the situation where this information is not accurate. We say that the algorithm resulting from this situation is *unconscious*.

Definition (unconsciousness). Algorithm A is *unconscious* if every run R is such that $R \in A$ if every partial run R_i of R is such that $R_i \in^\star A$.

Indulgent algorithms like in [7,19,4,23,21,8] are *conscious* because they rely on eventual information about at least one interleaving I. Any such algorithm A tolerates an interleaving I with a run $R \notin A$ such that $I(R) = I$ and all partial runs of R are in A. For instance, shared memory asynchronous algorithms are both indulgent and unconscious. Eventually synchronous algorithms are, on the other hand, indulgent but conscious. Indeed, consider a run R where every process p_i takes steps in rounds i, i^2, i^3, etc. Every partial run of R is eventually synchronous. However, R is not. Interestingly, by the definitions of the notions of stretched extensions and unconscious algorithm, we immediately get:

Proposition 3. *The stretched extension of any algorithm is an unconscious algorithm.*

For instance, the stretched extension of an eventually synchronous algorithm is asynchronous.

Proposition 2 and Proposition 3 say that if A solves some problem P while relying on some information about the interleaving of the processes (e.g., A assumes eventual synchrony), then A preserves the safety part of P even if the information turns out not to be accurate (e.g., even if the system ends up being asynchronous).

6   Uniformity

In the following, we show that indulgent algorithms are inherently *uniform*, in the intuitive sense that they are not sensitive to safety properties that restrict only the behavior of correct processes (which we call *correct-restrictions*). We will illustrate the idea of uniformity through the consensus problem and point out the fact that uniformity does not hold for algorithms that are not indulgent. Later, we will use the notion of uniformity to prove that certain problems do not have indulgent solutions. We first introduce below the notion of a *correct-restriction* of a property.

Correct Restriction of a Property

Informally, the *correct-restriction* of P, denoted $C(P)$, is the restriction of P to correct processes.

Definition (Correct-restriction). Let P be any property. We define the *correct-restriction* of P, denoted $C[P]$, as follows. For any run R, $C[P](R) = true$ if and only if $\exists R'$ such that $\forall p \in correct(R)$, $R/p = R'/p$ and $P(R') = true$.

Proposition 4. *Let P be any safety property and A any indulgent algorithm. If A satisfies $C[P]$ then A satisfies P.*

Proof. (Sketch) Let P be any safety property and A any indulgent algorithm that satisfies $C[P]$.

Assume by contradiction that A does not satisfy P. This implies that there is a run of A, say R, such that $P(R)$ is false. Because P is a safety property, there is a partial run of R, R', such that $P(R')$ is false.

By the indulgence of A, and our assumption that any interleaving has a failure-free extension, A has an extension of R', say R'', where all processes are correct.

Because P is a safety property and $P(R')$ is false, $P(R'')$ is also false. Hence, $C[P](R'')$ is false because all processes are correct in R'' and $C[P](R'') = P(R'')$. A contradiction with the fact that A satisfies $C[P]$.

Example: Consensus

An immediate corollary of Proposition 4 concerns for instance the *consensus* [9] and *uniform consensus* problems (resp. *total order broadcast* and *uniform total order broadcast*) [14]. Before stating our corollary, we recall below the consensus problem.

We assume here a set of values V. For every value $v \in V$ and every process $p \in \Pi$, there is an initial state e_p of p associated with v and e_p is no associated with any other value $v' \neq v$; v is called the initial value of p (in state e_p). Hence, each vector of n values (not necessarily different ones) correspond to an initial configuration of the system. We also assume that, among other distributed services used by the processes, a specific one models the act of *deciding* on a value. The service, called the *output* service, has an operation *output()*; when a process p invokes that operation with an input parameter v, we say that p decides v.

An algorithm A solves the consensus problem if, in any run $R = (C, S)$, the three following properties are satisfied.

- *Validity:* the value decided by any process p_i in R is the initial value of some process p_j in C.
- *Agreement:* no two processes decide different values in R;
- *Termination:* every correct process in R eventually decides in R.

Clearly, agreement and validity are safety properties whereas termination is a liveness property. Two weaker, yet orthogonal, variants of *consensus* have been studied in the literature. One, called *non-uniform consensus*, only requires that no two *correct* processes decide different values. (May be counter intuitively, this is a liveness property.) Another variant, called *k-agreement* [5], requires that the number of different values decided by all processes (in any run) is at most k.

The following is a corollary of Proposition 4.

Corollary 1. *Any indulgent algorithm that solves consensus also solves uniform consensus.*

This is not the case with non-indulgent algorithms as we explain below. Consider a system of 2 processes $\{p_1, p_2\}$ using two services: an atomic shared register and a perfect failure detector. The latter service ensures that any process is eventually informed about the failure of the other process and only if the other process has indeed failed. The idea of a non-indulgent algorithm solving non-uniform consensus is the following: process p_1 decides its initial value and then writes it in the shared register; process p_2 keeps periodically consulting its failure detector and reading the register until either (a) p_1 is declared faulty by the failure detector or (b) p_2 reads p_1's value. In the first case (a) p_2 decides its own value and in the second (b) p_2 decides the value read in the register. If both processes are correct, they both decide the value of p_1. If p_1 fails after deciding, p_2 might decide a different value.

7　Failure Sensitivity

In the following, we show that no indulgent algorithm can solve certain problems if at least one process can fail, even if this process can do so only initially, i.e., if the algorithm is 1^*-resilient. To simplify, we call a 1^*-resilient indulgent algorithm simply a 1^*-indulgent algorithm.

The problems we show impossible are those we call *failure sensitive*. In short, these are problems that resemble consensus with the particularity that the decision value might be considered valid or not depending on whether certain processes have failed. These problems include several classical problems in distributed computing like *terminating reliable broadcast*, *interactive consistency* and *non-blocking atomic commit* [14].

To prove our impossibility, we proceed as follows. We first define a simple failure sensitive problem, which we call *failure signal*, and which we show is impossible with a 1^*-indulgent algorithm. Then we show that any solution to *terminating reliable broadcast*, *interactive consistency* or *non-blocking atomic commit* solves *failure signal*: in this sense, *failure signal* is weaker than all those problems which are thus impossible with a 1^*-indulgent algorithm.

The Failure Signal Problem

In failure signal, just like in consensus, the goal is for processes to decide on a value based on some initial value. As we explain however, unlike consensus, no agreement is required and a process can decide different values.

More specifically, in failure signal, a specific designated process p has an initial binary value, 0 or 1, as part of p's initial state. The two following properties need to be satisfied: (1) every correct process eventually decides and (2) no process (a) decides 1 if p proposes 0, nor (b) decides 0 if p proposes 1 and p is correct.

Interestingly, we prove the impossibility of *failure signal* by reduction to our *uniformity* result (Proposition 4). We prove by contradiction that, if there is a 1^*-indulgent algorithm that solves failure signal, then there is an algorithm that ensures the corrected-restriction of a safety property, without ensuring the actual property.

Proposition 5. *There is no solution to failure signal using a 1*-indulgent algorithm.*

Proof. (Sketch) Assume by contradiction that there is a 1*-indulgent algorithm that solves failure signal. Consider the designated process p and some other process q. (Remember that we assume a system of at least two processes).

Define property P such that $P(R)$ is *false* in every run R where p proposes 1 and q decides 0 and *true* in all other runs. By definition of a correct-restriction, $C[P]$ is *false* in runs where p proposes 1, q decides 0 and all processes are correct, and *true* in all other runs.

We now show that if there is a 1*-indulgent algorithm that solves failure signal, then A ensures $C[P]$ but not P.

It is easy to show that A ensures $C[P]$. Indeed, because A solves *failure signal*, in any run R where p proposes 1 and all processes are correct, all processes decide 1.

We now show that A does not ensure P. Remember that A is a 1*-resilient algorithm: A tolerates at least one initial failure. Consider a run R where p proposes 0 and does not take any step whereas all other processes are correct (p initially fails). Any 1*-resilient algorithm that solves the failure signal problem has such a run R. In this run, every process that decides decides 0.

Consider now a run R' with the same schedule as R, except that p initially proposes 1 (and fails before taking any step). Such a run R is also a run of A and, because no process else that p, which fails initially, can distinguish R from R', all processes but p decide 0. This run R' is thus a run of A and $P(R')$ is false. This contradicts the uniformity of A.

Example 1: Terminating Reliable Broadcast

In *terminating reliable broadcast*, also called *Byzantine generals*, a specific designated process is supposed to *broadcast* one message $m \neq \perp$ that is a priori unknown to the other processes. (In our model, the process invokes a specific service with m as a parameter.) In a run R where the sender p does not fail, all correct processes are supposed to eventually receive m. If the sender fails, then the processes might or not receive m. If they do not, then they receive a specific message $\perp$ indicating that the sender has failed. More specifically, the following properties need to be satisfied. (1) Every correct process eventually receive one message; (2) No process receives more than one message; (3) No process receives a message different from $\perp$ or the message broadcast by the sender; (4) No two processes receive different messages; and (5) No process receives $\perp$ if the sender is correct.

The following is a corollary of Proposition 5.

Corollary 2. *No 1*-resilient algorithm solves terminating reliable broadcast.*

Proof. (Sketch) We simply show how any solution to *terminating reliable broadcast* can be used to solve *failure signal*. Assume there is an algorithm A that solves terminating reliable broadcast. Whenever the designated process p (in failure signal) proposes a value, 0 or 1, p broadcasts a message with that value to all, using *terminating reliable broadcast*. Any process that receives the message delivers the value in the message (0 or 1). A process that delivers $\perp$ decides 0.

Example 2: Non-blocking Atomic Commit

In non-blocking atomic commit, processes do all start with initial values 0 or 1, and are supposed to eventually decide one of these values. The following properties need to be satisfied. (1) Every correct process eventually decides one value (0 or 1); (2) no process decides two values; (3) No two processes decide different values; (4) No process decides 1 if some process proposes 0 and no process decides 0 if all processes propose 1 and no process fails.

The following is a corollary of Proposition 5.

Corollary 3. *No 1^*-resilient algorithm solves non-blocking atomic commit.*

Proof. (Sketch) Assume there is a solution to non-blocking atomic commit. We show how to obtain a solution to failure signal. All processes but p propose 1. Process p proposes exactly its initial value (of failure signal) to non-blocking atomic commit. The processes decide the output of non-blocking atomic commit. Because all processes but p propose 1, the decision can be 1 only if p proposes 1, and can be 0 only if p fails or proposes 0.

Example 3: Interactive Consistency

In interactive consistency, processes do all start with initial values, and are supposed to eventually decide a n-vector of values. The following properties need to be satisfied. (1) Every correct process eventually decides one vector; (2) No process decides two vectors; (3) No two processes decide different vectors; (4) If a process decides a vector v, then $v[i]$ should contain the initial value of p_i if p_i is correct. Otherwise, if p_i is faulty, $v[i]$ can be the initial value of p_i or $\perp$.

The following is a corollary of Proposition 5.

Corollary 4. *No 1^*-indulgent algorithm solves interactive consistency.*

Proof. (Sketch) Assume there is a solution to interactive consistency. Assume p is p_i. We show how to obtain a solution to failure signal. All processes propose to interactive consistency their identity, except p which proposes its initial value of failure signal. If a process q outputs a vector v such that $v[i] \neq \perp$, then q decides $v[i]$. Else, q decides 0.

8   Divergence

We now capture, in a general way, the traditional partitioning argument that is frequently used in distributed computing, e.g., [2]. This argument was traditionally used for message passing asynchronous algorithms where half of the processes can fail. In this case, the system can partition into two disjoint subsets that progress concurrently. We precisely state that argument here in the context of indulgent algorithms using timeless services which, as we pointed out, is a wider class than the class of asynchronous ones using message passing, and for systems with several possible partitions (the case with two partitions is just one particular case).

Definition (divergent property). We call a $k-divergent$ property P a property such that for any k disjoint non-empty subsets of processes Π_1, $\Pi_2,..\Pi_k$, there is a configuration C such that every k runs R_1, $R_2,..R_k$ of A, such that R_i involves only processes from Π_i, have respective partial runs R'_1, $R'_2,..,R'_k$ for which $S(P(R'_1.R'_2...R'_k))$ is false.

Remember that $S(P)$ denotes the safety part of P. We call configuration C the *critical configuration* for Π_1, $\Pi_2,..\Pi_k$ with respect to P. Note that, by construction, any property that is $k-$divergent is also $k+1-$divergent.

To intuitively illustrate the idea of a 2$-$divergent property, consider the specification of consensus in a system of 2 processes p_1 and p_2. Consider the initial configuration where p_1 has initial value 1 and p_2 has initial value 2. Starting from C, every run R_1 involving only p_1 eventually decides 1 and every run R_2 involving only p_2 eventually decides 2. Consider the partial run R'_1 of R_1 composed of all steps of R_1 until the decision of p_1 (1) is made, and the partial run R'_2 of R_2 until the decision of p_2 (2) is made. Clearly, the safety of consensus (in particular *agreement*) is violated in $R'_1.R'_2$.

Definition (timeless service). We say that an algorithm A uses *timeless* services if for any two partial runs R_1 and R_2 of A starting from the same initial configurations C and involving disjoint subsets of processes, if A has an extension of R_1, $R_1.R'_1$ such that $I(R'_1) = I(R_2)$, then $R_1.R_2$ is also a run of A.

Examples of timeless services include sequentially consistent shared objects [18] as well as reliable message passing or broadcast primitives [14]. To illustrate the underlying idea, consider an algorithm A in a system of 2 processes p_1 and p_2 using a message passing primitive which ensures that any message sent from process p_1 to process p_2 is eventually received by p_2, provided p_2 is correct. Assume that A has a partial run R_1 where p_1 executes steps alone and a partial run R_2 where p_2 executes steps alone. (Clearly, p_2 cannot have received any message from p_1 in R_2.) Provided that A does not preclude the possibility of p_2 to execute steps alone after R_1, and because there is no guarantee on the time after which the message of p_1 arrives at p_2, then $R_1.R_2$, the composition of both partial runs, is also a possible run of A. This captures the intuition that the message of p_1 can be arbitrarily delayed.

Proposition 6. *No $(n - \lfloor n/x \rfloor)$-indulgent algorithm ensures a $x-$divergent property using $x-$timeless services.*

Proof. (Sketch) Assume by contradiction that there is a $(n - \lfloor n/x \rfloor)$-resilient indulgent algorithm A that ensures a $x-divergent$ property P using *timeless* services.

Divide the set of processes Π of the system into k subsets $\Pi_1, \Pi_2,..\Pi_x$ of size at least $\lfloor n/x \rfloor$ such that all the subsets are disjoint and their union is Π. Consider the critical configuration C for $\Pi_1, \Pi_2,..\Pi_x$ with respect to P.

Because the algorithm A is $(n - \lfloor n/x \rfloor)$-resilient, and each Pi_i is of size at least $\lfloor n/x \rfloor$, then A has x runs $R_1, R_2,..R_x$ such that each such R_i involves only processes in Π_i, i.e., only processes of P_i take steps in R_i and every such R_i start from C.

Because P is $x-divergent$, these runs have respective partial runs $R'_1, R'_2,..,R'_k$ such that $S(P(R'_1.R'_2...R'_k))$ is false. We need to show that $R'_1.R'_2...R'_k$ is also a partial run of A. Because $S(P(R'_1.R'_2...R'_k))$ is false, this would contradict the very fact that A ensures P.

We first show that $R'_1.R'_2$ is a partial run of A. By the assumption that A is $(n - \lfloor n/x \rfloor)$-resilient, there is a partial run R_0 of A such that $I(R_0) = I(R'_1.R'_2)$. (Remember that a x-resilient algorithm is one that tolerates *all* interleavings where at least $n - x$ processes appear infinitely often).

By the indulgence of A, there is a partial run R''_2 such that $R'_1.R''_2$ is a partial run of A and $I(R'_1.R''_2) = I(R'_1.R'_2)$. By the assumption that A uses timeless services, $R'_1.R'_2$ is also a partial run of A. By a simple induction, $R'_1.R'_2...R'_k$ is also a run of A.

Because $S(P(R'_1.R'_2...R'_k))$ is false, P is false in every extension of $R'_1.R'_2...R'_k$: contradiction.

The following is a corollary of Proposition 6.

Corollary 5. *No $(n - \lfloor n/2 \rfloor)$-indulgent algorithm using message passing or sequentially consistent objects can implement a safe register.*

There are non-indulgent algorithms that implement a safe register with any number of failures and using only message passing. For instance, an algorithm assuming a perfect failure detector. The idea is to make sure every value written is stored at all processes that are not detected to have crashed and the value read can then simply be a local value. On the other hand, Corollary 5 means that an algorithm using eventually perfect failure detectors, and possibly also sequentially consistent registers or message passing, cannot implement a safe register if two disjoint subsets of processes can fail. This clearly also applies to problems like consensus.

The following is also a corollary of Proposition 6.

Corollary 6. *No $(n - \lfloor n/k \rfloor)$-indulgent algorithm using message passing or sequentially consistent objects can solve k-set agreement.*

9   Concluding Remarks

This paper presents a general characterization of indulgence. The characterization does not require any failure detector machinery [4], or timing assumptions [7]. It is furthermore not restricted to a specific communication scheme.

Instead, we consider a general model of distributed computation where processes might be communicating using any kind of services, including shared objects, be they simple read-write registers [18], or more sophisticated objects like compare-and-swap or consensus [15], as well as message passing channels and broadcast primitives [14].

May be interestingly, our characterization of indulgence abstracts the essence of the concept of *unreliable failure detection*. This concept, informally introduced in [4], captures the idea that failure detectors do not need to be accurate to be useful in solving interesting problems. This concept has however never been precisely defined.[4] Using our characterization, we can precisely define it by simply stating that a failure detector is *unreliable* if any algorithm that uses that failure detector is indulgent.

Generalizing the concept of a failure detector, one could also consider oracles that inform a process that certain processes will be scheduled before others. (Say an oracle that declares a run as being eventually synchronous.) Our characterization of indulgence also helps captures what it means for such oracles to be unreliable.

To conclude, it is important to notice that we focused in this paper on the computability of indulgent algorithms and did not discuss their complexity. There are many interesting open problems in measuring the inherent overhead of indulgence. This goes first through defining appropriate frameworks to measure the complexity of indulgent algorithms, e.g., [6,16,25].

References

1. Bowen Alpern and Fred B. Schneider. Defining liveness. *Information Processing Letters*, 21(4):181–185, October 1985.
2. Hagit Attiya, Amotz Bar-Noy, and Danny Dolev. Sharing memory robustly in message passing systems. *Journal of the ACM*, 42(2):124–142, January 1995.
3. Tushar Deepak Chandra, Vassos Hadzilacos, and Sam Toueg. The weakest failure detector for solving consensus. *Journal of the ACM*, 43(4):685–722, July 1996.
4. Tushar Deepak Chandra and Sam Toueg. Unreliable failure detectors for reliable distributed systems. *Journal of the ACM*, 43(2):225–267, March 1996.
5. Soma Chauduri. More choices allow more faults: Set consensus problems in totally asynchronous systems. *Information and Computation*, 105(1):132–158, 1993.
6. Partha Dutta and Rachid Guerraoui. The inherent price of indulgence. In *PODC '02: Proceedings of the annual ACM symposium on Principles of distributed computing*, pages 88–97, 2002.
7. Cynthia Dwork, Nancy A. Lynch, and Larry Stockmeyer. Consensus in the presence of partial synchrony. *Journal of the ACM*, 35(2):288–323, April 1988.
8. Christof Fetzer, Ulrich Schmid, and Martin Susskraut. On the possibility of consensus in asynchronous systems with finite average response times. In *International Conference on Distributed Computing Systems*, pages 271–280. ieee, 2005.
9. Michael J. Fischer, Nancy A. Lynch, and Michael S. Paterson. Impossibility of distributed consensus with one faulty process. *Journal of the ACM*, 32(2):374–382, April 1985.

---

[4] Except in [10] for the message passing context.

10. Rachid Guerraoui. Indulgent algorithms. In *Proceedings of the Nineteenth Annual ACM Symposium on Principles of Distributed Computing, Portland, Oregon, USA*, pages 289–297. ACM, July 2000.
11. Rachid Guerraoui. On the hardness of failure sensitive agreement problems. *Information Processing Letters*, 79, 2001.
12. Rachid Guerraoui. Non-blocking atomic commit in asynchronous distributed systems with failure detectors. *Distributed Computing*, 15(1):17–25, 2002.
13. Rachid Guerraoui and Michel Raynal. The information structure of indulgent consensus. *IEEE Trans. Computers*, 53(4):453–466, 2004.
14. Vassos Hadzilacos and Sam Toueg. Fault-tolerant broadcasts and related problems. In Sape J. Mullender, editor, *Distributed Systems*, chapter 5, pages 97–145. Addison-Wesley, 1993.
15. Maurice Herlihy. Wait-free synchronization. *ACM Transactions on Programming Languages and Systems*, 13(1):123–149, January 1991.
16. Idit Keidar and Alex Shraer. Timeliness, failure detectors and consensus peformance. In *PODC '06: Proceedings of the annual ACM symposium on Principles of distributed computing*, New York, NY, USA, 2006. ACM Press.
17. Leslie Lamport. Proving the correctness of multiprocessor programs. *Transactions on software engineering*, 3(2):125–143, March 1977.
18. Leslie Lamport. How to make a multiprocessor computer that correct executes multiprocess programs. *IEEE Transactions on Computers*, C-28(9):690–691, September 1979.
19. Leslie Lamport. The Part-Time parliament. *ACM Transactions on Computer Systems*, 16(2):133–169, May 1998.
20. Nancy A. Lynch. *Distributed Algorithms*. Morgan Kaufmann, 1996.
21. Achour Moustefaoui, Michel Raynal, and Corentin Travers. Crash-resilient time-free eventual leadership. In *Proceedings of the International Symposium on Reliable Distributed Systems*, pages 208–217. IEEE, 2004.
22. Livia Sampaio and Francisco Brasileiro. Adaptive indulgent consensus. In *Proceedings of the International Conference on Dependable Systems and Networks (DSN)*, pages 422–431, 2005.
23. Gadi Taubenfeld. Computing in the presence of timing failures. In *Proceedings of theInternational Conference on Distributed Computing Systems (DCS)*, 2007.
24. Pedro Vicente and Luis Rodrigues. An indulgent uniform total order broadcast algorithm with optimistic delivery. In *Proceedings of the International Symposium on Reliable Distributed Systems (SRDS)*, pages 92–80, 2002.
25. Piotr Zielinski. Optimistically terminating consensus. In *Proceedings of the Symposium on Parallel and Distributed Computing*, 2006.

Coverage, Connectivity, and Fault Tolerance Measures of Wireless Sensor Networks

Habib M. Ammari and Sajal K. Das

Center for Research in Wireless Mobility and Networking (CReWMaN)
Department of Computer Science and Engineering
The University of Texas at Arlington, Arlington, TX 76019, USA
{ammari, das}@cse.uta.edu

Abstract. Connectivity and sensing coverage are two fundamental concepts in the design of wireless sensor networks (WSNs). In this paper, we investigate the relationship between coverage and connectivity for *k-covered WSNs* (*k*CWSN), where every point in a field of interest is covered by at least k sensors. Furthermore, we compute the connectivity of *k*CWSN based on the degree of sensing coverage. We also propose measures of fault tolerance for *k*CWSN based on network connectivity and sensing coverage. Random distributions of the sensors in a field have been widely used in most of sensor networking protocols, in spite of the fact that these deployment techniques do not always provide complete, void-free coverage. On the contrary, we consider both deterministic and random sensor deployment strategies to meet coverage degree requirements of sensing applications. Using our *Augmented Equilateral Triangle* (AET) model, we prove that if the sensing coverage degree is k and $R \geq 2 \times r$, the network connectivity is higher than k . Precisely, our analysis of the geometric properties of deterministic sensor deployment strategies, demonstrates that sensing k-coverage and $R \geq \sqrt{3} \times r$ yield *k*CWSN connectivity that is higher than k. These findings are of practical use for network designers to build up sensing applications with prescribed degrees of sensing coverage, network connectivity and fault tolerance.

Keywords: *k*CWSN, coverage, connectivity, fault tolerance, measures.

1 Introduction

Sensing coverage is an important issue in the design of wireless sensor networks (WSNs), which does not exist in traditional ad hoc networks. It is a good indicator of the quality of surveillance of a field of interest (*field hereafter*) offered by a WSN. As pointed out in [13], coverage is a measure of the quality of service of a WSN. For several sensing applications, a full sensing coverage is one of the main requirements, which demands that every location in a field be covered by at least one sensor. Moreover, to cope with the problem of faulty sensors and guarantee network functionality, duplicate coverage of the same region is an appealing solution through appropriate sensor redundancy strategies. Sensor redundancy is

A.K. Datta and M. Gradinariu (Eds.): SSS 2006, LNCS 4280, pp. 35–49, 2006.
© Springer-Verlag Berlin Heidelberg 2006

strongly related to the *degree of sensing coverage* requested by sensing applications. Another fundamental aspect of WSNs is vertex connectivity (*connectivity* hereafter) by which the sensors can mutually interact through communication paths. Network connectivity implies the existence of at least one communication path between any pair of sensors. Similarly, some sensing applications are required to be fault tolerant, where any pair of sensors is connected by multiple communication paths. Hence, network fault tolerance is tightly dependent on the *degree of network connectivity*. In this paper, network connectivity refers to vertex connectivity.

While sensing coverage depends on the *sensing range* of the sensors and is an inherent property of all the locations in a field, network connectivity relates to the *transmission range* of the sensors and is a characteristic inherently associated with the locations of the sensors. Notice that the concepts of sensing coverage and network connectivity are not totally orthogonal. Wang, *et al.* [17] proved that sensing coverage implies network connectivity provided that $R \geq 2r$. They also proved that if the degree of sensing coverage provided by the network is k, the network connectivity is also k.

1.1 Contributions

In this paper, we consider isotropic sensors, where the sensing and transmission ranges of the sensors are modeled by disks of radii r and R, respectively. However, we consider both cases of homogeneous and heterogeneous sensors in our study of sensing coverage, connectivity and fault tolerance of WSNs in a unified framework. Precisely, we focus on both deterministic and random sensor deployment strategies, which provide us with a meaningful tool to perform a fine-grained analysis of the relationships between sensing coverage, network connectivity, and fault tolerance of WSNs. Using our proposed *Augmented Equilateral Triangle* (AET) model to guarantee sensing k-coverage, we prove that when the degree of sensing coverage is k and $R \geq 2r$ is satisfied, the network connectivity is larger than k. Furthermore, through analysis of the geometric properties of deterministic sensor placement strategies, we prove that when sensing coverage is guaranteed and the relationship, $R \geq \sqrt{3}r$, holds, the network connectivity is guaranteed. Similarly, we prove that sensing k-coverage and $R \geq \sqrt{3}r$ imply network connectivity higher than k. We also present measures of network connectivity for homogeneous and heterogeneous kCWSN based on the degree of sensing coverage and derive the corresponding network fault tolerance. We also propose a new measure of fault tolerance for kCWSN, called *field fault tolerance*, which helps maintain sensing coverage in spite of the sensor failures.

The remainder of this paper is organized as follows. Section 2 reviews related work on the combination of coverage and connectivity as well as fault tolerance of WSNs. Section 3 gives a few definitions. Section 4 discusses different relationships between the concepts of sensing coverage and network connectivity, and computes fault tolerance measures of kCWSN based on these two concepts. Section 5 concludes the paper.

2 Related Work

This section discusses existing studies on the combination of sensing coverage and network connectivity as well as fault tolerance of WSNs.

Ai and Abouzeid [1] proposed a directional sensors-based approach for sensor network coverage. While the coverage area of isotropic sensors depends on whether the event or target is within the sensing range of the sensors, the coverage region of a directional sensor depends on the location and the orientation of the sensors. Adlakha and Srivastava Cortes, et al. [3] proposed adaptive, distributed, and asynchronous coverage algorithms for mobile sensing networks. Cardei and Wu [4] surveyed different approaches addressing energy-efficient coverage problems. Du and Lin [7] proposed a differentiated coverage algorithm for heterogeneous sensor networks as different network areas may require different degrees of sensing coverage. Li, et al. [12] proposed efficient distributed algorithms to optimally solve the best-coverage problem with the least energy consumption. Ravelomanana [14] investigated several fundamental characteristics of randomly deployed wireless sensor networks regarding transmission and sensing range for connectivity and coverage in three-dimensional sensor networks. Shakkottai, et al. [15] gave necessary and sufficient conditions for a 1-covered, 1-connected wireless sensor grid network. A variety of algorithms have been proposed to maintain connectivity and coverage in large wireless sensor networks. Zhang and Hou [18] proposed a distributed algorithm, called *Optimal Geographical Density Control* (OGDC), to keep a smallest number of active sensors in a WSN regardless of the relationship between transmission and sensing ranges. Tian and Georganas [16] improved on the work of Wang, et al. [17] and Zhang and Hou [18] by proving that if the original network is connected and the identified active nodes can cover the same region as all the original nodes, then the network formed by the active nodes is connected when the transmission range is at least twice the sensing range. A more comprehensive survey on connectivity and coverage issues in WSNs can be found in [8]. Also, for more details about coverage processes, the interested reader is referred to [10]. Gupta, et al. [9] proposed algorithms for self-organization of a sensor network as a response to a query in order to reduce the communication cost incurred by its execution. Datta, et al. [6] proposed two self-stabilizing algorithms to the problem of minimal connected sensor cover [9]. These approaches were shown to be self-configuring and self-healing. Furthermore, the faults are contained within the neighborhood of the faulty nodes. Li and Hou [11] proposed centralized and localized fault-tolerant topology control protocols for WSNs based on a generalized version of Kruskal's algorithm to construct k-connected spanning subgraphs. Zhou, et al. [19] proposed a distributed and localized algorithm using the concept of the kth-order Voronoi diagram to provide fault tolerance and extend the network lifetime, while maintaining a required degree of coverage. Chelius, et al. [5] proposed an approach that considers both the transmission and reception costs in the evaluation of the energy consumption of a broadcasting task. They also presented lower and upper bounds on the energy consumption for covering a given region of the plane.

3 Definitions

This section gives useful terms to investigate different relationships between sensing coverage and connectivity and compute fault tolerance of kCWSN. Throughout this paper, we use the terms *sensor* and *node* interchangeably.

Definition 1 (Transmission range and neighbor set). *The transmission range of a sensor s_i is modeled as a disk of radius R_i including its boundary. A sensor s_j is said to be a neighbor of s_i if and only if $\delta(s_i, s_j) \leq R_i$, where $\delta(s_i, s_j)$ is the Euclidean distance between s_i and s_j. The neighbor set of s_i is denoted by $N(s_i)$.*

Definition 2 (Sensing range). *The sensing range of a sensor s_i is modeled as a disk of radius r_i including its boundary. A point p in a field Γ is said to be covered by a sensor s_i if and only if $\delta(s_i, p) \leq r_i$.*

Definition 3 (Homogeneous and heterogeneous sensors). *Two sensors s_i and s_j are said to be* homogeneous *if and only if they have the same sensing and transmission capabilities, i.e., $r_i = r_j$ and $R_i = R_j$. Otherwise, s_i and s_j are said to be* heterogeneous. *A WSN is said to be* homogeneous *if and only if all the sensors are homogeneous. Otherwise, it is said to be* heterogeneous.

Definition 4 (Communication graph). *A communication graph of a homogeneous (heterogeneous) WSN is an undirected (directed) graph $G = (S, E)$, where S is the set of vertices or sensors and E is the set of (directed) edges or links between sensors. Thus, $(s_i, s_j) \in E$ if $s_i, s_j \in S$ and s_j is a neighbor of s_i.*

Definition 5 (Mutually connected). *Two sensors $s_i, s_j \in S$ are said to be* mutually connected *in a communication graph $G = (S, E)$ if and only if $(s_i, s_j) \in E$ and $(s_j, s_i) \in E$.*

Definition 6 (k-coverage). *Let A be a geographical area of a field Γ and S_k a set of k sensors. The region A is said to be* k-covered *if and only if any point $p \in A$ belongs to the intersection of the sensing range of all the k sensors in S_k.*

Definition 7 (Vertex connectivity and fault tolerance). *The* vertex connectivity *(or* connectivity*) of a communication graph $G = (S, E)$ is equal to K if and only if G can be disconnected by the removal of at least K nodes. The* fault tolerance *of G (or the underlying WSN), denoted by $\eta(G)$, is computed as $\eta(G) = K - 1$.*

Definition 8 (Boundary and interior sensors). *A* boundary *sensor is a sensor whose sensing range does not lie entirely inside a field Γ. An* interior *sensor is a sensor whose entire sensing range lies inside the field Γ.*

Definition 9 (Width of a geographical area). *Let A be a closed convex area. The* width *of A, denoted by $w(A)$, is the maximum distance between parallel lines that bound it.*

4 Measuring Fault Tolerance of kCWSN

This section discusses optimal sensor deployment strategies to guarantee sensing k-coverage and computes connectivity and fault tolerance measures of kCWSN.

4.1 Why Is kCWSN Connectivity Higher Than k?

The approach used by Wang, et al. [17] to prove that a kCWSN is k-connected has a few shortcomings. To compute the connectivity of kCWSN, Wang, et al. [17] assumed that there are k coinciding sensors located at one point, which lies on the sensing range of another sensor, s_i, placed at one corner of a field. Notice that this assumption is not realistic in real-world sensor network setups. They also assumed that there is no other sensor whose sensing range intersects with that of s_i. This means that the closest sensors to s_i should be located at a distance equal to at least $2r + d$, where $d > 0$. For instance, consider a field which is a quarter of a circle of radius $2r$. If we apply Wang, et al.'s strategy, the field cannot be fully covered. Thus, sensing k-coverage of the network is not guaranteed. Otherwise, more sensors need to be thrown in the field and hence the actual network connectivity is larger than k. Also, if the field is just a circle of radius r, then it is impossible to throw k non-coinciding sensors in the field to achieve sensing k-coverage. Thus, Wang, et al.'s approach cannot always produce a connected kCWSN. Our results prove that the connectivity of kCWSN is larger than k and hence the network fault tolerance is higher than $k - 1$.

4.2 Homogeneous Wireless Sensor Networks

How Is Sensing k-Coverage Achieved? To guarantee sensing k-coverage, we should compute the maximum size of a geographical area, denoted by A_{max}, of a field Γ that is guaranteed to be k-covered. First, we prove theorem 1 which characterizes the width of any sensing k-covered area of a field, where $k \geq 3$.

Theorem 1 (Width of sensing k-covered areas). *If a geographical area A of a field Γ is k-covered with $k \geq 3$, then the width of A satisfies $w(A) \leq r$.*

Proof. Each point $q \in A$ is k-covered if $\delta(s_i, q) \leq r$, for all $1 \leq i \leq k$. For any pair of sensors s_i and s_j covering A, the maximum distance between s_i and s_j is r so that any location in A is covered by k sensors. Otherwise, there must be a pair of sensors s_i' and s_j' such that $\delta(s_i', s_j') > r$, meaning that there is at least one location that is not covered by both sensors at the same time. This contradicts the hypothesis that any $q \in A$ is covered by all k sensors, and in particular by s_i' and s_j'. Thus, the width of the region A cannot exceed r. □

Lemma 1 states a necessary and sufficient condition for the intersection of the sensing ranges of k sensors to be not empty.

Lemma 1 (Non-empty k-covered area). *Let Γ be a field covered by a homogeneous WSN. Assume $k \geq 3$ and let S_k be a set of k sensors. The area simultaneously covered by the k sensors in S_k is not empty if and only if the area simultaneously covered by any three sensors in S_k is not empty.*

Proof. " $\Rightarrow$ " Let A_k be an area simultaneously covered by k sensors in S_k and $D_r(s_i)$ the sensing range (disk of radius r) of the sensor s_i. Mathematically, $A_k = \cap_{1 \leq i \leq k} D_r(s_i)$. By definition of the intersection operator and since $A_k \neq \emptyset$, it implies that the intersection of any subset $S_{k'} \subseteq S_k$ of sensing ranges of k' sensors is not empty, where $k' \leq k$. In particular, this holds for $k' = 3$ and hence the area simultaneously covered by any three sensors in S_k is not empty.

" $\Leftarrow$ " Assume that the area covered by any three sensors in S_k is not empty. We proceed using a proof by construction. There are $\binom{k}{3}$ ways of choosing three sensors from the set S_k of k sensors, i.e., $S_k = \{s_1, ..., s_k\}$. Let $A_j = \cap_{1 \leq i \leq j} D_r(s_i)$ be the intersection of the sensing ranges of j distinct sensors. The case of three sensors is trivial, i.e., $A_3 = \cap_{1 \leq i \leq 3} D_r(s_i) \neq \emptyset$. Without loss of generality, we can build the sets, A_j, in an incremental manner by considering the next sensor in set, S_k. Consider the intersection of the sensing ranges of four sensors, i.e., $A_4 = \cap_{1 \leq i \leq 4} D_r(s_i)$, which can be rewritten as $A_4 = A_3 \cap D_r(s_4)$. There are four sets of three distinct sensors out of four sensors. By hypothesis, we have $D_r(s_{i1}) \cap D_r(s_{i2}) \cap D_r(s_{i3}) \neq \emptyset$, for any subset $\{s_{i1}, s_{i2}, s_{i3}\} \subset \{s_1, s_2, s_3, s_4\}$ with $s_{i1} \neq s_{i2} \neq s_{i3}$. In particular, $D_r(s_4) \cap D_r(s_{i1}) \cap D_r(s_{i2}) \neq \emptyset$, for any subset $\{s_{i1}, s_{i2}\} \subset \{s_1, s_2, s_3\}$. Using the hypothesis that $A_3 \neq \emptyset$, this implies that $A_4 = A_3 \cap D_r(s_4) \neq \emptyset$. We repeat the same reasoning for all sets A_j, $5 \leq j \leq k$. With the last set $A_k = \cap_{1 \leq i \leq k} D_r(s_i)$, we obtain $A_k \neq \emptyset$. Thus, the intersection of the sensing ranges of k sensors is not empty. $\square$

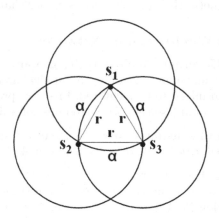

Fig. 1. Augmented Equilateral Triangle (AET) model

Theorem 2 (Maximum size of k-covered area). *Let $k \geq 3$, S_k a set of k sensors whose sensing range is r, and A a geographical area of a field Γ. The maximum size of A, denoted by $A_{max}(r)$, which is guaranteed to be simultaneously covered by all the sensors of S_k, is given by $A_{max}(r) = (\pi - \sqrt{3})\frac{r^2}{2}$.*

Proof. Let A be the intersection area of the sensing ranges of k sensors. From theorem 1 and using the Venn diagram given in Fig. 1, the maximum size of the intersection of the sensing ranges of the sensors s_1, s_2, and s_3, called *augmented equilateral triangle* and denoted by AET_r, is obtained when the sensors are symmetrically located from each other so that the distance between any pair of sensors is equal to their sensing range, r. Hence, the center of the sensing range of each sensor is located at the intersection of the other two. We refer to this model as the *Augmented Equilateral Triangle* (AET) model. Thus, The maximum area size of A is upper-bounded by the area of AET_r, which is given by $A_{max}(r) = A_1 + 3A_2 = (\pi - \sqrt{3})\frac{r^2}{2}$, where $A_1 = \frac{\sqrt{3}}{4}r^2$ is the area of the central equilateral triangle of side r and $A_2 = (\frac{\pi}{6} - \frac{\sqrt{3}}{4})r^2$ is the area of each of the circular segments delimited by an arc α and the corresponding side of the equilateral triangle. $\qquad\square$

The maximum size of a k-covered area, say A, is $A_{max}(r)$. Indeed, the sensors located at the boundary of A can only sense the locations within distance r from them. Corollary 2, which follows from theorem 2, computes the *node spatial density* of a homogeneous kCWSN under the assumption of a uniform sensor distribution.

Corollary 1 (Node spatial density). *Assume a uniform sensor distribution. The node spatial density of a homogeneous kCWSN, denoted by $\rho(r,k)$, is given by $\rho(r,k) = \frac{2k}{(\pi-\sqrt{3})r^2}$, where r is the sensing range of the sensors and $k \geq 3$.*

Proof. To achieve k-coverage, any area of the field Γ should be k-covered and in particular the AET_r area (theorem 2). Thus, k sensors should be deployed in AET_r and hence the node spatial density is equal to $\rho(r,k) = \frac{2k}{(\pi-\sqrt{3})r^2}$. $\qquad\square$

Computing Fault Tolerance of Homogeneous kCWSN. Lemma 2 computes the minimum size of the neighbor sets of interior and boundary sensors for guaranteeing sensing k-coverage.

Lemma 2 (Neighbor set size). *A field Γ is k-covered if the minimum size of the neighbor sets of interior and boundary sensors s_i and s_b, respectively, are given by $|N_{min}(s_i)| = \lceil \frac{8\pi}{\pi-\sqrt{3}}k - 1 \rceil$ and $|N_{min}(s_b)| = \lceil \frac{2\pi}{\pi-\sqrt{3}}k - 1 \rceil$.*

Proof. From corollary 1, the size of the neighbor set of an interior sensor, s_i, which should be an integer, is given by $|N(s_i)| = \lceil \frac{2k}{(\pi-\sqrt{3})r^2}\pi R^2 - 1 \rceil$. Since $R \geq 2r$, the minimum size of the neighbor set of s_i is $|N_{min}(s_i)| = \lceil \frac{8\pi}{\pi-\sqrt{3}}k - 1 \rceil$. Similarly, the minimum size of the neighbor set of a boundary sensor, s_b, located at one of the corners of the field Γ is $|N_{min}(s_b)| = \lceil \frac{2\pi}{\pi-\sqrt{3}}k - 1 \rceil$. $\qquad\square$

Theorem 3 computes the minimum numbers of nodes of a homogeneous connected kCWSN whose removal disconnect boundary and interior sensors.

Theorem 3 (Fault tolerance of homogeneous kCWSN). *Assume a uniform node spatial density. The fault tolerance of a connected homogeneous kCWSN with $k \geq 3$ and $R \geq 2r$ is given by $\kappa_b(G) - 1 \leq \eta(G) \leq \kappa_i(G) - 1$, where $\kappa_b(G) = \lceil \frac{2\pi}{\pi-\sqrt{3}}k - 1 \rceil$ and $\kappa_i(G) = \lceil \frac{8\pi}{\pi-\sqrt{3}}k - 1 \rceil$ are the minimum numbers of sensors whose removal disconnect boundary and interior sensors, respectively.*

Proof. Since we are interested in lower and upper bounds on network fault tolerance, we consider the following two extreme cases. Let s_b be a boundary sensor
located at one of the corners of a square field Γ and consider $R = 2r$. The
network could be disconnected by splitting it into at least two components, one
of them is trivial and containing s_b. To do so, all the neighbors of s_b should be
removed. By lemma 2, the size of the neighbor set of s_b is $|N(s_b)| = \lceil \frac{2\pi}{\pi-\sqrt{3}}k - 1 \rceil$.
Thus, a lower bound on network connectivity is given by $\kappa_b(G) = \lceil \frac{2\pi}{\pi-\sqrt{3}}k - 1 \rceil$.
To compute an upper bound on network connectivity, consider an interior sen-
sor, s_i. Disconnecting s_i would produce two components, where one of them
is trivial and including s_i. From lemma 2, the size of the neighbor set of s_i is
$|N(s_i)| = \lceil \frac{8\pi}{\pi-\sqrt{3}}k - 1 \rceil$. Therefore, an upper bound on network connectivity is
computed as $\kappa_i(G) = \lceil \frac{8\pi}{\pi-\sqrt{3}}k - 1 \rceil$. Hence, it follows from Definition 7 that
the fault tolerance of a connected homogeneous kCWSN satisfies the inequality
$\kappa_b(G) - 1 \leq \eta(G) \leq \kappa_i(G) - 1$.   □

Wang, *et al.* [17] proved that disconnecting a boundary node and an interior
node requires the removal of k sensors and $2k$ sensors, respectively.

4.3   Heterogeneous Wireless Sensor Networks

Condition Guaranteeing Connectivity. It is clear that, in general, the condition $R \geq 2r$ [17] does not guarantee network connectivity even when the
network is configured to provide sensing coverage [2]. Lemma 3 establishes a
condition that implies network connectivity provided that sensing coverage is
guaranteed.

Lemma 3 (Condition for connectivity in heterogeneous WSNs). *The
communication graph* $G = (S, E)$ *of a* kCWSN *is connected if for any node*
$s_i \in S$, $R_i \geq r_i + r_{max}$, *where* r_i *and* R_i *are the sensing and transmission
ranges, respectively, of node* s_i *and* $r_{max} = max\{r_j : s_j \in S\}$.

Proof. By hypothesis, each point of a field Γ is k-covered. Consider the extreme
case where the sensing ranges of the sensors s_i and s_j are tangent to each other
at a point, say p . Also, consider the case where $R_i = r_i + r_{max}$ and $R_j =
r_j + r_{max}$. This implies that $R_i \geq r_i + r_j$ and $R_j \geq r_i + r_j$, and hence $\delta(s_i, s_j) \leq
min\{R_i, R_j\}$. Therefore, s_i and s_j are mutually connected. This result applies
to any pair of sensors whose sensing ranges are either overlapping or tangent to
each other. Using the hypothesis of k-coverage of the field Γ and the above result,
there must be at least one communication path between any pair of sensors in
the network. We deduce that kCWSN is connected.   □

**Sensing k-Coverage, Connectivity, and Fault Tolerance of Heteroge-
neous kCWSN.** To guarantee sensing k-coverage, the *AET* model should be
applied to the least powerful sensors in terms of their sensing ranges. The following results for heterogeneous kCWSN correspond to theorem 1, theorem 2,
and theorem 3, which were established for homogeneous kCWSN.

Corollary 2 (Width of k-covered areas). *If a geographical area of a field Γ is k-covered with $k \geq 3$, then the width of A satisfies $w(A) \leq r_{min}$, where $r_{min} = min\{r_j : s_j \in S\}$.*

Proof. Any $AET_{r_{min}}$ with k sensors would guarantee k-coverage of the field Γ. Furthermore, $AET_{r_{min}}$ has a constant width equal to r_{min}. ☐

Corollary 3 (Maximum size of k-covered area and node spatial density). *Let S_k be a set of k heterogeneous sensors and A a geographical area of a field Γ. The maximum size of A, denoted by $A_{max}(r_{min})$, which is k-covered by the sensors of S_k with $k \geq 3$, is given by $A_{max}(r_{min}) = (\pi - \sqrt{3})\frac{r_{min}^2}{2}$ and the node spatial density to guarantee k-coverage is computed as $\rho(r_{min}, k) = \frac{2k}{(\pi - \sqrt{3})r_{min}^2}$, where $r_{min} = min\{r_j : s_j \in S\}$.*

Proof. The size of the largest area to be k-covered should depend on the least powerful sensors. Indeed, a given area could be covered by only the least powerful sensors. Hence, k-coverage will be guaranteed only if these k least powerful sensors are deployed in an area whose width cannot exceed r_{min}. Using the AET model, we can easily prove that $A_{max}(r_{min}) = (\pi - \sqrt{3})\frac{r_{min}^2}{2}$. Thus, the node spatial density required for achieving k-coverage is equal to $\rho(r_{min}, k) = \frac{2k}{(\pi - \sqrt{3})r_{min}^2}$. ☐

Network fault tolerance of connected heterogeneous kCWSN depends on the type of sensors to be disconnected (boundary or interior). Corollary 4 computes its tight lower and upper bounds, similar to the case of homogeneous kCWSN.

Corollary 4 (Fault tolerance). *The fault tolerance of a heterogeneous kCWSN with $R \geq 2r$ is given by $\kappa_b(G) - 1 \leq \eta(G) \leq \kappa_i(G) - 1$, where $\lceil \frac{\pi(r_{min}+r_{max})^2}{2(\pi - \sqrt{3})r_{min}^2}k - 1 \rceil \leq \kappa_b(G) \leq \lceil \frac{2\pi r_{max}^2}{(\pi - \sqrt{3})r_{min}^2}k - 1 \rceil$, $\lceil \frac{2\pi(r_{min}+r_{max})^2}{(\pi - \sqrt{3})r_{min}^2}k - 1 \rceil \leq \kappa_i(G) \leq \lceil \frac{8\pi r_{max}^2}{(\pi - \sqrt{3})r_{min}^2}k - 1 \rceil$, $r_{min} = min\{r_j : s_j \in S\}$, and $r_{max} = max\{r_j : s_j \in S\}$.*

Proof. To compute the lower and upper bounds on $\kappa_b(G)$, we consider a river containing only least powerful (minimum sensing range) and most powerful (maximum sensing range) boundary sensors, respectively. Hence, $\lceil \frac{\pi(r_{min}+r_{max})^2}{2(\pi - \sqrt{3})r_{min}^2}k - 1 \rceil \leq \kappa_b(G) \leq \lceil \frac{2\pi r_{max}^2}{(\pi - \sqrt{3})r_{min}^2}k - 1 \rceil$. Similarly, we consider the same scenario for interior sensors to compute the lower and upper bounds on $\kappa_i(G)$, thus giving $\lceil \frac{2\pi(r_{min}+r_{max})^2}{(\pi - \sqrt{3})r_{min}^2}k - 1 \rceil \leq \kappa_i(G) \leq \lceil \frac{8\pi r_{max}^2}{(\pi - \sqrt{3})r_{min}^2}k - 1 \rceil$. From Definition 7, it follows that $\kappa_b(G) - 1 \leq \eta(G) \leq \kappa_i(G) - 1$. ☐

Next, given kCWSN with $R < 2r$, we address the following questions:

- Are kCWSN connected under the assumption that $R < 2r$?
- Are kCWSN connected under the assumption that $R < r$?

We will show that using optimal sensor deployment strategies, sensing coverage guarantees network connectivity even though $R \geq 2r$, is not satisfied.

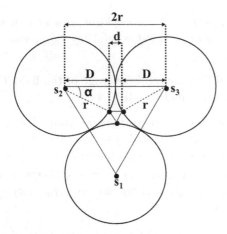
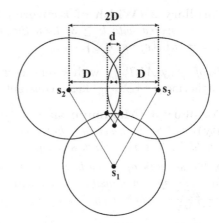

Fig. 2. Minimum gap between three tangential sensing ranges

Fig. 3. Optimal sensor deployment for 1-coverage

4.4   Are *k*CWSN Connected When $R < 2r$?

In this section, we investigate the case where $R < 2r$ and provide a configuration using a minimum number of sensors, thus minimizing the overlap between their sensing ranges, while achieving full sensing coverage. Theorem 4 proves that the deployment of the sensors according to the configuration in Fig. 3 is optimal in terms of minimum overlap between the sensing ranges of adjacent sensors.

Theorem 4 (Optimal sensor deployment for sensing 1-coverage). *The sensor deployment strategy according to the configuration in Fig. 3 is optimal.*

Proof. Consider the configuration given in Fig. 2. The equilateral triangle, Δ_d, in the gap area has a side length equal to d. In order to cover all the gap area, we need to cover Δ_d. To do so, both of the sensors s_2 and s_3 should be moved horizontally and in opposite directions until they intersect at the center of gravity, g, of the triangle Δ_d. This action will not be able to cover the whole gap as the triangle Δ_d is not fully covered. To cover the rest of Δ_d, the sensor s_1 should move vertically and bottom-up until its sensing range hits the intersection point of both sensing ranges of s_2 and s_3, i.e., the center of gravity, g. In fact, the farthest point from any of the locations of the sensors s_1, s_2, and s_3, is the point g. Hence, covering the entire gap area require covering its center of gravity, g. Therefore, the configuration given in Fig. 2, where any pair of sensing ranges of adjacent sensors have a constant overlap and any adjacent three sensing ranges intersect at only one point, is optimal. ☐

Theorem 5, which follows from theorem 4, states a condition that implies network connectivity provided that sensing coverage is guaranteed.

Theorem 5 (Condition for connectivity given sensing 1-coverage). *A homogeneous kCWSN with $k = 1$ is guaranteed to be connected if the sensing and transmission ranges of the sensors, r and R, respectively, satisfy $R \geq \sqrt{3}r$.*

Proof. Consider the configuration given in Fig. 2. The maximum distance between any pair of tangential sensors is $2r$. To cover the entire gap area of the tangential three sensing ranges of the sensors s_1, s_2, and s_3, the distance separating s_2 and s_3 should be equal to $2r - d$. We have $D = rcos(\alpha) = \frac{\sqrt{3}}{2}r$, where $\alpha = \frac{\pi}{6}$, and $d = 2r - 2D = r(2 - \sqrt{3})$. Hence, the distance between any pair of adjacent sensors, given by $2r - d$, is equal to $\sqrt{3}r$. Thus, if a field is sensing 1-covered, then the network is guaranteed to be connected if $R \geq \sqrt{3}r$ holds. $\square$

Theorem 6 proves that the network connectivity of a homogeneous kCWSN with $k \geq 3$ and $R \geq r$ is larger than k.

Theorem 6 (Fault tolerance of a homogeneous kCWSN with $R \geq r$).
Let $G = (S, E)$ be a communication graph corresponding to a homogeneous kCWSN and consider the case where $R \geq r$. The fault tolerance of a homogeneous kCWSN is given by $\kappa_b(G) - 1 \leq \eta(G) \leq \kappa_i(G) - 1$, where $\kappa_b(G) = \frac{\pi}{2(\pi - \sqrt{3})}k - 1$, $\kappa_i(G) = \frac{2\pi}{(\pi - \sqrt{3})}k - 1$, and $k \geq 3$.

Proof. Let us first assume that $k = 3$. From corollary 1, any AET_r region should contain k sensors. Thus, for any sensor located in AET_r, there is at least one sensor located in the same AET_r or in an adjacent one such that the distance between this pair of sensors cannot exceed r. Given that $R \geq r$, it implies that any sensor is connected to at least another sensor. Precisely, there is at least one communication path between any pair of sensors in the network. Thus, a kCWSN is connected. For the case $k > 3$, more sensors need to be thrown in any AET_r region to achieve sensing k-coverage. Hence, network connectivity is preserved and even increases. Thus, a kCWSN is connected, for all $k \geq 3$. It is easy to check that the minimum size of the neighbor set of a boundary sensor, s_b, is $|N(s_b)| = \lceil \frac{\pi}{2(\pi - \sqrt{3})}k - 1 \rceil$, and hence a lower bound on network connectivity is given by $\kappa_b(G) = \frac{\pi}{2(\pi - \sqrt{3})}k - 1$. Also, the minimum size of the neighbor set of an interior sensor, s_i, is $|N(s_i)| = \lceil \frac{2\pi}{(\pi - \sqrt{3})}k - 1 \rceil$, and hence an upper bound on network connectivity is computed as $\kappa_i(G) = \lceil \frac{2\pi}{(\pi - \sqrt{3})}k - 1 \rceil$. From definition 7, it follows that the fault tolerance of a connected homogeneous kCWSN satisfies $\kappa_b(G) - 1 \leq \eta(G) \leq \kappa_i(G) - 1$. Notice that $\kappa_b(G) > k$ and $\kappa_i(G) > k$, thus implying $\eta(G) > k-1$. Using the Hopital's theorem, we can prove that $lim_{k \to \infty} \frac{k}{\kappa(G)} = 0$, which implies that $\kappa(G) > k$ and hence $\eta(G) > k - 1$. $\square$

Corollary 5 establishes the previous result for heterogeneous kCWSN.

Corollary 5 (Fault tolerance of a heterogeneous kCWSN with $R \geq r$).
Let $G = (S, E)$ be a communication graph corresponding to a heterogeneous kCWSN with $R \geq r$. The fault tolerance of a heterogeneous kCWSN is given by $\kappa_b(G) - 1 \leq \eta(G) \leq \kappa_i(G) - 1$, where $\lceil \frac{\pi(r_{min}+r_{max})^2}{2(\pi - \sqrt{3})r_{min}^2}k - 1 \rceil \leq \kappa_b(G) \leq \lceil \frac{2\pi r_{max}^2}{(\pi - \sqrt{3})r_{min}^2}k - 1 \rceil$, $\lceil \frac{2\pi(r_{min}+r_{max})^2}{(\pi - \sqrt{3})r_{min}^2}k - 1 \rceil \leq \kappa_i(G) \leq \lceil \frac{8\pi r_{max}^2}{(\pi - \sqrt{3})r_{min}^2}k - 1 \rceil$, $r_{min} = min\{r_j : s_j \in S\}$, and $r_{max} = max\{r_j : s_j \in S\}$.

Proof. A boundary sensor can be either the least or the most powerful sensor in terms of the sensing range. Given that $R \geq r$, it is easy to find that the minimum numbers of nodes to remove to disconnect the least powerful boundary sensor and the most powerful boundary sensor are given by $\lceil \frac{\pi(r_{min}+r_{max})^2}{2(\pi-\sqrt{3})r_{min}^2}k - 1 \rceil$ and $\lceil \frac{2\pi r_{max}^2}{(\pi-\sqrt{3})r_{min}^2}k - 1 \rceil$, respectively. Thus, $\lceil \frac{\pi(r_{min}+r_{max})^2}{2(\pi-\sqrt{3})r_{min}^2}k - 1 \rceil \leq \kappa_b(G) \leq \lceil \frac{2\pi r_{max}^2}{(\pi-\sqrt{3})r_{min}^2}k - 1 \rceil$. We apply the same reasoning for interior sensors to establish that $\lceil \frac{2\pi(r_{min}+r_{max})^2}{(\pi-\sqrt{3})r_{min}^2}k - 1 \rceil \leq \kappa_i(G) \leq \lceil \frac{8\pi r_{max}^2}{(\pi-\sqrt{3})r_{min}^2}k - 1 \rceil$. Thus, the fault tolerance of a connected heterogeneous kCWSN satisfies $\kappa_b(G) - 1 \leq \eta(G) \leq \kappa_i(G) - 1$. Notice that $\kappa_b(G) > k$, $\kappa_i(G) > k$, and hence $\eta(G) > k - 1$. $\qquad\square$

4.5   Are kCWSN Connected When $R < r$?

Theorem 7 computes the distance between any pair of adjacent sensors leading to an optimal sensor deployment strategy, which guarantees sensing 2-coverage.

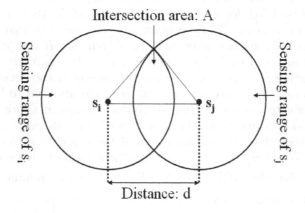

Fig. 4. Sensing range overlap and distance between sensors

Theorem 7 (Optimal sensor deployment for sensing 2-coverage). *An optimal deployment of the sensors to guarantee sensing 2-coverage requires that the distance, d, between any pair of adjacent sensors be equal to $d = 0.84r$.*

Proof. Our goal is to maximize the overlap between the sensing ranges of pairs of adjacent sensors, while minimizing the total number of deployed sensors. On the one hand, to maximize the area simultaneously covered by a pair of sensors, the distance between them should be minimized. This, however, would increase the number of sensors needed to 2-cover a field Γ. On the other hand, to minimize the number of sensors to 2-cover Γ, we need to maximize the distance between the sensors. As shown in Fig. 4, the size of the intersection area of the sensing ranges of two adjacent sensors, is given by $A(d) = 2r^2 cos^{-1}(\frac{d}{2r}) - \frac{d}{2}\sqrt{4r^2 - d^2}$. Then, we consider the objective function $g(d) = A(d) \times d$, which we want to maximize. Notice that $\frac{\partial^2 g(d)}{\partial^2 d} \leq 0$ for all $0 \leq d \leq 2r$. A theoretical solution, d_0, to $\frac{\partial g(d)}{\partial d} = 0$ is not straightforward. Indeed, to solve $\frac{\partial g(d)}{\partial d} = 0$, we need to solve $\frac{3d^3}{2} + 2r^2\sqrt{4r^2 - d^2}cos^{-1}(\frac{d}{2r}) - 6r^2d = 0$. We find that $g(d)$ reaches its maximum at $d_0 = 0.84r$ for $r = 50m$ and $d_0 = 0.836r$ for $r = 250m$, as shown in Fig. 5 and Fig. 6, respectively. Thus, $g(d)$ is maximum at approximately $d = 0.84r$. $\square$

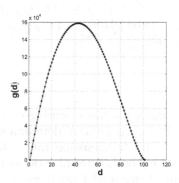

Fig. 5. $g(d)$ for $r = 50m$ **Fig. 6.** $g(d)$ for $r = 250m$

Theorem 8, which follows from theorem 7, states the condition that guarantees network connectivity given sensing 2-coverage and $R < r$.

Theorem 8 (Condition for connectivity given sensing 2-coverage and $R < r$). *Sensing 2-coverage guarantees network connectivity if the sensing and transmission ranges of the sensors, r and R, respectively, satisfy $R \geq 0.84r$.*

4.6 Coverage-Based Fault Tolerance Measure

We propose to define network fault tolerance in terms of the sensing coverage, which can be viewed as the fault tolerance of a monitored field. This means that any target area of a field should remain covered by at least one sensor in spite of the failure of a certain number of sensors. Next, we define a second measure of fault tolerance, called *field fault-tolerance*, and compute its value for kCWSN.

Definition 10 (Critical coverage and field fault tolerance). *Let $G = (S, E)$ be a communication graph of a WSN. The critical coverage, $\mu(\Gamma)$, of a field Γ, which is covered by a WSN, is the smallest number of sensors whose removal uncover Γ. The field fault-tolerance of a WSN is given by $\eta(G) = \mu(\Gamma) - 1$.*

Theorem 9 (Field fault tolerance). *Assume $k \geq 3$. The field fault-tolerance of a homogeneous kCWSN is given by $\eta_{hom}(G) = 4k - 1$ and that of a heterogeneous kCWSN is given by $4k - 1 \leq \eta_{het}(G) \leq \lceil 4k(\frac{r_{max}^2}{r_{min}}) - 1 \rceil$.*

Proof. Let AET_σ be the area of interest. The farthest location in AET_σ from any sensor on the boundary of AET_σ is its center of gravity, denoted by g. Thus, any sensor that is located at distance r from g should be removed so g becomes 0-covered. Hence, if all sensors located in AET_σ fail, where $\sigma = 2r + \epsilon$ and ϵ is an infinitesimal value, the location g is guaranteed to be uncovered. Assuming a uniform node spatial density, the minimum number of sensors ($\epsilon \to 0$) in AET_σ is given by $|AET_{2r}| = \rho(r,k) \times area(AET_{2r})$. Thus, the field fault-tolerance of a homogeneous kCWSN with $k \geq 3$ is given by $\eta(G) = |AET_{2r}| - 1 = 4k - 1$. It is also easy to check that the field fault-tolerance of a heterogeneous kCWSN with $k \geq 3$ is given by $|AET_{2r_{min}}| - 1 \leq \eta_{het}(G) \leq |AET_{2r_{max}}| - 1$, where $|AET_{2r_{min}}| = \rho(r_{min}, k) \times area(AET_{2r_{min}})$ and $|AET_{2r_{max}}| = \rho(r_{min},k) \times area(AET_{2r_{max}})$. Hence, $4k - 1 \leq \eta_{het}(G) \leq \lceil 4k(\frac{r_{max}^2}{r_{min}}) - 1\rceil$. □

5   Summary and Future Work

In this paper, we have investigated the relationships between sensing coverage, connectivity and fault tolerance of kCWSN. Precisely, we have determined different relationships between sensing range, r, and transmission range, R, for different degrees, k, of sensing coverage based on both deterministic and random sensor deployment strategies. Using our *Augmented Equilateral Triangle* (*AET*) model, which guarantees sensing k-coverage, we have proved that network connectivity of homogeneous and heterogeneous kCWSN is higher than k. We have also computed lower and upper bounds on network fault tolerance based on network connectivity and sensing coverage. Although the relationship $R \geq 2r$ seems at the first glance to be necessary to guarantee network connectivity provided that sensing coverage is guaranteed, our fine-grained analysis is able to give a tighter relationship, $R \geq \sqrt{3}r$. This result is based on the use of deterministic and optimal sensor deployment strategies. Compared to deterministic deployment strategies, which are more suitable for mathematical analysis and effective for small-scale wireless sensor networks, random sensor distributions cannot guarantee complete, void-free coverage. We should, however, mention the fact that random sensor deployment strategies are easier to use in inhospitable environments, such as military battle-fields, for instance, than deterministic deployment strategies.

Our findings are of practical use for wireless sensor network designers in developing sensing applications with prescribed degrees of sensing coverage, network connectivity and fault tolerance. We plan to extend these results for irregular sensing and transmission ranges. We also intend to exploit these results in the design of topology control and data dissemination protocols for WSNs.

Acknowledgments. The authors would like to thank the anonymous reviewers for their helpful comments. This work is partially supported by a grant from the NSF under award number IIS-0326505.

References

1. Ai, J., Abouzeid, A.: Coverage by Directional Sensors in Randomly Deployed Wireless Sensor Networks. Journal of Combinatorial Optimization 11(1) (2006) 21–41
2. Ammari, H. M., Das, S. K.: On Computing Conditional Fault-Tolerance Measures for k-Covered Wireless Sensor Networks. Proc. 9th ACM/IEEE Int. Symp. on Modeling, Analysis and Simulation of Wireless and Mobile Systems, Spain (2006)
3. Cortes, J., Martinez, S., Karatas, T., Bullo, F.: Coverage Control for Mobile Sensing Networks. IEEE Transactions on Robotics and Automation 20(2) (2004) 243–255
4. Cardei, M., Wu, J.: Energy-Efficient Coverage Problems in Wireless Ad-hoc Sensor Networks. Computer Communications 29(4) (2006) 413–420
5. Chelius, G., Fleury, E., Mignon, T.: Lower and Upper Bounds for Minimum Energy Broadcast and Sensing Problems in Sensor Networks. Proc. 11th Int. Conf. On Parallel and Distributed Systems (ICPADS), Fukuoka, Japan (2005)
6. Datta, A. K., Gradinariu, M., Linga, P., Raipin-Parvedy, P.: Self-* Distributed Query Region Covering in Sensor Networks. Proc. 24th IEEE Symp. on Reliable Distributed Systems (SRDS), Orlando, Florida, USA, (2005)
7. Du, X., Lin, F.: Maintaining Differentiated Coverage in Heterogeneous Sensor Networks. EURASIP Journal on Wireless Communications and Networking 5(4) (2005) 565–572
8. Ghosh, A., Das, S. K.: Coverage and Connectivity Issues in Wireless Sensor Networks. Mobile, Wireless and Sensor Networks: Technology, Applications and Future Directions, (Shorey, R., Ananda, A., Chan, M. C., Ooi, W. T. (ed.):), Wiley-IEEE Press (2006)
9. Gupta, H., Das, S.R., Gu, Q.: Connected Sensor Cover: Self-Organization of Sensor Networks for Efficient Query Execution. Proc. 4th ACM Int. Symp. on Mobile Ad Hoc Networking and Computing (MobiHoc), Annapolis, Maryland, USA (2003)
10. Hall, P.: Introduction to the Theory of Coverage Processes. John Wiley & Sons Inc., New York (1988)
11. Li, N., Hou, J.: A Fault-Tolerant Topology Control Algorithm for Wireless Networks. Proc. 10th Annual Int. Conf. on Mobile Computing and Networking (MobiCom), Pennsylvania, USA (2004)
12. Li, X.-Y., Wan, P.-J., Frieder, O.: Coverage in Wireless Ad-hoc Sensor Networks. IEEE Transactions on Computers 52 (2003) 753–763
13. Megerian, S., Koushanfar, F., Potkonjak, M., Srivastava, M.: Worst and Best-case Coverage in Sensor Networks. IEEE Transactions on Mobile Computing 4(1) (2005)
14. Ravelomanana, V.: Extremal Properties of Three-dimensional Sensor Networks with Applications. IEEE Transactions on Mobile Computing 3(3) (2004)
15. Shakkottai, S., Srikant, R., Shroff, N.: Unreliable Sensor Grids: Coverage, Connectivity and Diameter. Proc. 24th Annual Conf. IEEE Communications Societies (INFOCOM), San Fransisco, USA (2003)
16. Tian, D., Georganas, N.: Connectivity Maintenance and Coverage Preservation in Wireless Sensor Networks. Ad Hoc Networks 3 (2005) 744–761
17. Wang, X., Xing, G., Zhang, Y., Lu, C., Pless, R., Gill, C.: Integrated Coverage and Connectivity Configuration in Wireless Sensor Networks. Proc. 1st ACM Conf. on Embedded Networked Sensor Systems (SenSys), California, USA, (2003)
18. Zhang, H., Hou, J.: Maintaining Sensing Coverage and Connectivity in Large Sensor Networks. Ad Hoc & Sensor Wireless Networks 1(1-2) (2005) 89–124
19. Zhou, Z., Das, S., Gupta, H.: Fault Tolerant Connected Sensor Cover with Variable Sensing and Transmission Ranges. Proc. 2nd Annual conf. on Sensor and Ad Ho Communications and Networks (SECON), Santa Clara, California, USA (2005)

A Case Study on Prototyping Power Management Protocols for Sensor Networks*

Mahesh Arumugam, Limin Wang, and Sandeep S. Kulkarni

Department of Computer Science and Engineering
Michigan State University
East Lansing MI 488824
{arumugam, wanglim1, sandeep}@cse.msu.edu

Abstract. Power management is an important problem in battery powered sensor networks as the sensors are required to operate for a long time (usually, several weeks to several months). One of the challenges in developing power management protocols for sensor networks is prototyping. Specifically, existing programming platforms for sensor networks (e.g., nesC/TinyOS) use an event-driven programming model and, hence, require the designers to be responsible for stack management, buffer management, flow control, etc. Therefore, the designers simplify prototyping their solutions either by implementing their own discrete event simulators or by modeling them in specialized simulators. To enable the designers to prototype power management protocols in target platform (e.g., nesC/TinyOS), in this paper, we use *ProSe*, a programming tool for sensor networks. ProSe enables the designers to specify their programs in simple abstract models while hiding low-level challenges of sensor networks and programming-level challenges. As a case study, in this paper, we specify a power management protocol with ProSe, automatically generate the corresponding nesC/TinyOS code, and evaluate its performance. Based on the performance results, we expect that ProSe enables the designers to rapidly prototype, quickly deploy, and easily evaluate their protocols.

1 Introduction

In the recent years, sensor networks have become popular due to their wide variety of applications including border patrolling, hazard detection, habitat monitoring, and micro-climate monitoring. These applications require the network to operate for a long time (usually, several weeks to several months). However, the sensors are typically battery powered (e.g., Mica [1], XSM [2], Telos [3]) and, hence, they can operate continuously only for a few days. In addition, since the sensors are deployed in large numbers and mostly in inaccessible fields, it is difficult to change the batteries after deployment. Therefore, power management is crucial for extending the lifetime of the network.

---

* This work was partially sponsored by NSF CAREER CCR-0092724, DARPA Grant OSURS01-C-1901, ONR Grant N00014-01-1-0744, NSF Equipment Grant EIA-0130724, and a grant from Michigan State University.

One of the challenges in designing power management protocols for sensor networks is prototyping. Specifically, existing platforms (e.g., nesC/TinyOS [4]) for programming sensor networks use *event-driven programming model* and, hence, require the designer be responsible for stack management, buffer management, and flow control [5, 6]. Therefore, to rapidly prototype and quickly evaluate protocols, the designers of existing power management protocols (e.g., [7, 8, 9, 10, 11, 12, 13]) implement their own simulators or model their protocols in specialized simulators (e.g., GloMoSim [14]). However, it is desirable that the designers prototype their protocols in nesC/TinyOS platform as it provides a framework for generating both simulation as well as production code from the same source.

In this paper, we consider the problem of rapid prototyping of power management protocols in nesC/TinyOS platform. To deal with programming level challenges (e.g., stack management, buffer management, flow control, etc) and network level challenges (e.g., message collision, corruption, synchronization, etc) of sensor networks, we focus on *ProSe* [15], a programming tool for rapid prototyping of sensor network protocols and applications. ProSe is based on the theoretical foundation on computational model in sensor networks [16, 17]. It enables the designers to (i) specify programs in simple abstract models (e.g., shared-memory model, read/write model) that hide several challenges of sensor networks, (ii) automatically transform the programs into a model consistent with sensor networks, and (iii) automatically generate and deploy (nesC/TinyOS) binary.

In addition, we note that the transformation algorithms proposed in [16, 17] preserve self-stabilization and fault-tolerance properties of the programs in shared-memory model or read/write model in the transformed programs. Since we implement the transformation algorithms proposed in [16,17] in ProSe, ProSe automates the process of transformation of abstract programs. And, it preserves the self-stabilization and fault-tolerance properties of the transformed programs. (We refer the reader to [16, 17, 15] for more details on preserving properties of original programs.)

As a case study, we model *pCover* [13], a power management protocol that provides partial (but high) sensor coverage of the target field, in ProSe. We specify the pCover program in shared-memory model. We synthesize the corresponding nesC/TinyOS binary and study the performance of the generated code. Through simulations, we show that the generated program extends the lifetime of the network while providing a partial (but high) coverage.

Organization of the paper. The rest of the paper is organized as follows. In Section 2, we briefly discuss how programs are specified in ProSe. Then, in Section 3, we prototype pCover in ProSe. We present a brief overview of the protocol and discuss how we synthesized the nesC/TinyOS binary. Subsequently, we study the performance of the generated binary code. We show that the generated program extends the lifetime of the network. In Section 4, we discuss the lessons learned in prototyping power management protocols and in Section 5, we discuss the related work. Finally, in Section 6, we make the concluding remarks.

2   ProSe: Overview

In this section, we briefly outline the structure of programs in ProSe and discuss how nesC/TinyOS binaries are synthesized.

2.1   Structure of Programs

In ProSe, programs are specified in terms of guarded commands [18]; each command (or action) is of the form:

$$guard \quad \longrightarrow \quad statement,$$

where *guard* is a predicate over program variables, and *statement* updates program variables. An action $g \longrightarrow st$ is enabled when g evaluates to true and to execute that action, st is executed. A computation of this program consists of a sequence $s_0, s_1, \ldots$, where s_{j+1} is obtained from s_j by executing actions in the program $(0 \leq j)$.

Computation model. A computation model limits the variables that an action can read and write. Towards this end, we split the program actions into a set of processes (sensors). Each action is associated with one of the processes (sensors) in the program. We now describe how we model the restrictions imposed by shared-memory model and read/write model.

Shared-memory model. In this model, in one atomic step, a sensor can read its state as well as the state of its neighbors and write its own (*public* and *private*) variables.

Read/Write model. In this model, in one atomic step, a sensor can either (1) read the state of one of its neighbors and update its *private* variables, or (2) write its own variables.

Programs written in shared-memory model or read/write model, however, are not suitable for the constraints (and opportunities) provided by sensor networks. For this reason, in [16,17], the authors have modeled the computations in sensor networks as a *write all with collision* (WAC) model, discussed next.

Write all with collision (WAC) model. In this model, each sensor consists of write actions (to be precise, write-all actions). Specifically, in one atomic action, a sensor can update its own state and the state of all its neighbors. However, if two or more sensors simultaneously try to update the state of a sensor, say k, then the state of k remains unchanged. Thus, this model captures the fact that a message sent by a sensor is broadcast. But, if multiple messages are sent to a sensor simultaneously then, due to collision, it receives none.

To simplify programming sensor networks, recently, approaches have been proposed for transforming programs into WAC model. They can be classified as: (a) TDMA based deterministic transformation [16] and (b) CSMA based probabilistic transformation [17]. With the help of these transformation algorithms, ProSe allows the designer to specify programs in simple abstract models (e.g., shared-memory model, read/write model). Then, ProSe automatically transforms them into WAC model and, subsequently, generates the corresponding nesC/TinyOS code.

2.2   Input/Output of ProSe

The input to ProSe consists of the guarded commands program in shared-memory or read/write model, its initial states and (optionally) the topology of the network. We discuss the input/output of ProSe in the context of an example.

Input guarded commands program.   Consider a MAX program, where each process (i.e., sensor) maintains a public variable x. The goal of MAX is to eventually identify the maximum value of this variable across the network. We specify the actions of each process in this program as shown in Figure 1 (keywords are shown in bold font):

```
1 program max
2 sensor  j
3 var public  int x.j;
4 begin
5     (x.k > x.j) -> x.j = x.k;
6 end
7 init state x.j = j;
```

Fig. 1. MAX program in ProSe

The designer also specifies zero or more initial states of the program. If no initial states are specified, ProSe initializes the variables of the program to arbitrary values. If more than one initial states are specified, ProSe initializes the program to randomly selected state. In the above program, $x.j$ is initialized to j (i.e., ID of the sensor).

Auxiliary variables. ProSe provides abstractions to deal with failure of sensors and presence of Byzantine sensors. To determine whether a neighbor (say, k) is alive or failed, sensor j can just access the public variable $up.k$; if $up.k$ is $TRUE$ (respectively, $FALSE$) then k is alive (respectively, failed). Designers can use this abstract variable to simplify the design of sensor network protocols while ProSe provides implementation of this variable through heartbeat protocol (e.g., [19]). Similarly, ProSe also allows designers to model Byzantine sensors through abstract variables $(b.j)$.

Topology information. ProSe *wires* a component ($NeighborState$) that maintains the state information of the neighbors at each sensor, with the generated code. Towards this end, each sensor should identify its neighborhood. ProSe allows the designers to integrate a neighborhood abstraction layer (e.g., [20]) with the generated code. Such an abstraction layer allows a sensor to learn its neighborhood dynamically. Optionally, the designers can specify the static topology of the network as an input to ProSe using the *topology file*. This file includes the ID of the base station, size of the network, and the communication topology. Based on the neighborhood information, ProSe configures the MAC layer and NeighborState component.

Support for *local* component invocations in guarded commands. Since ProSe allows the designers to specify programs in guarded commands format, it makes protocol design highly intuitive and concise. However, it is not always desirable to use guarded commands to specify protocols. For example, consider the design of a routing protocol for sensor networks, where the sensors maintain a spanning tree rooted at the base station. In this program, whenever the parent of a sensor fails, it chooses one of its active neighbors for which the link quality is greater than a certain threshold, as its parent. Towards this end, the sensor has to compute the link quality of each of its neighbors. Specifying this action in guarded commands is difficult. Moreover, nesC/TinyOS components may exist that provide the desired functionality.

To simplify the design of sensor network protocols, ProSe allows component invocations in guarded commands. In the design of routing protocol, in order to find a neighbor that has a better link quality, the designer can invoke the component *LinkEstimator* to compute the quality estimate of a given link. Thus, parent update action in the routing protocol can be specified in guarded commands as shown in Figure 2.

```
1  // current parent (p.j) has failed and j-k link quality is greater than the threshold
2  (up.(p.j) == FALSE) && (up.k == TRUE) && (LinkEstimator.getQuality(k) > LINK_THRESHOLD)
3     -> p.j = k; currentParentLinkQuality.j = LinkEstimator.getQuality(k);
```

Fig. 2. Component invocation in ProSe

In the above action, the *getQuality(k)* method of LinkEstimator component returns the quality of the link $j-k$. This component may need certain variables to compute the quality estimate. For example, it may need counters that maintain the number of messages successfully transmitted over each link. The action by which the counters are updated would be specified in guarded commands. The variables used in the guarded commands program and the copies of the public variables of the neighbors (maintained in NeighborState) are made available to the invoked component.

The designer has to implement *LinkEstimator* in nesC/TinyOS platform. This component, however, uses only local data (i.e., it uses NeighborState). ProSe generates the code for NeighborState component. And, it wires the component implemented by the designer with the generated code.

Output nesC/TinyOS code. In the generated nesC/TinyOS program, the actions of the input program are executed whenever a timer fires. Once the sensor executes each action for which the corresponding guard is enabled, it marshals all the public variables as a message *wacMsg* and schedules it for transmission (broadcast). Depending on the transformation algorithm and the MAC layer selected by the user, it configures when the timer fires and how *wacMsg* is transmitted. For example, in case of a TDMA based transformation [16], ProSe configures the timer to fire in every TDMA slots assigned to the sensor. And, it uses the TDMA service (e.g., [16, 21, 22]) to broadcast the message. In case of a

CSMA based transformation [17], ProSe configures the timer to fire in a random interval whenever it receives a message containing values of public variables at the sender. And, it uses a CSMA service (e.g., [23]) to broadcast *wacMsg*.

Similarly, ProSe generates code for NeighborState component that maintains the state information of the neighbors whenever it receives an update message from one of its neighbors. Finally, ProSe also generates code to (1) initialize all the program variables, (2) configure network services (e.g., TDMA, CSMA), and (3) configure and start middleware services (e.g., Timer).

3   Case Study: Prototyping pCover with ProSe

In this section, we present a case study on prototyping power management protocols with ProSe. We model *pCover* [13], a simple power management protocol that provides partial (but high) sensor coverage of the target field. Specifically, pCover maintains a certain degree of coverage through sleep-awake scheduling of sensors. By trading little sensor coverage of the field, in [13], the authors show (using C++ discrete event simulator) that pCover substantially improves the network lifetime.

First, in Section 3.1, we discuss the pCover program (written in shared-memory model). Then, in Section 3.2, we show how we synthesize the corresponding nesC/TinyOS binary with ProSe. Finally, in Section 3.3, we evaluate the performance of the generated code.

3.1   pCover: Overview

The pCover program written in shared-memory model is shown in Figure 3. The basic idea of pCover is that a sensor should turn itself off if and only if its *local coverage* is higher than a certain threshold, called *OnThreshold*. Local coverage of a sensor is the percentage of the sensor's sensing area that is covered by other awake sensors.

Description of the program. In this program, each sensor is in one of 4 states: *probe*, *awake*, *readyoff*, and *sleep*. Each sensor j maintains one public variable $st.j$ that identifies the state of the sensor. In addition, j maintains a copy of the public variables of its neighbors (in NeighborState). We discuss the actions of the pCover program shown in Figure 3 in detail, next.

Probe state. A sensor in probe state probes the environment, determines whether it should stay awake or go to sleep. After a timeout Y, the sensor computes its local coverage. Note that the designer has to provide the *LocalCoverage* component that returns the local coverage of a sensor. This component acts only on the state information of the neighbors maintained at the sensor. The sensor starts working if its local coverage is lower than the OnThreshold. Otherwise, the sensor switches to sleep state. The timeout Y is used to ensure that when the sensor decides whether it should stay awake or go to sleep, it has the *fresh* state information of its neighbors.

```
 1 program pCover
 2 sensor j
 3 const int X, Y, Z, S, W, OnThreshold, OffThreshold;
 4 var
 5     public int st.j;
 6     private int timer.j;
 7 component LocalCoverage;
 8 begin
 9 (st.j == SLEEP) && (timer.j >= X)
10     -> st.j = PROBE; timer.j = 0;
11 | (st.j == PROBE) && (timer.j >= Y) && (LocalCoverage.compute() > OnThreshold)
12     -> st.j = SLEEP; timer.j = 0;
13 | (st.j == PROBE) && (timer.j >= Y) && (LocalCoverage.compute() <= OnThreshold)
14     -> st.j = AWAKE; timer.j = Random(0, S);
15 | (st.j == AWAKE) && (timer.j >= Z)
16     -> st.j = READYOFF; timer.j = 0;
17 | (st.j == READYOFF) && (timer.j >= W)
18     -> st.j = AWAKE; timer.j = Random(0, S);
19 | (st.j == READYOFF) && (LocalCoverage.compute() > OffThreshold)
20     -> st.j = SLEEP; timer.j = 0;
21 | ((st.j == SLEEP) && (timer.j <= X)) ||
22   ((st.j == PROBE) && (timer.j <= Y)) ||
23   ((st.j == AWAKE) && (timer.j <= Z)) ||
24   ((st.j == READYOFF) && (timer.j <= W))
25     -> timer.j = timer.j + 1;
26 end
```

Fig. 3. pCover program in ProSe

Awake state. A sensor in awake state actively monitors the area within its sensing range. It remains active until the timer reaches the timeout value Z. Since we do not want all awake sensors to timeout at the same time, the timer is initialized to a random value. Once the awake timer expires, the sensor changes its state to *readyoff*.

Readyoff state. In readyoff state, the sensor still provides sensing coverage. However, the neighbors of a readyoff sensor (say, j) consider j as a sleeping sensor. In other words, the neighbors of j do not count it when they compute local coverage. If a readyoff sensor finds that its local coverage is greater than *OffThreshold*, it will change its state to sleep. Also, if a sensor is in readyoff state for a long duration, it can switch to awake state. This action allows one to deal with the case where a lot of sensors are in readyoff state although none of them can go to sleep state (due to local coverage being less than OffThreshold).

Sleep state. A sensor in sleep state wakes up every X minutes. When it wakes up, it changes its state to probe and proceeds to execute actions in that state.

3.2   Transformation and Code Generation

We use ProSe to generate the nesC/TinyOS implementation of the pCover program and subsequently build the binary image. Towards this end, we use the TDMA based transformation from [16] to transform the program into WAC model and generate the nesC/TinyOS code. We integrate SS-TDMA [21] with the generated program to implement the write-all action. As mentioned in Section 2, since the pCover program includes component invocation (LocalCoverage) in the actions, we require the designer of the protocol to implement this component in nesC/TinyOS. We discuss how the designer implements this component and how ProSe integrates it with the generated code, next.

LocalCoverage component. Based on the state information of the neighbors of a sensor (say, j), LocalCoverage component computes the percentage of j's sensing area that is covered by its *awake* neighbors. This component provides a method (*compute()*) that could be invoked in the guarded commands program. This method returns the local coverage of the sensor.

In order to compute the local coverage of the sensor, LocalCoverage requires the state information of the neighbors of the sensor. This information is maintained by NeighborState component (as mentioned in Section 2). Since, ProSe wires NeighborState with LocalCoverage when generating the nesC/TinyOS code for pCover, LocalCoverage component can obtain the state information of the neighbors of the sensor by invoking NeighborState. Note that all accesses to NeighborState are local and ProSe is responsible for updating NeighborState with *fresh* values. Thus, the designer does not have to deal with programming level challenges of nesC/TinyOS platform and low-level challenges of sensor networks (e.g., communication, collisions, corruption, etc).

3.3   Evaluation of the Synthesized Program

We evaluate the performance of the generated nesC/TinyOS code for pCover with TOSSIM [24], a discrete event simulator for TinyOS sensor networks.

Simulation settings. We use the simulation setting similar to [13]. We deploy the sensors in a grid topology over a 100m X 100m area. We set the sensing range r of the sensors to 10m and the radio interference range to 50m. We did two simulations: one with network density of 1 node/r^2 and another with 2 nodes/r^2. Inter-sensor separation and the number of sensors deployed varies depending on the density. With 1 node/r^2 (respectively, 2 nodes/r^2), the inter-sensor separation is 10m (respectively, 7m) and the network size is 10x10 (respectively, 14x14). SS-TDMA [21] sets the TDMA period depending on the number of sensors falling in the interference range of a sensor. With 1 node/r^2 (respectively, 2 nodes/r^2), SS-TDMA sets the period to 50 (respectively, 100) slots, where one time slot = 30 ms.

We assume that the lifetime of a sensor is 20 minutes. We choose this value in order to ensure that the simulation completes within a reasonable time. (With density of 2 nodes/r^2, the simulation takes 3 days to complete. Typically, sensors are expected to work continuously for 1000 minutes. Simulating a sensor lifetime of 1000 minutes in TOSSIM, however, would approximately take 150 days to complete.) We simulate the lifetime of each sensor by maintaining a variable and decrementing it appropriately in each time slot.

In all our simulations, we set the timeout values for pCover as follows: X = 1 minute, Y = 2 TDMA slots, Z = 3 minutes, and S = W = 2 minutes. We randomly initialize the state of each sensor. We set OnThreshold and OffThreshold to 0.7 and 0.6. We consider that a network is "dead" when the *global coverage* of the network is less than a certain threshold even if all the alive nodes are working. Global coverage (or degree of coverage) is the percentage of the field that is covered by the working nodes. We define network lifetime as the duration from the beginning of deployment until the network is dead. We use 50% as the threshold in our simulations.

In our simulations, each link in the network has a bit error probability, representing the probability that a bit can be corrupted if it is sent along the link. Bit errors for each link is decided independently (using LossyBuilder, a Java program in TinyOS release) based on empirical loss data gathered from real world [25]. Next, we discuss our simulation results.

Coverage and network lifetime. In Figure 4, we show the degree of coverage and number of active sensors over time. In our simulations, we compute the global coverage for the entire 100m X 100m field and for the inner 80m X 80m field. The border sensors contribute only a part of their sensing range in the field and, hence, we consider the inner 80m X 80m field, where there is no such edge effect. As we can see from Figures 4(a) and 4(b), the sensors maintain the coverage at approximately the same level. With density $= 2$ nodes/r^2, initially (i.e., around 3 minutes), we observe a drop in the coverage. This is due to the fact that large number of sensors are initially set to active state (as a result of random initialization) and the number of active sensors fluctuate before converging to an appropriate number that maintains the coverage at a certain level (around 88.4%). Figure 4(c) shows the number of active sensors over time. As we can observe from the figure, this number remains at the same level until the point where the coverage starts dropping.

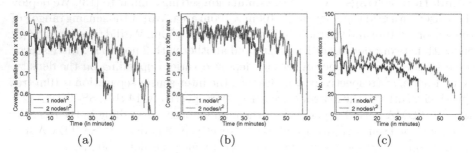

Fig. 4. Coverage and number of active sensors over time; (a) coverage of entire 100m X 100m area, (b) coverage of inner 80m X 80m area, and (c) number of active sensors

From Figures 4(a) and 4(b), we observe that the coverage is well maintained until one point, after which, the coverage drops suddenly, and the network dies in a short period. This shows that pCover maintains a balanced energy consumption as all sensors run out of power at around the same time. Also, we confirm the result in [13]; by sacrificing little coverage, the network lifetime is extended. Specifically, the lifetime with densities of 1 nodes/r^2 (respectively, 2 nodes/r^2) is around 39.55 minutes (respectively, 57.9 minutes).

Quality of coverage. As mentioned in [13], in partially covered sensor networks, quality of coverage is an important metric. For example, in surveillance networks, it is measured in terms of how fast the sensors detect a target object. Since the sleep interval (i.e., X) is 1 minute, time to detect stationary objects in the sensor field is bounded by 1 minute. Additionally, since the sensors rotate their roles (working vs. sleeping), the set of active sensors changes continuously. Hence, an undetected "hole" is likely to be detected as the set of active sensors changes. In Figure 5, we show the snapshots of the field at different times.

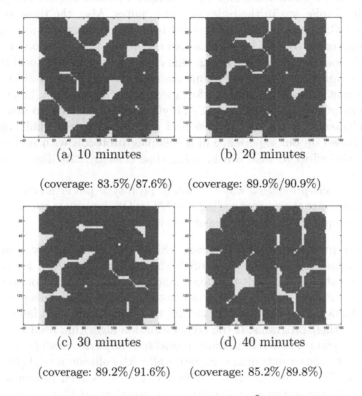

(a) 10 minutes   (b) 20 minutes

(coverage: 83.5%/87.6%)   (coverage: 89.9%/90.9%)

(c) 30 minutes   (d) 40 minutes

(coverage: 89.2%/91.6%)   (coverage: 85.2%/89.8%)

Fig. 5. Snapshot of the field with density = 2 nodes/r^2 (dark regions are covered). Coverage data below each subfigure shows the coverage of entire area and the coverage of inner 80m X 80m area respectively at that time.

From Figure 5, we observe that the location of "holes" change continuously. In surveillance networks, the intruder does not know the location of such holes. Hence, it is unlikely that the intruder can choose to move along the uncovered path. Therefore, the time to detect the intruder is small on average.

4   Lessons Learned in Prototyping Power Management Protocols

In this section, we discuss some of the lessons learned in prototyping power management protocols with ProSe.

Rapid prototyping and quick evaluation. Most of the power management protocols for sensor networks follow the event-driven model. For example, in pCover (cf. Section 3), we observe that a sensor switches to either working mode or sleeping mode whenever an event occurs (such as a timeout). Since guarded commands format is event-driven in nature, prototyping power management protocols with ProSe is straightforward. Furthermore, the time required to prototype protocols with ProSe is small. For example, the time required to prototype pCover with ProSe was in the order of few minutes. Also, the time required to specify LocalCoverage, a component used to compute the percentage of a sensor's sensing region covered by other active neighbors, was in the order of couple of hours. As mentioned in Section 3.2, this component uses only local data and, hence, we did not have to worry about communication. As a result, specifying this component in nesC/TinyOS platform was quick. By contrast, had we chosen to prototype pCover directly in nesC/TinyOS, we would have to deal with all low-level challenges of sensor networks and programming-level challenges of the platform. Based on our experience in developing protocols with nesC/TinyOS, we expect this effort to take considerable time (usually, few days to couple of weeks).

In short, ProSe provides a way to rapidly prototype power management protocols and generate the corresponding nesC/TinyOS implementation. Hence, the designers can quickly deploy and easily evaluate their protocols.

Preserving properties of interest. Since designers specify protocols in guarded commands format (with ProSe), they can analyze them for properties such as self-stabilization, fault-tolerance, and reliability. In addition, the designers can automatically add new properties to the guarded commands program. For example, the designers can use FTSyn [26] to automatically add fault-tolerance properties to their programs. If the transformation algorithm used to transform the input program (in shared-memory model or read/write model) into a model consistent with sensor networks (i.e., write all with collision model [16,17]) preserves properties of interest then ProSe also preserves such properties. ProSe implements the transformation algorithms proposed in [16,17] that preserve self-stabilization and fault-tolerance properties of the original programs. (We refer the reader to [15,16,17] for more details on how properties of interest are preserved in the transformed programs.) Thus, ProSe simplifies the design of power management protocols while ensuring that self-stabilization and fault-tolerance properties are preserved in the transformed programs.

5   Related Work

Work related to rapid prototyping of power management protocols can be categorized as: (i) programming platforms and (ii) power management protocols.

Programming platforms. Related work that deals with programming abstractions include [27,28,29,30] and tools for programming sensor networks include [31,32,20,33,34,35,36].

Programming abstractions. In [27], a state centric approach is proposed that captures algorithms such as sensor fusion, signal processing and control. In this model, the abstraction of *collaboration groups* hides the designer from issues such as communication protocols, event handling, etc. In [28, 29], *macroprogramming* primitives that abstract communication, data sharing and gathering operations are proposed. However, these primitives are application-specific (e.g., *abstract regions* for tracking and gathering [28] and *region streams* for aggregation [29]). And, in [30], *semantic services* programming model is proposed where users only specify the end goal on what semantic data to collect. Unlike [27,28,29,30], ProSe allows the designer to evaluate existing algorithms in the context of sensor networks. Moreover, since the programs are written in abstract models considered in distributed systems, ProSe permits the designer to verify the correctness of the programs as well as to manipulate the programs to meet new properties.

Programming tools. Techniques like virtual machine (e.g., *Maté* [31]), middleware (e.g., *EnviroTrack* [32]), library (e.g., *SNACK* [33]), and database (e.g., *TinyDB* [34]) are proposed for simplifying programming sensor network applications. However, these solutions are (i) application-specific, and/or (ii) restrict the designer to what is available in the virtual machine, middleware, library, or network. In [36], macroprogramming model, called *Kairos*, that hides the details of code-generation and instantiation, data management, and control is proposed. However, unlike [31,32,20,33,34,35,36], ProSe hides low-level details such as message collisions, corruption, sensor failures, etc. Moreover, ProSe does not require any runtime support.

Power management protocols. Related work on power management protocols for sensor networks include [7,9,8,11,10,12,13]. In [9], a sensor is allowed to go to sleep if and only if one of its neighbors can completely cover its sensing area. As identified by [7], this approach underestimates the coverage provided by neighboring sensors and, hence, it leads to energy waste. Additionally, both [7] and [9] require a global synchronization service. In [10], a coverage configuration protocol is proposed where a sensor can switch to sleep state if all *intersection* points inside its sensing range are at least k-covered (i.e., a point is covered by at least k sensors). However, unlike [13], this approach requires more number of active sensors.

Power management protocols proposed in [8,11,13] follow similar design principles. However, unlike [13, 11], in [8], a working sensor is awake continuously until its failure or depletion of power. In [8,11], by controlling the range of messages transmitted, the density of working sensors is controlled. However, online estimation of transmission ranges and the number of working sensors are often difficult and inaccurate.

6   Conclusion

In this paper, we considered the problem of rapid prototyping of power management protocols for sensor networks. Since existing programming platforms (e.g., nesC/TinyOS) require the designers to be responsible for stack management, buffer management, and flow control, the designers of power management protocols prototype the protocols either by implementing a discrete event simulator or by modeling in a specialized simulator such as GloMoSim [14]. To enable rapid prototyping and quick evaluation of power management protocols in the target platform (e.g., nesC/TinyOS for Mica, XSM, or Telos based sensor networks), in this paper, we used ProSe, a programming tool for sensor networks. As a case study, we specified the power management program from [13] with ProSe, generated the corresponding nesC/TinyOS code, and evaluated its performance on TOSSIM [24]. We showed that the synthesized program provides partial (but high) coverage of the sensor field.

Since ProSe hides low-level challenges of sensor networks (e.g., message collision, corruption, synchronization, etc) and programming level challenges (e.g., buffer management, stack management, etc), the designers can rapidly prototype their protocols and generate code in the target platform. As a result, the development time and deployment time are small. In this paper, we illustrated this by prototyping pCover program [13]. We have also prototyped and evaluated the differentiated surveillance program [7] with ProSe (cf. [37]). Thus, with ProSe, we expect that the designers can rapidly prototype, quickly deploy and easily evaluate power management protocols in the target platform.

References

1. J. Hill and D. E. Culler. Mica: A wireless platform for deeply embedded networks. *IEEE Micro*, 22(6), 2002.
2. P. Dutta, M. Grimmer, A. Arora, S. Bibyk, and D. Culler. Design of a wireless sensor network platform for detection of rare, random, and ephemeral events. *In Proceedings of the Conference on Information Processing in Sensor Networks (IPSN)*, April 2005.
3. J. Polastre, R. Szewczyk, and D. Culler. Telos: Enabling ultra-low power wireless research. *In Proceedings of the Fourth International Conference on Information Processing in Sensor Networks, SPOTS track*, 2005.
4. D. Gay, P. Levis, R. von Behren, M. Welsh, E. Brewer, and D. Culler. The nesC language: A holistic approach to networked embedded systems. *In Proceedings of Programming Language Design and Implementation*, 2003.
5. A. Adya, J. Howell, M. Theimer, W. J. Bolosky, and J. R. Douceur. Cooperative task management without manual stack management or, event driven programming is not the opposite of threaded programming. *In Proceedings of 2002 USENIX Annual Technical Conference*, June 2002.
6. O. Kasten and K. Römer. Beyond event handlers: Programming sensor networks with attributed state machines. *In Proceedings of the Fourth Internation Conference on Information Processing in Sensor Networks (IPSN)*, 2005.
7. T. Yan, T. He, and J. A. Stankovic. Differentiated surveillance for sensor networks. *In Proceedings of the First ACM Conference on Embedded Networked Sensing Systems (SenSys)*, November 2003.
8. F. Ye, G. Zhong, J. Cheng, S. W. Lu, and L. X. Zhang. PEAS: A robust energy conserving protocol for long-lived sensor networks. *In Proceedings of the International Conference on Distributed Computing Systems*, 2003.

9. D. Tian and N. D. Georganas. A node scheduling scheme for energy conservation in large wireless sensor networks. *Wireless Communications and Mobile Computing Journal*, May 2003.

10. X. Wang, G. Xing, Y. Zhang, C. Lu, R. Pless, and C. Gill. Integrated coverage and connectivity configuration in wireless sensor networks. *In Proceedings of the Conference on Embedded Networked Sensing Systems*, 2003.

11. C. Gui and P. Mohapatra. Power conservation and quality of surveillance in target tracking sensor networks. *In Proceedings of the Tenth Annual International Conference on Mobile Computing and Networking*, 2004.

12. S. Ren, Q. Li, H. Wang, X. Chen, and X. Zhang. Analyzing object detection quality under probabilistic coverage in sensor networks. *In Proceedings of the International Workshop on Quality of Service (IWQoS)*, June 2005.

13. L. Wang and S. S. Kulkarni. Sacrificing a little coverage can substantially increase network lifetime. *In Proceedings of Third Annual IEEE Communications Society Conference on Sensor, Mesh, and Ad Hoc Communications and Networks (SECON)*, September 2006, to appear.

14. X. Zeng, R. Bagrodia, and M. Gerla. GloMoSim: A library for parallel simulation of large scale wireless networks. *In Proceedings of the Workshop on Parallel and Distributed Simulations*, May 2002.

15. M. Arumugam and S. S. Kulkarni. Programming sensor networks made easy. Technical Report MSU-CSE-05-25, Department of Computer Science, Michigan State University, September 2005.

16. S. S. Kulkarni and M. Arumugam. Transformations for write-all-with-collision model. *Computer Communications (Elsevier)*, 29(2):183–199, January 2006.

17. T. Herman. Models of self-stabilization and sensor networks. *In Proceedings of the 5th International Workshop on Distributed Computing (IWDC)*, LNCS:2918:205–214, December 2003.

18. E. W. Dijkstra. *A Discipline of Programming*. Prentice Hall PTR, 1997.

19. M. G. Gouda and T. M. McGuire. Accelerated heartbeat protocols. *In Proceedings of the International Confernece on Distributed Computing Systems (ICDCS)*, 1998.

20. K. Whitehouse, C. Sharp, E. Brewer, and D. Culler. Hood: A neighborhood abstraction for sensor networks. *In Proceedings of the ACM International Conference on Mobile Systems, Applications, and Services*, 2004.

21. S. S. Kulkarni and M. Arumugam. SS-TDMA: A self-stabilizing MAC for sensor networks. In S. Phoha, T. F. La Porta, and C. Griffin, editors, *Sensor Network Operations*. Wiley-IEEE Press, May 2006.

22. T. Herman and S. Tixeuil. A distributed TDMA slot assignment algorithm for wireless sensor networks. *In Proceedings of the Workshop on Algorithmic Aspects of Wireless Sensor Networks*, 2004.

23. A. Woo and D. Culler. A transmission control scheme for media access in sensor networks. *In Proceedings of the Seventh Annual International Conference on Mobile Computing and Networking*, pages 221–235, 2001.

24. P. Levis, N. Lee, M. Welsh, and D. Culler. TOSSIM: Accurate and scalable simulation of entire tinyOS applications. *In Proceedings of the Conference on Embedded Networed Sensor Systems*, 2003.

25. D. Ganesan, B. Krishnamachari, A. Woo, D. Culler, D. Estrin, and S. Wicker. An empirical study of epidemic algorithms in large scale multihop wireless networks. Technical Report IRB-TR-02-003, Intel Research, 2002.

26. S. S. Kulkarni and A. Ebnenasir. A framework for automatic synthesis of fault-tolerance. Technical Report MSU-CSE-03-16, Michigan State University, 2003.

27. J. Liu, M. Chu, J. Liu, J. Reich, and F. Zhao. State-centric programming for sensor-actuator network systems. *Pervasive Computing*, 2(4):50–62, 2003.
28. M. Welsh and G. Mainland. Programming sensor networks using abstract regions. *In Proceedings of the First USENIX/ACM Symposium on Networked Systems Design and Implementation (NSDI)*, March 2004.
29. R. Newton and M. Welsh. Region streams: Functional macroprogramming for sensor networks. *In Proceedings of the First Workshop on Data Management for Sensor Networks (DMSN)*, August 2004.
30. K. Whitehouse, F. Zhao, and J. Liu. Semantic streams: A framework for declarative queries and automatic data interpretation. Technical Report MSR-TR-2005-45, Microsoft Research, April 2005.
31. P. Levis and D. Culler. Maté: A tiny virtual machine for sensor networks. *ACM SIGOPS Operating Systems Review*, 36(5):85–95, December 2002.
32. T. Abdelzaher et al. EnviroTrack: Towards an environmental computing paradigm for distributed sensor networks. *In Proceedings of the International Conference on Distributed Computing Systems*, 2004.
33. B. Greenstein, E. Kohler, and D. Estrin. A sensor network application construction kit (SNACK). *In Proceedings of the Second ACM Conference on Embedded Networked Sensing Systems (SenSys)*, November 2004.
34. S. Madden, M. Franklin, J. Hellerstein, and W. Hong. TinyDB: An acquisitional query processing system for sensor networks. *ACM Transactions on Database Systems (TODS)*, 2005.
35. R. Newton, Arvind, and M. Welsh. Building up to macroprogramming: An intermediate language for sensor networks. *In Proceedings of the International Conference on Information Processing in Sensor Networks*, 2005.
36. R. Gummadi, O. Gnawali, and R. Govindan. Macro-programming wireless sensor networks using kairos. *In Proceedings of the International Confernece on Distributed Computing in Sensor Systems (DCOSS)*, 2005.
37. M. Arumugam, L. Wang, and S. S. Kulkarni. Rapid prototyping of power management protocols for sensor networks: A case study. Technical Report MSU-CSE-06-26, Department of Computer Science, Michigan State University, July 2006.

Unconscious Eventual Consistency with Gossips

Roberto Baldoni[1], Rachid Guerraoui[2,3], Ron R. Levy[2],
Vivien Quéma[1], and Sara Tucci Piergiovanni[1]

[1] DIS, Università di Roma "La Sapienza", 00198 Roma, Italy
[2] LPD, EPFL, CH 1015 Lausanne, Switzerland
[3] CSAIL, MIT, Cambridge, MA 02139, USA

Abstract. This paper combines various self-stabilization techniques within a replication protocol that ensures eventual consistency in large-scale distributed systems subject to network partitions and asynchrony. A simulation study shows that the resulting protocol is scalable and achieves high throughput under load.

Our protocol does not rely on any form of consensus, which would lead to block the replicas in case of partitions and asynchrony. Our protocol instead ensures that (1) updates are continuously applied to the replicas and (2) no two updates are ever performed in a different order. Gaps might occur during periods of unreliable communication. They are filled whenever connectivity is provided, and consistency is then eventually ensured, but without any conscious commitment. That is, there is no point in the computation when replicas know that consistency is achieved. This unconsciousness is the key to tolerating perpetual asynchrony with no consensus support.

1 Introduction

A new class of so-called *interactive* distributed applications is emerging: distributed virtual environments, interactively steered scientific applications, collaborative design systems, etc [3]. These applications may need to run in a wide area asynchronous environment with widely distributed users and resources and no central authority. In such settings it is important for each user to have access to a local copy (replica) of every object of interest. This is key to allowing local progress without constantly relying on the network. The main technical challenge is then to maintain some form of consistency among all replicas of the same object [17].

Traditionally, many systems running on local area networks provide so-called single copy semantics that gives the user the illusion of accessing a single, highly available object. Typical solutions require users to access a quorum of replicas, to acquire exclusive locks on data they wish to update or to agree on a total order of updates to be applied at each replica. Maintaining single-copy semantics in a worldwide deployed system is practically very expensive and theoretically impossible [10]. It is thus necessary to use (weaker) consistency criteria. This is precisely what *eventual consistency* [19] provides. It guarantees that whatever

A.K. Datta and M. Gradinariu (Eds.): SSS 2006, LNCS 4280, pp. 65–81, 2006.
© Springer-Verlag Berlin Heidelberg 2006

the current state of the replica, if no new updates are issued and replicas can communicate freely for a long enough period, the contents of all replicas eventually become identical. From an implementation point of view, the issues to solve in order to guarantee eventual consistency are [17]: (1) *update dissemination*: each update must eventually reach all replicas, and (2) *update ordering*: all updates must be *eventually* applied in the same order at each replica.

Some solutions (Bayou [19], OceanStore [15]) have updates disseminated based on epidemic (gossip) protocols. Update ordering [15,19,14,20,18] is achieved by having replicas deliver updates locally in any order (tentative order) and using *rollbacks* to eventually reach a total order. Total ordering is typically computed *a posteriori* using some form of consensus. This requires a "synchrony island" where agreement can be achieved to ensure that all replicas eventually agree on the exact update order. When that happens, each replica is *conscious* of the fact that total order has been reached.

This paper combines various self-stabilization techniques within a replication protocol that achieves eventual consistency in large-scale distributed environments subject to network partitions and asynchrony. These techniques include merging partition, electing stable processes and gossip-based propagation. Update dissemination is performed using a classical gossip-based strategy [8]. Our replication protocol differs from others by the fact that it does not use any form of consensus, even only eventual. It defines an *a priori* total order that is never explicitly agreed upon among replicas. Updates are disseminated using gossips and subsequently delivered. In the case that some old update arrives after already having delivered subsequent messages, the replica has to roll back to the old state, apply the old update and re-deliver all subsequent messages. This means that, in theory, each replica should keep all delivered updates forever. However, in practice, it is possible to reach consistency with high probability without keeping all delivered updates.

A fundamental aspect of our protocol is that replicas are *unconscious* of when total order is reached, i.e. when they are in a consistent state. This unconsciousness is the key to reaching eventual consistency even if the network is permanently asynchronous. Our protocol has the following characteristics:

- *Non-blocking:* the protocol enables update delivery even during periods when the network is asynchronous or partitioned.
- *Self-stabilizing:* the protocol exploits periods of (even partial synchrony) and merging of partitions to reduce the number of rollbacks. (Note that the periods of synchrony are not relied on in order to reach consistency).
- *Scalable:* the protocol encompasses a self-sizing mechanism that guarantees high throughput when the number of broadcasters and/or the rate at which they broadcast updates increase.

Our simulations convey the fact that our protocol achieves reasonable latency during synchronous periods (due to a small number of rollbacks) and achieves high throughput under high load.

This paper is organized as follows. Section 2 presents the ramifications underlying unconscious eventual consistency. Section 3 describes our protocol.

A performance evaluation is presented in Section 4. Finally, related work is presented in Section 5, before concluding the paper in Section 6.

2 Ensuring Unconscious Eventual Consistency

Roughly speaking, eventual consistency stipulates that all replicas eventually converge to the same state, i.e. deliver the same set of updates in the same total order. Eventual consistency can be achieved by having replicas (called processes in the rest of the paper) deliver updates in their order of arrival and then eventually re-order already delivered updates using a rollback mechanism. This section starts by discussing few points that must be taken into account while implementing eventual consistency. We then describe a naive implementation. Finally, we discuss the drawbacks of this naive implementation to introduce the improvements that are brought by the protocol presented in this paper.

2.1 Few Comments on Eventual Consistency Implementations

Update Ordering. As explained before, achieving eventual consistency requires every process to eventually deliver updates in the same order. Since updates can continuously be applied (i.e. processes can *re*-deliver updates until the total order is reached), it is only needed that each two updates be univocally associated to unique sequence numbers. On the other hand, it is not necessary that assigned sequence numbers be *consecutive* (i.e. *gaps* in the sequence are allowed). Nevertheless, for avoiding rollbacks, it is better that they be consecutive as this allows processes to know whether it is worth waiting for updates.

Update Dissemination. Eventual consistency requires that all updates eventually reach all processes. Reliable communication is therefore necessary. However, in a large scale environment, ensuring strong reliable communication can be very expensive. Consequently, most solutions [15,19] rely on epidemic dissemination [13,4,7], even if they do not provide strong reliability. Therefore, just like [15,19], our protocol only provides eventual consistency with high probability.

Unconscious Consistency. The total order used to achieve eventual consistency can be defined *a priori* (by associating to each update a pair composed of ID of the process that issued the update and a local sequence number). This allows achieving eventual consistency without relying on consensus. On the other hand, not relying on consensus implies that processes never know when a consistent state has been reached. As a consequence, we say that eventual consistency is implemented in an *unconscious* manner.

2.2 A Naive Implementation

Eventual consistency can be naively implemented as follows. Consider a finite and ordered set of processes $\{p_1, \ldots, p_n\}$. Each process acts as a *sequencer*; it keeps a local sequence number that is increased before broadcasting a new message (update). Along with the sequence number, each process tags the message m with its id. The resulting message (m, id, seq) is then disseminated to all processes. A total order is defined on these messages using the sequence number and id. More precisely: for any pair of messages m and m', m precedes m' iff (i) $seq < seq'$ or (ii) $seq = seq'$ and $id < id'$.

Upon reception of a message, a process cannot possibly know if it will ever receive another message preceding it in the total order. Indeed, there may exist *gaps* in the sequence of broadcast messages. It therefore doesn't make sense for a process to wait for other messages. Consequently, processes deliver messages upon reception. If a message m_1 is received after a message m_2 preceding it in the total order, a rollback is performed on m_2. Subsequently, m_1 and m_2 are delivered in the correct (total) order.

2.3   Towards a Better Implementation

The drawback of the naive implementation is that there is no mechanism to reduce the number of rollbacks. In particular, with a large number of sequencers, the number of rollbacks in the system drastically increases. Consider that there are N sequencers in the system identified by $s_1 < \ldots < s_N$. Each sequencer sequences k messages. Moreover, consider that messages are broadcast using a reliable FIFO broadcast primitive. If $N = 1$, all messages are received in the correct order by all processes. Thus, no rollbacks are necessary. However, with a larger number of sequencers, the number of possible rollbacks increases. Consider the case $N = 2$ with s_1 and s_2 starting to broadcast at the *same time* and *same rate*. Moreover, consider that messages sent by s_2 are systematically received before messages sent by s_1. Messages arrive at each process in the following order: $(m_2, s_2, 1)$, $(m_1, s_1, 1)$, $(m_4, s_2, 2)$, $(m_3, s_1, 2)$, etc. Consequently, each process needs to rollback k messages (those sent by s_2). Extending the previous example to a system with $N = m$ sequencers, it is trivial to demonstrate that each process performs $(m - 1) \times k$ rollbacks.

The protocol described in the next section exploits periods of synchrony to reduce the possible number of sequencers (and hence reduce the number of rollbacks) and to assure that each sequencer (actually implemented by a set of processes) gives consecutive sequence numbers.

3   Protocol

This section starts by an overview of the protocol. We then describe its basic behaviour. Follow the presentation of a self-stabilization mechanism and the description of a self-sizing mechanism that improves the protocol's scalability.

3.1   Overview

For scalability and fault-tolerance reasons, the protocol we propose implements each sequencer as a pool of processes organized in a *coalition*. Each process wishing to disseminate an update has access to a primitive called ecBroadcast. This primitive first requests a sequence number from *the coalition the process relies on* and then uses gossiping to disseminate the update together with its sequence number.

Coalition Creation. If a process p_i that does not rely on a coalition wants to ecBroadcast a message, it first tries to discover an already existing coalition. If it does not find one, it creates a new coalition including itself and some other processes (to get the desired size of the coalition) in a new coalition.

Sequencing Using Coalitions. A coalition c_k is a set of processes (called *members*) acting as a common sequencer. Within a coalition, processes are sorted using their identifiers. We note $c_k[x]$ the xth process in c_k (x is called *rank* of process $c_k[x]$) and we note $card(c_k)$ the cardinality of coalition c_k. Processes belonging to a coalition issue sequence numbers as follows: let c_k be a coalition and let p_j be a process belonging to c_k, $p_j = c_k[x]$. Process p_j assigns monotonically increasing sequence numbers belonging to the sequence $SN^{c_k[x]} = (sn_n)_{n \in \mathbb{N}}$ with $sn_n = n \times card(c_k) + x$. Along with this sequence number, messages are tagged with the id of the process that issued the sequence number.

Note that the above-described mechanism ensures that a coalition issues *distinct*, totally-ordered sequence numbers. Moreover, the protocol is such that each process requests sequence numbers to coalition members in a round-robin way. This allows (1) balancing the load over all coalition members and (2) increasing the probability that successively issued sequence numbers be *consecutive*.

Dissemination. We rely on a gossip-based protocol for message dissemination [8]. It has been shown that these protocols are able to ensure high delivery ratios. Moreover, for improving reliability during periods when the network is highly asynchronous or partitioned, the protocol uses a *pull* mechanism similar to the one presented in [19].

Message Delivery. Processes try to deliver messages in sequence. This is done by waiting until the preceding messages have been delivered before delivering the current one. However, a process cannot possibly know about all preceding messages for three reasons: (1) there might be other coalitions issuing sequence numbers, (2) the sequence numbers issued by the coalition the process relies on are not necessarily consecutive, and (3) the gossiping mechanism used for dissemination is not reliable. Therefore, a process only waits for a given period of time before delivering received messages. Consequently, a message can be received after consecutive messages have already been delivered. In this case a rollback mechanism is used to undeliver messages and re-deliver them in the correct order. Our experiments show that in the case when only one coalition is present in the system, the number of rollbacks is close to zero.

Self-stabilization. As explained above, it is desirable to have a single coalition in the entire system. The protocol encompasses a self-stabilization mechanism that aims at leading to a system with only one coalition. Members of different coalitions get to know each other when they receive messages sequenced by a different coalition. If a member p_i of a coalition A receives a message coming from another coalition B, then it builds a new coalition C including all members of A and B. As explained below, the size of the resulting coalition is readjusted after the merger. Note that this sizing mechanism tries to select the most *stable* processes, i.e. the processes that have been in the system for the longest time.

Each time a coalition member switches to another coalition, it starts issuing new sequence numbers as explained above. Therefore a process could reissue the same sequence number twice. This problem is solved by adding an epoch number to each sequenced message. When a process joins a coalition, it associates an epoch number to this new coalition. This epoch number must be greater than the epoch number of the last coalition the process was a member of. Epoch numbers do not change the way processes deliver messages. We just need to change the way the total order on messages is defined such that the epoch number takes precedence over the sequence number and finally the process id.

Coalition Self-sizing. Scalability of the sequencing service is obtained by dynamically adjusting coalition size according to the load on coalition members. This load depends on the number of broadcasters and the rate at which they broadcast. These two parameters are often impossible to determine a priori in the target environments. The self-sizing mechanism described in Section 3.4 dynamically modifies the size of coalitions, based on the average number of sequence number requests that coalition members receive during a period of time.

3.2   Main Protocol

Data Structures. Each process p executing the algorithm contains the following set of data structures. *coalition* represents the coalition process p relies on. It is a list of processes. *optimalSize* is the size that the *coalition* must have. *epoch* represents the epoch process p is in. *nextSN* is the next sequence number from the coalition that p relies on and expects to deliver next. *pending* is the list of messages that process p received but did not yet deliver. Each entry in the *pending* list contains $[m, sn, ts]$, where m is the message to be delivered, sn is its sequence number (integrating the process id, epoch number and sequence number attributed by the sequencing service), and ts the time at which message m was received. The *deliveryTimeout* parameter indicates the time process p should wait before delivering the first message in *pending*. All messages that have been delivered so far are stored in the *delivered* list. Finally, *nbOfRetries* refers to the number of attempts to retrieve a coalition process p must do before creating its own coalition.

Note that for the sake of clarity, some functions (resp. messages) that are described below take a parameter, named *info*, that is a data structure carrying various data on the process that called the function (resp. sent the message). For instance *info.coalition* contains the coalition the process relies on; *info.epoch* carries its epoch; etc.

The isNext() Function. To ease the reading of the algorithm, we have isolated the isNext() function (Figure 1), whose role is to indicate if a message must be delivered (returns true) or if it must stay in the *pending* list. This function enforces the following policy: the protocol can only wait for messages that are sequenced by the coalition the process relies on and at the same epoch as the one the process is currently in. All other messages are delivered as soon as they are received.

```
1: function isNext(sn, ts)
2:    if (sn.pid ∈ coalition) ∧ (sn.epoch = epoch) then
3:       if (sn.number = nextSN) ∨ (ts + deliveryTimeout < getTime()) then
4:          nextSN := sn.number + 1
5:          return true
6:       else
7:          return false
8:    return true
```

Fig. 1. The isNext() function

Algorithm Executed by Any Process. Figure 2 depicts the algorithm executed by any process p_i. The coalitionUpdate() function aims at updating the knowledge p_i has about existing coalitions. It is called each time a new message is received. It simply changes p_i's coalition if p_i's epoch is lower than the epoch of the coalition given in parameter.

For each process p_i

```
1: procedure ecBroadcast(m)
2:    ⟨sn⟩ := getSN()
3:    gossip ⟨m, sn, info⟩
4:    pending.add([m, sn, getTime()])

5: function getSN()
6:    repeat nbOfRetries times
7:       ⟨info⟩ := getCoalition()
8:       if info ≠ ∅ then
9:          coalitionUpdate(info)
10:         return snRequest()
11:   info.coalition = {p_i}
12:   info.epoch = epoch + 1
13:   coalitionUpdate(info)
14:   return snRequest()

15: upon gossip⟨m, sn, info⟩ from p_j do
16:   coalitionUpdate(info)
17:   pending.add([m, sn, getTime()])
```

For each process p_i

```
18: upon pending.first = [m, sn, ts]
         with isNext(sn, ts) do
19:   rolledback = ∅
20:   while m ≺ delivered.last do
21:      rollback(delivered.last)
22:      rolledback.add(delivered.removeLast())
23:   ecDeliver (m)
24:   delivered.add(m)
25:   while rolledback ≠ ∅ do
26:      ecDeliver (rolledback.removeFirst())
27:   pending.remove([m, sn, ts])

28: procedure coalitionUpdate(info)
29:   if info.epoch > epoch then
30:      coalition := info.coalition
31:      epoch := info.epoch
32:      nextSN := 0
```

Fig. 2. Algorithm executed by any process p_i

Process p_i can use the ecBroadcast() function to initiate the broadcast of a message m. This function first gets a sequence number using the getSN()

function; it then gossips the message together with its sequence number and information about p_i (coalition and epoch); finally, it adds message m to the *pending* list. The getSN() function first tries to retrieve a coalition using the getCoalition()[1] function. Then, it uses the snRequest()[2]. function to get a sequence number from the coalition returned by the getCoalition() function. Note that each time the snRequest function is invoked, it sends the request to a different member in order to balance the load over all coalition members and to increase the probability to successively issue consecutive sequence numbers. After *nbOfRetries* unsuccessful tries, the getSN() function creates a coalition.

When process p_i receives a gossip message m, it first updates its coalition if necessary; it then adds m to the *pending* list. Messages stored in the *pending* list are delivered as soon as they are first in the list and that the isNext() function returns true. Note that the delivery of a message may require rolling back and re-delivering previously delivered messages (Lines **??-??** and **??-??**).

3.3   Self-stabilization

The mechanism described in this section aims at leading to a system with only one coalition. We start by describing a protocol executed by coalition members to merge coalitions. Then, we present an age-based mechanism that allows selecting stable processes, i.e. processes that remained in the system for the longest time. Finally, we show how faults impacting coalition members are handled.

Coalition Merging. Each coalition member p_i executes an algorithm in charge of merging coalitions. This algorithm differs from the one executed by standard processes by the coalitionUpdate() function (Figure 3). Its behavior is the following: when the coalition given in parameter is the same as p_i's coalition, the function simply updates p_i's epoch if it is lower than the one passed as a parameter. When coalitions differ, the function merges the two coalitions and uses the size() function to try to reach the coalition's optimal size. This function either truncates the coalition using the truncate() function, or adds processes returned by the getProcess() function. Next paragraph explains how processes are selected by these two functions.

Aging Mechanism. To improve the stability convergence time, the protocol encompasses an *aging* mechanism[3] that aims at selecting the most *stable* members. The aging mechanism shares similarities with the mechanism used to improve the reliability of epidemic broadcast algorithms [8]. The basic idea underlying this mechanism is that each process has an age that reflects the number

---

[1] For space reasons, the getCoalition() function is not described. This function either returns the coalition p_i relies on (if such a coalition exists), or broadcasts a "coalition request" message to discover a coalition.

[2] For space reasons, the snRequest() function is not described. This function simply requests a sequence number from one member of the coalition p_i relies on.

[3] For space reasons, we do not provide the pseudo-code of this mechanism.

For each coalition member p_i	For each coalition member p_i
1: **procedure** coalitionUpdate($info$)	11: **procedure** merge($c1, c2$)
2: **if** $info.coalition = coalition$ **then**	12: $c1 := c1 \cup c2$
3: **if** $info.epoch > epoch$ **then**	
4: $epoch := info.epoch$	13: **procedure** size(c)
5: $nextSN := 0$	14: **if** card(c) $> optimalSize$ **then**
6: **else**	15: truncate(c)
7: merge($coalition, info.coalition$)	16: **else**
8: size($coalition$)	17: **while** (card(c) $<$ $optimalSize$) $\wedge$
9: $epoch := \max(epoch, info.epoch) + 1$	hasMoreProcesses()
10: $nextSN := 0$	18: $c := c \cup$ getProcess()

Fig. 3. Algorithm executed by any coalition member p_i

of messages the process delivered (the age is incremented every N deliveries). Each process stores the age of coalition members and propagates them with each message (in the *coalition* list). Then, the truncate() function selects the members with highest age. Eventually, stable processes will have a higher age than all other processes, which guarantees that all coalition members will be stable.

Note that there is no guarantee that two executions of the truncate() function by two different coalition members will produce the same result. Indeed, this depends on the knowledge that these two members have about the ages of all coalition members. Nevertheless, this is not an issue because the probability of having different knowledge can be decreased by increasing N.

Moreover, to further increase the speed at which stability is reached, the getProcess() function returns "old" processes. This is achieved by having each coalition member maintain a (short) list of the oldest processes it knows.

Handling Faults in Coalitions. As described, the protocol does not handle faulty coalition members. This does not affect the correctness of the protocol, but it alters its stability convergence time. Faulty members are handled using a *heartbeat* protocol among coalition members (Figure 4). Each member periodically (δ) sends a $PING$ message to other members in the coalition. Members maintain two data structures: *alive* is the list of processes from which a $PING$ message has been received. This list is reset periodically. *suspected* is the list of processes that the member suspects. This list is built by adding members of the coalition that are not in *alive* after $(2 * \delta)$ ms (Line **??**), and by adding members suspected by other members (Line **??**). Processes that are in the *suspected* list of a process p_i will no longer be added by p_i in a coalition (Line **??**).

The above-described behavior requires some additional comments: the *heartbeat* protocol does not prevent *false suspicions*. On the contrary, once a member is suspected by some process p_i, it will eventually be suspected by all other coalition members. Nevertheless, if *suspected* lists were not propagated, coalitions would oscillate as long as one process falsely suspects another member. Moreover, propagating *suspected* lists is not a real issue since (1) timeouts can be set sufficiently large to prevent most cases of false suspicions and (2) it is possible

For each coalition member p_i	For each coalition member p_i
1: $suspected := \emptyset$	9: **task** coalitionMaintenance **every** $(2 * \delta)$ ms
2: $alive := \emptyset$	10: $info.epoch = epoch + 1$
	11: **if** $alive \neq coalition$ **then**
3: **task** heartBeat **every** δ ms	12: $suspected$.add($coalition \backslash alive$)
4: send$\langle PING, info \rangle$ to all $p_j \in coalition$	13: $info.coalition = alive$
	14: coalitionUpdate($info$)
5: **upon** receive$\langle PING, info \rangle$ from p_j **do**	15: $alive := \emptyset$
6: $alive := alive \cup \{p_j\}$	
7: $suspected$.add($info.suspected$)	16: **procedure** merge($c1, c2$)
8: coalitionUpdate($info$)	17: $c1 := (c1 \cup c2) \backslash suspected$

Fig. 4. Extension for handling coalition members faults

to remove processes from the *suspected* lists after some (long enough) period of time, in order to allow falsely suspected processes to re-integrate coalitions.

3.4   Coalition Self-sizing

This section describes a mechanism in charge of improving the protocol's scalability. In our context, ensuring scalability consists in being able to handle a large number of nodes and to guarantee high throughput in message deliveries under high load. The protocol described so far already deals with scalability issues by (1) using a gossip protocol to disseminate messages, (2) distributing the sequencer role among several processes (coalition), and (3) balancing the load among coalition members by requesting sequence numbers in a round-robin fashion. Nevertheless, one limitation of the protocol is that it assumes a priori knowledge of the *optimal* coalition size.

We have extended the protocol with a *self-sizing* mechanism[4] that aims at dynamically computing the optimal coalition size. This mechanism is based on the fact that during a long enough period of time, all coalition members experience the same load (due to the round-robin load balancing mechanism). Therefore, computing the optimal size can be done by a specific member (i.e. the member that has rank 0, which we will call the "smallest member"), by simply looking at the load it experienced during the last *sizing period*. If the node is overloaded, it adds processes to the coalition; otherwise, it removes processes. This is the responsibility of the application deployer to decide the maximal load (in terms of request/seconds) a node in the system can support.

When two coalitions merge, the optimal size is set to the sum of the optimal sizes of both coalitions. This is the only case when the optimal size can be changed by a member other than the smallest one. Note that it is necessary to determine if the optimal size is the one set by the smallest member or by the process that executed the merger. This decision can easily be done by propagating a *sizing number* together with the optimal size sent in each message. This sizing number allows knowing if a sizing decision precedes or not another one.

---

[4] For space reasons, the pseudo-code of this extension is not shown.

4   Performance

In this section, we present the performance results obtained by simulating our algorithm. We start by describing the simulation settings and then give the actual performance measurements. The goal of the simulations is to show that the protocol is (1) self-stabilizing, (2) non-blocking, and (3) scalable.

4.1   Simulation Environment

We simulated our algorithm using the Peersim simulator [1]. Peersim allows cycle-based simulations of distributed algorithms in large-scale environments. Processes are connected using a random graph topology: every process knows a fixed number of random processes. Moreover, processes disseminate messages using an LPBCast-like broadcast protocol [8]. Note that we extended the simulator in order to be able to simulate asynchrony: we can vary the time (i.e. number of cycles) it takes for a message to be transferred from one process to another. In our experiments, this time is bounded by *maxLatency*, and every message transfer takes a random number of cycles ranging from 1 to *maxLatency*.

Finally, we model churn (i.e. continuous joining and leaving of processes) by periodically replacing a percentage of processes. All experiments are run with 1000 processes, with a PING period (δ) of 20 cycles and a sizing period of 40 cycles. All the experiments start with a warm-up phase (first 100 cycles) in which processes progressively join.

4.2   Self-stabilization

The first experiment illustrates the fact that the protocol is able to select stable processes. It consists in simulating 1000 processes that randomly broadcast messages. The self-sizing mechanism was disabled and the optimal coalition size was set to 8. The goal of the experiment is to show how the average number of stable members in each coalition evolve. For the sake of clarity, the average was only computed on coalitions that stayed in the system for longer than 20 cycles.

Figure 5 depicts the average number of stable processes in each coalition as a function of time (i.e. cycle number). We varied both the latency (through the *maxLatency* parameter) and the churn rate. The *maxLantecy* parameter ranges from 1 to 15; the churn rate ranges from 4% to 8% every 15 cycles. We observe that without any aging mechanism, the protocol does not reach stability (last plot). On the contrary, the aging mechanism ensures that stability is reached (first four plots), i.e. that eventually there will be 8 stable processes in the coalition. Nevertheless, the speed at which stability is reached depends on the level of asynchrony and churn.

- The stability time increases with asynchrony for two reasons: (1) more time is necessary for coalitions to meet, and (2) asynchrony alters the knowledge that processes have about the age of other processes. Therefore, the protocol has a higher probability of selecting processes that are not stable.

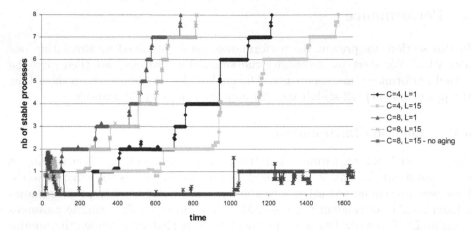

Fig. 5. Stable processes selection

– Increasing churn decreases the time it takes to reach stability. This result
  might seem surprising, but it can easily be explained by the fact that: (1)
  unstable members in the coalition have higher probability to fail (and thus
  to be replaced), and (2) stable processes are proportionally older (and thus
  have higher probability to be selected).

4.3   Non-blocking Behavior

The second experiment illustrates the fact that our protocol is non-blocking.
In particular, we show that it still provides service during periods when the
network is partitioned. The experiment consists in simulating 1000 processes
that randomly broadcast messages. The *maxLatency* parameter is set to 10.
Moreover, there is no churn. In order to simulate 3 network partitions, we group
processes into 3 groups. The interconnection graph is built in such a way that
each process has an equal number of (randomly chosen) neighbors in each group.
A network partition is simulated by disconnecting the groups.

Figure 6 plots the average latency of a message broadcast as a function of
the time at which the broadcast was initiated. The experiment starts with three
network partitions that merge at cycle 300. As explained in Section 3.1, messages
that are not delivered by the gossip primitive are retrieved using a *pull* mechanism. In the depicted experiment, this is the case of most messages sent between
cycles 0 and 300. Indeed, our protocol keeps providing service, but the gossip
primitive only delivers messages to processes belonging to the same partition
as the one the message's broadcaster is in. Other processes wait until the partitions have merged to retrieve these messages using the pull mechanism. Messages
broadcast after cycle 300 have an average latency ranging from 5 to 40 cycles.
This is reasonable considering that the maximum latency of a point-to-point
communication is equal to 10 cycles.

Figure 7 plots the average number of rollbacks that were done before delivering a message as a function of the time at which the broadcast was initiated.

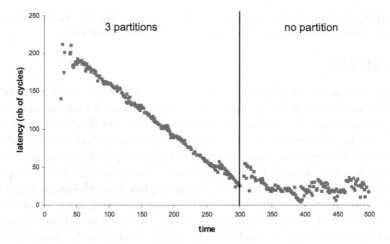

Fig. 6. Average message latency

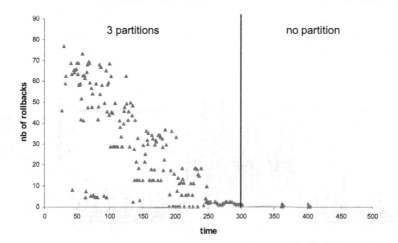

Fig. 7. Average number of rolled-back messages

The experiment is the same as the previously described one. We observe that messages broadcast between cycles 0 and 300 require rollbacks before being delivered. This can be explained by the fact that these messages were previously delivered in the partition of their respective broadcasters. After the network merger, these messages are retrieved using the pull mechanism. Their delivery requires rolling-back part of messages that were delivered during the network partition. We also observe that messages sent after cycle 300 do (almost) not require any rollback before being delivered. This shows that our protocol behaves like a traditional total ordering protocol when the network is not partitioned.

As a consequence, it is possible in such periods to truncate the memory, while still ensuring eventual consistency with a very high probability.

4.4 Scalability

The last experiment we present demonstrates that the protocol is scalable. In particular, we show that the protocol ensures (almost) constant throughput even during periods when the number of initiated broadcasts drastically increases.

The experiment consists in simulating 1000 processes that have a probability to broadcast messages that varies over time. In this experiment, the *maxLatency* parameter is set to 10 and there is no churn. Moreover, the warm-up phase is not represented for the sake of clarity. Figure 8 plots both the average number of sequence number (SN) requests received by each coalition member at the start of each round (first Y axis) and the average number of broadcasts initiated at the start of each round (second Y axis). Each "coalition X" plot depicts the life cycle of a coalition (i.e. the cycle at which it is created/destroyed) and the average number of SN requests received by each member.

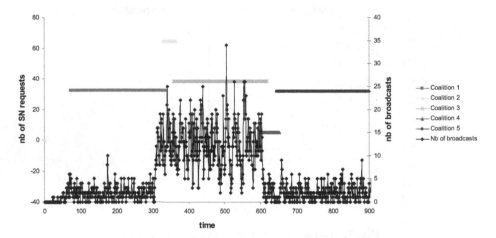

Fig. 8. Self-sizing mechanism

The self-sizing mechanism was parameterized to maintain the average number of SN requests by member between 30 and 40. From cycle 0 to cycle 300, processes have a low probability to initiate a new broadcast. During this period, messages are sequenced by coalition 1, which contains 3 members that handle (on average) 32,5 SN requests per cycle. Then, the broadcast rate significantly increases between cycles 300 and 600. Coalition 1 is first replaced by coalition 2 (6 members and 64,7 SN requests per cycle). Thus coalition 2 does not yet have enough members to handle the load. Consequently, coalition 2 is replaced by coalition 3 (12 members and 38,5 SN requests per cycle) after a short period of time. At time 600, the broadcast rate suddenly decreases. Coalition 3 is first replaced by coalition 4 (7 members and 15 SN requests per cycle), and then by coalition 5 (4 members and 31,3 SN requests per cycle). This experiment shows that the self-sizing ensures that coalitions can sustain a constant throughput, regardless of the broadcast rate.

5   Related Work

Update ordering for eventual consistency can be ensured by using total order protocols like the ones described in [6]. However, only optimistic total order protocols can efficiently support eventual consistency in a large scale setting [20,18]. Other approaches to total ordering are too strong and would decrease responsiveness.

A interesting work is the one presented in [9] that presents a formalization of a related problem (eventual serializability) and an algorithm that solves it. Nevertheless, targeted environments are much smaller scale than the one we target and it is assumed that each replica is able to know if an update is stable (i.e. has been applied to every replica). Thus, the algorithm would not work correctly in highly asynchronous systems. Another work related to our work is the one done by Golding who proposes protocols for weak consistency group communications [11]. Proposed protocols assume a knowledge of the number of replicas in the system. Thus, they are not usable in the environments we target.

Moreover, several optimistic total order protocols have been proposed. They distinguish between tentative delivery and committed delivery of messages. This approach has been proposed by Kemme et al. in [14] to improve the responsiveness of the system in a LAN. The optimistic approach in this case is based on the spontaneous total ordering in LANs. The protocol proposed by Vincente and Rodrigues in [20,18] guarantees that the tentative order is equal to the committed one during synchrony periods of the network. During periods of asynchrony rollbacks might occur. Finally, the protocol proposed by Sousa et al. in [18] does its best to guarantee that the tentative order is equal to the committed by artificially delaying messages received at a process before delivery through a mechanism called delay compensation. This delay based approach aims at creating the right conditions for spontaneous total ordering in WANs. All these protocols deterministically guarantee eventual consistency by relying on strong reliable update dissemination. As a consequence, they do not scale and cannot be employed in weakly connected environments. This is contrary to our protocol that uses epidemic dissemination.

There exist other examples of protocols relying on epidemic dissemination [19,15,16,2]. For instance, Bayou [19] is a storage system designed for a weakly connected computing environment. In Bayou, one server, designated as the primary, takes responsibility for totally ordering updates and thus for deciding the committed order. Each secondary replica executes updates in a tentative order while the committed order is being decided. Update propagation follows an anti-entropy [7] mechanism: pairs of replicas periodically exchange information to update their states. This pair-wise communication copes with arbitrary network connectivity and after an arbitrary number of communication exchanges, replicas converge to an identical state.

Oceanstore [15] targets extremely wide distributed environments with huge numbers of users. Consistency is reached using a two-tier architecture: a specific small set of untrusted servers, called the inner ring of the object, store the primary object replicas (primary tier). Other replicas, called secondaries, are deployed on a large number of nodes, mostly for caching reasons (secondary tier). The inner-ring totally orders updates coming from any node hosting a replica using a Byzantine agreement protocol [5]. Contrarily to our protocol, in Oceanstore and Bayou, consistency is achieved in a *conscious* manner. Note that a similar notion of unconsciousness has been introduced in the context of self-stabilizing communication protocols [12].

6   Concluding Remarks

This paper combines various self-stabilization techniques within a replication protocol that ensures *unconscious* eventual consistency. The protocol is stable, non-blocking, and scalable. Our simulations convey the reasonable latency of the protocol during synchronous periods, and its high throughput under load.

In contrast to a conscious notion of eventual consistency, where the replicas would know when they reached a stable consistent state, the guarantee we provide can be implemented in permanently asynchronous environments, while still supporting important classes of distributed applications such as interactive applications based on continuous shared data.

References

1. PeerSim: A Peer-to-Peer Simulator, 2006. http://peersim.sourceforge.net/.
2. Karl Aberer, Magdalena Punceva, Manfred Hauswirth, and Roman Schmidt. Improving data access in p2p systems. *IEEE Internet Computing*, 6(1):58–67, 2002.
3. Sumeer Bhola and Mustaque Ahamad. 1/k phase stamping for continuous shared data. In *Proceedings of the Symposium on Principles of Distributed Computing*, pages 181–190, 2000.
4. Kenneth P. Birman, Mark Hayden, Oznur Ozkasap, Zhen Xiao, Mihai Budiu, and Yaron Minsky. Bimodal multicast. *ACM Transactions on Computer Systems*, 17(2):41–88, 1999.
5. Miguel Castro and Barbara Liskov. Practical Byzantine Fault Tolerance and Proactive Recovery. *ACM Trans. Comput. Syst.*, 20(4):398–461, 2002.
6. Xavier Defago, Andre Schiper, and Peter Urban. Total Order Broadcast and Multicast Algorithms: Taxonomy and Survey. *ACM Comput. Surv.*, 36(4):372–421, 2004.
7. A. Demers, D. Greene, C. Hauser, W. Irish, J. Larson, S. Shenker, H. Sturgis, D. Swinehart, and D. Terry. Epidemic algorithms for replicated database maintenance. In *Proceedings of the Symposium on Principles of Distributed Computing*, pages 1–12, 1987.

8. P. Th. Eugster, R. Guerraoui, S. B. Handurukande, P. Kouznetsov, and A.-M. Kermarrec. Lightweight Probabilistic Broadcast. *ACM Transanctions on Computer Systems*, 21(4):341–374, 2003.

9. A. Fekete, D. Gupta, V. Luchangco, N. Lynch, and A. Shvartsman. Eventually-serializable data services. *Theoretical Computer Science*, 220(1):113–156, 1999.

10. M. Fischer, N. Lynch, and M. Paterson. Impossibility of Distributed Consensus with One Faulty Process. *Journal of the ACM*, 32(2):374–382, 1985.

11. R. Golding. A weak-consistency architecture for distributed information services. *Computing Systems*, 5(4):379–405, 1992.

12. M. Gouda and N. Multari. Stabilizing communication protocols. *IEEE Trans. Comput.*, 40(4):448–458, 1991.

13. I. Gupta, K. Birman, and R. van Renesse. Fighting fire with fire: using randomized gossip to combat stochastic scalability limits. *Journal of Quality and Reliability Engineering International*, 2002.

14. B. Kemme, F. Pedone, G. Alonso, and A. Schiper. Processing Transactions over Optimistic Atomic Broadcast Protocols. In *Proceedings of International Conference on Distributed Computing Systems*, 1999.

15. J. Kubiatowicz, D. Bindel, Y. Chen, P. Eaton, D. Geels, R. Gummadi, S. Rhea, H. Weatherspoon, W. Weimer, C. Wells, and B. Zhao. Oceanstore: An architecture for global-scale persistent storage. In *Proceedings of ASPLOS*, November 2000.

16. Y. Saito, C. Karamanolis, M. Karlsson, and M. Mahalingam. Taming Aggressive Replication in the Pangaea Wide-area File System. *ACM SIGOPS Operating Systems Review*, 36, 2002.

17. Yasushi Saito and Marc Shapiro. Optimistic Replication. *ACM Computing Survey*, 37(1):42–81, 2005.

18. Antonio Sousa, Jos Pereira, Francisco Moura, and Rui Oliveira. Optimistic Total Order in Wide Area Networks. In *Symposium on Reliable Distributed Systems*, pages 190–199, October 2002.

19. D. B. Terry, M. M. Theimer, Karin Petersen, A. J. Demers, M. J. Spreitzer, and C. H. Hauser. Managing update conflicts in bayou, a weakly connected replicated storage system. In *Proceedings of the Symposium on Operating Systems Principles*, pages 172–182. ACM Press, 1995.

20. Pedro Vicente and Luís Rodrigues. An Indulgent Uniform Total Order Algorithm with Optimistic Delivery. In *21st Symposium on Reliable Distributed Systems (SRDS 2002)*, pages 92–101, Osaka, Japan, 2002.

All *k*-Bounded Policies Are Equivalent for Self-stabilization

Joffroy Beauquier, Colette Johnen, and Stéphane Messika

L.R.I./C.N.R.S., Université Paris-Sud 11, bat 490, 91405 Orsay Cedex, France
jb@lri.fr, colette@lri.fr, messika@lri.fr

Abstract. We reduce the problem of proving the convergence of a randomized self-stabilizing algorithm under k-bounded policies to the convergence of the same algorithm under a specific policy. As a consequence, all *k*-bounded schedules are equivalent: a given algorithm is self-stabilizing under one of them if and only if it is self-stabilizing under any of them.

Keywords: randomized algorithms, distributed algorithm, self-stabilizing system, scheduler.

1 Introduction

By their very nature, distributed algorithms have to deal with a non-deterministic environment. The speeds of the different processors (machines) or the message delays are generally not known in advance and may vary substantially from one execution to the other.

For representing the environment in an abstract way, the notion of scheduler (also called deamon or adversary) has been introduced. The scheduler is in particular responsible of which machines take a step in a given configuration or of which among the messages in transit arrives first. It is well known that the correctness of a distributed algorithm depends on the considered scheduler. This remark also holds for self-stabilizing distributed algorithm.

Different classes of schedulers have been considered in the literature on self-stabilization. Very often, the scheduler is viewed as a machine that chooses the subset of activable machines to be activated. For instance the synchronous scheduler chooses all enabled machines which take an elementary step concurrently, the central scheduler (central demon) chooses a single machine and then the machines take their steps one after the other, the distributed scheduler chooses a subset of enabled machines which take a step concurrently and the probabilistic scheduler draws randomly a subset of enabled machines. It can be assumed that the scheduler disposes of no memory at all, or of a bounded finite memory, or of an infinite memory. The second case corresponds to bounded schedulers (that can be either centralized or distributed).

If the synchronous scheduler is able to produce one policy, there is infinity of policies produced by the distributed schedulers (corresponding to all possible choices of subsets along the computation). Then stating that an algorithm is correct under a given scheduler means it is correct for each policy 'produced'

A.K. Datta and M. Gradinariu (Eds.): SSS 2006, LNCS 4280, pp. 82–94, 2006.
© Springer-Verlag Berlin Heidelberg 2006

by the scheduler. A "proof" that does not take into account all policies can hardly be considered as correct even if the algorithm is deterministic, and it is still worst for probabilistic algorithms, since the probabilistic measure of the executions depends on the considered policy. For instance under some policies the algorithm converges in a finite bounded number of steps (the stabilization time) while with others it can not converge at all. Even when the stabilization time is always finite, it can differ according to the policy.

Since it is not feasible to have a special proof for each policy, a convenient way to treat correctly the problem would be to prove general equivalence properties for some classes of policies. These properties would express that if an algorithm is correct for a particular policy of the class, then it is correct for any policy in the class. The aim of this paper is to present such an equivalence property.

We prove that all bounded policies are equivalent for self-stabilization for a large class of protocols. That means that if an algorithm can be proved to be self-stabilizing under a particular bounded policy, then it is also self-stabilizing for any bounded policy. Note that this class contains the synchronous policy. The class contains all potential stable protocols (see Definition 10) such that every computation step is serializable, although several machines concurrently perform a action during the computation step. Any distributed protcol may be transformed into a potential stable protocol (the converse is not true). The requirement that a computation step is serializable, is a strong requirement that is not verified by all protocols. For instance, a protocol that converges only under the centralized deamon has some computation steps that are not serializable.

We also establish a bound of the convergence time in any bounded policy according to the convergence time in a specific policy.

Then, as a corollary we get that self-stabilization under the synchronous policy implies self-stabilization under any bounded policy. This leads to drastic simplifications in the proofs of already known results. For instance the result of [1], can be deduced directly from [2].

Related works. In [3], Dolev, Israeli and Moran introduced the idea of a two players game between the scheduler and what they call luck, i.e. random values, without defining formally the probabilistic space of computations. The structure (informally presented) behind a scheduler-luck game is a policy (formally defined in this paper) where some branches have beeen cut. In [4], [5], and [6], Lynch, Pogosyants and Segala present a formal method for analyzing probabilistic I/O automata which model distributed systems. A clear distinction between the algorithm, which is probabilistic, and the scheduler, which is non-deterministic, is made. The notion of cone, that is at the basis of the probabilistic space, is also used. These works do not consider self-stabilization. In [7,8] the notion of randomized distributed algorithms under a fixed policy is studied using methods issued from Markov theory, in [8] the authors adapt these methods to Markov Decision Processes. In [9], we reduce the problem of computing the convergence time of a probabilistic self-stabilizing algorithm to an instance of the Stochastic Shortest Path problem (SSP). The reduction gives us a way to compute automatically the stabilization time against the worst and the best policy.

2 Notion of Markov Decision Process

In this section we adopt the notation of de Alfaro [10].

Informally, a Markov Decision Process is a generalization of the notion of Markov chain in which a set of possible actions is associated with each state. To each state-action pair corresponds a probability distribution on the states, which is used to select the successor state. A Markov chain corresponds thus to a Markov decision process in which there is exactly one action associated with each state. The formal definition is as follows.

Definition 1 (Markov Decision Process). *A Markov decision process (MDP) (S, Act, A, p) consists of a finite set S of states, a finite set Act of actions, and two components A, p that specify the transition structure.*

- *For each $s \in S$, $A(s)$ is the non-empty finite set of actions available at s.*
- *For each $s, t \in S$ and $a \in A(s)$, $p_{st}(a)$ is the probability of a transition from s to t when action a is selected. Moreover, p verifies the following property :*
  $\forall s, \forall a \in A(s) \sum_{t \in S} p_{st}(a) = 1$.

Definition 2 (Behavior of MDP). *A behavior of a Markov decision process is an infinite sequence of alternating states and actions, constructed by iterating a two phases selection process. First, given the current state s, an action $a \in A(s)$ is selected non deterministically; second the successor state t of s is chosen according to the probability distribution $P(t|s,a) = p_{st}(a)$.*

Given a state s we denote Ω_s the set of all the behaviors starting in s.

Definition 3 (cylinder sets). *The basic cylinder associated with the sequence $h = s_0 a_0 s_1 a_1 ... s_n$ contains all behaviors of a MDP starting at s_0 and having the same prefix h: $C_h = \{hw \in \Omega_{s_0}\}$.*

Now, we define some measurable sets of behaviors. For every state s, let $B_s \in 2^{\Omega_s}$ be the smallest algebra of subsets of Ω_s, that contains all the basic cylinder sets and that is closed under complement and countable unions and intersections. This algebra is called the Borel σ-algebra of the basic cylinder sets and its elements are the measurable sets of behaviors (see [10]).

To be able to talk about the probability of behaviors, we associate with each $\omega \in B_s$ a probability measure $P(\omega)$. However this measure is not well defined, since the probability that a behavior belongs to ω depends on how the actions have been nondeterministically chosen.

To represent these choices, we use the concept of policy (see [10]). Policies are closely related to the adversaries of Segala and Lynch [4] to the schedulers of Lehman and Rabin [11], Vardi [12] and Pnueli and Zuck [13], and to the notion of strategy [14]. Informally, a policy defines the probabilities with which the actions are chosen knowing the history of the machine states.

Definition 4 (Policy). *A policy η is a set of conditional probabilities $Q_\eta(a|s_0 s_1 ... s_n)$, for all $n \geq 0$, all possible sequences of states $s_0, ..., s_n$ and all $a \in A(s_n)$, such that*

$$0 \leq Q_\eta(a|s_0, s_1 ..., s_n) \leq 1 \ and \ \sum_{a \in A(s_n)} Q_\eta(a|s_0, s_1 ..., s_n) = 1.$$

Definition 5 (Probability measure of a cylinder under a policy). *Let η be a policy. Let $h = s_0 a_0 s_1 a_1 ... s_n$ be a sequence of computation steps. In η, the probability of the basic cylinder associate with the history h is*

$$P_s^\eta(w \in C_h) = \prod_{k=0}^{n-1} p_{s_k s_{k+1}}(a_k) Q_\eta(a_k|s_0, s_1 ..., s_k)$$

It is well-known that there is an unique extension of the probabilistic measure P_s^η to any element of B_s. Thus the triple (η, B_s, P_s^η) defines a probabilistic space on B_s.

Note that a policy of a randomized distributed algorithm can be seen as a Markov chain.

3 Randomized Distributed Algorithms as Markov Decision Processes

We present how we model a randomized distributed algorithm as a Markov Decision Process (see [7,8]for more details).

In a distributed system, the topology of the network of machines is usually given under the form of a communication graph $G = (V, E)$, where the set $V = \{1, ..., N\}$ corresponds to the machine set. There is an edge between two vertices when the corresponding machines can communicate directly. We assume that all the machines are finite state machines. A configuration X of the distributed system is the N-tuple of all the states of the machines. Given a configuration X, the state of the ith machine is written $X(i)$. The code is a finite set of guarded rules: (i.e. label:: guard $\rightarrow$ action). The guard of a rule on p is a boolean expression involving p's state. The action of a p rule updates the p state. A machine p is *enabled* in a configuration c, iff a rule guard of p is true, in c. The simultaneous execution by several machines of rules is called a *computation step*.

The MDP associated with a distributed algorithm is defined by (i) S, the set of configurations, (ii) Act, the set of machine sets, (iii) $A(c)$, contain all subsets of enabled machines in c, (iv) $p_{st}(a)$, the probability to reach the configuration t from a configuration s by a computation step where all machines in a execute a rule.

Scheduler. A scheduler (adversary) is a mechanism which selects, at each step, a nonempty subset of enabled machines for applying the guarded rules of the algorithm. Basically, a scheduler is intended to be an abstraction of the external non-determinism. Because the effect of the environment is unknown in advance, the scheduler must have the ablility to formalize any external behavior.

Definition 6. *Let DS be a distributed system. A scheduler D is a set of DS policies.*

The *synchronous daemon* [2] is the scheduler which "chooses" all enabled machines. This scheduler is a memoryless scheduler (see Definition 7). A single deterministic policy is produced by the synchronous scheduler.

A computation is *k-bounded* [15] if along any sequence where a machine p is continuously enabled, any other machine p' performs at most k actions before p performs an action. A policy is *k-bounded* if it contains only k-bounded computations. For a randomized distributed algorithm, an infinity of k-bounded policies exist. For instance, for any positif value of f, $Policy(f)$ (defined in Section 6) is a 2-bounded policy. Because all enabled machines execute a rule during an even-numbered computation steps.

The k-bounded scheduler is the set of k-bounded policies. The memory k-bounded scheduler is the set of memory k-bounded policies (defined below). In Section 6, we compare the memory k-bounded scheduler with the k-bounded scheduler. We prove that a memory k-bounded policy is a k-bounded policy. But there are some k-bounded policies that are not memory K-bounded policies, for any value of K.

Definition 7. *A policy is deterministic iff for each state s there is an action $a \in A(s)$ such that $Q_\eta(a|s_0, s_1..., s_n) = 1$.*
A policy η is a memory k-bounded policy if for all $n \geq 0$, all possible sequences of states $s_0, ..., s_n$ we have $Q_\eta(a|s_0, s_1..., s_n s'_1 s'_2..., s'_k) = Q_\eta(a|s'_1 s'_2..., s'_k)$.
A policy is called memoryless if it is a memory 1-bounded policy.

3.1   Probabilistic Convergence of a Randomized Protocol

The main idea behind these definitions is simple : to analyze a self-stabilizing algorithm under a scheduler, one has to analyze every Markov chain derived from the MDP associated with the algorithm combined with each policy "produced" by the scheduler.

Definition 8 (Probabilistic convergence). *Let L be a predicate defined on configurations. A probabilistic distributed algorithm A under a scheduler D probabilistically converges to L iff : in any policy η of D, from any configuration c, the probability of the set of computations reaching a configuration satisfying L is equal to 1.*
Formally, $\lim_{n \to \infty} P_c^\eta(\exists m \leq n \mid X_m \in L) = 1$ where X_m is the reached state after m computation steps in the Markov chain defined as the MDP associated with A, c and η.

4 Extension to All k-Bounded Policies

We will show in the sequel that, under some simple conditions, the probabilistic convergence under **a** policy guarantees the probabilistic convergence under **any** k-bounded policies. After that, it is only needed to prove the convergence under **a** policy to formally prove the probabilistic convergence under the k-bounded scheduler for any value of k.

The first hypothesis we will assume is the serializability, a classical concurrency notion. It ensures that a schedule for executing concurrent machine rules is equivalent to one that executes the machine rule serially in some order.

Definition 9. *A computation step sas' is serializable iff s' is reachable from s by a series of computation steps where only a machine performs an action.*

An history $h = s_0a_0s_1a_1...s_l$ is serializable iff each computation step of h is serializable.

The second hypothesis is a property of probabilistic algorithms.

Definition 10. *A probabilistic distributed algorithm is potentially stable if and only if for each guarded rule there is a no zero probability that the execution of the rule does not change the machine state.*

Observation 1. *For a potentially stable distributed algorithm, there exists a real number ε_b, such that for any rule performed by any machine, the probability that this machine state does not change, is at least ε_b. (Because, the number of rules is finite). Thus, in any case, the probability that no machine changes its state during a computation step is at least $\varepsilon_b{}^N$ where N is the number of machines in the system.*

Notice that any distributed algorithm $\mathcal{A}$ can be transformed into a potential stable algorithm accoding the the following recIpe. Each rule of $\mathcal{A}$ $G \rightarrow A$ is remplaced by the rule

$$G \rightarrow if \ (random(1,0) == 0) \ then \ A.$$

Notation 1. $|h|$ *denotes the length of the sequence h.*

N *is the number of machines in the system.*

Sketch of the proof. The proof is almost constructive. We suppose that for a policy the algorithm converges, and then under the two assumptions desccripted above we find a bound in which the algorithm will be convergent for any arbitrary policy. To make it clearer we've done it step by step (first, when the action performed is only a one state action and then for any serializable algorithm). The conclusion is given in the last theorem.

Lemma 1. *Let A be a potentially stable algorithm. Assume that there exist two configurations s, s', and an action a such that $p_{ss'}(a) > 0$ and a contains a machine. Then, there is a real number $\varepsilon > 0$ such that in any k-bounded policy η, for any initial configuration s_0, for any history h ending at the configuration s, there exists a sequence h' of computation steps such that* *(i)* $P_{s_0}^{\eta}(w \in C_{hh'}) > P_{s_0}^{\eta}(w \in C_h)\varepsilon$, *(ii)* $|h'| \le kN$, *(iii)* $\varepsilon \ge \varepsilon_b{}^{kN^2} p_{ss'}(a)$, *and (iv) the last configuration of h' is s'.*

Proof. We prove that under any policy, it possible to reach s' after an history reaching s, in less that kN computation steps with a probability greater than ε.

Let η be a k-bounded policy. Let h be an history $s_0a_0s_1a_1s_2...a_ms$ such that $P_{s_0}^{\eta}(w \in C_h) \ne 0$.

An action a is the set of machines that perform a rule during the associated computation step. We study the case where only one machine performs a rule; we name it machine 1.

The η policy is k-bounded, thus there exists an action a_i in which the machine 1 executes a rule such that (i) $Q_{\eta}(a_i|s_0, s_1 ..., s_{m+i-1}) > 0$ assuming that $s_{m+j} = s \; \forall j \in [0, i-1]$, and (ii) $1 \le i < kN$. Note that by definition of a k bounded policy, we have the following property: $\forall l \in [0, i-1]$ there exists an action a_l such that $Q_{\eta}(a_i|s_0, s_1 ..., s_{m+1}) > 0$ assuming that $s_{m+j} = s \; \forall j \in [0, l]$.

We denote by h' the sequence $sa_1sa_2..sa_is'$ defined as: (i) during the execution of a_j where $j < i$ no machine changes its state, and (ii) during the execution of a_i only the machine 1 changes its states. We have (i) $P_{s_0}^{\eta}(w \in C_{hh'}) > P_{s_0}^{\eta}(w \in C_h)\varepsilon$, (ii) $\varepsilon > \varepsilon_b{}^{i+1N^2} p_{ss'}(a)$, (iii) $|h'| < kN$.

Lemma 2. *Let A be a potentially stable algorithm. Assume that there exist two configurations s, s', and an action a such that $p_{ss'}(a) > 0$ and $cs = sas'$ is serializable. Then, there is a real number $\varepsilon > 0$ such that in any k-bounded policy η, for any initial configuration s_0, for any history h ending at the configuration s, there exists a sequence h' of computation steps such that*

(i) $P_{s_0}^{\eta}(w \in C_{hh'}) > P_{s_0}^{\eta}(w \in C_h)\varepsilon$, *(ii)* $|h'| \le kN^2$, *(iii)* $\varepsilon \ge \varepsilon_b{}^{kN^3} p_{ss'}(a)$, *and (iv) the last configuration of h' is s'.*

Proof. We prove that under any policy, it possible to reach s' after an history reaching s, in less that kN^2 computation steps with a probability greater than ε.

$cs = sas'$ is serializable thus there exists a sequence of computation steps $s_0a'_1s'_1a'_2s'_2..a'_ns'_n$ of length $n < N$ that reaches s' from s and along this sequence, at most one machine performs an action at a time. We call i the machine executing a rule during a_i. $\forall i \in [0, n-1]$, we have $p_{s'_is'_{i+1}}(a'_i) > 0$ and, by definition, $p_{ss'}(a) = \prod_{i=0}^{n-1} p_{s'_is'_{i+1}}(a'_i)$.

Let η be a k-bounded policy. Let h be an history $s_0a_0s_1a_1s_2...s$ such that $P_{s_0}^{\eta}(w \in C_h) \ne 0$.

According to Lemma 1, for $1 \le i \le n$, there exists an history $h_i = h_{i-1}a_1s_2a_2...$ having the following properties :

(i) $h_0 = h$, (ii) $P_{s_0}^{\eta}(w \in C_{h_i}) > P_{s_0}^{\eta}(w \in C_{h_{i-1}})\varepsilon_i > 0$, (iii) $|h_i| < h_{i-1} + kN$, (iv) $\varepsilon_i \ge \varepsilon_b{}^{kN^2} p_{s_{i-1}s'_i}(a'_i)$, and (v) the last configuration of h_i is s'_i.

We conclude that the history h_n has the following properties (i) $P_{s_0}^{\eta}(w \in C_{h_n}) > P_{s_0}^{\eta}(w \in C_h)\varepsilon$ (ii) $|h_n| < |h| + kN^2$, (iii) $\varepsilon \ge \varepsilon_b{}^{kN^3} p_{ss'}(a)$, and (iv) the last configuration of h_n is s'.

Lemma 3. *Let A be a potentially stable algorithm. Assume that there exists η_s, a policy such that there is an history h_s of length l reaching a legitimate configuration and there is a real number $\varepsilon_s > 0$ such that (i) $P_{s_0}^{\eta_s}(w \in C_{h_s}) > \varepsilon_s$, and (ii) h_s is serializable.*

Then, there is a real number $\varepsilon > 0$ such that in any k-bounded policy η, for any initial configuration c, for any history h ending at the configuration s_0, there is a sequence h' such that (i) $P_c^{\eta}(w \in C_{hh'}) > P_c^{\eta}(w \in C_h)\varepsilon$, (ii) $|h'| \leq lkN^2$, (iii) $\varepsilon > \varepsilon_b^{lkN^3}\varepsilon_s$, and (iv) h' reaches a legitimate configuration.

Proof. We prove that under any policy, it possible to reach a legitimate configuration after an history reaching s_0, in less that lkN^2 computation steps with a probability greater than $\varepsilon_b^{lkN^3}\varepsilon_s$.

There exists a sequence $h_s = s_0 a_0 s_1 a_1 s_2 .. a_{l-1} s_l$ such that $P_{s_0}^{\eta_s}(w \in C_{h_s}) > \varepsilon_s$ and s_l is a legitimate configuration. We have $\varepsilon_s = \prod_{i=1}^{l} p_{s_{i-1}s_i}(a_{i-1}) > 0$. Thus $\forall i \in [1, l]$, we have $p_{s_{i-1}s_i}(a_{i-1}) > 0$. Moreover, $s_{i-1}a_{i-1}s_i$ is serializable, $\forall i \in [1, n]$.

Let η be a k-bounded policy. Let h be an history such that $P_s^{\eta}(w \in C_h) \neq 0$ and the last configuration of h is s_0.

According to Lemma 2, for $1 \leq i \leq n$, there exists an history h_i having the following properties (i) $P_c^{\eta}(w \in C_{h_i}) > P_c^{\eta}(w \in C_{h_{i-1}})\varepsilon_i > 0$ where $h_0 = h$ (ii) $\varepsilon_i > \varepsilon_b^{kN^3} p_{s_{i-1}s_i}(a_{i-1})$, (iii) $i < kN^2$ and (iii) the last configuration of h_i is s_i.

We conclude that the history h_l has the following properties (i) $P_c^{\eta}(w \in C_{h_l}) > P_c^{\eta}(w \in C_h)\varepsilon$, (ii) $|h_l| < |h| + lkN^2$, (iii) $\varepsilon > \varepsilon_b^{lkN^3}\varepsilon_s$, and (iv) the last configuration of h_l is legitimate.

Lemma 4. *Let A be a potentially stable algorithm. Assume that there exist a policy η_s, a real number $\varepsilon_s > 0$ and an integer l such that from any initial configuration c there is an history h reaching a legitimate configuration with (i) $P_c^{\eta_s}(w \in C_h) > \varepsilon_s$, (ii) h is serializable, and (iii) $|h| \leq l$.*

Then there is a real number $\varepsilon > 0$ such that in any k-bounded policy η, for any initial configuration c, for any history h there is an sequence h' such that (i) $P_c^{\eta}(w \in C_{hh'}) > P_c^{\eta}(w \in C_h)\varepsilon$, (ii) $|h'| \leq lkN^2$, (iii) $\varepsilon > \varepsilon_b^{lkN^3}\varepsilon_s$, and (iv) h' reaches a legitimate configuration.

Proof. We prove that under any policy, it possible to reach a legitimate configuration after any history, in less that lkN^2 computation steps with a probability greater than $\varepsilon_b^{lkN^3}\varepsilon_s$.

Let η be a k-bounded policy. Let h be an history such that $P_c^{\eta}(w \in C_h) \neq 0$; we name s_0 the reached configuration after the execution of h.

According to the hypothesis, there is an history h_s of length lesser than l reaching a legitimate configuration such that (i) $P_{s_0}^{\eta_s}(w \in C_{h_s}) > \epsilon_s$ and (ii) h_s is serializable.

According to Lemma 3, there exists a sequence h' having the following properties (ii) $P_c^{\eta}(w \in C_{hh'}) > P_c^{\eta}(w \in C_h)\epsilon > 0$, (iii) $\varepsilon > \varepsilon_b^{lkN^3}\varepsilon_s$, (iv) $|h'| < klN^2$ and (iii) the last configuration of h' is legitimate.

Theorem 1. *Let A be a potentially stable algorithm. Assume that there exist a policy η_s, a real number $\varepsilon_s > 0$ and an integer l such that from any initial configuration c there is an history reaching a legitimate configuration with (i) $P_c^{\eta_s}(w \in C_h) > \epsilon_s$, (ii) h is serializable, and (iii) $|h| \leq l$.*

Under the k-bounded scheduler, Algorithm A probabilistically converges to the legitimate configuration set.

The expected number of computation steps for reaching a legitimate configuration is bounded by $\frac{lkN^2}{\varepsilon_b^{lkN^3}\varepsilon_s}$.

Proof. Let η be a k-bounded policy. Let c be a configuration.

According to Lemma 4, there is a real number $\varepsilon > 0$ and an integer D such that for any history h there is an sequence h' such that (i) $P_c^{\eta}(w \in C_{hh'}) > P_c^{\eta}(w \in C_h)\varepsilon$, (ii) $|h'| \leq D$, (iii) h' reaches a legitimate configuration.

Let L be the set of legitimate configurations.

Thus we have $P_c^{\eta}(X_n \text{ reaches } L) > 1 - (1 - \varepsilon)^n$ where X_n contains all the histories of length lesser or equal to Dn.

We conclude that $\lim_{n \to \infty} P_c^{\eta}(X_n \text{ reaches } L) = 1$. Under the policy η, Algorithm A probabilistically converges to the legitimate configurations set.

In summary under any k-bounded policy, algorithm A probabilistically converges to the legitimate configurations set. The expected number of computation steps for reaching a legitimate configuration is bounded by $\frac{D}{\varepsilon}$. Notice that $1 > \varepsilon > \varepsilon_b^{lkN^3}\varepsilon_s$ and $D \leq lkN^2$, according Lemma 4.

5 Examples

The aim of these examples is to illustrate how our results can be used. For each algorithm, we exhibit a particular k-bounded policy for which the stabilization proof is easy. Then, we get, than the algorithm is stabilizing for any k-bounded policy.

5.1 Self-stabilizing Vertex Coloring

In this section, we study a very simple self-stabilizing vertex coloring algorithm (Algorithm 1). The algorithm converges from any configuration to a configuration where neighboring machines do not have the same color. A machine that has the same color as one of its neighbors is enabled. An enabled machine can randomly choose any color in the colors set (i.e. execute the $\mathcal{R}$ action). All

---

Algorithm 1. Self-stabilizing vertex coloring algorithm

Constant in p:
  B is a constant in N, we assume that $B > \Delta$ (the degree)

Variable on p: c_p color of p machine, taking its values in B

Action on p:
  $\mathcal{R}::\ \exists q \in N_p$ such that $c_p = c_q \longrightarrow c_p = random(1, B)$

colors have the same probability to be chosen: $1/B$ (B being the color set size). We assume that B is greater than the maximum machine degree, denoted Δ.

Let us study the algorithm under the memoryless policy η that chooses at each computation step one of the enabled machine. At each computation step, the probability that the executing machine chooses a color distinct of its neighbor colors is at least $\frac{B-\Delta}{B}$. Using the *measure* technique proposed in [16], one proves that from any initial configuration c, there is an history h reaching a legitimate configuration such that (i) $P_c^\eta(w \in C_h) > (\frac{B-\Delta}{B})^{N-1}$, and (ii) $|h| \leq N - 1$.

Using the Theorem 1, we directly establish that the vertex coloring algorithm converges under any k-bounded policy.

5.2 Token Circulation

Consider the following property:

Proposition 1. *there is a real $\varepsilon_s > 0$ and an integer l such that from any initial configuration c, there is an history h reaching a legitimate configuration such that (i) $P_c^{\eta_s}(w \in C_h) > \epsilon_s$, (ii) h is serializable, and (iii) $|h| \leq l$.*

We showed in the previous section that once this proposition is true for a policy η then the algorithms converges to its legitimate configuration under any k-bounded policy.

Herman [2] has proposed a token circulation algorithm under unidirectional rings of size 2N+1. This algorithm is a randomly delayed circulation (see code in Algorithm 2). Only a machine holding a token can take a step. A step consists in tossing a coin (probability $1/2$ for head and tail) and if head to transmit the token. Finally, the specification is that eventually, only one token circulates in the ring. In [2], the algorithm was proven under the synchronous policy. This algorithm is very interesting to analyse because there exists memoryless policy under which the algorithm does not converge. For instance, under the memoryless policy that chooses at each computation step one of the token in the set FAR, the set of tokens at maximum distance of predecessor.

Algorithm 2. Token circulation on anonymous and unidirectional rings

Variables on p: v_p is a boolean variable;

Random Variables on p:
$rand\_bool_p$ taking value in $\{1, 0\}$. Each value has a probability $1/2$.

Action on p: lp is the machine preceeding p
$\mathcal{R}$:: $v_p == v_{lp} \rightarrow$ if $rand\_bool_p = 1$ then $v_p := (v_p + 1) \bmod 2$;

Let us study the algorithm under the memoryless policy η that chooses at each computation step one of the tokens in the set $NEAR$, the set of tokens at minimum distance from teh predecessor. All computations under this policy are serializable, because in a computation step, a single machine performs an action. Using the *measure* technique proposed in [16], it can be proven that from any initial configuration c, there is an history h reaching a legitimate configuration such that (i) $P_c^\eta(w \in C_h) > \frac{1}{2^{2N}}$, and (ii) $|h| \leq 2N$.

Using the Theorem 1, we directly establish that Herman's algorithm converges under any k-bounded policy. Note that the policy η is not a k-bounded policy. Five years after the publication of this algorithm, Beauquier and al., [1], have proven the convergence of this algorithm under any memory k-bounded policy, Beauquier and al., in [15], have proven the convergence of this algorithm under any k-bounded policy.

6   Comparison of k-Bounded and Memory k-Bounded Policies

In this section, we assume that all policies are fair. Informally, a fair policy is a policy that "produces" only fair computations. The notion of fair/unfair computation is well known; but we need to define the meaning of the expression "produced computations by a policy η". If the probability of any prefix of a computation is not null in η the we say that η "produces" this computation.

A policy η is unfair if (i) there is an infinite computation in which a machine is continously enabled and never activated (ii) any prefix of this computation has a positive probability in η.

Definition 11 (Fairness). *Let η be a policy. Let comp be a computation where p is always enabled. η is said fair iff it exists n_{comp} such that $p \in a$ and $Q_\eta(a|\text{prefix of length } n_{comp} \text{ of comp})> 0$ or P^η (prefix of length n_{comp} of comp)$= 0$.*

Proposition 2. *Let A be an algorithm such that any machine has a bounded number T of states. Any fair memory k-bounded policy is α-bounded with $\alpha = T^{N^k} + k + 1$.*

Proof. Let η be a fair memory k-bounded policy.

Note that the number of distincts configuration sequences of length k is bounded by T^k.

Consider a computation *comp* of length $\alpha = T^{N^k} + k + 1$ where some machine p is always enabled and never performs a rule with $P^\eta(comp) > 0$. If no such computation exists then the algorithm is α-bounded. In *comp*, A same sequence of length k, s necesseraly appears twice: Thus $comp = s_0, s, s', s, s_f,$. We have $P^\eta(s, s') > 0$. Let us study the computation $comp' = (s, s)^*$. p is always enabled during *comp'*, for any value of n we have P^η(prefix of length n of comp')> 0. η is not fair because p is never in the set of selected machines by the policy along *comp'*: if $Q_\eta(a|\text{prefix of length } n_{comp} \text{ of comp}) > 0$ then p is not an element of a. There is a contradiction: η is a fair policy.

This proves that the class of memory k-bounded policies is included in the class of k-bounded policies.

There are k-bounded policies that are not memory K-bounded policies. For any value of f, $Policy(f)$ ($Policy(f)$ defined below) are 2-bounded, because all enabled machines execute a rule during even computation steps, but it is not memory K-bounded for any K. A possible sequence of choices of $Policy(2)$ is:

$$(\{p1,p2\},p1)^{2^1}, (\{p1,p2\},p2)^{2^2}, (\{p1,p2\},p1)^{2^3}, (\{p1,p2\},p1)^{2^4}, ...$$

A possible sequence of choices of $Policy(3)$ is:

$$(\{p1,p2\},p1)^{3^1}, (\{p1,p2\},p2)^{3^2}, (\{p1,p2\},p1)^{3^3}, (\{p1,p2\},p1)^{3^4}, ...$$

Policy 1. Policy(f)

Constant: N: the network size

Initialisation: counter0 := 1; counter1 := 0; pn := 0;

Policy(f) where f is an positif integer :
if the history length is an even number then all enabled machines are selected;
else
  if (count1 == 0) **then**
    counter0 := counter0*f; counter1 := counter0-1; np := np+1 mod N;
  else counter1 := counter1-1;
  fi
  while machine np is not enabled **do** np:=np+1 mod N; **done**
  The machine np is selected;
fi

---

7 Conclusion

In this paper we show that under assumptions all the k-bounded policies are equivalent for self-stabilization. Then, when an algorithm can be proven to be self-stabilizing for a particular k-bounded policy, it is also self-stabilizing for any k-bounded policy. This property is specially interesting when the self-stabilization proof is easy for a particular policy. The more obvious choice is the synchronous policy, but as we demonstrate it in the examples, some othe policies may be used in each particular case. The property allows to simplify existing proofs, to make some of them unnecessary (Herman's example). An important future work issue will be now to compare the convergence time between all these policies.

References

1. Beauquier, J., Cordier, S., Delaët, S.: Optimum probabilistic self-stabilization on uniform rings. In: Second Workshop on Self-Stabilizing Systems (WSS95). (1995) 15.1–15.15
2. Herman, T.: Probabilistic self-stabilization. Information Processing Letters **35** (1990) 63–67
3. Dolev, S., Israeli, A., Moran, S.: Analyzing expected time by scheduler-luck games. IEEE Transactions on Software Engineering **21** (1995) 429–439

4. Segala, R., Lynch, N.: Probabilistic simulations for probabilistic processes. In: 5th International Conference on Concurrency Theory (CONCUR'94), Springer-Verlag, LNCS:836. (1994) 481–496
5. Pogosyants, A., Segala, R.: Formal verification of timed properties of randomized distributed algorithms. In: 14th Annual ACM Symposium on Principles of Distributed Computing (PODC95). (1995) 174–183
6. Pogosyants, A., Segala, R., Lynch, N.: Verification of the randomized concensus algorithm of Aspnes and Herlihy: a case study. In: 11th International Workshop in Distributed Algorithms (WDAG97), Springer-Verlag, LNCS:1320. (1997) 22–36
7. Fribourg, L., Messika, S., Picaronny, C.: Coupling and Self-stabilization. In: 18th International Conference on Distributed Computing (DISC'04), Springer-Verlag, LNCS 3274, Springer (2004) 201–215
8. Fribourg, L., Messika, S.: Brief announcement: Coupling for markov decision processes - application to self-stabilization with arbitrary schedulers. In: 24th Annual ACM Symposium on Principles of Distributed Computing (PODC'05). (2005) 322
9. Beauquier, J., Johnen, C., Messika, S.: Brief announcement: Computing automatically the stabilization time against the worst and the best schedulers. In: 20th International Conference on Distributed Computing (DISC'06). (2006)
10. de Alfaro, L.: Formal Verification of Probabilistic systems. PhD Thesis, Stanford University (1997)
11. Lehmann, D., Rabin, M.O.: On the advantages of free choice: a symmetric and fully-distributed solution to the dining philosophers problem. In: 8th Annual ACM Symposium on Principles of Programming Languages (POPL'81). (1981) 133–138
12. Vardi, M.Y.: Automatic verification of probabilistic concurrent finite-state programs. In: 26th Annual Symposium on Foundations of Computer Science, IEEE Computer Society (FOCS'85). (1985) 327–338
13. Pnueli, A., Zuck, L.: Verification of multiprocess probabilistic protocols. Distributed Computing 1(1) (1986) 53–72
14. Johnen, C.: Service time optimal self-stabilizing token circulation protocol on anonymous unidirectional rings. In: 21th Symposium on Reliable Distributed Systems (SRDS 2002), IEEE (2002)
15. Beauquier, J., Gradinariu, M., Johnen, C.: Memory space requirements for self-stabilizing leader election protocols. In: 18th Annual ACM Symposium on Principles of Distributed Computing (PODC'99). (1999) 199–208
16. Duflot, M., Fribourg, L., Picaronny, C.: Finite-state distributed algorithms as markov chains. In: 15th International Symposium on Distributed Computing (DISC'01), Springer-Verlag LNCS:2180. (2001) 240–254

A 1-Strong Self-stabilizing Transformer

Joffroy Beauquier, Sylvie Delaët, and Sammy Haddad

Université Paris-Sud, PCRI, LRI (CNRS UMR 8623), INRIA Futurs, Orsay, France
jb@lri.fr,
{delaet, haddad}@lri.fr

Abstract. In this paper we study k-strong self-stabilizing systems, which satisfy the properties of strong confinement and of k-linear time adaptivity. Strong confinement means that a non faulty processor has the same behavior with or without the presence of faults elsewhere in the system (in other words faults are confined). k-linear time adaptivity means that after k or less faults hitting the system in a correct state, the recovery takes a number of rounds linear in k.

We show, under some conditions, how an asynchronous self-stabilizing system can be automatically transformed into an equivalent synchronous 1-strong self-stabilizing system where the recovery takes at most 3 rounds. We present in detail the transformer as well as a 1-strong synchronous unison algorithm. We also discuss how the construction can be extended to the k-strong case, for an arbitrary k.

Keywords: Self-stabilization, Fault Containment, k-strong, Transformer.

1 Introduction

Self-stabilization was introduced by Dijkstra in 1974 under the form of three algorithms for mutual exclusion. Nowadays this notion has been proven to be one of the most important in the field of fault tolerance for distributed systems. The reason is that self-stabilization guarantees, regardless of its initial state, that a system will eventually reach a legitimate state (a state from which the executions satisfy the specification), in particular when the initial state results from transient faults.

One of the actual challenge for stabilization is scalability. Most of the existing self-stabilizing algorithms are not scalable, in the sense that, even if a single processor is corrupted in a legitimate state, the convergence time may be proportional to the size of the system. In fact if no particular care is taken, a correct processor that has a faulty neighbor, detecting then an inconsistency, can "think" it is the culprit and change its state. Then in some sense the fault has been propagated and the same phenomenon can possibly be repeated again with the neighbors of the neighbors and so on. Thus even if the property of self-stabilization will take back the system in a legitimate state, first it will take a long time (especially in large systems), second a large number of processors (possibly all) will be involved in the recovery. For obvious reasons such systems are not scalable. Fault-containment is a major issue for the scalability of self-stabilizing solutions. Being able to confine the effect of the faults in a small perimeter

A.K. Datta and M. Gradinariu (Eds.): SSS 2006, LNCS 4280, pp. 95–109, 2006.
© Springer-Verlag Berlin Heidelberg 2006

is a necessary condition for translating theoretical solutions into real world solutions. But being able to confine the faults is not enough for most applications, because when a fault hits a self-stabilizing system, as long as a legitimate state is not reached, the behavior is incorrect and some safety conditions may not hold. Thus the best solution one could think of is to regain the consistency in a very small number of transition. As soon as a single fault appears, it is immediately corrected but if multiple faults hit simultaneously several processors, then the general self-stabilizing mechanism is used. Such a system would be instantaneously stabilizing for isolated faults and at the same time stabilizing for the most serious situations. Such a solution would be very high priced in terms of stabilization time and memory enlargement because every single move of the system should be carefully controlled. We choose here a trade-off between correction efficiency, memory enlargement and stabilization slow down. The systems will stabilize in 3 rounds or less in the former situation and be self-stabilizing in the latter.

Related works. The first time adaptive algorithms, as well as the notion of fault locality, were both introduced in [20] and [17], in the context of non reactive problems. These articles present algorithms for the persistent bit task. They stabilize in a time proportional to the number of corrupted nodes in the initial state of the system if that number does not exceed a fixed value. A first asynchronous fault containing algorithm for the same problem was introduced in [18]. General methods for transforming silent self-stabilizing algorithms into time adaptive algorithms were studied in [11], [17] and [14]. In [11] the authors present a transformation with a stabilization time in $\theta(1)$ if $k = 1$ and in $\theta(ST.D)$ for $k \geq 2$, where k is the number of faults, ST the stabilization time of the non transformed algorithm and D the diameter of the network. In [17], the idea is to replicate data and to use a voting strategy to repair data corrupted by transient faults. This transformation has an output stabilization time in $\theta(k)$ for a number of corrupted nodes lower or equal to $n/2$ (where n is the number of nodes in the system). Otherwise it stabilizes in $\theta(diam)$. [14] extends the idea of [17] to any number of corrupted nodes. In [6] appears the first time adaptive solution to a reactive problem, the mutual exclusion, but if the number of faults exceeds a predefined value then the system does not stabilize. Two algorithms for broadcast are presented in [19] and [4]. The algorithm of [19] is used to prove that any non silent algorithm in synchronous systems has an adaptive solution. In [4] the measure of agility which quantifies the strength of a reactive algorithm against state corrupting faults, is also defined and a broadcast algorithm is proven to guarantee error containment with optimal agility within a constant factor.

Other approaches of fault containment can be found in [1], [9], [15] and [21]. In [1] and [9] the notion of superstabilization is presented. A superstabilizing algorithm is a self-stabilizing algorithm that satisfies a passage predicate during recovery and thus restrains the effect of the faults. In [1] a local stabilizer transforming any algorithm into a self-stabilizing algorithm that stabilizes in $\theta(k)$ is presented. This transformation was the first to introduce the use of snapshots in order to locally detect and correct inconsistencies due to transient failures. The correction was performed by a system of votes based on the snapshots. The first algorithms for the problems of graph coloring and the dining philosophers locally resistant to Byzantine faults are presented in [21]. In this article a definition of fault containment in regard to a certain class of faults that limits the effect of a fault within a certain diameter is also presented. An interesting impossibility result can be found in [10]. In this article it is proven that a large class of reactive problems do not have an adaptive solution in asynchronous networks. The first article to introduce the problem of correcting a single failure in one computation step is [13]. The authors present a transformer of self-stabilizing algorithms into algorithms that may correct the fault in the next transition (with a certain probability given by the transformer) or stabilizes normally otherwise.

Our contribution. The first non-probabilistic 1-adaptive algorithm is presented in [5]. In this article the definition of 1-adaptivity is given, together with necessary and sufficient conditions for a self-stabilizing algorithm to be 1-adaptive under the asynchronous demon. A 1-adaptive self-stabilizing system is a self-stabilizing system that corrects any memory corruption of a single process in just one computation step. In other words it is a 1-strong self-stabilizing algorithm with an optimal convergence time of 1 transition if the system is hit by a single fault. Two algorithms (election on hypercubes and naming) show how the conditions can be used for building by hand 1-adaptive algorithms. In the present paper we go one step further in presenting an automatic transformer. We introduce k-strong self-stabilizing systems, which satisfy the properties of strong confinement and of k-linear time adaptivity. Strong confinement means that the execution of the algorithm by a non faulty processor from a legitimate configuration has the same behavior with or without the presence of faults in the system. k-linear time adaptivity means that after k or less faults hitting the system in a correct state, the recovery takes a number of rounds linear in k. We show, under some conditions, how an asynchronous self-stabilizing system can be automatically transformed into an equivalent synchronous 1-strong self-stabilizing system, becoming then resilient to the effect of scattered faults and so more likely to be used in real large systems.

The input of the transformer is a self-stabilizing algorithm under the asynchronous demon, the output an equivalent 1-strong self-stabilizing algorithm, correct under the synchronous demon. Roughly speaking the transformer manages for each processor a local snapshot (the view is reduced to the processor and its neighbors). The idea of using snapshots is not new, but previous works used to manage a complete snapshot of the system, while we use a memory enlargement only proportional to the degree of the network. Thanks to these snapshots, a corrupted processor can detect inconsistencies and regain its consistency by consensus with the neighbor's snapshots. On the contrary, the neighbors, that also detect the inconsistency, are made unable to take any step and then the corruption is not propagated. We restrain our attention to the case of a single fault. Note that the general case of k faults, for an integer k, could be treated with the same basic ideas, but in a more complicated way (Cf. conclusion).

2 Model

We will use in this article the widely adopted state reading model for self-stabilizing systems. It is inspired from [3] for the description of the communication network and from [22] for its representation by a transition system. A distributed algorithm is a set of processors connected by communication links. It is represented by a **communication graph** $G = (\mathcal{P}, \mathcal{E})$ where $\mathcal{P}$ is a set of processors and $\mathcal{E}$ a set of edges, $l = (p_i, p_j)$, where $(p_i, p_j) \in \mathcal{P}^2$ and $p_i \neq p_j$. Two processors p_i and p_j of G are said to be **neighbors** and can communicate in G if and only if $(p_i, p_j) \in \mathcal{E}$ or $(p_j, p_i) \in \mathcal{E}$. We note $\mathcal{N}_{p_i}$ the set of p_i's neighbors in G and $\delta_{p_i} = |\mathcal{N}_{p_i}|$ the number of this neighbors. A **processor** p_i is a state machine. Its state, noted e_{p_i}, is the vector of all the values of its variables. The set of all the possible state of a processor p_i is noted S_{p_i}. A processor has a set of **guarded rules** also called moves and noted $A_{p_i} = \{l_{p_i}^1, ..., l_{p_i}^{\alpha_{p_i}}\}$, where each rule is of the form $< label >::< guard > \rightarrow < action >$, $label$ is the identifier of the rule, $label \in A_{p_i}$, $guard$ is a boolean expression over p_i's and p_i's neighbors' variables and $action$ updates the values of p_i's variables.

A distributed system is a **transition system** $S = (\mathcal{C}, \mathcal{T})$, where $\mathcal{C}$ is the set of configurations of the system and $\mathcal{T}$ the set of its transitions. A **configuration** of the system $C \in \mathcal{C}$ is a vector $C = (e_{p_i}, ..., e_{p_j})$ of the processors' states of S. We note $C_{|P}$ the restriction of the configuration C to a set of processors $P = \{p_i, ..., p_j\}$, $P \subset \mathcal{P}$ and $Dist(C, C')$, the **distance** between two configurations C and C' ($Dist(C, C')$ is the number of processors which have a different state in C and C'). We say that a guarded rule $l_{p_i}^j \in A_{p_i}$ is **executable** in a configuration C if and only if its guard is true in C. We consider that every processor p_i has for each guarded rule $l_{p_i}^k \in A_{p_i}$ a function $g_{p_i}^k : S_{p_i} \times \prod_{p_j \in \mathcal{N}_{p_i}} S_{p_j} \rightarrow \{true, false\}$ where $g_{p_i}^k(C_{|p_i}, \{C_{|p_j} \mid p_j \in \mathcal{N}_{p_i}\})$ returns true if the guard $l_{p_i}^k$ of p_i is evaluated to true in C and false otherwise. A **transition** of $\mathcal{T}$ is a triple (C, t, C'), where $(C, C') \in \mathcal{C}^2$ and t is a set of label $l_{p_i}^j$ such that $l_{p_i}^j \in A_{p_i}$ and $g_{p_i}^j(C_{|p_i}, \{C_{|p_j} \mid p_j \in \mathcal{N}_{p_i}\}) = true$. C' is obtained by updating the state in C of every processor p_i by executing the action $a_{p_i}^j$ of the guarded rule $l_{p_i}^j$, $l_{p_i}^j \in t$, where $a_{p_i}^j$ is a function, $a_{p_i}^j : S_{p_i} \times \prod_{p_j \in \mathcal{N}_{p_i}} S_{p_j} \rightarrow S_{p_i}$ and $a_{p_i}^j(C_{|p_i}, \{C_{|p_j} \mid p_j \in \mathcal{N}_{p_i}\}) = C'_{|p_i}$. We say that a processor p_i is **enabled** in a configuration C if and only if one of its guarded rule is executable in C, formally: $\exists l_{p_i}^j \in A_{p_i}, g(C_{|p_i}, \{C_{|p_k} \mid p_k \in \mathcal{N}_{p_i}\}, l_{p_i}^j) = true$. An **execution** E_α of a system S is a maximal sequence of configurations, $E_\alpha = (C_0, C_1, ...)$, so either the sequence is infinite or the last configuration is terminal (no processor is enabled). We have $C_0 = \alpha$ and for every configuration $C_i \in E_\alpha$ there is a t such that $(C_{i-1}, t, C_i) \in \mathcal{T}$.

It is well known that the two models of distributed algorithms and distributed systems are canonically equivalent (the variables of the algorithm yield the configurations of the system, the actions yield the transitions). We will freely use this two models in the sequel.

The set of the possible executions of a system is restricted by the **demon**. The **distributed demon** chooses for each transition any subset of the enabled processors in C to apply one of their executable rules. A system that works under the distributed demon is said to be asynchronous. The **synchronous demon** chooses for each transition the set of all the enabled processors.

The **specification** of a problem is a predicate over the system executions. The specification of a **static problem** is a predicate over the system configurations. We call **output variables** of a system the set of variables which have to verify the specification. Let $S = (\mathcal{C}, \mathcal{T})$ be a transition system and Spe be a specification of a problem. Then S is **self-stabilizing** for Spe if and only if there is a subset $\mathcal{L}$ of configurations, called **legitimate configurations** such that: (i) Every execution that starts in a configuration of $\mathcal{L}$ satisfies Spe; *(ii)* Every execution reaches a configuration of $\mathcal{L}$. A **silent** self-stabilizing system is a self-stabilizing system such that all the legitimate configurations are terminal. A self-stabilizing system S has the property of **strong confinement** if and only if for any pair of configurations (C, C') of S such that $C \in \mathcal{L}$, $C' \notin \mathcal{L}$ and C' is obtained by corrupting any number of processors (arbitrarily changing their state), there is for every execution $E_{C'}$ of S an execution E_C of the system such that for every processor p_i having the same state in C and C', the projection of the execution on the output variables of p_i are identical in E_C and $E_{C'}$. A self-stabilizing system has the property of **k-linear adaptivity** if and only if, for every execution of S starting in an illegitimate configuration at distance at most k from the nearest legitimate configuration, these executions reach a legitimate configuration in a number of transition smaller or equal to $\alpha \times k$, where α is a constant. Finally we define a self-stabilizing system S as being **k-strong** if and only if it has the property of strong confinement for any configuration with no more than k faulty process and the property of linear k-adaptivity. By extension we say that an algorithm associated to a distributed system S is synchronous, asynchronous, self-stabilizing or 1-strong if and only if S is synchronous, asynchronous, self-stabilizing or 1-strong.

3 Transformer

We present in this article a general transformer of asynchronous silent self-stabilizing algorithms into synchronous silent 1-strong self-stabilizing algorithms. Both, the original and the transformed algorithm, work on the same identified communication graphs with no processor of degree 1. The transformed algorithm is composed of a set of snapshots actions (Cf. section 3.2), noted $Snap$, and a set of modified actions of the input algorithm, noted $Stab$ (Cf. section 3.3). The transformed algorithm alternates synchronous rounds of stabilization with rounds of snapshots (respectively named: **snapshot round** and **stabilization round**). This alternation is obtained by the composition of the transformed algorithm with a 1-strong synchronous unison algorithm that can regain the unison after a single fault in a single round (Cf. section 3.1). This algorithm stabilizes in at most $4D$ rounds where D is the diameter of the system. The final transformed algorithm has then, after the stabilization of the unison, a stabilization time of 2 times the stabilization time of the input algorithm (because of the alternation of rounds). In the case of a single fault the system will correct the output variables of the faulty process as soon as it will make a transition involving the output variables (that is in at most 2 rounds) and regain a legitimate configuration during the following round, in the snapshot part.

The assumption on the topology is made for the sake of performance. Consider a processor of degree one and assume it detects an inconsistency on its output variables. There are at least two possible reasons for that: it has been the only processor hit by a fault or its unique neighbor is the only processor hit by a fault. The isolated processor cannot distinguish between the two situations by itself. It has to wait that its neighbors take a step (we exclude the case of a network of two processors of degree 1). That would imply that the general correction mechanism would take 5 rounds instead of 3 when the hypothesis is made, as we need an idle stabilization round before the correction.

The hypothesis for the algorithm to be silent is used for the same reason. The main difference between silent and not silent is that, for the latter, a processor cannot know immediately whether one of its neighbor has changed its state because of a normal step or because of a corruption. In the case of a normal step the processor must execute the algorithm normally, and perhaps take a step itself in the next round, but in the case of a corruption it has to freeze, waiting for the corrupted processor to be corrected. Clearly the processor has not enough information to distinguish between the two cases, but this information will be allowable to him during the next round, if it decides not to do anything during the present one. This case can be treated by adding an idle round after each effective round (a round in which the algorithm is executed) and then an extra dilatation factor passing from 2 to 3 for each execution step.

The need to identify the processors comes from the use of snapshots. Finally the hypothesis of asynchrony for the input algorithm comes from the fact that we cannot avoid that some processor has to be frozen sometimes for not taking the risk to propagate a fault. Thus the processors may sometimes move asynchronously. We can note that many common topologies have no processor of degree one like rings, grids, hypercubes, etc. Moreover most of the common problems concerning in distributed systems have silent self-stabilizing asynchronous solutions (leader election, topology construction, processor naming, construction of routing tables, etc.).

3.1   Synchronous Unison

To be able to alternate synchronously this succession of rounds we need to use a synchronizer. Several self-stabilizing algorithms for the problem of synchronous unison already exist ([12], [2], [16] and [7]). The unison algorithm has to correct immediately a single corruption so that the faulty processor can recover immediately the unison. Otherwise the fault would be propagated as the processors would start to move asynchronously.

We use the synchronous unison presented in [7] with slight modifications (Cf. algorithm 1-Strong-SS-MinSU). The general self-stabilizing mechanism is still the same. We have added a correction action for the faulty processor (in case of a single local fault), action $1A$, and a specific action of no propagation of fault for its neighbors, action RF. Action RF has the property that it cannot be executed two rounds in a row. Thus a processor is not affected by a fault (in case of a single fault) and is not blocked for the stabilization, having the same behavior as in the input algorithm afterwards. Due to the lack of space we do not give the proof here but this algorithm verifies the two following theorems.

Theorem 1. *Algorithm 1-Strong-SS-MinSU is self-stabilizing and has a stabilization time of $4D$, where D is the diameter of the system.*

Theorem 2. *Algorithm 1-Strong-SS-MinSU is 1-strong and recover the unison in a single transition in the case of a single fault.*

We have now a 1-strong self-stabilizing synchronous unison algorithm (here we chose K=1). We will compose this algorithm with the actions of *Snap* and *Stab* produced

Algorithm 1. 1-Strong-SS-MinSU

Constants and Variables:
$\mathcal{N}_p$: set of neighbors of process p;
$\mathcal{N}_p^+$: $\mathcal{N}_p^+ = \mathcal{N}_p \cup \{p\}$;
r : synchronizer value in $\chi = (tail_\varphi^* = \{-(2D), ..., -1\}) \cup (stab_\varphi = \{0, ..., K\})$;
RPF : counter in $\{0, 1\}$ indicating the possible non-propagation of a reset in the past round;

Boolean Functions:
$LocalUnison \equiv \forall q \in \mathcal{N}_p : (r = q.r)$;
$NormalStep \equiv r \in Stab_\varphi \wedge LocalUnison$;
$TailStep \quad \equiv \exists q \in \mathcal{N}_p^+ : q.r \in tail_\varphi^*$;
$ResetInit \quad \equiv (\forall q \in \mathcal{N}_p^+ : q.r \in stab_\varphi \wedge \neg LocalUnison)$
$ResetFrozen \equiv \exists q \in \mathcal{N}_p : r \neq q.r, \forall k \in \mathcal{N}_p \setminus \{q\} : (r = k.r) \wedge r \in Stab_\varphi \wedge RPF = 0$;
$1\text{-}faulty \quad \equiv \forall q \in \mathcal{N}_p, \forall k \in \mathcal{N}_p \setminus \{q\}, (r \neq q.r) \wedge (q.r = k.r) \wedge q.r \in Stab_\varphi$;
$1\text{-}local\text{-}fault \quad \equiv 1\text{-}faulty \vee ResetFrozen$

Functions:
$RPF\text{-}Reset \equiv$ if $(RPF = 1)$ then $RPF := 0$;
$RPF\text{-}Set \quad \equiv$ if $(RPF = 0)$ then $RPF := 1$;
$\varphi(r) \qquad \equiv$ if (r = 1) then r:=0 else r := r+1 ;

Actions:
NA : $NormalStep$ $\qquad\qquad \to r := \varphi(r), RPF\text{-}Reset$;
TA : $TailStep \wedge \neg\ 1\text{-}local\text{-}fault \to r := \varphi(min\{q.r, q \in \mathcal{N}_p^+\}), RPF\text{-}Reset$;
RA : $ResetInit \wedge \neg\ 1\text{-}local\text{-}fault \to r := -2D, RPF\text{-}Reset$; (*Reset*)
RF : $ResetFrozen \qquad\qquad \to r := \varphi(r), RPF\text{-}Set$;
1A : $1\text{-}faulty \qquad\qquad\qquad \to r := \varphi(q.r), q \in \mathcal{N}_p, RPF\text{-}Reset$;

by the transformer by using a fair composition (Cf. [8]). The transformer will alternate two types of rounds by checking that either r is equal to 0 for stabilization rounds ($Stab$ actions) or 1 for snapshot rounds ($Snap$ actions). If r is negative then the transformed algorithm only executes stabilization rounds to let the system stabilize faster.

3.2 Local Snapshots

The principle of the transformation is to keep in every processor an image of the local partial configuration of the system. Then, because the system is assumed to be silent, a faulty processor is able to detect and correct a fault in a legitimate state by detecting an inconsistency between its state and the image of its past state that its neighbors have stored in their snapshots.

In the sequel we will use the following notations and definitions. We call **partial state** of a processor p_i for a transformed algorithm in a configuration C the projection of $C_{|p_i}$ on the variables of the input algorithm and we note it $e_{p_{p_i}}$. We call **local partial configuration** of the system for a processor p_i in a configuration C the set of the partial states of p_i and all of its neighbors.

Each processor maintains three local views of the system named $StabSnap$, Cur-$Snap$ and $LastSnap$. $CurSnap$ contains a local partial image of the system at the beginning of the current round. $LastSnap$ contains the local partial image of the system at the beginning of the past snapshot round. Finally $StabSnap$ is updated if and only if the system locally stays in the same local partial configuration during two stabilization rounds. This corresponds to the fact that a processor detects that the

Algorithm 2. Snap

Functions:

/* CorrectSnaps() returns true if the 3 snapshots of p_i contain the current local partial configuration of the system. */

CorrectSnaps():

return($StabSnap = CurSnap = LastSnap \land StabSnap[p_i] = e_{p_{p_i}}$
$\land \; \forall p_j \in \mathcal{N}_{p_i}, StabSnap[p_j] = e_{p_{p_j}}$ **);**

/* SnapCorCond() returns true if all the snapshots of all the neighbors of p_i are consistent and they all contains the current local partial configuration of the system. */

SnapCorCond():

return($\forall p_j \in \mathcal{N}_{p_i}, p_j.StabSnap = p_j.LastSnap \land p_j.StabSnap[p_i] = e_{p_{p_i}}$
$\land p_j.StabSnap[p_j] = e_{p_{p_j}}$
$\forall p_k \in \mathcal{N}_{p_i} \cap \mathcal{N}_{p_j}, p_j.StabSnap[p_k] = e_{p_{p_k}}$
$\forall p_l \in \mathcal{N}_{p_j} \cap \mathcal{N}_{p_k}, p_j.StabSnap[p_l] = p_k.StabSnap[p_l]$ **);**

Actions:

$Snap1$ **(Snapshots Correction 1):**
  $\neg CorrectSnaps() \land SnapCorCond()$
$\rightarrow CurSnap := StabSnap, LastSnap := StabSnap, \forall p_j \in \mathcal{N}_{p_i} \cup \{p_i\},$
  $StabSnap[p_j] := e_{p_{p_j}};$

$Snap2$ **(Snapshots Correction 2):**
  $g_{p_i}^{Snap1}(e_{p_i}, \{e_{p_j} \mid p_j \in \mathcal{N}_{p_i}\}) = false \land \neg CorrectSnaps()$
$\land \; \forall p_j \in \mathcal{N}_{p_i} \cup \{p_i\}, StabSnap[p_j] = LastSnap[p_j] = e_{p_{p_j}}$
$\land \; \forall p_k \in \mathcal{N}_{p_i} \cup \{p_i\} \setminus \{p_j\} StabSnap[p_k] = CurSnap[p_k] = LastSnap[p_k] = e_{p_{p_k}}$
$\rightarrow CurSnap := StabSnap;$

$Snap3$ **(Snapshots):**
  $g_{p_i}^{Snap1}(e_{p_i}, \{e_{p_j} \mid p_j \in \mathcal{N}_{p_i}\}) = false \land g_{p_i}^{Snap2}(e_{p_i}, \{e_{p_j} \mid p_j \in \mathcal{N}_{p_i}\}) = false$
$\land \; \neg CorrectSnaps() \land \forall p_j \in \mathcal{N}_{p_i} \cup \{p_i\}, CurSnap[p_j] = e_{p_{p_j}}$
$\rightarrow StabSnap := CurSnap, LastSnap := CurSnap;$

$Snap4$ **(Snapshots):**
  $g_{p_i}^{Snap1}(e_{p_i}, \{e_{p_j} \mid p_j \in \mathcal{N}_{p_i}\}) = false \land g_{p_i}^{Snap2}(e_{p_i}, \{e_{p_j} \mid p_j \in \mathcal{N}_{p_i}\}) = false$
$\land \; g_{p_i}^{Snap3}(e_{p_i}, \{e_{p_j} \mid p_j \in \mathcal{N}_{p_i}\}) = false \land \neg CorrectSnaps()$
$\rightarrow LastSnap := CurSnap, \forall p_j \in \mathcal{N}_{p_i} \cup \{p_i\}, CurSnap[p_j] := e_{p_{p_j}};$

---

system may be in a legitimate configuration. The snapshots are the key points of the transformer. They are taken after each executions of the actions of *Self-Stab* and are maintained thanks to the actions of *Snap*. *Snap* is composed of four actions, respectively named $Snap1$, $Snap2$, $Snap3$ and $Snap4$ (Cf. algorithm 3.2). Here are their intuitive descriptions. *Snap1: If a processor p_i detects that the systems seems to be in a configuration where only p_i's snapshots are corrupted,* then p_i corrects its snapshots by replacing the corrupted values of its snapshots by the current local partial states. *Snap2: If p_i detects that the system was in a legitimate state (or seemed so) and that there has been one corrupted processor in its neighborhood that has already been corrected,* then it replaces its $CurSnap$ view by the current local partial configuration, in order to remove from $CurSnap$ the corrupted state of its neighbor. *Snap3: If the system has not locally moved during the past round and so seems to be stabilized,* then p_i puts in its three snapshots the current local partial view of the system if they do not already contain it. *Snap4: If at least one processor in the neighborhood of p_i (including p_i) has changed its partial state during the last transition,* then it puts in its *LastSnap* view the value of its *CurSnap* view and it puts in its *CurSnap* view the local view of the system.

If no processor has changed its partial state and all the snapshots of the processors contain the current value of the local partial configuration, then the processor executes no action and do not change the snapshots. The actions are mutually exclusive.

As already said in the introduction, the idea of taking snapshots to detect and correct an inconsistency is not new in the field of self-stabilization. But here, contrary to what was done before ([1], [5]) we just keep a local (not global) snapshot of the system. Indeed we enlarge the memory of a processor p_i by a factor $3 * \delta_{p_i}$. The global memory space used by the algorithm is enlarged by a factor not greater than $3 * \delta$, where δ is the degree of the system.

3.3 Transformed Actions of the Input Algorithm

The second step of the transformation consists in slightly modifying the actions of the input algorithm (actions T_{A_k}) and adding a correction action (CA) such that the system becomes 1-strong. CA detects a possible inconsistency between the current state of the processor and the partial local configuration stored in its neighbor snapshot. This action is executed by the faulty processor in case of a single local fault. The corrupted processor is corrected thanks to a consensus on its neighbors snapshots that contain its former correct partial state.

All the other actions are the actions of the original algorithm to which we add the test of the function $Freeze$, that is used to block any fault propagation. All the functions used by the transformer are presented here. *Transition():* The function $Transition$ tests wether or not the current partial state of the processor is reachable by a normal transition of the system from the last local partial state stored in the snapshots of its neighbors. *Consensus():* The function Consensus() tests wether or not in every $StabSnap$ view of a neighbor there is a same partial state different from the current one. If it is the case then $Consensus()$ returns this partial state, $\emptyset$ otherwise. *(δ)-CNS():* The function (δ)-CNS() tests wether or not the snapshots of the neighbors are mutually consistent and also consistent with the current local partial configuration, more specifically if all the values in the snapshots are equal to the current partial state of every common neighbor. *InconsistentSnapshot():* The function InconsistentSnapshot() returns true if a processor in the neighborhood of p has a different value in its snapshots that the value stored in p's $CurSnap$ view or $LastSnap$ view for a common neighbor q. *PSCC:* The function PSCC() returns true if $Consensus$ returns a partial state different from the current partial state of p_i and all its neighbors snapshots are consistent with each other and either its snapshots are not consistent with their snapshots. or its partial state cannot be obtained by a normal transition of the system from the local partial configuration of the past round stored in the snapshots. *Freeze:* If, thanks to the local snapshots in the neighborhood of the processor p_i, p_i detects that only one of its neighbors, p_j, has made a move during the last two stabilization rounds, whereas all the other processors did not move, then p_i presumed that p_j might be faulty and $Freeze$ returns true.

Algorithm 3. Stab

Variables:

V_{algo}: Set of variables of the original algorithm;

LastSnap: array of $PartialStates$ of size δ;

CurSnap: array of $PartialStates$ of size δ;

StabSnap: array of $PartialStates$ of size δ;

Functions:

Transition($e'_{p_{p_i}}, \{e_{p_{p_j}} \mid p_j \in \mathcal{N}_{p_i}\}$):

$return\ (\ \exists l_{p_i}^k \in A_{p_i},$
$\qquad g_{p_i}^k(e_{p_{p_i}}, \{e_{p_{p_j}} \mid p_j \in \mathcal{N}_{p_i}\}) = true \wedge a_i^j(e'_{p_{p_i}}, \{e_{p_{p_j}} \mid p_j \in \mathcal{N}_{p_i}\}) = e_{p_{p_i}}\ );$

Consensus():

if ($\forall p_j \in \mathcal{N}_{p_i}, \forall p_k \in \mathcal{N}_{p_i},$
$\qquad p_k \neq p_j \wedge p_j.StabSnap[p_i] = p_k.StabSnap[p_i] \wedge p_j.StabSnap[p_i] \neq e_{p_{p_i}}$)

then $\ return(p_j.StabSnap[p_i]);$

else $\ return(\emptyset);$

(δ)-CNS():

$\quad return(\ \forall p_j \in \mathcal{N}_{p_i}, p_j.StabSnap = p_j.LastSnap$
$\qquad\qquad \wedge p_j.StabSnap[p_j] = p_j.CurSnap[p_j] = e_{p_{p_j}}$
$\qquad\qquad \forall p_k \in \mathcal{N}_{p_i} \cap \mathcal{N}_{p_j} \setminus \{p_i\}, p_j.StabSnap[p_k] = p_j.CurSnap[p_k]$
$\qquad\qquad \forall p_l \in \mathcal{N}_{p_j} \cap \mathcal{N}_{p_k}, p_j.StabSnap[p_l] = p_k.StabSnap[p_l]$
$\qquad\qquad \forall p_l \in \mathcal{N}_{p_i} \cap \mathcal{N}_{p_j} \cap \mathcal{N}_{p_k} \setminus \{p_i\}, p_j.StabSnap[p_l] = e_{p_{p_l}}\qquad\ );$

InconsistentSnapshot():

$return(\ \exists p_j \in \mathcal{N}_{p_i}, \exists p_k \in \mathcal{N}_{p_i} \cap \mathcal{N}_{p_j} \cup \{p_i\} \cup \{p_j\},$
$\qquad\qquad CurSnap[p_k] \neq p_j.CurSnap[p_k] \vee LastSnap[p_k] \neq p_j.LastSnap[p_k]\ );$

PSCC():

$return\ (\ Consensus() \neq 0 \wedge (\delta) - CNS() \wedge (InconsistentSnapshot()$
$\qquad\qquad \vee \neg transition(Consensus, \{e_{p_{p_j}} \mid p_j \in \mathcal{N}_{p_i}\}))\qquad\qquad\qquad);$

Freeze():

return($\ StabSnap = LastSnap$
$\qquad\qquad \wedge \exists p_j \in \forall p_k \in \mathcal{N}_{p_i} \setminus \{p_j\},$
$\qquad\qquad p_k.StabSnap = p_k.LastSnap, \wedge p_k.StabSnap[p_i] = e_{p_{p_i}}$
$\qquad\qquad \wedge StabSnap[p_k] = CurSnap[p_k] = e_{p_{p_k}} \wedge StabSnap[p_j] \neq e_{p_{p_j}}$
$\qquad\qquad \forall p_l \in \mathcal{N}_{p_i} \cap \mathcal{N}_{p_k} \setminus \{p_j\}, StabSnap[p_l] = p_k.StabSnap[p_l]\qquad\ );$

Correction Actions:

CA **(Partial State Correction):**

$PSCC()$

$\rightarrow e_{p_{p_i}} := Consensus(), \forall p_j \in \mathcal{N}_{p_i} \cup \{p_i\}, CurSnap[p_j] := e_{p_{p_j}};$

Stabilisation Actions:

$\forall l_{p_i}^k \in A_{p_i},$

T_{A_k} **(Stabilisation):**

$\neg Freeze \wedge g_{p_i}^{CA}(e_{p_i}, \{e_{p_j} \mid p_j \in \mathcal{N}_{p_i}\}) = false \wedge g_{p_i}^{l_{p_i}^k}(e_{p_{p_i}}, \{e_{p_{p_j}} \mid p_j \in \mathcal{N}_{p_i}\}) = true$

$\rightarrow a_{l_i};$

3.4   Proof

Due to the lack of space we do not give the complete proof here. In the sequel we need and assume the following notations and hypothesis. Let $G = (\mathcal{P}, \mathcal{E})$ be an identified communication graph with no processor of degree 1. Let Alg be a self-stabilizing algorithm for the problem specification Spe that is correct under the distributed demon. Let $\mathcal{L}_A$ be the set of legitimate configurations of Alg. Let $S_A = (\mathcal{C}_A, \mathcal{T}_A)$ be its associated transition system. Let Alg_t be the transformation of Alg by the transformer 3.3 for the communication graph G. Let $S_{Alg_t} = (\mathcal{C}_{Alg_t}, \mathcal{T}_{Alg_t})$ be its associated transition system under the synchronous demon. We first prove that the transformed algorithm is self-stabilizing.

Lemma 1. *At most 4 rounds after the first round of unison, in which for every processor* $r = RPF = 0$ *(Cf. section 3.1), then every processor p_i of S_{Alg_t} has in its $CurSnap$ view the current partial local configuration, in its $LastSnap$ view the partial local configuration at the end of the second last stabilization round (except possibly for one processor of its snapshots).*

Sketch of the proof. After at most 4 rounds after the unison we have that the snapshots of all the processors are almost correct. The only possibility for a snapshot not to be correct is when a processor in the neighborhood changed its state during one round and regained the previous state in the following round.

Every round of snapshot, every processor puts in its $CurSnap$ view the current value of its partial state and of the partial state of its neighbors, whatever action of $Snap$ is executed (Cf. $Snap1$, $Snap2$, $Snap3$, $Snap4$ p. 102). Otherwise if a processor does not execute any action of $Snap$ then its $CurSnap$ view already contains this value.

Let $T_1 = (C_i, t_1, C_{i+1})$, $T_2 = (C_{i+1}, t_2, C_{i+2})$, $T_3 = (C_{i+2}, t_3, C_{i+3})$, $T_4 = (C_{i+3}, t_4, C_{i+4})$, $T_1, T_2, T_3, T_4 \in \mathcal{T}_{Alg_t}$ such that in C_i: $\forall p_i \in \mathcal{P}$, $p_i.r = p_i.RPF = 0$. We get that in C_{i+2} every processor has in its $CurSnap$ view the current local partial state of the system. Thus if a processor p_i executes in T_4 the action $Snap4$, then by definition there is at least one processor in the neighborhood of p_i that changed its state during T_3. Thus p_i puts in its $CurSnap$ view the current local partial configuration and in its $LastSnap$ view the former value of its $CurSnap$ view. We get for p_i: $\forall p_j \in \mathcal{N}_{p_i} \cup \{p_i\}$, $C_{i+4|p_i}.CurSnap[p_j] - C_{i|3|e_{p_{p_j}}} = C_{i+4|e_{p_{p_j}}}, C_{i+4|p_i}.LastSnap[p_j] - C_{i+1|e_{p_{p_j}}} = C_{i+2|e_{p_{p_j}}}$.

Now if p_i executes $Snap1$, $Snap2$ or $Snap3$ then at most one processor in the neighborhood of p_i changed its state during T_3. Then either we get the same property as above if no processor changed its state during T_3 or if processor p_j did, we get: $\exists p_j \in \mathcal{N}_{p_i} \cup \{p_i\}, C_{i+4|p_i}.LastSnap[p_j] = C_{i+3|e_{p_{p_j}}} \neq C_{i+1|e_{p_{p_j}}}, \forall p_k \in \mathcal{N}_{p_i} \cup \{p_i\}, C_{i+4|p_i}.StabSnap[p_k] = C_{i+1|e_{p_{p_k}}} = C_{i+3|e_{p_{p_k}}}, C_{i+4|p_i}.CurSnap[p_k] = C_{i+3|e_{p_{p_k}}}, \forall p_k \in \mathcal{N}_{p_i} \cup \{p_i\} \setminus \{p_j\}, C_{i+4|p_i}.LastSnap[p_k] = C_{i+1|e_{p_{p_k}}}$. □

Lemma 2. *At most 4 rounds after the first round of unison, in which for every processor* $r = RPF = 0$, *no processor in the system can execute the correction action, CA.*

Sketch of the proof. From the first lemma we have that no processor evaluates the function $Transition$ to false after the fourth round following the unison.

In fact, let $T_1 = (C_i, t_1, C_{i+1}), T_2 = (C_{i+1}, t_2, C_{i+2}), T_3 = (C_{i+2}, t_3, C_{i+3}), T_4 = (C_{i+3}, t_4, C_{i+4})$, $T_1, T_2, T_3, T_4 \in \mathcal{T}$ such that in C_i: $\forall p_i \in \mathcal{P} p_i.r = RPF = 0$. Suppose that p_i evaluates the guard of CA to true in C_{i+4}. Then p_i evaluates $PSCC()$

to true and thus $Consensus()$ to $e_{p_{p_i}}$, $e_{p_{p_i}} \neq C_{i+4|e_{p_{p_i}}}$ and (δ)-CNS() to true which means that: $\forall p_j \in \mathcal{N}_{p_i}, p_j.StabSnap[p_i] = p_j.LastSnap[p_i] = e_{p_{p_i}}$ and $p_j.Stab\text{-}$ $Snap[p_j] = p_j.CurSnap[p_j] = C_{i+4|p_{p_j}}$. By lemma 1 we get that $e_{p_{p_i}} = C_{i+2|e_{p_{p_i}}} =$ $C_{i+2|e_{p_{p_i}}}$ (no processor changes its partial state in T_3) and $\forall p_j \in \mathcal{N}_{p_i}, C_{i+2|p_{p_j}} =$ $C_{i+4|p_{p_j}}$. Finally, as there has been no fault or corruption during the transitions T_1, T_2, T_3 and T_4 we get that p_i evaluates $Transition(C_{i+2|e_{p_{p_i}}}, \{C_{i+2|e_{p_{p_i}}} \mid p_j \in \mathcal{N}_{p_i}\})$ to true in C_{i+4} and consequently the guard of CA to false.   □

Theorem 3. *Alg_t is self-stabilizing.*

Sketch of the proof. From section 3.1 we have that the system reaches after at most $4D$ rounds a configuration in which all processor are in unison (and their variables RPF are equal to 0). Thus from theorem 2 we get that after the first stabilization round that follows the unison the only actions that the system can execute are the actions of the input algorithm. The only difference with a synchronous execution of this algorithm is that once in a while a processor can slow down. A processor can evaluate the function $Freeze$ to true if in the past stabilization rounds only one of its neighbors moved after a locally stable period. But a processor cannot evaluate two rounds in a row the function $Freeze$ to true (Cf. $Freeze$ p. 104). Thus the projection of the execution on V_{alg} for the stabilization rounds corresponds to an execution under the distributed demon. But by assumption the input algorithm is self-stabilizing under this demon. We get that the transformed algorithm is still self-stabilizing.   □

From the proof above we get that the upper bound for the stabilization time is $4D$ plus twice the normal stabilization time of the original algorithm (alternation of snapshots rounds and stabilization round). Note that during the stabilization of the unison the system is also executing actions of stabilization, and then is already converging to a legitimate configuration. When the system is stabilized for the unison it might possibly be already stabilized. Let us prove now that the transformed algorithm is 1-strong.

1-corrupted configurations. The aim of our transformer is to get in particular a 1-strong algorithm, that is restraining the effect of a single corruption to the output variables of the faulty processor. Due to the alternation of rounds if one processor is corrupted during a stabilization round, at the end of the next snapshot round the corrupted value of that processor is stored in its neighbor snapshot. Due to the fact that the unison algorithm stabilizes in one round, a processor cannot change its output variables before the next stabilization round. Then we will only consider executions starting from such a round. Thus we have to consider the configurations reached after 1 corruption as being as follows:

Definition 1. *An illegitimate configuration C of S_{Alg_t} is 1-Corrupted with respect to the legitimate configuration C', noted $1\text{-}Cor(C, C') = true$ if and only if either $Dist(C, C') = 1$ or $Dist(C, C') = \delta_{p_i} + 1$ (where δ_{p_i} is the number of neighbors of p_i) and : $Dist(C_{|V_{Alg}}, C'_{|V_{Alg}}) = 1 \wedge C_{|e_{p_{p_i}}} \neq C'_{|e_{p_{p_i}}} \wedge \forall p_j \in \mathcal{N}_{p_i}, C_{|p_j}.StabSnap = C'_{|p_j}.StabSnap \wedge C_{|p_j}.LastSnap = C'_{|p_j}.LastSnap, \forall p_k \in \mathcal{N}_{p_j} \setminus \{p_i\}, C_{|p_j}.CurSnap[p_k] = C'_{|p_j}.CurSnap[p_k] = C_{|e_{p_{p_i}}} \wedge C'_{|p_j}.CurSnap[p_i] = C'_{|e_{p_{p_i}}}.*$

Lemma 3. *Let C be an illegitimate configuration of S_{Alg_t}, then if C' is a legitimate configuration of S_{Alg_t} such that 1-$Cor(C, C') = true$ and $C_{|e_{p_{p_i}}} \neq C'_{|e_{p_{p_i}}}$ (p_i is the only corrupted processor in C and its partial state is corrupted) and all the processors but p_i are in a stabilization round in C, then in at most two rounds, any execution starting from C reaches C' and we have the property of strong confinement.*

Sketch of the proof. Let C_i be an illegitimate configuration of S_{Alg_t} and C'_i a legitimate configuration of S_{Alg_t} such that 1-$Cor(C_i, C'_i) = true$, $C_{i|e_{p_{p_i}}} \neq C'_{i|e_{p_{p_i}}}$ and $\forall p_j \in \mathcal{P}, p_j.r = RPF = 0$. Let $T_1 = (C_i, t_1, C_{i+1}), T_2 = (C_{i+1}, t_2, C_{i+2}), T_1, T_2 \in T_{Alg_t}$.

If the corrupted processor has its partial state corrupted in C_i, then it evaluates $SnapCorCond()$ to true and so the guard of CA to true. All its neighbors see that it is the only one that changed its partial state during the last transition. Their snapshots contain the partial state of their neighbors different from p_i that did not move. Thus they evaluate the function $Freeze$ to true and they have no action enabled in C_i. The action CA puts p_i in its former state because $Consensus()$ returns the value that all its neighbors have in their $StabSnap$ view which is by definition of C_i the partial state that p_i had in C_i. We get that the projection of the configurations C_{i+1} and C'_i on V_{Alg_t} are the same. Thus we have the property of strong confinement. Moreover in C_{i+1} the neighbors of p_i evaluate the guard of $Snap2$ if their $CurSnap$ views contain the corrupted state of p_i, $C_{i|e_{p_{p_i}}}$ and thus correct their snapshots. p_i evaluates in C_{i+1}, $Snap1$ to true if its snapshots have been corrupted and thus also correct its snapshots. Finally we have $C_{i+2} = C_i$. □

Lemma 4. *Let C be an illegitimate configuration of a system executing the transformed algorithm, then if C' is a legitimate configuration such that 1-$Cor(C, C') = true$ and $C_{|e_{p_{p_i}}} \neq C'_{|e_{p_{p_i}}}$ (p_i is the only corrupted processor in C and only its snapshots are corrupted) and all the processors but p_i are in a stabilization round in C, then in at most two rounds any execution starting from C reaches C'.*

Sketch of the proof. If just the snapshots of a processor are corrupted, then $Consensus()$ returns 0 for p_i and as the projection of C_i on V_{Alg_t} corresponds to a legitimate configuration of Alg we get that no processor is enabled in C. Moreover p_i regains its correct state thanks to the execution of the guarded rule $Snap1$ of $Snap$ and no other processor in the system can make any move. Thus we have the property of strong confinement as no processor changed its output variables, $t_1 = \emptyset$ and $C_{i+2} = C_i$. □

Theorem 4. *Alg_t is 1-strong.*

Sketch of the proof. From theorems 3 and 4 we get that for any pair of configurations C_i illegitimate and C'_i legitimate, 1-$Cor(C_i, C'_i) = true$ and $C_{i|e_{p_{p_i}}} = C'_{i|e_{p_{p_i}}}$, we have for any pair of transitions $T_1 = (C_i, t_1, C_{i+1}), T_2 = (C_{i+1}, t_2, C_{i+2}), T_1, T_2 \in T$ such that in C_i: $\forall p_i \in \mathcal{P}, p_i.r = 0$ the property of strong confinement and $C_{i+2} = C_i$. Thus for any single corruption of the system we have the property of strong confinement and the system recovers a legitimate state in a constant time (at most three rounds). Thus the transformed algorithm is 1-strong.

4 Conclusion

In this paper we introduce the notion of k-strong self-stabilization which implies the property of strong confinement and the property of linear k-time-adaptivity. We present the first 1-strong synchronous unison algorithm. We show how, under some conditions, a self-stabilizing system can be automatically transformed into a 1-strong self-stabilizing system, although 1-strongness also takes into account the case of multiple faults hitting simultaneously the system, provided that two faulty processors are at distance at least 3. Thus we obtain thanks to the transformer an algorithm with a slower convergence time in the case of a badly corrupted initial configuration. But once the system is stabilized, if it is only hit by faults scattered in space and time (what usually happens in large systems), it becomes optimal in terms of fault containment and very efficient in terms of stabilization time as it recovers a legitimate state in from 1 to 3 rounds (depending of the type of fault and when it occurs).

As a matter of fact the construction can be extended to the general case of k faults. We will briefly describe how a general transformer could be built and how the construction made in the case k = 1 can be generalized. The first issue is strong confinement. In the case k = 1, when a processor discovers an inconsistency, it can learn from the snapshots of its neighbors, that contain its state before the fault, whether or not it is faulty. The hypothesis that there is no processor of degree 1 ensures that a non faulty processor gets always a majority of correct views. In the general case we make the hypothesis that every ball of radius k (a ball contains a processor, the center, and all the processors at distance at most k) has at least 2k+1 processors. Note that this hypothesis generalizes the hypothesis on the degree in the case k= 1. Now the snapshots contain more information, namely the past local states of the processors at distance k or less. When a processor detects an inconsistency, it freezes for k rounds, the time for the snapshots in its ball of radius k to reach it. Then, like before, the processor has a majority of correct information about its state before the faults and does not change its state if it appears non faulty. The dilatation factor of the transformed system is k+2 (instead of 1+2= 3). The k first rounds are described above and it is still needed one stabilization round for the correction of the partial state of the faulty processors and one snapshot round for the correction of all the corrupted view or views containing the corrupted states of the faulty processors.

A last issue is to know whether or not it is possible to build a general transformer into a totally adaptive strong self-stabilizing system (strong confinement and a dilatation factor linear in the exact number f of faults, when f is unknown, but inferior to some fixed integer k). We conjecture that the answer is negative and that getting strong confinement in this case needs a dilatation factor of at least k+2.

References

1. Y. Afek and S. Dolev. Local stabilizer. In *Israel Symposium on Theory of Computing Systems*, pages 74–84, 1997.
2. A. Arora, S. Dolev, and M. Gouda. Maintaining digital clocks in step. *Parallel Processing Letters*, 1(1):11–18, September 1991.

3. H. Attiya and J. L. Welch. *Distributed computing: fundamentals, simulations and advanced topics*. McGraw-Hill, Inc., Hightstown, NJ, USA, 1998.
4. Y. Azar, S. Kutten, and B. Patt-Shamir. Distributed error confinement. In *Proceedings of the twenty-second annual symposium on Principles of distributed computing*, pages 33–42, Boston, Massachusetts, July 2003.
5. J. Beauquier, S. Delaët, and S. Haddad. Necessary and sufficient conditions for 1-adaptivity. In *IPDPS*, page 96, 2006.
6. J. Beauquier, C. Genolini, and S. Kutten. Optimal reactive k-stabilisation: the case of mutual exclusion. In *18th Annual ACM Symposium on Principles of Distributed Computing (PODC'99)*, May 1999.
7. Boulinier, Petit, and Villain. Synchronous vs. asynchronous unison. In *WSS: International Workshop on Self-Stabilizing Systems, LNCS*, 2005.
8. S. Dolev. *Self-Stabilization*. MIT Press, Cambridge, MA, 2000. Ben-Gurion University of the Negev, Israel.
9. S. Dolev and T. Herman. Superstabilizing protocols for dynamic distributed systems. In *PODC '95: Proceedings of the fourteenth annual ACM symposium on Principles of distributed computing*, page 255, New York, NY, USA, 1995. ACM Press.
10. C. Genolini and S. Tixeuil. A lower bound of dynamic k-stabilization in asynchronous systems. In *21st IEEE Symposium on Reliable Distributed Systems (SRDS'02)*, pages 212–222, Osaka University, Suita, Japan, Octobre 2002.
11. S. Ghosh, A. Gupta, T. Herman, and S.V. Pemmaraju. Fault-containing self-stabilizing algorithms. In *Symposium on Principles of Distributed Computing*, pages 45–54, 1996.
12. Mohamed G. Gouda and Ted Herman. Stabilizing unison. *Information Processing Letters*, 35(4):171–175, 7 August 1990.
13. Herman and Pemmaraju. Error-detecting codes and fault-containing self-stabilization. *IPL: Information Processing Letters*, 73, 2000.
14. T. Herman. Observations on time-adaptive self-stabilization, October 15 1997.
15. T. Herman. Superstabilizing mutual exclusion. *Distributed Computing*, 13(1):1–17, 2000.
16. Ted Herman and Sukumar Ghosh. Stabilizing phase-clocks. *Information Processing Letters*, 54(5):259–265, 9 June 1995.
17. S. Kutten and B. Patt-Shamir. Time-adaptive self stabilization. In *Proceedings of the 16th Annual ACM Symposium on Principles of Distributed Computing (PODC'97)*, pages 149–158, 1997.
18. S. Kutten and B. Patt-Shamir. Asynchronous time-adaptive self stabilization. In *PODC*, page 319, 1998.
19. S. Kutten and B. Patt-Shamir. Adaptive stabilization of reactive protocols. *FSTTCS: Foundations of Software Technology and Theoretical Computer Science*, 24, 2004.
20. S. Kutten and D. Peleg. Fault-local distributed mending. In *Proceedings of the 14th Annual ACM Symposium on Principles of Distributed Computing (PODC'95)*, pages 20–27, August 1995.
21. M. Nesterenko and A. Arora. Tolerance to unbounded byzantine faults. In *The 21th IEEE Symposium on Reliable Distributed Systems, (SRDS '02)*, pages 22–31, Washington - Brussels - Tokyo, October 2002. IEEE.
22. G. Tel. *Introduction to distributed algorithms*. Cambridge University Press, New York, NY, USA, 1994.

Optimal Message-Driven Implementation of Omega with Mute Processes

Martin Biely* and Josef Widder**

Technische Universität Wien, Embedded Computing Systems Group 182/2
Treitlstraße 3/2, A-1040 Wien, EU
{biely, widder}@ecs.tuwien.ac.at

Abstract. We consider the complexity of algorithms in message-driven models, i.e., models of distributed computations where events can only be caused by message receptions but not by the passage of time. Hutle and Widder (2005) have shown that there is no self-stabilizing implementation of the eventually strong failure detector, and thus the eventual leader oracle Ω in such models under certain assumptions. Under stronger assumptions it was shown that even the eventually perfect failure detector can be implemented in systems consisting of at least $f + 2$ processes — f being the upper bound on the number of processes that crash during an execution.

In this paper we show that $f + 2$ is in fact a lower bound in message-driven systems, even if non stabilizing algorithms are considered. This contrasts time-driven models where $f + 1$ is sufficient for failure detector implementations. After that, we provide an efficient message-driven implementation of Ω. Our algorithm is efficient in the sense that not all processes have to send messages forever, which is an improvement to previous message-driven failure detector implementations.

1 Introduction

Fault-tolerant agreement problems are crucial for both practical applications of distributed algorithms, as well as for understanding the principles of distributed computations. In this context, specifically the role of time — or rather synchrony — is heavily researched, for example with respect to consensus, the problem of agreeing on a common value despite faults [1,2,3,4]. As a result of research on consensus, it was shown that if just crash faults are contemplated, synchrony can be encapsulated by failure detectors [4] and that the eventual leader oracle Ω is the weakest failure detector (FD) to allow solving consensus [5]. Intuitively, Ω is a distributed oracle that provides processes with the name of a process guaranteeing that eventually all processes will be provided with the name of a unique correct process. Obviously, implementing Ω presents a problem on its own that can be solved with synchrony assumptions, and much work focused on contemplating timing models to that end and in fact very weak models

---

* Supported by the Austrian BM:vit FIT-IT project *TRAFT* (proj. no. 812205).
** Partially supported by the Austrian FWF project *Theta* (proj. no. P17757).

A.K. Datta and M. Gradinariu (Eds.): SSS 2006, LNCS 4280, pp. 110–121, 2006.

have been established [6,7,8]. But timing is not the sole parameter of distributed computing models: others are for example atomicity of events (broadcast vs. unicast) and event generation.

In this paper we do not focus on the timing of an execution but we investigate the orthogonal issue of how the events that constitute a distributed computation are triggered. Here we distinguish two possibilities: time-driven and message-driven models. In time-driven models, events can be triggered locally by the passage of time, i.e., by clocks or timers. In the message-driven model of execution, events can only occur as immediate reaction to the reception of a message. Therefore message-driven algorithms do not need to have access to a clock. In other words, in message-driven executions, processes only perform computations when necessary. Algorithms that perform steps only upon message receptions were discussed in [9] and named "asynchronous" there (similar to asynchronous network protocols that operate by explicit handshaking).

Although it might appear that message-driven models are artificially restrictive when considering the traditional systems under consideration in distributed computing research — i.e., computers linked by a network — it is nevertheless the case that message-driven models appear to be the natural choice when considering new application domains for distributed algorithms like the design of asynchronous (delay insensitive [10]) circuits. Asynchronous hardware differs from synchronous one in the way computations are triggered. In synchronous designs, there exists a central clock whose ticks trigger each component (flip-flop) conceptually simultaneously. The inputs of a component are ready when the tick is generated, and its outputs are present at the next stage of the logic at the beginning of the next tick. The concept of periodically executed steps is not appropriate for asynchronous chip design (due to the lack of a central clock). In [11] it was shown how a message-driven algorithm can be implemented in asynchronous hardware. It was shown that the central clock can be replaced by a VLSI implementation of a message-driven fault-tolerant clock generation algorithm. Consequently, there is a requirement to understand possibilities and restrictions of the message-driven model.

Most of the algorithms that solve consensus or implement a failure detector (although often presented in a message-driven style) are based on time-driven execution models, i.e., steps can be taken whether messages are in the incoming buffers or not. Only little work exists in the context of consensus that considers how events in a distributed computation are triggered [12]. In [13] it was shown that there is a difference between the expressiveness of time-driven and message-driven execution models, by showing that Ω cannot be implemented with a self-stabilizing message-driven protocol under certain assumptions where self-stabilizing time-driven protocols [14] can solve the problem. By strengthening the assumptions it was shown that the problem has message-driven implementations as well. The question of whether the choice of message-driven vs. time-driven algorithms has consequences with respect to the complexity and resilience of solutions for non stabilizing systems was not analyzed. With the present paper, we intend to contribute to closing this gap: The aforementioned message-driven implementations of Ω require a system of at least $f + 2$ processes — f being the upper bound on the number of processes that may fail during an execution (by crashing). Time-driven implementations of Ω are known that require just $f + 1$ processes, therefore the question arises whether the algorithms in [13] are optimal regarding the required number of processes. In this paper we answer this question in the affirmative. We present an $f + 2$ lower bound on the number of processes required for message-driven implementations of Ω.

Additionally, we consider efficiency issues: It is known that for time-driven systems, communication efficient failure detector implementations are possible [15]. Here, communication efficiency refers to the number of processes that have to keep sending messages forever. All known message-driven failure detector implementations [13,16,17,18] require all correct processes to keep sending messages forever. We show that this is not necessary for implementing Ω. Our algorithm requires at most $f + 2$ processes to send messages while the other ones may remain mute. Our lower bound theorem does also hold for such communication efficient algorithms, that is, our algorithm is optimal in this respect.

This reduced complexity may not seem particularly relevant at first sight, but the remarkable fact is that for solving consensus with Ω one requires $2f + 1$ processes, while — with our algorithm — only $f + 2$ have to actively participate in doing failure detection. It follows that only in the case where $n = 3$ and $f = 1$ all processes have to send messages. In all other systems in which consensus can be solved, our implementation of Ω allows $n - f - 2 > \frac{n}{2} - 2 \geq 0$ processes to remain silent.

1.1   Contribution

To the best of our knowledge, this paper establishes for the first time a lower bound on the number of processes required to solve problems in the area of fault-tolerant distributed computing with message-driven protocols. To this end, we employ a rather conservative synchrony assumption in order to make explicit the peculiarities of message-driven models. Even under our strong assumptions, the difference in the lower bound follows — although time-driven protocols are known that implement Ω with $f + 1$ processes even under far less restrictive synchrony assumptions [15].

We also present an algorithm that shows that this bound is tight. Additionally, the algorithm allows some processes to remain silent throughout the execution. We thus contribute to the comparison of time-driven and message-driven protocols.

Knowing message-driven implementations of failure detectors [13], our results appear to be obvious: Failure detection is done by comparing round-trips with at least $f + 1$ other processes. This ensures that there will always be timely (bounded by lower and upper bounds) communication between at least 2 correct processes. This communication establishes some kind of time-base — or a source of synchrony — for these two processes that allows to solve certain problems (like timing out crashed processes).

We believe that our results contributes to the general understanding of the term "synchrony". What are sources of synchrony? How many do we need to solve certain problems in a fault-tolerant manner? What semantics do these sources have? We believe that due to the interleaving of event generation with synchrony assumptions, the basic properties of synchrony are not perfectly understood by now. By investigating different models and observing the commonalities, we hope that it is possible to eventually get an abstract notion of synchrony (or time) in fault-tolerant distributed computations.

1.2   Road Map

In the following section we introduce our model which we use to show our lower bound theorem in Section 3. In Section 4, we present an efficient implementation of Ω that is optimal with respect to the derived resilience bound.

2   Model

We consider a system consisting of N distributed processes, which run on a number of processors connected by a communication network. We assume the existence of a reliable (logically) fully connected message-passing network between the processes. Every process has a unique name out of the set $\{1, 2, \ldots, N\}$. The set of all processes will be denoted $\Pi = \{p \mid 1 \leq p \leq N\}$.

The processes perform a distributed computation which proceeds by the computational steps of processes in Π. Since we consider only message-driven computations, a computational *step* is either the initial step (by which the computation is started at every process) or a *message reception step*. In a message reception step a process must receive at least one message, performs a local computation, and may send zero or more messages. The initial step is the only step a process can ever take without receiving a message, and consists only of a local computation and sending of messages.

Processes may fail by permanently crashing, i.e., they do not take any steps after they have crashed. More precisely, the behavior of a faulty process p is described by the fact that p only takes finitely many steps in an execution although infinitely many messages are sent to p during this execution. A process that does not crash in an execution is called *correct* in this execution. At most f out of the N processes in Π may fail during an execution. Since we are interested in FD implementations where only some processes ever send messages, we introduce $\Lambda = \{p \mid 1 \leq p \leq n\}$, which is the set of $n \leq N$ active processes, i.e., processes that send messages. The set of silent processes will be called $\Sigma = \Pi - \Lambda$. We define $s = |\Sigma| \geq 0$ and since $N = |\Pi|$, we have $N = n + s$.

For our algorithm we assume that $n = f + 2$ and in our lower bound result in Section 3 we show that this is optimal. Further, for the algorithm analysis, we assume the existence of a global Newtonian real-time clock. The processes, however, do not have a way to access this clock, neither do they have any other means of measuring passage of time locally. This does not only imply the absence of local clocks but also that there are no lower or upper bounds that only restrict the time for a computational step — these times are accounted for in the end-to-end delays (read on).

2.1   Timing

Every communication network is bound to cause delays between the time a message is sent in some step by some process p and the time when it causes a message reception step at some other process $q \neq p$. For simplicity we assume for our algorithm the existence of some unknown upper and lower bounds on these end-to-end delays, i.e., time to transmit and queue the message (at both ends) plus the time to process the message. We denote by $\tau^+ < \infty$ the upper and by $\tau^- > 0$ the lower bound on the end-to-end delay between processes p and q with $p \neq q$, where $p, q \in \Lambda$; that is, the delays of all links involving a process $s \in \Sigma$ just have to be finite. Our algorithm does not know these values. Indeed the knowledge of the values would be useless as processes cannot measure time. Instead we assume the knowledge of the ratio $\Theta = \tau^+/\tau^-$. In our analysis we also use the transmission uncertainty $\varepsilon = \tau^+ - \tau^-$. It has been shown in [19] that algorithms designed for this model also work in a model where no bounds on end-to-end delays exists, while just the ratio between the delays of messages concurrently in transit must be bounded by some Θ. In other words, τ^+ and τ^- may change during the execution, as long as their ratio continues to be bounded by Θ. Note that Θ is in fact the only (time-related) value that processes can observe.

Until now we have assumed that $p \neq q$ for a message sent from p to q. For the other case, i.e., self-receptions, we only assume that the transmission is reliable (in order to strengthen our lower bound result in Section 3) while we do not assume any bounds on transmission times except that they are finite. In fact, transmission delays may as well be 0 (which would model writing the message into memory directly instead of sending it over the network). Our algorithms, however, do not use self-receptions.

2.2   Events

For our lower bound (Section 3) we require the following definitions to discriminate between different types of steps. Let p be some process that receives a set M of messages in a message reception step. If all messages in M were sent by p, we call the step a *self reception step*. If at least one message in M was sent by some process $q \neq p$ then the step is called *extrinsic reception step*.

We further need the following definitions: An extrinsic reception step of message m at some process p, where it is locally impossible for p to determine that m was not the last message received by p in the execution is called *potentially final extrinsic reception step*. By *potentially final non self reception step* we denote all steps that are either a potentially final extrinsic reception step or an initial step. (A potentially final extrinsic reception step occurs at p when p has received all messages that causally precede the message that caused the step. In the case of $f + 1$ active processes, it could be the case that there is only one surviving process p, and no message except those sent by p will ever be received by p after this event.)

2.3   Failure Detectors

We consider two kinds of failure detectors, both of which will only output failure information about processes in Λ. The failure detector Ω [5] outputs a single process (its leader estimate), which eventually must be the same correct process at all processes. The formal definition for Ω reads as follows.

(EL) *Eventual Leadership.* There is a time after which all the correct processes always trust the same correct process.

Additionally we will consider a variant of a stronger FD, i.e., the perfect FD $\mathcal{P}$. It was defined [4] to fulfill the following two properties:

(SC) *Strong Completeness.* Eventually, every process that crashes is permanently suspected by every correct process.

(SA) *Strong Accuracy.* No process is suspected before it crashes.

As mentioned above, the FDs considered in this paper only output information about Λ. Therefore we define the following generalization of the perfect FD. Thus we define $\mathcal{P}_\Lambda$ via two following properties:

(LSC) *Limited Strong Completeness.* Eventually, every process $p \in \Lambda$ that crashes is permanently suspected by every correct process $q \in \Lambda$.

(LSA) *Limited Strong Accuracy.* No process $p \in \Lambda$ is suspected by any process $q \in \Lambda$ before it crashes.

Guerraoui and Schiper introduced Γ-accurate FDs [20] which are similar to $\mathcal{P}_\Lambda$. $\mathcal{P}_\Lambda$, however, restricts both accuracy *and* completeness to some fixed subset Λ of all processes while Γ-accurate FDs only restrict accuracy properties to some fixed subset Γ.

We do not restrict the semantics of the algorithms that use our FDs, i.e., classic query based execution models [4] can be employed as well as interrupt based models; discussions on the respective expressiveness can be found in [12]. If the whole distributed computation (FDs and applications) should be message (i.e., interrupt) driven as described in our model, the FDs have to be an additional source of events for the application. That is, in addition to message reception steps, applications can also take steps whenever the output of the FD — the leader estimate in case of Ω — changes.

3 Lower Bound on the Number of Processes

We show that it is impossible to implement Ω with a message-driven algorithm when only $n = f + 1$ processes are active.

The proof of the following theorem is done by contradiction. We will assume that there exists an implementation $\mathcal{I}$ of Ω. In the following, we show how $\mathcal{I}$ must behave if $n - 1$ processes in Λ crash during an execution. Then we consider executions where just $n - 2$ processes in Λ crash. By indistinguishability to the first execution, $\mathcal{I}$ violates the properties of Ω thus providing the required contradiction.

Theorem 1 (Lower Bound). *There is no correct message-driven implementation of Ω in our model if $n \leq f + 1$.*

Proof. Assume by contradiction that there exists a message-driven implementation $\mathcal{I}$ of Ω, for a system where $n \leq f + 1$.

Let $\mathcal{E}_1$ be the set of all executions of $\mathcal{I}$ where $n - 1$ processes in Λ crash. In all these executions there is a final extrinsic reception step or (at least) the initial step at the sole correct processes $p \in \Lambda$ such that there must be at least one potentially final non self reception step at p after which p takes a possibly infinite number of self reception steps. By (EL), however, after some finite number $\ell \geq 0$ of self reception steps, p must set $leader_p = p$ or $leader_p = r \in \Sigma$ permanently—in both cases the leader estimate of p satisfies (EL).

Let $\mathcal{E}_2$ be the set of all executions of $\mathcal{I}$ where $n - 2$ processes in Λ crash initially and there are two correct processes $p, q \in \Lambda$, $p \neq q$. Note that just $n - 2 < f$ processes in Λ are faulty such that there can be faulty processes also in Σ in $\mathcal{E}_2$. Let all executions in $\mathcal{E}_2$ be such that all message end-to-end delays between the processes p and q are equal. From this timing behavior it follows directly that all extrinsic reception steps are potentially final extrinsic reception steps as causally dependent events are perceived in temporal order.

We now consider finite prefixes of $\mathcal{E}_2$. Let these finite executions $\mathcal{E}_2'$ have some potentially final non self reception step s at some process p as their final step. For p, every execution $e \in \mathcal{E}_2'$ is indistinguishable from some finite prefix execution $e_1 \in \mathcal{E}_1$ that is identical to e except that either (1) q crashes in e_1 directly after sending the message that is the cause of s at p, if s is a potentially final extrinsic reception step, or (2) q is initially crashed in e_1, if s is the initial step at p. As there are no synchrony assumptions on self receptions, we can construct a finite execution e' by extending e with $\ell \geq 0$ self reception steps. By indistinguishability of e' to execution e_1, p must set $leader_p = p$ or $leader_p = r \in \Sigma$ for some ℓ. This constructive argument can be applied to every potentially final non self reception step at any of the two correct processes in Λ, such that these processes p and q have to set their leader estimate as described above.

Since, by (EL), all correct processes must permanently trust one process, $v \in \{p, q\}$ must either set $leader_v = v$ or $leader_v = r \in \Sigma$ upon every (following) potentially final extrinsic reception step. It follows that they cannot set $leader_p = p$ and $leader_q = q$ permanently, as this would violate the "the same correct process" requirement. Thus, $v \in \{p, q\}$ must set $leader_v = r \in \Sigma$. If $|\Sigma| = 0$, we have already reached a contradiction since p and q cannot reach the same leader estimate. If $|\Sigma| > 0$, we observe that only less than f processes in Λ crash in all $\mathcal{E}_2$ executions. That is, at least one process in Σ can crash in such executions. Since r is in Σ, it never sends messages such that p and q cannot distinguish executions where r is correct from ones where r crashes. It follows that there exist executions where permanently $leader_p = r$ but r is crashed which violates (EL). We again reach a contradiction.   □

Corollary 1. *There is no correct message-driven implementation of Ω in our model if $N \leq f + 1$.*

Corollary 2. *There is no correct message-driven implementation of Ω if $N \leq f + 1$ where processes never send messages to themselves.*

Corollary 1 shows that the self-stabilizing algorithms in [13] are optimal regarding the number of processes required. (The impossibility of [13], however, even holds if there are synchrony assumptions on self-receptions.) Note that self-stabilization was not used in the proof of Theorem 1, such that the complexity gap is due to the difference in the expressiveness of message-driven respectively time-driven models (and not due to self-stabilization). Since the algorithms of this paper do not create self receptions, Corollary 2 shows that our algorithms are optimal as well.

4 A Matching Algorithm

The algorithm has different code for the processes of Λ and Σ. The code for processes $p \in \Lambda$ is a variant of the bounded memory algorithm of [13]. Each active process p exchanges (p, ph, k) messages with the other processes in Λ, where ph is the phase number and k is an integer that is increased with every round trip. When an active process q receives such a message, q just returns it to p (line 21). For all $q \in \Lambda$, p holds a variable $lastmsg_p[q]$, where it stores the highest integer k received in a (p, ph, k) reply from q. If Φ is chosen properly, p can correctly suspect a process q of being crashed upon termination of Φ round trips if there was no round trip terminated by q.

The code for processes $q \in \Sigma$ simply sets the leader upon reception of an estimate sent by some $p \in \Lambda$. We assume that eventually all messages sent over links from process $p \in \Lambda$ to process $q \in \Sigma$ are received after some finite time (no message loss). Trivially, this algorithm works also in systems where links between processes in Λ and Σ also obey the Θ assumption (cf. Section 2.1).

Lemma 1. *For Algorithm 1 with $\Phi > \Theta$ it holds that the set $suspects_p$ implements a perfect failure detector $\mathcal{P}_\Lambda$ with respect to the set of potential leaders Λ.*

Proof. To show that $suspects_p$ acts as a perfect failure detector for processes in Λ, we have to show (LSC) and (LSA).

We first show that no correct process $q \in \Lambda$ is ever suspected by some process $p \in \Lambda$. Assume by contradiction that some process p adds the correct process q to its suspect list $suspects_p$. Then p must have performed Φ round-trips (via line 11 and line 7) since the beginning of the current phase with some other process, while not receiving a response from q to the message p has sent in line 6 or line 17. This, however, is impossible due to the definition of Θ in Section 2.1, the fact that $\Phi > \Theta$ and the fact that q is not crashed.

It remains to show that, when some process q does crash, p will eventually add it to $suspects_p$. At some time after q crashes, p will start a new phase, and subsequently perform Φ round-trips with some other correct process r, after which line 13 will be executed for a phase during which q remained silent, therefore $lastmsg_p[q] = 0$ and q will be in the new $suspects_p$ set. $\qquad\square$

Algorithm 1. Failure Detector Implementation

Code for processes $p \in \Lambda$:

1: $phase_p \in \{0, 1\} \leftarrow 0$
2: $leader_p \in \Lambda \leftarrow \min_r \{r \in \Lambda\}$
3: $suspects_p \subset \Lambda \leftarrow \{\}$
4: $\forall q \in \Lambda : lastmsg_p[q] \in \{0, \dots, \Phi\} \leftarrow 0$

5: **upon** initialization **do**
6:    send $(p, phase_p, 1)$ to Λ

7: **upon** reception of (p, ph, k) from q **do**
8:    **if** $ph = phase_p$ and $k > lastmsg_p[q]$ **then**
9:       $lastmsg_p[q] \leftarrow k$
10:      **if** $k < \Phi$ **then**
11:         send $(p, phase_p, k + 1)$ to q
12:      **else**
13:         $suspects_p \leftarrow \{r \mid r \in \Lambda \wedge lastmsg_p[r] = 0\}$
14:         $leader_p \leftarrow \min_r \{r \mid r \in (\Lambda - suspects_p)\}$
15:         $phase_p \leftarrow 1 - phase_p$
16:         $\forall r \in \Lambda : lastmsg_p[r] \leftarrow 0$
17:         send $(p, phase_p, 1)$ to Λ a
18:         **if** $p = leader_p$ **then**
19:            send (p) to Σ

20: **upon** reception of (q, ph, k) from q **do**
21:    send (q, ph, k) to q

Code for processes $p \in \Sigma$:
22: $leader_p \in \Lambda \leftarrow \min_r \{r \in \Lambda\}$
23: **upon** reception of (q) from some $q \in \Lambda$ **do**
24:    $leader_p \leftarrow q$

Note that implementing $\mathcal{P}_\Lambda$ is not identical to implementing $\mathcal{P}_\Pi$, i.e., a perfect FD for all processes including the mute ones, since crashes by mute processes cannot be detected. This is obviously different for implementing Ω: Since Ω only outputs one correct process, it is sufficient to choose the leader from a (large enough) subset of all processes. Therefore $\Omega_\Lambda = \Omega_\Pi$.

Lemma 2. *For Algorithm 1 with $\Phi > \Theta$ it holds that eventually all correct processes $p \in \Lambda$ have the same correct process $q \in \Lambda$ as their leader.*

Proof. Let t be the time the last process in Λ crashes during an execution and let process q be such that

$$q = \min_r \{r \mid r \in \Lambda \wedge r \text{ is correct}\}.$$

From line 14 we see that the leader is selected out of the set of non suspected processes $r \in \Lambda$. By Lemma 1, all crashed processes in Λ will eventually be suspected, and therefore at some time after t all correct processes in Λ suspect the same processes, consequently all will determine the same minimum, i.e., the same leader, that is q. □

Lemma 3. *Algorithm 1 ensures that processes in Σ will choose the process $q \in \Lambda$ as leader if q is the only process in Λ that keeps sending messages to Σ forever.*

Proof. Since there is only one process q that keeps sending (q) messages to Σ forever, eventually all messages (p) with $p \neq q$ are received. From then on, only (q) messages remain and by line 24 processes in Σ will select q as leader whenever such message arrives.

Theorem 2. *Algorithm 1 with $\Phi > \Theta$ implements the eventual leader oracle Ω.*

Proof. By Lemma 2, eventually there is only one unique leader among Λ, let q denote this leader. It remains to show that the same processes becomes leader of the processes in Σ.

By line 19 the leader $q \in \Lambda$ keeps sending (q) messages forever. Thus (by Lemma 3) q will also become the leader of the silent processes Σ. □

5 Discussions

Note that Lemma 3 shows that the leader of Σ emerges from the message pattern alone, and does not depend on the state of the processes. It can therefore be argued that the code for processes in Σ is self-stabilizing, while the code for Λ is not. To arrive at a self-stabilizing overall solution for message-driven leader election with silent processes, it would be sufficient to adapt the algorithm for Λ. Indeed one could use any self-stabilizing implementation of Ω that fulfills the requisite in the lemma. In particular, the algorithms of [13,21] can be adapted in this way by requiring every leader to broadcast its identifier, whenever it elects itself as leader.

Another interesting point is that the dissemination of the leader to the processes in Σ is not restricted by the impossibility result of [13] in the same way as it is the case for the election of the leader in Λ. It follows that additional assumptions that are required to circumvent the impossibility result of [13] only have to consider processes in Λ respectively the links that connect them.

6 Conclusions

In this paper we explored the required properties for implementing the eventual leader oracle Ω in the context of message-driven algorithms. For this, we found limits for algorithms that implement Ω under the given system requirements: We showed that it is harder to implement the failure detector Ω in message-driven systems than it is in time-driven systems by proving that strictly more processes are required to tolerate a given number of faults. The analysis reveals that the absence of synchrony or timing assumptions regarding self-receptions is central for our results. It is quite obvious that an assumption like some lower bound on self-receptions would allow to implement a simulation for partially synchronous models like the FAR model [22].

Previous results [13] showed that message-driven semantics are weaker than time-driven semantics with respect to self-stabilization. Here we have shown that message-driven semantics are weaker in non self-stabilizing systems as well. Apart from resilience, to implement Ω other assumptions have to be stronger as well: In order to guarantee liveness, message-driven solutions require reliable links or bounded message-loss, such that enough messages always remain to trigger computational steps. In contrast, time-driven solutions typically only demand the eventual absence of message-loss to allow accurate discrimination between crashed and alive processes; see e.g. [4,6,15].

References

1. Fischer, M.J., Lynch, N.A., Paterson, M.S.: Impossibility of distributed consensus with one faulty process. Journal of the ACM **32**(2) (1985) 374–382
2. Dolev, D., Dwork, C., Stockmeyer, L.: On the minimal synchronism needed for distributed consensus. Journal of the ACM **34**(1) (1987) 77–97
3. Dwork, C., Lynch, N., Stockmeyer, L.: Consensus in the presence of partial synchrony. Journal of the ACM **35**(2) (1988) 288–323
4. Chandra, T.D., Toueg, S.: Unreliable failure detectors for reliable distributed systems. Journal of the ACM **43**(2) (1996) 225–267
5. Chandra, T.D., Hadzilacos, V., Toueg, S.: The weakest failure detector for solving consensus. Journal of the ACM **43**(4) (1996) 685–722
6. Aguilera, M.K., Delporte-Gallet, C., Fauconnier, H., Toueg, S.: On implementing Omega with weak reliability and synchrony assumptions. In: Proceeding of the 22nd Annual ACM Symposium on Principles of Distributed Computing (PODC'03). (2003)
7. Malkhi, D., Oprea, F., Zhou, L.: Ω meets paxos: Leader election and stability without eventual timely links. In: Proceedings of the 19th Symposium on Distributed Computing (DISC'05). Volume 3724 of LNCS., Cracow, Poland, Springer Verlag (2005) 199–213
8. Hutle, M., Malkhi, D., Schmid, U., Zhou, L.: Chasing the weakest system model for implementing omega and consensus. Research Report 74/2005, Technische Universität Wien, Institut für Technische Informatik, Treitlstr. 1–3/182-2, 1040 Vienna, Austria (2005) (appears as brief announcement at SSS 2006).
9. Fischer, M., Lamport, L.: Byzantine generals and transaction commit protocols. Technical Report 62, SRI International (1982)
10. Ebergen, J.C.: A formal approach to designing delay-insensitive circuits. Distributed Computing **5** (1991) 107–119
11. Fuegger, M., Schmid, U., Fuchs, G., Kempf, G.: Fault-Tolerant Distributed Clock Generation in VLSI Systems-on-Chip. Sixth European Dependable Computing Conference (EDCC-6) (2006)
12. Gärtner, F.C., Pleisch, S.: (Im)possibilities of predicate detection in crash-affected systems. In: 5th International Workshop on Self-Stabilizing Systems. Volume 2194 of LNCS., Springer Verlag (2001) 98–113

13. Hutle, M., Widder, J.: On the possibility and the impossibility of message-driven self-stabilizing failure detection. In: Proceedings of the Seventh International Symposium on Self Stabilizing Systems (SSS 2005). Volume 3764 of LNCS., Barcelona, Spain, Springer Verlag (2005) 153–170 Appeared also as brief announcement in *Proceedings of the 24th ACM Symposium on Principles of Distributed Computing (PODC'05)*.
14. Beauquier, J., Kekkonen-Moneta, S.: Fault-tolerance and self-stabilization: Impossibility results and solutions using self-stabilizing failure detectors. International Journal of Systems Science **28**(11) (1997) 1177–1187
15. Aguilera, M.K., Delporte-Gallet, C., Fauconnier, H., Toueg, S.: Communication-efficient leader election and consensus with limited link synchrony. In: PODC '04: Proceedings of the twenty-third annual ACM symposium on Principles of distributed computing, St. John's, Newfoundland, Canada, ACM Press (2004) 328–337
16. Le Lann, G., Schmid, U.: How to implement a timer-free perfect failure detector in partially synchronous systems. Technical Report 183/1-127, Department of Automation, Technische Universität Wien (2003)
17. Widder, J., Le Lann, G., Schmid, U.: Failure detection with booting in partially synchronous systems. In: Proceedings of the 5th European Dependable Computing Conference (EDCC-5). Volume 3463 of LNCS., Budapest, Hungary, Springer Verlag (2005) 20–37
18. Hermant, J.F., Widder, J.: Implementing reliable distributed real-time systems with the Θ-model. In: Proceedings of the 9th International Conference on Principles of Distributed Systems (OPODIS 2005). Volume 3974 of LNCS., Pisa, Italy, Springer Verlag (2005) 334–350
19. Widder, J.: Distributed Computing in the Presence of Bounded Asynchrony. PhD thesis, Vienna University of Technology, Fakultät für Informatik (2004)
20. Guerraoui, R., Schiper, A.: "Γ-accurate" failure detectors. In Babaoğlu, Ö., ed.: Proceedings of the 10th International Workshop on Distributed Algorithms (WDAG'96). Volume 1151 of LNCS. (1996) 269–286
21. Hutle, M., Widder, J.: Self-stabilizing failure detector algorithms. In: Proc. IASTED International Conference on Parallel and Distributed Computing and Networks (PDCN'05), Innsbruck, Austria (2005)
22. Fetzer, C., Schmid, U., Süßkraut, M.: On the possibility of consensus in asynchronous systems with finite average response times. In: Proceedings of the 25th International Conference on Distributed Computing Systems (ICDCS'05), Columbus, Ohio, USA (2005) 271–280

Incremental Synthesis of Fault-Tolerant Real-Time Programs*

Borzoo Bonakdarpour and Sandeep S. Kulkarni

Department of Computer Science and Engineering
Michigan State University
East Lansing, MI 48824, USA
{borzoo, sandeep}@cse.msu.edu
http://www.cse.msu.edu/~{borzoo, sandeep}

Abstract. In this paper, we focus on the problem of automated addition of fault-tolerance to an existing fault-intolerant *real-time* program. We consider three levels of fault-tolerance, namely *nonmasking*, *failsafe*, and *masking*, based on safety and liveness properties satisfied in the presence of faults. More specifically, a nonmasking (respectively, failsafe, masking) program satisfies liveness (respectively, safety, both safety and liveness) in the presence of faults. For failsafe and masking fault-tolerance, we consider two additional levels, *soft* and *hard*, based on satisfaction of timing constraints in the presence of faults. We present a polynomial time algorithm (in the size of the input program's region graph) that adds *bounded-time recovery* from an arbitrary given set of states to another arbitrary set of states. Using this algorithm, we propose a sound and complete synthesis algorithm that transforms a fault-intolerant real-time program into a nonmasking fault-tolerant program. Furthermore, we introduce sound and complete algorithms for adding soft/hard-failsafe fault-tolerance. For reasons of space, our results on addition of soft/hard-masking fault-tolerance are presented in a technical report.

Keywords: Fault-tolerance, Real-time, Bounded-time recovery, Program synthesis, Program transformation, Formal methods.

1 Introduction

Automated program synthesis is the problem of designing an algorithmic method to find a program that satisfies a required set of properties. Such automated synthesis is desirable, as it ensures that the synthesized program is correct-by-construction. In existing specification-based synthesis methods, a change in the specification requires us to redo synthesis from scratch. Thus, it would be advantageous, if we could reuse the previous efforts made to synthesize real-time programs and somehow *incrementally add* properties (e.g., fault-tolerance) to them. Moreover, such incremental synthesis is especially useful if the given real-time program is designed manually, e.g., for ensuring that the

---
* This work was partially sponsored by NSF CAREER CCR-0092724, DARPA Grant OSURS01-C-1901, ONR Grant N00014-01-1-0744, NSF grant EIA-0130724, and a grant from Michigan State University.

A.K. Datta and M. Gradinariu (Eds.): SSS 2006, LNCS 4280, pp. 122–136, 2006.

original program is efficient. More importantly, incremental synthesis is crucial when the existing real-time program satisfies properties whose automated synthesis is undecidable (e.g., precise eventuality $\Diamond_{=\delta}q$) or lies in highly complex classes of complexity.

In this paper, we focus on designing incremental synthesis algorithms that solely add fault-tolerance to existing fault-intolerant real-time programs, where processes can read and write all program variables in one atomic step. In particular, we concentrate on algorithms with manageable time and space complexity such that they can be used in tools for synthesizing fault-tolerant real-time programs. To characterize such manageable complexity, we require that the complexity of our algorithms are comparable to that of existing model checking techniques in the dense real-time model.

In order to characterize fault-tolerance requirements of programs, in our work, we consider three levels of fault-tolerance, namely *nonmasking* (respectively, stabilizing), *failsafe*, and *masking*, based on safety and liveness properties satisfied in the presence of faults. Furthermore, we propose two additional levels, namely *soft* and *hard* fault-tolerance, based on satisfaction of timing constraints in the presence of faults. Precisely, in the absence of faults, both soft and hard fault-tolerant programs are required to satisfy their timing constraints. However, in the presence faults, a soft fault-tolerant program is *not* required to satisfy its timing constraints while a hard fault-tolerant program is required to do so. In this sense, for instance, a hard-failsafe program satisfies its safety specification as well as its timing constraints in the presence of faults.

1.1 Related Work

In the literature of real-time computing, fault-tolerance has mostly been addressed in the context of scheduling theory (e.g., [1, 2]). In fault-tolerant real-time scheduling, the objective is to find the optimal schedule of a set of tasks on a set of processors *dynamically*, such that the largest possible number of tasks meet their deadlines. Since time complexity is a critical issue in dynamic scheduling, most of the proposed algorithms are in the form of heuristics designed for specific platforms and special types of faults (e.g., transient, fail-stop, Byzantine, etc.).

Recently, we studied the problem of incremental synthesis of timed automata in the absence of faults in [3]. More specifically, we developed synthesis algorithms and hardness results for adding different types of bounded response properties to a given timed automaton. We also studied the problem of incremental addition of UNITY [4] properties to untimed programs in [5].

The problem of synthesizing *untimed* fault-tolerant programs has been studied in the literature from different perspectives. In [6, 7, 8], the authors propose synthesis methods for adding fault-tolerance and multitolerance to existing untimed programs. In [9], Attie, Arora, and Emerson study the problem of synthesizing fault-tolerant concurrent untimed programs from temporal logic specifications expressed in CTL formulas.

Synthesis of real-time systems has mostly been studied in the context of controller synthesis and game theory [10, 11, 12, 13, 14, 15]. In these papers, the common assumption is that the existing program (called a plant) and/or the given specification are *deterministic*. Moreover, since the authors consider highly expressive specifications, the complexity of proposed methods is very high. For example, synthesis problems presented in [15, 10, 11, 14] are EXPTIME-complete. Moreover, deciding the existence of a solution (called a controller) in [12, 13] is 2EXPTIME-complete.

1.2 Contributions

In this paper we (i) introduce a generic fault-tolerance framework for real-time programs independent of platform, architecture, and type of faults; (ii) extend the previous work by Kulkarni and Arora [6] to the context of real-time programs; (iii) consider a general notion of real-time programs that covers both deterministic and nondeterministic programs in both synchronous and asynchronous models; and (iv) introduce various levels of fault-tolerance for real-time systems based on satisfaction of properties and timing constraints in the presence of faults. Furthermore, we present a class of specifications where we can express typical requirements for specifying real-time and fault-tolerant systems and we show that the complexity of synthesis algorithms for this class of specifications is comparable to existing model checking techniques for real-time programs [16]. Moreover, since we follow the standard model of timed automata [17], many of the problems in fault-tolerant scheduling theory can be modeled in our framework [18].

The main results in this paper are as follows. First, we present a polynomial time algorithm (in the size of the input program's region graph) that adds bounded-time recovery from an arbitrary given set of states to another arbitrary set of states. Then, using this algorithm, we propose sound and complete synthesis algorithms that transform a fault-intolerant real-time program into a (1) nonmasking or soft-failsafe fault-tolerant programs, or (2) hard-failsafe fault-tolerant program where the synthesized fault-tolerant program is required to satisfy at most one bounded response property in the presence of faults. For reasons of space, in a technical report [19], we also present a synthesis algorithm for adding soft-masking fault-tolerance. Moreover, we show that the problem of adding hard-masking fault-tolerance where the synthesized program is required to satisfy at least two bounded response properties in the presence of faults is NP-hard.

Organization of the paper. In Section 2, we present formal definitions of real-time programs, specifications, and regions graphs. We introduce the notions of faults and fault-tolerance in the context of real-time programs in Section 3. In Section 4, we formally state the problem of adding fault-tolerance to real-time programs. We present our synthesis algorithms for adding nonmasking, soft-failsafe, and hard-failsafe fault-tolerance in sections 5, 6, and 7, respectively. Finally, in Section 8, we make the concluding remarks.

2 Real-Time Programs, Specifications, and Region Graphs

In our framework, programs are specified in terms of their state space and their transitions [20]. The definition of specifications is adapted from Henzinger [21]. Finally, the notion of region graph is due to Alur and Dill [17].

2.1 Real-Time Program

Let V be a finite set of *discrete variables* and X be a finite set of *clock variables*. Each discrete variable is associated with a finite *domain D* of values. A *location* is a function that maps each discrete variable to a value from its respective domain. A *clock constraint* over the set X of clock variables is a Boolean combination of formulas of the form $x \preceq c$ or $x - y \preceq c$, where $x, y \in X$, $c \in \mathbb{Z}_{\geq 0}$, and $\preceq$ is either $<$ or $\leq$. We denote the set of all clock constraints over X by $\Phi(X)$. A *clock valuation* is a function $\nu : X \to \mathbb{R}_{\geq 0}$ that assigns a real value to each clock variable. Furthermore, for $\tau \in \mathbb{R}_{\geq 0}$, $\nu + \tau = \nu(x) + \tau$ for every clock x. Also, for $\lambda \subseteq X$, $\nu[\lambda := 0]$ denotes the clock valuation for X which assigns 0 to each $x \in \lambda$ and agrees with ν over the rest of the clock variables in X.

A *state* (denoted σ) is a pair (s, ν), such that s is a location and ν is a clock valuation for X at location s. A *transition* (denoted (σ_0, σ_1)) is of the form $(s_0, \nu_0) \to (s_1, \nu_1)$. Transitions are classified into two types:

- **Delay:** for a state $\sigma = (s, \nu)$ and a time *duration* $\delta \in \mathbb{R}_{\geq 0}$ (denoted (σ, δ)), $(s, \nu) \to (s, \nu + \delta)$.
- **Jump:** for a state (s_0, ν), a location s_1, and a set λ of clock variables, $(s_0, \nu) \to (s_1, \nu[\lambda := 0])$.

A *program* $\mathcal{P}$ is a tuple $\langle S_p, \psi_p \rangle$, where S_p is the *state space*, and ψ_p is a set of transitions. Let ψ_p^s and ψ_p^d denote the set of jump and delay transitions in ψ_p, respectively. A *state predicate* is a subset of S_p such that it is definable by the above syntax of clock constraints, i.e., in the corresponding Boolean expression clock variables are only compared to nonnegative integers. A state predicate S is *closed* in program $\mathcal{P}$ if $((\forall (\sigma_0, \sigma_1) \in \psi_p^s : (\sigma_0 \in S \Rightarrow \sigma_1 \in S)) \land (\forall (\sigma, \delta) \in \psi_p^d : (\sigma \in S \Rightarrow \forall \epsilon \leq \delta : \sigma + \epsilon \in S)))$. A timed state sequence $\langle (\sigma_0, \tau_0), (\sigma_1, \tau_1), \cdots \rangle$, where $\tau_i \in \mathbb{R}_{\geq 0}$, is a *computation* of $\mathcal{P}$ if the following conditions are satisfied: (1) $\forall j > 0 : (\sigma_{j-1}, \sigma_j) \in \psi_p$, (2) if it is finite and terminates in (σ_l, τ_l) then there does not exist state σ such that $(\sigma_l, \sigma) \in \psi_p$, and (3) the sequence $\langle \tau_0, \tau_1, \cdots \rangle$ satisfies the following constraints:

Monotonicity: $\tau_i \leq \tau_{i+1}$ for all $i \in \mathbb{N}$.
Divergence: For all $t \in \mathbb{R}_{\geq 0}$, there exists j such that $\tau_j \geq t$.

The *projection* of a set of program transitions ψ_p on state predicate S (denoted $\psi_p | S$) is the set of transitions $\{ (\sigma_0, \sigma_1) \in \psi_p^s \mid \sigma_0, \sigma_1 \in S \} \cup \{ (\sigma, \delta) \in \psi_p^d \mid \sigma \in S \land (\forall \epsilon \leq \delta : \sigma + \epsilon \in S) \}$.

2.2 Specification

A *specification* (or *property*), denoted Σ, is a set of timed state sequences of the form $\langle (\sigma_0, \tau_0), (\sigma_1, \tau_1), \cdots \rangle$. Following Henzinger [21], we require that the sequence $\langle \tau_0, \tau_1, \cdots \rangle$ satisfies monotonicity and divergence. We now define what it means for a program $\mathcal{P}$ to satisfy a specification Σ. Given a program $\mathcal{P}$, a state predicate S, and a specification Σ, we write $\mathcal{P} \models_S \Sigma$ and say that program $\mathcal{P}$ *satisfies* Σ *from* S iff (1) S is closed in $\mathcal{P}$, and (2) every computation of $\mathcal{P}$ that starts where S is true is in Σ. If $\mathcal{P} \models_S \Sigma$ and $S \neq \{\}$, we say that S is an *invariant* of $\mathcal{P}$ for Σ.

Notation. Whenever the specification is clear from the context, we will omit it; thus, "S is an invariant of $\mathcal{P}$" abbreviates "S is an invariant of $\mathcal{P}$ for Σ".

We say that program $\mathcal{P}$ *maintains* Σ iff for all finite timed state sequences α of $\mathcal{P}$, there exists a timed state sequence β such that $\alpha\beta \in \Sigma$. We say that $\mathcal{P}$ *violates* Σ iff it is not the case that $\mathcal{P}$ maintains Σ. Note that, the definition of *maintains* identifies the property of finite timed state sequences, whereas the definition of *satisfies* expresses the property of infinite timed state sequences.

Following Alpern and Schneider [22] and Henzinger [21], we let the specification consist of a *liveness specification* and a *safety specification*. The liveness specification is represented by a set of infinite computations. A program satisfies the liveness specification, if every computation prefix of the program has a suffix that is in the liveness specification.

Remark 2.1: In the synthesis problem, we begin with an initial fault-intolerant program that satisfies its specification (including the liveness specification) in the absence of faults. We will show that our synthesis algorithms *preserve* liveness specification. Hence, the liveness specification need not be specified explicitly.

In this paper, with abuse of notation, we let the safety specification consist of (1) a set Σ_{bt} of location switch *bad transitions* that should not occur in the program computation, and (2) a conjunction of zero or more *bounded response* properties of the form $\Sigma_{br} \equiv ((P_1 \mapsto_{\leq \delta_1} Q_1) \wedge (P_2 \mapsto_{\leq \delta_2} Q_2) \wedge \ldots \wedge (P_m \mapsto_{\leq \delta_m} Q_m))$, i.e., it is always the case that a state in P_i is followed by a state in Q_i within δ_i time units, where P_i and Q_i are state predicates and $\delta_i \in \mathbb{Z}_{\geq 0}$, for all i such that $1 \leq i \leq m$. Observe that we abuse the $\models$ notation for the set Σ_{bt} of bad transitions. This is because it is possible to trivially translate this concise representation of safety into the corresponding set of infinite computations. The same concept applies to definitions of *maintains* and *violates*.

2.3 Region Graph

Real-time programs can be analyzed with the help of an equivalence relation of finite index on the set of states [17]. Given a real-time program $\mathcal{P}$, for each clock $x \in X$, let c_x be the largest constant in the guards of transitions and invariant of $\mathcal{P}$ that involve x, where $c_x = 0$ if x does not occur in any guard or invariant of $\mathcal{P}$. Two clock valuations ν, μ are *clock equivalent* if (1) for all $x \in X$, either $\lfloor \nu(x) \rfloor = \lfloor \mu(x) \rfloor$ or both $\nu(x), \mu(x) > c_x$, (2) the ordering of the fractional parts of the clock variables in the set $\{x \in X \mid \nu(x) < c_x\}$ is the same in μ, and (3) for all $x \in \{y \in X \mid \nu(y) < c_y\}$, the clock value $\nu(x)$ is an integer if and only if $\mu(x)$ is an integer. A *clock region* ρ is a clock equivalence class. Two states (s_0, ν_0) and (s_1, ν_1) are region equivalent, written $(s_0, \nu_0) \equiv (s_1, \nu_1)$, if (1) $s_0 = s_1$ and (2) ν_0 and ν_1 are clock equivalent. A *region* is an equivalence class with respect to $\equiv$. Using the region equivalence relation, we construct the *region graph* of $\mathcal{P}\langle S_p, \psi_p \rangle$ (denoted $R(\mathcal{P})\langle S_p^r, \psi_p^r \rangle$) as follows. Vertices of $R(\mathcal{P})$ (denoted S_p^r) are regions. Edges of $R(\mathcal{P})$ (denoted ψ_p^r) are of the form $(s_0, \rho_0) \rightarrow (s_1, \rho_1)$ iff for some clock valuations $\nu_0 \in \rho_0$ and $\nu_1 \in \rho_1$, $(s_0, \nu_0) \rightarrow (s_1, \nu_1)$ is a transitions in ψ_p. We say that a region (s_0, ρ_0) of region graph $R(\mathcal{P})$ is a *deadlock region* iff for all regions (s_1, ρ_1), there does not exist an edge of the form $(s_0, \rho_0) \rightarrow (s_1, \rho_1)$. A *region predicate* S^r with respect to a state predicate S is defined by $S^r = \{(s, \rho) \mid \exists(s, \nu) : ((s, \nu) \in S \wedge \nu \in \rho)\}$. Likewise, the region predicate with respect to invariant S of a program $\mathcal{P}$ is called *region invariant* S^r. The projection of a set of edges ψ_p^r on region predicate S^r (denoted $\psi_p^r | S^r$) is the set of edges $\{(r_0, r_1) \in \psi_p^r \mid r_0, r_1 \in S^r\}$.

Region graphs are time-abstract bisimulation of real-time programs [17]. In our synthesis algorithms in section 5, 6, and 7, we transform a real-time program $\mathcal{P}\langle S_p, \psi_p \rangle$ into its corresponding region graph $R(\mathcal{P})\langle S_p^r, \psi_p^r \rangle$ by invoking the procedure ConstructRegionGraph. We also let this procedure take state predicates and sets of transitions in $\mathcal{P}$ (e.g., S and Σ_{bt}) and return the corresponding region predicates and sets of edges in $R(\mathcal{P})$ (e.g., S^r and Σ_{bt}^r). Likewise, we transform a region graph $R(\mathcal{P})$ back to a real-time program by invoking the procedure ConstructRealTimeProgram.

A clock region β is a *time-successor* of a clock region α iff for each $\nu \in \alpha$, there exists $\tau \in \mathbb{R}_{\geq 0}$, such that $\nu + \tau \in \beta$, and $\nu + \tau' \in \alpha \cup \beta$ for all $\tau' < \tau$. We call a region (s, ρ) a *boundary region*, if for each $\nu \in \rho$ and for any $\tau \in \mathbb{R}_{\geq 0}$, ν and $\nu + \tau$ are not equivalent. A region is *open*, if it is not a boundary region. A region (s, ρ) is called an *end region*, if $\nu(x) > c_x$ for all $\nu \in \rho$ and for all clocks $x \in X$.

3 Faults and Fault-Tolerance in Real-Time Programs

In this section, we extend formal definitions of faults and fault-tolerance due to Arora and Gouda [23] to the context of real-time programs. The faults that a program is subject to are systematically represented by transitions. A class of *faults* f for program $\mathcal{P}\langle S_p, \psi_p \rangle$ is a subset of the set $S_p \times S_p$. Faults are also categorized into *delay faults* and *jump faults*. We use $\psi_p[] f$ to denote the transitions obtained by taking the union of the transitions in ψ_p and the transitions in f.

We say that a state predicate T is an f-span (read as *fault-span*) of $\mathcal{P}$ from S iff the following conditions are satisfied: (1) $S \subseteq T$, and (2) T is closed in $\psi_p[] f$. Observe that for all computations of $\mathcal{P}$ that start from states where S is true, T is a boundary in the state space of $\mathcal{P}$ up to which (but not beyond which) the state of $\mathcal{P}$ may be perturbed by the occurrence of the transitions in f. As we defined the computations of $\mathcal{P}$, we say that a timed state sequence, $\langle (\sigma_0, \tau_0), (\sigma_1, \tau_1), \cdots \rangle$, is a *computation of $\mathcal{P}$ in the presence of f* iff the following four conditions are satisfied: (1) $\forall j > 0 : (\sigma_{j-1}, \sigma_j) \in (\psi_p \cup f)$, (2) if it is finite and terminates in state (σ_l, τ_l) then there does not exist state σ such that $(\sigma_l, \sigma) \in \psi_p$, (3) $\langle \tau_0, \tau_1, \cdots \rangle$ satisfies monotonicity and divergence, and (4) $\exists n \geq 0 : (\forall j > n : (\sigma_{j-1}, \sigma_j) \in \psi_p)$.

We consider three levels of fault-tolerance, namely nonmasking, failsafe, and masking based on satisfaction of safety and liveness properties in the presence of faults. For failsafe and masking fault-tolerance, we propose two additional levels, namely *soft* and *hard*, based on satisfaction of timing constraints in the presence of faults. Intuitively, a *soft fault-tolerant* real-time program is not required to satisfy its timing constraints in the presence of faults. A *hard fault-tolerant* real-time program must satisfy its timing constraints even in the presence of faults.

Let specification Σ consist of Σ_{bt} and Σ_{br}. Since a nonmasking fault-tolerant program need not satisfy safety in the presence of faults, $\mathcal{P}$ is *nonmasking f-tolerant from S for Σ with recovery time δ*, where $\delta \in \mathbb{Z}_{\geq 0}$, iff (1) $\mathcal{P} \models_S \Sigma_{bt}$, (2) $\mathcal{P} \models_S \Sigma_{br}$, and (3) there exists T such that T is an f-span of $\mathcal{P}$ from S, and every computation of $\mathcal{P}\langle S_p, \psi_p[] f \rangle$ that starts from a state in T, reaches a state in S within δ time units. We say that $\mathcal{P}$ is *soft-failsafe f-tolerant from S for Σ* iff (1) $\mathcal{P} \models_S \Sigma_{bt}$, (2) $\mathcal{P} \models_S \Sigma_{br}$, and (3) there exists T such that T is an f-span of $\mathcal{P}$ from S, and $\mathcal{P}\langle S_p, \psi_p[] f \rangle$ maintains

Σ_{bt} from T. A program $\mathcal{P}$ is *hard-failsafe f-tolerant from S for* Σ iff $\mathcal{P}$ is soft-failsafe f-tolerant from S for Σ and $\mathcal{P}\langle S_p, \psi_p[]f\rangle$ maintains Σ_{br} from T. A program $\mathcal{P}\langle S_p, \psi_p\rangle$ is *soft-masking f-tolerant from S for* Σ *with recovery time* δ, where $\delta \in \mathbb{Z}_{\geq 0}$, iff (1) $\mathcal{P} \models_S \Sigma_{bt}$, (2) $\mathcal{P} \models_S \Sigma_{br}$, (3) there exists T such that T is an f-span of $\mathcal{P}$ from S and $\mathcal{P}\langle S_p, \psi_p[]f\rangle$ maintains Σ_{bt} from T, and (4) every computation of $\mathcal{P}\langle S_p, \psi_p[]f\rangle$ that starts from a state in T, reaches a state in S within δ time units. A program $\mathcal{P}\langle S_p, \psi_p\rangle$ is *hard-masking f-tolerant from S for* Σ *with recovery time* δ, where $\delta \in \mathbb{Z}_{\geq 0}$, iff $\mathcal{P}$ is soft-masking f-tolerant from S for Σ with recovery time δ, and $\mathcal{P}\langle S_p, \psi_p[]f\rangle$ maintains Σ_{br} from T.

Notation. Whenever the specification Σ and the invariant S are clear from the context, we omit them; thus, "f-tolerant" abbreviates "f-tolerant from S for Σ".

Assumption 3.1: Since $\mathcal{P}$ satisfies $\Sigma_{br} \equiv ((P_1 \mapsto_{\leq \delta_1} Q_1) \wedge ... \wedge (P_m \mapsto_{\leq \delta_m} Q_m))$ in the absence of faults (cf. Remark 2.1), without loss of generality, we assume that for each bounded response property $(P_i \mapsto_{\leq \delta_i} Q_i)$, where $1 \leq i \leq m$, the intolerant program already has a clock variable that is reset on transitions that go from a state in $\neg P_i$ to a state in P_i to keep track of time as soon as P_i becomes true.

Assumption 3.2: We assume that faults are immediately detectable and that given a state of the program, we can determine the number of faults that have occurred in reaching that state. This assumption is needed only for addition of hard fault-tolerance and is realistic in many commonly considered systems. For instance, in multiprocessor scheduling theory, a processor-crash is immediately detectable and its number of occurrences is easily traceable.

Assumption 3.3: We assume that the number of occurrence of faults in a program computation is bounded by a pre-specified value n. This assumption is required since for commonly considered faults, it can be shown that *bounded-time recovery* in the presence of unbounded occurrence of faults is impossible.

4   Problem Statement

Given are a fault-intolerant real-time program $\mathcal{P}\langle S_p, \psi_p\rangle$, its invariant S, a set of faults f, and a safety specification Σ such that $\mathcal{P} \models_S \Sigma$. Our goal is to synthesize a real-time program $\mathcal{P}'\langle S_p, \psi_p'\rangle$ with invariant S' such that $\mathcal{P}'$ is f-tolerant from S' for Σ. As mentioned in the introduction, our synthesis methods obtain $\mathcal{P}'$ from $\mathcal{P}$ by adding fault-tolerance *alone* to $\mathcal{P}$, i.e., $\mathcal{P}'$ does not introduce new behaviors to $\mathcal{P}$ when no faults have occurred. Observe that:

1. If S' contains states that are not in S then, in the absence of faults, $\mathcal{P}'$ may include computations that start outside S. Since we require that $\mathcal{P}' \models_{S'} \Sigma$, it would imply that $\mathcal{P}'$ is using a new way to satisfy Σ in the absence of faults.
2. If $\psi_p'|S'$ contains a transition that is not in $\psi_p|S'$ then $\mathcal{P}'$ can use this transition in order to satisfy Σ in the absence of faults.

Thus, the synthesis problem is as follows (we instantiate this problem for soft/hard-failsafe, nonmasking, and soft/hard-masking f-tolerance in the obvious way):

Problem Statement 4.1. Given $\mathcal{P}\langle S_p, \psi_p \rangle$, S, Σ, and f such that $\mathcal{P} \models_S \Sigma$. Identify $\mathcal{P}'\langle S_p, \psi'_p \rangle$ and S' such that

    (C1) $S' \subseteq S$
    (C2) $\psi'_p | S' \subseteq \psi_p | S'$, and
    (C3) $\mathcal{P}'$ is f-tolerant from S' for Σ.

Soundness and completeness. We say that an algorithm for the synthesis problem is *sound* iff its output meets the constraints of the Problem Statement 4.1. We say that an algorithm for the synthesis problem is *complete* iff it finds a solution to the Problem Statement 4.1 iff there exists one.

5 Adding Nonmasking Fault-Tolerance

Algorithm sketch. Since a nonmasking program is not required to satisfy its safety specification in the presence of faults, it only suffices to provide bounded-time recovery from the fault-span $S_p - S$ to the invariant S. We develop a general procedure that adds bounded-time recovery to a given region graph from any arbitrary given state predicate P to another state predicate Q within δ time units (i.e., $P \mapsto_{\leq \delta} Q$). Notice that bounded-time recovery from fault-span to the invariant can be formally defined by $\mathcal{R} \equiv (S_p - S) \mapsto_{\leq \delta} S$. The algorithm has four main steps. First, we transform the region graph to a weighted directed graph (called MaxDelay digraph [24]), in which the length of a path from vertex v_s to v_t is equivalent to the maximum delay for reaching the region that corresponds to v_t from the region that corresponds to v_s. We use this property to remove the computations that violate $P \mapsto_{\leq \delta} Q$. To this end, in Step 2, we rank vertices of the MaxDelay digraph by simply applying an *adjusted* Dijkstra's shortest path algorithms. For instance, suppose that a computation starts from a state $\sigma_0 \in P$. If a fault perturbs the program to a state σ_j where "something" should be *redone*, the maximum delay of that computation to reach Q is obviously increased. Hence, we adjust the length of the shortest path from σ_0 to Q such that the amount of time wasted by every occurrence of faults is considered (cf. Figure 1). In Step 3, we include regions and edges whose rank is at most the required response time δ. Then, in Step 4, we transform the synthesized MaxDelay digraph back into a region graph.

Construction of MaxDelay digraph. We now describe the procedure Construct-MaxDelayGraph that transforms a region graph to a MaxDelay digraph. The procedure takes a region graph $R(\mathcal{P})\langle S_p^r, \psi_p^r \rangle$ and a set f^r of fault edges as input, and constructs a MaxDelay digraph $G\langle V, A \rangle$ as follows. Vertices of G consist of the regions in $R(\mathcal{P})$.

Notation. We denote the weight of an arc (v_0, v_1) by $Weight(v_0, v_1)$. Let γ denote a bijection that maps each region $r \in S_p^r$ to its corresponding vertex in G; i.e., $\gamma(r)$ is a vertex of G that represents region r of $R(\mathcal{P})$. Also, let γ^{-1} denote the inverse of γ; i.e., $\gamma^{-1}(v)$ is the region of $R(\mathcal{P})$ that corresponds to vertex v in V. Let Γ be a function that maps a region predicate in $R(\mathcal{P})$ to the corresponding set of vertices of G and let

Γ^{-1} be its inverse. Finally, for a boundary region r with respect to clock variable x, we denote the value of x by $r.x$ (equal to some nonnegative integer in $\mathbb{Z}_{\geq 0}$).

Arcs of G consist of the following:

- Arcs of weight 0 from v_0 to v_1, if $\gamma^{-1}(v_0) \to \gamma^{-1}(v_1)$ represents a jump transition in $R(\mathcal{P})$.
- Arcs of weight $c' - c$, where $c, c' \in \mathbb{Z}_{\geq 0}$ and $c' > c$, from v_0 to v_1, if $\gamma^{-1}(v_0)$ and $\gamma^{-1}(v_1)$ are both boundary regions with respect to clock variable x_i, such that $\gamma^{-1}(v_0).x_i = c$, $\gamma^{-1}(v_1).x_i = c'$, and there is a path in $R(\mathcal{P})$ from $\gamma^{-1}(v_0)$ to $\gamma^{-1}(v_1)$, which does not reset x_i.
- Arcs of weight $c' - c - \epsilon$, where $c, c' \in \mathbb{Z}_{\geq 0}$, $c' > c$, and $0 < \epsilon \ll 1$, from v_0 to v_1, if (1) $\gamma^{-1}(v_0)$ is a boundary region with respect to clock x_i, (2) $\gamma^{-1}(v_1)$ is an open region whose time-successor $\gamma^{-1}(v_2)$ is a boundary region with respect to clock x_i, (3) $\gamma^{-1}(v_0) \to \gamma^{-1}(v_1)$ represents a delay transition in $R(\mathcal{P})$, and (4) $\gamma^{-1}(v_0).x_i = c$ and $\gamma^{-1}(v_2).x_i = c'$.
- Self-loop arcs of weight ∞ at vertex v, if $\gamma^{-1}(v)$ is an end region.

In order to compute the maximum delay between regions in P^r and Q^r, it suffices to find the longest distance between $\Gamma(P^r)$ and $\Gamma(Q^r)$ in G.

We now describe the procedure Add_BoundedRecovery (cf. Figure 2) in detail. Given a region graph $R(\mathcal{P})$, we first transforms it into a MaxDelay digraph $G\langle V, A \rangle$ (Line A1). Recall that, by Assumption 3.2, faults are detectable and $\mathcal{P}$ has a variable that shows how many faults have occurred in a computation. Thus, let $G^i\langle V^i, A^i \rangle$ be the portion of G, in which $n - i$ faults have occurred, where $0 \leq i \leq n$. More specifically, initially, a computation starts from the portion G^n where no faults have occurred. If a fault occurs in a computation that is currently in portion G^i, the computation will proceed in portion G^{i-1}. We use these portions to see whether it is possible to reach a vertex in $\Gamma(Q^r)$ from each vertex in $\Gamma(P^r)$ within δ time units.

Next, we rank vertices of all portions of G using a modified Dijkstra's shortest path algorithm, which takes state perturbations into account (lines A2-A9 and A22-A23). More specifically, since no faults occur in G^0, we first let the rank of each vertex $v \in V^0$ be the length of Dijkstra's shortest path from v to $\Gamma(Q^r)^0$ (Line A2). Now, let v_0 be a vertex in V^i where $1 \leq i \leq n$, and let v_1 be a vertex in V^{i-1}, such that $(\gamma^{-1}(v_0), \gamma^{-1}(v_1))$ is a fault edge in $R(\mathcal{P})$ and both v_0 and v_1 are on a path from $\Gamma(P^r)$ to $\Gamma(Q^r)$. There exist two cases: (1) the fault edge $(\gamma^{-1}(v_0), \gamma^{-1}(v_1))$ decreases or

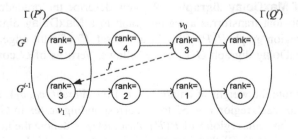

Fig. 1. Adjusted shortest path

---

procedure Add_BoundedRecovery($R(\mathcal{P})\langle S_p^r, \psi_p^r\rangle$: region graph, f^r: set of edges,
$\qquad\qquad\qquad\qquad\qquad\qquad P^r, Q^r$: region predicate, n, δ: **integer**)
// Adds bounded-time recovery from P^r to Q^r in the presence of f^r
{
step 1: $G\langle V, A\rangle := \text{ConstructMaxDelayGraph}(R(\mathcal{P})\langle S_p^r, \psi_p^r\rangle, f^r);$ (A1)
    Let $G^i\langle V^i, A^i\rangle$ be the portion of G, in which $(n-i)$ faults have occurred, where $0 \le i \le n$;
step 2: **for** each vertex $v \in V^0$: $Rank(v) := $ Length of the shortest path from v to $\Gamma(Q^r)^0$; (A2)
    for $i = 1$ **to** n (A3)
      for each vertex $v_0 \in V^i$:   (A4)
        $V_f := \{v_1 \mid (v_1 \in V^{i-1} \land (\gamma^{-1}(v_0), \gamma^{-1}(v_1)) \in f^r)\};$ (A5)
        if $V_f \ne \{\}$ **then** $MinRank(v_0) :=$ (A6)
          $\max\{(Rank(v_1) + Weight(v_0, v_1)) \text{ for all } v_1 \in V_f\};$ (A7)
        else $MinRank(v_0) := 0;$ (A8)
        $\text{AdjustShortestPaths}(G^i\langle V^i, A^i\rangle, \Gamma(P^r)^i, \Gamma(Q^r)^i);$ (A9)
// Constructing a subgraph of each portion such that the longest distance between $\Gamma(P^r)$ and $\Gamma(Q^r)$ is at most δ
and then adding the arcs and vertices that do not appear on paths from $\Gamma(P^r)$ to $\Gamma(Q^r)$
step 3: **for** $i = 0$ **to** n (A10)
      $G'^i\langle V'^i, A'^i\rangle = \{\};$ (A11)
      for each vertex $v \in \Gamma(P^r)^i$:   (A12)
        if $Rank(v) \le \delta$ **then**   (A13)
          $\Pi := $ the shortest path from v to $\Gamma(Q^r)^i$;   (A14)
          $V'^i := V'^i \cup \{u \mid u \text{ is on } \Pi\};$ (A15)
          $A'^i := A'^i \cup \{a \mid a \text{ is on } \Pi\};$ (A16)
        $A'^i := A'^i \cup \{(u, v) \mid (u, v) \in A^i \land (u \notin V'^i \lor (u \in \Gamma(Q^r)^i))\};$ (A17)
        $V'^i := (V'^i \cup \{u \mid (\exists v : (u, v) \in A'^i \lor (v, u) \in A'^i)\};$ (A18)
// Transforming weighted digraph G into a region graph
step 4: $\psi_p'^r := \{(r_0, r_1) \mid (r_0, r_1) \in \psi_p^r \land (\gamma(r_0), \gamma(r_1)) \in A'\} \cup$
      $\{(r_1, r_2) \mid (r_1, r_2) \in \psi_p^r \land (\gamma(r_1), \gamma(r_2)) \notin A' \land$
       $\exists r_0 : Weight(\gamma(r_0), \gamma(r_1)) = 1 - \epsilon\};$ (A19)
    $ns := \{r \mid \gamma(r) \in (V - V')\};$ (A20)
    return $\psi_p'^r, ns$ (A21)
}
procedure AdjustShortestPaths($G^i\langle V^i, A^i\rangle$: directed weighted graph, V_q: set of vertices)
// Adjusts the rank of each vertex based on the ranks computed in Add_BoundedRecovery
{
    for each vertex $v \in V^i$ apply Dijkstra's shortest path with the following change:
      if Dijkstra's shortest path computes a length less than $MinRank(v)$ **then**
        $Rank(v) := MinRank(v);$ (A22)
      else $Rank(v) := $ length of Dijkstra's shortest path from v to V_q
        using the assigned rank of other vertices   (A23)
}
algorithm Add_Nonmasking($\mathcal{P}\langle S_p, \psi_p\rangle$:real-time program f :transitions, S: state predicate, n, δ: **integer**)
{
    $R(\mathcal{P})\langle S_p^r, \psi_p^r\rangle, S^r, f^r := \text{ConstructRegionGraph}(\mathcal{P}\langle S_p, \psi_p\rangle, S, f);$ (B1)
    $\psi_p^r := \psi_p^r \cup \{((s_0, \rho_0), (s_1, \rho_1)) \mid (s_0, \rho_0) \notin S^r \land$
      $\exists \rho_2 \mid \rho_2 \text{ is a time-successor of } \rho_0 : (\exists \lambda \subseteq X : \rho_1 = \rho_2[\lambda - \{t\} := 0])\};$ (B2)
    $\psi_p^r, ns := \text{Add\_BoundedRecovery}(R(\mathcal{P})\langle S_p^r, \psi_{p_1}^r\rangle, f^r, S_p^r - S^r, S^r, n, \delta);$ (B3)
    $rs := \{r_0 \mid \exists r_1, r_2, ...r_n : (\forall j : 0 \le j < n : (r_j, r_{j+1}) \in f^r) \land r_n \in (ns \cap P^r)\};$ (B4)
    $rt := \{(r_0, r_1) \mid (r_0, r_1) \in \psi_p^r \land r_1 \in rs)\};$ (B5)
    $S'^r, \psi_p'^r := S^r - rs, \psi_p^r - rt;$ (B6)
    $\psi_p'^r := \text{EnsureClosure}(\psi_p'^r, S'^r);$ (B7)
    $\mathcal{P}'\langle S_p, \psi_p'\rangle, S' := \text{ConstructRealTimeProgram}(R(\mathcal{P})\langle S_p^r, \psi_p'^r\rangle, S'^r)$ (B8)
}
procedure EnsureClosure(ψ_p^r : set of edges, S^r : region predicate)
  { **return** $\psi_p^r - \{(r_0, r_1) \mid r_0 \in S^r \land r_1 \notin S^r\}\}$

Fig. 2. Adding Bounded-Time Recovery/Nonmasking Fault-Tolerance

---

does not change the computation delay, i.e, the shortest distance from v_1 to $\Gamma(Q^r)^{i-1}$ is less than or equal to the shortest distance from v_0 to $\Gamma(Q^r)^i$, and (2) the fault edge $(\gamma^{-1}(v_0), \gamma^{-1}(v_1))$ increases the computation delay, i.e., the shortest distance from v_1

to $\Gamma(Q^r)^{i-1}$ is greater than the shortest distance from v_0 to $\Gamma(Q^r)^i$ (cf. Figure 1 for an example). While the former case does not cause violation of $P \mapsto_{\leq \delta} Q$ in the presence of faults, the later may do. Hence, the rank of $v_0 \in V^i$ must be at least the rank of $v_1 \in V^{i-1}$. Moreover, if there exist multiple fault edges at $\gamma^{-1}(v_0)$ then we take the maximum rank (Line A7). After computing the rank of vertices from where faults may occur, we adjust the rank of the rest of vertices from where faults do not occur by invoking the procedure AdjustShortestPath (Line A9).

Now, for each portion G^i, we construct a subgraph of G^i whose longest distance from each vertex in $\Gamma(P^r)^i$ to $\Gamma(Q^r)^i$ is at most δ as follows (lines A11-A16). We begin with an empty digraph $G'^i \langle V'^i, A'^i \rangle$ and we first include the shortest paths from each vertex $v \in \Gamma(P^r)^i$ to $\Gamma(Q^r)^i$, provided $Rank(v) \leq \delta$ (lines A13-A16). Next, we include the remaining arcs and vertices in G'^i, so that no arcs of the form (v_0, v_1), where v_0 is on a path from $\Gamma(P^r)^i$ to $\Gamma(Q^r)^i$ are added (lines A17-A18).

Now, we transform the digraph G' back into a region graph (Line A19). Finally, we return the set $\psi_p'^r$ of edges from where $P \mapsto_{\leq \delta} Q$ is not violated even in the presence of faults, and the set ns of regions from where $P \mapsto_{\leq \delta} Q$ may be violated in the presence of faults (lines A20-A21).

Using Add_BoundedRecovery to Add Nonmasking Fault-Tolerance. In order to add nonmasking fault-tolerance with bounded-time recovery δ, we first transform the real-time program $\mathcal{P}\langle S_p, \psi_p \rangle$, invariant S, and the set of fault transitions f into a region graph $R(\mathcal{P})\langle S_p^r, \psi_p^r \rangle$, region invariant S^r, and fault edges f^r by invoking the procedure ConstructRegionGraph (Line B1), as described in Subsection 2.3. Next, in order to ensure that S' is reachable from all the states in $S_p - S'$, we add *recovery edges* that start from each region in $S_p^r - S^r$ and go to regions where the time monotonicity condition is preserved, i.e., time is not decreased (Line B2). Notice that the algorithm allows arbitrary clock resets (except the clock that keeps track of the recovery time time δ) during recovery, which is fine according to the definition of nonmasking fault-tolerance (such "new" clock resets occur only in states outside the invariant). Then we invoke the procedure Add_BoundedRecovery. This invocation identifies the set rs of regions and the set rt of edges from where faults alone may violate $\mathcal{R}$ (lines B4-B5). Then, it removes such regions (respectively, edges) from S^r (respectively, ψ_p^r). Finally, the algorithm ensures the closure of the invariant (Line B7) and transforms the synthesized region graph $R(\mathcal{P}')$ back to a real-time program $\mathcal{P}'$ (Line B8).

6 Adding Soft-Failsafe Fault-Tolerance

As mentioned in Subsection 2.2, the safety specification identifies a set Σ_{bt} of bad transitions and a conjunction Σ_{br} of multiple bounded response properties. Also, recall that in the presence of faults, a soft-failsafe program is required to maintain Σ_{bt} only.

Algorithm sketch. We adapt the proposed algorithm in [6], which adds failsafe fault-tolerance to *untimed* programs. Intuitively, our algorithm, consists of three main steps. First, we prohibit the program from reaching the set ms of states from where a sequence of faults takes the program to a state where safety (Σ_{bt}) is violated. Since our goal is to synthesize a *maximal* program, we find ms by computing the smallest fixpoint of states from where safety may be violated. In step 2, after removing ms from the program invariant S, we make sure that this removal do not create new finite computations in the absence of faults. To this end, we remove deadlock states from the invariant which is in turn computing the largest fixpoint of the invariant. Finally, in step 3, we ensure that removal of transitions from where safety may be violated does not violate the closure of the output program.

We now describe the algorithm Add_SoftFailsafe (cf. Figure 3). We first transform the program $\mathcal{P}$ into its region graph $R(\mathcal{P})$ (Line C1). Then, the algorithm adds failsafe fault-tolerance to $R(\mathcal{P})$, so that no edge of Σ_{bt}^r occurs in computations of $R(\mathcal{P})$ in the presence of faults by invoking the procedure Add_UntimedFailsafe (Line C2). This procedure first finds the set ms of regions and the set mt of edges from where safety of $\mathcal{P}$ may be violated by faults alone (lines E1-E2). Next, it removes such regions (respectively, edges) from the region invariant S^r (respectively, set of edges ψ_p^r) of $R(\mathcal{P})$. Then, it removes deadlock regions from S^r (Line E3), ensures the closure of ψ_p^r in S^r (Line E5), and returns a failsafe region graph $R(\mathcal{P}')\langle S_p^r, \psi_p^{\prime r}\rangle$ (Line E6). Finally, we transform the region graph $R(\mathcal{P}')$ back into a real-time program $\mathcal{P}'$ (Line C3) as described in Subsection 2.3.

7 Adding Hard-Failsafe Fault-Tolerance with One Bounded Response Property

In this section, we present our algorithm Add_HardFailsafe (cf. Figure 3) for the case where the synthesized hard-failsafe program is required to satisfy at most one bounded response property in the presence of faults, i.e., $\Sigma_{hr} \equiv P \mapsto_{\leq \delta} Q$.

Algorithm sketch. Intuitively, the algorithms works in five main steps. First, we add soft-failsafe to $R(\mathcal{P})$ to ensure that a transition in Σ_{bt} occurs in no computation of $\mathcal{P}'$. Note that, the outcome of adding soft-failsafe is a maximal program and every transition that is removed by Add_SoftFailsafe has to be removed, i.e., such transitions cannot be in any fault-tolerant program that satisfies the constraints of Problem Statement 4.1. In Step 2, we remove the behaviors that violate the bounded response property $\Sigma_{br} \equiv P \mapsto_{\leq \delta} Q$ in the presence of faults using the procedure Add_BoundedRecovery. In step 3, we remove deadlock states due to removal of states and transitions in step 2. In Step 4, if a state $\sigma_1 \in Q$ is removed and some state, say σ_0, in P uses σ_1 to satisfy $P \mapsto_{\leq \delta} Q$ then another path from σ_0 must be provided to satisfy $P \mapsto_{\leq \delta} Q$. Hence, we remove σ_1 from Q and repeat steps 2, 3, and 4 until no such Q-states exist. Finally, in Step 5, we ensure the closure of the output program.

We now describe the pseudo-code of the algorithm. In order to ensure that $\mathcal{P}'$ maintains Σ_{bt}, we first add soft-failsafe fault-tolerance to $R(\mathcal{P})$ (Line D1). Next, we transform $\mathcal{P}$ into its region graph $R(\mathcal{P})$ (Line D2). Next, we modify $R(\mathcal{P})$, such that any computation that starts from a region in P^r, reaches a region in Q^r in at most δ time units even in the presence of faults. Towards this end, we compute the set of regions and edges from where Σ_{br} is maintained (lines D3-D14). Precisely, in order to ensure that Q is reachable from all the states in $P \wedge \neg S$, we first include edges that start from each region in $S_p^r - S^r$ and go to regions where the time monotonicity condition is preserved, i.e., time is not decreased (Line D4). Notice that the algorithm allows arbitrary

---

algorithm Add_SoftFailsafe($\mathcal{P}\langle S_p, \psi_p \rangle$:real-time program f :transitions, S: state predicate, Σ_{bt}: specification)
{

$\quad R(\mathcal{P})\langle S_p^r, \psi_p^r \rangle, S^r, f^r, \Sigma_{bt}^r := \text{ConstructRegionGraph}(\mathcal{P}\langle S_p, \psi_p \rangle, S, f, \Sigma_{bt});$ (C1)

$\quad \psi_p^{\prime r}, S^{\prime r} := \text{Add\_UntimedFailsafe}(R(\mathcal{P})\langle S_p^r, \psi_p^r \rangle, f^r, S^r, \Sigma_{bt}^r);$ (C2)

$\quad \mathcal{P}'\langle S_p, \psi_p' \rangle, S' := \text{ConstructRealTimeProgram}(R(\mathcal{P})\langle S_p^r, \psi_p^{\prime r} \rangle, S^{\prime r});$ (C3)

$\quad$ **return** $\mathcal{P}'\langle S_p, \psi_p' \rangle, S';$ (C4)

}

algorithm Add_HardFailsafe($\mathcal{P}\langle S_p, \psi_p \rangle$:real-time program f :transitions,
$\qquad\qquad\qquad\qquad S, P, Q$: state predicate, Σ_{bt}: specification, n, δ: **integer**)
{

step 1: $\quad \mathcal{P}\langle S_p, \psi_p \rangle, S := \text{Add\_SoftFailsafe}(R(\mathcal{P})\langle S_p^r, \psi_p^r \rangle, f^r, S^r, \Sigma_{bt}^r);$ (D1)

$\qquad\qquad R(\mathcal{P})\langle S_p^r, \psi_p^r \rangle, S^r, P^r, Q^r, f^r, \Sigma_{bt}^r :=$

$\qquad\qquad\qquad \text{ConstructRegionGraph}(\mathcal{P}\langle S_p, \psi_p \rangle, S, P, Q, f, \Sigma_{bt});$ (D2)

$\qquad$ **repeat**

$\qquad\qquad IsQRemoved := false;$ (D3)

step 2: $\quad \psi_p^r := \psi_p^r \cup \{((s_0, \rho_0), (s_1, \rho_1)) \mid (s_0, \rho_0) \notin S^r \land$

$\qquad\qquad \exists \rho_2 \mid \rho_2 \text{ is a time-successor of } \rho_0 : (\exists \lambda \subseteq X : \rho_1 = \rho_2[\lambda - \{t\} := 0])\} - mt;$ (D4)

$\qquad\qquad \psi_p^r, ns := \text{Add\_BoundedRecovery}(R(\mathcal{P})\langle S_p^r, \psi_p^r \rangle, f^r, P^r, Q^r, n, \delta);$ (D5)

$\qquad\qquad rs := \{r_0 \mid \exists r_1, r_2, \dots r_n :$

$\qquad\qquad\qquad (\forall j : 0 \le j < n : (r_j, r_{j+1}) \in f^r) \land r_n \in (ns \cap P^r)\};$ (D6)

$\qquad\qquad rt := \{(r_0, r_1) \mid (r_0, r_1) \in \psi_{p_1}^r \land r_1 \in rs)\};$ (D7)

step 3: $\quad S^{\prime r} := \text{RemoveDeadlocks}(S^r - (ns \cup rs), \psi_p^r - rt);$ (D8)

$\qquad$ **if** $(S^{\prime r} = \{\})$ **then**

$\qquad\qquad$ declare no hard-failsafe f-tolerant program $\mathcal{P}'$ exists; **exit**; (D9)

step 4: $\quad$ **if** $(Q^r \cap (S^r - S^{\prime r}) \ne \{\})$ **then**

$\qquad\qquad IsQRemoved := true;$ (D11)

$\qquad\qquad S^r := S^{\prime r};$ (D12)

$\qquad\qquad \psi_p^r := \psi_p^r - \{(r, r_0), (r_0, r) \mid r_0 \in Q^r \cap (S^r - S^{\prime r})\};$ (D13)

$\qquad\qquad Q^r := Q^r \cap (S^r - S^{\prime r});$ (D14)

$\qquad$ **until** $(IsQRemoved = false);$

step 5: $\quad \psi_p^{\prime r} := \text{EnsureClosure}(\psi_p^r, S^{\prime r});$ (D15)

$\qquad\qquad \mathcal{P}'\langle S_p, \psi_p' \rangle, S' := \text{ConstructRealTimeProgram}(R(\mathcal{P})\langle S_p^r, \psi_p^{\prime r} \rangle, S^{\prime r})$ (D16)

}

procedure Add_UntimedFailsafe($R(\mathcal{P})\langle S_p^r, \psi_p^r \rangle$: region graph, f^r : set of edges,
$\qquad\qquad\qquad S^r$: region predicate, Σ_{bt}^r : specification)
{

step1: $\quad ms := \{r_0 \mid \exists r_1, r_2, \dots r_n :$

$\qquad\qquad (\forall j \mid 0 \le j < n : (r_j, r_{j+1}) \in f^r) \land (r_{n-1}, r_n) \in \Sigma_{bt}^r\};$ (E1)

$\qquad\qquad mt := \{(r_0, r_1) \mid (r_1 \in ms) \lor ((r_0, r_1) \in \Sigma_{bt}^r)\};$ (E2)

step2: $\quad S^r := \text{RemoveDeadlocks}(S^r - ms, \psi_p^r - mt);$ (E3)

$\qquad$ **if** $(S^r = \{\})$ **then**

$\qquad\qquad$ declare no soft/hard-failsafe f-tolerant program $\mathcal{P}'$ exists; **exit**; (E4)

step3: $\quad \psi_p^r := \text{EnsureClosure}(\psi_p^r - mt, S^r);$ (E5)

$\qquad$ **return** ψ_p^r, S^r (E6)

}

procedure RemoveDeadlocks(S^r : region predicate, ψ_p^r : set of edges)
// Returns the largest subset of S^r from where all computations of $R(\mathcal{P})$ are infinite
{

$\qquad$ **while** $(\exists r_0 \mid r_0 \in S^r : (\forall r_1 \in S^r : (r_0, r_1) \notin \psi_p^r))$

$\qquad\qquad S^r := S^r - \{r_0\};$

$\qquad$ **return** S^r

}

Fig. 3. Adding Failsafe Fault-Tolerance

clock resets as long as safety is not violated (by excluding the edges in mt). Then, we
invoke the procedure Add_BoundedRecovery to ensure that $P \mapsto_{\le \delta} Q$ is maintained
in the presence of faults (Line D5). Then, we identify the set rs of regions and rt of
transitions from where Σ_{br} may be violated (lines D6-D7). We remove such regions
and edges along with the deadlock regions from S^r in the same fashion that we did for
adding soft-failsafe (Line D8). However, we need to consider a special case where a

region, say r_1, in Q^r becomes a deadlock region. In this case, it is possible that all the regions along the paths that start from a region, say r_0, in P^r and end in r_1 become deadlock regions. Hence, we need to find another path from r_0 to a region in Q^r other than r_1. Thus, in this case, we remove r_1 (and similar regions) from S^r and Q^r and start over (lines D10-D14). Finally, the algorithm ensures closure of the invariant (Line D15) and transforms the synthesized region graph $R(\mathcal{P}')$ back to a real-time program $\mathcal{P}'$ (Line D16).

Theorem 7.1. The algorithms Add_Nonmasking and Add_Soft/HardFalisafe are sound and complete. □

Theorem 7.2. The problem of adding nonmasking and soft/hard-failsafe fault-tolerance to a real-time program, where the synthesized program is required to satisfy at most one bounded response property in the presence of faults, is PSPACE-complete in the size of the input program. □

8 Conclusion

In this paper, we focused on the problem of automatic addition of fault-tolerance to real-time programs. We considered three levels of fault-tolerance, namely failsafe, non-masking, and masking. For failsafe and masking, we proposed two cases, soft and hard, based on satisfaction of timing constraints in the presence of faults. We first introduced a generic framework to formally define the notions of faults and fault-tolerance in the context of real-time programs. Then, we presented sound and complete algorithms for transforming fault-intolerant real-time programs into soft-failsafe and nonmasking fault-tolerant programs. We also proposed a sound and complete algorithm that synthesizes hard-failsafe fault-tolerant real-time programs, where the fault-tolerant program is required to satisfy at most one bounded response property in the presence of faults. The complexity of our algorithms are in polynomial time in the size region graphs. The results on synthesis of soft/hard-masking fault-tolerance are presented in a technical report [19].

References

1. M. Pandya and M. Malek. Minimum achievable utilization for fault-tolerant processing of periodic tasks. *IEEE Transactions on Computers*, 47(10):1102–1112, 1998.
2. D. Mossé, R. G. Melhem, and S. Ghosh. A nonpreemptive real-time scheduler with recovery from transient faults and its implementation. *IEEE Transactions on Software Engineering*, 29(8):752–767, 2003.
3. B. Bonakdarpour and S. S. Kulkarni. Automated incremental synthesis of timed automata. In *International Workshop on Formal Methods for Industrial Critical Systems (FMICS)*, 2006.
4. K. M. Chandy and J. Misra. *Parallel Program Design: A Foundation.* Addison-Wesley, 1988.
5. A. Ebnenasir, S. S. Kulkarni, and B. Bonakdarpour. Revising UNITY programs: Possibilities and limitations. In *9th International Conference on Principles of Distributed Systems (OPODIS)*, 2005.
6. S. S. Kulkarni and A. Arora. Automating the addition of fault-tolerance. In *Formal Techniques in Real-Time and Fault-Tolerant Systems (FTRTFT)*, pages 82–93, 2000.

7. S. S. Kulkarni, A. Arora, and A. Chippada. Polynomial time synthesis of Byzantine agreement. In *20th Symposium on Reliable Distributed Systems (SRDS)*, pages 130–140, 2001.
8. S. S. Kulkarni and A. Ebnenasir. Automated synthesis of multitolerance. In *International Conference on Dependable Systems and Networks (DSN)*, pages 209–219, 2004.
9. P. C. Attie, A. Arora, and E. A. Emerson. Synthesis of fault-tolerant concurrent programs. *ACM Transactions on Programming Languages and Systems*, 26(1):125–185, 2004.
10. E. Asarin, O. Maler, A. Pnueli, and J. Sifakis. Controller synthesis for timed automata. In *IFAC Symposium on System Structure and Control*, pages 469–474, 1998.
11. E. Asarin and O. Maler. As soon as possible: Time optimal control for timed automata. In *Hybrid Systems: Computation and Control (HSCC)*, pages 19–30, 1999.
12. D. D'Souza and P. Madhusudan. Timed control synthesis for external specifications. In *19th Annual Symposium on Theoretical Aspects of Computer Science (STACS)*, pages 571–582, 2002.
13. P. Bouyer, D. D'Souza, P. Madhusudan, and A. Petit. Timed control with partial observability. In *Computer Aided Verification (CAV)*, pages 180–192, 2003.
14. L. de Alfaro, M. Faella, T. A. Henzinger, R. Majumdar, and M. Stoelinga. The element of surprise in timed games. In *14th International Conference on Concurrency Theory (CONCUR)*, 2003.
15. M. Faella, S. LaTorre, and A. Murano. Dense real-time games. In *Logic in Computer Science (LICS)*, pages 167–176, 2002.
16. R. Alur, C. Courcoubetis, and D. Dill. Model-checking in dense real-time. *Information and Computation*, 104(1):2–34, 1993.
17. R. Alur and D. Dill. A theory of timed automata. *Theoretical Computer Science*, 126(2):183–235, 1994.
18. Y. Abdeddam. *Scheduling with Timed Automata*. PhD thesis, INPG, Grenoble, November 2002.
19. B. Bonakdarpour and S. S. Kulkarni. Automatic addition of fault-tolerance to real-time programs. Technical Report MSU-CSE-06-13, Department of Computer Science and Engineering, Michigan State University, 2006.
20. R. Alur and T. A. Henzinger. Real-time system = discrete system + clock variables. *International Journal on Software Tools for Technology Transfer*, 1(1-2):86–109, 1997.
21. T. A. Henzinger. Sooner is safer than later. *Information Processing Letters*, 43(3):135–141, 1992.
22. B. Alpern and F. B. Schneider. Defining liveness. *Information Processing Letters*, 21:181–185, 1985.
23. A. Arora and M. G. Gouda. Closure and convergence: A foundation of fault-tolerant computing. *IEEE Transactions on Software Engineering*, 19(11):1015–1027, 1993.
24. C. Courcoubetis and M. Yannakakis. Minimum and maximum delay problems in real-time systems. In *Computer-Aided Verificaion (CAV)*, pages 399–409, 1991.

Toward a Time-Optimal Odd Phase Clock Unison in Trees

Christian Boulinier, Franck Petit, and Vincent Villain

LaRIA, CNRS FRE 2733
Université de Picardie Jules Verne, France

Abstract. We address the self-stabilizing unison problem in tree networks. We propose two self-stabilizing unison protocols without any reset correcting system. The first one, called Protocol SU_Min, being scheduled by a synchronous daemon, is self-stabilizing to synchronous unison in at most D steps, where D is the diameter of the network. The second one, Protocol WU_Min, being scheduled by an asynchronous daemon, is self-stabilizing to asynchronous unison in at most D rounds. Moreover, both are optimal in space. The amount of required space is independent of any local or global information on the tree. Furthermore, they work on dynamic trees networks, in which the topology may change during the execution.

1 Introduction

We consider the problem of *phase synchronization* [1] in uniform distributed systems liable to transient faults. Phase synchronization consists in designing a synchronization mechanism devoted to a distributed protocol made of a sequence of phases $0, 1, \ldots$ such that no process starts to execute its phase $i+1$ before all processes have completed their phase i. In a distributed environment, each process maintains its own copy of the phase clock. Therefore, the problem consists in the design of a protocol insuring that all the phase clocks are in phase. The phrase "in phase" has a natural meaning in *synchronous* systems.

In asynchronous systems, there is no global signal. So, one can at most ensure that no process starts to execute its phase $i+1$ before all processes have completed their phase i. But this kind of synchronization needs $O(D)$ rounds between two phases. So, in general, the synchronization requirement is relaxed as follows: the clocks are in phase if the value of two neighboring processes does not differ by no more than 1, and the clock value of each process is incremented by 1 infinitely often. The *asynchronous unison* [2] deals with this criteria.

Unison can be used as an underlayer mechanism to solve many local synchronization problems like, Local Mutual Exclusion, Local Reader-Writers, Local Group Mutual Exclusion, or Local Resource Allocation [3,4]. Recently, unison was also used in the design of a Publish/Subscribe protocol in peer-to-peer networks [5].

Self-stabilization [6,7] is the most general technique to design a system that tolerates arbitrary transient faults, i.e., faults that may corrupt the state of

A.K. Datta and M. Gradinariu (Eds.): SSS 2006, LNCS 4280, pp. 137–151, 2006.
© Springer-Verlag Berlin Heidelberg 2006

processes or links. Regardless of the initial state of the system, the self-stabilizing unison consists to settle all clocks in phase—the clocks are in phase after a finite number of steps—, and to keep all clocks in phase thereafter—the clocks are infinitely often incremented in phase.

1.1   Related Works

Numerous works in the area of self-stabilization deals with the phase synchronization problem. In this paper, we focus on deterministic solutions for uniform systems only. Moreover, we limit our discussion to trees. In the rest of this section, K is the size of the clock, S is the number of states the processes are required to have, D is the diameter of the network, n the number of processes, and Δ is the maximum degree of a process.

Self-stabilizing Synchronous Unison in trees. The first self-stabilizing synchronous unison is given in [8]. It works on a general graph but it requires unbounded clocks. The first protocol with a bounded memory space is proposed in [9]. It needs $K \geq 2\Delta D$, and stabilizes in $3\Delta D$ steps. As it is noticed in [10], the Δ factor is due to the model: it is assumed that a process cannot read more than the state of one neighbor at a time. From now on, all the protocols we discuss will be assumed to work on a model where every process can read the state of all its neighbors at a time. In this model, the solution in [9] needs $K \geq 2D$ ($S = K$) and stabilizes in at most $3D$ steps only. [11] gives a new solution which needs $K \geq 2$ ($S \geq n + K$) and stabilizes in at most $2D$ steps only.

A solution for tree networks is proposed in [10]. It requires $K = 3^m$ ($m > 0$), $S = K$, and stabilizes in $(D(K - 1))/2$ steps. Note that the stabilization time is equal to D only for $m = 1$ ($K = 3$), but is greater than $2D$ when $m \geq 2$. Thus, in the case $3^m \geq 2D$, the solution in [9] is better. In terms of stabilization time, the best solution in trees is proposed in [12]. It stabilizes in at most D steps only. Moreover, this protocol is *"universal"*, meaning that K can take any value greater than or equal to 2. But, the state requirement depends on Δ only: $S = (\Delta + 1)K$. In [11], we provide a universal self-stabilizing synchronous unison for trees which is optimal in memory space. It works with any $K \geq 3$, $S = K$, and stabilizes within $2D$ steps. We can also remark that for $K = 3$, the stabilization time is equal to D only, i.e., that reaches the performance of [10].

Self-stabilizing Asynchronous Unison in trees. The self-stabilizing asynchronous unison was introduced in [2]. Two deterministic protocols are proposed. The former works assuming unbounded clock, the latter needs $K \geq n^2$ (according to our model) ($S = K$). The second and last solution is proposed in [3]. The authors show that in trees K must be greater than 2, and S, the amount of space, must be greater than K. The stabilization time is upper bounded by $2D$ rounds. D rounds in the case $K = 3$. In the same paper, they present an algorithm reaching these bounds. This protocol is optimal in terms of state requirement.

1.2   Contribution

In this paper the contribution is twofold. We give a new self-stabilizing synchronous unison (resp. asynchronous unison) in trees which is optimal in space and better than, or as good than all known algorithms in terms of self-stabilization time.

More precisely. Let K be an odd integer, greater than 1, and let M be such that $(K = 2M + 1)$. Let $\chi = \{0, ..., K - 1\}$ and Let $b \in \chi$. We are able to define a total order $\leq_b$ on χ defined by the ordered sequence $\overline{b - M} \leq_b ... \leq_b b \leq_b ... \leq_b \overline{b + M}$. Where $\overline{U}$ is the unique element $a \in \chi$ such that $a \equiv U$ to modulus K. Consequently, from $\leq_b$ we are able to define a minimum notion denoted by min_b.

Let $\mathcal{N}_p$ be the set of neighbors of a process p and $\mathcal{CN}_p = \mathcal{N}_p \cup \{p\}$ is the closed neighbor set of p . We define on a tree of processes, each process p labeled by $p.r \in \chi$, the distributed algorithm defined on each process p by

$$cond \longrightarrow p.r := \overline{min_{p.r}\{q.r, q \in \mathcal{CN}_p\} + 1}$$

We claim that:

1. If $cond \equiv \mathbf{true}$ then the protocol, being scheduled by a synchronous daemon, is self-stabilizing to synchronous unison in at most D steps.
2. If $cond \equiv p.r \neq \overline{min_{p.r}\{q.r, q \in \mathcal{CN}_p\} + 1} \land (\forall q \in N_p, q.r \leq_{p.r} p.r + 1)$ then the protocol, being scheduled by an asynchronous daemon, is self-stabilizing to asynchronous unison in at most D rounds.

Example 1. Consider the graph G in Figure 1, with $K = 7$. For Process p_1 the total order defined by its register $r = 6$ is $3 <_6 4 <_6 5 <_6 6 <_6 0 <_6 1 <_6 2$, and for the process p_2 the total order is $6 <_2 0 <_2 1 <_2 2 <_2 3 <_2 4 <_2 5$. It is easy to calculate the minimum in each case: $min_{p_1.r}\{q.r, q \in \mathcal{CN}_{p_1}\} = min_6 \{5, 2, 6\} = 5$ and $min_{p_2.r}\{q.r, \mathcal{CN}_{p_2}\} = min_2 \{1, 4, 0, 5, 6, 2, \} = 6$. It follows that $\overline{min_{p_1.r}\{q.r, q \in \mathcal{CN}_{p_1}\} + 1} = 6$ and $\overline{min_{p_2.r}\{q.r, q \in \mathcal{CN}_{p_2}\} + 1} = 0$. We can see an execution of the protocol in the synchronous case in Figure 2.

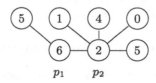

$$p_1 \qquad p_2$$

Fig. 1. A configuration with register values, for K=7

This algorithms are without reset correcting system. The definition of this protocols is quasi-trivial. But the correction proofs are not. Moreover, both are optimal in space. The amount of required space is independent of any local or global information on the tree. Furthermore, they work in dynamic tree networks, in which the topology may change during the execution. In this family of protocols in trees, only the case $K = 3$ was studied [11]. This case is trivial, any configuration is correct for asynchronous unison. In the synchronous case, the convergence is a consequence of Theorem "$WU \triangleright SU$" in [11] under a synchronous Daemon. We can say that this paper is a generalization of this case to any odd phase clocks. The difficulty (and the originality) is that this algorithms are without reset, and so the proof methods of [11] cannot be used directly. An improvement of the methods is necessary. The success of this improvement shows the robustness and the generality of the methods developed in [11,3].

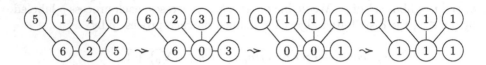

Fig. 2. A synchronous protocol execution on the example

1.3 Paper Outline

In Section 2, we first present the algebraic framework needed in the paper. In the same section, we describe the distributed system and the model. We also state what it means for a protocol to be self-stabilizing, we present the unison problem, and we generalize the framework developed in [3] and [11]. An Unison Protocol working in a synchronous environment in presented in Section 3, followed by the Asynchronous Unison Protocol—Section 4. Finally, we make concluding remarks in Section 5.

2   Preliminaries

In this section, we define congruence and local comparison relationship. Then we introduce the distributed systems considered in this paper. We state what it means for a protocol to be self-stabilizing.

2.1   Congruence to Modulus K, Local Comparison Relationship

Let $\mathbb{Z}$ be the set of integers. Let M be a strictly positive integer and let $K = 2M + 1$. We say that a and b are congruent to modulus K, denoted by $a \equiv b\,[K]$, if and only if there exists λ in $\mathbb{Z}$ such that $b = a + \lambda K$. We denote $\bar{a}$ the only element of $[0, K[$ such that $a \equiv \bar{a}\,[K]$. We define $d_K(a, b) = \min\left(\overline{a - b}, \overline{b - a}\right)$, it is a distance on $[0, K[$. In the following $\chi = \{0, ..., K - 1\}$.

A local order on a set χ is an antisymmetric and reflexive binary relation on χ. For every integers a and b, we have $d_K(x, y) \leq M$. Let us define the local order relation $\leq_l$ as follows: $a \leq_l b \overset{\text{def}}{\Leftrightarrow} 0 \leq \overline{b-a} \leq M$. Note that this relation is not transitive, nor a total order on χ. We define a local minimum as follows: Let $a_1, a_2...a_n$ be a sequence of elements of χ, and let $b \in \chi$. Every element a_i is locally comparable to b. This remark suggests the following definition:

Definition 1. *If a_i and a_j are two integers in χ, then we say that $a_i \leq_b a_j$ if and only if one of the three following propositions is satisfied: (1) $a_i \leq_l b$ and $b \leq_l a_j$, (2) $a_i \leq_l b$ and $a_j \leq_l b$ and $a_i \leq_l a_j$, or (3) $b \leq_l a_i$ and $b \leq_l a_j$ and $a_i \leq_l a_j$.*

Proposition 1. *Let a and b be two items in χ, then the binary relation induced by $\leq_b$ is a total order on χ and we have $a \leq_a b \Longleftrightarrow a \leq_b b \Longleftrightarrow a \leq_l b$. Denote by $\min_b$ the min operator defined by the total order $\leq_b$ on χ.*

Definition 2. *We define $b \ominus a$ by: if $a \leq_l b$ then $b \ominus a \overset{\text{def}}{=} \overline{b-a}$ else $b \ominus a \overset{\text{def}}{=} -\overline{a-b}$.*

Clearly, $b \ominus a \equiv b-a \; [K]$. Let $a_0, a_1, a_2, ...a_\alpha$ be a sequence of integers. The *local variation* of this series is the sum $S = \sum\limits_{i=0}^{\alpha-1} (a_{i+1} \ominus a_i)$.

Obviously, $S \equiv a_\alpha - a_0 \; [K]$.

2.2   Self-stabilizing Distributed System and Unison

Distributed System. A *distributed system* is an undirected connected graph, $G = (V, E)$, where V is a set of nodes—$|V| = n$, $n \geq 2$—and E is the set of edges. Nodes represent *processes*, and edges represent *bidirectional communication links*. A communication link (p, q) exists iff p and q are neighbors. The set of neighbors of every process p is denoted as $\mathcal{N}_p$. The *degree* of p is the number of neighbors of p, i.e., equal to $|\mathcal{N}_p|$. The program of a process consists of a set of registers (also referred to as variables) and a finite set of guarded actions of the following form: $< label >:: < guard > \longrightarrow < statement >$. Each process can only write to its own registers, and read its own registers and registers owned by the neighboring processes. The guard of an action in the program of p is a boolean expression involving the registers of p and its neighbors. The statement of an action of p updates one or more registers of p. An action can be executed only if its guard evaluates to true. The actions are atomically executed, meaning, the evaluation of a guard and the execution of the corresponding statement of an action, if executed, are done in one atomic step. We assume that each transition from a configuration to another is driven by a *distributed scheduler* called *daemon*. In this paper, we consider two types of distributed daemons:

- The *synchronous daemon* (D_s) chooses all enabled processes to execute an action in each computation step;
- The *asynchronous daemon* (D_a) chooses any nonempty set of enabled processes to execute an action in each computation step (*unfair Daemon*).

The space of states of the network is denoted by Γ. Structured by possible transitions by a given distributed algorithm and a given Daemon, we obtain an oriented graph $S = (\Gamma, \rightarrow)$ called transition graph. To study dynamic of a distributed algorithm scheduled by a given daemon, is to give topological properties of its transition graph.

A sequence $e = \gamma_0, \gamma_1, \ldots, \gamma_i, \gamma_{i+1}, \ldots$ is called an *execution* of $\mathcal{P}$ iff $\forall i \geq 0, \gamma_i \rightarrow \gamma_{i+1}$ holds. A process p is said to be *enabled* in a configuration γ ($\gamma \in \Gamma$) if there exists an action A such that the guard of A is true for p in γ. When there is no ambiguity, we will omit γ. We consider that any enabled process p is *neutralized* in the computation step $\gamma_i \rightarrow \gamma_{i+1}$ if p is enabled in γ_i and not enabled in γ_{i+1}, but does not execute any action between these two configurations. (The neutralization of a process occurs when p is enabled in γ_i, but at least one neighbor of p changes its state during $\gamma_i \rightarrow \gamma_{i+1}$, and this change effectively made the guard of all actions of p false in γ_{i+1}.)

The distributed systems considered in this paper are assumed to be uniform. A distributed protocol is *uniform* if every process with the same degree executes the same program. In particular, we do not assume unique process identifier or some consistent orientation of links in the network such that any dynamic deterministic election of a master clock can be feasible.

In order to compute the time complexity, we use the definition of *round* [13]. This definition captures the execution rate of the slowest process. Given an execution e, the *first round* of e (let us call it e') is the minimal prefix of e containing the execution of one action of the protocol or the neutralization of every enabled process from the first configuration. Let e'' be the suffix of e, i.e., $e = e'e''$. Then *second round* of e is the first round of e'', and so on.

Self-Stabilization. Let $\mathcal{X}$ be a set. A *predicate* P is a function that has a Boolean value—true or false—for each element $x \in \mathcal{X}$. A predicate P is *closed* for a transition graph Γ iff every state of an execution e that starts in a state satisfying P also satisfies P. A predicate Q is an attractor of the predicate P, denoted by $P \rhd Q$, iff Q is closed for Γ and for every execution e of Γ, beginning by a state satisfying P, there exists a configuration of e for which Q is true. A transition graph Γ is *self-stabilizing* for a predicate P iff P is an attractor of the predicate true, i.e., true $\rhd P$.

Distributed Unison. We assume that each process p maintains a clock register $p.r \in \chi$. Let γ a system configuration, we define the two predicates:

$$SU(\gamma) \overset{\text{def}}{\equiv} \forall p \in V, \ \forall q \in \mathcal{N}_p : p.r = q.r \text{ in } \gamma.$$

$$WU(\gamma) \overset{\text{def}}{\equiv} \forall p \in V, \forall q \in \mathcal{N}_p : d_K(p.r, q.r) \leq 1 \text{ in } \gamma.$$

In the remainder, we will abuse notation, referring to the corresponding set of configurations simply by SU, or WU.

The *synchronous (distributed) unison* problem is specified as follows:

Unison (Safety): SU is closed;
No Lockout (Liveness): In SU, every process p increments its clock variable infinitely often.

With a synchronous daemon, the problem is trivially solved by:

$$true \longrightarrow p.r := \overline{(p.r+1)};$$

The *asynchronous* (*distributed*) *unison* problem is to design a uniform protocol so that the following properties are true in every execution:

Unison (Safety): WU is closed;
Synchronization: In WU, a process can increment its clock $p.r$ only if the value of $p.r$ is lower than or equal to the clock value of all its neighbors;
No Lockout (Liveness): In WU, every process p increments its clock $p.r$ infinitely often.

With a asynchronous daemon, the problem is trivially solved by :

$$\forall q \in \mathcal{N}_p : (q.r = p.r) \vee (q.r = \overline{p.r+1}) \longrightarrow p.r := \overline{(p.r+1)}; \qquad (1)$$

The only interesting question is to stabilize these protocols, i.e., to solve the above problems with the extra global specification: $\mathbf{true} \triangleright SU$ (resp. $\mathbf{true} \triangleright WU$).

2.3   Local Variation and Delay

We call *delay* on the path $c = p_0 p_1....p_k$, noted $\triangle_c$ the *local variation* of the series $p_0.r, p_1.r, ..., p_k.r$: $\triangle_c = \sum_{i=0}^{k-1} (p_{i+1}.r \ominus_l p_i.r)$, and $\triangle_c = 0$ if the length of the path is 0.

The delay is intrinsic if for every couple of vertices (p, q) and every paths μ and v from the vertex p to the vertex q there is the equality: $\triangle_\mu = \triangle_\nu$. Roughly, delay is intrinsic iff it is independent of the choice of the path between two vertices. In this paper, delay is always intrinsic because G is a tree. Let γ_t be a configuration, then $p^t.r$ denotes the value of the register $p.r$ at time t, and $\triangle_\mu^t$ denotes the local variation along the path μ at time t. Let $\gamma_t \rightarrow \gamma_{t+1}$ be a transition. Let μ a path $p_0...p_k$ then the following congruence holds:

$$\triangle_\mu^{t+1} \equiv \triangle_\mu^t + p_k^{t+1}.r \ominus p_k^t.r - p_0^{t+1}.r \ominus p_0^t.r[K]$$

Definition 3. *Distributed algorithm scheduled by the daemon D_i ($i_i n\{a, s\}$) is path-compatible if and only if for any state $\gamma_t \in \Gamma$ and any transition $\gamma_t \rightarrow \gamma_{t+1}$ scheduled by D_i and any path $\mu = p_0 p_1...p_k$ there is the equality $\triangle_\mu^{t+1} = \triangle_\mu^t + p_k^{t+1}.r \ominus p_k^t.r - p_0^{t+1}.r \ominus p_0^t.r$.*

Let γ be an element in Γ. Denote $\triangle_{pq}$ the value of delay on the path from p to q. We say that p "*precedes*" q in a configuration γ iff $\triangle_{pq} \leq 0$. Similarly, p and q are "γ-*synchronous*" if $\triangle_{pq} = 0$ in γ. Since the network is connected, the precedence relation is a preorder. According to precedence relation, minimal processes are γ-synchronous. The set of minimal processes is never empty because the network is finite. We denote by V_0 the set of minimal processes at each state.

3   Protocol for Synchronous Daemon

Let G be a tree network. $M \in \mathbb{N} - \{0\}$ and $K = 2M + 1$. The notion of min_p is defined in Proposition 1. We are able to define the operation $min_{p.r}\{q.r, q \in \mathcal{CN}_p\}$ for every $p \in V$.

Algorithm 1. SU_Min algorithm for process p

Action:

  $NA : True \longrightarrow p.r := \overline{min_{p.r}\{q.r, q \in \mathcal{CN}_p\} + 1};$

Under a synchronous daemon, the algorithm SU_Min has a nice property, it is *path-compatible*, this property assures the stability of the set of minimal processes V_0 . Thus, to prove the convergence to SU, it is sufficient to prove that V_0 is strictly increasing until $V_0 = V$. In the example, we can see this phenomenon on the Figure 3. We first prove the path-compatibility, afterwards we prove the convergence.

An immediate consequence of the definition of the protocol is the following lemma:

Lemma 1. *Let $\gamma_t \rightarrow \gamma_{t+1}$ a transition and p a process. There exists $\alpha \in \{0, ..., M\}$ such that $p^{t+1}.r = p^t.r - \alpha + 1$.*
  Let $q_1 \in \mathcal{CN}_p$ such that $q_1^t.r = min_{p.r}\{q^t.r, q \in \mathcal{CN}_p\}$. Then $\alpha = p^t.r \ominus q_1^t.r$ and $p^{t+1}.r \ominus p^t.r = -\alpha + 1$.

In the following, we consider the transition $\gamma_t \rightarrow \gamma_{t+1}$. To lighten the notations, we define $p.r = p^t.r$, $q.r = q^t.r$, $p.r' = p^{t+1}.r$, and $q.r' = q^{t+1}.r$. From Lemma 1 there exists α and β in $\{0, .., M\}$ such that $p.r' = \overline{p.r - \alpha + 1}$ and $q.r' = \overline{q.r - \beta + 1}$. Trivially $q.r' \ominus p.r' \equiv q.r \ominus p.r + \alpha - \beta \, [K]$. The crux of the proof is to show that under a synchronous daemon this congruence is an equality. We have to explore four cases.

Lemma 2. *Under a synchronous daemon, if $q.r \geq_l p.r$ and $q.r' \geq_l p.r'$ then the equality $q.r' \ominus p.r' = q.r \ominus p.r + \alpha - \beta$ holds.*

Proof.   From the hypothesis, $q.r \ominus p.r = \overline{q.r - p.r} \in \{0, ..., M\}$ and $q.r' \ominus p.r' = \overline{q.r' - p.r'} \in \{0, ..., M\}$. But, $q.r' \ominus p.r' = \overline{q.r - p.r - \beta + \alpha}$. It follows that $\overline{q.r - p.r - \beta + \alpha} \in \{0, ..., M\}$. Since $q.r \geq_l p.r$, we deduce that $q.r' \leq_l p.r + 1$. So, $\beta \in \{\overline{q.r - p.r}, ..., M\}$, it follows $\alpha - \beta \in \{-M, ..., M - \overline{q.r - p.r}\}$. So, $\overline{q.r - p.r} - \beta + \alpha \in \{-M + \overline{q.r - p.r}, ..., M\}$. Assume that $\overline{q.r - p.r} - \beta + \alpha \in \{-M + \overline{q.r - p.r}, ..., -1\}$. Then, $\overline{q.r - p.r} - \beta + \alpha \in \{M + 1 + \overline{q.r - p.r}, 2M\}$, which is impossible since $\overline{q.r - p.r} - \beta + \alpha \in \{0, ..., M\}$. Thus, $\overline{q.r - p.r} - \beta + \alpha \in \{0, ..., M\}$. We conclude that $q.r - p.r - \beta + \alpha = \overline{q.r - p.r} - \beta + \alpha$ and the lemma holds.   □

Lemma 3. *Under a synchronous daemon, if $q.r \geq_l p.r$ and $q.r' \leq_l p.r'$ then the equality $q.r' \ominus p.r' = q.r \ominus p.r + \alpha - \beta$ holds.*

Proof. From the hypothesis, $q.r \ominus p.r = \overline{q.r - p.r} \in \{0, ..., M\}$ and $q.r' \ominus p.r' = \overline{-p.r' - q.r'} = \overline{-p.r - q.r + \beta - \alpha} \in \{-M, ..., 0\}$. From $q.r \geq_l p.r$ we deduce $\beta \in \{\overline{q.r - p.r}, ..., M\}$ and $\beta - \alpha \in \{-M + \overline{q.r - p.r}, ..., M\}$. From $q.r' \leq_l p.r'$ we deduce $\beta - \alpha \geq \overline{q.r - p.r}$ and $\beta - \alpha \in \{\overline{q.r - p.r}, ..., M\}$. So, $\overline{p.r - q.r} + \beta - \alpha \in \{\overline{q.r - p.r} + \overline{p.r - q.r}, ..., M + \overline{p.r - q.r}\}$. If $p.r = q.r$ then the lemma holds, else $\overline{q.r - p.r} + \overline{p.r - q.r} = 2M + 1$ and $\overline{p.r - q.r} + \beta - \alpha \in \{2M + 1, ..., M + \overline{p.r - q.r}\}$. So $\overline{p.r - q.r} + \beta - \alpha = \overline{p.r - q.r} + \beta - \alpha - (2M + 1)$. From $\overline{q.r - p.r} + \overline{p.r - q.r} = 2M + 1$ we deduce $\overline{-p.r - q.r + \beta - \alpha} = \overline{q.r - p.r} - \beta + \alpha$. We conclude that $q.r' \ominus p.r' = q.r \ominus p.r - \beta + \alpha$. The lemma holds. □

Lemma 4. *In each case, under a synchronous daemon, $q.r' \ominus p.r' = q.r \ominus p.r + \alpha - \beta$.*

Proof. There are two cases. If $q.r \geq_l p.r$, then by Lemmas 2 and 3, the lemma is proved. Otherwise $(p.r \geq_l q.r)$, by exchanging the processes p and q, remark that $q.r \ominus p.r = -p.r \ominus q.r$. So, this case is identical to the first case. □

An important corollary is the following proposition:

Proposition 2 (Path-compatibility). *Scheduled by a synchronous daemon, the SU_Min algorithm is path − compatible.*

Proof. We prove the proposition by induction on the length of the path μ. If length(μ) $= 0$ the proposition holds. Assume that the proposition is true for the path $\mu = p_0 p_1 ... p_k$, let $\mu_1 = \mu p_{k+1}$ be a new path then: $\Delta^t_{\mu p_{k+1}} = \Delta^t_\mu + p^t_{k+1}.r \ominus p^t_k.r$ and $\Delta^{t+1}_{\mu p_{k+1}} = \Delta^{t+1}_\mu + p^{t+1}_{k+1}.r \ominus p^{t+1}_k.r$. Let α be such that $p^{t+1}_k.r \ominus p^t_k.r = 1 - \alpha$. Let β be such that $p^{t+1}_{k+1}.r \ominus p^t_{k+1}.r = 1 - \beta$.

Induction hypothesis: $\Delta^{t+1}_\mu = \Delta^t_\mu + p^{t+1}_k.r \ominus p^t_k.r - p^{t+1}_0.r \ominus p^t_0.r$. We have: $\Delta^{t+1}_{\mu p_{k+1}} = \Delta^{t+1}_\mu + p^{t+1}_{k+1}.r \ominus p^{t+1}_k.r$. By induction:

$$\Delta^{t+1}_{\mu p_{k+1}} = \Delta^t_\mu + p^{t+1}_k.r \ominus p^t_k.r - p^{t|1}_0.r \ominus p^t_0.r + p^{t+1}_{k+1}.r \ominus p^{t+1}_k.r$$

$$= (\Delta^t_\mu + p^t_{k+1}.r \ominus p^t_k.r) + p^{t+1}_{k+1}.r \ominus p^t_{k+1}.r - p^{t+1}_0.r \ominus p^t_0.r + R$$

$$= \Delta^t_{\mu^\wedge p_{k+1}} + p^{t+1}_{k+1}.r \ominus p^t_{k+1}.r - p^{t+1}_0.r \ominus p^t_0.r + R$$

with $R = -p^t_{k+1}.r \ominus p^t_k.r + (p^{t+1}_k.r \ominus p^t_k.r + p^{t+1}_{k+1}.r \ominus p^{t+1}_k.r - p^{t+1}_{k+1}.r \ominus p^t_{k+1}.r)$.

From Lemma 4, we have: $p^{t+1}_{k+1}.r \ominus p^{t+1}_k.r = p^t_{k+1}.r \ominus p^t_k.r + \alpha - \beta$. By definition of α and β, we have: $p^{t+1}_k.r \ominus p^t_k.r = 1 - \alpha$ and $p^{t+1}_{k+1}.r \ominus p^t_{k+1}.r = 1 - \beta$. We deduce: $R = -p^t_{k+1}.r \ominus p^t_k.r + 1 - \alpha + p^t_{k+1}.r \ominus p^t_k.r + \alpha - \beta - 1 + \beta = 0$. The proposition follows by induction. □

Proposition 3 (Stability of V_0). *For every transition $\gamma_t \rightarrow \gamma_{t+1}$ scheduled by the synchronous daemon: if $p \in V_0$ in γ_t, then $p \in V_0$ in γ_{t+1} and $p^{t+1}.r = p^t.r + 1$.*

Proof. With the same notations than above, let p be a minimal process in γ_t. From the minimality of p, we deduce $\Delta^t_{pq} \geq 0$ in γ_t for any process q in V. p is minimal in γ_t, thus for the transition to $t+1$, so $\alpha = 0$ and $p^{t+1}.r = \overline{p^t.r + 1}$. The equality $\Delta_{pq}^{t+1} = \Delta_{pq}^t - \beta$ holds from the $path - compatibility$ (Proposition 2).

If $\beta = 0$ then $\Delta_{pq}^{t+1} \geq 0$. If $\beta > 0$ then there exists $q_1 \in \mathcal{N}_q$ such that $q^t.r \ominus q_1^t.r = \beta$. So $\Delta_{pq_1}^t = \Delta_{pq}^t - \beta$, and the fact that p is minimal in γ_t, we deduce that $\Delta_{pq}^t \geq \beta$ and that $\Delta_{pq}^{t+1} \geq 0$. The proposition follows. □

The distance between two processes p and q, denoted by $d\,(p,q)$ is the length of the shortest path between p and q. Let $p \in V$, we define δ_p as $\max_{q \in V} d(p,q)$. Let k be a positive integer. Define $B(p,k)$ as the set of processes such that $d(p,q) \leq k$.

Theorem 1 (Self-stabilization). *For every execution starting from any $\gamma \in \Gamma$ and scheduled by the synchronous daemon, SU is an attractor for Γ. The time of convergence from Γ to SU is tightly upper bounded by D.*

Proof.   Consider an infinite execution $e = \gamma_{t_0}, \gamma_{t_1}, \ldots$. Let V_0^t be the set of minimal processes at time t. Let p be an element of $V_0^{t_0}$ with the lowest $\delta_p = w$.

We prove by induction that: $\forall i \in \mathbb{N}, B(p,i) \subseteq V_0^{t_0+i}$. This will prove that for $i = w$, then $V_0^{t_0+i} = V$. Hence, the time convergence is less than or equal to w, which is less than or equal to D.

If $i = 0$ then $p \subseteq V_0^{t_0}$. Assume that $i \geq 0$ and $B(p,i) \subseteq V_0^{t_0+i}$. Let $q \in B(p,i+1)$. Then, q is a neighbor of an element q' of $B(p,i)$. There are two cases:

1. $q \in V_0^{t_0+i}$. From Proposition 3 then $q \in V_0^{t_0+i+1}$.
2. $q \notin V_0^{t_0+i}$. Then, $q'.r = min_{q.r}\{s.r, s \in \mathcal{CN}_p\}$ and from Proposition 3 $q \in V_0^{t_0+i+1}$.

In both cases, $q \in V_0^{t_0+i+1}$. We deduce $B(p,i+1) \subseteq V_0^{t_0+i+1}$. And by induction $\forall i \in \mathbb{N}, B(p,i) \subseteq V_0^{t_0+i}$. The first part of the theorem follows.

Let p be one extremity on a diameter of G ($\delta_p = \max_{q \in V} \delta_q$). Assume that $p.r = 0$ in γ_0. We define for each q such that $d(q,p) = \alpha$ ($\alpha \in \{1, ..., D\}$), $q.r = \overline{\alpha}$. Starting from such a configuration γ_0, SU is reached in at least D steps. We showed that D can be reached, and the second part of the theorem is proved. □

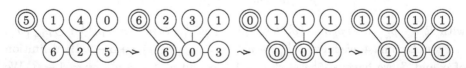

Fig. 3. Growth of the V_0 set in the example

4   Protocol for Asynchronous Daemon

The algorithm defined in the previous part is not self-stabilizing for an asynchronous daemon. It is not *path-compatible* for the distributed asynchronous daemon. A counter-example is given by the asynchronous transition $\gamma_t \to \gamma_{t+1}$ shown in Figure 4.

Let $\mu = p_0p_1p_2$. p_0 and p_2 are invariant. But $\Delta^t_\mu = 2M$ and $\Delta^{t+1}_\mu = -1$. There are not equal but only congruent to modulus $K = 2M + 1$.

Fig. 4. Counter-example for an asynchronous transition

4.1   The Protocol

As we have seen, the correction proof in the synchronous case cannot help us in the asynchronous case. In the synchronous case the predicate of the guard is *true*. First, to avoid starvation in our asynchronous model, we must add in the following predicate: $p.r \neq \overline{min_{p.r}\{q.r, q \in C\mathcal{N}_p\} + 1}$. But it is not sufficient. If we keep only this condition, there is possibility of livelock. So we must add a second condition which requires an order between the local adjustments. This condition is: $\forall q \in N_p, q.r \leq_{l_p} p.r + 1$.

We can remark that this predicate is true on WU. It is why our new predicate *Move* is the conjunction of both above conditions.

Algorithm 2. WU_Min algorithm for process p

Predicate:
   $Move \equiv (p.r \neq \overline{min_{p.r}\{q.r, q \in C\mathcal{N}_p\} + 1}) \wedge (\forall q \in N_p, q.r \leq_p p.r + 1)$
Action:
   $NA : Move \longrightarrow p.r := \overline{min_{p.r}\{q.r, q \in C\mathcal{N}_p\} + 1};$

Note that in WU, Predicate *Move* is equivalent to Predicate (1)—refer to Subsection 2.2. Also, when the predicate *Move* is satisfied in WU we have the equality: $\overline{min_{p.r}\{q.r, q \in C\mathcal{N}_p\} + 1} = \overline{p.r + 1}$.

We deduce that the safety property and the no lockout property are satisfied in WU. There is still to prove the convergence property: $\mathbf{true} \triangleright WU$.

4.2   Liveness and Self-stabilization

Because the protocol WU_Min is not path-compatible, we cannot use the delay notion. We must be perceptive. We will use Occam razor to eliminate incrementing actions and we will link the others actions by a causal relationship, the *adjustment DAG*. When an action is not an incrementing action, it is an *adjustment action*. Let us define a notion of *adjustment action*.

Definition 4. *Let $e = \gamma_0\gamma_1...\gamma_k....$ be a maximal execution of WU_Min. An adjustment is an ordered pair (p, t) where p is a process and $t = 0$, or $t > 0$ such that p executes action NA at time t with $\alpha \neq 0$. Namely, $p^t.r \ominus p^{t-1}.r \neq 1$ (Lemma 1). If $t > 0$, we say that p adjusts at time t.*

We now prove the liveness property. Then, we prove the convergence to WU.

Theorem 2 (Liveness). *In trees, WU_Min is without any deadlock.*

Proof. Let $\gamma \in \Gamma$, a configuration, we define from γ a binary relation on V by:

$$\forall (p,q) \in V^2, p \hookrightarrow_\gamma q \overset{\text{def}}{\Leftrightarrow} \begin{cases} q \in N_p \\ p.r <_p q.r - 1 \end{cases}$$

Remark that if $p \hookrightarrow_\gamma q$ then $p.r <_p q.r - 1$, and from Proposition 1 we have $p.r <_q q.r - 1$ and consequently $q \hookrightarrow_\gamma p$ is not true. There is no *stutter* for this relation which defines a directed graph on a tree, thus it is an acyclic directed graph on V.

Let $p_1 \hookrightarrow_\gamma p_2 \hookrightarrow_\gamma .... \hookrightarrow_\gamma p_k$ be a maximal path on this graph. If $k = 1$ then $\gamma \in WU$ and γ is not a deadlock configuration. If $k > 1$ then p_k is enable for an adjustment action. The proposition follows. □

We introduce now the notion of *adjustment DAG*. This structure contains all the information about the propagation of the adjustments on the tree. The task is to prove that during a maximal execution, this structure is finite.

Lemma 5. *If (p, t_1) is an adjustment with $t_1 > 0$, then there exists $q \in N_p$ and $t_0 < t_1$ such that: (1) $p^{t_1}.r \ominus q^{t_1-1}.r = 1$, (2) $\forall \tau \in [t_0, t_1[, q^{\tau+1}.r = q^\tau.r$ or $q^{\tau+1}.r = \overline{q^\tau.r + 1}$ i.e. there are only incrementing actions for q during $]t_0, t_1]$, and (3) $t_0 = 0$ or q adjusts at time t_0.*

Proof. Let (p, t_1) be an adjustment, with $t_1 > 0$. By definition, there exists a neighbor q of p such that $p^{t_1}.r \ominus q^{t_1-1}.r = 1$. We proved the first claim. Let t_0 the smallest date such that: $\forall \tau \in [t_0, t_1[, q^{\tau+1}.r = q^\tau.r$ or $q^{\tau+1}.r = \overline{q^\tau.r + 1}$. t_0 is defined. Then either $t_0 = 0$ or $t_0 > 0$. In this last case, because the minimality of t_0, q adjusts at time t_0 this proved the third property. □

Remark that, in Lemma 5, q is not necessarily unique.

Definition 5. *Let (p_0, t_0) and (p_1, t_1) two adjustments.*
We say that (p_0, t_0) adjusts (p_1, t_1), denoted by $(p_0, t_0) \rightsquigarrow (p_1, t_1)$ if and only if: (1) $t_0 < t_1$, (2) $\forall \tau \in [t_0, t_1[, p_0^{\tau+1}.r = p_0^\tau.r$ or $p_0^{\tau+1}.r = \overline{p_0^\tau.r + 1}$, i.e. only incrementing action for p_0 during $[t_0, t_1[$, and (3) $p_1^{t_1}.r \ominus p_0^{t_1-1}.r = 1$.

From this definition and Lemma 5, we obtain the following proposition:

Proposition 4. *For every adjustment (p_1, t_1) with $t_1 > 0$ there exists an adjustment (p_0, t_0) such that $(p_0, t_0) \rightsquigarrow (p_1, t_1)$.*

Since $(p_0, t_0) \rightsquigarrow (p_1, t_1)$ implies $t_0 < t_1$, the relation $\rightsquigarrow$ defines a Directed Acyclic Graph, called *adjustment DAG*. An adjustment (p_1, t_1) is not generate by an other one if and only if $t_1 = 0$.

To prove self-stabilization of *WU_Min* algorithm, it is sufficient to prove that the *adjustment DAG* is always finite. To reach this task, we must prove that there is no stutter on the *adjustment DAG*, that is to say that there is no path of the following form: $(p_0, t_0) \rightsquigarrow (p_1, t_1) \rightsquigarrow (p_0, t_2)$.

Proposition 5. *If $(p_0, t_0) \rightsquigarrow (p_1, t_1)$ then for every $t \in \,]t_0, t_1[$, neither p_0 nor p_1 do any action and at time t_1, only p_1 does an action, which is an adjustment. Namely:* (1) $\forall \tau \in [t_0, t_1[, p_0^{\tau+1}.r = p_0^{\tau}.r$ and $\forall \tau \in \,]t_0, t_1[, p_1^{\tau}.r = p_1^{\tau-1}.r$, (2) $p_1^{t_1} r \ominus p_0^{t_0}.r = 1$.

Proof. Assume that $(p_0, t_0) \rightsquigarrow (p_1, t_1)$. The question is: What happens during the period $[t_0, t_1]$? Let t_0' be the smallest time such that during the period $]t_0', t_1[$, there is no action for p_0 and p_1. We have: $t_0 \leq t_0'$. If $t_0 = t_0'$ the proposition is proved. We suppose now that $t_0 < t_0'$. By assumption, there is one action for p_0 or p_1 at time t_0'. In fact, there are only 2 possible actions for p_0 and p_1. Remark that, due to the added condition in the guard, if a process p increments at time $t_0 + 1$ then at time t_0 we have: $\forall q \in \mathcal{N}_p, q.r \in \{p.r, \overline{p.r + 1}\}$. We discuss from p_0 at time t_0':

1. p_0 does no action. So, p_1 does an action and there are two cases:
   (a) If p_1 increments at time t_0' then, because p_0 does not do any action, p_1 is correct with p_0 at this time and $p_1.r \in \{p_0.r, p_0.r + 1\}$. Because there is no action for p_1 and p_0 until the date t_1. p_1 cannot adjust from p_0 at time t_1. So this case is impossible.
   (b) If p_1 adjusts at time t_0' then at this time $p_1.r \leq_{p_1.r} \overline{p_0.r + 1}$ and so p_1 cannot adjust from p_0 at time t_1. So this case is impossible.
2. p_0 increments at time t_0'. There are three cases:
   (a) If p_1 does nothing, then at this time: $p_0.r \in \{p_1.r, p_1.r + 1\}$ Because there is no action for p_1 and p_0 until the date t_1, p_1 cannot adjust from p_0 at time t_1. So this case is impossible.
   (b) If p_1 does an incrementing action, then at time t_0' we have $p_1.r = p_0.r$ which is impossible.
   (c) If p_1 adjusts. First we note that, because p_0 increments at time t_0' then at time $t_0' - 1$: $p_0^{t_0'-1}.r \in \left\{ p_1^{t_0'-1}.r - 1, p_1^{t_0'-1}.r \right\}$ and at time t_0': $p_0^{t_0'}.r \in \left\{ p_1^{t_0'-1}.r, p_1^{t_0'-1}.r + 1 \right\}$. Secondly, since p_1 adjusts from p_0, then we have $p_1^{t_0'}.r \in \left\{ p_1^{t_0'-1}.r - M, ..., p_1^{t_0'-1}.r \right\}$. We deduce that at time $t_0' - 1$, we have $p_1.r \leq_l p_0.r$. Once again, because there is no action for p_1 and p_0 until the date t_1, p_1 cannot adjust from p_0 at time t_1. So this case is impossible.
3. p_0 adjusts is the only possibility. By definition of the adjustment relation, we obtain $t_0 = t_0'$.

Moreover at t_1, p_0 is locked by p_1, so p_0 does not do any action at time t_1. $\square$

An immediate consequence of Proposition 5 is the following lemma:

Lemma 6. *The adjustment DAG is without any stutter. If $(p_0, t_0) \rightsquigarrow (p_1, t_1)$ is an adjustment then $]t_0, t_1]$ is less than or equal to a round.*

Theorem 3 (Self-stabilization). *The adjustment DAG is finite, and the protocol WU_Min is self-stabilizing to WU. The Stabilization time is less than or equal to D Rounds.*

Table 1. Performances of Self-stabilizing Unison in Synchronous Trees

	Number of Clock Values (K)	Number of States per Process (S)	Stabilization Time (worst case)
Specific Algorithms			
[10]	$K = 3^m (m > 0)$	$S = K$	$\frac{D(K-1)}{2}$
[10]	$K = 3$	$S = K$	D
[12]	$K \geq 2$	$S = (\Delta + 1)K$	D
Algorithm SU_Min	$K = 2M + 1; M > 0$	$S = K$	D
General Algorithms			
[9]	$K \geq 2D$	$S = K$	$3D$
Algorithm SS [3]	$K > 3$	$S = K$	$2D$
Algorithm $SSAU$ [3]	$K = 3$	$S = 3$	D
Algorithm $SS\text{-}MinSU$ [11]	$K \geq 2$	$S = K + D$	$2D$

Table 2. Performances of Self-stabilizing Unison in Asynchronous Trees

	Number of Clock Values (K)	Number of States per Process (S)	Stabilization Time (Worst case in Round)
[2]	$K \geq n^2$	$S = K$	$O(nD)$
Algorithm $SSAU$ [3]	$K \geq 3$	$S \geq K$	$2 + 2D$
Algorithm WU_Min	$K = 2M + 1; M > 0$	$S = K$	D

Proof.   Let $(p_0, t_0) \rightsquigarrow (p_1, t_1) \ldots \rightsquigarrow (p_k, t_k) \ldots$ be a maximal path on the *adjustment DAG*. Then, by Proposition 4, $t_0 = 0$. From Lemma 6, there is no stutter. So, since G is a tree, the length of the path is at most D. So, the DAG is finite, and after D rounds (Lemma 6), there no adjustment and states are in WU.   □

5   Concluding Remarks

We discussed the self-stabilizing unison problem in trees. We proposed two protocols: Protocol SU_Min, being scheduled by a synchronous daemon, is self-stabilizing to synchronous unison in at most D steps. Protocol WU_Min, being scheduled by an asynchronous daemon, is self-stabilizing to asynchronous unison in at most D rounds. Moreover, both are optimal in space. Comparisons of the results of this paper are presented in Tables 1 and 2 for tree general synchronous networks, and tree generals asynchronous networks, respectively.

Remark that, following [11], the second algorithm converges to SU under a synchronous daemon, but we cannot assure the convergence in D steps, but only in $2D$ steps. It is possible to give a proof of the convergence of the first algorithm to SU by using a kind of proof like for the second algorithm. Unfortunately, this possible proof is not able to tighten the upper bound of the time convergence. Actually, with this approach we obtain only $2D$ steps as a bound, which is not enough tightened. It is why the mathematical analysis of each algorithm is different.

We believe that, due to the presence of cycles, this protocols cannot be generalized directly to the general graphs. This question remains open. Improving the time complexity of unison on the general graph should require to explore other ways. An important question arising from this study is the following: "Is the self-stabilization time optimal for both algorithms?"

References

1. Misra, J.: Phase synchronization. Information Processing Letters **38(2)** (1991) 101–105
2. Couvreur, J., Francez, N., Gouda, M.: Asynchronous unison. In: Proceedings of the 12th IEEE International Conference on Distributed Computing Systems (ICDCS'92). (1992) 486–493
3. Boulinier, C., Petit, F., Villain, V.: When graph theory helps self-stabilization. In: PODC '04: Proceedings of the twenty-third annual ACM symposium on Principles of distributed computing. (2004) 150–159
4. Cantarell, S., Datta, A., Petit, F.: Self-stabilizing atomicity refinement allowing neighborhood concurrency. In Springer-Verlag, ed.: DSN SSS'03 Workshop: 6th Symposium on Self-Stabilizing Systems (SSS '03). Volume 2704 of Lecture Notes in Computer Science. (2003) 102–112
5. Xu, Z., Srimani, P.: Self-stabilizing publish/subscribe protocol for P2P networks. In: Seventh International Workshop on Distributed Computing (IWDC 2005), LNCS 3741. (2005) 129–140
6. Dijkstra, E.: Self stabilizing systems in spite of distributed control. Communications of the Association of the Computing Machinery **17** (1974) 643–644
7. Dolev, S.: Self-Stabilization. The MIT Press (2000)
8. Gouda, M., Herman, T.: Stabilizing unison. Information Processing Letters **35** (1990) 171–175
9. Arora, A., Dolev, S., Gouda, M.: Maintaining digital clocks in step. Parallel Processing Letters **1** (1991) 11–18
10. Herman, T., Ghosh, S.: Stabilizing phase-clocks. Information Processing Letters **54** (1995) 259–265
11. Boulinier, C., Petit, F., Villain, V.: Synchronous vs. asynchronous unison. In: 7th Symposium on Self-Stabilizing Systems (SSS'05), LNCS 3764. (2005) 18–32
12. Nolot, F., Villain, V.: Universal self-stabilizing phase clock protocol with bounded memory. In: IPCCC '01, 20th IEEE International Performance, Computing, and Communications Conference. (2001) 228–235
13. Dolev, S., Israeli, A., Moran, S.: Uniform dynamic self-stabilizing leader election. IEEE Transactions on Parallel and Distributed Systems **8**(4) (1997) 424–440

Recovery Oriented Programming*
(Extended Abstract)

Olga Brukman and Shlomi Dolev

Department of Computer Science, Ben-Gurion University of the Negev,
Beer-Sheva, 84105, Israel
{brukman, dolev}@cs.bgu.ac.il

Abstract. Writing a perfectly correct code is a challenging and a nearly impossible task. In this work we suggest the *recovery oriented programming* paradigm in order to cope with eventual Byzantine programs. The program specification composer enforces the program specifications (both the safety and the liveness properties) in run time using predicates over input and output variables. The component programmer will use these variables in the program implementation. We suggest using the "sand-box" approach in which every instruction of the program that changes a specification variable, is executed first with temporary variables and that is in order to avoid execution of an instruction that violates the specifications. In addition, external monitoring is used for coping with transient faults and for ensuring convergence to a legal state. The implementation of these ideas includes the definition of new instructions in the programming language with the purpose of allowing addition of predicates and recovery actions. We suggest a design for a tool that extends the Java programming language. In addition to that, we provide a correctness proof scheme for proving that the code combined with the predicates and the recovery actions is self-stabilizing and, under the restartability assumption, eventually fulfills its specifications.

Keywords: self-stabilization, autonomic computing.

1 Introduction

Writing a perfectly correct code is a challenging and a nearly impossible task. Paradigms, tools and programming environments, including structured programming, object oriented programming, design patterns and others, were created to assist the programmer in writing a manageable and correct code. Tools that ensure testing during the programming phase complement the above effort [2,5,13]. Still, in many cases the program specifications are not fulfilled [19] – a situation that can cause a great deal of damage. In our previous work on self-stabilizing autonomic recoverer [4], we suggested a formal framework for the recovery oriented paradigm [20]. The suggested approach fitted existing (black box) software

---

* Partially supported by the Lynn and William Frankel Center for Computer Sciences, by Deutsche Telecom grant, by IBM faculty award, the Israeli Ministry of Science, and the Rita Altura Trust Chair in Computer Sciences.

A.K. Datta and M. Gradinariu (Eds.): SSS 2006, LNCS 4280, pp. 152–168, 2006.

packages, which resulted in high overhead, as each IO action had to be intercepted to detect a faulty state.

Fault tolerance paradigms and eventual Byzantine software. Self-stabilization [9] is a strong fault tolerance property for systems that ensures automatic recovery once faults stop occurring. A self-stabilizing system is able to start from any possible configuration in which processors, processes, communication links, communication buffers and any other process-related components are in an arbitrary state (e.g., arbitrary variable values, arbitrary program counter). The designer can only assume that the system's programs are executed. Based on that assumption, he or she proves that the system converges to a legal state, i.e., to a state in which the system satisfies its specifications. If the system is started from a legal initial state, the execution will ensure that the system remains in a legal state. This is called "closure property". In case the system is started in an illegal state (possibly after encountering transient faults), the execution of the self-stabilizing program will ensure that eventually (within a finite number of steps) a legal state will be reached. This is called "convergence property". Again, once the program reaches a legal state, it will continue running and will remain in a legal state until a (transient) fault reoccurs. A self-stabilizing algorithm never terminates. The algorithm does not necessarily need to "identify" the failure occurrence and to recover, but rather it continues to be executed and brings the system into a legal state. The time complexity of a self-stabilizing algorithm is the number of steps required for an algorithm started in an arbitrary state to converge to a legal state. Note that when all the processors execute incorrect programs (programs with bugs), they may exhibit any kind of behavior and, therefore, there is no guarantee for convergence.

The Byzantine fault model [16,10] is used for modeling arbitrary (in fact, malicious) behavior of a program that contains bugs and, therefore, does not obey the specifications. Systems that tolerate a bounded number of Byzantine processors (typically, less than one third of the processors can be Byzantine) were designed and proved to be correct.

Research on self-stabilizing systems and systems that model faults through Byzantine behavior has not yet provided solutions for systems in which software packages contain bugs with a very high probability. We observe that software packages usually function as required for a long period of time after being started from an initial state. The initial correct behavior can be attributed to the testing done by the software manufacturer. Therefore, programs started from an initial state run correctly for bounded length executions. System administrators and users occasionally restart such software in order to cope with failures.

Our contribution. Our goal is to incorporate the program predicates and the recovery actions provided by the program specification composer with the program code so that the predicates violation would be detected and avoided during run-time. Both predicates and recovery actions will be an integral part of the program specification. In this scope we are interested in a new programming paradigm that complements the case of black box software packages (addressed in [4]).

This approach alters the responsibility of the program specification composer (e.g., project manager). In addition to providing complete formal specifications, the composer has to state critical safety and liveness properties, and provide recovery actions for each property (there can be a few recovery actions for each property). The recovery actions will be executed if the predicate is violated. The programmer will make the best effort to write a program that satisfies these specifications. Still, the program may encounter some unpredicted states due to bugs or transient faults. Our framework automatically generates additional code for the program. This code will enforce the program satisfactory behavior (assuming the restartability property of programs [20]) by checking the predicates supplied by the program specification composer during runtime and by executing recovery actions, e.g., restart, in case of predicates failures.

Execution of an instruction that violates the specifications should be avoided. We suggest using the "sand-box": every instruction of the program that changes a specification variable will be first executed on temporary variables. In case the predicates are not violated with regard to the temporary variables, the instruction is executed. Otherwise, the execution of this instruction is stalled and a recovery action takes place.

A program may be in an illegal state (possibly, infinite loop), executing portions in which no predicate variable is updated. Therefore, the specifications may not be checked, possibly ever. In such cases external monitoring is required in order to cope with transient faults and to ensure convergence to a legal state. The external monitor will check the specifications periodically and enforce a state in which the specifications hold.

We suggest a design for a generic tool that extends an object oriented language, e.g., the Java programming language. The pre-compiler is designed to support new primitives for recovery oriented programming. Moreover, we provide a correctness proof scheme for proving that under the assumption of *rsf-execution* (Definition 1) the code combined with the predicates and the recovery actions fulfills its specifications.

Our framework is the first, to the best of our knowledge, to ensure the eventual validity of the specifications starting in any initial state. This is achieved by relying on self-stabilizing software platform, by using sandbox and by using external monitoring. We address full monitoring of liveness properties, while other works consider safety properties only.

While full specifications define in fact a program [22], we consider abstract task specifications, that leaves freedom to the programmer to choose the (efficient) way to write the program, including the specific data structures and algorithms. The abstract task specifications reflect the minimal desired functionality of the system.

The suggested framework is able to cope with transient faults. In addition, we assume that the software is either correct or *eventually Byzantine*. The software is called *eventually Byzantine* if, after being restarted, it can be trusted to perform correctly throughout the execution for a significant portion of the execution. The correct execution after restart is attributed to the testing and debugging process the software undergoes when being released. Our framework is not intended for dealing with totally incorrect (Byzantine) programs, such as empty programs (programs with no code).

The suggested approach is more efficient than the approach proposed in our previous work [4] as we now assume that we have access to the program. In our previous work we had to intercept all IO actions in order to detect a faulty state – a feature that implied a substantial overhead. In this work we consider the case in which the code is given and we are able to avoid this overhead by monitoring the variables, mainly when their values are changed.

Related work. There are tools that monitor safety by augmenting the programs with monitoring code for safety problems [13,7] and making some kind of recovery, e.g., throwing exception or executing predefined recovery action.

The well known and widely used exception mechanism [14] is a technique for handling illegal input or underlying system failures. In [23] transactions are used as a tool for achieving atomic actions and use exceptions as a recovery tool in case a transaction fails. However, practice shows that exceptions are not practical for programming an alternative flow of the program in case of a failure [12].

The *recovery block* concept [21] suggested to use component redundancy (e.g., N-programming) for dealing with failures in critical parts of the system. The recovery block concept does not support full monitoring of liveness properties and does not provide guarantees for stability of a monitoring mechanism.

There are several well known languages, Nurpl [8], ASM [15] and IO Automata [18], that provide a formal language for writing program specifications and framework for gradually and manually translating them into a fully verified program. Still, since the process is not fully automated, there is no guarantee that the resulting code is correct.

Writing a program as a collection of SRC (Software Cost Reduction) specifications (detailed specification describing in full the program automata) and then automatically transforming them into the code is suggested in [22]. However the produced program may have the same problems as the same program written from scratch by a programmer due to mistake in the detailed SRC specifications, which is, in fact, the program.

The work in [1,17] attempts to model a monitoring and correcting middleware layer for arbitrary faulty software. The correcting actions are arbitrary. Thus, the system original software can be completely ignored or its private state can be altered by the correcting layer. Therefore, the programmer of the component correcting actions is, in fact, the component programmer. In our work we limit ourselves only to non-intruding recovery actions, such as restarting.

The rest of the paper is organized as follows. The system architecture appears in the Section 2. The design and implementation details of our framework are presented in Section 3. Section 4 presents a study case that uses our framework.

In this study case we investigate the producer-consumer classical problem. Conclusions appear in Section 5.

2   The System Architecture

A *processor* is a multitasking entity that may execute several *processes*. Each *process* is modeled by a state machine that executes *atomic steps* of a *program* that might be faulty. An *atomic step* $a = \langle j, s, s', io \rangle$ of a *process* is a transition from state s to state s' by a process p_j. The transition consists of internal calculations and of a single interaction of p_j with other processes by an input/output operation (io). The communication capabilities of the processes are defined by a directed communication graph $G(V, E)$. An edge (i, j) in $G(V, E)$ denotes the ability of a process p_j to receive information from a process p_i by means of messages or shared memory. The *system configuration* consists of a vector $\langle s_1, s_2, \ldots, s_n \rangle$, where s_i is a state of a process p_i in the system, and of the contents of the communication devices. The contents of the communication devices are either the contents of the messages queues $\langle m_{1,2}, m_{1,3}, \ldots, m_{i,j}, \ldots \rangle$, where $m_{i,j}$ is a queue for messages sent by a process p_i to a process p_j, or the shared communication registers $\langle r_{1,2}, r_{1,3}, \ldots r_{i,j}, \ldots \rangle$, where $r_{i,j}$ is a register shared by processes p_i and p_j. An *execution* is a sequence $E = c_1, a_1, c_2, a_2, \ldots$ of configurations c_i and atomic steps a_i so that c_{i+1} is reached from c_i by the execution of a_i. An execution E is *fair* if every process executes a step infinitely often in E.

A *subsystem* is a set of dependent processes that may include one or more processes. Subsystems can be nested according to a *directed acyclic graph* (DAG) defined by the system designer. The composition of subsystems is required to ensure that both the state of each subsystem component and the combined state of the subsystem components are legal. The DAG hierarchy implies conclusive recovery scenario, where a cyclic dependencies graph may cause infinite recovery loop. Further discussions concerning processes and subsystems will be in terms of subsystems.

The *software/task specification function* is a function $sf(I)=IO$, where $I \in \mathcal{I}$ is a particular sequence of inputs in the set $\mathcal{I}$ of all possible (finite and infinite) sequences of inputs, and $IO \in \mathcal{IO}$ is a particular sequence $\langle i_1, o_1, i_2, o_2, \ldots \rangle$ of alternating inputs and outputs in the set $\mathcal{IO}$. The set $\mathcal{IO}$ defines the desired behavior of the software. A (sub)system sub_i *respects its specification function* sf_i in an execution E with input/output sequence IO if $IO \in \mathcal{IO}$.

A *legal state* of a process/subsystem is a state in which process/subsystem does not violate any safety properties and in which any fair execution that starts in this state does not violate any safety or liveness properties.

For the sake of a correctness proof we assume that a recovery action of a process/subsystem results in a process/subsystem that respects its specification function sf forever, i.e., after executing the recovery action the process/subsystem will be in a legal state. Once a process/subsystem reaches a legal state, the process will continue and stay in a legal state.

We suggested modeling the behavior of software as eventually Byzantine, and to use restarts as recovery actions that bring the system to a legal state.

Definition 1 (Rsf-execution). *An execution E is a recovery supporting fair execution (rsf-execution) iff E is a fair execution in which every subsystem sub_i that executes a recovery action during E, respects its specification function sf_i.*

We are now ready to state the system requirement.

Requirement 1. *Every rsf-execution E has a suffix in which the system respects its specification function sf.*

We will prove that any process or subsystem that starts from an arbitrary state will satisfy Requirement 1 in every sufficiently long execution. This proof technique is frequently used for proving self-stabilization [9].

3 Recovery Oriented Programming

Subsystems configuration file. A program specification composer provides a file with the subsystems dependencies graph. A process is the name of a thread or of an object (phantom process) instance. Each process forms a (minimal) subsystem. For each subsystem sub the following information is provided: the subsystem name and the list of all the subsystems names that constitute sub.

Recovery tuple. We suggest that the code contract between the specification composer and the programmer will be in the form of recovery tuples for subsystems. There might be more than one recovery tuple for a subsystem. Each recovery tuple is a list consisting of a *triggering event*, a *snapshot instruction*, a *predicate*, a list of *recovery actions*, and a *rule for trimming the history log*. The recovery tuples are used for augmenting the program with monitoring and recovery code. Next, we elaborate on each field of the recovery tuples.

• *Triggering event.* A triggering event is defined by the name of a specification (input/output) variable and a method used for modifying the variable value. The augmented code produced for this tuple is activated whenever there is a modification of the variable value using the method.

• *Snapshot instruction.* The snapshot instruction is a tuple $\langle sub_{tag}, \{var_1, \ldots var_k\}, \{var_{k+1}, \ldots, var_l\}\rangle$, where sub_{tag} is the name of the subsystem the recovery tuple is for, and var_i is a variable that its value should be recorded during the snapshot. The variables in the first clause ($\{var_1, \ldots var_k\}$) are recorded before the triggering event is executed. The variables from the second clause ($\{var_{k+1}, \ldots var_l\}$) are recorded immediately after the triggering event execution. After the snapshot is completed a new entry is added to the history log of the subsystem sub_{tag} and to the history log of each subsystem sub_j, such that $sub_{tag} \subset sub_j$. That is, $history_{tag}$ is an ordered list consisting of snapshots made for subsystem sub_{tag} and for all subsystems that sub_{tag} consists of. This is done to ensure that the recovery tuple predicate for some subsystem sub_i would use history log of sub_i only and would not need access to the history log of some sub_j, where $sub_j \subset sub_i$.

• *Predicate.* The predicate is a linear temporal logic (LTL) expression specifying the required program behavior using the input and output variables of the program. In addition, the linear temporal logic expression may have the history log as one of its variables.

For the sake of simplicity, we assume that a predicate that contains the LTL operator *eventually* is a *liveness predicate*. Otherwise, it is a *safety predicate*. The predicate can be either a process predicate or a subsystem predicate. A process predicate is a logical expression on process variables and the process history only. The subsystem predicate is a logical expression on variables from several different processes and on the subsystem history log entries. A recovery tuple with a safety predicate can be either for an event-driven check or for external monitoring. The recovery tuple with safety predicate for external monitoring will have an empty triggering event field.

The scope of the recovery tuple is the scope of the tuple snapshot instruction and of the predicate.

Recovery tuples are classified according to their predicate to be either a liveness recovery tuple or a safety recovery tuple.

• *Recovery actions.* The recovery actions field of a recovery tuple is a list of several procedure calls or actual code segments. Whenever the activated augmented monitoring code discovers that a predicate of a recovery tuple does not hold, some recovery action is invoked. Typical recovery action procedures use non-intrusive actions such as rolling back to a safe state, waiting, rescheduling or restarting.

The recovery actions of a recovery tuple are listed in the severity order. Each time the predicate of the recovery tuple does not hold, the next more severe recovery action from the list is invoked. The last recovery action in the list of recovery actions is always the restart of the whole subsystem and the initialization of the subsystem history.

The programmer must implement the *Restartable* interface for each process that might be restarted. The *Restartable* interface provides the structure for implementing several recovery action functions. A recovery action for a process is a call for one of its recovery action function.

• *History trimming rule.* A history trimming rule is a (simple) function on the history log of a subsystem sub_i, where the scope of the recovery tuple, for which the history trimming field belongs to, is sub_i as defined by the tag in the snapshot field.

Roughly speaking, history trimming is used for efficiency reasons and as a way for supporting a liveness indication. A *liveness event* (such as entrance to the critical section) associated with a recovery tuple is identified during run time when (1) the triggering event of the recovery tuple occurs and (2) the liveness predicate of the tuple holds. Whenever the liveness event occurs, the history log is trimmed according to the function defined in the history trimming field. Lack of liveness is detected when the subsystem is in the same state twice, executing steps in between, without making progress. This implies that the system can repeat this behavior forever.

Theoretically, since non-terminating computation can infinitely increase a variables, an unbounded history log might be required. In reality, the possible values of variables are bounded by the type of the variable. Therefore, the history log can be considered to be bounded. Moreover, a program specifications composer that would like to have an efficient liveness detection, may choose variables with very limited possible values. The bounded history log implies that if there is a failure of a liveness property it will be detected.

Next we will elaborate on the way recovery tuples are used in creation of the monitoring augmented code.

Monitoring of a subsystem. The augmented monitoring code has two main components: a code for event driven monitoring and a code for the external monitoring. The external monitoring of a subsystem is required for two reasons. The first reason is to ensure that the system would be able to recover from transient faults. That is, even if the subsystem does not reach a triggering event that activates augmented monitoring code (possibly due to its state corruption), the predicates will be checked, and the specifications will be enforced by invoking a recovery action. The second reason is the fact that the detection of livelock is sometimes impossible from within the subsystem.

Each subsystem has an external monitor process (thread). The existence of the external monitor threads and their scheduling is ensured by a self-stabilizing OS [11] and by the framework of the self-stabilizing autonomic recoverer [4]. The external monitor of the subsystem repeatedly checks the subsystem recovery tuples.

An external monitor will have an additional responsibility, namely, checking the syntax and the length bounds (that may be related to the number of possible states of the subsystem) of the history log entries.

Next we describe the augmented code for each type of the recovery tuple.

Liveness recovery tuple. Every liveness recovery tuple has a triggering event, a snapshot instruction, a predicate, and a history trimming rule. Event driven monitoring for liveness recovery tuples only trims the subsystem history log upon the predicate satisfaction.

The external monitor uses only the snapshots recorded in the history and the recovery actions. Namely, in case the value of the variables of this set appear twice in the history, while the subsystem has been scheduled to execute steps in between, the external monitor invokes a recovery action.

For each recovery tuple with a liveness predicate event the pre-compiler (Figure 1) inserts a code for checking the predicate each time the triggering event takes place.

Event driven safety recovery tuple. If a safety recovery tuple has a triggering event, then such an event driven safety recovery tuple yields augmented code for monitoring that uses temporary variables for checking the predicate before the actual modification. For each such recovery tuple the pre-compiler (Figure 1) inserts code for checking the predicate in a "sand-box" and only if the predicate is satisfied the actual assignment takes place. Otherwise, a recovery action is invoked.

Externally checked safety recovery tuple. A non event driven safety recovery tuple yields a code for the external monitor only. The generated code implies repeated snapshots, a predicate check and recovery action when needed.

Pre-compiler. The pseudocode for the pre-compiler is presented in Figure 1. The pre-compiler receives as an input the program file F and the file G with a definition of the subsystems hierarchy. The pre-compiler output is the transformed program file F' and files with code for external monitors, $em_1, em_2, \ldots, em_N$, where N is the number of subsystems in the system as stated in G. We denote the augmented code inserted by the pre-compiler during the program file transformation by $\{\}$ brackets.

In line 1 the pre-compiler analyzes G and forms data structures for subsystems according to the information stated in G. For each subsystem sub_i, the pre-compiler declares a new variable for the subsystem history log – $history_i$ (line 3). Then, the pre-compiler adds $history_i$ as an additional constructor parameter for each process in sub_i (lines 4-5).

Next, the pre-compiler iterates over each recovery tuple rt (line 6). If the recovery tuple has a non-empty event trigger field, the pre-compiler

```
Pre-Compiler
input: F, G
output: F', EM₁, EM₂, ..., EMₙ
1  analyze G and form subsystems sub₁, ..., subₙ
Transforming code of subᵢ processes
2  ∀subᵢ
3    { new historyᵢ }
(* Add new parameter, historyᵢ,
         to the constructor of each process in subᵢ *)
4    ∀pⱼ ⊆ subᵢ
5      { linkHistory(constructorⱼ, historyᵢ) }
6  ∀ rt = ⟨event = {var, method};
         ⟨tag, {var₁, ..., var_k}, {var_{k+1}, ..., var_l}⟩;
         pred;
         actions = {ra₁, ra₂, ..., ra_m};
         trimmingRule⟩
(* Event Driven Recovery Tuple *)
7    if rt.event ≠ ∅
8      { new global int rai_rt := 0 }
(* Safety Recovery Tuple *)
9    if evetually ⊄ rt.pred
10     replace rt.event in F with
11       { snapshot(var₁, ..., var_k)
12         temp=rt.event.var
13         if (!pred(rt.event.method(temp)))
14           ra_{rai_rt}
15           rai_rt = (rai_rt + 1)%m
16         else
17           snapshot(var_{k+1}, ..., var_l)
18           ∀sub_k : sub_{rt.tag} ⊆ sub_k
19             history_k = history_k∘
                   ⟨rt.tag, snapshot(var₁, ..., var_l)⟩
20           trimmingRule()
21           rt.event.method(rt.event.var) }
(* Liveness Recovery Tuple *)
22   else
23     replace rt.event in F with
24       { history_tag = history_tag∘
                 ⟨tag, snapshot(var₁, ..., var_l)⟩
25         if (rt.pred)
26           trimmingRule() }
Creating external monitors
27 ∀ subᵢ
28   create an instance of external
     monitor for the subsystem,
     EMᵢ(code in Figure 2)
```

Fig. 1. Pre-compiler pseudocode

declares a new global variable – recovery action index rai_{rt} (lines 7-8). If the recovery tuple predicate is a safety predicate, the pre-compiler replaces the triggering event execution according to the code in lines 11-21, i.e., by taking a snapshot of some variable before the event execution, by creating a variable *temp* and by assigning it with the current value of the variable from the triggering event and by checking if the predicate still holds with regards to the *temp* variable after the execution of the triggering event method on *temp* (lines 12-13). If the predicate does hold, the snapshot of the rest of the variables from the snapshot field is made (line 17). If the predicate does not hold, then the current recovery action is invoked and the recovery action index is updated (lines 14-15). The new entry is added to the history log of $sub_{rt.tag}$ and to all history logs of subsystems sub_k, that contain the $sub_{rt.tag}$ subsystem (line 19). Next, the trimming rule is executed (line 20). Finally, the triggering event is executed on the triggering event variable (line 21).

If the recovery tuple predicate is a liveness predicate, the pre-compiler adds code according to lines 24-26 after the execution of the triggering event. The augmented code checks the predicate; if the predicate holds, the history trimming rule is executed.

In lines 27-28, the pre-compiler creates a file called EM_i with code for the external monitor for each subsystem sub_i.

The pseudocode for the external monitor for a subsystem is presented in Figure 2. The parameter of the external monitor is the subsystem to monitor. The monitor declares a new variable rai_{rt} for each recovery tuple rt in the subsystem (lines 1-2). Next, the monitor repeatedly executes the loop in lines 3-17. For each recovery tuple in the subsystem, the monitor creates a snapshot according to the snapshot instruction field in the recovery tuple and adds

```
External monitor thread
input: subᵢ
(* Declaring recovery action index
      variable for each tuple *)
1  ∀ rt = ⟨event;
           ⟨tag, {var₁,..., varₖ}, {varₖ₊₁,..., varₗ}⟩;
           pred;
           actions = {ra₁, ra₂,..., raₘ};
           trimmingRule) : subₜₐg ⊆ subᵢ
2       new int raiᵣₜ := 0
(* Monitoring loop *)
3  do forever
4     ∀rt = ⟨event; ⟨tag, var₁, ..., varₗ⟩; pred;
           actions = {ra₁, ra₂, ..., raₘ};
           trimmingRule⟩ : subₜₐg ⊆ subᵢ
5        snap := snapshot(var₁,..., varₗ)⟩ ∈ subᵢ
6        ∀subₖ : subᵣₜ.ₜₐg ⊆ subₖ
7           historyₖ = historyₖ ∘ ⟨rt.tag, snap⟩
(* Safety Repeated Recovery Tuple *)
8        if eventually ∉ rt.pred & rt.event = ∅
9           if (!rt.pred)
10              raᵣₐᵢᵣₜ
11              raiᵣₜ := (raiᵣₜ + 1)%m
12           else
13              trimmingRule()
(* Liveness Recovery Tuple *)
14        if eventually ∈ rt.pred
15           if ∃j, k : j ≠ k:
                 historyₜₐg[j] − historyₗₐg[k]
                 & stepsₛᵤbₜₐg (j, k)
16              raᵣₐᵢᵣₜ
17              raiᵣₜ := (raiᵣₜ + 1)%m
```

Fig. 2. Pseudocode for an external monitor of a subsystem

the snapshot to the history log of the $sub_{rt.tag}$ subsystem and to all history logs of subsystems sub_k that contain $sub_{rt.tag}$ (lines 6-7).

Next, if the recovery tuple predicate is a safety predicate and if the recovery tuple is intended for external monitoring, i.e., the event field is empty (line 8), the monitor checks that the predicate is satisfied (line 9). If the predicate is unsatisfied, the current recovery action is executed and the recovery action index is updated (lines 10-11). If the predicate is satisfied, the history trimming rule from the recovery tuple is applied on the subsystem history log (line 13).

If the recovery tuple predicate is a liveness predicate, the monitor checks the subsystem history log for identical entries. In case there are identical entries and between these entries the subsystem processes were scheduled to make steps, then the subsystem is in a livelock. Thus, the recovery action is executed and the recovery action index is updated (lines 14-17).

The snapshot instruction for a subsystem is equivalent to making a distributed snapshot of (part of) the system. There are several algorithms, e.g., [6], for making a distributed snapshot. Another possible solution is to enable the external monitor to request the operating system scheduler to activate solely the monitor (while not activating the processes that are the snapshot subjects) for a number of steps that suffices for executing the snapshot.

Proof outline of an automatic recovery for a transformed program.
Next we prove that a system satisfies the requirements for automatic recovery with relation to the specifications after the program was transformed by the pre-compiler using the recovery tuples. The system is a collection of processes $p_1, \ldots, p_n$ with code in the file F. The processes form subsystems $sub_1, \ldots, sub_N$, where $sub_i = \{sub_{i_1}, sub_{i_2}, \ldots, sub_{i_k}\}$. In order to show that a system eventually satisfies Requirement 1, we need to demonstrate that the super-subsystem containing all other subsystems (there is such super-subsystem as we use a DAG hierarchy) respects Requirement 1. This implies that each subsystem respects Requirement 1 too. A subsystem respects its specification function if it respects the subsystem safety and the liveness requirements, i.e., if there is an execution suffix $E' = \{c_j, a_j, \ldots\}$, such that for each configuration c_k the subsystem safety predicates are satisfied and there are infinitely many configurations $c_k \in E'$ in which the liveness predicates are satisfied. Lemma 1 formalizes the claim that need to be proven for each subsystem.

Lemma 1. *Every rsf-execution has a suffix in which a subsystem sub_i eventually satisfies Requirement 1, i.e., the subsystem satisfies its safety and liveness requirements.*

Note that our framework uses event-driven approach for recording predefined state changes and for trimming the histories log for detecting liveness. The specification composer has to include event-driven snapshot instructions in order for the history log to have enough information for liveness detection. The alternative approach that does not use event driven history trimming is to use a flag variable for each recovery tuple with a liveness predicate. Initially, the flag would be set to *false*. Each time the liveness predicate variables are updated, the liveness predicate is checked. If the predicate holds, the flag is updated to be *true*. Each time an external monitor of a subsystem is scheduled, the monitor checks the flag. If the flag is *true*, the monitor executes the history trimming rule and resets the flag to *false*, so the liveness would be identified further on. If the flag is set to *false*, the history log has two or more identical entries, and the subsystem processes execute several steps, the monitor regards this situation as livelock and initiates recovery.

Lastly, we remark that the predicate verification that occurs while some predicate variables are being updated, may yield a false negative, since the predicate will be satisfied only after the updates completion. The programmer may use *record assignment* in order to overcome this technicality. The predicate variables are stored in a record data structure *rec*. We accomplish simultaneous update of several predicate variables by creating a copy of the record, *copy*. Then, we execute all the assignments on the *copy* variable. Finally, we assign record *rec* with the updated *copy* variable.

4 Producer-Consumer Example

In this section we describe in detail how the classical producer-consumer task is enhanced by our framework. The code produced by our framework is a recovery oriented code for the producer-consumer task. We present the original code with the recovery tuples. We provide the formal correctness proof for the claim that the system with the transformed program is able to recover from any initial state automatically.

The producer-consumer task consists of two threads and a shared queue object. The producer thread repeatedly produces an item and enqueues the item into the queue. The enqueue attempt can be unsuccessful if the queue is full. The consumer thread repeatedly dequeues an item from the queue (and consumes it). The dequeue attempt can be unsuccessful if the queue is empty. The liveness requirements for the producer and the consumer processes are stated in Requirement 2 and 3 respectively.

Requirement 2 (Producer Liveness). *Every rsf-execution has a suffix in which there are infinitely many enqueue events (either successful or unsuccessful).*

Requirement 3 (Consumer Liveness). *Every rsf-execution has a suffix in which there are infinitely many dequeue events (either successful or unsuccessful).*

The producer-consumer task liveness and safety requirements are stated in Requirements 4 and 5 respectively.

Requirement 4 (Liveness). *Every rsf-execution has a suffix in which there are infinitely many successful enqueue and successful dequeue events.*

Requirement 5 (Safety). *Every rsf-execution E has a suffix $E' = c_i, a_i, ...$ in which every item dequeued by the consumer thread has been in the queue, i.e.,*
$a_j = \{dequeue, item\} \Rightarrow \left[\exists k \; i \leq k \leq j : \forall l \; k \leq l < j \;\; item \in c_l(queue) \right]$
and items are dequeued in the same order they were enqueued:
$a_k = \{dequeue, item_1\}, a_l = \{dequeue, item_2\}, k < l \Rightarrow \left[\exists m, n : \; m < n < k < l \wedge \forall j \; m \leq j \leq k \;\; item_1 \in c_j(queue) \wedge \forall j \; n \leq j \leq l \;\; item_2 \in c_j(queue) \right]$

In this system there are two processes: the producer and the consumer threads. In addition, we have one "phantom" process: the queue object. The queue object is not a real process, but rather a collection of related variables. We choose treating the queue object as a process. These three processes form six subsystems. The first three subsystems are the processes themselves: the producer is sub_1, the consumer is sub_2 and the queue is sub_3. The producer thread (sub_1) and the queue object (sub_3) form subsystem sub_4. The consumer thread (sub_2) and the queue object (sub_3) form subsystem sub_5. The subsystem sub_4 and sub_5 form the subsystem sub_6. The subsystems configuration graph G for the system is presented in Figure 3. Each of these subsystems has an external monitor as presented in Figure 2.

Next we present the code for the task processes. The interface for the *Queue* object is presented in Figure 4. The *Queue* object implements the *Restartable* interface (i.e., implements the function *restart()*) in order to meet the requirements of our framework. The *Queue* is implemented as a limited size cyclic queue based on an array. The *Queue* is a non-blocking queue: the *dequeue* function returns *null* if the queue is empty and *enqueue* function returns *false* if the queue is full. The *Queue* object has a public variable N – the queue capacity.

```
sub1: producer
sub2: consumer
sub3: queue
sub4: sub1, sub3
sub5: sub2, sub3
sub6: sub4, sub5
```

Fig. 3. Subsystem configuration graph for the Producer-Consumer task

The producer thread is implemented by the *Producer* class (Figure 5). The *Producer* class implements the *Restartable* interface. Therefore, it implements the function *restart* (lines 7-10), in which the thread is suspended and then is started again.

```
Queue implements Restartable
1   int N;
2   Queue(n);
3   boolean enqueue(item);
4   item dequeue();
5   void restart(){this = new Queue(N);}
```

Fig. 4. Pseudocode for the queue object

We denote *initHistory* to be the function that receives a subsystem sub_i as a parameter and initializes the history logs of sub_i and of each sub_j, such that $sub_j \subseteq sub_i$.

Recovery tuple I is a liveness recovery tuple for the producer thread. The tuple predicate checks that eventually the producer makes some enqueue attempts. The event trigger variable is the queue object and the event trigger method is an invocation of the enqueue function of the queue object. Upon execution of the event the snapshot adds a new record with label "sub_1" to the history log of the producer thread. The first recovery action is to restart the producer thread (sub_1) and to initialize the producer process history. The second recovery action is to restart the whole system and to initialize all history logs. If the predicate holds, the history log of sub_1 is initialized.

The predicate of recovery tuple II is a safety predicate for sub_4 (the producer thread and the queue). As in recovery tuple I, the event trigger variable is the queue object and the event trigger method is an invocation of the enqueue function of the queue object. The snapshot records the values of the variable *success* and the hash code value of *item* immediately after the triggering event. The predicate checks whether the number of successful enqueue events in the history log of sub_4 (which equals to the number of currently enqueued items in the queue) is less than the queue capacity. If so, the executed enqueue event must have been successful. The first recovery action is to restart sub_4 and to initialize all sub_4 history logs. The second recovery action is to restart the whole system and to initialize all history logs. The history trimming rule is empty.

The items in the queue are normally large pieces of data. Having items recorded in the history log would be expensive. Thus, we record a certain key instead of an item, e.g., hash code of the item object.

The consumer thread is similar to the producer thread. The predicate of recovery tuple I is a liveness predicate for the consumer process that checks that eventually the consumer makes some dequeue attempts. The event trigger variable is the queue object and the event trigger method is an invocation of the dequeue function of the queue object. The first recovery action is to restart the consumer process (sub_2) and to initialize the history log of sub_2. The second recovery action is to restart the whole system and to initialize all history logs. If the predicate holds, the history log of sub_2 is initialized.

```
Producer implements Restartable
//Liveness for sub₁
I⟨queue.enqueue;
   ⟨"sub₁",{},{}⟩;
   eventually ⟨"sub₁";{};{}⟩ ∈ historyₛᵤᵦ₁;
   {{this.restart(); initHistory(sub₁); },
   {queue.restart(); this.restart();
      consumer.restart(); initHistory(sub₆);}};
   {initHistory(sub₁);}⟩
//Safety for sub₄
II⟨queue.enqueue;
   ⟨"sub₄",{},{success,item.hashCode()}⟩
   |⟨"sub₄";{};{true,¬null}⟩ ∈ historyₛᵤᵦ₄|
      < queue.N ⇒ success;
   {{this.restart(); queue.restart();
      initHistory(sub₄)};
   {queue.restart(), this.restart(),
      consumer.restart(); initHistory(sub₆);}};
   {}⟩
1  Producer(Queue queue, Consumer consumer);
2  void run() {
3     do forever
4        item = produce_item();
5        success=queue.enqueue(item);
6  }
7  void restart() {
8     this.suspend();
9     this.start();
10 }
```

Fig. 5. Pseudocode for the producer thread

The predicate of recovery tuple II is a safety predicate for sub_5 (the consumer thread and the queue). The event trigger variable is the queue object and the event trigger method is an invocation of the dequeue function of the queue object. The predicate checks whether the number of the history entries of sub_4 that reflect successful enqueue events is bigger than zero (i.e., the number of currently enqueued items in queue is bigger than zero). If so, the last dequeue event should have been successful. The first recovery action is to restart sub_5 and to initialize the history logs of sub_5. The second recovery action is to restart the whole system and to initialize all of the history logs. The history trimming rule is empty.

The predicate of recovery tuple III is the safety predicate for the whole system. The event trigger variable is the queue object and the event trigger method is an invocation of the dequeue function of the queue object. The predicate checks that each dequeued item has been previously enqueued and that the dequeued item is the first successfully enqueued item from the current queue. The recovery action is a restart of the whole system and an initialization of all history logs. The trimming rule is to remove the enqueue event entries of the successfully dequeued item from the history log of sub_6.

The correctness proof of the producer-consumer task is based on the guidelines provided in Lemma 1. The proofs for Lemmas 2, 3 and 4 appear in [3].

Lemma 2 (Liveness of Producer Thread). *In any rsf-execution E the producer thread executes a call for the queue.enqueue function infinitely often.*

Lemma 3 (Liveness of Consumer Thread). *In any rsf-execution E, the Consumer thread executes a call for the queue.dequeue function infinitely often.*

Lemma 4 (Producer-Consumer Task Correctness). *The Producer-Consumer task that uses the pseudocode presented in Figures 4, 5, and 6, eventually satisfies Requirements 4 and 5.*

The code produced by our framework for the producer-consumer task is self-stabilizing only if the uniqueness of the object hash codes is guaranteed. Otherwise, the produced code is pseudo self-stabilizing [9] with regards to the safety property as explained in [3].

5 Conclusions

In this work we have combined fault tolerance paradigms such as self-stabilization and (eventual) Byzantine faults with the restartability recovery paradigm into a single framework for writing recovery oriented programs.

We view the new

```
Consumer implements Restartable
//Liveness for sub₂
I⟨queue.dequeue;
    ⟨"sub₂"{}; {}⟩
    eventually  ⟨"sub₂"{}; {}⟩ ∈ history_{sub₂};
    {{this.restart(); initHistory(sub₂)},
    {queue.restart(); this.restart();
        consumer.restart(); initHistory(sub₆)}};
    {initHistory(sub₂)}⟩
//Safety for sub₅
II⟨queue.dequeue;
    ⟨⟩
    |⟨"sub₄"; {}; {true, item.hashCode}⟩ ∈ history_{sub₄}| > 0 ⇒
        item ≠ null;
    {{this.restart(); queue.restart(); initHistory(sub₅)},
    {queue.restart(); this.restart();
        consumer.restart(); initHistory(sub₆)}};
    {}⟩
Safety for sub₆
III⟨queue.dequeue;
    ⟨⟩
    item ≠ null ⇒
        ∃i : history_{sub₆}[i] = ⟨"sub₄", {}, {true, hashCode_{item}}⟩∧
        ∀j < i history_{sub₆}[j] = ⟨"sub₄", {}, {false, hashCode_{item}}⟩
    {{queue.restart(); this.restart(); consumer.restart();
        initHistory(sub₆)}}
    {history_{sub₆} = history_{sub₆} \ history_{sub₆}[1, ..., i]}⟩
1  Consumer(Queue queue, Producer producer);
2  void run(){
3    do forever
4      item = queue.dequeue();
5      consume_item(item);
6  }
7  void restart() {
8    this.suspend();
9    this.start();
10}
```

Fig. 6. Pseudocode for the consumer thread

framework as an important infrastructure that allows the specification composer to monitor the specifications on-line and to act upon violation of the safety and the liveness specifications. There is no doubt that such an approach is vitally important for gaining autonomous, robust and fault-tolerant systems.

Acknowledgment. We thank Marcelo Sihman for discussions during the first stage of this research.

References

1. A. Arora and M. Theimer. "On Modeling and Tolerating Incorrect Software". Microsoft Research Technical Report MSR-TR-2003-27, 2003.
2. K. Beck, C. Andres. " Extreme Programming Explained : Embrace Change". Second Edition, Addison-Wesley, 1999.
3. O. Brukman, S. Dolev. "Recovery Oriented Programming". Technical Report #06-06, Department of Computer Science, Ben-Gurion University, Israel, June 2006.
4. O. Brukman, S. Dolev, E. K. Kolodner. "Self-Stabilizing Autonomic Recoverer for Eventual Byzantine Software". *Proc. of the IEEE SWSTE*, pp. 20-29, 2003.
5. L. Burdy, Y. Cheon, D. Cok, M. Ernst, J. Kiniry, G. T. Leavens, K. R. M. Leino, E. Poll. "An overview of JML tools and applications". *International Journal on Software Tools for Technology Transfer*, vol. 7(3), pp. 212-232, June 2005.
6. K. M. Chandy, L. Lamport. "Distributed snapshots: Determining global states of distributed systems". *ACM TOCS*, vol. 3(1), pp. 63-75, February 1985.
7. F. Chen, G. Rosu. "Java-MOP: A Monitoring Oriented Programming Environment for Java". *Proc. of the TACAS* , pp. 546-550, Edinburgh, U.K., April 2005.
8. R. L. Constable, T. B. Knoblock, J. L. Bates . "Writing Programs that Construct Proofs ". *Journal of Automated Reasoning*, vol. 1(3), pp. 285-326, 1984.
9. S. Dolev. *Self-stabilization*. The MIT press, March 2000.
10. S. Dolev, J. L. Welch. "Self-Stabilizing Clock Synchronization in the Presence of Byzantine Faults". *Journal of the ACM*, vol. 51(5), pp. 780-799, September 2004.
11. S. Dolev, R. Yagel. "Toward Self-Stabilizing Operating Systems". *Proc. of the SAACS* , pp. 684-688, 2004.
12. *Thinking in Java*. Prentice Hall PTR, December 2002.
13. Eiffel. Eiffel Programming Language. http://www.eiffel.com.
14. D. P. Friedman, M. Wand, C. T. Haynes. "Essentials of Programming Languages". The MIT press, 2nd edition, 2001.
15. Y. Gurevich, B. Rossman, W. Schulte. "Semantic Essence of AsmL". Microsoft Research Technical Report MSR-TR-2004-27, March 2004.
16. L. Lamport, R. Shostak, and M. Pease. "The Byzantine Generals Problem". *ACM Trans. on Programming Languages and Systems*, vol. 4(3), pp. 382-401, 1982.
17. W. Leal, A. Arora. "Scalable self-stabilization via composition". *Proc. of the ICDCS*, Tokyo, Japan, March 2004.
18. N. Lynch *Distributed Algorithms*. Morgan Kaufmann Publishers, 1996.
19. P. G. Neumann. "Computer-Related Risks". Addison-Wesley/ACM Press, 1995.
20. D. Patterson, A. Brown, P. Broadwell, G. Candea, M. Chen, J. Cutler, P. Enriquez, A. Fox, E. Kiciman, M. Merzbacher, D. Oppenheimer, N. Sastry, W. Tetzlaff, J. Traupman, and N. Treuhaft. "Recovery Oriented Computing(ROC): Motivation, Definition, Techniques and Case Studies". UC Berkeley Computer Science Technical Report UCB/CSD-02-1175, Berkeley, CA, March 2002.

21. B. Randell, J. Xu. "The Evolution of the Recovery Block Concept". *Software Fault Tolerance*, pp. 1-22, 1994.
22. T. Rothamel, Y. A. Liu, C. L. Heitmeyer, E. I. Leonard. "Generating Optimized Code from SCR Specifications". *Proc. of the LCTES*, pp. 135-144, Ottawa, Ontario, Canada ,June 2006.
23. J. Xu, B. Randell, A. Romanovsky, R. J. Stroud, A. F. Zoro. "Rigorous Development of a Safety-Critical System Based on Coordinated Atomic Actions". *IEEE Transactions on Computers*, vol. 51(2), pp. 164-179, 2002.

Evaluation of a Tracking Architecture in Wireless Sensor Networks

Florent Claerhout

IRISA, Université de Rennes 1, France
fclaerho@irisa.fr

Abstract. A wireless sensor network is a collection of tiny and cheap devices deployed over a physical surface and able to gather and process in a collaborative way some information about a specified phenomenon occuring in their surroundings. Particularly, in tracking applications, the end-user is interested in the statistics of mobile targets crossing the region monitored by the network (i.e. trajectory forecast, speed, etc.). Those statistics share the common need for causally and temporally correlated data. In this paper, we evaluate the energetics cost of TRAC, a high level tracking architecture designed to respond to the requirements of tracking applications. We compare TRAC to a basic flooding-based mechanism, which does not offer any guarantee on the correlation of the disseminated data. Via theoritical analysis and simulations we show that the complexity of TRAC is $O(2^x)$ while the complexity of the flooding-based solution is $O(x^3)$ (where x^2 is the number of nodes in the network). These results emphasize the extra cost of high level properties. We conjecture that a careful aggregation of the data managed by TRAC drops its complexity to $O(x^2)$ and we provide some hints to implement these optimizations.

1 Introduction

A wireless sensor is a tiny and cheap electronic device equipped with several modules including a *processing* module, a *wireless communication* module, a *sensing module* and an *energy source*. Some wireless sensors may be also equipped with *actuators* allowing it to interact with its environment. The main idea is that even if such a device is very versatile, its resources are always limited: its processing power, communication bandwidth and additional parameters are weak, and in particular its energy source (typically a mere battery) can last only for a limited amount of time (we do not consider the possibility of recharging it). Once deployed over the *region of interest* the set of sensors implicitly form a network through the wireless communication links, and therefore, they are able to cooperate at a higher-level in order to achieve their task(s). In the following, we will use the term *node* instead of *wireless sensor*.

The applications considered in this paper are tracking applications. The term 'tracking application' is in fact a language abuse refering to an *application* (running on each node, and corresponding, for instance, to the 7th layer in the OSI model) using a *tracking service* (also running on each node); In the following

A.K. Datta and M. Gradinariu (Eds.): SSS 2006, LNCS 4280, pp. 169–183, 2006.

the term *application* will designate the top-level application. In this context, a wireless sensor network is expected to detect all the targets crossing the covered region and to report various statistics (past trajectory, estimated trajectory, velocity, etc.) to the end-users (interfaced to the network by some fixed *base stations* or mobile devices like a pda or a phone). The targets, as well as the reported statistics are application-dependent (the application specifies to the tracking service which are the requirements). A general specification of the tracking service can be found in [3].

A lot of works can be found in the literature concerning the traking problem, but in general those works are focused only on a specific sub-problem of a complete architecture ([2] focuses on the classification part, for instance). A tracking service brings together several specific problems (detection, estimation, classification, etc.) but also requires a lot of additional basic protocols (time synchronization, communication, etc.), thus also importing the difficulties related to those supplementary protocols. An interesting description of the method to design and implement such an architecture can be found in [1] along with the presentation of each specific component (detection, estimation, classification).

In this paper we will consider two architectures: the most simple one, based only on a flooding mechanism, and a more complicated one, TRAC [3], based on two levels of overlays designed to optimize some network metrics. In particular, we expect with this second architecture, a diminution of the energy expense, but possibly a worse latency. The interesting problem is: how to evaluate the design of a wireless sensor network (including hardware and software)? There exists a lot of established metrics [4,7] (including the network lifetime, the average energy consumption, the accuracy, etc.). Unfortunately, those metrics are all influenced by multiple parameters caracterizing the protocols, the nodes, the network, and its expected activity (including the nodes communication and sensing scopes, the number of targets and their trajectory, etc.). In fact, the main metrics can only be evaluated according to a 'fixed' scenario corresponding to a particular activity in the covered region.

Contribution − In this paper, we are interested in the energy consumption of two tracking architectures, TRAC (a complex assembly using the combination of two overlays) and a flooding-based approach. In order to evaluate those two solutions, a general scenario has been defined, with several parameters fixed and some variable ones (e.g. the network size). For each solution, we provide a formal analysis (of the general case and the specific case in our scenario); the analysis corresponding to our scenario is checked against simulations. We show in this paper that a basic implementation of a complex system like TRAC results in performances less interesting than the ones of the flooding-based approach (except that the flooding-based solution requires post-processing as explained later, this cost is not taken into account in our evaluation). We explain, first, how to optimize the implementation to achieve better results, and second, in which cases TRAC should be preferred.

Paper Overview − The paper is organized as follows: we start by describing the sensor network used for the evaluations and the simulation tool. The next part consists in the presentation of the two architectures as well as their respective models (of energy consumption). The results are then discussed and the paper concludes on the future works to be done.

2   Case Study

The case study for the evaluation, called *S1*, is the following: we consider a simple square-shaped network with an uniform distribution of the nodes as shown on the following figure. The side of the network is denoted x (so the network contains x^2 nodes). A single target appears at the bottom of the network and moves in a straight line alongside it and until it leaves the covered region: the sensing scope (cs) of the nodes has been limited to 0.5 so the target is only detected by the x nodes at the bottom of the network. There is a single sink at the top-right. The communication scope (ss) is set to 1.5 (each node is separated from its side and up/down neighbors (if any) by 1 'space unit' (the real unit is of no importance). It will be considered that all the nodes are active (their sensing and communication devices always on).

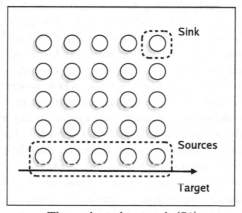

The evaluated network (S1)

We use the communication energy cost model proposed in [5,6]:

$$E_{tx} = P_{tx} \cdot (\frac{s}{W} + T_{startup}) + \alpha_{amp} \cdot cs^2 \cdot \frac{s}{W} \qquad (1)$$

$$E_{rx} = P_{rx} \cdot (\frac{s}{W} + T_{startup}) \qquad (2)$$

E_{tx} is the energy cost of the transmission of a packet of size s bytes, using a channel of bandwidth W, where the power of the modulator (roughly) is P_{tx} and the power of the amplifier is $\alpha_{amp} \cdot cs^2$. Similarly, E_{rx} is the energy cost of the reception of a packet of size s, with P_{rx} as the power of the demodulator. In our case, this model has been simplified to the following equations:

$$E_{tx} = s \cdot (p_{tx} + \alpha_{amp} \cdot cs^2) = s \cdot \epsilon_{tx} \qquad (3)$$

$$E_{rx} = s \cdot (p_{rx}) = s \cdot \epsilon_{rx} \qquad (4)$$

The following values have been arbitrary used (a set of coherent values has been chosen but the individual values do not necessarily correspond to real ones, as we only wish to do comparisons):

ss	cs	p_{tx}	p_{rx}	α_{amp}	ϵ_{tx}	ϵ_{rx}
0.5	1.5	0.1	0.1	0.1	0.325	0.1

Additionally, the initial battery capacity of each node is set to 2400 'units of capacity' (the real unit for battery capacities is the mAh). Communications are considered as perfect (no collisions, no fading, no delay) and a node can send/received as many packets as it wishes at the same time.

3 Simulator

In order to check the theoritical results and test more complex protocols, a simulator as be developped, allowing to put aside some low-level details which are not interesting for our study and difficult to manage (i.e. communication protocol, clock synchronisation, etc.) The simulator (WSNS[1]) allows to design accurately a network topology (including the sinks location) and to describe an approximation of each target trajectory and speed through a polygonal line associated with the speed on each segment; this whole description constitutes a so-called *scenario*. As most distributed systems simulators, a simple evolution model is used: a simulation is a sequence of *cycles* during which each node is allowed to perform the actions described by its protocol. These actions include the emission/reception of messages, target detection and the protocol specific inner tasks. Concerning communications, collisions are not taken into account (a node can send/ receive as many packets as it wishes at the same time) and there are, by default, no loss or corruptions. Besides, transmissions and propagation delays are all considered to be negligeable. The energy consumption and packet emissions are always interesting statistics, so the simulator records their progression. The simulator communication energy cost model is the one described previously. Additionally, the usage of the sensing and communication devices is not free, the cost per cycle and per node has been arbitrary fixed to the following values:

$\epsilon_{sensing}$	ϵ_{com}
0.1	0.1

The other parameters are fixed as detailed in the previous section. At last, for our experiments, the number of cycles has been fixed to 1000 and the target enters the region at cycle 400.

---

[1] WSNS (Wireless Sensor Network Simulator) can be freely provided on demand.

4   Notations

We will use the following notations: $\mathcal{N}$ is the the set of nodes in the network, its cardinal $|\mathcal{N}|$ corresponds to the number of nodes in the network. $\mathcal{S}$ the set of sources and $\mathcal{K}$ the set of sinks ($(\mathcal{S} \cup \mathcal{K}) \subset \mathcal{N}$). $\forall n \in \mathcal{N}, d(n)$ is the degree of the node n (its number of neighbors) and $N(n)$ is the set of neighbors of n ($|N(n)| = d(n)$). Additional (specific) notations are added later. All those values might vary with time but we will only consider situations in which time doesn't affect anything.

5   Flooding

The very obvious algorithm (we can barely speak of an 'architecture') for a tracking service consists in sending the raw data packets as soon as a node sensed a target; then each packet is broadcast/forwarded in the entire network. Thanks to the symplifying hypothesis on the communications, we are guaranteed that each node will indeed receive each packet (in particular, the sinks will receive it). However, in addition to the classical flooding problems (duplication of packets, network overload, supplementary energy consumption, etc.) the problem of infinite looping occurs because a node doesn't record which packet it has already sent. There are two possible solutions: the first one consists in adding the equivalent of a TTL[2] field to each packet, but the initial value of this field is proportional to the network diameter, which is not known by a node in advance (in the general case); the second solution, more simple, consists in recording in each node a trace of each packet it has already sent (so a packet is sent only once by a node). The main drawback of this algorithm (at the end-user level) is that the sinks only get back unordered information implying the necessity of a post-processing either at the application level or before it.

The energy cost model of this algorithm is fairly simple: as explained before, each node in the network will emit/forward exactly one time each packet. There are $|\mathcal{S}|$ packets emitted initially (one per source) so the number of packets emitted and forwarded is:

$$P = |\mathcal{S}| \cdot |\mathcal{N}| \qquad (5)$$

According to our implementation, a packet has a size of 4 bytes[3], so the total emission cost is:

$$E_{tx} = 4 \cdot P \cdot \epsilon_{tx} \qquad (6)$$

The reception cost is less trivial as it depends on each node number of neighbors, this total number of neighbors is: $A = \sum_{n \in \mathcal{N}} d(n)$, so:

$$E_{rx} = 4 \cdot |\mathcal{S}| \cdot A \cdot \epsilon_{rx} \qquad (7)$$

---

[2] TCP/IP TTL (Time To Live).

[3] In WSNS a byte is an unsigned long integer, the exact size is platform-dependent.

Those functions show that, in the general case, the energy expense of the flooding algorithm only depends on the total number of nodes, the total number of neighbors and the number of sources.

We can now rewrite everything for S1, our case study. Let's denote $\alpha(x) = x^2$. The emission cost is now:

$$E_{tx}(x) = 4 \cdot x \cdot \alpha(x) \cdot \epsilon_{tx} \tag{8}$$

A can be calculated easily with a square-shaped network: the 4 nodes in the corners have 3 neighbors, the others nodes on the sides have 5 neighbors and they are exactly $4 \cdot (x-2)$, at last, all the nodes except the ones on the side have 8 neighbors: $8 \cdot (x-2)^2$.

$$A(x) = \begin{cases} 0 & \text{if } x \leq 1 \\ 12 & \text{if } x = 2 \\ 12 + 20 \cdot (x-2) + 8 \cdot (x-2)^2 & \text{if } x \geq 3 \end{cases}$$

Hence the total reception cost:

$$E_{rx}(x) = 4 \cdot x \cdot A(x) \cdot \epsilon_{rx} \tag{9}$$

To those costs, we must add the sensing and communication devices usage costs. As initially all the devices are off (they are enabled when the node starts up) then they cost something only during 999 cycles on the 1000, so the total cost for a network of side x is:

$$E(x) = E_{tx}(x) + E_{rx}(x) + 999 \cdot (\epsilon_{sensing} + \epsilon_{com}) \cdot \alpha(x) \tag{10}$$

The final function can be rewritten as:

$$E(x) = 4.5 \cdot x^3 + 195 \cdot x^2 + 1.6 \cdot x \tag{11}$$

Which means that we obtain, for example, with a network of 100 nodes ($x = 10$), the emission of $x \cdot \alpha(x) = 1000$ packets and a total cost of $E(10) = 24016$ 'units of energy' (the standard unit is the Joule, [J]), those results are confirmed by the simulations. The following graph shows the energy consumption for an increasing number of nodes.

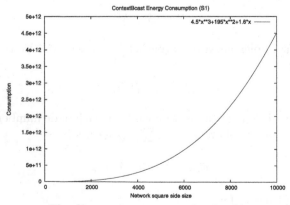

Flooding energy consumption for S1

6 TRAC

A detailed description of the TRAC architecture can be found in [3]. The essential points are presented below. TRAC is an architecture built from 4 modules: the *detection* module, the *neighbor probing* module, the *optimization* block (built from the *trajectory overlay manager* module and the *trajectory overlay builder* module) and, at last, the *publish/subscribe* block (built from the *notification overlay manager* module and the *notification overlay builder* module), as represented on the following figure.

The *detection* module (which abstracts the detection, the estimation and the classification sub-modules) provides *detection reports* (the target signature and the detection time) to the optimization block. When a detection report is submitted to this last block, the *trajectory module builder* first tries to find out whether the current node has a neighbor which has detected the same target before[4]. If this is the case, the *trajectory overlay manager* sends a 'delegation packet' (a packet containing the local data) to the previous node (on the target trajectory) which simply concatenates the delegated data to its own data; this is considered as a new detection report and the process is restarted from the beginning on this new node.

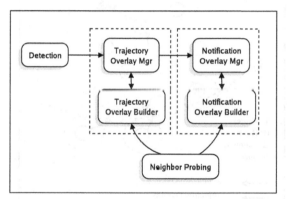

TRAC Architecture

If a node doesn't have any 'previous' node (which is the case for border nodes, or if the concerned neighbor is crashed, for instance) then the local data (a detection report or concatenated data) is handed off to the publish/subscribe block. The goal of the *notification overlay builder* is simply to create an overlay allowing to publish the data to the sinks. Once this overlay is built, the local data are distributed to the sinks thanks to the *notification overlay manager*.

An example is shown on the following figure: all the nodes having detected the target are linked together (each source node knows the previous source node on the target trajectory, according to the detection time, there can be several possible 'previous' node, a simple election based on the node id is done

---

[4] This is based on the locality principle: it a node has sensed a target, then at least one of its neighbors has sensed the same target before (assuming the target cannot jump). This is true except for the border nodes.

in this case). A single node, the first one having detected the target is responsible to publish all the data to the sinks, this is done thanks to the second overlay (the 'notification overlay'). This last overlay is, for instance, a spanning tree between the sinks and the root, intermediate nodes are marked as gateways.

It should be emphasized here that TRAC is an architecture, thus, as explained already, the algorithms can be changed easily (in particular the both overlays). However we need a concrete implementation for our evaluation, so we stick to the initial choices.

The delegation mechanism form a so-called *trajectory overlay* which links together all the source nodes: the interest is first to perform some filtering/smoothing to ensure the coherency and the order of data and second to perform some compression operation to reduce the amount of data sent. The aggregation operations are not considered in this paper to keep it simple, but these are major advantages when considering data processing (which cannot easily be achieved with a flooding-based design for instance).

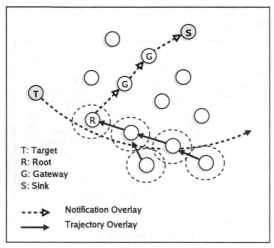

T: Target
R: Root
G: Gateway
S: Sink

- - - ▷ Notification Overlay
———▶ Trajectory Overlay

TRAC overview

Fault-tolerance – The algorithms associated to this architecture are self-stabilizing, but to keep the evaluation simple, the stabilization part has been removed, except for the neighor probing: it simply means that we tolerate crash-type faults (due to battery exhaustion for instance) but no longer transient faults. Crashes, however, won't be considered.

Packets sizes – At last, each algorithm (described in the next sections) of the standard implementation of TRAC uses different types of packets. We will need those packets size for the analytical model (in the following table, L is the 'useful' size of data, i.e. the data collected by the nodes, the other values are the overheads):

Message Type	Size
PING	3
PONG	3
TARGETADV	5
TARGETACK	6
PUBDELEGREQ	$7+L$
PUBDELEGACK	6
ROUTEIN	8
ROUTEACK	5
ROUTEMSG	$6+L$

Neighbor Probing (NP) – This proactive algorithm maintains for each node the list of its neigbors (with which the communication link is bidirectional). Initially a node doesn't know its neigbors, so it begins by broadcasting a PING message and its neigbors reply by a PONG. However the neighbors don't know whether their link with this node is bidirectional or not for themselves so they also send a PING message. The initial node reply to the PINGs by a PONG to each of its neighbors. Up to now, the number of emitted packets is:

$$P^{init} = |\mathcal{N}| + 2 \cdot A + A \tag{12}$$

Which results in the following emission and reception costs:

$$E_{tx}^{init} = 3 \cdot P \cdot \epsilon_{tx} \tag{13}$$

$$E_{rx}^{init} = 3 \cdot (A + 2 \cdot \Gamma + \Gamma) \cdot \epsilon_{rx} \tag{14}$$

Where Γ is the number of neighbors of order 2 (i.e. the number of neighbors of each neighbor of a node: $\Gamma(\mathcal{N}) = \sum_{n\in\mathcal{N}} \sum_{m\in N(n)} d(m)$). Besides, as a node is prone to fail (from energy exhaustion in our case), each node must update its neighbor list. This is simply done by broadcasting periodically a PING to which the already known neighbors reply by a PONG. The new packet emission number is:

$$P^{stab} = |\mathcal{N}| + \Lambda \tag{15}$$

The emission/reception costs are thus:

$$E_{tx}^{stab} = 3 \cdot P \cdot \epsilon_{tx} \tag{16}$$

$$E_{rx}^{stab} = 3 \cdot (A + \Gamma) \cdot \epsilon_{rx} \tag{17}$$

Therefore, by denoting f the update frequency, we obtain as total cost:

$$E_{NP} = E_{tx}^{init} + E_{rx}^{init} + f \cdot (E_{tx}^{stab} + E_{rx}^{stab}) \tag{18}$$

Clearly, and as expected, this algorithm cost depends only on the total number of nodes in the network, the number of neighbors (of order 1 and 2), and the update frequency f.

Applied to our case study, we get:

$$\Gamma(x) = \begin{cases} 0 & \text{if } x \leq 1 \\ 36 & \text{if } x = 2 \\ 200 & \text{if } x = 3 \\ 492 & \text{if } x = 4 \\ 492 + 356 \cdot (x - 4) + 64 \cdot (x - 4)^2 & \text{if } x \geq 5 \end{cases}$$

$$P^{init}(x) = \alpha(x) + 2 \cdot A(x) + A(x) \tag{19}$$

The other functions are similar. For $p = 10$ and $c = 1000$, $f = floor((c-1)/p) = 99$, the final function can be rewritten as:

$$E_{NP}(x) = 3091.5 \cdot x^2 - 6327 \cdot x + 3333 \tag{20}$$

And the simulations confirm this result.

Trajectory Overlay Builder (TB) – As quickly explained before, this algorithm tries to find the previous neighbor source node on the target trajectory (from the current node point of view), so each source node, after having detected the target, starts by emitting a TARGETADV message containing its detection parameters, the number of packets is:

$$P^{ADV} = |\mathcal{S}| \tag{21}$$

The emission/reception costs are:

$$E_{tx}^{ADV} = 5 \cdot P^{ADV} \cdot \epsilon_{tx} \tag{22}$$

$$E_{tx}^{ADV} = 5 \cdot A_\mathcal{S} \cdot \epsilon_{rx} \tag{23}$$

Where $A_\mathcal{S}$ denotes the number of neighbors of the sources: $A_\mathcal{S} = \sum_{n \in \mathcal{S}} d(n)$. Each source node, except the ones not having a successor on the trajectory (i.e. all the last nodes having detected the target) will reply by a TARGETACK message (including the root nodes). Let's denote $\mathcal{F}$ the set of nodes without a successor (without a 'next' node). Let $\mathcal{R}$ denotes the set of root nodes. the number of packets is:

$$P^{ACK} = |\mathcal{S} \cup \mathcal{R} - \mathcal{F}| \tag{24}$$

The emission/reception costs are:

$$E_{tx}^{ACK} = 6 \cdot P^{ACK} \cdot \epsilon_{tx} \tag{25}$$

$$E_{rx}^{ACK} = 6 \cdot A_{\mathcal{S} \cup \mathcal{R} - \mathcal{F}} \cdot \epsilon_{rx} \tag{26}$$

Where $A_{\mathcal{S} \cup \mathcal{R} - \mathcal{F}} = \sum_{n \in (\mathcal{S} \cup \mathcal{R} - \mathcal{F})} d(n)$. The total cost E_{TB} is the sum of the four functions:

$$E_{TB} = E_{tx}^{ADV} + E_{rx}^{ADV} + E_{tx}^{ACK} + E_{rx}^{ACK} \tag{27}$$

Applied to S1, we get respectively:

$$P^{ADV} = x, \ P^{ACK} = (x - 1), \ A_\mathcal{S} = 2 \cdot 3 + 5 \cdot (x - 2), \ A_{\mathcal{S} \cup \mathcal{R} - \mathcal{F}} = 3 + 5 \cdot (x - 2)$$

In a 'real' case, with more sources and a less simple topology, a node may select temporarily a wrong 'previous' node. We can ignore this case here. The total cost for S1 (confirmed by the simulations) can be rewritten as:

$$E_{TB}(x) = 9.075 \cdot x - 8.150 \tag{28}$$

Trajectory Overlay Manager (TM) – This algorithm simply makes a node to delegate its local data to the previous source node on the trajectory if it knows it, or hand off the data to the publish/subscribe block otherwise. The idea, here, is that we try first the optimized method to publish the data but if it doesn't work, as a node must do its publication, it falls back on a basic method to do it (achieved thanks to the publish/subscribe block). In our case, first we are guaranteed that each node indeed knows it previous node and second, we will assume there is no aggregation, so a node re-send its data augmented with the delegated data recursively until the border node.

The trick here is that the expression of this recursive delegation highly depends on the form of the trajectory overlay. Due to space limitation, and as this part is quite long to explain, we will limit ourselves to the particular expressions of the case study.

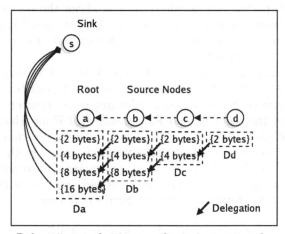

Delegation mechanism on the trajectory overlay

Each node delegates its currently possessed set of data, and each time a node get back some delegated data, it concatenates this new data to its local data to create a new data packet (the size is the size of the both concatenated packets) which will be, in turn, delegated at the next step. For the delegation part, we get:

$$E_{tx}^{DRQ}(x) = \sum_{i=1}^{x-1}\sum_{j=1}^{i} (7 + 2^j) \cdot \epsilon_{tx} \tag{29}$$

$$E_{rx}^{DRQ}(x) = 3 \cdot (7 + 2) \cdot \epsilon_{rx} + 5 \cdot \sum_{i=2}^{x-1}\sum_{j=1}^{i} (7 + 2^j) \cdot \epsilon_{rx} \tag{30}$$

And for the acknowlegments:

$$E_{tx}^{DACK}(x) = \sum_{i=1}^{x-1} \sum_{j=1}^{i} 6 \cdot \epsilon_{tx} \tag{31}$$

$$E_{rx}^{DACK}(x) = 3 \cdot \sum_{j=1}^{x-1} 6 \cdot \epsilon_{rx} + 5 \cdot \sum_{i=1}^{x-2} \sum_{j=1}^{i} 6 \cdot \epsilon_{rx} \tag{32}$$

Clearly this part is really expensive (with a complexity in $O(2^x)$ for the total cost).

Notification Overlay Builder (NB) – The objective of this module is to built a spanning tree between the current node (the root of the tree) and the sinks distributed in the network (and which locations are unknown). The node starts by emitting a ROUTEIN packet to advertise the entire network about the fact it possesses some information about a target (the ROUTEIN packet contains only *meta-data*[5]). Those packets allow each node in the network to select its parent ensuring the shortest path between itself and the root, so each time a ROUTEIN packet is forwarded, its data about the parent and distance to the root is updated. As, in the general case, there are possibly several targets crossing the region of interest, there are possibly several root nodes (there is at least one root node per target[6]).

The sinks will also receive the ROUTEIN packets, and, as they are interested they reply by a ROUTEACK to activate the shortest path between itself and the root. Let $\mathcal{P}$ denotes the set of nodes belonging to the shortest paths between the sinks in $\mathcal{K}$ and the roots $\mathcal{R}$, and $\mathcal{P}_r$ the subset of $\mathcal{P}$ for which $r \in \mathcal{R}$ is the root. In our case study there is only one sink in the upper-right corner of the network, and only one root node at the bottom-left corner so the ROUTEACK messages are forwarded on the diagonal of the square-shaped network. Due to space limitation, we won't detail this part, however, in our case study, the total cost (confirmed by simulation results) can be rewritten as:

$$E_{NB}(x) = 9 \cdot x^2 - 3.975 \cdot x - 4.925 \tag{33}$$

Notification Overlay Manager (NM) – At last, once a notification tree is ready, it remains to send the data to the sinks. The trick is that, as we didn't considered aggregation, we have to send the progressive concatenation of the packets (as explained for the trajectory overlay manager).

---

[5] In our case the meta-data about a target is simply reduced to its signature as returned by the sensing device of the node, however it may be much more complicated in a 'real' case.

[6] Ideally, there is exactly one root node per target, which is our case as we do not consider node failures.

In the particular case of S1, there is only one root ($\mathcal{R} = \{r\}$), and only one set of node forming a shortest path to the sink (the diagonal of the network):

$$|\mathcal{P}| = |\mathcal{P}_r| = x - 2 \text{ and } A_\mathcal{P} = A_{\mathcal{P}_r} = 8 \cdot (x - 2)$$

Therefore, we obtain the following simplified functions:

$$E_{tx}^{MSG}(x) = (x - 1) \cdot \sum_{i=1}^{x} (6 + 2^i) \cdot \epsilon_{tx} \tag{34}$$

$$E_{rx}^{MSG}(x) = (3 + 8 \cdot (x - 2)) \cdot \sum_{i=1}^{x} (6 + 2^i) \cdot \epsilon_{rx} \tag{35}$$

TRAC – The total cost for the architecture is the sum of each algorithm total cost plus the usage of the sensing and communication devices during the simulation cycles.

$$E_{TRAC}(x) = E_{NP}(x) + E_{TB}(x) + E_{TM}(x) +$$

$$E_{NB}(x) + E_{NM}(x) + 999 \cdot (\epsilon_{sensing} + \epsilon_{com}) \cdot \alpha(x) \tag{36}$$

This function has a complexity of $O(2^x)$.

7   Optimization

TRAC for the case study S1, with its default algorithms has a complexity of $O(2^x)$ (where x is the network square side size) against a complexity of $O(x^3)$ for the flooding. So the immediate conclusion is that TRAC is much more expensive when the number of nodes increases, as shown on the following figure.

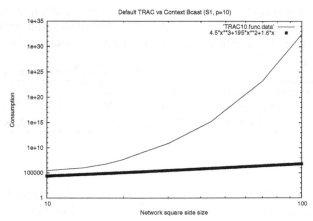

Comparison of the consumption of TRAC with the default algorithms ($p = 10$) and the flooding method for S1 (log scale)

However, as explained before, the used algorithms are not optimized and there's plenty of room for improvement:

- *Neighbor Probing* – A reactive version of the algorithm may be more attractive according to the hypothesis on the fault occurences;
- *Trajectory Overlay Manager* – This is one of the expensive parts, with a complexity in $O(2^x)$. The fact that all the local data, augmented with the delegated data are re-emitted recursively is good relatively to the fault-tolerance as it ensures redundancy, but this is expensive. The redundancy dropped, in the best case, each source node should simply delegate data packets with a (small) constant size, in our case, without considering aggregation, only 2 bytes should be recursively delegated along the trajectory overlay:

$$E_{tx}^{DRQ}(x) = \sum_{i=1}^{x-1}\sum_{j=1}^{i}(7+2)\cdot\epsilon_{tx} \qquad (37)$$

Which makes us fall back on a complexity in $O(x^2)$;
- *Notification Overlay Builder* – This is an algorithm based on a broadcast so it fundamentally depends on the network size, its complexity in $O(x^2)$ may not be improved much, however there are different publish algorithms which could be used instead;
- *Notification Overlay Manager* – The expensive complexity of this part (also in $O(2^x)$) is due to the Trajectory Overlay Manager, but in the ideal case a single packet (containing all the data) will be emitted by the root nodes, so the complexity is proportional to the number of nodes on the paths between the roots and the sinks, in our case study, this is $O(x)$. So this part is interesting if $|\mathcal{K}| \ll |\mathcal{N}|$.

Concretely with the modifications suggered above, the TRAC complexity falls back in $O(x^2)$ which become much more interesting and less expensive than the standard flooding method for S1. In the general case, TRAC is more interesting when the supplementary overlays are justified, which corresponds, at least, to the following condition: $|\mathcal{S} \cup \mathcal{K}| \ll |\mathcal{N}|$. The following table summarizes the different characteristics of the architectures studied in this paper:

	Flooding	Default TRAC	Optimized TRAC
S1 Consumption Complexity	x^3	2^x	x^2
Data Correlation	No	Yes	Yes
Aggregation	Difficult	Easy	Easy

8   Conclusion

In this paper, we evaluated two types of architectures, a simple flooding-based mechanism and a more complicated architecture based on two levels of overlays (called TRAC), in order to determine whether a simple design is more interesting or not from the energy consumption viewpoint. Those evaluations were conducted in a well-defined case study, consisting of, mainly, a square-shaped network crossed by a single target. With TRAC, the expectations were that the overall consumption expense should be better than the simple solution and, additionally, TRAC allows to achieve easily data processing (ensuring, in particular, the correlation properties needed by the application). Our first conclusion is that, despite the different components of TRAC were assembled to optimize the tracking service, it clearly appears that this is not sufficient: each component itself must be carefully optimized to, indeed, improve the global performances. From a complexity in $O(2^x)$, we show how to optimize the algorithms to achieve a complexity in $O(x^2)$ for the general consumption, which is better than the flooding-based method, which complexity is in $O(x^3)$. We also show that using our optimization mechanism is interesting only if the number of source and sink nodes is smaller than the size of the network $|\mathcal{S} \cup \mathcal{K}| \ll |\mathcal{N}|$ or if ensuring the data correlation properties is more critical than the consumption metric.

In our future works, we intend to evaluate the cost of the fault-tolerance in the algorithms, with more complex scenarios, and to evaluate TRAC with different combinations of algorithms (adding also the additional components left aside in this paper: the time synchronization and the communication protocols).

References

1. Anish Arora, Prabal Dutta, Sandip Bapat, Vinod Kulathumani, Hongwei Zhang, Vinayak Naik, Vineet Mittal, Hui Cao, Murat Demirbas, Mohamed G. Gouda, Young ri Choi, Ted Herman, Sandeep S. Kulkarni, Umamaheswaran Arumugam, Mikhail Nesterenko, Adnan Vora, and M. Miyashita. A line in the sand: A wireless sensor network for target detection, classification, and tracking. *Computer Networks*, 46(5):605–634, 2004.
2. R.R. Brooks, P. Ramanathan, and A.M. Sayeed. Distributed target classification and tracking in sensor networks. In *Proceedings of the IEEE*, volume 91, pages 1163 1171, aug 2003.
3. F. Claerhout, A.K. Datta, M. Gradinariu, and M. Hurfin. Self-* architecture for trajectory tracking in wireless sensor networks. In *The 5th IEEE International Symposium on Network Computing and Applications*, 2006. To be published.
4. D. Estrin. An introduction to wireless sensor networks: Applications and challenges. Course Slides.
5. W.R. Heinzelman, A. Chandrakasan, and H. Balakrishnan. Energy efficient communication protocol for wireless microsensor networks. In *Proceedings of the 33rd Annual Hawaii International Conference on System Sciences (HICSS)*, pages 3005–3014, jan 2000.
6. E. Shih, B.H. Calhoun, H.C. Seong, and A.P. Chandrakasan. Energy efficient link layer for wireless microsensor networks. In *Proceedings of the IEEE Computer Society Workshop on VLSI*, pages 16–21, 2001.
7. S. Tilak, N.B. Abu Ghazaleh, and W. Heinzelman. A taxonomy of wireless microsensor network models. In *ACM Mobile Computing and Communications Review (MC2R)*, 2002.

Self-protection for Distributed Component-Based Applications

Benoit Claudel[1], Noël De Palma[1], Renaud Lachaize[2], and Daniel Hagimont[3]

[1] Institut National Polytechnique de Grenoble, France
[2] Université Joseph Fourier, Grenoble, France
[3] Institut National Polytechnique de Toulouse, France

Abstract. The complexity of today's distributed computing environments is such that the presence of bugs and security holes is statistically unavoidable. A very promising approach to this issue is to implement a self-protected system, similarly to a natural immune system which has the ability to detect the intrusion of foreign elements and react while it is still in progress.

This paper describes an approach relying on component-based software engineering to ease the protection of distributed systems. The knowledge of the application architecture is used to detect foreign activities and to trigger counter measures. We focus on a mean to recognize known and unknown attacks independently from legacy software and avoiding false positives. Hence, the scope of the detected attacks is, for the moment, limited to the detection of illegal communications. We describe how this approach can be applied to provide self-protection for clustered J2EE applications with a very low overhead.

1 Introduction

Today, human activity is getting ever more dependent on computing systems. They are used extensively to process and store confidential information. However, computers remain fragile systems: in addition to hardware breakdowns, other troubles threaten them, especially when they are connected to an open network such as the Internet.

Modern software is plagued by security flaws at many levels. In this context, hackers and intruders make successful attempts to attack company networks and web services on a daily basis. Hence, security is now a major concern for any IT infrastructure.

Enforcing the security of a computing system lies on some key abilities. First, as preventive measures, it is important to define tight access control policies, so that hackers can hardly break into the system and hide their tracks. Second, one should be able to distinguish suspicious activities from the normal operations of the system. Third, once detected, the malicious processes must be stopped in a comprehensive and efficient way.

Unfortunately, these goals are very hard to meet in practice, for several reasons.

A.K. Datta and M. Gradinariu (Eds.): SSS 2006, LNCS 4280, pp. 184–198, 2006.

1. It is notoriously complex to specify and maintain access policies that are effective, globally consistent (across different programs and computers) and not overly restrictive for users.
2. The complexity of today's software components (and their interactions) is such that the presence of bugs and security holes is statistically unavoidable. This leaves the opportunity for hackers to develop new hijacking techniques ("exploits") at a very high pace. Keeping up with the appropriate security patches requires a continuous vigilance.
3. Detecting malicious activities within the system is, in general, far from trivial and relies almost exclusively on human expertise. For this reason, most intrusions are only noticed once much damage has been done.

Overall, most problems stem from the fact that (human) administrators are unable to cope with the amount of work required to properly secure a computing infrastructure at the age of the Internet.

We propose to address the above problem through the construction and implementation of a self-protected system. As a first step towards the fulfillment of this vision, this paper addresses two main goals: (i) simplifying the configuration (and reconfiguration) of security components according to the knowledge of the system structure and (ii) easing the development of automated counter measures to various classes of attacks. As a first case study, we focus on the context of multi-tier applications (such as clustered J2EE servers) hosted in a data center.

Section 2 presents the concepts of *autonomic computing* and *self-protection*. Section 3 describes related work. The design principles of a self-protected system are presented in section 4. Section 5 describes our implementation of such a system for clustered J2EE applications. Section 6 presents our experimental results. The limitations of our prototype and the perspectives of our work are presented in section 7. We conclude in section 8.

2   Autonomic Computing

Self-protection is the ability of an autonomic system to secure itself against attacks, i.e. to detect illegal activities and to trigger counter measures in order to stop them. This section describes the main concepts of autonomic computing (2.1), as well as the more specific concern of self-protection (2.2).

2.1   General Principles

As computing systems have become more complex and distributed, the human resources involved in managing and administrating them have considerably grown. Autonomic computing [7] aims at enabling computing infrastructures to perform administration tasks without (or with minimal) human intervention; such tasks include application deployment, platform configuration, reaction to events like node failures, wide variation in load, and various kind of attacks. Successful autonomic systems require to be self-configuring, self-optimizing, self-healing and self-protecting.

One approach to build an *autonomic system* [1] is to implement a control loop that regulates (according to high level policies) a part of the system, called the *managed system*. The *managed system* may consist of a single elementary hardware or software component, or may be a complex system itself, such as a cluster of machines, or a distributed middleware infrastructure. An *autonomic manager* adjusts the behavior of the system according to its constraints. It relies on two connections to the managed system: sensors to watch the state of the system, and actuators to modify it. In order to manage themselves, these systems must be able to discover and act on their own structure through introspection and adaptation.

2.2 Self-protection

In order to prevent network intrusions, many methods have been developed (section 3.1) notably firewalls and intrusion detection systems (IDS). But these techniques have a certain number of limitations. First of all, most of these tools report abnormal behaviors (perhaps attacks) to administrators, who must then carry out a manual analysis of the problem. These analysis may take time and allow the pirate to freely exploit the flaw whereas a fast answer would have stopped the attack while it was still in an early stage. Moreover, current security tools can often only protect systems against known attacks and pirates are always a length ahead. Finally, security tools are very difficult to configure in a distributed computing environment and errors from administrators are becoming a significant source of security flaws.

A very promising approach to address this issue is to implement a self-protected system which has the ability to detect illegal activities within the system and to trigger counter measures without human intervention. The purpose of our work is not to replace the existing tools but rather to provide a systematic approach that allows more closely-coupled interactions between them, so that the cluster-wide, coordinated reaction against an attack can become automated, and thus, more efficient.

3 Related Work

This section briefly reviews (3.1) the main tools and techniques currently used by security experts to fight against intrusions (some of these techniques can be used as basic building blocks to implement a self-protected system) and the existing systems that implement a self-protected behavior (3.2).

3.1 Common Security Tools

We make the distinction between different functions (protection filters, detectors of suspicious activity, logging and backtracking tools) although many available solutions integrate several of them.

Protection filters are used to restrict interactions among machines (or, more generally, distributed processes/resources) to a given set of limited, well established set of patterns. For instance, a firewall acts as a network filter that checks if any given packet can be forwarded according to its related protocol, source/destination addresses and ports.

Detectors (or scanners) used to recognize malicious activity fall generally into two categories [13,6]: (i) *misuse intrusion detection* and (ii) *anomaly detection intrusion.*The former approach compares the data packets passing through the detector with a library of patterns typical of known attacks, while the latter tries to spot irregular behaviors of the system. In addition, scanners can sometimes react themselves against the intrusion, but their action is usually limited in scope (block offending request/packet, quarantine suspect resource) and context (no coordination between the different servers). Thus, (quick) human intervention is generally required anyway for further study and containment of the problem.

Loggers record detailed data about the system activity so that once an intrusion attempt has been detected, it is possible to determine the sequence of events that led to the intrusion and the potential extent of the damage (e.g. data theft/loss).

3.2 Self-protected Systems

The Vigilante system [5] is an antivirus system where detectors are based on the immune system analogy and are able to find unknown viruses. Furthermore, when a new virus is found, its signature is spread across the network to all other protected computers.

Self-cleansing [9] is another solution to build self-protected software. This pessimistic approach makes the assumption that all intrusions cannot be detected and blocked. In fact, the system is considered to be compromised after a certain time. Hence, this approach periodically reinstalls a part of the system from a secure repository. However, this solution only applies to stateless components.

When a computer is compromised, another important function is the ability to restore the system in a trusted state. The Taser system [8] provides the file system with a selective self-recovery capability. Taser logs all file system access for each process. If a process is compromised, Taser computes illegal access for each file and is able to rollback illegal modification. However if a dependency is found between an illegal and a legal access, Taser requires a human intervention.

3.3 Summary

As we have seen, most security tools can only protect the system against known attacks. Furthermore, human administrators are heavily solicited by the alarms produced by the scanners. In particular, after checking the relevance of alarms, they are usually in charge of initiating lots of actions, both for coordinated defense at the cluster scale (e.g. through reconfiguration of the filters and scanners) and investigation (e.g. with backtracking tools). As a consequence, the human resources still represent the main bottleneck of the security infrastructure, which tends to increase the vulnerability of a system exposed to a new kind of attack. Besides, very little research has been performed on how to combine well-known security tools to create an autonomic security system.

4 Design Principles

Research on self-protected systems is a recent initiative, still in its prospective stage. The self-protection approach is notably inspired by the operations of the human body and has led to the concept of *computer immune system*, in the mid 90s.

The main goal of natural immune systems is to protect a live being from dangerous foreign pathogens. This mission relies on a key ability, the *sense of self*, that is, the capacity to detect the intrusion of foreign elements within the "system" (in this case, the body), through the distinction of *self* from *nonself*. Once an intruder is properly detected, measures can be taken to destroy it (or at least contain its damages and progression). In the context of a computing system, *nonself* may correspond to the activity of a malicious program or an unauthorized user.

Inspired by this principle, we propose architectural patterns to improve the coordination between multiple elements which compose a security infrastructure. Our focus is not on the development of new specific techniques for access control, intrusion detection or backtracking but rather on the mechanisms that allow an efficient and flexible integration of these various tools within a global, automated control process.

Furthermore, many studies have shown that the magnitude of the damages caused by an attack increases with the time afforded to an intruder within the system. However, as we have seen previously, the human administrators are the main bottleneck of the security infrastructure and, thus, the intruder residence time in the system is often relatively long. The most generic intrusion detectors (i.e. those able to detect new kinds of attacks) rely on statistical methods and generate a non negligible amount of false positives. As a consequence, it is not possible to use such detectors in order to trigger counter-measures autonomously and we aim at developing new means to detect abnormal behaviors while avoiding false positives.

4.1 Requirements

The main design principles required to build a self-protected system are summarized below:

1. An autonomic system needs to be able to detect intrusions. It requires a definition of its own operations: this is the *sense of self* capacity or the *self-knowledge* aspect. In other words, it must be able to distinguish legal behaviors from illegal behaviors. As the countermeasures are triggered autonomously, this distinction must be done while avoiding false positives. Moreover, the legal operations or the system structure could evolve over time: as a consequence, self-knowledge requires dynamic introspection capabilities.
2. The system must have the ability to respond to attacks. This capacity relies on the capacity for the system to reconfigure all its individual components.
3. A wide variety of systems must be protected, including legacy software not designed to be autonomic.

4. The components, involved in the self-protection of the system, can become themselves a target of attacks. Those, if compromised, can be used by the attackers in an unintended way. Hence, the system must prevent the self-protection components from being compromised.

The remainder of this paper describes our propositions to partially address the first three challenges mentioned above. We more particularly investigate how some "sense of self" abilities can be derived from the architecture of a distributed application (which can easily be obtained from its deployment/monitoring infrastructure). Note that this generic technique is not sufficient to protect a system against all kinds of attacks and should thus be combined with more application-specific mechanisms. More generally, the current limitations of our work are discussed in section 7.

4.2   Context

As a first application domain, we have chosen to focus on data servers, which have very high security requirements since they host sensible data and services in every organization. Before describing our approach, we briefly introduce J2EE, a popular platform for multi-tier, server-side applications and Jade, the middleware on which we built our self-protection logic.

Multi-tier applications. J2EE (Java 2 Enterprise Edition) [11] platforms allow the construction of web application services, which typically include e-commerce, on line banking, web portals and so on. Such applications are generally organized in 3 or 4 tiers: a web server tier, a presentation tier, a business tier (optional), and a database tier.

The *web tier* is an HTTP server (such as Apache). Its function is to receive and process the client's requests. If the answer to a request is a static content page, it is directly delivered by this tier; if dynamic content needs to be provided, the request is dispatched to a server of the next tier. The function of the *presentation tier* (e.g. a Tomcat server) is to manage the execution of *Servlets*, which drive the execution of the application and synthesize its results in the form of dynamic pages. The (optional) *business tier* (e.g. EJB Enterprise Java Beans) implements the application logic (data access and processing) if it is not provided by the presentation tier. Last, the *database tier* (e.g. a MySQL server) is to provide persistent storage and access functions for the information needed by the application.

J2EE multistage applications allow a separation of concerns and can be easily clustered. The different tiers may run on distinct nodes and be replicated for increased performance and robustness.

Middleware for autonomic applications. Our approach is based on the knowledge of the system operation and its architectural representation. We aim to provide such a representation of the environment using a component model. According the overall organization proposed for autonomic computing, we designed and implemented JADE, a framework for building autonomic systems. It

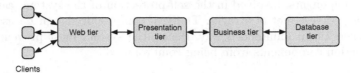

Fig. 1. Architecture of a J2EE platform

relies on the Fractal component architecture [3] to reconfigure applications according to observed events. JADE provides abilities for encapsulation of legacy entities, introspection, deployment and reconfiguration. Next, we detail the features of Fractal and JADE, and explain how they can ease the development of self-protection mechanisms.

Fractal Component Model. The component model we use in JADE is Fractal [3], a reflective component model intended for the construction of dynamically configurable and monitored systems.

A Fractal component is a run-time entity that is encapsulated and communicates with its environment through well-defined access points called interfaces. Fractal components communicate through explicit bindings. A binding corresponds to a communication path between two or more components. The Fractal specification specifies several useful controllers: the binding controller allows creating or removing bindings between components; the life-cycle controller allows starting and stopping the component; the attribute controller allows setting and getting configuration attributes.

Jade. The choice of a component model is justified by needs for encapsulation of legacy software, system representation and reconfiguration.

Wrapping Legacy Software. JADE uses Fractal to manage legacy entities using a uniform model, instead of relying on resource-specific, hand-managed, configuration files.

This approach is illustrated in the case of a clustered J2EE architecture. In figure 2, an L5-switch balances the requests between two replicated (Apache) web servers. The latter are connected to two (Tomcat) servlet engines. The Tomcat servers are both connected to the same (MySQL) database server.

The vertical dashed arrows represent management relationships between components and the wrapped software entities. In the legacy layer, the dashed lines represent relationship (or bindings) between legacy entities, whose implementations are proprietary. These bindings are represented in the management layer by component bindings (full lines in the figure).

In the management layer, all components provide the same (uniform) management interface for the encapsulated resources, and the corresponding implementation is specific to each resource (e.g. in the case of J2EE: Apache, Tomcat, MySQL, ...). The interface allows managing the attributes, bindings and life cycle of the resources.

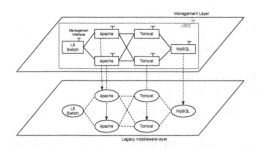

Fig. 2. Component-based management of legacy applications with JADE

Relying on this management layer, sophisticated administration programs can be implemented, without having to deal with complex, proprietary configuration interfaces, which are hidden in the wrappers.

Introspection and System Representation. An introspection interface enables the monitoring of the managed resources and the expression of the system structure in terms of components. For instance, an administration program can inspect an Apache managed resource (i.e. the component encapsulating the Apache server) to discover that this server runs on *node1:port80* and is bound to a Tomcat server running on *node2:port66*. It can also inspect the overall J2EE infrastructure, considered as a single managed resource, to discover that it is composed of two Apache servers interconnected with two Tomcat servers connected to the same MySQL server. This introspection ability provides an architectural representation of the system, which can be leveraged to define a set of legal operations for the system.

Reconfiguration. A reconfiguration interface allows the control over the component architecture. In particular, this interface allows to modify component attributes and bindings. These changes are reflected onto the legacy layer. For instance, an administration program can add or remove an Apache replica in the J2EE infrastructure to adapt the available resources according to the workload variations.

4.3   Architecture-Based Configuration and Protection

Sense of Self Capacity. Since JADE maintains an architectural representation of the system in terms of components and communication channels, it provides a notion of *sense of self* independently of the legacy software.

For instance, Figure 3 represents a clustered J2EE application in terms of components. This representation is autonomously generated during the deployment. The J2EE component contains node components which themselves contain the application tiers (i.e. Apache, Tomcat and MySQL servers). A legal communication between two nodes is represented by a binding between two components (full lines in the figure), the port on which the application is running (in the application wrapper) and the addresses of the nodes (in the components encapsulating the nodes).

Any communication attempt that is not associated with a legal channel is considered as an attack. This allows the detection of any attack breaking the structural rules of an application, with no false positives.

Sensors and Actuators. As we have previously mentioned, JADE is built according to the overall organization proposed for autonomic computing (section 2.1). Hence, it uses sensors to observe the *managed system* and actuators to manipulate it.

In the context of self-protection, sensors are used to detect attacks. They use the system's self-knowledge in order to distinguish illegal operations from legal ones. For instance, in the context of our architecture-based protection scheme, they must detect illegal communications.

Actuators, in a self-protected system, allow fighting against attacks by manipulating the *managed system* according to the decisions from the *autonomic manager*. For instance, they can isolate a node, apply more thorough checks to the packets that it sends or even force the reboot and reinstall of a node (assuming that we are in a controlled environment with the proper hardware support).

In order to prevent a compromised node from bypassing the protection filters thanks to spoofed reconfiguration requests, the orders emitted by the autonomic manager are authenticated thanks to asymmetric cryptography.

Control Loops for Self-protection. We describe here a simple control loop for self-protection that we implemented in JADE (section 5). It is aimed at isolating compromised nodes from the rest of the system. The actuators are able

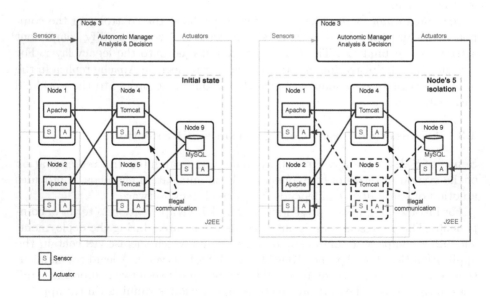

Fig. 3. Detection of an illegal communication and isolation of a node

to allow certain types of traffic, or disallow others on each node. The sensors detect illegal communications and provide information about the dropped network packets to the *autonomic manager*. The latter can then take the decision to isolate the node that sparked off the attack. For this purpose, it removes, at the management layer level, all the bindings towards the component encapsulating the compromised machine. These modifications are reflected onto the system by the actuators.

For instance, in the J2EE architecture represented in figure 3, no communication is allowed between nodes 4 and 5. However, the sensor on node 4 detects an illegal communication and sends this information to the *autonomic manager*, which decides to isolate node 5 (considered as compromised). This results in a reconfiguration of the actuators on nodes 1,2 and 9 (figure 3).

5   Implementation Details

This section presents the implementation details of the control loop described previously (4.3). Actuators and sensors are based on communications over TCP/ IP channels. The *autonomic manager* must be able to isolate nodes in reaction to alarms. This component has two interfaces: the first one receives alert notifications from sensors while the second one outputs reconfiguration directives to the actuators.

The goals of our prototype can be summarized as follows:

1. Auto-configuration: the security components should be automatically deployed and (re)configured according to the description of the application.
2. Low overhead: the security mechanisms must not significantly impact the performance of server-class applications.

To implement the actuators and sensors, we used Netfilter [12], a packet filtering framework provided by the Linux kernel. Iptables is used as a front-end to add or remove configuration rules. Next, we describe how to use this tool to build sensors able to detect illegal communications and actuators for filtering and isolation.

5.1   Actuators

In our prototype, the actuators allow (i) to automatically configure the Netfilter firewall running on each node of the cluster and (ii) to isolate compromised machines. A modification at the administrated level (e.g. a new binding between components, the change of an application's port number, ...) is reflected onto the Netfilter configuration by the actuators.

The automatic configuration of security components by the *actuators* and the *autonomic manager* lowers the burden of the human administrators as well as the risks of errors. Let us now describe the required rules for a subset of the configuration from figure 3 (nodes 2, 4 and 9):

Rules Required to Enforce the Overall Security Policy. First, it is necessary to enforce an efficient security policy: all the packets not explicitly allowed are blocked. The following rules allow to drop all the packets by default:

```
1. iptables -t filter -P INPUT DROP
2. iptables -t filter -P OUTPUT DROP
3. iptables -t filter -P FORWARD DROP
```

This set of rules is required on each node.

Rules on the Apache Node. In order to communicate with clients and the Tomcat server, the Apache server needs the four following rules:

```
1. iptables -t filter -A INPUT -j ACCEPT -p tcp --dport 8080
   -m state --state NEW,ESTABLISHED
2. iptables -t filter -A OUTPUT -j ACCEPT -p tcp -d 192.168.0.4
   --dport 8098 -m  state --state NEW,ESTABLISHED
3. iptables -t filter -A INPUT  -j ACCEPT -p tcp -s 192.168.0.4
   --sport 8098 -m  --state ESTABLISHED
4. iptables -t filter -A OUTPUT  -j ACCEPT state-p tcp
   --sport 8080 -m state --state ESTABLISHED
```

These rules are generated thanks to the system representation. A binding between two components at the administration level involves two filtering rules in order to allow a bidirectional communication between two legacy software. The first rule (arrow number 1) allows node 2 to accept connections from clients on the port 8080. The second one (arrow number 2) allows the machine 192.168.0.2 to establish a connection towards the machine 192.168.0.4 on the port 8098. This rule represents the binding between the Apache component and the Tomcat component in the "Apache towards Tomcat" direction. The third rule represents the same binding but from Tomcat towards Apache. Finally, the last rule allows the Apache server to answer client requests. The rules for the other nodes are not presented here but are in the same vein that the above-mentioned ones.

The configuration of a set of firewalls, even more in a complex distributed environment, is a difficult task. The *autonomic manager* and actuators allow to automate this task from the information provided by the deployment and introspection features of JADE. In addition, it is possible to randomly choose on the port number for a given service. In this way, the security level is improved because attackers must then resort to port scanning, and are thus more likely to be discovered.

5.2   Sensors

In our prototype, the sensors are able to detect illegal communications. For this, they use a special feature of Netfilter, which provides a mechanism for passing packets out of the network stack for queuing in userspace, then receiving these packets back into the kernel with a verdict specifying what to do with the packets (such as ACCEPT or DROP). These packets may also be modified in userspace prior to reinjection back into the kernel. In this way, the sensors are able to send the illegal packets to the *autonomic manager* before these packets are destroyed.

6   Evaluation

We evaluated our prototype in a J2EE cluster running RUBiS [2], a standard benchmark modeled according to an online auction service such as eBay. RUBiS provides a load injector to emulate clients.

Experiments ran on the *grillon* cluster [4], with a switched Gigabit Ethernet network and nodes featuring two 2Ghz AMD Opteron processors and 2GB of RAM.

Protection Level. As we have seen, our sensors detect all the communication not explicitly authorized in the system representation without any false positive. Hence, it is possible to react to all kind of attacks (known and unknown) using an illegal communication channel. For instance, it is possible to detect a port scanner and block the attack before the real intrusion.

Control Loop Reactivity. This experience aims at measuring the time between the detection of an illegal communication and the isolation of compromised nodes. We implemented the scenario described in section 4.3. The average time measured (over 1000 runs) is 2.133 ms with a 0.146 ms standard deviation. Hence, our prototype is very reactive and can quickly block an intruder.

Performance overhead. The following experience aims at measuring the impact of the protection control loop on the performance of RUBiS. The deployed J2EE architecture corresponds to the one on figure 3.

The load injector of RUBiS emulates a variable number of clients (from 0 to 3000 in our experiments) sending a series of requests.

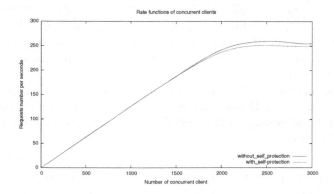

Fig. 4. Scalability of the RUBiS benchmark with and without self-protection

As shown in figure 4, the overhead induced by the use of a firewall on each cluster node is very low (less than 2%).

As the netfilter processing time increases according to the number of filtering rules, we checked the scalability of our solution by adding a hundred fictive rules to each firewall. The overhead, induced by this experimental setup, remained very low (less than 3%). Furthermore, even in a complex J2EE platform, the number of rules should not reach such a number.

7   Limitations and Perspectives

Limitations. We have designed and implemented a self-protected system for clustered J2EE applications. Our approach relies on a software component architecture to provide a *sense of self* to the system (i.e. to distinguish illegal behaviors from legal ones). For the moment, the scope of the detected attacks is limited to illegal communications over TCP/IP. We are thus unable to spot intruders respecting the expected control flow and/or targeting different protocols.

Our work mostly targets controlled environments such as server rooms (where most nodes are trusted) and "silent" attacks (aimed at quietly stealing or destroying data) rather than open grids and denial-of-service attacks. Our approach is well suited to the context of multi-tier applications deployed in a data center because an attacker knows a priori little about the structure of the system and will likely have to expose itself while exploring the network and trying to hijack other nodes. However, our current proposition may not be very helpful for peer-to-peer systems, where anyone acts as a router and can easily determine the architecture of the application.

Currently, the only counter-measure implemented in the *autonomic manager* is the isolation of compromised nodes. Our prototype nonetheless provides an easy way to develop various counter-measures (e.g. reinstalling compromised nodes, starting an intrusion backtracking procedure, etc.).

Besides, self-protected systems, similarly to natural immune systems, must not have a unique point of failure (i.e. several security components must be distributed over the network). However, our implementation relies on a single *security manager*. Hence, this crucial component must be fault-tolerant. Indeed, in addition to hardware of software breakdowns (*fail-stop failures*), it can become a victim of attacks or complex bugs and become compromised or corrupted (*byzantine failures*).

Last, in our prototype, the communications between security components are not fully authenticated. Hence, attackers with a good knowledge of our middleware could take advantage of this this flaw to control sensors and actuators in an unintended way.

Future work. As mentioned in section 4, we propose to define *self-knowledge* of legal operations in the system at two levels: (i) in a legacy independent way at a system's architecture level and (ii) in a more specific way at a legacy software level. This paper focuses on our work at the former level but we also intend to investigate the latter, i.e. develop mechanisms to spot and block attacks targeted at legacy software (buffer overflows, SQL injection, etc.). Since, in our model, legacy software are wrapped by manageable components, it is possible to encapsulate information about their normal behaviors. For instance, one could specify the children processes expected from a particular application in order to block an illegal *fork/exec*. We may also add the definition of well formed requests to prevent exploits like *SQL injections* on the database.

The main weakness of our prototype is the security of the self-protection mechanisms themselves. Existing solutions [10] have not been implemented and evaluated yet. The *autonomic manager* must be replicated ($m + 2$ replicas to detect the presence of m compromised *autonomic manager*) and any decision will require majority voting (and a more elaborate authentication scheme).

8   Conclusion

Today, distributed computing environments are increasingly complex and difficult to administrate. This complexity is such that the presence of bugs and security holes is statistically unavoidable. Therefore, access control policies become very difficult to specify and to enforce.

Following the autonomic computing vision, a very promising approach to deal with this issue is to implement a self-protected system which is able to distinguish legal (*self*) from illegal (*nonself*) operations. The detection of an illegal behavior triggers a counter-measure to isolate the compromised resources and prevent further damages.

In this vein, we have designed and implemented a system called JADE which allows the construction of autonomous administration programs. JADE relies on a component model for wrapping administrated resources and provides support for the definition of autonomic managers which capture significant events from the computing environment and trigger relevant actions.

In this paper, we investigated the application of JADE features to implement a self-protected system. We showed how to take advantage of the knowledge of a component-based application to provide a means of distinction between legal and illegal operations. We implemented a prototype system for a realistic use case, clustered J2EE applications. Our prototype is able to configure a firewall on each cluster node according to the system representation. When an illegal communication is detected, the *autonomic manager* quicly isolates the compromised nodes. Moreover, the overhead induced by our approach is very low and acceptable for high-performance data servers.

References

1. An architectural blueprint for autonomic computing. *IBM and Autonomic Computing*, April 2003. http://www-306.ibm.com/autonomic/pdfs/ACwpFinal.pdf.
2. C. Amza, E. Cecchet, A. Chanda, Alan L. Cox, S. Elnikety, R. Gil, J. Marguerite, K. Rajamani, and W. Zwaenepoel. Specification and Implementation of Dynamic Web Site Benchmarks. In *5th Annual IEEE Workshop on Workload Characterization*, 2002.

3. E. Bruneton, T. Coupaye, and J.B. Stefani. Recursive and dynamic software composition with sharing. In *Proceedings of the 7th ECOOP International Workshop on Component-Oriented Programming (WCOP'02)*, June 2002.

4. F. Cappello, F. Desprez, M. Dayde, E. Jeannot, Y. Jegou, S. Lanteri, N. Melab, R. Namyst, P. Primet, O. Richard, E. Caron, J. Leduc, and G. Mornet. Grid'5000: A large scale, reconfigurable, controlable and monitorable grid platform. In *Grid2005 6th IEEE/ACM International Workshop on Grid Computing*, 2005.

5. M. Costa, J Crowsoft, M. Castro, A. Rowstron, L. Zhou, L. Zhang, and P. Barham. Vigilante: end-to-end containment of Internet worms. In *SOSP '05: Proceedings of the Twentieth ACM Symposium on Operating Systems Principles*, pages 133–147, New York, NY, USA, 2005. ACM Press.

6. H. Debar, M. Dacier, and A. Wespi. Towards a taxonomy of intrusion-detection systems. *Computer Networks*, 31(9):805–822, 1999.

7. A.G. Ganek and T.A. Corbi. The dawning of the autonomic computing era. *IBM Systems Journal*, 40(1), 2003.

8. A. Goel, K. Po, K. Farhadi, Z. Li, and E. de Lara. The Taser intrusion recovery system. In *SOSP '05: Proceedings of the Twentieth ACM Symposium on Operating Systems Principles*, pages 163–176, New York, NY, USA, 2005. ACM Press.

9. Y. Huang and Sood A. Self-cleansing systems for intrusion containment. In *Workshop on Self-Healing, Adaptive and self-MANaged Systems (SHAMAN)*, 2002.

10. L. Lamport, R. Shostak, and M. Pease. The byzantine generals problem. In *Advances in Ultra-Dependable Distributed Systems, N. Suri, C. J. Walter, and M. M. Hugue (Eds.), IEEE Computer Society Press*. 1995.

11. Sun Microsystems. Java 2 platform enterprise edition (J2EE). http://java.sun.com/j2ee/.

12. Netfilter. Firewalling, NAT, and packet mangling under linux. http://www.nefilter.org.

13. A. Sundaram. An introduction to intrusion detection. *ACM Crossroads Student Magazine*, 2(4):3–7, 1996.

From Self- to Snap- Stabilization

Alain Cournier, Stéphane Devismes, and Vincent Villain

LaRIA CNRS FRE 2733
University of Picardie Jules Verne, Amiens, France
firstname.lastname@u-picardie.fr
http://www.laria.u-picardie.fr/~lastname

Abstract. A *snap-stabilizing* protocol, starting from any configuration, always behaves according to its specification. In this paper, we propose a light semi-automatic method allowing to snap-stabilize self-stabilizing wave protocols for arbitrary networks with a unique initiator. To that goal, we consider such a self-stabilizing protocol $\mathcal{A}$. We then slightly update $\mathcal{A}$ to obtain a protocol $\mathcal{B}$ that can be automatically transformed, using a black box protocol, into a snap-stabilizing protocol. $\mathcal{B}$ is easy to obtain from $\mathcal{A}$ compared to the design of a snap-stabilizing protocol.

1 Introduction

The quality of a distributed system depends on its tolerance to faults. Many fault-tolerant schemes have been proposed. For instance, *self-stabilization* [1] allows to design a system tolerating arbitrary transient faults. A self-stabilizing system, regardless of the initial states of the processors and messages initialy in the links, is guaranteed to converge into the intended behavior in finite time. Recently, a new paradigm called *snap-stabilization* has been introduced in [2]. A *snap-stabilizing* protocol guarantees that, starting from any configuration, it always behaves according to its specification. In other words, a snap-stabilizing protocol is a self-stabilizing protocol which stabilizes in 0 time unit. Designing and proving self- or snap- stabilizing protocols is usually a complicated task. That is why some protocols, called *transformers*, were proposed to automatically perform such a task, e.g., [3,4]. In [3], Katz and Perry design a protocol that transforms almost all non-self-stabilizing protocols into self-stabilizing protocols. In [4], the authors propose a *transformer* providing a snap-stabilizing version of any protocol which can be self-stabilized with the transformer of [3], but, this transformer is designed in a higher level model than the one used in [3]. The transformers of [3,4] use heavy mechanisms to transform an initial protocol into a self- or snap- stabilizing protocol and the overcost of the stabilization is often difficult to evaluate. Indeed, they use snapshots to regulary evaluate a predicate defined on the variables of the protocol to transform. This predicate characterizes the normal configurations of the system. This technique is used for preventing the system from deadlocks and livelocks. The main drawbacks of these solutions are: (*i*) such a predicate is generally difficult to formalize; (*ii*) the number of snapshots used by the transformer protocol cannot be bounded compared to

A.K. Datta and M. Gradinariu (Eds.): SSS 2006, LNCS 4280, pp. 199–213, 2006.
© Springer-Verlag Berlin Heidelberg 2006

the number of actions of the initial protocol. In this paper, we propose a light semi-automatic method allowing to snap-stabilize self-stabilizing wave protocols for arbitrary networks with a unique initiator. To that goal, we consider such a self-stabilizing protocol $\mathcal{A}$. We then slightly update $\mathcal{A}$ to obtain a protocol $\mathcal{B}$ that can be automatically transformed, using a black box protocol, into a snap-stabilizing protocol. $\mathcal{B}$ is easy to obtain from $\mathcal{A}$ compared to the design of a snap-stabilizing protocol. In contrast with the solution in [4], our black box does not use any snapshot to snap-stabilize $\mathcal{B}$ and keeps the same fairness as the protocol to transform. Finally, to show the feasibility of our method, we propose to transform a self-stabilizing depth-first token circulation of Huang and Chen [5] into a snap-stabilizing token circulation.

The rest of the paper is organized as follows. In Section 2, we describe the model. In Section 3, we present and justify how our black box works. A sketch of proof and the complexity analysis are provided in Section 4. We show in Section 5 how to snap-stabilize the protocol of [5]. Finally, we conclude in Section 6.

2   Preliminaries

We consider a *network* as an undirected connected rooted graph $G = (V,E,r)$ where V is a set of *processors*, E is the set of *bidirectional asynchronous commu-nication links*, and $r \in V$. The particular processor r, called *root*, corresponds to the protocol initiator. In the network, a communication link (p,q) exists if and only if p and q are neighbors. Every processor p can distinguish all its links. To simplify the presentation, we refer to a link (p,q) of a processor p by the *label* q. We assume that the labels of p, stored in the set Ng_p, are locally ordered by $\prec_p$. We also use the following notations: respectively, N is the size, Δ the degree, and D the diameter of the network. Our protocols are *semi-uniform*, i.e., each processor executes the same program except r. We consider a local shared memory model of computation (see [6]) where the program of every processor consists in a set of *shared variables* (henceforth, referred to as variables) and an *ordered finite set of actions* inducing a *priority*. This priority follows the order of appearance of the actions into the text of the protocol. A processor can write to its own variable only, and read its own variables and that of its neighbors. Each action is constitued as follows: $< label > :: < guard > \rightarrow < statement >$. The guard of an action in the program of p is a boolean expression involving variables of p and its neighbors. The statement of an action of p updates one or more variables of p. An action can be executed only if its guard is satisfied. The *state* of a processor is defined by the value of its variables. The *state* of a system is the product of the states of all processors. We will refer to the state of a processor and the system as a *(local) state* and *(global) configuration*, respec-tively. We note $\mathcal{C}$ the set of all configurations of the system. Let $\gamma \in \mathcal{C}$ and A an action of p ($p \in V$). A is said *enabled* at p in γ if and only if the guard of A is satisfied by p in γ. Processor p is said to be *enabled* in γ if and only if at least one action is enabled at p in γ. When several actions are simultaneously enabled at a processor p: only the priority enabled action can be activated. Let a distributed protocol $\mathcal{P}$ be a collection of binary transition relations denoted by $\mapsto$, on $\mathcal{C}$. An *execution* of a protocol $\mathcal{P}$ is a *maximal* sequence of configurations $e = (\gamma_0, \gamma_1, ..., \gamma_i, \gamma_{i+1}, ...)$ such that, $\forall i \geq 0$, $\gamma_i \mapsto \gamma_{i+1}$ (called a *step*) if γ_{i+1} exists, else γ_i is a terminal configuration. *Maximality* means that the sequence is either finite (and no action of $\mathcal{P}$ is enabled in the terminal configuration) or infinite. All executions considered here are assumed to be maximal. $\mathcal{E}$ is the set of all executions of $\mathcal{P}$. As we already said, each execution is decomposed into steps. Each step is shared into three sequential phases atomically executed: (i) every processor evaluates its guards, (ii) a *daemon* chooses some enabled processors, (iii) each chosen processor executes its priority enabled action. When the three phases are done, the next step begins. A *daemon* can be defined in terms of *fairness* and *distribution*. There exists several kinds of fairness assumption. In this paper, we consider the *strongly fairness*, *weakly fairness*, and *unfairness* assumption. Under a *strongly fair* daemon, every processor that is enabled infinitively often is chosen by the daemon infinitely often to execute an action. When a daemon is *weakly fair*, every continuously enabled processor is eventually chosen by the daemon. Finally, the *unfair* daemon is the weakest scheduling assumption: it can forever prevent a processor to execute an action except if it is the only enabled processor. To simplify the notation, we will denote (when necessary) the strongly fair, weakly fair, and unfair daemon by SF, WF, and UF. Concerning the *distribution*, we assume that the daemon is *distributed* meaning that, at each step, if one or more processors are enabled, then the daemon chooses at least one of these processors to execute an action. We consider that any processor p is *neutralized* in the step $\gamma_i \mapsto \gamma_{i+1}$ if p was *enabled* in γ_i and not enabled in γ_{i+1}, but did not execute any action in $\gamma_i \mapsto \gamma_{i+1}$. To compute the time complexity, we use the definition of *round* [7]. This definition captures the execution rate of the slowest processor in any execution. The 1st *round* of $e \in \mathcal{E}$, noted e', is the minimal prefix of e containing the execution of one action or the neutralization of every enabled processor from the initial configuration. Let e'' be the suffix of e such that $e = e'e''$. The 2nd *round* of e is the 1st round of e'', and so on.

Definition 1 (Wave Protocol [6]). *A* wave protocol *is a protocol $\mathcal{P}$ that satisfies the following requirements: (i) each execution of $\mathcal{P}$ (called* wave*) is finite and contains at least an action of* decision*; (ii) each action of* decision *is causally preceded by an action of each processor.*

Definition 2 (Snap-stabilization). *Let $\mathcal{T}$ be a task, and $\mathcal{S}_\mathcal{T}$ a specification of $\mathcal{T}$. A protocol $\mathcal{P}$ is snap-stabilizing for $\mathcal{S}_\mathcal{T}$ if and only if $\forall e \in \mathcal{E}$, e satisfies $\mathcal{S}_\mathcal{T}$.*

Consider a wave protocol having a unique initiator, r, and performing a specific task in a safe system. In the safe system, starting from a pre-defined configuration called *normal starting configuration*, r initiates the protocol by executing a special action called *initialization action*. This initialization occurs upon an external (w.r.t. the protocol) request. Before this request, all the processors are "asleep" (i.e., disabled). In particular, r is on standby of a request. Similary, at the termination of the protocol, the processors become asleep again until the next request occurs at the initiator. In contrast, in a self-stabilizing system, the protocols achieve a convergence to a specified behavior of the system in a finite time. So, the execution of the first waves of such a protocol may not satisfy its specification and, as a consequence, the waves have to be repeated so that the system eventually satisfies its specification. Hence, self-stabilizing protocols are inherently cyclic and the notion of request is simply kept in the background. On the contrary, the snap-stabilization guarantees that after the first initialization action, the execution of the protocol works as expected (i.e., according to its specification). Thus, snap-stabilization does not require to design cyclic protocols and the initialization of the protocols is similar to the one in a safe system, i.e., the initialization is assumed to occur only upon an external request (see [4] for further details). So, in our protocols, we will explicitly mention this external request using the shared variable $Req_r \in \{W,I,O\}$ (noted $\mathcal{P}.Req_r$ for the specific protocol $\mathcal{P}$). We consider Req_r as an input into the algorithm of the protocol initiator (r). $Req_r = W$ means that an execution of the protocol is required. When the initialization of the protocol occurs, Req_r switches from W to I meaning that r has taking in account of the request. Finally, Req_r switches from I to O at the termination of the wave meaning that the system is now ready to receive another request. Of course, the switching of Req_r from W to I and from I to O is managed by the task itself while the switching from O to W (which means that another execution of the protocol is required) is managed externally. Note that all other transitions (for instance, I to W) are forbidden. The external action, noted IR, that manages the switching from O to W is of the following form:

$$IR :: AppliReq(r) \wedge (Req_r = O) \rightarrow Req_r := W; AppliRelease_r;$$

$AppliReq(r)$ is a predicate which is true when an application of the initiator r needs an execution of the snap-stabilizing protocol. $AppliRelease_r$ is a macro which contains the code of the application that has to be executed when the system takes the request into account. In particular, this macro has to make $AppliReq(r)$ false. In the following, we will assume that, since satisfied, $AppliReq(r)$ is continuously satisfied until IR is executed.

From Definitions 1, 2, and the above discussion, follows:

Remark 1. Let $\mathcal{T}$ be a task, $\mathcal{S}_\mathcal{T}$ a specification of $\mathcal{T}$, and $\mathcal{P}$ a wave protocol with one initiator, r. To prove that $\mathcal{P}$ is snap-stabilizing for $\mathcal{S}_\mathcal{T}$, we must show that any execution of $\mathcal{P}$ satisfies two conditions: (i) since r requests a $\mathcal{P}$ wave, the requested $\mathcal{P}$ wave is initiated in a finite time; (ii) from any configuration where r has initiated a $\mathcal{P}$ wave, the system computes $\mathcal{T}$ according to $\mathcal{S}_\mathcal{T}$.

3   The Approach

Principle. Let $\mathcal{A}$ be a self-stabilizing protocol with a unique initiator, r, designed for stabilizing to a specific task $\mathcal{T}$. In addition, assume that the decision actions are at the root only. We want to snap-stabilize $\mathcal{A}$ without using the snapshot

---

Algorithm 1. $Reset(\mathcal{B})$ for $p = r$

Input: Ng_p: set of (locally) ordered neighbors of p;

Constants: $P_p = \perp$; $L_p = 0$;

Variables: $S_p \in \{B,F,P,C\}$; $Que_p \in \{Q,R,A\}$;

Macro: $Cld_p = \{q \in Ng_p :: (S_q \neq C) \wedge (P_q = p) \wedge (L_q = L_p + 1) \wedge [(S_q \neq S_p) \Rightarrow (S_p \in \{B,P\} \wedge S_q = F)]\}$;

Predicates:

$CF(p)$ ≡ $(\forall q \in Ng_p :: S_q \neq C)$

$Leaf(p)$ ≡ $[\forall q \in Ng_p :: (S_q \neq C) \Rightarrow (P_q \neq p)]$

$BLeaf(p)$ ≡ $(S_p = B) \wedge [\forall q \in Ng_p :: (P_q = p) \Rightarrow (S_q = F)]$

$AnsOk(p)$ ≡ $(Que_p = A) \wedge [\forall q \in Ng_p :: (S_q \neq C) \Rightarrow (Que_q = A)]$

$Bst(p)$ ≡ $(S_p = C) \wedge Leaf(p)$

$Fck(p)$ ≡ $BLeaf(p) \wedge CF(p) \wedge AnsOk(p)$

$PreC(p)$ ≡ $(S_p = F) \wedge [\forall q \in Ng_p :: (P_q = p) \Rightarrow (S_q \in \{F,C\})]$

$Clean(p)$ ≡ $(S_p = P) \wedge Leaf(p)$

$Requi(p)$ ≡ $(S_p \in \{B,F\}) \wedge [(S_p = B) \Rightarrow CF(p)] \wedge [[(Que_p = Q) \wedge (\forall q \in Ng_p :: (S_q \neq C) \Rightarrow (Que_q \in \{Q,R\}))]$
   $\vee\ [(Que_p = A) \wedge (\exists q \in Ng_p :: (S_q \neq C) \wedge ((Que_q = Q) \vee (q \in Cld_p \wedge Que_q = R)))]]$

$Ans(p)$ ≡ $(S_p \in \{B,F\}) \wedge [(S_p = B) \Rightarrow CF(p)] \wedge (Que_p = R)$
   $\wedge\ (\forall q \in Cld_p :: Que_q \in \{W,A\}) \wedge [\forall q \in Ng_p :: (S_q \neq C) \Rightarrow (Que_q \neq Q)]$

Actions:

PIF Part:

B-action ::	$(\mathcal{B}.Req_p = W) \wedge \mathcal{B}.End_p \wedge Bst(p)$	$\rightarrow S_p := B$; $Que_p := Q$; $\mathcal{B}.Req_p := I$;
F-action ::	$Fck(p)$	$\rightarrow S_p := F$; $\mathcal{B}.Init_p$; $\mathcal{B}.End_p := false$;
P-action ::	$PreC(p)$	$\rightarrow S_p := P$;
C-action ::	$Clean(p)$	$\rightarrow S_p := C$;
T-action ::	$(\mathcal{B}.Req_p = I) \wedge \mathcal{B}.End_p \wedge (S_p = C)$	$\rightarrow \mathcal{B}.Req_p := O$;

Question Part:

QR-action ::	$Requi(p)$	$\rightarrow Que_p := R$;
QA-action ::	$Ans(p)$	$\rightarrow Que_p := A$;

---

techniques. In [3,4], the snapshots are used for detecting deadlocks and livelocks in the execution of the initial protocol. Since $\mathcal{A}$ is self-stabilizing, we know that, starting from any configuration, it will never generates deadlocks or livelocks. We now propose to slightly modify $\mathcal{A}$ to obtain a protocol $\mathcal{B}$ which is automatically snap-stabilized by a black box protocol. From now on, we note $SSBB(\mathcal{B})$ the snap-stabilizing version of $\mathcal{B}$ obtained with our Snap-Stabilizing Black Box ($SSBB$). By Remark 1, the code of $\mathcal{B}$ must insure the following property:

(i) Starting from any configuration and upon an external request on r, r eventually initiates $SSBB(\mathcal{B})$.

(ii) As soon as $SSBB(\mathcal{B})$ is initiated, it executes the task $\mathcal{T}$ as expected.

First, by (i), starting from any configuration, the system must reach a configuration from which $SSBB(\mathcal{B})$ can properly start. This implies that when the root requests an execution of $SSBB(\mathcal{B})$, $SSBB(\mathcal{B})$ must start in a finite time but without aborting a previously initiated computation of $\mathcal{T}$. One way to get this property is to use in $\mathcal{B}$ a variable $\mathcal{B}.End_r$ such that when r is ready to decide in $\mathcal{A}$, then r is also ready to decide in $\mathcal{B}$ and sets $\mathcal{B}.End_r$ to true. Also, since $\mathcal{B}.End_r$ is equal to true, the initialization actions of $\mathcal{B}$ (at r) have to be disabled until $SSBB(\mathcal{B})$ can execute the computation of $\mathcal{T}$ as expected (ii). To that goal, we have just to modify the guards of the initialization actions of $\mathcal{A}$ so that they become disabled when $\mathcal{B}.End_r = true$. $\mathcal{B}.End_r$ will be set to false by $SSBB(\mathcal{B})$ when the system will be in a configuration from which $SSBB(\mathcal{B})$ can execute the computation of $\mathcal{T}$ as expected (ii). Assuming the existence of

$\mathcal{B}.End_r$ and the associated modifications in $\mathcal{B}$, we now just need to reset the variables of $\mathcal{B}$ since $\mathcal{B}.End_r$ is true in order to verify (ii). To that goal, $\forall p \in V$, all the variables assignments required to generate a *normal starting configuration* of $\mathcal{A}$ have to be stored in a macro of $\mathcal{B}$ noted $\mathcal{B}.Init_p$. For sake of clarity, we note $\mathcal{B}.Init$ the set of the macros $\mathcal{B}.Init_p$ defined on all the processors p. Using $\mathcal{B}.Init$, the reset phase is trivially initiated at the initialization action of $\mathcal{SSBB}(\mathcal{B})$ and, as soon as the reset terminates, $\mathcal{B}.End_r$ is set to false and $\mathcal{B}$ executes the task $\mathcal{T}$ as $\mathcal{A}$ in a non-faulty situation. In particular, this means that the initialization action of $\mathcal{SSBB}(\mathcal{B})$ corresponds to the the initialization action of reset and, of course, $\mathcal{SSBB}(\mathcal{B})$ will take in account of the requests for $\mathcal{B}$ (using $\mathcal{B}.Req_r$) instead of $\mathcal{B}$ itself. $\mathcal{SSBB}(\mathcal{B})$ will reset the $\mathcal{B}$ variables (using $\mathcal{B}.Init$) so that the system reaches a *normal starting configuration* of $\mathcal{A}$ and, then, give the execution control to $\mathcal{B}$ so that it performs the task $\mathcal{T}$. A well-known technique to perform a reset in distributed systems is based on the *Propagation of Information with Feedback* (PIF). Some PIF protocols for arbitrary networks have been proposed in the snap-stabilizing literature, e.g., [8,9]. A PIF scheme can be informally described as follows: the initiator, r, starts the protocol by broadcasting a message m (*broadcast phase*), then, $\forall p \in V \setminus \{r\}$, p will send an acknowledgment to r for the receipt of m (*feedback phase*). Using the PIF scheme, the reset protocol can be performed as follows: (i) r broadcasts an "abort" message, (ii) upon the reception of the message, the processors abort the execution of $\mathcal{B}$, (iii) finally, the processors reset their $\mathcal{B}$ variables during the feedback phase. To implement $\mathcal{SSBB}$, we need to use a snap-stabilizing PIF protocol working under a distributed unfair daemon. Indeed, we want to apply our technique to self-stabilizing protocols working with any daemon, so, we need a reset protocol that works with the most general daemon. Such a protocol is provided in [9].

Snap-Stabilizing PIF. A snap-stabilizing PIF protocol satisfies the following specification: starting from any configuration, when r has a message m to broadcast, it starts the broadcast in a finite time. Then, $\forall p \in V \setminus \{r\}$, p will both receive m and send an acknowledgment (for the receipt of m) which will reach r in a finite time.

Theorem 1 ([9]). *The PIF protocol proposed in [9] is snap-stabilizing under a distributed unfair daemon.*

As the distributed unfair daemon is the most general daemon, Theorem 1 implies that the protocol of [9], called $\mathcal{PIF}$, works with any daemon. The another important consequence of Theorem 1 is that, starting from any configuration, each PIF wave performed by $\mathcal{PIF}$ is bounded in terms of steps. We now roughly present the main actions and variables of $\mathcal{PIF}$ (see [9] for details). $\mathcal{PIF}$ is divided in three parts: the PIF, question, and correction parts. The PIF part is the most important part of the protocol because it contains the actions related to the three phases of a PIF wave: the broadcast phase, the feedback phase following the broadcast phase, and the cleaning phase which cleans the trace of the feedback phase so that the root is ready to broadcast a new message.

The two other parts of the algorithm implement two mechanisms allowing the snap-stabilization of the PIF part. Due to the lack of space, we do not present these mechanisms here. Informally, the PIF part maintains in every processor p a variable crucial for $\mathcal{SSBB}$: S_p. Indeed, S_p allows to know in which phase of the PIF the processor p is. S_p is set to B when p switches to the broadcast phase (B-action). Then, S_p is set to F when p switches to the feedback phase (F-action). The cleaning phase is managed with two states: P and C. After r detects the end of the feedback phase (r is the last processor which switches to the feedback phase), r initiates the propagation of the P value into the S variables following the computed spanning tree in order to inform all the processor of this termination (P-action). Then, the processors successively switches to C (C-action) in a bottom up fashion (from the leaves of the spanning tree to r) meaning that they now ready to receive another broadcast message. Hence, the PIF wave terminates when r sets S_r to C (C-action). Finally, note that two more states exists in S_p for $p \neq r$: EB and EF. But, they are used by the correction part only. So, we do not explain the goal of these states here.

Property 1. From [9], follows:

1. After r initiates a broadcast (B-action), the system eventually reaches a configuration where every processor is in the feedback phase associated to the broadcast of r.
2. From any configuration, r executes B-action in at most $9N - 1$ rounds and $O(\Delta \times N^3)$ steps.
3. From any configuration, a complete PIF wave costs at most $15N - 3$ rounds and $O(\Delta \times N^3)$ steps.

Remark 2. By Property 1, from any configuration, r executes B-action at most $9N - 1$ rounds. Actually, this time complexity corresponds to the following worst case: the maximal number of rounds starting from any configuration before the system reaches a configuration where B-action at r is the only enabled action of the system (see the technical report for details [10]).

SSBB Protocol. To build $\mathcal{SSBB}(\mathcal{B})$, we use the following composition technique. This composition technique is closed to the *hierarchical composition* of Gouda and Herman [11]. Let P_1 and P_2 be two protocols. The composition of P_1 and P_2, noted $P_2 \circ_{|G} P_1$, is the program satisfying the following conditions:

- $P_2 \circ_{|G} P_1$ contains all the variables and actions of P_1 and P_2.
- G is a predicate defined on the variables of P_1.
- Any action $L_i :: H_i \to S_i$ in P_2 is replaced by $L_i :: G \wedge H_i \to S_i$ in $P_2 \circ_{|G} P_1$.

Following these rules, $\mathcal{SSBB}(\mathcal{B}) = \mathcal{B} \circ_{|Ok(p)} Reset(\mathcal{B})$ with $Ok(p) \equiv (S_p = C)$. $Reset(\mathcal{B})$ is a slightly modified $\mathcal{PIF}$ (Algorithms 1 and 2). It is used for resetting the $\mathcal{B}$ variables when it is necessary. To that goal, we modify the guard of its initialization action: B-action at r (the initialization action of $\mathcal{SSBB}(\mathcal{B})$) so that it is enabled only when a request for $\mathcal{B}$ occurs at the root ($\mathcal{B}.Req_r = W$) and $\mathcal{B}.End_r = true$ (to avoid the aborting a previous initiated wave of $\mathcal{B}$). Also, we modify the F-action to reset the $\mathcal{B}$ variables using $\mathcal{B}.Init_p$ ($\forall p \in V$) and to set $\mathcal{B}.End_r$ to false (for the root only and so that the actions of $\mathcal{B}$ at r will be unlocked at the end of the reset) during the feedback phase. We use the predicate $Ok(p)$ in the composition so that any processor p aborts its local execution of $\mathcal{B}$ when receiving the reset and until the local termination of the reset at p. Indeed, we already know that p continuously satisfies $S_p \neq C$ during its participation to a reset. So, while p participates to a reset, $Ok(p)$ is false and any action of $\mathcal{B}$ in $SSBB(\mathcal{B})$ is disabled at p. Finally, we add an action, noted $T\text{-}action$, so that r switches $\mathcal{B}.Req_r$ from I to O at the termination of each wave of $SSBB(\mathcal{B})$.

Algorithm 2. $Reset(\mathcal{B})$ for $p \neq r$

Input: Ng_p: set of (locally) ordered neighbors of p;

Variables: $S_p \in \{B,F,P,C,EB,EF\}$; $P_p \in Ng_p$; $L_p \in \mathbb{N}$; $Que_p \in \{Q,R,W,A\}$;

Macros:
$Cld_p \ = \{q \in Ng_p :: (S_q \neq C) \wedge (P_q = p) \wedge (L_q = L_p + 1) \wedge [(S_q \neq S_p) \Rightarrow ((S_p \in \{B,P\} \wedge S_q = F) \vee (S_p = EB))]\}$;
$PPot_p = \{q \in Ng_p :: S_q = B \}$;
$Pot_p \ = \{q \in Ng_p :: \forall q' \in PPot_p, L_q \leq L_{q'} \}$;

Predicates:
$CF(p) \qquad \equiv (\forall q \in Ng_p :: S_q \neq C)$
$Leaf(p) \qquad \equiv [\forall q \in Ng_p :: (S_q \neq C) \Rightarrow (P_q \neq p)]$
$BLeaf(p) \quad \equiv (S_p = B) \wedge [\forall q \in Ng_p :: (P_q = p) \Rightarrow (S_q = F)]$
$AnsOk(p) \quad \equiv (Que_p = A) \wedge [\forall q \in Ng_p :: (S_q \neq C) \Rightarrow (Que_q = A)]$
$GoodS(p) \quad \equiv (S_p = C) \vee [(S_{P_p} \neq S_p) \Rightarrow ((S_{P_p} = EB) \vee (S_p = F \wedge S_{P_p} \in \{B,P\}))]$
$GoodL(p) \quad \equiv (S_p \neq C) \Rightarrow (L_p = L_{P_p} + 1)$
$AbR(p) \qquad \equiv \neg GoodS(p) \vee \neg GoodL(p)$
$EFAbR(p) \equiv (S_p = EF) \wedge AbR(p) \wedge [\forall q \in Ng_p :: (P_q = p \wedge L_q > L_p) \Rightarrow (S_q \in \{EF,C\})]$
$EBst(p) \qquad \equiv (S_p \in \{B,F,P\}) \wedge [\neg AbR(p) \Rightarrow (S_{P_p} = EB)]$
$EFck(p) \qquad \equiv (S_p = EB) \wedge [\forall q \in Ng_p :: (P_q = p \wedge L_q > L_p) \Rightarrow (S_q \in \{EF,C\})]$
$Bst(p) \qquad \equiv (S_p = C) \wedge (Pot_p \neq \emptyset) \wedge Leaf(p)$
$Fck(p) \qquad \equiv BLeaf(p) \wedge CF(p) \wedge AnsOk(p)$
$PreC(p) \qquad \equiv (S_p = F) \wedge (S_{P_p} = P) \wedge [\forall q \in Ng_p :: (P_q = p) \Rightarrow (S_q \in \{F,C\})]$
$Clean(p) \qquad \equiv (S_p = P) \wedge Leaf(p)$
$Requi(p) \qquad \equiv (S_p \in \{B,F\}) \wedge [(S_p = B) \Rightarrow CF(p)] \wedge [[(Que_p = Q) \wedge (\forall q \in Ng_p :: (S_q \neq C) \Rightarrow (Que_q \in \{Q,R\}))] \vee [(Que_p \in \{W,A\}) \wedge (\exists q \in Ng_p :: (S_q \neq C) \wedge ((Que_q = Q) \vee (q \in Cld_p \wedge Que_q = R)))]]$
$Wait(p) \qquad \equiv (S_p \in \{B,F\}) \wedge [(S_p = B) \Rightarrow CF(p)] \wedge (Que_p = R) \wedge (Que_{P_p} = R) \wedge (\forall q \in Cld_p :: Que_q \in \{W,A\}) \wedge (\forall q \in Ng_p :: (S_q \neq C) \Rightarrow (Que_q \neq Q))$
$Ans(p) \qquad \equiv (S_p \in \{B,F\}) \wedge [(S_p = B) \Rightarrow CF(p)] \wedge (Que_p = W) \wedge (Que_{P_p} = A) \wedge (\forall q \in Cld_p :: Que_q \in \{W,A\}) \wedge (\forall q \in Ng_p :: (S_q \neq C) \Rightarrow (Que_q \neq Q))$

Actions:
Correction Part:
$\quad EC\text{-}action :: EFAbR(p) \rightarrow S_p := C$;
$\quad EB\text{-}action :: EBst(p) \quad \rightarrow S_p := EB$;
$\quad EF\text{-}action :: EFck(p) \quad \rightarrow S_p := EF$;
PIF Part:
$\quad B\text{-}action \quad :: Bst(p) \qquad \rightarrow S_p := B; P_p := \min_{\prec_p}(Pot_p); L_p := L_{P_p} + 1; Que_p := Q$;
$\quad F\text{-}action \quad :: Fck(p) \qquad \rightarrow S_p := F; \mathcal{B}.Init_p$;
$\quad P\text{-}action \quad :: PreC(p) \quad \rightarrow S_p := P$;
$\quad C\text{-}action \quad :: Clean(p) \quad \rightarrow S_p := C$;
Question Part:
$\quad QR\text{-}action :: Requi(p) \quad \rightarrow Que_p := R$;
$\quad QW\text{-}action :: Wait(p) \qquad \rightarrow Que_p := W$;
$\quad QA\text{-}action :: Ans(p) \qquad \rightarrow Que_p := A$;

---

4   Correctness

Let $\mathcal{A}$ be self-stabilizing wave protocol under a daemon $\mathcal{D}$ such that $\mathcal{A}$ has a unique initiator (r) and such that the decision actions of $\mathcal{A}$ are at r only. Let $\mathcal{T}$ be the task solved by $\mathcal{A}$ in a self-stabilizing manner. Let $\mathcal{B}$ the modified version of $\mathcal{A}$ according to the explanation provided in Section 3. We now prove that $SSBB(\mathcal{B})$ is snap-stabilizing for the specification of $\mathcal{T}$ under $\mathcal{D}$ ($\mathcal{D} \in \{SF, WF, UF\}$). First, as $\mathcal{A}$ is designed to solve the specific task $\mathcal{T}$ only, we make the following remark about $\mathcal{B}$:

Remark 3. $\mathcal{B}$ does not write into the $Reset(\mathcal{B})$ variables.

We now show that $SSBB(\mathcal{B})$ is a *fair composition* of $Reset(\mathcal{B})$ and $\mathcal{B}$.

Definition 3 (Fair Execution [6]). *An execution e of the composite protocol $P_2 \circ_{|G} P_1$ is fair w.r.t. P_i ($i \in \{1,2\}$), if one of these conditions holds: (i) e is finite, (ii) e contains infinitely many steps of P_i, or (iii) e contains an infinite suffix in which no step of P_i is enabled.*

From Assumption 3, it is easy to see that the number of steps of each protocol in a wave of the composition is finite, so we can deduce the following theorem.

Theorem 2. *$SSBB(\mathcal{B})$ is a fair composition of Algorithms $Reset(\mathcal{B})$ and $\mathcal{B}$.*

Since Algorithm $\mathcal{A}$ allows r to restart the protocol infinitely often it is clear that $\mathcal{B}$ sets $\mathcal{B}.End_r$ to $false$ in a finite time. So, the system needs a computation of $\mathcal{T}$, $SSBB(\mathcal{B})$ is initiated in a finite time and the two next lemmas are proved.

Lemma 1. *Starting from any configuration where $\mathcal{B}.Req_r = W$, $SSBB(\mathcal{B})$ is initiated in a finite time.*

The next lemma shows that since r requests a computation of $\mathcal{T}$, the system eventually takes this request into account by executing $\mathcal{B}.Req_r := W$.

Lemma 2. *Starting from any configuration where r requests a $SSBB(\mathcal{B})$ wave, r executes IR in a finite time.*

By Lemmas 1 and 2, the following theorem holds. This theorem means that, since r requests an execution of $SSBB(\mathcal{B})$, $SSBB(\mathcal{B})$ is initiated in a finite time.

Theorem 3. *Starting from any configuration where r requests a $SSBB(\mathcal{B})$ wave, the requested $SSBB(\mathcal{B})$ wave is eventually initiated.*

The next theorem shows that each computation of $\mathcal{T}$ initiated by r is executed as expected. This result is based on the snap-stabilizing reset of $\mathcal{B}$ when r initiates $SSBB(\mathcal{B})$.

Theorem 4. *From any configuration where r initiates $SSBB(\mathcal{B})$, the system computes $\mathcal{T}$ as expected.*

By Remark 1, Theorems 3 and 4, follows:

Theorem 5. *$SSBB(\mathcal{B})$ is snap-stabilizing for the specification of $\mathcal{T}$ under $\mathcal{D}$.*

4.1   Complexity Analysis

Space Complexity. Let $\mathcal{M}(\mathcal{A})$ be the memory requirement of $\mathcal{A}$. $\mathcal{B}$ differs from $\mathcal{A}$ by just a boolean at r. So, the memory requirement of $\mathcal{B}$ is in the same order than $\mathcal{A}$ and by taking into account of $Reset(\mathcal{B})$, follows:

Theorem 6. *The memory requirement of $SSBB(\mathcal{B})$ is $O(\log(N) + \log(\Delta) + \mathcal{M}(\mathcal{A}))$ bits per processor.*

Time Complexity. In the following, we assume that $\mathcal{A}$ is self-stabilizing under $\mathcal{D}$ such that $\mathcal{D} \in \{WF, UF\}$. So, let $R_1(\mathcal{A})$ be the maximal number of rounds starting from any configuration before r decides in $\mathcal{A}$ and let $R_2(\mathcal{A})$ be the maximal number of rounds that $\mathcal{A}$ requires to perform $\mathcal{T}$ starting from the configuration generated by $\mathcal{B}.Init$.

Theorem 7. *If $\mathcal{A}$ is self-stabilizing under $\mathcal{D}$ such that $\mathcal{D} \in \{WF, UF\}$, then, starting from any configuration where r requests a $SSBB(\mathcal{B})$ wave, the requested $SSBB(\mathcal{B})$ wave is initiated in $O(N + R_1(\mathcal{A}) + R_2(\mathcal{A}))$ rounds.*

Proof. Assume that, from a configuration γ_i, r requests a wave of $SSBB(\mathcal{B})$ (i.e., $AppliReq(r)$ is satisfied). According to $\mathcal{B}.Req_r$, three cases are possible:

- $\mathcal{B}.Req_r = O$ in γ_i. In such a configuration, IR is enabled (the guard of IR is $AppliReq(r) \wedge (\mathcal{B}.Req_r = O)$). Also, no action of $SSBB(\mathcal{B})$ can modify $\mathcal{B}.Req_r$ until $\mathcal{B}.Req_r$ is set to W by IR (see Algorithms 1 and 2). So, IR is continuously enabled at r and, r executes IR, i.e., $\mathcal{B}.Req_r := W$, in at most one round. Then, $\mathcal{B}.Req_r$ is continuously equal to W until r initiates $SSBB(\mathcal{B})$ by $B\text{-}action$ (see Algorithms 1 and 2). Also, as $\mathcal{B}$ does not write into the $Reset(\mathcal{B})$ variables (Assumption 3), in the worst case, the system reaches a configuration γ_j from which $Bst(r)$ is continuously satisfied and no action of $Reset(\mathcal{B})$ different of $B\text{-}action$ at r is enabled until r executes $B\text{-}action$ in at most $9N - 2$ rounds by Property 1 (Claim 2) and Remark 2. This configuration corresponds to a configuration of $\mathcal{PIF}$ where every processor are waiting for a new broadcast, i.e., $\forall p \in V, S_p = C$. Now, in at most $R_1(\mathcal{A})$ rounds from γ_j, the system reaches a configuration γ_k from which $\mathcal{B}.End_r$ is continuously true. Thus, $B\text{-}action$ becomes continuously enabled at r from γ_k and r executes $B\text{-}action$ in the next round. Hence, starting from any configuration where $\mathcal{B}.Req_r = O$, $SSBB(\mathcal{B})$ is initiated in at most $9N + R_1(\mathcal{A})$ rounds.
- $\mathcal{B}.Req_r = I$ in γ_i. As $\mathcal{B}$ does not write into the $Reset(\mathcal{B})$ variables (Assumption 3), in the worst case, the system reaches a configuration γ_j from which $Bst(r)$ is continuously satisfied and no action of $Reset(\mathcal{B})$ different of $B\text{-}action$ at r is enabled until r executes $B\text{-}action$ in at most $9N - 2$ rounds by Property 1 (Claim 2) and Remark 2. This configuration corresponds to a configuration of $\mathcal{PIF}$ where every processor are waiting for a new broadcast, i.e., $\forall p \in V, S_p = C$. Then, in at most $R_1(\mathcal{A})$ rounds from γ_j, the system reaches a configuration from which $\mathcal{B}.End_r$ is continuously true. As $B\text{-}action$ is disabled until $\mathcal{B}.Req_r = W$, two rounds are necessary so that

$B.Req_r$ switches from I to O by T-action $(Bst(r) \Rightarrow (S_r = C))$ and from O to W by Action IR. Then, B-action will be continuously enabled at r and r will execute it in the next round. Hence, starting from any configuration where $B.Req_r = I$, $SSBB(\mathcal{B})$ is initiated in at most $9N + R_1(\mathcal{A}) + 1$ rounds.

- $B.Req_r = W$ in γ_i. In this case, the system has to perform a complete $SSBB(\mathcal{B})$ wave before r satisfies $B.Req_r = O$. A $SSBB(\mathcal{B})$ wave becomes by a reset of the $\mathcal{B}$ variables (a $Reset(\mathcal{B})$ wave). $\mathcal{B}$ does not write into the $Reset(\mathcal{B})$ variables by Assumption 3. So, actions of $Reset(\mathcal{B})$ are executed like in PIF except for B-action at r (which now also depends on $B.End_r$). So, compared to the round complexities of a complete PIF wave (at most $15N - 3$ rounds, by Property 1 (Claim 3) and similarly to the previous cases, we have an additional cost of $R_1(\mathcal{A})$ rounds before $SSBB(\mathcal{B})$ starts. After the initialization action (B-action at r), $B.Req_r = I$ and $Reset(\mathcal{B})$ works with a same cost than PIF. So, the cost of the reset is globally at most $15N + R_1(\mathcal{A}) - 3$ rounds. After the reset, the system is in the configuration generated by $B.Init$ ($SSBB(\mathcal{B})$ is snap-stabilizing by Theorem 5) and $R_2(\mathcal{A})$ additional rounds are necessary to perform the specific task $\mathcal{T}$. Finally, after performing $\mathcal{T}$, $SSBB(\mathcal{B})$ terminates the wave with T-action: $B.Req_r := O$ (this latter action is executed in at most one round). After T-action, the system is in a configuration where $\forall p \in V$, $S_p = C$, i.e., the normal starting configuration of PIF (indeed, Property 1 implies that the abnormal behavior related to PIF are erased from the system during the first wave), $B.Req_r = O$, and $B.End_r = true$. From such a configuration, the root executes IR followed by B-action in the two next steps (resp. rounds): they are the only enabled action of the system. Hence, starting from any configuration where $B.Req_r = W$, $SSBB(\mathcal{B})$ is initiated in at most $15N + R_1(\mathcal{A}) + R_2(\mathcal{A})$ rounds.

□

Corollary 1. *If $\mathcal{A}$ is self-stabilizing under $\mathcal{D}$ such that $\mathcal{D} \in \{WF, UF\}$, then, starting from any configuration, a complete requested $SSBB(\mathcal{B})$ wave is executed in $O(N + R_1(\mathcal{A}) + R_2(\mathcal{A}))$ rounds.*

For the following result, we assume that $\mathcal{A}$ is self-stabilizing under $\mathcal{D} = UF$. We have proved that, if $\mathcal{A}$ is self-stabilizing under $\mathcal{D} = UF$, then $SSBB(\mathcal{B})$ is snap-stabilizing under $\mathcal{D} = UF$. This means, in particular, that $\mathcal{B}$ can only execute a finite number of actions between each action of $Reset(\mathcal{B})$. Actually, this number of actions, noted $S(\mathcal{A})$, is equal to the maximal number of steps starting from any configuration so that $\mathcal{A}$ decides and then reaches a configuration from which r executes an initialization action (n.b., in the worst case, the unfair daemon prevents $\mathcal{A}$ to execute an initialization action until the system reaches a configuration where only the initialization actions are enabled). Actually, in $\mathcal{B}$, this number corresponds to the maximal number of actions that $\mathcal{B}$ can execute to set $B.End_r$ to $true$ and then reaches a configuration where none of its actions are enabled (the initialization actions are disabled because $B.End_r = true$).

Theorem 8. *If $\mathcal{A}$ is self-stabilizing under $\mathcal{D} = UF$, then, starting from any configuration where r requests a $SSBB(\mathcal{B})$ wave, the requested $SSBB(\mathcal{B})$ wave is initiated in $O(\Delta \times N^3 \times S(\mathcal{A}))$ steps.*

Proof. In the proof of Theorem 7, we have seen that, in the worst case, a requested $SSBB(\mathcal{B})$ wave is initiated after a complete non-requested wave of $SSBB(\mathcal{B})$. By Property 1 (Claim 3), we know that this non-requested wave contains $O(\Delta \times N^3)$ actions of $Reset(\mathcal{B})$ (i.e., the steps complexities of $\mathcal{PIF}$ provided in [10] except for a constant factor due to the T-action). Also, we have stated that at most $S(\mathcal{A})$ actions of $\mathcal{B}$ are executed between each action of $Reset(\mathcal{B})$. Hence, a loose estimate of the delay to start a requested $SSBB(\mathcal{B})$ wave is the product of these two complexities and the theorem holds. $\square$

Corollary 2. *If $\mathcal{A}$ is self-stabilizing under $\mathcal{D} = UF$, then, starting from any configuration, a complete requested $SSBB(\mathcal{B})$ wave is executed in $O(\Delta \times N^3 \times S(\mathcal{A}))$ steps.*

5   Example

In this section, we propose to snap-stabilize the self-stabilizing depth-first token circulation $(DFTC)$ protocol of Huang and Chen [5] using our transformer. In the following, the protocol of Huang and Chen will be denoted by $\mathcal{DFS}$.

Protocol $\mathcal{DFS}$. In arbitrary rooted networks, a $DFTC$ protocol works as follows: a token is first created at the root and, then, is passed from one processor to another in the depth-first order such that every processor eventually gets it during a single traversal. From [5], follows:

Theorem 9 ([5]). *$\mathcal{DFS}$ is a self-stabilizing $DFTC$ protocol assuming a weakly fair daemon.*

Informally, $\mathcal{DFS}$ is divided in two parts. The first part manages the token circulation strictly speaking. The other part handles abnormal behaviors due to the initial configuration. We first focus on the token circulation part. This part maintains two variables: D and C. D is a *descendant* pointer variable; C, a *color* variable. The token circulation uses two colors: 1 and 2. At the beginning of a new circulation, the root switches to a color different from the color of all the other processors. A processor having the token searches its neighbors to find one with a different color. The processor then passes the token to the neighbor if such a neighbor exists. Otherwise, it backtracks the token to its parent - the processor which passed the token to it. A processor changes its color to the color of its parent when its receives the token. In this way, all visited processors in the current circulation have the same color of the root, and all unvisited processors have a different color. The descendant relationship is indicated by variable D and this relationship is destroyed by letting $D_p := NULL$ when the token backtracks from p. Starting from the root and tracing through the descendant pointers, a *segment* of processors can be described with the token on the *front* of it. The segment lengthens when the token moves to an unvisited processor, and shrinks when the token backtracks. The token finally backtracks to the root when all the processors are visited. The root then changes its color and initiates a new circulation. We now explain the error handling strategy. First, due to the initial configuration, the D value of some processors may describe a cycle. A *level* variable L is thus used for detecting such cycles. The level of the root is fixed to 0. Levels of others processors have a value from 1 to $n-1$. During a circulation, a processor computes its level when it receive the current token for the first time: its level is set to one plus the level of its parent. When a processor p is in a segment and does not satisfy $L_p = L_q + 1$ where q is its parent, it know that it is in a cycle. So, p break the circle by setting D_p to $NULL$. Then, the system may contain some illegal segments, i.e., the segment rooted at another processor than r. To erase such illegal segments, the protocol uses an additionnal color: $ERROR$. The root of an illegal segment knows it is in an error state and hence changes its color to $ERROR$. The error color then propagates along the D pointers to the front of the segment. When the parent of the front processor sees the color of the front processor is already changed to $ERROR$, it drops the front processor away by setting the pointer D to $NULL$. The dropped processor then recovers itself by changing its color to a normal one. Repeating the dropping and recovering process will correct the processors on the illegal segments.

How to snap-stabilize $\mathcal{DFS}$ using $\mathcal{SSBB}$. First, we know that:

- $\mathcal{DFS}$ is a protocol with a unique initiator: r.
- The decision actions of $\mathcal{DFS}$ occurs at r only: the token finally backtracks to the root when all the processors are visited.

So, by Theorem 5, we know that a slightly modified version of $\mathcal{DFS}$ can be snap-stabilized by $\mathcal{SSBB}$. According to the principles exposed in Section 3, we now explain how to modify $\mathcal{DFS}$ into $\mathcal{DFS}'$ such that $\mathcal{SSBB}(\mathcal{DFS}')$ is a snap-stabilizing $DFTC$ protocol assuming a weakly fair daemon:

1. A boolean variable End_r must be declared in $\mathcal{DFS}$.
2. In $\mathcal{DFS}$, r decides when setting D_r to $NULL$. So, we must modify each action of $\mathcal{DFS}$ such that $D_r := NULL$ appears in its statement so that each time $D_r := NULL$ is executed, $End_r := true$ is also executed.
3. We add the condition $\neg End_r$ at the guard of the initialization of the token circulation action at r.
4. Finally, we know that a normal starting configuration of $\mathcal{DFS}$ satisfies $\forall p, q \in V$, $D_p = NULL \land C_p = C_q \land C_p \neq ERROR$. So, a normal starting configuration of $\mathcal{DFS}$ can be the following: $\forall p \in V$, $D_p = NULL \land C_p = 1$. Hence, we can define in $\mathcal{DFS}$ the macro $Init_p$ $(\forall p \in V)$ with the following assignments: $D_p := NULL; C_p := 1$.

With such modifications, we obtain a protocol $\mathcal{DFS}'$ and, by Theorem 5, the following theorem holds:

Theorem 10. $\mathcal{SSBB}(\mathcal{DFS}')$ *is a snap-stabilizing $DFTC$ protocol assuming a weakly fair daemon.*

$\mathcal{DFS}$ of Huang and Chen does not works assuming an unfair daemon. Indeed, under an unfair daemon, a possible execution of $\mathcal{DFS}$ is the following: the protocol can perform infinitively often uncomplete token circulation because some isolated processors p satisfying $D_p = NULL \land C_p = ERROR$ remains in the network. This is due to the fact that a processor that holds the token from the root simply ignores its neighbors such that $D = NULL \land C = ERROR$. However, starting from any configuration, if the unfair daemon eventually blocks the progression the legal segment, then this blocking can last only a finite number of steps because the number of actions that can be executed, the actions on the legal segment apart, is finite. So, this means that the unfair daemon cannot prevent forever the tokens from the root to circulate in the network. This also implies that the unfair daemon cannot prevent forever the root to decide. Transposed to $\mathcal{DFS}'$, these properties insures that:

1. Only a finite number of actions of $\mathcal{DFS}'$ can be executed before $End_r :=$ true.
2. Since $End_r = true$, only a finite number of actions of $\mathcal{DFS}'$ can be executed before $Reset(\mathcal{DFS}')$ moves (indeed, since $End_r = true$, the initialization action of $\mathcal{DFS}'$ are disabled until F-action at r sets End_r to false).

Clearly, 1. and 2. implies the following theorem:

Theorem 11. $SSBB(\mathcal{DFS}')$ is a snap-stabilizing DFTC protocol assuming an unfair daemon.

By Theorem 7, we know that, starting from any configuration, a requested wave of $SSBB(\mathcal{DFS}')$ is initiated in $O(N + R_1(\mathcal{DFS}) + R_2(\mathcal{DFS}))$ where $R_1(\mathcal{DFS})$ is the maximal number of rounds starting from any configuration before r decides in $\mathcal{DFS}$ and $R_2(\mathcal{DFS})$ be the maximal number of rounds that $\mathcal{DFS}$ requires to perform a $DFTC$ starting from a configuration γ_i where $\forall p \in V$, $D_p = NULL \land C_p = 1$. In the same way, by Corollary 1, starting from any configuration, a complete requested wave of $SSBB(\mathcal{DFS}')$ is executed in $O(N + R_1(\mathcal{DFS}) + R_2(\mathcal{DFS}))$. Clearly, starting from any configuration, r decides in $\mathcal{DFS}$ in $O(N)$ rounds and starting from γ_i, a $DFTC$ is also performed in $O(N)$ rounds. So, $R_1(\mathcal{DFS})$ and $R_2(\mathcal{DFS})$ are both in $O(N)$ rounds and follows:

Theorem 12. Starting from any configuration, a requested DFTC is initiated (resp. performed) using $SSBB(\mathcal{DFS}')$ in $O(N)$ rounds.

This latter result is very surprising because $\mathcal{DFS}$ alone stabilizes in $\Omega(D \times N)$ rounds. Actually, Theorems 11 and 12 show that our transformer ($SSBB$) allows not only to snap-stabilize some self-stabilizing protocols but also, in some case, it enhances the fairness and the time complexity of the protocols. We conjecture that we can obtain the same results with the self-stabilizing protocols in [12,13].

6   Conclusion

We propose a semi-automatic method to snap-stabilize self-stabilizing wave protocols for arbitrary networks with one initiator and such that their decision actions are at the initiator only. The snap-stabilizing solution we obtain with our technique works at least with the same daemon than the self-stabilizing protocol to snap-stabilizing. But, in some case like the $DFTC$ protocol of [5], we obtain a solution working with a weaker scheduling assumption. Also, the solution we obtain could be better in time complexities than the self-stabilizing protocol we want to transform. For instance, despite the $DFTC$ protocol of [5] stabilizes in $\Omega(D \times N)$ rounds, its snap-stabilizing version executes a requested $DFTC$ (as expected) in $O(N)$ rounds.

References

1. Dijkstra, E.: Self stabilizing systems in spite of distributed control. Communications of the Association of the Computing Machinery **17** (1974) 643–644
2. Bui, A., Datta, A., Petit, F., Villain, V.: State-optimal snap-stabilizing PIF in tree networks. In: Proceedings of the Fourth Workshop on Self-Stabilizing Systems, Austin, Texas, USA, IEEE Computer Society Press (1999) 78–85
3. Katz, S., Perry, K.: Self-stabilizing extensions for message-passing systems. Distributed Computing **7** (1993) 17–26
4. Cournier, A., Datta, A., Petit, F., Villain, V.: Enabling snap-stabilization. In: 23th International Conference on Distributed Computing Systems (ICDCS 2003), Providence, Rhode Island USA, IEEE Computer Society Press (2003) 12–19
5. Huang, S., Chen, N.: Self-stabilizing depth-first token circulation on networks. Distributed Computing **7** (1993) 61–66
6. Tel, G.: Introduction to distributed algorithms. Cambridge University Press, Cambridge, UK (Second edition 2001)
7. Dolev, S., Israeli, A., Moran, S.: Uniform dynamic self-stabilizing leader election. IEEE Transactions on Parallel and Distributed Systems **8**(4) (1997) 424–440
8. Blin, L., Cournier, A., Villain, V.: An improved snap-stabilizing PIF algorithm. In: DSN SSS'03 Workshop: Sixth Symposium on Self-Stabilizing Systems (SSS'03), LNCS 2704 (2003) 199–214
9. Cournier, A., Devismes, S., Villain, V.: Snap-stabilizing PIF and useless computations. In: The Twelfth International Conference on Parallel and Distributed Systems (ICPADS'06). Volume 1., Minneapolis, USA, IEEE Computer Society Press P2612 (2006) 39–46
10. Cournier, A., Devismes, S., Villain, V.: Snap-stabilizing PIF and useless computations. Technical Report LaRIA-2006-04, LaRIA, CNRS FRE 2733 (2006) Available at www.laria.u-picardie.fr/~devismes/LaRIA-2006-04.pdf.
11. Gouda, M.G., Herman, T.: Adaptive programming. IEEE Trans. Softw. Eng. **17**(9) (1991) 911–921
12. Johnen, C., Beauquier, J.: Space-efficient distributed self-stabilizing depth-first token circulation. In: Proceedings of the Second Workshop on Self-Stabilizing Systems, Las Vegas (UNLV), USA, Chicago Journal of Theoretical Computer Science (1995) 4.1–4.15
13. Datta, A., Johnen, C., Petit, F., Villain, V.: Self-stabilizing depth-first token circulation in arbitrary rooted networks. In: SIROCCO'98, The 5th International Colloquium On Structural Information and Communication Complexity Proceedings, Carleton University Press (1998) 229–243

Self-stabilizing Philosophers with Generic Conflicts

Praveen Danturi[1], Mikhail Nesterenko[1,*], and Sébastien Tixeuil[2,**]

[1] Department of Computer Science, Kent State University, Kent, OH, USA
{pdanturi, mikhail}@cs.kent.edu
[2] LRI-CNRS UMR 8623 & INRIA Grand Large Université Paris Sud, France
tixeuil@lri.fr

Abstract. We generalize the classic dining philosophers problem to separate the conflict and communication neighbors of each process. Communication neighbors may directly exchange information while conflict neighbors compete for the access to the exclusive critical section of code. This generalization is motivated by a number of practical problems in distributed systems including problems in wireless sensor networks. We present a self-stabilizing deterministic algorithm — $\mathcal{KDP}$ that solves a restricted version of the generalized problem where the conflict set for each process is limited to its k-hop neighborhood. Our algorithm is terminating. We formally prove $\mathcal{KDP}$ correct and evaluate its performance. We then extend $\mathcal{KDP}$ to handle fully generalized problem. We further extend it to handle a similarly generalized drinking philosophers problem. We describe how $\mathcal{KDP}$ can be implemented in wireless sensor networks and demonstrate that this implementation does not jeopardize its correctness or termination properties.

1 Introduction

Self-stabilization (or just stabilization) [12,17] is an elegant approach to forward recovery from transient faults as well as initializing a large-scale system. Regardless of the initial state, a stabilizing system converges to the legitimate set of states and remains there afterwards. In this paper we present a stabilizing solution to our generalization of the dining philosophers problem.

The dining philosophers problem [11] is a fundamental resource allocation problem. The name of the problem is frequently shortened to *diners* [27]. The diners, as well as its generalization — the drinking philosophers problem [8], has a variety of applications. In diners, a set of processes (philosophers) request access to the critical section (CS) of code. For each process there is a set of neighbor processes. Each process has a conflict with its neighbors: it cannot share the CS

* This author was supported in part by DARPA contract OSU-RF #F33615-01-C-1901 and by NSF CAREER Award 0347485.
** This author was supported in part by the FNS grants FRAGILE and SR2I from ACI "Sécurité et Informatique". Some of the research for this paper was done while the author was visiting Kent State University.

A.K. Datta and M. Gradinariu (Eds.): SSS 2006, LNCS 4280, pp. 214–230, 2006.
© Springer-Verlag Berlin Heidelberg 2006

with any of them. In spite of the conflicts, each requesting process should eventually execute the CS. To coordinate CS execution, the processes communicate. In classic diners it is assumed that each process can directly communicate with its conflict neighbors. In other words, for every process, the conflict neighbor set is a subset of the communication neighbor set.

However, there are applications where this assumption does not hold. Consider, for example, wireless sensor networks. A number of problems in this area, such as TDMA slot assignment, cluster formation and routing backbone maintenance can be considered as instances of resource allocation problems. Yet, due to radio propagation peculiarities, the signal's interference range may exceed its effective communication range. Moreover, radio networks have so called hidden terminal effect. The problem is as follows. Let two transmitters t_1 and t_2 be mutually out of reception range, while receiver r be in range of them both. If t_1 and t_2 broadcast simultaneously, due to mutual radio interference, r is unable to receive either broadcast. The potential interference pattern is especially intricate if the antennas used by the wireless sensor nodes are directional (see for example [23]). Such transmitters can be modeled as conflict neighbors that are not communication neighbors. To accommodate such applications, we propose the following extension. Instead of one, each process has two sets of neighbors: the conflict neighbors and the communication neighbors. These two sets are not necessarily related. The only restriction is that each conflict-neighbor has to be reachable through the communication neighbors.

Some solutions to classic diners can potentially be extended to this problem. Indeed, if a separate communication channel is established to each conflict neighbor the classic diners program can be applied to the generalized case. However, such a solution may not be efficient. The channels to conflict neighbors go over the communication topology of the system. The channels to multiple neighbors of the same process may overlap. Moreover, the sparser the topology, the greater the potential overlap. Yet, in a diners program, the communication between conflict neighbors is only of two kinds: a process either requests the permission to execute the CS from the neighbors, or releases this permission. Due to channel overlap, communicating the same message to each conflict neighbor separately leads to excessive overhead. This motivates our search for a solution to generic diners that effectively combines communication to separate conflict neighbors.

Related work. There exist a number of deterministic self-stabilizing solutions to classic diners [1,4,5,16,20,21,25,26]. Cantarell et al [7] solve the drinking philosophers problem. Datta et al [10] solve a specific extension of diners. None of these solutions separate conflict and communication neighbors.

Meanwhile, researchers working in the area of self-stabilization studied specific problems that require such separation. A few studies [3,18,22] address the aforementioned problem of TDMA slot assignment in the presence of the hidden terminal effect. This problem requires the processes to agree on a fixed schedule of time intervals (slots) such that each slot is allocated exclusively to a single process in the conflict neighborhood. Herman and Tixeuil [18] present a self-stabilizing probabilistic TDMA slot assignment algorithm for wireless sensor networks. They deal with channel conflicts that may arise between nodes that cannot communicate directly by assuming an underlying probabilistic CSMA/CA mechanism that provides constant time correct transmission with high probability. The authors assume that the network is tightly synchronized so that the phases that use the CSMA/CA mechanism are clearly distinguished from the phases that use TDMA mechanism. Arumugam and Kulkarni [3,22] propose deterministic solutions to the same problem. In [3], to avoid conflicts they propose to serialize channel assignments by circulating a single assignment token (privilege) throughout the network. In [22], they consider a regular grid topology where each node is aware of its position in the grid. Gairing et al [13] propose an interesting stabilizing algorithm for conflict neighbor sets containing the communication neighbors of distance at most two. They apply their algorithm to a number of graph-theoretical problems. However, their algorithm cannot solve the diners as it is not designed to allow each requesting process to enter the CS if its continuously request as well. That is, their program allow unfair computations. Goddard et al [14] propose a solution to the conflict neighbor sets of communication neighbors at most k-hops away. Their solution recursively extends Gairing's algorithm. It is unfair as well.

Our contribution and paper outline. We generalize the diners problem to separate the conflict and communication neighbor sets of each process. We formally state this problem, as well as describe our notation and execution model in Section 2. To the best of our knowledge, this problem has not been defined or addressed before either inside or outside of context of self-stabilization. In Section 3, we present a self-stabilizing deterministic terminating solution to a restricted version of this problem where the conflict set comprises the set of processes that are at most a fixed number of hops k away from the process. We call this program $\mathcal{KDP}$. In the same section we provide a formal correctness proof of $\mathcal{KDP}$ and discuss its stabilization performance. We extend $\mathcal{KDP}$ to solve generalized diners in Section 4. In Section 5 we describe how $\mathcal{KDP}$ can be implemented in wireless sensor networks without compromising its correctness or performance properties. We describe a number of further extensions to $\mathcal{KDP}$ in Section 6. Specifically, we generalize $\mathcal{KDP}$ to handle arbitrary conflict neighbor sets, as well as solve generalized drinking philosophers; we simplify our solution to handle problems that do not require fairness of CS access.

2   Preliminaries

Program model. For the formal description of our program we use simplified UNITY notation [9,15]. A program consists of a set of processes. A process contains a set of *constants* that it can read but not update. A process maintains a set of *variables*. Each variable ranges over a fixed domain of values. We use small case letters to denote singleton variables, and capital ones to denote sets.

An action has the form $\langle name \rangle : \langle guard \rangle \longrightarrow \langle command \rangle$. A *guard* is a Boolean predicate over the variables of the process and its communication neighbors. A *command* is a sequence of statements assigning new values to the variables of the process. We refer to a variable *var* and an action *ac* of process p as $var.p$ and $ac.p$ respectively. A *parameter* is used to define a set of actions as one parameterized action. For example, let j be a parameter ranging over values 2, 5, and 9; then a parameterized action $ac.j$ defines the set of actions: $ac.(j := 2) \; [\,] \; ac.(j := 5) \; [\,] \; ac.(j := 9)$.

A *state* of the program is the assignment of a value to every variable of each process from the variable's corresponding domain. Each process contains a set of actions. An action is *enabled* in some state if its guard is **true** at this state. A *computation* is a maximal fair sequence of states such that for each state s_i, the next state s_{i+1} is obtained by executing the command of an action that is enabled in s_i. Maximality of a computation means that the computation is infinite or it terminates in a state where none of the actions are enabled.

In a computation the action execution is *weakly fair*. That is, if an action is enabled in all but finitely many states of an infinite computation then this action is executed infinitely often.

A state *conforms* to a predicate if this predicate is **true** in this state; otherwise the state *violates* the predicate. By this definition every state conforms to predicate **true** and none conforms to **false**. Let R and S be predicates over the state of the program. Predicate R is *closed* with respect to the program actions if every state of the computation that starts in a state conforming to R also conforms to R. Predicate R *converges* to S if R and S are closed and any computation starting from a state conforming to R contains a state conforming to S. The program *stabilizes* to R iff **true** converges to R.

Problem statement. An instance of the generalized diners problem defines for each process p a set of *communication neighbors* $N.p$ and a set of *conflict neighbors* $M.p$. Both relations are symmetric. That is for any two processes p and q if $p \in N.q$ then $q \in N.p$. Same applies to $M.p$. Throughout the computation each process requests CS access an arbitrary number of times: from zero to infinity. A program that solves the generalized diners satisfies the following two properties for each process p: **safety** — if the action that executes the CS is enabled in p, it is disabled in all processes of $M.p$; **liveness** — if p wishes to execute the CS, it is eventually allowed to do so.

A desirable performance property of a solution to diners is **termination**: if a computation contains finitely many states where processes wish to execute the CS, then this computation is itself finite. To put another way, if there are no requests for the CS, a terminating solution to diners should eventually arrive at a state with all actions disabled.

A restriction of the generalized diners problem which we call *k-hop diners* specifies that $M.p$ for each process p contains the processes whose distance to p in the graph formed by the communication topology is no more than k.

process p
const
    M: k-hop conflict neighbors of p
    N: communication neighbors of p
    $(\forall q : q \in M : dad.p.q \in N, KIDS.p.q \subset N)$
                parent id and set of children ids for each k-hop neighbor
parameter
    $r : M$
var
    $state.p.p : \{\textbf{idle}, \textbf{req}\}$,
    $(\forall q : q \in M : state.p.q : \{\textbf{idle}, \textbf{req}, \textbf{rep}\})$,
    $YIELD : \{\forall q : q \in M : q > p\}$ lower priority processes to wait for
    $needcs : \textbf{boolean}$, application variable to request the CS

$$*[$$

join: $needcs \wedge state.p.p = \textbf{idle} \wedge YIELD = \varnothing \wedge$
                $(\forall q : q \in KIDS.p.p : state.q.p = \textbf{idle}) \longrightarrow$
                    $state.p.p := \textbf{req}$

        $[\!]$

enter: $state.p.p = \textbf{req} \wedge$
                $(\forall q : q \in KIDS.p.p : state.q.p = \textbf{rep}) \wedge$
                $(\forall q : q \in M \wedge q < p : state.p.q = \textbf{idle}) \longrightarrow$
                  /* CS */
                  $YIELD := \{\forall q : q \in M \wedge q > p : state.p.q = \textbf{rep}\}$,
                  $state.p.p := \textbf{idle}$

        $[\!]$

forward: $state.p.r = \textbf{idle} \wedge state.(dad.p.r).r = \textbf{req} \wedge$
                $((KIDS.p.r = \varnothing) \vee (\forall q : q \in KIDS.p.r : state.q.r = \textbf{idle})) \longrightarrow$
                  $state.p.r := \textbf{req}$

        $[\!]$

back: $state.p.r = \textbf{req} \wedge state.(dad.p.r).r = \textbf{req} \wedge$
                $((KIDS.p.r = \varnothing) \vee (\forall q : q \in KIDS.p.r : state.q.r = \textbf{rep})) \vee$
                $state.p.r \neq \textbf{rep} \wedge state.(dad.p.r).r = \textbf{rep} \longrightarrow$
                  $state.p.r := \textbf{rep}$

        $[\!]$

stop: $(state.p.r \neq \textbf{idle} \vee r \in YIELD) \wedge$
                $state.(dad.p.r).r = \textbf{idle} \longrightarrow$
                  $YIELD := YIELD \setminus \{r\}$,
                  $state.p.r := \textbf{idle}$

$$]$$

Fig. 1. Process of $\mathcal{KDP}$

3 $\mathcal{KDP}$ Algorithm

3.1 Description

Algorithm overview. The main idea of the algorithm is to coordinate CS request notifications between multiple conflict neighbors of the same process. We assume that for each process p there is a tree that spans $M.p$. This tree is rooted in p. A stabilizing breadth-first construction of a spanning tree is a relatively simple task [12].

The processes in this tree propagate CS request of its root. The request reflects from the leaves and informs the root that its conflict neighbors are notified. This mechanism resembles information propagation with feedback [6].

The access to the CS is granted on the basis of the priority of the requesting process. Each process has an identifier that is unique throughout the system. A process with lower identifier has higher priority. To ensure liveness, when executing the CS, each process p records the identifiers of its lower priority conflict neighbors that also request the CS. Process p then waits until all these processes access the CS before requesting it again.

Detailed description. Each process p has access to a number of constants. The set of identifiers of its communication neighbors is N, and its conflict neighbors is M. For each of its conflict neighbors r, p knows the appropriate spanning tree information: the parent identifier — $dad.p.r$, and a set of ids of its children — $KIDS.p.r$.

Process p stores its own request state in variable $state.p.p$ and the state of each of its conflict neighbors in $state.p.r$. Notice that p's own state can be only **idle** or **req**, while for its conflict neighbors p also has **rep**. To simplify the description, depending on the state, we refer to the process as being idle, requesting or replying. In $YIELD$, process p maintains the ids of its lower priority conflict neighbors that should be allowed to enter the CS before p requests it again. Variable *needcs* is an external Boolean variable that indicates if CS access is desired. Notice that CS entry is guaranteed only if *needcs* remains **true** until p requests the CS.

There are five actions in the algorithm. The first two: *join* and *enter* manage CS entry of p itself. The remaining three: *forward*, *back* and *stop* — propagate CS request information along the tree. Notice that the latter three actions are parameterized over the set of p's conflict neighbors.

Action *join* states that p requests the CS when the application variable *needcs* is **true**, p itself, as well as its children in its own spanning tree, is idle and there are no lower priority conflict neighbors to wait for. As action *enter* describes, p enters the CS when its children reply and the the higher priority processes do not request the CS themselves. To simplify the presentation, we describe the CS execution as a single action[1].

---

[1] In Section 6, we demonstrate how to extend our algorithm to perform CS entry and exit in separate actions.

Action *forward* describes the propagation of a request of a conflict neighbor r of p along r's tree. Process p propagates the request when p's parent — $dad.p.r$ is requesting and p's children are idle. Similarly, *back* describes the propagation of a reply back to r. Process p propagates the reply either if its parent is requesting and p is the leaf in r's tree or all p's children are replying. The second disjunct of *back* is to expedite the stabilization of $\mathcal{KDP}$. Action *stop* resets the state of p in r's tree to idle when its parent is idle. This action removes r from the set of lower-priority processes to await before initiating another request.

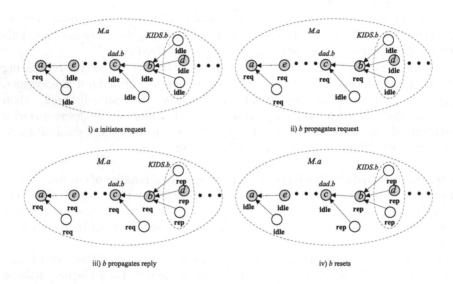

Fig. 2. Phases of $\mathcal{KDP}$ operation

Example operation. The operation of $\mathcal{KDP}$ in legitimate states is illustrated in Figure 2. We focus on the conflict neighborhood $M.a$ of a certain node a. We consider representative nodes in the spanning tree of $M.a$. Specifically, we consider one of a's children — e, a descendant — b, b's parent — c and one of b's children — d.

Initially, the states of all processes in $M.a$ are idle. Then, a executes *join* and sets $state.a.a$ to **req** (see Figure 2, i). This request propagates to process b, which executes *forward* and sets $state.b.a$ to **req** as well (Figure 2, ii). The request reaches the leaves and bounces back as the leaves change their state to **rep**. Process b then executes *back* and changes its state to **rep** as well (Figure 2, iii). After the reply reaches a and if none of the higher priority processes are requesting the CS, a executes *enter*. This action resets $state.a.a$ to **idle**. This reset propagates to b which executes *stop* and also changes $state.b.a$ to **idle** (Figure 2, iv).

3.2   Proof of Correctness

Proof outline. We present $\mathcal{KDP}$ correctness proof as follows. We first state a predicate we call $InvK$ and demonstrate that $\mathcal{KDP}$ stabilizes to it in Theorem 1.

We then proceed to show that if $InvK$ holds, then $\mathcal{KDP}$ satisfies the safety and liveness properties of the k-hop diners in Theorems 2 and 3 respectively.

Proof notation. Throughout this section, unless otherwise specified, we consider the conflict neighbors of a certain node a (see Figure 2). That is, we implicitly assume that a is universally quantified over all processes in the system. We focus on the following nodes: $e \in KIDS.a.a$, $b \in M.a$, $c \equiv dad.b.a$ and $d \in KIDS.b.a$.

Since we discuss the states of e, b, c and d in the spanning tree of a, when it is clear from the context, we omit the specifier of the conflict neighborhood. For example, we use $state.b$ for $state.b.a$. Also, for clarity, we attach the identifier of the process to the actions it contains. For example, $forward.b$ is the $forward$ action of process b.

Our global predicate consists of the following predicates that constrain the states of each individual process and the states of its communication neighbors. The predicate below relates the states of the root of the tree a to the states of its children.

$$(state.a = \mathbf{idle}) \Rightarrow (\forall e : e \in KIDS.a : state.e \neq \mathbf{req}) \qquad (Inv.a)$$

The following sequence of predicates relates the state of b to the state of its neighbors.

$$state.b = \mathbf{idle} \wedge state.c \neq \mathbf{rep} \wedge (\forall d : d \in KIDS.b : state.d \neq \mathbf{req}) \qquad (I.b.a)$$
$$state.b = \mathbf{req} \wedge state.c = \mathbf{req} \qquad (R.b.a)$$
$$state.b = \mathbf{rep} \wedge \qquad\qquad (\forall d : d \in KIDS.b : state.d = \mathbf{rep}) \qquad (P.b.a)$$

We denote the disjunction of the above three predicates as follows:

$$I.b.a \vee R.b.a \vee P.b.a \qquad (Inv.b.a)$$

The following predicate relates the states of all processes in $M.a$.

$$(\forall a :: Inv.a \wedge (\forall b : b \in M.a : Inv.b.a)) \qquad (InvK)$$

To aid in exposition, we mapped the states and transitions for individual processes in Figure 3. Note that to simplify the picture, for the intermediate process b we only show the states and transitions if Inv holds for each ancestor of b. For b, the $I.b$, $R.b$ and $P.b$ denote the states conforming to the respective predicates. While the primed versions $I'.b$ and $P'.b$ signify the states where b is respectively idle and replying but $Inv.b.a$ does not hold. Notice that the primed version of R does not exist if $Inv.c$ holds for b's parent c. Indeed, to violate R, b should be requesting while c is either idle or replying. However, if $Inv.c$ holds and c is in either of these two states, b cannot be requesting.

For a, $IR.a$ and $RR.a$ denote the states where a is respectively idle and requesting while $Inv.a$ holds. In states $IR'.a$, a is idle while $Inv.a$ does not

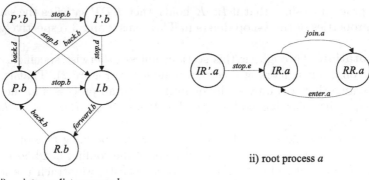

i)   intermediate process b
       if *Inv* holds for ancestors

ii) root process a

Fig. 3. State transitions for an individual process

hold. Notice that since $state = \mathbf{req}$ falsifies the antecedent of $Inv.a$, the predicate always holds if a is requesting. The state transitions in Figure 3 are labeled by actions whose execution effects them. Loopback transitions are not shown.

Theorem 1 (Stabilization). Program $\mathcal{KDP}$ stabilizes to $InvK$.

Proof: By the definition of stabilization, $InvK$ should be closed with respect to the execution of the actions of $\mathcal{KDP}$, and $\mathcal{KDP}$ should converge to $InvK$. We prove the closure first.

Closure. To aid in the subsequent convergence proof, we show a property that is stronger than just the closure of $InvK$. We demonstrate the closure of the following conjunction of predicates: $Inv.a$ and $Inv.b.a$ for a set of descendants of a up to a certain depth of the tree. To put another way, in showing the closure of $Inv.b.a$ for b we assume that the appropriate predicates hold for all its ancestors. Naturally, the closure of $InvK$ follows.

By definition of a closure of a predicate, we need to demonstrate that if the predicate holds in a certain state, the execution of any action in this state does not violate the predicate.

Let us consider $Inv.a$ and a root process a first. Notice that the only two actions that can potentially violate $Inv.a$ are *enter.a* and *forward.e*. Let us examine each action. If *enter.a* is enabled, each child of a is replying. Hence, when it is executed and it changes the state of a to **idle**, $Inv.a$ holds. If *forward.e* is enabled, a is requesting. Thus, executing the action and setting the state of e to **req** does not violate $Inv.a$.

Let us now consider $Inv.b.a$ for an intermediate process $b \in M.a$. We examine the effect of the actions of b, b's parent — c, and one of b's children — d in this sequence.

We start with the actions of b. If $I.b$ holds, *forward.b* is the only action that can be enabled. If it is enabled, c is requesting. Thus, if it is executed, $R.b$ holds and $Inv.b.a$ is not violated. If $R.b$ holds then $back.b$ is the only action that can be enabled. However, if $back.b$ is enabled and $R.b$ holds, then all children of b are replying. If $back.b$ is executed, the resultant state conforms to $P.b$. If $P.b$ holds, then $stop.b$ can exclusively be enabled. If $P.b$ holds and $stop.b$ is enabled, then c is idle and all children of b are replying. The execution of $back.b$ sets the state of b to **idle**. The resulting state conforms to $I.b$ and $Inv.b.a$ is not violated.

Let us examine the actions of c. Recall that we are assuming that $Inv.c$ and the respective invariants of all of b's ancestors hold. If $I.b$ holds, $forward.c$ and $join.c$ (in case b is a child of a) are the actions that can possibly be enabled. If either is enabled, b is idle. The execution of either action changes the state of c to **req**. $I.b$ and $Inv.b.a$ still hold. If $R.b$ holds, none of the actions of c are enabled. Indeed, actions $forward.c$, $back.c$, $join.c$ and $enter.c$ are disabled. Moreover, if $R.b$ holds, c is requesting: since $Inv.c$ holds, c must be in $R.c$. Which means that c's parent is not idle. Hence, $stop.c$ is also disabled. Since $P.b$ does not mention the state of c, the execution of c's actions does not affect the validity of $P.b$.

Let us now examine the actions of d. If $I.b$ holds, the only possibly enabled action is $stop.d$. The execution of this action changes the state of d to **idle**, which does not violate $I.b$. $R.b$ does not mention the state of d. Hence, its action execution does not affect $R.b$. If $P.b$ holds, all actions of d are disabled. This concludes the closure proof of $InvK$.

Convergence. We prove convergence by induction on the depth of the tree rooted in a. Let us show convergence of a. The only illegitimate set of states is $IR'.a$. When a conforms to $IR'.a$, a is idle and at least one child e is requesting. In such state, all actions of a that affect its state are disabled. Moreover, for every child of a that is idle, all relevant actions are disabled as well. For the child of a that is not idle, the only enabled action is $stop.e$. After this action is executed, e is idle. Thus, eventually $IR.a$ holds.

Let a conform to $Inv.a$. Let also every descendant process f of a up to depth i confirm to $Inv.f$. Let the distance from a to b be $i+1$. We shall show that $Inv.b.a$ eventually holds. Notice that according to the preceding closure proof, the conjunction of $Inv.a$ and $Inv.f$ for each process f in the distance no more than i is closed.

Note that according to Figure 3, there is no loop in the state transitions containing primed states. Hence, to prove that b eventually satisfies $Inv.b.a$ we need to show that b does not remain in a single primed state indefinitely. Process b can satisfy either $I'.b$ or $P'.b$. Let us examine these cases individually.

Let $b \in I'.b$. Since $Inv.c$ holds, if b is idle, c cannot satisfy $P.c$. Thus, for b to satisfy $I'.b$, at least one child d of b must be requesting. However, if b is idle then $stop.d$ is enabled. Notice that when b is idle, none of its non-requesting children can start to request. Thus, when this $stop$ is executed for every requesting child of b, b leaves $I'.b$.

Suppose $b \in P'.b$. This means that there exists at least one child d of b that is not replying. However, for every such process d, $back.d$ is enabled. Notice that when b is replying, none of its replying children can change state. Thus, when $back$ is executed for every non-replying child of b, b leaves $P'.b$.

Hence, $\mathcal{KDP}$ converges to $InvK$.   □

Theorem 2 (Safety). If $InvK$ holds and $enter.a$ is enabled, then for every process $b \in M.a$, $enter.b$ is disabled.

Proof: If $enter.a$ is enabled, every child of a is replying. Due to $InvK$, this means that every descendant of a is also replying. Thus, for every process x whose priority is lower than a's priority, $enter.x$ is disabled. Note also, that since $enter.a$ is enabled, for every process y whose priority is higher than a's, $state.a.y$ is **idle**. According to $InvK$, none of the ancestors of a in y's tree, including y's children, are replying. Thus, $enter.y$ is disabled. In short, when $enter.a$ is enabled, neither higher nor lower priority processes of $M.a$ have $enter$ enabled. The theorem follows.   □

Lemma 1. If $InvK$ holds, and some process a is requesting, then eventually either a stops requesting or none of its descendants are idle.

Proof: Notice that the lemma trivially holds if a stops requesting. Thus, we focus on proving the second claim of the lemma. We prove it by induction on the depth of a's tree. Process a is requesting and so it is not idle. By the assumption of the lemma, a will not be idle. Now let us assume that this lemma holds for all its descendants up to distance i. Let b be a descendant of a whose distance from a is $i + 1$. And let b be idle.

By inductive assumption, b's parent c is not idle. Due to $InvK$, if b is idle, c is not replying. Hence, c is requesting. If there exists a child d of b that is not idle, then $stop.d$ is enabled at d. When $stop.d$ is executed, d is idle. Notice that when b and d are idle, all actions of d are disabled. Thus, d continues to be idle. When all children of b are idle and its parent is requesting, $forward.b$ is enabled. When it is executed, b is not idle. Notice, that the only way for b to become idle again is to execute $stop.b$. However, by inductive assumption c is not idle. This means that $stop.b$ is disabled. The lemma follows.   □

Lemma 2. If $InvK$ holds and some process a is requesting, then eventually all its children in $M.a$ are replying.

Proof: Notice that when a is requesting, the conditions of Lemma 1 are satisfied. Thus, eventually, none of the descendants of a are idle. Notice that if a process is replying, it does not start requesting without being idle first (see Figure 3). Thus, we have to prove that each individual process is eventually replying. We prove it by induction on the height of a's tree.

If a leaf node b is requesting and its parent is not idle, $back.b$ is enabled. When it is executed, b is replying. Assume that each node whose longest distance to a leaf of a's tree is i is replying. Let b's longest distance to a leaf be $i + 1$. By assumption, all its children are replying. Due to Lemma 1, its parent is not idle. In this case *back.b* is enabled. After it is executed, *b* is replying. By induction, the lemma holds. □

Lemma 3. If *InvK* holds and the computation contains infinitely many states where *a* is idle, then for every descendant there are infinitely many states where it is idle as well.

Proof: We first consider the case where the computation contains a suffix where *a* is idle in every state. In this case we prove the lemma by induction on the depth of *a*'s tree with *a* itself as a base case. Assume that there is a suffix where all descendants of *a* up to depth *i* are idle. Let us consider process *b* whose distance to *a* is $i + 1$ and this suffix. Notice that this means that *c* remains idle in every state of this suffix. If *b* is not idle, *stop.b* is enabled. Once it is executed, no relevant actions are enabled at *b* and it remains idle afterwards. By induction, the lemma holds.

Let us now consider the case where no computation suffix of continuously idle *a* exists. Yet, there are infinitely many states where *a* is idle. Thus, *a* leaves the idle state and returns to it infinitely often. We prove by induction on the depth of the tree that every descendant of *a* behaves similarly. Assume that this claim holds for the descendants up to depth *i*. Let *b*'s distance to *a* be $i + 1$.

When *InvK* holds, the only way for *b*'s parent *c* to leave **idle** is to execute *forward.c* (see Figure 3). Similarly, the only way for *c* to return to **idle** is to execute *stop.c* while *c* is replying [2]. However, *forward.c* is enabled only when *b* is idle. Also, according to *InvK* when *c* is requesting, *b* is not idle. Thus, *b* leaves **idle** and returns to it infinitely many times as well. By induction, the lemma follows. □

Lemma 4. If *InvK* holds and process *a* is requesting such that and *a*'s priority is the highest among the processes that ever request the CS in *M.a*, then *a* eventually executes the CS.

Proof: If *a* is requesting, then, by Lemma 2, all its children are eventually replying. Therefore, the first and second conjuncts of the guard of *enter.a* are **true**. If *a*'s priority is the highest among all the requesting processes in *M.a*, then each process *z*, whose priority is higher than that of *a* is idle. According to Lemma 3, *state.a.z* is eventually **idle**. Thus, the third and last conjunct of *enter.a* is enabled. This allows *a* to execute the CS. □

Lemma 5. If *InvK* holds and process *a* is requesting, *a* eventually executes the CS.

Proof: Notice that by Lemma 2, for every requesting process, the children are eventually replying. According to *InvK*, this implies that all the descendants of the requesting process are also replying. For the remainder of the proof we assume that this condition holds.

---

[2] The argument is slightly different for $c = a$ as it executes *join.a* and *enter.a* instead.

We prove this lemma by induction on the priority of the requesting processes. According to Lemma 4, the requesting process with the highest priority eventually executes the CS. Thus, if process a is requesting and there is no higher priority process $b \in M.a$ which is also requesting then, by Lemma 4, a eventually enters the CS.

Suppose, on the contrary, that there exists a requesting process $b \in M.a$ whose priority is higher than a's. If every such process b enters the CS finitely many times, then, by repeated application of Lemma 4, there is a suffix of the computation where all processes with priority higher than a's are idle. Then, by Lemma 4, a enters the CS. Suppose there exists a higher priority process b that enters the CS infinitely often. Since a is requesting, $state.b.a = $ **rep**. When b executes the CS, it enters a into $YIELD.b$. We assume that b enters the CS infinitely often. However, b can request the CS again only if $YIELD.b$ is empty. The only action that takes a out of $YIELD.b$ is $stop.b$. However, this action is enabled if $state.b.a$ is **idle**. Notice that, if $InvK$ holds, the only way for the descendants of a to move from replying to idle is if a itself moves from requesting to idle. That is a executes the CS. Thus, each process a requesting the CS eventually executes it.   □

Lemma 6. If $InvK$ holds and process a wishes to enter the CS, a eventually requests.

Proof: We show that a wishing to enter the CS eventually executes $join.a$. We assume that a is idle and $needcs.a$ is **true**. Then, $join.a$ is enabled if $YIELD.a$ is empty. a adds a process to $YIELD$ only when it executes the CS. Thus, as a remains idle, processes can only be removed from $YIELD.a$.

Let us consider a process $b \in YIELD.a$. If b executes the CS finitely many times, then there is a suffix of the computation where b is idle. According to Lemma 3, for all descendants of b, including a, $state.a.b$ is idle. If this is the case $stop.a$ is enabled. When it is executed b is removed from $YIELD.a$.

Let us consider the case, where b executes the CS infinitely often. In this case, b enters and leaves **idle** infinitely often. According to Lemma 3, $state.a.b$ is idle infinitely often. Moreover, a moves to idle by executing $stop.a$, which removes b from $YIELD.a$. The lemma follows.   □

The theorem below follows from Lemmas 5 and 6.

Theorem 3 (Liveness). If $InvK$ holds, a process wishing to enter the CS is eventually allowed to do so.

We draw the following corollary from Theorems 1, 2 and 3.

Corollary 1. Program $\mathcal{KDP}$ is a self-stabilizing solution to the k-hop diners problem.

Due to the space restrictions we state the following theorem without proof.

Theorem 4 (Termination). *Program $\mathcal{KDP}$ is terminating.*

3.3 Stabilization Efficiency Evaluation

Observe (see Figure 3) that each process executes at most two of its own actions before satisfying the stabilization predicate. Each of these action executions may only be interleaved by the action execution of the process neighbors. Let δ be the maximum degree of a process. Since stabilization proceeds from the root, there could be at most $2(\delta + 1)k$ executions of actions in the conflict neighborhood before it stabilizes. If δ is not related to the number of processes in the system, the stabilization time of $\mathcal{KDP}$ depends only on k and thus independent of the system size.

Notice that the stabilization of one conflict neighborhood is independent of stabilization of another. Thus, the spacial extent of the state corruption is at most $2k$. Notice also that the locality extends to the trees used by $\mathcal{KDP}$. The individual tree construction is independent of construction of other trees. Thus, these trees can be built or stabilized in parallel.

4 Solution to Generalized Dining Philosophers

Notice that we presented $\mathcal{KDP}$ for the case of a rather strictly defined conflict neighborhood. However, $\mathcal{KDP}$ can be extended to handle an arbitrary symmetric conflict neighborhood relation.

In this case, each process p still has to have a spanning tree to all its conflict neighbors. Notice that, unlike $\mathcal{KDP}$, it is possible that some conflict neighbor q is only reachable through a process r that is not a conflict neighbor of p. In this case, r is included in p's spanning tree. Process r still propagates the requests and replies along p's tree. However, r ignores the state of p for its own CS access. For instance, r never enters p in $YIELD.r$.

Notice, that it may happen that some branches of the constructed tree for some process of p do not contain its conflict neighbors at all. The CS request propagation from p to such a branch is not necessary. To avoid such propagation our program can be further optimized as follows. If a leaf of a tree is not a conflict neighbor of p, it so informs its parent. If process q does not have conflict neighbors of p in a certain branch, q does not forward p's requests to that branch. If process q does not have any conflict neighbors of p at all among its descendants and q itself is not a conflict neighbor of p, q informs its parent about it. Thus, the tree is pruned to contain only p's conflict neighbors and their ancestors which further improves the efficiency of our program.

5 Implementation in Wireless Sensor Networks

As we motivated $\mathcal{KDP}$ by the problems arising in wireless sensor networks, we would like to discuss implementing our algorithm in this environment. From algorithm correctness standpoint, this environment is a variant of a message-passing system with lossy channels. The broadcast nature of the radio signal allows certain performance gains.

In implementing $\mathcal{KDP}$ in this environment the concern is to preserve its correctness and termination properties. We discuss the modifications to preserve the algorithm's correctness first. Note that in order to satisfy non-trivial liveness properties we assume that our environment conforms to *transmission fairness*: if a process attempts to send infinitely many messages, all of its communication neighbors will receive infinitely many of them. Note that this assumption is weaker than used previously for self-stabilizing algorithms in sensor networks [19,24]: it is usually assumed that the expected message transmission time for one hop neighbors is constant. Our idea is to use the timeouts such that the lost messages are recovered. There are two phases where the message recovery is important: request and release propagation. In case of request propagation, when the parent changes its state to **req**, it sends a message to its children and starts a timeout. When the timeout expires, the parent resubmits the request. Upon the receipt of the request, the child's actions differ depending on its state. As in the original algorithm, in case the child is in **idle**, it switches to **req** and further propagates the request; similarly, if the child is in **req**, it ignores the request. In case the child is in **rep**, it sends back the message informing the parent of its state. These actions ensure that the request will be propagated along the routing tree and the reply will be collected. As an efficiency optimization, a child may acknowledge the request message from its parent. This acknowledgment is done either explicitly or by broadcasting the its own request to its children. The parent then resubmits its request only to the children that have not acknowledged it yet. Recall that for release propagation, the parent needs to ascertain that its children are **idle** before switching to **req** and starting to propagate the next request. Similar to the case of request propagation, the parent has to keep the list of its non-idle children and keep informing its children of its idle state until all of its children acknowledge (explicitly or implicitly) that they also switched to **idle**. When all its children are **idle** the parent can turn of its notification timeout.

Let us now address termination preservation of $\mathcal{KDP}$. Note that co-satisfaction of stabilization and termination in message-passing systems is a rather difficult objective. However, Arora and Nesterenko [2] demonstrated that mutual exclusion and, by extension, diners admits a solution with both of these properties. Notice that, as described, it is possible that the algorithm refined to operate in wireless sensor networks starts in an illegitimate terminal state where some child is in **rep** and its parent is in **idle**. This state is illegitimate: if there is a further request and the parent switches to **req**, then the parent may mistake the child's reply as the answer to its new request. This mistake may result in a safety violation (see [2] for a detailed discussion of this issue). A stabilizing algorithm cannot terminate in an illegitimate state. Thus, this particular terminal state has to be eliminated. The mechanism is as follows. If a process is in **req**, it periodically informs its parent about its state. If parent is in **idle**, it messages back with its state and forces the child to switch to **idle** as well. With this modification, the only terminal state is the one where every process is in **idle**. This is a legitimate state and our algorithm remains terminating and stabilizing.

6   Further Extensions

Extension to generic drinking philosophers. In the classic drinking philosophers problem, the set of conflict neighbors for each process p may vary with each CS access. This problem can be extended to the generic case of conflict neighbors in a straightforward manner.

$\mathcal{KDP}$ can be extended to solve the generalized drinking philosophers problem as well. In this case, p has to construct a spanning tree to the union of all of its possible conflict neighbors. Each process q in the tree has the list of all its descendants. Thus, p has the list of all its potential conflict neighbors. When p requests the CS, it advertises the list of the actual conflict neighbors for this request. The child of p propagates the request only if it has a descendant in this set. The process repeats at each node.

Simplification to unfair case. Notice that some problems, such as distance-k vertex coloring, maximal irredundant sets, etc. [14] do not require fairness of CS access specified by the diners: in any computation of such a problem there are only finitely many CS accesses. If $\mathcal{KDP}$ is to be used for such a problem, it can be simplified. In the unfair case, an idle higher priority process does not have to wait for a lower priority neighbor. This obviates the need for *YIELD* and simplifies actions *stop*, *enter* and *join*. Moreover, the computations of such program are finite. Thus, this program is capable of operating without the weak fairness assumption about action execution.

Future research directions. It is unclear if $\mathcal{KDP}$ is an optimal solution to generalized diners with respect to space complexity. If the communication topology is dense, statically maintaining spanning trees may be expensive. Hence, the construction of a more space-efficient algorithm is an attractive area of future.

References

1. G. Antonoiu and P.K. Srimani. Mutual exclusion between neighboring nodes in an arbitrary system graph that stabilizes using read/write atomicity. In *EuroPar'99*, volume 1685 of *LNCS*, pages 823–830. Springer-Verlag, 1999.
2. A. Arora and M. Nesterenko. Unifying stabilization and termination in message-passing systems. *Distributed Computing*, 17(3):279–290, March 2005.
3. M. Arumugam and S.S. Kulkarni. Self-stabilizing deterministic TDMA for sensor networks. Technical Report MSU-CSE-05-19, Michigan State University, 2005.
4. J. Beauquier, A.K. Datta, M. Gradinariu, and F. Magniette. Self-stabilizing local mutual exclusion and daemon refinement. In *14th International Symposium on Distributed Computing*, volume 1914 of *LNCS*, pages 223–237. Springer, 2000.
5. C. Boulinier, F. Petit, and V. Villain. When graph theory helps self-stabilization. In *PODC '04: Proceedings of the twenty-third annual ACM symposium on Principles of distributed computing*, pages 150–159, New York, NY, USA, 2004. ACM Press.
6. A. Bui, A.K. Datta, F. Petit, and V. Villain. Space optimal PIF algorithm: self-stabilized with no extra space. In *IEEE International Conference on Performance, Computing and Communications*, pages 20–26, 1999.
7. S. Cantarell, A.K. Datta, and F. Petit. Self-stabilizing atomicity refinement allowing neighborhood concurrency. In *6th International Symposium on Self-Stabilizing Systems*, volume 2704 of *LNCS*, pages 102–112. Springer, 2003.

8. K.M. Chandy and J. Misra. The drinking philosophers problem. *ACM Transactions on Programming Languages and Systems*, 6(4):632–646, October 1984.
9. K.M. Chandy and J. Misra. *Parallel Program Design: a Foundation*. Addison-Wesley, Reading, Mass., 1988.
10. A.K. Datta, M. Gradinariu, and M. Raynal. Stabilizing mobile philosophers. *Information Procesing Letters*, 95(1):299–306, 2005.
11. E. Dijkstra. *Cooperating Sequential Processes*. Academic Press, 1968.
12. S. Dolev. *Self-Stabilization*. MIT Press, 2000.
13. M. Gairing, W. Goddard, S.T. Hedetniemi, P. Kristiansen, and A.A. McRae. Distance-two information in self-stabilizing algorithms. *Parallel Processing Letters*, 14(3-4):387–398, 2004.
14. W. Goddard, S.T. Hedetniemi, D.P Jacobs, and V Trevisan. Distance-k information in self-stabilizing algorithms. to appear in the Proceedings of the 13th Colloquium on Structural Information and Communication Complexity (SIROCCO'06).
15. M.G. Gouda. *Elmnts. of Network Protocol Design*. John Wiley & Sons, Inc., 1998.
16. M.G. Gouda and F. Haddix. The alternator. In *Proceedings of the Fourth Workshop on Self-Stabilizing Systems*, pages 48–53. IEEE Computer Society, 1999.
17. T. Herman. A comprehensive bibliography on self-stabilization (working paper). *CJTCS: Chicago Journal of Theoretical Computer Science*, 1995.
18. T. Herman and S. Tixeuil. A distributed TDMA slot assignment algorithm for wireless sensor networks. In *Proceedings of the First International Workshop on Algorithmic Aspects of Wireless Sensor Networks*, pages 45–58, 2004.
19. Ted Herman and Sébastien Tixeuil. A distributed TDMA slot assignment algorithm for wireless sensor networks. In *Proceedings of the First Workshop on Algorithmic Aspects of Wireless Sensor Networks (AlgoSensors'2004)*, number 3121 in LNCS, pages 45–58. Springe, July 2004.
20. S.T. Huang. The fuzzy philosophers. In J. Rolim et al., editor, *Proceedings of the 15th IPDPS 2000 Workshops*, volume 1800 of *Lecture Notes in Computer Science*, pages 130–136, Cancun, Mexico, May 2000. Springer-Verlag.
21. C. Johnen, L.O. Alima, A.K. Datta, and S. Tixeuil. Optimal snap-stabilizing neighborhood synchronizer in tree networks. *Parallel Processing Letters*, 12(3-4):327–340, 2002.
22. S.S. Kulkarni and M. Arumugam. Collision-free communication in sensor networks. In *Proceedings of the Symposium on Self-Stabilizing Systems (SSS), Springer-Verlag LNCS:2704*, pages 17–31, San Francisco,CA, June 2003.
23. M. Malhotra, M. Krasniewski, C. Yang, S. Bagchi, and W. Chappbell. Location estimation in ad-hoc networks with directional antennas. In *the 25th IEEE International Conference on Distributed Computing Systems*, pages 633–642, 2005.
24. Nathalie Mitton, Eric Fleury, Isabelle Guérin-Lassous, Bruno Séricola, and Sébastien Tixeuil. On fast randomized colorings in sensor networks. In *Proceedings of ICPADS 2006*, page to appear. IEEE Press, July 2006.
25. M. Mizuno and M. Nesterenko. A transformation of self-stabilizing serial model programs for asynchronous parallel computing environments. *Information Processing Letters*, 66(6):285–290, 1998.
26. M. Nesterenko and A. Arora. Stabilization-preserving atomicity refinement. *Journal of Parallel and Distributed Computing*, 62(5):766–791, 2002.
27. P.A.G. Sivilotti, S.M. Pike, and N. Sridhar. A new distributed resource-allocation algorithm with optimal failure locality. In *Proceedings of the 12th IASTED International Conference on Parallel and Distributed Computing and Systems*, volume 2, pages 524–529. IASTED/ACTA Press, November 2000.

Selfish Stabilization

Anurag Dasgupta[1], Sukumar Ghosh[2,*], and Sébastien Tixeuil[3,**]

[1] University of Iowa, USA
adasgupt@cs.uiowa.edu
[2] University of Iowa, USA
ghosh@cs.uiowa.edu
[3] LRI, Université Paris-Sud, France
tixeuil@lri.fr

Abstract. Stabilizing distributed systems expect all the component processes to run predefined programs that are externally mandated. In Internet scale systems, this is unrealistic, since each process may have selfish interests and motives related to maximizing its own payoff. This paper formulates the problem of selfish stabilization that shows how competition blends with cooperation in a stabilizing environment.

1 Introduction

Motivation. Current research on the design of self-stabilizing (*a.k.a.* stabilizing) distributed systems [4,5] assumes that all processes run predefined programs mandated by an external agency who is the owner or the administrator of the entire system. The model is acceptable only when processes cooperate with one another, and the goal is purely a global one. The model falls apart when the distributed system spans over multiple administrative domains or processes have private goals too. On Internet-scale distributed systems, each process or each administrative domain may have selfish motives to maximize its own *payoff*. In fact, payoffs or cost functions have been the major driving force behind *game theory*, but individual payoffs never figured into the realm of stabilizing distributed systems. There are many applications where individual payoffs are relevant, but the spirit of competition need not conflict with the general spirit of cooperation that is the driving force behind stabilizing algorithms. To clarify this issue, consider that a system of n processes for which a legal configuration is any element of the set of configurations $\{L_0, L_1, \cdots, L_k\}$, but different processes have different preferences about their ideal legal configurations. Attaining the individual goal may be possible via the use of asymmetric cost functions that are statically defined, or by the use of specific strategies that may be adopted at run time. Such strategies refine the basic move, for example, to execute the step of choosing a neighbor, different processes may adopt different strategies for choosing the

---

* This author's research was supported in part by the Alexander von Humboldt Foundation, Germany.
** This author was supported in part by the FRAGILE, SR2I, and SOGEA projects. Part of this work was done while the author was visiting University of Iowa.

A.K. Datta and M. Gradinariu (Eds.): SSS 2006, LNCS 4280, pp. 231–243, 2006.
© Springer-Verlag Berlin Heidelberg 2006

neighbor. While the choice will impact the payoffs, it will not affect the global goal, or the stabilization mechanism. As an example, consider the stabilizing token circulation protocols that have been widely studied by the stabilization community. If there are two kinds of processes with competing interests, then in addition to the common goal of reducing the number of tokens to one, each class may try to retain the token among themselves more often than their competitors. Maximizing individual payoffs under the umbrella of stabilization characterizes the notion of *selfish stabilization*.

Related Work. Selfish stabilization blends game theory with self-stabilization. There are some strong similarities between the two paradigms, but there are significant differences too. Considering the *players* in games to be equivalent to *processes* in a stabilizing system, the equilibrium in games is comparable to the legal configuration of stabilizing systems in as much as both satisfy the condition of convergence and closure. However, unlike stabilizing systems, games start from predefined initial configurations, and largely ignore faulty moves or transient state corruptions. An exception is the notion of *bounded rationality* (see Herbert Simon [17]) that suggests that economic agents employ the use of heuristics to make decisions rather than a strict rigid rule of optimization in light of the complexity of the situation. In the context of distributed systems, the anarchic behavior of processes for meeting selfish goals can be viewed as a weaker variation of byzantine failure. So far, game theory has been a hotbed of activities in computational economics (like auctions) and algorithm design. It is also receiving attention in interdomain routing protocols like BGP. For example, in the *stable path problem* [8], each process has to choose the best path according to some local routing policy, and conflicts between local interests can lead to unstable or oscillating behavior. Cobb et al [3] proposed a stabilizing solution to the stable path problem. In [12], Moscibroda, Schmid and Wattenhofer studied the formation of the topology of a P2P network by selfish peers. In [13] the same authors analyzed the impact of allowing some processes to be malicious or byzantine whereas others are selfish, and determined the price of malice. Mavronicolas [11] used a game-theoretic view to model security in wireless sensor networks as a game between the attackers and the defenders. Halpern [9] presented a perspective of game theory for distributed systems researchers. Other than these approaches, mixing game theory with distributed computing is certainly on a fast growing curve [16], yet no specific work has addressed the self-stabilizing setting. This paper aims at bridging the gap.

Contributions. This paper introduces the notion of selfish stabilization, and addresses a specific problem in this domain. Given a graph $G = (V, E)$, assume that there are two different classes of nodes, *white* and *black*. For each class, there is a separate cost function that maps the set of edges to the set of positive integers. Starting from an arbitrary initial configuration, the two classes of nodes cooperate with one another to form a spanning tree rooted at a designated node, and at the same time compete against each other to minimize their cost of communication with the root node. The communication cost may depend on various factors: for example, ownership of the routers may be a factor in determining the cost of routing traffic for any class of nodes. The processes are free to choose a strategy from a given set of strategies, and may switch strategy to satisfy their individual needs. We demonstrate how the two different classes of processes stabilize to an equilibrium configuration after which no process can unilaterally decrease its communication cost.

The paper has four sections. Section 2 introduces the model and the notations. Section 3 describes a stabilizing algorithm for constructing the shortest path tree by the competing classes of processes. Section 4 further analyzes various aspects of the problem, and provides some food for thought.

2   Model and Notations

We model the topology of the network by a graph $G = (V, E)$ where $V = \{0, 1, 2, \ldots, n - 1\}$ denotes the set of nodes (processes) and E denotes the set of edges connecting pairs of processes. All the nodes in V have a common goal: to form a spanning tree with a given node designated as the root. We divide V into two disjoint subsets of nodes: W (*white* nodes) and B (*black* nodes)[1]. $V = (W \cup B)$. In addition to the common goal, these subsets have their own agenda: we call them *private* goals. The private goals of the two subsets may be conflicting - for example, the two sets of nodes may want to split a common resource. To illustrate such private goals, let us first convert G into a weighted graph by defining two *cost functions* (here $\mathbb{N}^*$ is the set of positive integers):

$$w : E \longrightarrow \mathbb{N}^*$$
$$b : E \longrightarrow \mathbb{N}^*$$

For each node in W, $w(e)$ is the cost of using the edge e, and for each node in B, $b(e)$ is the cost of using the same edge. Once a spanning tree is generated, for each node (black or white) there is a unique path leading to the root node. Let $\{e_1, e_2, \cdots, e_m\}$ be the edges belonging to such a path p from a node i to the root. Then the communication cost (or simply the *cost*) of the node i depends on its color. Thus

$$cost(i) = \begin{cases} \sum_{e \in p} w(e) \text{ if } i \text{ is white} \\ \sum_{e \in p} b(e) \text{ if } i \text{ is black} \end{cases}$$

The private goal for each node i (black or white) is to minimize $cost(i)$. In meeting these goals, the two classes of nodes will compete with one another in choosing the tree edges. Unlike traditional stabilization algorithms where all processes execute the same algorithm, here processes are allowed to choose different algorithms, or switch algorithms from a set $\Sigma = \{P_0, P_1, \cdots, P_m\}$ (each P_i reflects a different strategy), to meet their goals. Let S_v denote the global state space of all the processes in V. A *computation* is a sequence of states $(s_0, s_1, s_2, \cdots)$, where $\forall i \geq 0 : s_i \in S_v$, and the state transition (s_i, s_{i+1}) is caused by an action of some algorithm $P_j \in \Sigma$.

---

[1] Call (W, B) the composition of V.

Our goal is to devise a stabilizing mechanism for the construction of such a tree – the computation should lead to a tree configuration so that the conflicting private goals of cost minimization do not interfere with the common goal of tree formation. The two components of the mechanism are:

1. **Equilibrium.** The goal configuration corresponds to an equilibrium configuration such that no process can unilaterally decrease the cost of its own color by any other means.
2. **Convergence.** Starting from an arbitrary initial configuration, the system of processes must converge to an equilibrium configuration.

We add a few clarifications to explain the above two mechanisms:

Clarification 1. The equilibrium need not always correspond to a quiescent state in which all guards are false. It can also represent the dynamic behavior of a reactive system (like a token-passing system). For the current problem however, a quiescent equilibrium state will suffice, and it naturally reflects a Nash equilibrium.

Clarification 2. In principle, the equilibrium condition can be further generalized to the case where no coalition of processes can decrease the cost of a subset of them.

Clarification 3. Compared to the closure property [1] used in traditional stabilizing systems, the equilibrium criteria is more general in as much as it allows the processes to try out a different strategy that does not conflict with the spirit of cooperation.

Indeed, a selfish strategy without cooperation (such as arbitrarily picking an edge whose cost is minimal for its own color) can result in a graph that is not a tree towards the destination, as is exemplified by Figure 1. Even if nodes have global knowledge about other edge costs of their own color (*e.g.* they are aware of the minimum costs path towards the destination), the resulting graph may not be a tree, as is exemplified by Figure 2.

Let $N(i)$ be the set of neighbors of a node i. Also, for each node $i \in V$, define two variables $p(i)$ and $L(i)$ (commonly called the *parent* and the *label* or *distance* variables). By definition, for the root node r, $p(r)$ is non-existent. Every other node picks a neighboring node as its parent. The label $L(i)$ for each node has two components $L(i).w$ and $L(i).b$. By definition, $L(r).w = L(r).b = 0$, which is also represented as $L(r) = (0,0)$ [2]. For all $i \neq r$, draw a directed edge from i to $p(i)$. In our shortest-path tree, the following three conditions must hold:

1. The set of edges $\{(i, p(i)) : i \neq r\}$ induce a spanning tree in G.
2. $\forall i \neq r : L(i) = L(p(i)) + (w(i, p(i)), b(i, p(i)))$. For a white node i, $L(i).w$ denotes its communication cost, and for a black node j, $L(j).b$ represents its communication cost.
3. For each white node i, the value of $L(i).w$, and each black node j, the value of $L(j).b$, reflect the equilibrium condition introduced earlier, i.e. it cannot be unilaterally lowered by choosing a different action or a different strategy.

---

[2] By convention, the first component of L is always for the white nodes.

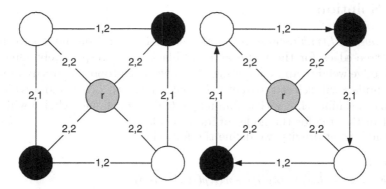

Fig. 1. Pure selfish strategies may not yield a tree. Each node picks an edge whose cost is minimal for its own color, and this results in a cycle.

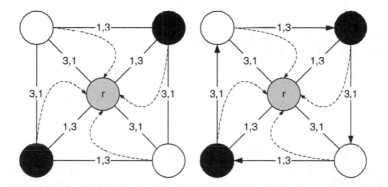

Fig. 2. Pure selfish strategies may not yield a tree. Each node picks an edge whose path towards the root has minimal cost for its own color, and this results in a cycle.

In networks with selfish peers, the costs influencing decision-making are often of commercial nature, and are thus kept private to the participating nodes. To accommodate this feature in our framework, we assume that for each node, the value of each component of L and the weights of the edges incident on it will be stored in an encrypted form. All black nodes share a common secret key, and all white nodes share another secret key. Thus, no node can access the component of the costs of a different color from a neighboring node or link to decide its course of action. However every node can securely extract the component of the variables corresponding to its own color. This authentication mechanism preserves fairness of the game and prevents possible foul play by deliberately tampering the variables of the nodes of opposing color. We will designate the encrypted version of a variable x by $\hat{x}$. For the sake of simplicity, we assume that

$$\hat{x} + \hat{y} = \widehat{x+y}$$

Homomorphic encryptions like Pallier's scheme [14] satisfy this property.

3　A Solution

Let $L(i).w$ and $L(i).b$ denote the total cost of the path from node i to the root via the tree edges for the white and the black nodes respectively. Due to the variable edge weights and competing goals, we first propose a greedy approach: a black node i will select a parent $p(i)$ that minimizes $L(i).b$ and a white node will make a similar choice that minimizes $L(i).w$. Each such choice will reduce the cost of the tree for the nodes of its own color.

For the sake of brevity, we define the following:

Conditions

$LabelOK(i) \equiv \quad \widehat{L(i)} = \widehat{L(p(i))} + w\widehat{(i, p(i))}, b\widehat{(i, p(i))}$

$ParentOK(i) \equiv \quad (i = white) \wedge$
$\qquad\qquad\qquad p(i) = j : L(j).w + w(i, j) = min\{L(k).w + w(i, k) : k \in N(i)\} \vee$
$\qquad\qquad\qquad (i = black) \wedge$
$\qquad\qquad\qquad p(i) = j : L(j).b + b(i, j) = min\{L(k).b + b(i, k) : k \in N(i)\}$

Actions

$FixLabel(i) \equiv \quad \widehat{L(i)} := \widehat{L(p(i))} + w\widehat{(i, p(i))}, b\widehat{(i, p(i))}$

$FixParent(i) \equiv \quad$ **if** i is white $\rightarrow p(i) := j :$
$\qquad\qquad\qquad\qquad L(j).w + w(i, j) = min\{L(k).w + w(i, k) : k \in N(i)\}$
$\qquad\qquad\quad \square\ i$ is black $\rightarrow p(i) := j :$
$\qquad\qquad\qquad\qquad L(j).b + b(i, j) = min\{L(k).b + b(i, k) : k \in N(i)\}$
$\qquad\qquad$ **fi**

The algorithm that we will propose here reflects only the greedy strategy, but there could be other strategies too: we will discuss such alternatives shortly. Regardless of these, we show that once an equilibrium is reached, no process can reduce the cost for their group by switching strategies unless at least one process from its competitors switches strategies as well.

The proposed algorithm has a single guarded action $R0$. The root r does not execute any action. The action for node $i \neq r$ is described in the following algorithm:

Program for process i

do
{R0: Correct the label}
$(\neg\ LabelOK(i) \vee \neg\ ParentOK(i)) \longrightarrow$
$\qquad\qquad FixParent(i);$
$\qquad\qquad FixLabel(i);$
od

3.1　Proof of Correctness

Fig 3 shows a graph and three corresponding spanning trees that could be obtained at some point of a computation (none of these necessarily denotes the terminal configuration). For example, the cost of tree *(b)* is $(10, 9)$, while the cost of tree *(c)* is $(9, 9)$ and the cost of tree *(d)* $(11, 8)$. So different trees yield different costs for different teams.

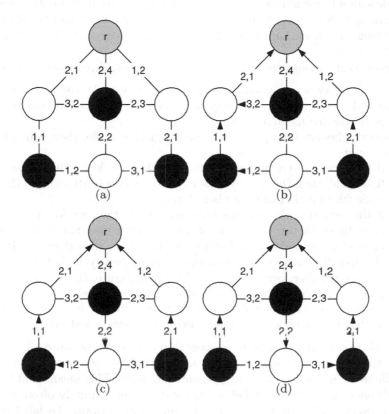

Fig. 3. Various spanning trees of the graph in part (a) (note that not all trees are terminal configurations)

Theorem 1. *The system of processes executing the proposed algorithm stabilizes to an equilibrium configuration, and the edges connecting the processes with their parents form a spanning tree of G.*

Proof. The proof consists in two parts: first, we show that every execution is finite, and then we show that in any terminal configuration, a spanning tree is constructed towards the root and is an equilibrium configuration.

Finite executions. Assume for the purpose of contradiction that the execution is infinite. This implies that there exists at least a node that executes an infinite number of actions. In turn, either this node changes its parent an infinite number of times, or it adjusts its label an infinite number of times (or both). If this node changes its parent an infinite number of times (and since it has finitely many potential parents) or updates its label an infinite number of times, at least one of its neighbors makes an infinite number of actions as well. By induction on the (finite) size of the network, and the fact that the root node takes no action, this implies that there exists at least one cycle of nodes in the network where every node takes an infinite number of actions. Such cycles are in finite numbers, and all remaining nodes (in set S, for silent) execute only a finite number of actions. Assume that the execution has reached the point where all nodes in S execute no further action.

If a node that belongs to a cycle changes its parent, three cases may occur:

1. The node chooses as a parent a node in the same cycle, then the size of the cycle is decreased (as a node may only choose a new parent that decreases the path cost for its color),
2. The node chooses as a parent a node in another cycle, then two sub-cases may occur:
   (a) if the second cycle only contains costs that are lower than those in the first cycle, then the first cycle is cut and a chain is attached to the other cycle (the number of cycles is reduced),
   (b) if the second cycle contains both path costs that are lower and higher than those in the first cycle, it may happen that two new cycles are created while nodes from both cycles attach to the other one. However the overall number of nodes in the resulting two cycles is lower than the original number, because nodes with the highest path cost never become new parents (the size of at least one cycle decreases).
3. The node chooses as a parent a node in S, then the cycle is cut and a chain is attached to the nodes in S (the number of cycles is reduced).

Overall, there can only be a finite number of parent changes, since all cycles are of finite size and in finite number. Now, assume that the execution has reached a point where all nodes do not change parents any more. This means that in every cycle, all nodes execute only label adjustment actions infinitely often. Since all nodes in every cycle execute only label adjustment actions, the label of each node in a cycle grows in an unbounded manner. Now, at least one node u of a cycle is a neighbor to a node s in S, yet executes an infinite number of label adjustments. After the label is larger than the label of s plus the cost of the edge (u, s), u changes its parent to s, which contradicts the fact that no node changes its parent from this point of the execution.

Overall, the hypothesis that the execution is infinite leads to a contradiction.

Final Equilibrium. Assume that the system has reached a terminal configuration, where no node may execute an action. This means that for every node i, $LabelOK(i)$ and $ParentOK(i)$ hold. Now consider the subgraph of G induced by the edges connecting the nodes of G to their parents. By the strictly increasing property of the labels, every path towards the parent is strictly decreasing, so there can be no cycles in this subgraph. Also, by construction, every node except the root has a parent. Thus, the induced subgraph is a tree that leads towards the root. Now, since $parentOK(i)$ holds for every node i, no node may change its parent to minimize further the cost of the tree, implying that the final state is an equilibrium. □

Once the stable configuration is reached, all guards are false, and the closure property trivially holds. This proves the stabilization property.

3.2 Alternative Strategies

If there exists a set of strategies (synonymous with algorithms) with the property that no process can lower its cost by changing its strategy while the other processes keep their strategies unchanged, then that set of strategies and the corresponding costs constitute the *Nash Equilibrium*.

To prove that the stable configuration reflects a Nash equilibrium, we need to consider various strategies that can be adopted by the processes to lower their costs. The algorithm we proposed uses a *greedy strategy*, (call it *Strategy A*) but it is, by no means, the only possible strategy. Let us examine a second strategy for cost minimization by the individual processes. It is an *altruistic strategy*: each node picks a parent that lowers the communication cost of the nodes of the opposite color (call it *Strategy B*). As a result, black processes will help lower the cost of the white processes, and vice versa. To implement Strategy B, we modify the definition of *ParentOK* and *FixParent* as follows[3]:

$ParentOK(i) \equiv$ $(i = white) \land p(i) = j :$
$$L(j).b + b(i,j) = min\{L(k).b + b(i,k) : k \in N(i)\} \lor$$
$(i = black) \land p(i) = j :$
$$L(j).w + w(i,j) = min\{L(k).w + w(i,k) : k \in N(i)\}$$

$FixParent(i) \equiv$ **if** i is white $\rightarrow p(i) := j :$
$$L(j).b + b(i,j) = min\{L(k).b + b(i,k) : k \in N(i)\}$$
$\Box$ i is black $\rightarrow p(i) := j :$
$$L(j).w + w(i,j) = min\{L(k).w + w(i,k) : k \in N(i)\}$$
fi

Once these are appropriately defined, the main algorithm remains unchanged. Using the same line of arguments, we can show that this algorithm also stabilizes the system, but to a different configuration. This leads to the following observation:

Observation 1. *Using Strategy B, the system of processes stabilizes to an equilibrium configuration, and the edges connecting the processes with their parents form a spanning tree.*

The observation trivially follows from Theorem 1 if we swap the costs of the white and the black nodes for each edge.

The Cost of Equilibrium. A natural component of such an exercise is to analyze the quality of the equilibrium configuration: How bad is the cost of this

---

[3] This apparently weakens the encryption mechanism since it requires $x > y \Rightarrow \hat{x} > \hat{y}$. However, using the altruistic protocol, white processes lower their cost by helping the black processes and vice versa, and this is more conducive to building a trust relationship. So we will disregard the encryption symbol.

configuration in comparison with the "optimal" configuration? For the nodes of a given color, define the cost of a configuration as the sum of weights of all the tree edges for that color. Define the *optimal* cost as the cost of the tree when all nodes are of the same color. The issue is: By what extent will it increase if some of the nodes belong to a different color? Here is an upper bound. Let $e_{max} = max\{w(e), b(e) : e \in E\}$ and $e_{min} = min\{w(e), b(e) : e \in E\}$. Then the following theorem holds.

Theorem 2. *For any set of processes of a given color, the ratio of the cost of the equilibrium configuration to the cost of the optimal configuration is bounded from above by $\frac{e_{max}}{e_{min}}$.*

Proof. A tree with N nodes has $(N-1)$ edges, so the cost of the optimal configuration has a lower bound of $(N-1).e_{min}$. To determine the maximum possible weight of the tree in an equilibrium configuration under any of the algorithms A or B (or a mix of the two), think of an adversary that can switch the color of zero or more processes so that each node chooses the edge with largest weight as its link to its parent node. The cost of the resulting configuration is bounded from above by $(N-1).e_{max}$. The ratio of the two costs will not exceed

$$\frac{e_{max}}{e_{min}}. \hspace{3cm} \square$$

This is a loose upper bound. In general, when the number of white processes is much larger than the number of black processes, Strategy A will lead to a lower cost for the white processes, and Strategy B will lead to a lower cost for the black processes. This is quite intuitive, since in Strategy A, each step by the majority (i.e. white) processes helps lower their own cost at the expense of the competitors' cost, whereas in Strategy B, each step by the majority processes lowers the cost of the competitors at the expense of their own cost.

Simulations support this observation, although the costs do not necessarily decrease (or increase) monotonically with the number of processes switching strategies. The topology and the cost distribution play deciding roles. That said, based on the knowledge acquired during the progress of the communication, processes may be tempted to use different strategies. However, we will demonstrate that the system is robust enough to guarantee convergence to a Nash equilibrium, where all processes choose Strategy A, and no process can unilaterally lower its cost of communication with the root node.

Observation 2. *The cost of the white(black) processes will be minimum when they use Strategy A while the black(white) processes use strategy B.*

Viewed from the perspective of the white processes, the validity of the above observation is based on the fact that that every node picks the best edge for the white processes, so the algorithm reduces to the classical stabilizing shortest path algorithm (*e.g.* [10,6]) for the white nodes.

Theorem 3. *For a given graph $G = (V, E)$ with a given composition of the processes in V, and the set of strategies (A, B), the equilibrium configuration is unique, and it reflects the Nash equilibrium.*

Proof. Assume that using whatever strategy the processes choose, the system of processes stabilizes to some configuration that determines the payoffs for the black and the white processes. Now consider three different cases:

1. Assume that all processes use Strategy B. Observe that one or more processes of a certain group will switch to Strategy A, since this will lower their cost (Observation 2). However the other group might apprehend this, they will also switch from Strategy B to Strategy A.
2. Assume that the white processes use Strategy B, while the black processes use Strategy A. However, altruism does not pay off unless everyone is altruistic. Since the white processes do not know what strategy the black processes are using, they will switch to Strategy A, and their cost will go down.
3. Assume that all processes use Strategy A. Now no process will be motivated to switch to Strategy B, since such a switch will imply lowering the cost of the other group even if it increases the cost of its own group. Thus this is a stable configuration.

Thus, regardless of the initial strategies chosen by the black and the white processes, all processes will eventually switch to Strategy A, and regardless of the initial values of L and p, the system will stabilize in a bounded number of steps. Furthermore, since no process can unilaterally lower its cost by switching to a different strategy, the stable configuration will reflect a Nash equilibrium. □

Note. Both strategies (A and B) can be further optimized as follows. Consider A first. There may be cases in which a white node i finds multiple neighbors j satisfying the condition $L(j).w + w(i,j) = min\{L(k).w + w(i,k) : k \in N(i)\}$. Instead of arbitrarily choosing one such node, i will choose a $p(i) = j$ for which the cost of the black component of $L(i)$ is the lowest. A similar step can be taken by the black nodes too, i.e. when a black node i finds multiple neighbors j satisfying $j : L(j).b + b(i,j) = min\{L(k).b + b(i,k) : k \in N(i)\}$, it will pick a $p(i) = j$ such that the cost of the white component of $L(i)$ is the lowest. Similarly, for B, whenever a node i has more than one choice for the parent node, it will break the tie by picking one that lowers the component of $L(i)$ corresponding to its own color.

The interesting aspect of this exercise is that not only does the network state stabilize to a desirable configuration, but the strategies stabilize too, in as much as regardless of the starting strategies, all processes end up using the same final strategy. This does not rule out the invention of new strategies beyond what has been considered for this exercise.

4 Conclusion

Selfish stabilization reduces to classical stabilization when the private goals of the constituent processes do not conflict. The following issues are relevant about the approach taken in this paper:

The first is the separation of *cooperation* and *competition*. Assume that processes first cooperate to form a spanning tree, then try to optimize it to improve their individual payoffs. In presence of arbitrary initializations, failures, and selfish motives, such segregation of actions is difficult to implement.

The uniqueness of the equilibrium point is another significant issue. For the current problem, under each strategy, the system of processes reaches a unique equilibrium point, and the resulting Nash equilibrium is also unique. If this were not true, then there could be multiple trees, possibly of different costs, where the system of processes could stabilize to, the choice being determined by the schedule and the relative speeds of actions. However, once reaching an equilibrium point, an unhappy (or ambitious) process could deliberately introduce a perturbation (by corrupting a local variable) to possibly reach a different equilibrium point with a better payoff, and jeopardize the common goal. There is no guarantee that this will happen. But the uniqueness of the equilibrium point will prevent the constituent processes from using deliberate perturbation as a strategy to improve payoff, or at least probe the possibility of a better payoff.

Non-compliance to global mandates can have an overall negative impact on the payoffs when the Nash equilibrium corresponds to an inferior equilibrium. One approach can be the development of a payment scheme to reward compliance. Another approach involves detecting cheaters and appropriately penalizing them to force compliance. Quantification of these issues is an open problem, and is a topic of future research.

The paradigm of selfish stabilization can easily be extended in several ways. First, it can easily be extended to systems involving more than two competing groups, in the extreme case, each process caring for itself and no one else. Second, the metric used here (simple additive metric) could be replaced by any strictly monotonic metric, such as those presented in [7,6]. This would extend those previous results on stabilizing generic routing, since our scheme allows the possibility to use different metrics for different groups of players. This would also subsume previous approaches that investigated a specific metric [3].

References

1. Arora, A., Gouda, M.G.: Closure and Convergence: A foundation of fault-tolerant computing. IEEE Trans. Software Engineering **19**, (1993) 1015–1027.
2. Chen, N.S., Yu, H.P., Huang, S.T.: A self-stabilizing algorithm for constructing a spanning tree. Information Processing Letters **39** (1991) 147–151.
3. Cobb, J.A., Gouda, M.G, Musunuri, R.: A stabilizing solution to the stable path problem. Workshop on Self-stabilizing Systems (2003) 169–183.
4. Dijkstra, E.W.: Self-stabilization in spite of distributed control. Communications of the ACM **17** (1974), 643–644.

5. Dolev, S.: Self-stabilization. MIT Press (2000).
6. Ducourthial, B., Tixeuil S.: Self-stabilization with r-operators. Distributed Computing **14** (2001) 147–162.
7. Gouda, M.G., Schneider, M.: Stabilization of maximal metric trees. Workshop on Self-stabilizing Systems (1999) 10–17.
8. Griffin, T.G., Shepherd, F.B., Wilfong, G.: The stable paths problem and interdomain routing. IEEE/ACM Transactions on Networking **10** (2002).
9. Halpern, J.Y.: A computer scientist looks at game theory. Invited talk at *Games 2000*. Available from http://www.econwpa.wustl.edu/listings/0411.html.
10. Huang, T.C.: A self-stabilizing algorithm for the shortest path problem assuming read/write Atomicity. J. Computer and System Sciences **71** (2005) 70–85.
11. Mavronicolas, M., Papadopoulou, V.G., Philippou, A., Spirakis, P.: A graph-theoretic network security game. First International Workshop in Internet and Network Economics (WINE 2005) 969–978.
12. Moscibroda, T., Schmid, S., Wattenhofer, R.: On the topology formed by selfish peers. ACM Conference on Principles of Distributed Computing (PODC), Denver, 2006.
13. Moscibroda, T., Schmid, S., Wattenhofer, R.: When selfish meets evil: Byzantine players in a virus inoculation game. ACM Conference on Principles of Distributed Computing (PODC), Denver, 2006.
14. Pallier, P.: Public-key cryptosystems based on composite degree residue classes. Eurocrypt (1999).
15. Osborne, M.J., Rubinstein, A.: A course in game theory. MIT Press (1994).
16. Roughgarden, T., Tardös E.: How bad is selfish routing? Journal of the ACM **49** (2002) 236–259.
17. Simon, H.: Models of Bounded Rationality: Volumes 1 and 2. MIT Press (1982)

Reliability and Availability Analysis of Self-stabilizing Systems*

Abhishek Dhama, Oliver Theel, and Timo Warns

Carl von Ossietzky University of Oldenburg,
Department of Computing Science,
D-26111 Oldenburg, Germany

Abstract. Self-stabilizing systems are often only evaluated in terms of worst-case time and space complexities for the recovery from arbitrary state disruptions. In this paper, we interpret and formalize well-known fault tolerance measures for masking fault-tolerant systems, namely reliabilty, instantaneous availability, and limiting availability in the context of self-stabilizing systems. This allows to additionally evaluate self-stabilizing systems by these well-accepted measures. The calculation is challenging due to a large (and possibly infinite) state space. We present an analysis procedure that comprises a suitable state abstraction thereby making the calculation tractable. Exemplarily, we apply the procedure to a system that constructs a depth-first search spanning tree showing that our approach is feasible and yields meaningful results.

1 Introduction

Forms of fault tolerance can be divided into four categories, two important categories thereof being *masking fault tolerance* and *non-masking fault tolerance* [1]. A system that is masking fault-tolerant with respect to a given fault class $\mathcal{F}$ "covers" the appearance of failures of sub-components from an outside observer who inspects the system at it's application interface, at least as long as the assumptions stated by $\mathcal{F}$ hold. If the fault class holds, a service provided by the system to the environment at the application interface behaves in accordance to its *problem specification*. The problem specification consists of a *safety* and a *liveness property*. A system is correct with respect to the problem specification if the liveness as well as the safety property hold. In order for the system to be masking fault-tolerant with respect to fault class $\mathcal{F}$, the liveness as well as the safety property must not be compromised by any fault in $\mathcal{F}$. In other words: the system does not fail. Only if the fault class is left, a violation of the problem specification may occur and incorrectness of the system could potentially be observed in the manner stated. Examples of masking fault-tolerant systems are data replication services [2] and distributed consensus services [3]: they behave correctly as long as a certain number of sub-components do not fail.

---

* This work was supported by the German Research Foundation (DFG) under grants GRK 1076/1 "TrustSoft" and SFB/TR 14 "AVACS."

A.K. Datta and M. Gradinariu (Eds.): SSS 2006, LNCS 4280, pp. 244–261, 2006.

In non-masking fault-tolerant systems with respect to a fault class $\mathcal{F}$ – even if the fault class has not been not left – an observer may recognize a particular incorrectness of the system: the safety property is violated but the liveness property still holds. For ease of description, let $\mathcal{P}_S$ be a configuration predicate that specifies all system configurations in which the safety property holds. Let $\mathcal{P}_A \supseteq \mathcal{P}_S$ be a configuration predicate that specifies all possible configurations of the system assuming fault class $\mathcal{F}$. Consequently, in $\mathcal{P}_A$ the liveness property must hold.

Note that due to $\mathcal{P}_A \supseteq \mathcal{P}_S$, configurations of the system may be observed where $\mathcal{P}_A$ holds but not $\mathcal{P}_S$. In those cases, the system has not completely failed with respect to $\mathcal{F}$ but is nevertheless not performing "useful work." In order to still make productive use of such systems, situations in which $\mathcal{P}_A \wedge \neg \mathcal{P}_S$ hold must be bounded in space and/or time. Being in those configurations, the system must somehow itself – in the way it is implemented – correct its configuration such that the bounds are guaranteed and $\mathcal{P}_S$ (and implicitly $\mathcal{P}_A$) finally holds. Examples of non-masking fault-tolerant systems are self-stabilizing systems [4] and asymptotically stable systems [5]. In the context of self-stabilizing systems, the fault class covers transient faults affecting program variables only and $\mathcal{P}_A$ includes the entire configuration space [1].

Usually, different solutions to a problem are available forcing a developer to choose a solution from the set of all possible solutions. Ideally, he or she thoroughly evaluates all possible solutions to support the design decision and to find the solution that is best suited for given requirements. In order to differentiate "good" from "bad" fault-tolerant systems that provide the same service using the same fault class, *measures of fault tolerance* are used. The most prominent measures are *reliability, instantaneous availability*, and *limiting availability* [6]. The latter is often referred to as simply *availability* (see details in Sect. 2).

These three fault tolerance measures are widely used and well understood in the context of masking fault-tolerant systems [6,7,8,9,10]. In contrast, self-stabilizing systems are commonly evaluated in terms of worst-case time and space complexities only. These measures alone might be not expressive enough in practice, because different solutions to the same problem may have an equal worst-case complexity, but exhibit differing average case complexities: often average case complexity has a more significant impact in real-world settings. In particular, the three fault tolerance measures given above address average case complexities and, therefore, enable to identify suitable solutions in those settings. But how can these measures be applied to *non-masking* fault-tolerant systems in general and to self-stabilizing systems in particular? What do they mean in such a context? How can they be derived and, finally, how can these measures help to improve the quality of non-masking fault-tolerant and self-stabilizing systems? We are unaware of any treatment of these issues in literature.

In this paper, we answer some of the above questions. In particular, we make the following contributions. 1) We interpret and formalize classic fault tolerance measures, namely reliability, instantaneous availability, and limiting availability, for self-stabilizing systems enabling a meaningful evaluation of such systems. 2)

We present a system analysis procedure that makes the problem of calculating fault tolerance measures tractable by abstracting configurations to configuration classes. In particular, the procedure exhibits a trade-off between costs of system analysis and achievable accuracy. This trade-off can be adapted to the actual requirements by choosing an appropriate level of abstraction. 3) We exemplarily apply the analysis procedure to a self-stabilizing system constructing a depth-first search spanning tree and discuss the results.

The paper is structured as follows. In Sect. 2, we present our system model and interpret and formalize fault tolerance measures for self-stabilizing systems. Section 3 gives the basic ideas of the system analysis procedure, which is detailed and – exemplarily – applied to a system constructing a depth-first search (DFS) spanning tree in Sect. 4. Section 5 describes related work followed by a conclusion in the final section.

2   Basic Notions and Preliminaries

System Model of a Self-Stabilizing System. Our system model is based on the *asynchronous shared-memory* computation model [4]. A *distributed application* (hereafter synonymously referred to as "system") consists of a finite set of processes, $\Pi = \{p_1, \ldots, p_n\}$. The system executes a *distributed algorithm* that consists of a set of *sub-algorithms*. Each process in the system executes a sub-algorithm and is perceived as a (possibly infinite) state machine.

A process may communicate with certain other processes, called its *neighbors*. Communication takes place using *shared communication registers*. Each process has two sets of communication registers: *read* and *write* registers. A process *owns* its *write* registers and uses them to communicate part of its local state to its neighbors. The *read* registers are used to gather information about the states of its neighbors. The communication structure of the system can be represented by a *communication graph* that has a node for each process and a directed link between each pair of neighboring processes: the graph has a link l_i^j from process p_i to process p_j iff p_i may read from a register of p_j. Each process p_i has a total ordering $\alpha_i = \langle l_i^u, \ldots, l_i^z \rangle$ of its links that induces a total ordering of its neighbors. Besides the communication registers, a process may use additional *local variables* that cannot be accessed by other processes.

The local variables together with the communication registers of a process p_i form the *local state space* of p_i, denoted by S_i. A *configuration* c of the entire system is a vector composed of the local states of all the constituent processes of Π. The set of all possible system configurations is denoted by $C = S_1 \times \ldots \times S_n$.

The execution semantics is modeled using a central *scheduler*. The scheduler selects one of the processes in Π in a *random* manner and the selected process, in turn, executes a single *computation step*. We assume *read/write atomicity* for computation steps, that is, a computation step of a process consists of a computation on the process' local variables and either an atomic read or an atomic write operation on a process' communication register.

An *observed execution* of the system is a sequence of configurations $e = \langle c_1, c_2, \ldots \rangle$ such that a configuration c_{i+1} follows from configuration c_i either due to the execution of a single computation step by a constituent process or due to a manifestation of a transient fault called a *fault step*. Compared to the classical theory of self-stabilization [4], we generalize executions that can be perceived by an observer to factor in intermittent transient faults to determine fault tolerance measures.

We assume that the scheduler is *fair*, in the sense that it activates each process infinitely often in every infinite execution. The executions that result using a fair scheduler are called *fair executions*. Furthermore, we assume that the scheduler can be described by a tuple of probability values $\langle Q_S(p_1), \ldots, Q_S(p_n) \rangle$ representing a probability density function, where $Q_S(p_i)$ denotes the probability that the scheduler activates process p_i[1]. As the scheduler always chooses a process, $\sum_{i=1}^{n} Q_S(p_i) = 1$. In order to fulfill the fairness requirement, it is necessary that $\forall p \in \Pi : Q_S(p) \neq 0$.

Due to our system model, time proceeds in discrete "time ticks", that is, one tick per computation step or per fault step. Therefore, we represent a point in time with respect to the model simply by a non-zero number k. Furthermore, for ease of presentation, we assume that any execution starts at time $k = 0$.

The system is assumed to be self-stabilizing, that is, eventually, the system reaches a configuration that is in a set of *safe* configurations even if started in an arbitrary configuration and stays in this set of safe configurations thereafter in absence of faults leading to errors. The set of safe configurations is defined using a configuration predicate $\mathcal{P}_S$. A configuration $c \in C$ of a system is called *safe* with respect to $\mathcal{P}_S$ iff it satisfies the predicate $\mathcal{P}_S$. We denote the set of all safe configuration by C_S, that is, $C_S := \{c : c \in C \wedge c \text{ satisfies } \mathcal{P}_S\}$.

As already indicated, we augment the system model with additional fault assumptions. A *fault* is a configuration transition that is not caused by a computation step of a constituent process: within an execution, a fault may lead to a configuration c_{i+1} from c_i even if c_{i+1} may not be reached by a computation step of a process. The manifestation of a fault is regarded as a fault step that – in correspondence to a computational step – requires one time tick to be realized. We can differentiate types of faults depending on whether the predicate $\mathcal{P}_S$ holds for the configurations it maps to or not. Figure 1 shows the configuration space of a self-stabilizing system where solid arcs represent transitions due to faults and dashed arrows represent the transitions due to computations by the processes. For example, if a fault is a transition from a safe configuration to a non-safe configuration such as transition 1 in Fig. 1, the fault leads to a partial failure of the system in the sense that an outside observer perceives a violation of the safety property $\mathcal{P}_S$. Other faults like transition 2 that lead from a non-safe configuration to a safe configuration even help to correct the configuration. As we only consider those safety properties which can be expressed by configuration

---

[1] The approach does not exclude that Q_S varies over time. However, the associated computations become significantly more involved such that we assume fixed Q_S for ease of presentation.

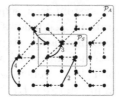

Fig. 1. Illustration of the four different fault types that may occur in a self-stabilizing system

predicates, a transition from a safe configuration to another safe configuration (transition 3) owing to a fault does not constitute a failure. Transition 4, finally, represents the effects of a fault leading the system from an non-safe to another non-safe configuration. We describe faults by a probability $q_{\mathcal{F}}$ denoting that a fault occurs *instead* of the execution of a computation step. Next, we present how to adapt the fault tolerance measures referred to in the introduction to self-stabilizing systems.

Fault Tolerance Measures for Self-Stabilizing Systems. As already said, we want to apply fault tolerance measures to self-stabilizing systems. We briefly summarize the notions of reliability and availability and give formalizations and interpretations in terms of our system model. Note that all fault tolerance measures are only given for discrete time points due to this model. Refer to, for example, Trivedi [6, p. 124–129, 319–328] for a more detailed discussion of reliability and availability in general.

We formalize the notions of reliability and availability for self-stabilizing systems whose safety property can be expressed in terms of a configuration predicate. We assume that a self-stabilizing system is designed such that it does something "useful" (i.e., it is functioning) when it is in a safe configuration or transits between safe configurations. Therefore, the fact that a system is in an "up" phase means that the system is in a safe configuration.

Intuitively, *reliability* is defined as the "continuity of correct service" of a system [11]. Reliability analysis is done for systems where components are not repaired on a failure. Hence, the lifetime of these systems consists of a single "up" phase from system start to failure and a subsequent permanent "down" phase. Formally, the reliability of a general system $R(t)$ is the probability that the system has not failed in the continuous time interval $[0, t], t > 0$, with respect to the problem specification under the constraint that is was correct at time $t = 0$ (i.e., $R(0) = 1$). Based on our model, the reliability $R(k)$ of a self-stabilizing system is the probability

$$R(k) := P(\mathcal{P}_S \text{ holds at time } l = 0, \dots, k) \tag{1}$$

In contrast to reliability, availability analysis is done for systems where components are repaired on failures. Hence, the lifetime of a system can be divided into alternating periods of "up" and "down" phases. Intuitively, availability is defined as the "readiness for correct service" of a system [11]. Formally, the *instantaneous availability* of a system $A(t)$ is defined as the probability that a system is in an "up" phase at time t under the constraint that it was correct at time $t = 0$ (i.e., $A(0) = 1$). Note that instantaneous availability is equivalent to reliability in the absence of repair operations. Consequently, instantaneous availability $A(k)$ of a self-stabilizing system in our model is the probability

$$A(k) := P(\mathcal{P}_S \text{ holds at time } k \mid \mathcal{P}_S \text{ holds at time } k = 0) \qquad (2)$$

Availability analysis often comprises the probability that the system is in an "up" phase after a "sufficiently long time" after system start when looking at it at an arbitrary point in time. In general, the *limiting availability* of a system A is defined as the limiting value of $A(t)$ as t approaches infinity. Consequently, we define the limiting availability of a self-stabilizing system in our model as the probability

$$A := \lim_{k \to \infty} A(k) \qquad (3)$$

These three fault tolerance measures allow to differentiate self-stabilizing systems in terms of the degree of dependability they provide. For example, having multiple self-stabilizing system solutions to the same problem, high availability solutions can be identified and preferably be used in safety-critical application environments. However, the problem of determining concrete values for these measures given a concrete system is challenging due to a large, possibly infinite configuration space. Next, we present how we approach this problem.

3   Basic Ideas for Calculating Fault Tolerance Measures

For the calculation of fault tolerance measures, one would ideally consider every possible configuration and all possible transitions between configurations. However, the configuration space of a system may consist of an infinite number of configurations drawing such an approach infeasible. The problem can be made tractable if the configuration space is reduced into a finite number of partitions such that only these partitions and transitions between partitions are considered. The scalability of the approach can be further improved if we perceive a distributed algorithm as a set of sub-algorithm classes where instances of a class may be instantiated and executed by processes. If the analysis is based on sub-algorithm classes instead of instances and classes are used by multiple processes (as it is usually the case), we only need to analyze each sub-algorithm class rather than each process. We now discuss the reduction of the configuration space and the analysis of sub-algorithm classes in detail.

Reduction of Configuration Space. We reduce the possibly infinite set of all possible configurations to a finite set of configuration classes by dividing the configuration space into configuration classes such that such that the classes are non-overlapping and completely and exactly cover the configuration space. All configurations belonging to a class are characterized by *local predicates* defined over the states of the individual processes.

A *configuration class* $\mathcal{C}_i$ is the set of all configurations $c \in C$ satisfying a *configuration predicate* $\mathcal{P}_i$. The configuration space C is partitioned into g configuration classes, $\mathcal{C}_1, \ldots, \mathcal{C}_g$. We subsume all safe configurations into a single configuration class C_g by defining define $\mathcal{P}_g := \mathcal{P}_S$. This implies that the system is in an "up" phase iff the system configuration belongs to configuration class C_g.

$\mathcal{P}_i$ can be defined using a "bottom-up" approach, that is in terms of *local predicates*, because every predicate $\mathcal{P}_i$ is a configuration predicate and every configuration is a tuple of local states. A local predicate for a process p_i is defined as a state predicate on the local state of p_i. In particular, we define a finite number of local predicates for each sub-algorithm class thereby partitioning the local state space of each process that executes the sub-algorithm class.

Therefore, each configuration class predicate $\mathcal{P}_i, i = 1, \ldots, g - 1$, is defined as conjunction of n local predicates $\mathcal{P}_{ij}, j = 1, \ldots, n$, one local predicate $\mathcal{P}_{ij}$ for each process $p_j \in \Pi$:

$$\forall i \in \{1, \ldots, g-1\} : \mathcal{P}_i := \bigwedge_{j=1}^{n} \mathcal{P}_{ij}. \tag{4}$$

Depending on the system specification, it may be the case that the configuration predicate $\mathcal{P}_g \equiv \mathcal{P}_S$ is defined as a disjunction of multiple conjunction terms rather than a single conjunction term. However, this does not affect the analysis.

The partitioning into configuration classes effectively reduces the possibly infinite configuration space of a system to a finite number of configuration classes. For example, if we define l local predicates for each sub-algorithm and the safety predicate can be expressed by a single conjunction term, the configuration space is reduced to l^n configuration classes. The "bottom-up" approach of defining configuration class predicates is highly advantageous, since it tremendously eases the analysis of sub-algorithms: based on the knowledge of local states of processes only – mirrored by $\mathcal{P}_{ij}$ – one can quite conveniently identify all the possible transitions from a configuration class.

Exemplarily, we calculate the fault tolerance measures for self-stabilizing systems whose safety predicate $\mathcal{P}_S$ can be expressed by a single conjunction term of local predicates, that is, $\mathcal{P}_g \equiv \mathcal{P}_S \equiv \mathcal{P}_{g1} \wedge \ldots \wedge \mathcal{P}_{gn}$. Such systems allow to partition the state space of each process p_i into only two partitions leading to 2^n configuration classes. In general, if the safety predicate can be expressed as a single conjunction term, this – obviously – is the least number of configuration classes with non-trivial partitionings of each process' state space. The two partitions of the state space can be characterized by two local predicates $\mathcal{S}_i$ and $\mathcal{N}_i$, which are defined as follows. If none of the local variables or communication registers of p_i contains a value that violates the system's safety predicate $\mathcal{P}_S$, then p_i satisfies $\mathcal{S}_i$. Otherwise, p_i satisfies $\mathcal{N}_i$. Thus, $\mathcal{S}_i \equiv \neg \mathcal{N}_i$ always holds. Obviously, $\mathcal{P}_S \equiv \mathcal{S}_1 \wedge \ldots \wedge \mathcal{S}_n$ holds for our example system.

For simplifying the presentation in subsequent sections, we adopt the following convention. Due to fact that the state of each process is characterized by two local predicates, one can represent a configuration class as a binary number with n bits such that 0 (or alternatively: 1) in the ith position corresponds to process p_i satisfying local predictae $\mathcal{N}_i$ (or $\mathcal{S}_i$ respectively). This "encoding" also defines a total ordering on configuration classes which may be used to assign classes unambigiously to lines and rows of particular matrices. We define a distance function $d(\mathcal{C}_i, \mathcal{C}_j)$ that gives the number of local predicates $\mathcal{P}_{il}, l = 1, \ldots, n$, that define $\mathcal{P}_i$, but do not hold for $\mathcal{P}_j$. For our examples with two partitions of each state space, we can define $d(\mathcal{C}_i, \mathcal{C}_j)$ as being the Hamming distance [12] between the binary notation of configuration classes. For example, for a three process system, 110_2 (equivalent to 6_{10}) "encodes" a configuration class $\mathcal{C}_6$ corresponding to $\mathcal{S}_1 \wedge \mathcal{S}_2 \wedge \mathcal{N}_3$. The value of $d(\mathcal{C}_3, \mathcal{C}_6)$ is 2 implying that two local predicates change between $\mathcal{P}_3 \equiv \mathcal{N}_1 \wedge \mathcal{S}_2 \wedge \mathcal{S}_3$ and $\mathcal{P}_6 \equiv \mathcal{S}_1 \wedge \mathcal{S}_2 \wedge \mathcal{N}_3$.

Analysis of Distributed Algorithms. Depending on the distributed algorithm, the individual processes either execute the same or different sub-algorithms. As all processes that are an instance of the same sub-algorithm class behave in a similar way, an analysis that is performed on a per-class basis and not on a per-process basis facilitates the overall analysis. In particular, an analysis of a sub-algorithm class that abstracts from concrete neighbors by differentiating between the algorithm and its communication structure (given, for example, via a communication graph), can be re-used for all the processes using this class.

We now describe the analysis of a particular sub-algorithm class: The result of a computation step of a process p_i depends on the current values of p_i's local state and, possibly, on the value of a neighbor's communication register. Thus, a computation step of p_i only affects the local predicates of p_i since the step changes only the state of p_i but local states of other processes are unchanged. However, the result of the step may be affected by the current state of a neighboring process. For example, if p_i satisfies the predicate $\mathcal{S}_i$ and reads a communication register of a neighbor p_j satisfying $\mathcal{N}_j$, then p_i itself may reach a state satisfying $\mathcal{N}_i$ owing to error propagation.

For the analysis of a sub-algorithm class, we consider a generic process p_i that instantiates and executes the corresponding sub-algorithm. We determine the probability that a computation step of p_i leads from a state satisfying $\mathcal{P}_x$ to a state satisfying $\mathcal{P}_y$ for each pair of local predicates $\mathcal{P}_x$ and $\mathcal{P}_y$ of p_i. This analysis requires detailed knowledge about the sub-algorithm and is challenging. However, it needs to be performed only once per sub-algorithm class – and not per process – since it is performed on the basis of a generic process.

For an example with two state partitions per process, we only need to determine the following four probabilities:

$$P(\mathcal{N}_i^k \mid p_i \text{ executes step } k \text{ and } \mathcal{N}_i^{k-1}), \tag{5}$$

$$P(\mathcal{N}_i^k \mid p_i \text{ executes step } k \text{ and } \mathcal{S}_i^{k-1}), \tag{6}$$

$$P(\mathcal{S}_i^k \mid p_i \text{ executes step } k \text{ and } \mathcal{N}_i^{k-1}), \text{ and} \tag{7}$$

$$P(\mathcal{S}_i^k \mid p_i \text{ executes step } k \text{ and } \mathcal{S}_i^{k-1}), \tag{8}$$

where $\mathcal{S}_i^k$ and $\mathcal{N}_i^k$ denote that predicates $\mathcal{S}_i$ and $\mathcal{N}_i$ immediately hold after step k, respectively.

Trading Analysis Feasibility vs. Accuracy. The two techniques presented above allow for a quite convenient analysis of a self-stabilizing system. However, these technique-inherent abstractions trade accuracy for feasibility. In particular, we make the following additional assumptions that interfere with accuracy:

In our examples, we pessimistically assume error propagation between processes if the communication register of a neighboring process p_j is read whose predicate $\mathcal{N}_j$ holds. That is, whenever a communication register of a process that is erroneous is read, we assume that the reading process becomes erroneous as well even if the particular value read from the communication register is not affected by an error. Note that there is the possibility that an erroneous process corrects itself if it overwrites erroneous values in its communication registers or local variables by correct values (e.g., by writing a fixed correct value to a communication register). Furthermore, we assume that the result of an internal computation is erroneous if one or more of the local variables or communication registers that are read during the computation are erroneous. Note that we obtain a lower bound on reliability and availability under this assumption.

Due to lack of further information, we adopt – as a best effort estimation – a uniform distribution assumption for the probability that the system is in a certain configuration of a configuration class $\mathcal{C}_i$ if it is known that the system is in a configuration of $\mathcal{C}_i$.

Clearly, the trade-off between accuracy and analysis feasibility can be adjusted by the "granularity" of the local predicates. The finer granular the predicates are chosen, the higher the accuracy of the results. However, finer granular local predicates complicate the analysis of sub-algorithm classes and increase the number of configuration classes to be considered in subsequent processing steps.

4   System Analysis Procedure

We will now describe the system analysis procedure in order to calculate the fault tolerance measures of a self-stabilizing system both, generally and in terms of an example. The procedure consists of three steps. First, each sub-algorithm class is analyzed with respect to probabilities of configuration class transitions that are caused by a computation step of a corresponding process. (Sect. 4.1). Second, these probabilities are used to determine a Markov chain that characterizes the overall system (Sect. 4.2). In addition to the probabilities identified in the first step, the identification of an appropriate Markov chain also takes the influence of the scheduler and of fault steps into account. Finally, the fault tolerance measures are calculated based on the obtained Markov chain (Sect. 4.3).

Exemplarily, we apply the procedure to a system that executes the self-stabilizing depth first search (DFS) distributed spanning tree algorithm of Collin and Dolev [13]. Informally, the system calculates a DFS tree of the system's communication graph where the DFS tree is encoded as paths in communication registers. The distributed algorithm comprises two sub-algorithm classes: Figure 2 gives the sub-algorithm for a root process and Fig. 3 gives the sub-algorithm used by non-root processes.

Both sub-algorithms are equivalent to the ones of Collin and Dolev [13] except being written in terms of guarded commands. We consider a system with

```
1  do
2      true   →   write(path₁ := ⊥)
3  od
```

Fig. 2. DFS sub-algorithm for the root process p_1

```
1  do
2      j ∉ {0, ..., δ}      →    j := random value in {0, ..., δ}
3      j ∈ {0, ..., δ}      →
4      do
5          j ∈ {0, ..., δ − 1}   →    j := j + 1;   read(read_path_j := path_{α_i(j)})
6          j = δ    →    j := 0;   write(path_i := min{|read_path_l ∘ α_i(l)|_N, 1 ≤ l ≤ δ})
7      od
8  od
```

Fig. 3. DFS sub-algorithm for non-root process $p_i, i > 0$

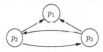

Fig. 4. Communication graph of the DFS example

three processes, $\Pi = \{p_1, p_2, p_3\}$, where process p_1 executes the sub-algorithm of Fig. 2, and the processes p_2 and p_3 execute the sub-algorithm given in Fig. 3. Figure 4 shows the communication graph of the system illustrating which process can read the communication registers from what other process. As indicated, the distributed algorithm encodes the DFS tree as paths in communication registers. A path is denoted by $\perp$ followed by a sequence of links. Each process p_i owns a single communication register $path_i$ that contains the path from p_i to the root process p_1. The constant δ denotes the number of neighbors of a process. The process p_1 repeatedly writes the empty path denoted by "$\perp$" to its communication register. The processes p_2 and p_3 repeatedly read the communication registers of their neighbors and store these values in their local $read\_path$ variable. Both processes calculate different paths to the root from the values in the $read\_path$ variables, which contain paths read from neighbors and information about the link ordering. Finally, they determine the correct path with respect to the DFS tree and write it to their communication register. The correct path is the shortest path of the calculated paths. The iteration over the neighbors and the final calculation is done using the local variable j.

4.1   Analysis of Sub-algorithm Classes

First, we characterize the behavior of the system if no faults occur by analyzing each class of sub-algorithms with respect to probabilities of configuration class transitions that are caused by a *single* computation step of a process that executes a corresponding sub-algorithm as given by Eqs. (5)–(8) in Sect. 3.

In the scope of the example, for a generic process p_i that executes the sub-algorithm given in Fig. 2, $\mathcal{S}_i$ holds iff $path_i = \perp$. Thus,,

$$\forall k \in \mathbb{N}: \; P(\mathcal{S}_i^k \mid p_i \text{ exec. step } k) = 1,$$

because p_i always overwrites the $path_i$ register by the correct value $\perp$ no matter whether $\mathcal{S}_i^{k-1}$ or $\mathcal{N}_i^{k-1}$.

For a generic process p_i that executes the sub-algorithm given in Fig. 3, the analysis is more complex: The predicate $\mathcal{S}_i$ holds iff the $read\_path$ variables and the $path_i$ communication register of p_i contain correct values as given by the problem specification of the DFS spanning tree problem. This is obvious for $path_i$ as it is a part of the encoding of the spanning tree. The $read\_path$ variables must contain correct values as well, because an erroneous value can affect computations to determine the value of $path_i$ and, therefore, lead to a violation of the system's safety predicate $\mathcal{P}_S$. However, the local variable j may contain an arbitrary value as j does not affect the problem specification.

If $\mathcal{S}_i^{k-1}$ and $\mathcal{N}_i^k$, an error propagation must have occurred. Error propagation to p_i occurs iff p_i reads an erroneous value from a neighbor in line 5. This happens if the value of the local variable j, which has $\delta + 1$ possible values, is such that a value from a neighbor with $\mathcal{N}^{k-1}$ is read. Let f denote the number of neighbors with $\mathcal{N}^{k-1}$. Thus, the probability that $\mathcal{N}_i^k$ if $\mathcal{S}_i^{k-1}$ is $f/(\delta + 1)$ assuming every neighbor being equally probable as the source. More precisely,

$$\forall k \in \mathbb{N}: P(\mathcal{N}_i^k \mid p_i \text{ exec. step } k \text{ and } \mathcal{S}_i^{k-1}) = \frac{f}{\delta + 1}.$$

Obviously,

$$\forall k \in \mathbb{N}: P(\mathcal{S}_i^k \mid p_i \text{ exec. step } k \text{ and } \mathcal{S}_i^{k-1}) = 1 - P(\mathcal{N}_i^k \mid p_i \text{ exec. step } k \text{ and } \mathcal{S}_i^{k-1}).$$

Let us assume that $\mathcal{N}_i^{k-1}$ and p_i executes step k. $\mathcal{S}_i^k$ can only hold due to the execution of line 5 or 6. The probability of $\mathcal{S}_i$ becoming true due to line 5 is

$$\forall k \in \mathbb{N}: P(\mathcal{S}_i^k \mid p_i \text{ exec. line 5 in step } k \text{ and } \mathcal{N}_i^{k-1})$$
$$= \frac{\delta}{2^{\delta+1} - 1} \cdot \frac{\delta - f}{\delta} \cdot \frac{1}{\delta + 1} = \frac{\delta - f}{(\delta + 1) \cdot 2^{\delta+1} - \delta - 1}$$

for the following reasons that are given term by term from left to right: 1) Only the local variable $read\_path_l$ of the overall δ $read\_path$ variables may contain an incorrect value and $path_i$ must contain a correct value. The process p_i has δ local variables and one communication register that influence the predicates $\mathcal{S}_i$ and $\mathcal{N}_i$. There are $2^{\delta+1}$ overall combinations of the local variables and communication register being correct or incorrect. However, as $\mathcal{N}_i^{k-1}$, the combination with all local variables and communication registers being correct cannot occur after step k. Therefore, the probability for a single incorrect $read\_path_l$ variable and a correct communication register is $\delta/(2^{\delta+1} - 1)$. 2) The predicate $\mathcal{S}$ must hold for the neighboring process, whose communication register is read. The probability for this is $(\delta - f)/\delta$ as p_i has δ neighbors with $\mathcal{N}^{k-1}$ holding for f of them. 3) The local variable j must be equal to l. Thus, the according probability calculates to $1/(\delta + 1)$ as $j \in \{0, \ldots, \delta\}$. The probability of $\mathcal{S}_i$ becoming true due to line 6 is

$$\forall k \in \mathbb{N}: P(\mathcal{S}_i^k \mid p_i \text{ exec. line 6 in step } k \text{ and } \mathcal{N}_i^{k-1})$$
$$= \frac{1}{2^{\delta+1} - 1} \cdot \frac{1}{\delta + 1} = \frac{1}{(\delta + 1) \cdot 2^{\delta+1} - \delta - 1}$$

for the following reasons (again given term by term): 1) The $path_i$ register must contain an incorrect value and all $read\_path$ variables must contain a correct value. Likewise to the arguments from above, the probability of such a situation is $1/(2^{\delta+1}-1)$. 2) The local variable j must be equal to δ which is probable with $1/(\delta+1)$ as $j \in \{0, \dots, \delta\}$. Therefore, the probability that $\mathcal{S}_i$ holds at time k if $\mathcal{N}_i$ held at time $k-1$ and p_i executes step k is

$$\forall k \in \mathbb{N} : P(\mathcal{S}_i^k \mid p_i \text{ exec. step } k \text{ and } \mathcal{N}_i^{k-1}) = \frac{\delta - f + 1}{(\delta + 1) \cdot 2^{\delta+1} - \delta - 1}.$$

Finally, the probability that $\mathcal{N}_i$ remains true from $k-1$ to k is

$$\forall k \in \mathbb{N} : P(\mathcal{N}_i^k \mid p_i \text{ exec. step } k \text{ and } \mathcal{N}_i^{k-1}) = 1 - P(\mathcal{S}_i^k \mid p_i \text{ exec. step } k \text{ and } \mathcal{N}_i^{k-1}).$$

4.2 Markov Chain Identification

We now determine the Markov chain for a system to be used for calculating the fault tolerance measures. In Step 1, we calculate the transition probability matrix for transitions between configuration classes due to a single computation step of a process. In Step 2, we determine the transition probability matrix for transitions between configuration classes due to fault steps. Finally, in Step 3, we combine both matrices and obtain a transition probability matrix representing an appropriate Markov chain of the entire system.

Step 1. The computation step probability matrix $E := (e_{i,j})$ describes the probabilities of transitions due to computation steps. An element $e_{i,j}$ gives the probability that the system reaches a configuration in the configuration class $\mathcal{C}_j$ from a configuration of $\mathcal{C}_i$ if a process executes a single computation step. This captures the behavior of the distributed algorithm in the absence of faults leading to errors. We determine this matrix using the analysis of the sub-algorithm classes, the communication graph, and the information about the scheduler.

In our example, E is a $2^n \times 2^n$ matrix as we have 2^n overall configuration classes. For a transition from a configuration of $\mathcal{C}_i$ to a configuration of $\mathcal{C}_j$, let $T_l(\mathcal{C}_i, \mathcal{C}_j)$ denote the probability that has been derived in the analysis of the sub-algorithms executed by process $p_l \in \Pi$ and for the local predicates of p_l in $\mathcal{C}_i$ and $\mathcal{C}_j$. For the example,

$$T_l(\mathcal{C}_i, \mathcal{C}_j) = \begin{cases} P(\mathcal{N}_i^k \mid p_i \text{ exec. step } k \text{ and } \mathcal{N}_i^{k-1}) & \text{if } \mathcal{N}_l \text{ holds in } \mathcal{C}_i \wedge \mathcal{N}_l \text{ holds in } \mathcal{C}_j \\ P(\mathcal{N}_i^k \mid p_i \text{ exec. step } k \text{ and } \mathcal{S}_i^{k-1}) & \text{if } \mathcal{S}_l \text{ holds in } \mathcal{C}_i \wedge \mathcal{N}_l \text{ holds in } \mathcal{C}_j \\ P(\mathcal{S}_i^k \mid p_i \text{ exec. step } k \text{ and } \mathcal{N}_i^{k-1}) & \text{if } \mathcal{N}_l \text{ holds in } \mathcal{C}_i \wedge \mathcal{S}_l \text{ holds in } \mathcal{C}_j \\ P(\mathcal{S}_i^k \mid p_i \text{ exec. step } k \text{ and } \mathcal{S}_i^{k-1}) & \text{if } \mathcal{S}_l \text{ holds in } \mathcal{C}_i \wedge \mathcal{S}_l \text{ holds in } \mathcal{C}_j \end{cases}$$

Moreover, let f be substituted by the number of neighboring processes of p_l whose predicate $\mathcal{N}_l$ hold in $\mathcal{C}_i$. For example, consider the configuration classes $\mathcal{C}_4$ and $\mathcal{C}_6$, given by $\mathcal{P}_4 \equiv \mathcal{S}_1 \wedge \mathcal{N}_2 \wedge \mathcal{N}_3$ and $\mathcal{P}_6 \equiv \mathcal{S}_1 \wedge \mathcal{S}_2 \wedge \mathcal{N}_3$. In this case, $\mathcal{N}_l$ holds for $f = 1$ of $\delta = 2$ neighbors of process p_2 in $\mathcal{C}_4$ and, therefore, according to Sect (4.1),

$$T_2(\mathcal{C}_4, \mathcal{C}_6) = P(\mathcal{S}_2^k \mid p_2 \text{ exec. step } k \text{ and } \mathcal{N}_2^{k-1}) = \frac{2 - 1 + 1}{(2 + 1) \cdot 2^{2+1} - 2 - 1} = \frac{2}{21}$$

We can now give the matrix E with

$$e_{i,j} = \begin{cases} \sum_{p_l \in \Pi} Q_S(p_l) \cdot T_l(\mathcal{C}_i, \mathcal{C}_j) & \text{if } d(\mathcal{C}_i, \mathcal{C}_j) = 0 \\ Q_S(p_l) \cdot T_l(\mathcal{C}_i, \mathcal{C}_j) & \text{if } d(\mathcal{C}_i, \mathcal{C}_j) = 1 \wedge \mathcal{C}_i, \mathcal{C}_j \text{ differ in a local predicate of } p_l \\ 0 & \text{if } d(\mathcal{C}_i, \mathcal{C}_j) > 1 \end{cases}$$

This corresponds to the following facts stated case by case from above to below: 1) If no local predicate changes by a computation step, each process may be responsible for the transition under the constraint that the scheduler chooses the process. 2) If only the local predicate for process p_l changes by a computation step, this step must be executed by p_l, because only p_l itself can affect its local predicate. However, the probability for such a transition is constrained by the probability that the scheduler chooses p_l. 3) No computation step can affect more than one local predicate. The resulting computation step probability matrix characterizes the behavior of the self-stabilizing system in the absence of faults leading to errors. For the DFS example, matrix E is as follows (all matrices given are rounded to four decimals after the decimal point)

$$E = \begin{pmatrix} 0.6349 & 0.0159 & 0.0159 & 0 & 0.3333 & 0 & 0 & 0 \\ 0.2222 & 0.4127 & 0 & 0.0317 & 0 & 0.3333 & 0 & 0 \\ 0.2222 & 0 & 0.4127 & 0.0317 & 0 & 0 & 0.3333 & 0 \\ 0 & 0.1111 & 0.1111 & 0.4444 & 0 & 0 & 0 & 0.3333 \\ 0 & 0 & 0 & 0 & 0.9365 & 0.0317 & 0.0317 & 0 \\ 0 & 0 & 0 & 0 & 0.1111 & 0.8413 & 0 & 0.0476 \\ 0 & 0 & 0 & 0 & 0.1111 & 0 & 0.8413 & 0.0476 \\ 0 & 0 & 0 & 0 & 0 & 0 & 0 & 1.0000 \end{pmatrix}$$

Step 2. Next, the transient faults that may occur are characterized. A fault may cause an *arbitrary* transition between configuration classes. Due to our system model, we assume that one occurrence of a transient fault causes a single transition either into a different or the same configuration class. We specify the faults by a fault step probability matrix $F := (f_{i,j})$ with the same dimensions as matrix E, where the element $f_{i,j}$ gives the probability that the system transits into a configuration of configuration class $\mathcal{C}_j$ from a configuration of configuration class $\mathcal{C}_i$ in the event of a fault step.

There are different ways to arrive at a fault step probability matrix for a system. Due to lack of more refined information, we adopt equal probabilities for every transition from a configuration class, that is, $\forall i, j \in \{1, \ldots, 2^n\}$: $f_{i,j} = 1/2^n$. For the DFS example, we use a fault step probability matrix F with $f_{i,j} = 1/2^3 = 0.125$. An alternative is to use a specific probability density function to derive the transition probability between configuration classes. Such a density function could be obtained by observing real-world systems.

Step 3. Using both, the computation step probability matrix E and the fault step probability matrix F, we can determine the Markov chain that characterizes the overall system by its corresponding system step probability matrix M. With the probability $q_{\mathcal{F}}$ that a fault occurs,

$$M := (m_{i,j}) = (1 - q_{\mathcal{F}}) \cdot E + q_{\mathcal{F}} \cdot F \tag{9}$$

The element $m_{i,j}$ gives the probability that the system reaches a configuration in configuration class C_j from a configuration in configuration class C_i if the system performs a single computation or fault step. The matrix for the DFS example is

$$M = \begin{pmatrix} 0.6344 & 0.0160 & 0.0160 & 0.0001 & 0.3331 & 0.0001 & 0.0001 & 0.0001 \\ 0.2221 & 0.4124 & 0.0001 & 0.0318 & 0.0001 & 0.3331 & 0.0001 & 0.0001 \\ 0.2221 & 0.0001 & 0.4124 & 0.0318 & 0.0001 & 0.0001 & 0.3331 & 0.0001 \\ 0.0001 & 0.1111 & 0.1111 & 0.4441 & 0.0001 & 0.0001 & 0.0001 & 0.3331 \\ 0.0001 & 0.0001 & 0.0001 & 0.0001 & 0.9357 & 0.0318 & 0.0318 & 0.0001 \\ 0.0001 & 0.0001 & 0.0001 & 0.0001 & 0.1111 & 0.8406 & 0.0001 & 0.0477 \\ 0.0001 & 0.0001 & 0.0001 & 0.0001 & 0.1111 & 0.0001 & 0.8406 & 0.0477 \\ 0.0001 & 0.0001 & 0.0001 & 0.0001 & 0.0001 & 0.0001 & 0.0001 & 0.9991 \end{pmatrix}$$

for $q_{\mathcal{F}} = 0.001$. In order to calculate steady-state probabilities, it must be checked whether M is irreducible. If it is not in a particular case, the fault step probability matrix F may be transformed to make M irreducible. Such transformations are possible without significantly affecting the overall accuracy. Furthermore, M always is finite, because the configuration space is abstracted to a finite set of configuration classes. If M is irreducible, M is aperiodic in non-trivial cases (i.e., $q_{\mathcal{F}} < 1$), because the system is self-stabilizing, that is, $m_{g,g} > 0$. If M is irreducible, finite, and aperiodic, the unique steady-state probabilities of the corresponding Markov chain exist [6, p. 347–352]. Next, we describe how the fault tolerance measures can be calculated from the Markov chain.

4.3 Determination of Fault Tolerance Measures

Based on the system analysis procedure described above and the system step probability matrix M in particular, we will now determine lower bounds of the discussed fault tolerance measures of self-stabilizing systems.

Reliability. For a self-stabilizing system, a lower bound for reliability $\hat{R}(k)$ at time $k = 1$ is

$$\hat{R}(1) = P(\mathcal{P}_S^1 \text{ holds} \mid \mathcal{P}_S^0 \text{ holds}) \tag{10}$$

which is given by the element $m_{g,g}$ of the system step probability matrix M (as the configuration class C_g contains all and only safe configurations). Note that this probability not only comprises the probability of being in a safe configuration and remaining there while executing a computation step *in the absence of a fault* (which would calculate to $(1 - q_{\mathcal{F}})$), but additionally the probability that a fault step actually occurs *instead* of a computation step that carries the system configuration from a safe configuration belonging to C_g into a possible but not necessarily different safe configuration of C_g. For the DFS example, the latter amounts for an additional probability mass of $q_{\mathcal{F}} \cdot 1/2^n$ and, for the fault probability of $q_{\mathcal{F}} = 0.001$, $\hat{R}(1)$ calculates to 0.999125 as given by element $m_{8,8}$ of the matrix M. Generally, $\hat{R}(k)$ calculates as follows:

$$\hat{R}(k) = (\hat{R}(1))^k, \qquad k > 0 \tag{11}$$

This correctly takes into account that the configuration class C_g has never been left in the course of k steps. Thus, the term expresses a lower bound of the probability that the systems was correctly functioning and did not cease doing so in the discrete time interval $[0, 1, \ldots, k]$.

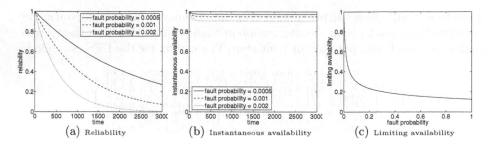

(a) Reliability   (b) Instantaneous availability   (c) Limiting availability

Fig. 5. Reliability and availability of the DFS system

Figure 5(a) shows $\hat{R}(k)$ for the DFS example with fault probabilities $q_{\mathcal{F}}$ of 0.0005, 0.001, and 0.002 over the course of 3000 steps. For example, when assuming a fault probability of 0.001, the reliability of the DFS system is at most 0.1122 after 2500 steps and with every further step not more than 1% are lost. In other words, in the absence of activating any "repair actions," the system will cease to deliver correct service with a probability of 0.8879 no later than after 2500 steps. For a critical service, reliability might not be high enough. Fortunately – except as in a trivial case where $\mathcal{P}_S \equiv \mathcal{P}_A$ – self-stabilizing systems *inherently* own those "repair actions." Their effect on the probability that the system can provide correct service is shown next.

Instantaneous availability. The lower bound for instantaneous availability $\hat{A}(k)$ can be derived for a given system by means of the system model as follows.

$$\hat{A}(k) = v_g^k \qquad \text{with } v^k = (M^T)^k \cdot v^0, \quad k > 0 \text{ and } v^0 = (0, \ldots, 0, 1)^T \qquad (12)$$

Thus, $\hat{A}(1)$ is the probability that the system remains in configurations belonging to configuration class $\mathcal{C}_g$ either due to program or fault actions until the end of step 1. This value is given by the entry in the g-th dimension of configuration vector v^1. Thus, $\hat{A}(1)$ is always equal to $\hat{R}(1)$.

For further steps, always remaining in $\mathcal{C}_g$ is not necessarily required: the values in dimensions 1 to $g-1$ of vector v state the probabilities that faults cause specific configuration class transitions that all leave class $\mathcal{C}_g$. The probability mass associated with these vector entries has positive impact on $\hat{A}(k)$ for $k > 1$, since either due to 1) faults or 2) program "repair actions" executed in subsequent steps. Configuration class transitions from classes *into* configuration class $\mathcal{C}_g$ may occur with some probability leading to a possible increase of the availability value at time k. Thus – in contrast to reliability – repair actions occurring until time k actually help to achieve a high probability level. The impact of faults can be negative as well as positive: faults leading out of configuration class $\mathcal{C}_g$ decrease availability whereas faults directly or indirectly leading into it cause an increase. By "indirectly" we mean that certain combinations of subsequent repair actions and/or faults might "steer the system" back into configuration class $\mathcal{C}_g$.

Figure 5(b) shows $\hat{A}(k)$ for the DFS example with fault probabilities $q_{\mathcal{F}}$ of 0.0005, 0.001, and 0.002 during 3000 steps. As expected, when comparing the appropriate lower bounds of availability and reliability (see Fig. 5(a)), the positive impact of repair actions of a self-stabilizing systems is clearly visible: Even for $q_{\mathcal{F}} = 0.002$, the instantaneous availability is always above 0.9. Compared to a reliability of 0.1122 after 2500 steps, the instantaneous availability is 0.9072.

Limiting availability. Limiting availability A is defined as $\lim_{t \to \infty} A(t)$ if the limit exists. Thus, the lower bound on limiting availability $\hat{A}$ for a given system using the discrete time model evaluates to

$$\hat{A} = \lim_{k \to \infty} \hat{A}(k) \tag{13}$$

if the limit exists. If the system step probability matrix M is aperiodic, finite, and irreducible then $\hat{A}$ can also be obtained by calculating the g-th dimension of the steady-state probability vector v^* of the system, that is,

$$\hat{A} = v_g^* \quad \text{with } v^* \text{ being the solution of } v^* = M^T \cdot v^* \tag{14}$$

Note that in (14), under the assumptions given, only a single solution of v^* exists. Consequently, there exists only a single, unique steady-state probability vector and, therefore, also only a single, unique value for $\hat{A}$ given a particular system. Thus, $\hat{A}$ is independent of any initial probability vector v^0. This is important to note, since a self-stabilizing system generally does not exhibit any fixed initial configuration.

The steady-state probability vector of the DFS example is

$$v^* = (0.0007, 0.0003, 0.0003, 0.0003, 0.0323, 0.0078, 0.0078, 0.9507)^T$$

Thus, the availability of the DFS example is 0.9507 denoting the probability that a system is in safe configuration if the external observer inspects the system. Figure 5(c) gives the availability of the DFS example when the fault probability $q_{\mathcal{F}}$ ranges from 0 to 1. As can be expected, the availability exponentially decreases with increasing $q_{\mathcal{F}}$. However, the availability does not asymptotically approach 0 as faults may take a system into a safe configuration. Such faults have a positive impact on availability amounting to $1/2^n$ for $q_{\mathcal{F}} = 1$ under the assumption of equal transition probabilities due to faults.

5 Related Work

Infinite state systems can be abstracted to finite state systems using *predicate abstraction* as firstly proposed in [14]. This technique is commonly used in model checking to prove the correctness of a system. Predicate abstraction is used in [15] for verifying multiprocessor cache coherence protocol. Predicate diagrams [16] are used to abstract infinite state systems and have been applied to verify Dijkstra's self-stabilizing mutual exclusion algorithm [17] in [18]. The reduction of configurations to configuration classes in our approach can be seen as an application of predicate abstraction. In particular, we apply predicate abstraction to serve the purpose of making a quantitatively evaluation tractable.

In [19] a method to calculate fault tolerance measures for a system given by CSP processes [20] is presented. They give an algorithmic method to derive an automaton from a CSP process specification and, subsequently, transform this automaton to a Markov process. Using this Markov process, they calculate some fault tolerance measures such as reliability and expected time to a catastrophic failure. In particular, they only address systems that eventually suffer from a permanent failure, that is, a failure that cannot be corrected. In contrast, in our approach, we consider self-stabilizing systems that suffer from transient faults. Such a difference in fault assumptions determines the applicable fault tolerance measures. Obviously, the calculation of limiting availability is useless under the assumption of an eventual permanent failure. Furthermore, in [19], too, abstraction has been applied. In contrast to our approach, the authors abstract from traces and not from system states and they address finite state systems, only.

6   Conclusions

We presented an approach for evaluating self-stabilizing systems (representing instances of particular non-masking fault-tolerant systems) in terms of well-accepted fault tolerance measures for masking fault-tolerant systems, namely reliability, instantaneous availablity, and limiting availablity.

The analysis procedure presented can also be used to systematically optimize a system. For example, consider the fundamental matrix $M' := (I-Q)^{-1}$, where Q is the submatrix of the matrix E omitting the last row and the last column and I is the identity matrix. The elements of the matrix M' can be used to calculate the *mean time to repair* (while faults may occur) of a system (cf. [6, p. 392–396]). This allows to systematically add repair operations to a self-stabilizing system hence optimizing its availability. Likewise, the analysis procedure allows to optimize the communication graph of a system in a systematic fashion, for example, by reducing the number of neighbors of a process to limit error propagation.

In the scope of this paper, we restricted ourselfs to the use of a fixed system model, for example, by assuming read/write atomicity. However, this is not an inherent limitation of our approach. The approach can be extended to other system models which will be a part of our future work.

References

1. Gärtner, F.C.: Fundamentals of fault-tolerant distributed computing in asynchronous environments. ACM Computing Surveys **31**(1) (1999) 1–26
2. Helal, A.A., Heddaya, A.A., Bhargava, B.B.: Replication Techniques in Distributed Systems. Kluwer Academic Publishers (1996)
3. Pease, M., Shostak, R., Lamport, L.: Reaching Agreement in the Presence of Faults. Journal of the ACM **27**(2) (1980) 228–234
4. Dolev, S.: Self-Stabilization. MIT Press (2000)
5. Khalil, H.K., Teel, A.R., Georgiou, T.T., Praly, L., Sontag, E.: Stability. In Levine, W.S., ed.: The Control Handbook. CRC Press, Inc (1995) 889 – 908

6. Trivedi, K.S.: Probability and Statistics with Reliability, Queuing and Computer Science Applications. 2nd edn. John Wiley and Sons Ltd. (2002)
7. Somani, A.K., Vaidya, N.H.: Understanding Fault Tolerance and Reliability. Computer **30**(4) (1997) 45–50
8. Suri, N., Hugue, M.M., Walter, C.J.: Reliability Modeling of Large Fault-tolerant Systems. In: 22nd Intern. Fault-Tolerant Comp. Symp. IEEE (1992) 212–220
9. Amir, Y., Wool, A.: Optimal Availability Quorum Systems: Theory and Practice. IPL **65**(5) (1998) 223–228
10. Babaoğlu, Ö.: On the reliability of consensus-based fault-tolerant distributed computing systems. ACM Transactions on Computer Systems **5**(4) (1987) 394–416
11. Avižienis, A., Laprie, J.C., Randell, B., Landwehr, C.E.: Basic Concepts and Taxonomy of Dependable and Secure Computing. IEEE ToDSC **1**(1) (2004) 11–33
12. Hamming, R.W.: Error-detecting and Error-correcting Codes. Bell System Technical Journal **29**(2) (1950) 147–160
13. Collin, Z., Dolev, S.: Self-stabilizing Depth First Search. IPL **49**(6) (1994) 297–301
14. Graf, S., Saïdi, H.: Construction of Abstract State Graphs with PVS. In: 9th Intern. Conf. on CA Verification. No. 1254 in LNCS (1997) 72–83
15. Das, S., Dill, D.L., Park, S.: Experience with Predicate Abstraction. In: 11th Intern. Conf. on CA Verification, Springer-Verlag (1999)
16. Cansell, D., Méry, D., Merz, S.: Predicate Diagrams for the Verification of Reactive Systems. In: 2nd Intl. Conf. Integrated Formal Methods (IFM 2000). Vol. 1945 of LNCS., Springer-Verlag (2000) 380–397
17. Dijkstra, E.W.: Self-stabilizing Systems in Spite of Distributed Control. CACM **17**(11) (1974) 643–644
18. Cansell, D., Méry, D., Merz, S.: Formal Analysis of a Self-stabilizing Algorithm using Predicate Diagrams. In Wirsing, M., ed.: Workshop Integrating Diagrammatic and Formal Spec. Techniques (GI-/ÖCG-Jahrestagung). Vol. 157/I. (2001) 39–45
19. Sorensen, E.V., Nordahl, J., Hansen, N.H.: From CSP mMdels to Markov Models. IEEE ToSE **19**(6) (1993) 554 – 570
20. Hoare, C.A.R.: Communicating Sequential Processes. Prentice Hall Int. (1985)

Circle Formation of Weak Mobile Robots

Yoann Dieudonné[1], Ouiddad Labbani-Igbida[2], and Franck Petit[1]

[1] LaRIA CNRS FRE 2733, University of Picardie Jules Verne, Amiens, France
[2] CREA, University of Picardie Jules Verne, Amiens, France

Abstract. The Circle Formation Problem (CFP) consists in the design of a protocol insuring that starting from an initial arbitrary configuration, n robots eventually form a regular n-gon. In this paper, we present the first protocol which deterministically solves CFP in finite time for any number of robots, provided that $n \notin \{4, 6, 8\}$. The proposed protocol works in the semi-synchronous model introduced in [1]. The robots are assumed to be uniform, anonymous, oblivious, and they share no kind of coordinate system nor common sense of direction.

1 Introduction

In this paper, we address the class of distributed systems where the computing units are *autonomous mobile robots* (also sometimes referred to as *sensors* or *agents*), i.e., devices equipped with sensors which do not depend on a central scheduler and designed to move in a two-dimensional plane. Also, we assume that the robots cannot remember any previous observation nor computation performed in any previous step. Such robots are said to be *oblivious* (or *memoryless*). The robots are also *uniform* and *anonymous*, i.e, they all have the same program using no local parameter (such that an identity) allowing to differentiate any of them. Moreover, none of them share any kind of common coordinate mechanism or common sense of direction, and they communicate only by observing the position of the others.

The motivation behind such a weak and unrealistic model is the study of the minimal level of ability the robots are required to have in the accomplishment of some basic cooperative tasks in a deterministic way, e.g., [2,3,4,5]. Among them, the *Circle Formation Problem* (CFP) has received a particular attention [6,7,8,9,10,11]. The CFP consists in the design of a protocol insuring that starting from an initial arbitrary configuration, all n robots eventually form a circle with equal spacing between any two adjacent robots. In other words, the robots are required to form a *regular n-gon* when the protocol terminated.

Related Works. An informal CFP algorithm is presented in [6] to show the relationship between the class of pattern formation algorithms and the concept of self-stabilization in distributed systems [12]. In [7], an algorithm based on heuristics is proposed for the formation of a circle approximation. A CFP protocol is given in [3] for non-oblivious robots with an unbounded memory. Two deterministic algorithms are provided in [8,9]. In the former work, the robots asymptotically converge toward a configuration in which they are uniformly distributed on

A.K. Datta and M. Gradinariu (Eds.): SSS 2006, LNCS 4280, pp. 262–275, 2006.
© Springer-Verlag Berlin Heidelberg 2006

the boundary of a circle. This solution is based on an elegant Voronoi Diagram construction. The latter work avoid this construction by making an extra assumption on the initial position of robots. In [13], properties on Lyndon words are used to achieve a Circle Formation Protocol (the exact n-gon is eventually built) for a prime number of robots. All the above solutions work in the semi-synchronous model introduced in [1]. The solution in [11] works in a fully asynchronous model, but when n is even, the robots may only achieve a biangular circle—the distance between two adjacent robots is alternatively either α or β.

A common strategy in order to solve a non trivial problem as CFP is to combine subproblems which are easier to solve. In general, CFP is separated into two distinct parts: The first subproblem consists in placing the robots along the boundary of a circle C, without considering their relative positions. The second subproblem, called *uniform transformation problem* (UTP), consists in starting from there, and arranging robots, without them leaving the circle C, evenly along the boundary of C. In [8], the authors present an algorithm, for the second subproblem which converges toward a homogeneous distribution of robots, but it does not terminate deterministically. They conjecture that there is no deterministic solution solving UTP in finite time in the semi-synchronous model in [1]—the robots being uniform, anonymous, oblivious, and none of them sharing any kind of coordinate system or common sense of direction. In a recent paper [14], the validity of the conjecture is proven. In the same paper, the authors propose two deterministic solutions for UTP by assuming an extra assumption: The robots agree on a clockwise direction of the circle. The first solution solves UTP by assuming that the desired final distance d between two robots is know to them. The second solution does not require that the robots knows d. This solution leads the system in an ϵ-approximate regular n-gon, i.e., the actual distance between the robots is eventually equal to d' such that $|d - d'| \leq \epsilon$ for a given $\epsilon > 0$.

Contribution. We propose the first protocol which deterministically solves CFP in finite time for any number n of weak robots, provided that $n \notin \{4, 6, 8\}$. The proposed protocol works in the semi-synchronous model introduced in [1]. By weak, we mean that the robots are assumed to be uniform, anonymous, oblivious, and they share no kind of coordinate system nor common sense of direction. Our protocol is not based on UTP, but it is based on concentric circles formed by the robots.

Outline of the Paper. In the next section (Section 2), we describe the distributed systems and the model we consider in this paper. In the same section, we present the problem considered in this paper. The algorithm is proposed in Section 3. Finally, we conclude this paper in Section 4.

2 Preliminaries

In this section, we define the distributed system, basic definitions and the problem considered in this paper.

Distributed Model. We adopt the model introduced in [1], in the remainder referred to as *SSM*. The *distributed system* considered in this paper consists of n robots $r_1, r_2, \cdots, r_n$—the subscripts $1, \ldots, n$ are used for notational purpose only. Each robot r_i, viewed as a point in the Euclidean plane, moves on this two-dimensional space unbounded and devoid of any landmark. When no ambiguity arises, r_i also denotes the point in the plane occupied by that robot. It is assumed that the robots never collide and that two or more robots may simultaneously occupy the same physical location. Any robot can observe, compute and move with infinite decimal precision. The robots are equipped with sensors allowing to detect the instantaneous position of the other robots in the plane. Each robot has its own local coordinate system and unit measure. The robots do not agree on the orientation of the axes of their local coordinate system, nor on the unit measure. They are *uniform* and *anonymous*, i.e, they all have the same program using no local parameter (such that an identity) allowing to differentiate any of them. They communicate only by observing the position of the others and they are *oblivious*, i.e., none of them can remember any previous observation nor computation performed in any previous step.

Time is represented as an infinite sequence of time instant $t_0, t_1, \ldots, t_j, \ldots$ Let $P(t_j)$ be the multiset of the positions in the plane occupied by the n robots at time t_j $(j \geq 0)$. For every t_j, $P(t_j)$ is called the *configuration* of the distributed system at time t_j. $P(t_j)$ expressed in the local coordinate system of any robot r_i is called a *view*, denoted $v_i(t_j)$. At each time instant t_j $(j \geq 0)$, each robot r_i is either *active* or *inactive*. The former means that, during the computation step (t_j, t_{j+1}), using a given algorithm, r_i computes in its local coordinate system a position $p_i(t_{j+1})$ depending only on the system configuration at t_j, moves towards $p_i(t_{j+1})$ during (t_j, t_{j+1}), and takes place on the computed position $p_i(t_{j+1})$ at time t_{j+1}—$p_i(t_{j+1})$ can be equal to $p_i(t_j)$, making the location of r_i unchanged. In the latter case, r_i does not perform any local computation and remains at the same position.

The concurrent activation of robots is modeled by the interleaving model in which the robot activations are driven by a *fair scheduler*. At each instant t_j $(j \geq 0)$, the scheduler arbitrarily activates a (non empty) set of robots. Fairness means that every robot is infinitely often activated by the scheduler.

The Circle Formation Problem. In this paper, the term *"circle"* refers to a circle having a radius strictly greater than zero. Consider a configuration at time t_k $(k \geq 0)$ in which the positions of the n robots are located at distinct positions on the circumference of a circle C. At time t_k, the *successor* r_j, $j \in 1 \ldots n$, of any robot r_i, $i \in 1 \ldots n$ and $i \neq j$, is the single robot such that no robot exists between r_i and r_j on C in the clockwise direction. Given a robot r_i and its successor r_j on C centered in O:

1. r_i is said to be the *predecessor* of r_j;
2. r_i and r_j are said to be *adjacent*;
3. $\widehat{r_i O r_j}$ denotes the angle centered in O and with sides the half-lines $[O, r_i)$ and $[O, r_j)$ such that no robots (other than r_i and r_j) is on C inside $\widehat{r_i O r_j}$.

Definition 1 (regular n-gon). *A cohort of n robots $(n \geq 2)$ forms (or is arranged in) a regular n-gon if the robots take place on the circumference of a circle C centered in O such that for every pair r_i, r_j of robots, if r_j is the successor of r_i on C, then $\widehat{r_i O r_j} = \delta$, where $\delta = \frac{2\pi}{n}$. The angle δ is called the* characteristic angle *of the n-gon.*

The problem considered in this paper, called CFP (*Circle Formation Problem*) consists in the design of a distributed protocol which arranges a group of n $(n > 2)$ mobile robots with initial distinct positions into a *regular n-gon* in finite time. (We ignore the trivial cases $n \leq 2$ because in that cases, they always form a regular n-gon.)

3   Circle Formation Protocol

In this section, we present the main result of this paper. We first provide particular configurations of the system which we use for simplifying the design and proofs of the protocol. Next, the protocol is presented.

3.1   Definitions and Basics Properties

Definition 2 (Biangular circle). *A cohort of n robots $(n \geq 2)$ forms (or is arranged in) a biangular circle if the robots take place on the circumference of a circle C centered in O and there exist two non zero angles α, β such that for every pair r_i, r_j of robots, if r_j is the successor of r_i on C, then $\widehat{r_i O r_j} \in \{\alpha, \beta\}$ and α and β alternate in the clockwise direction.*

Remark 1. In a biangular circle, $\alpha + \beta = \frac{4\pi}{n}$.

Obviously, if $\alpha = \beta$ then, for any n value, the n robots form a regular n-gon. If $\alpha \neq \beta$, then n must be even $(n = 2p, \; p > 1)$. In that case, the biangular circle is called a *strict* biangular circle—refer to Figure 1.

Definition 3 (regular (k, n)-gon). *A cohort of k robots $(0 < k \leq n)$ forms a regular (k, n)-gon if their positions coincide with a regular n-gon such that $n - k$ robots are missing.*

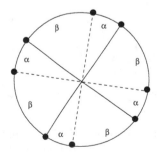

Fig. 1. An example showing a strict biangular circle ($\alpha \neq \beta$)

An example of a (k,n)-gon is given in Figure 2 (Case (b)). Given a (k,n)-gon such that $k \geq 2$, if p robots are missing (w.r.t. the corresponding n-gon) between two adjacent robots, then $\widehat{rOr'} = (p+1)\frac{2\pi}{n}$. Given a $(1,n)$-gon, the number of missing robots is equal to $n-1$. Remark that, since the uniqueness of any circle is guaranteed by passing through only 3 points, there is an infinity of circles passing through 1 or 2 robots. So, if $k \leq 2$, then there is an infinity of (k,n)-gon passing through k robots.

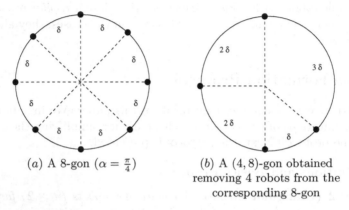

(a) A 8-gon $(\alpha = \frac{\pi}{4})$

(b) A $(4,8)$-gon obtained removing 4 robots from the corresponding 8-gon

Fig. 2. An example showing a (k,n)-gon

Let C_1 and C_2 be two circles having their radius greater than 0. C_1 and C_2 are said to be *concentric* if they share the same center but their radii are different. Without loss of generality, in the remainder, given a pair (C_1, C_2) of concentric circles, C_1 (resp. C_2) indicates the circle with the greatest radius (resp. smallest radius).

Definition 4 (Concentric Configuration). *The system is said to be in a concentric configuration if there exists a pair of concentric circles (C_1, C_2) and a partition of the n robots into two subsets A and B such that every robot of A (respectively B) is located on C_1 (resp. C_2).*

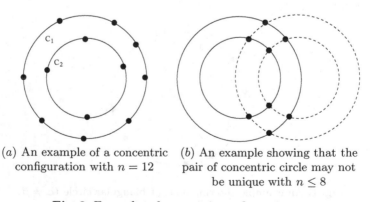

(a) An example of a concentric configuration with $n = 12$

(b) An example showing that the pair of concentric circle may not be unique with $n \leq 8$

Fig. 3. Examples of concentric configurations

Remark 2. $A \neq \emptyset$ and $B \neq \emptyset$.

Remark 3. If $n \leq 8$, then the pair (C_1, C_2) may not be unique.

An example illustrating Remark 3 is given in Figure 3.

Lemma 1. *If the system is in a concentric configuration and if $n > 8$, then there exists a single pair (C_1, C_2) in which all the robots are located.*

Proof. Assume by contradiction, that the system is in a concentric configuration, $n > 8$ and there exists two pairs $\gamma = (C_1, C_2)$ and $\gamma' = (C'_1, C'_2)$ such that $\gamma \neq \gamma'$ (i.e., $C_1 \neq C'_1$, $C_1 \neq C'_2$, $C_2 \neq C'_1$ and $C_2 \neq C'_2$) and in which all the robots are located. Since two different circles share at most two points, the pairs γ can share at most eight robots with γ' (refer to Case (b) in Figure 3). Since by assumption $n \geq 9$, there exists at least one robot which is located on either C_1 or C_2, but which is located on neither C'_1 nor C'_2. This contradicts the fact that each robot is located either on C'_1 or on C'_2. $\qquad\square$

So, from Lemma 1, when the system is in a concentric configuration and $n \geq 9$, the pair (C_1, C_2) is unique. In such a configuration, given a robot r, $proj(r)$ denotes the projection of r on C_1, i.e., the intersection between the half-line $[O, r)$ and C_1, where c is the center of (C_1, C_2). Obviously, if r is located on C_1, then $proj(r) = r$. We denote by Π the projection set of the n robots. In a concentric configuration, if $|\Pi| = n$, then the radii passing through the robots on C_1 split up the disk bounded by C_1 into *sectors*. Note that the condition "$|\Pi| = n$" induces that the sectors are defined if and only if, for any robot r located on C_2, no robot on C_1 occupies $proj(r)$—refer to Figure 4.

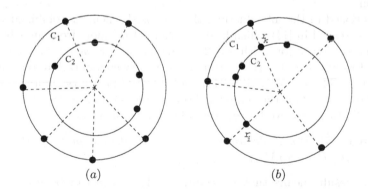

(a) $\qquad\qquad\qquad\qquad\qquad\qquad$ (b)

Fig. 4. The concentric configuration shown in Case (a) is split up into sectors, whereas the one in Case (b) is not because robots on C_1 are located on the projections of r_i and r_k

Definition 5 (quasi n-gon). *A cohort of n robots ($n \geq 9$) forms an (arbitrary) quasi n-gon iff the three following conditions hold:*

1. *The robots form a concentric configuration divided into sectors;*
2. *The robots on C_1 form a regular (k,n)-gon;*
3. *In each sector, if p robots are missing on C_1 to form a regular n-gon, then p robots are located on C_2 in the same sector.*

A quasi n-gon is said to be *aligned* iff Π coincides with a regular n-gon. Two quasi n-gon are shown in Figure 5, the first one is arbitrary, the other one is aligned.

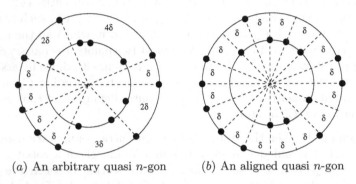

(a) An arbitrary quasi n-gon   (b) An aligned quasi n-gon

Fig. 5. Two quasi n-gon with $n = 16$

3.2 The Protocol

Let us consider the overall scheme of our protocol presented in Algorithm 1. It is mainly based on the particular configurations presented in the previous subsection.

As mentioned in the introduction, the proposed scheme is combined with the protocol presented in [11] which leads a cohort of n robots from an arbitrary to a biangular configuration, with $n \geq 2$. In the remainder, we refer to the protocol in [11] as Procedure $< A \rightsquigarrow B >$—from an *A*rbitrary configuration to a *B*iangular configuration. The model used in [11], called Corda [5], allows more asynchrony among the robots than the semi-synchronous model used in this paper—let us call it SSM. However, we borrow the following result from [5]:

Theorem 1. *[5] Any algorithm that correctly solves a problem P in Corda, correctly solves P in SSM.*

The above result means that Procedure $< A \rightsquigarrow B >$ can be used in SSM. Obviously, Procedure $< A \rightsquigarrow B >$ trivially solves the CFP if the number of robots n is odd. So, to solve CFP for any number of robots, it remains to deal with a system in a strict biangular configuration when n is even.

In the remainder, we consider that the system is in an arbitrary configuration if the robots do not form either (1) a regular n-gon, (2) a quasi n-gon, or (3) a strict biangular circle. Let us describe the general scheme provided by Algorithm 1.

Procedure $<A \rightsquigarrow B>$ excluded, the protocol mainly consists of three procedures. The first one, called Procedure $<aQ \rightsquigarrow Ngon>$ is used when the system form an aligned quasi n-gon. It leads the system into a regular n-gon. The aim of Procedure $<Q \rightsquigarrow aQ>$ is to transform the cohort from an arbitrary quasi n-gon into an aligned quasi n-gon. The last procedure, Procedure $<B \rightsquigarrow Q>$, is used when the robots form a biangular circle and arranges them into either a regular n-gon or an arbitrary quasi n-gon, depending on the synchrony of the robots. The details of those procedures are given in the remainder of this section.

Let us explain how the procedures are used by giving the overall scheme of Algorithm 1. Starting from an arbitrary configuration, using Procedure $<A \rightsquigarrow B>$, the system is eventually in a biangular circle. If n is odd, then the robots form a regular n-gon, i.e., CFP is solved. Otherwise (n is even), the robots form either a regular n-gon or a strict biangular circle. Starting from the latter case, each robot executes Procedure $<B \rightsquigarrow Q>$. As mentioned above, the resulting configuration can be either a regular n-gon or a quasi n-gon. From a quasi n-gon, the robots execute either Procedure $<aQ \rightsquigarrow Ngon>$ or Procedure $<Q \rightsquigarrow aQ>$, depending on whether the quasi n-gon is aligned or not. Both procedures $<aQ \rightsquigarrow Ngon>$ and $<Q \rightsquigarrow aQ>$ require no ambiguity on the concentric configuration forming the quasi n-gon, i.e $n \geq 9$. However, since $<aQ \rightsquigarrow Ngon>$ and $<Q \rightsquigarrow aQ>$ are called when n is even only, only the cases $n = 4, 6$ and 8 are not solved by our algorithm. So, in the remainder, we assume that $n \notin \{4, 6, 8\}$. Finally, starting from an aligned quasi n-gon, the resulting configuration of the execution of Procedure $<aQ \rightsquigarrow Ngon>$ is a regular n-gon. Otherwise, the quasi n-gon becomes aligned by executing Procedure $<Q \rightsquigarrow aQ>$.

Algorithm 1. Procedure $< A \rightsquigarrow Ngon >$ for any r_i in a cohort of n robots $(n \neq 4, 6,$ or $8)$

---

n:= the number of robots;
if n is even
then   if the robots do not form a regular n-gon
      then   if the robots form a quasi n-gon
      then   if the robots form an aligned quasi n-gon
            then Execute $<aQ \rightsquigarrow Ngon>$;
            else Execute $<Q \rightsquigarrow aQ>$;
      else   if the robots form a strict biangular circle
            then Execute $<B \rightsquigarrow Q>$;
            else Execute $<A \rightsquigarrow B>$;
**else   ** Execute $<A \rightsquigarrow B>$;

Theorem 2. *Procedure $< A \rightsquigarrow Ngon >$ is a deterministic Circle Formation Protocol for any number n of robots such that $n \notin \{4, 6, 8\}$.*

The above theorem follows from Procedure $<A \rightsquigarrow Ngon>$—Algorithm 1, [11], Lemmas 2, 4, and 7. In the remainder of this section, the procedures and the proofs of the three above lemmas are presented in separate paragraphs.

Procedure $<\text{a}Q \rightsquigarrow \text{Ngon}>$. Starting from an aligned quasi n-gon, each robot on C_2 needs to move toward its projection on C_1 whereas it is required that any robot on C_1 remains at the same position because it is located on its projection. This obvious behavior is made of the following single instruction:

$$\text{move to } proj(r_i)$$

Since we have $n \geq 9$ in quasi n-gon, from Lemma 1, the pair (C_1, C_2) is unique. Moreover, it remains unchanged while the regular n-gon is not formed. So, the following result holds:

Lemma 2. *Starting from an aligned quasi n-gon, Procedure* $< \text{a}Q \rightsquigarrow N\text{gon} >$ *solves the Circle Formation Problem.*

Procedure $< Q \rightsquigarrow \text{a}Q >$. The idea behind Procedure $< Q \rightsquigarrow \text{a}Q >$ consists in changing a quasi n-gon into an aligned quasi n-gon by arranging the robots on C_2 in each sector—refer to Figure 5.

In the following of the paragraph, denote a quasi n-gon by the corresponding pair of concentric circles (C_1, C_2). Two quasi n-gons (C_1^α, C_2^α) and (C_1^β, C_2^β) are said to be *equivalent* if $C_1^\alpha = C_1^\beta$, $C_2^\alpha = C_2^\beta$ and the positions of the robots on C_1^α and C_1^β are the same ones. In other words, the only allowed possible difference between two equivalent quasi n-gons (C_1^α, C_2^α) and (C_1^β, C_2^β) is different positions of robots between C_2^α and C_2^β in each sector.

Procedure $< Q \rightsquigarrow \text{a}Q >$ is shown Algorithm 2. This procedure assumes that the initial configuration is an arbitrary quasi n-gon. In such a configuration, we build, a partial order among the robots on C_2 belonging to a common sector to eventually form an aligned quasi n-gon.

Algorithm 2. Procedure $< Q \rightsquigarrow \text{a}Q >$ for any robot r_i in an arbitrary quasi n-gon

---

$C_1 :=$ greatest concentric circle; $C_2 :=$ smallest concentric circle;
if r_i are located on C_2
then *MySector* := sector wherein r_i is located;
$\qquad PS := FindFinalPos(Mysector)$;
$\qquad FRS :=$ set of robots in MySector which are not located on a position in PS;
$\qquad$ **if** $FRS \neq \emptyset$
$\qquad$ **then** $EFR := ElectFreeRobots(FRS)$;
$\qquad\qquad$ **if** $r_i \in EFR$ **then** move to Position $Associate(r_i)$;

Let $p_1, \ldots, p_s$ be the final positions on C_2 in the sector S in order to form the aligned quasi n-gon. Let B_1, B_2 be the two points located on C_2 at the boundaries of S. Of course, if only one robot is located on C_1 (i.e. there exists only one sector), then $B_1 = B_2$. For each $i \in 1 \ldots s$, p_i is the point on C_2 in S such that $\widehat{B_1 O p_i} = \frac{2i\pi}{n}$, $p_i \neq B_1$ and $p_i \neq B_2$. Clearly, while the distributed system remains in an equivalent quasi n-gon, all the final positions remain unchanged for every robot. A final position p_i, $i \in 1 \ldots s$, is said to be *free* if no robot takes place at p_i. Similarly, a robot r_i on C_2 in S is called a *free* robot if its current position does not belong to $\{p_1, \ldots, p_s\}$.

Define Function $FindFinalPos(S)$ which returns the set of final positions on C_2 in S with respect to B_1. Clearly, in S all the robots compute the same set of final positions, stored in PS. Each robot also temporarily stores the set of free robots in the variable called FRS. Of course, since the robots are oblivious, each active robot on C_2 re-compute PS and FRS each time Procedure $< Q \rightsquigarrow aQ >$ is executed. Basically, if $FRS = \emptyset$ all the robots occupy a final position in the sector S. Otherwise, the robots move in waves to the final positions in their sector following the order defined by Function $ElectFreeRobots()$. In each sector, the elected robots are the closest free robots from B_1 and B_2. Clearly, the result of Function $ElectFreeRobots()$ return the same set of robots for every robot in the same sector. Also, the number of elected robots in each sector is at most equal to 2, one for each point B_1 and B_2. Note that it can be equal to 1 when there is only one free robot, i.e., when only one robot in S did not reach the last free position.

Function $Associate(r)$ assigns a unique free position to an elected robot as follows:

If $ElectFreeRobots()$ returns only one robot r_i, then r_i is associated to the single free remaining position p_i in its sector. This allows r_i to move to p_i. If $ElectFreeRobots()$ returns a pair of robots $\{r_i, r_{i'}\}$ ($r_i \neq r_{i'}$), then the closest robot to B_1 (respectively, B_2) is associated with the closest position to B_1 (resp., B_2) in S. Note that, even if the robots may have opposite clockwise directions, r_i, $r_{i'}$, and their associated positions are the same for every robot in S.

Lemma 3. *According to Procedure $< Q \rightsquigarrow aQ >$, if the robots are in a quasi n-gon at time t_j ($j \geq 0$), then at time t_{j+1}, the robots are in an equivalent quasi n-gon.*

Proof. By assumption, at each time instant t_j, at least one robot is active. So, by fairness, starting from a quasi n-gon, at least one robot executes Procedure $< Q \rightsquigarrow aQ >$. Assume first that no robot executing Procedure $< Q \rightsquigarrow aQ >$ moves from t_j to t_{j+1}. In that case, since the robots are located on the same positions at t_j and at t_{j+1}, the robots are in the same quasi n-gon at t_{j+1}. Hence, the robots remains in an equivalent quasi n-gon seeing that any quasi n-gon is equivalent to itself. So, at least one robot moves from t_j to t_{j+1}. However, in each sector at most two robots are allowed to move toward distinct free positions on C_2 only inside their sector. Thus, the robots remains in an equivalent quasi n-gon.   □

The following lemma follows from Lemma 3 and fairness:

Lemma 4. *Procedure $< Q \rightsquigarrow aQ >$ is a deterministic algorithm transforming an arbitrary quasi n-gon into an aligned n-gon in finite time.*

Procedure $< B \rightsquigarrow Q >$. We assume that initially, the robots form a strict biangular circle. In such a configuration, every active robot r_i applies the following scheme:

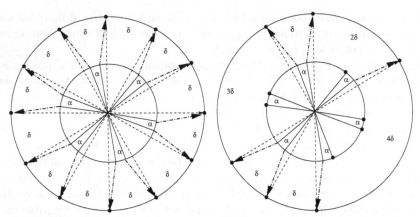

(a) If all the robots are active at t_j, (b) If some robots are inactive at t_j,
then the robots form a regular n-gon then the robots form a quasi n-gon at
at t_{j+1} t_{j+1}

Fig. 6. An example showing the principle of Procedure $<B \rightsquigarrow Q>$

1. Robot r_i computes the concentric circle C' whose radius is twice the radius of the strict biangular circle C;
2. Robot r_i considers its neighbor $r_{i'}$ such that $\widehat{r_i O r_{i'}} = \alpha$ and r_i moves away from r_i' to the position $p_i(t_{j+1})$ on C' with an angle equal to $\frac{\pi}{n} - \frac{\alpha}{2}$. More precisely, $\widehat{p_i(t_{j+1})Op_i(t_j)} = \frac{\pi}{n} - \frac{\alpha}{2}$ and $\widehat{p_i(t_{j+1})Op_{i'}(t_j)} = \frac{\pi}{n} + \frac{\alpha}{2}$ —refer to Figure 6.

Let us consider two possible behaviors depending on the synchrony of the robots.

1. Assume that every robot in the strict biangular circle is active at time t_j. In that case, at t_{j+1}, the robots form a regular n-gon—see Case (a) in Figure 6. Indeed, there are two cases:
   (a) If $\widehat{p_i(t_j)Op_{i'}}(t_j) = \alpha$, then $\widehat{p_i(t_{j+1})Op_{i'}}(t_{j+1}) = \alpha + 2(\frac{\pi}{n} - \frac{\alpha}{2})$.
       So, in that case, $\widehat{p_i(t_{j+1})Op_{i'}}(t_{j+1}) = 2\frac{\pi}{n}$.
   (b) If $\widehat{p_i(t_j)Op_{i'}}(t_j) = \beta$, then $\widehat{p_i(t_{j+1})Op_{i'}}(t_{j+1}) = \beta - 2(\frac{\pi}{n} - \frac{\alpha}{2})$.
       So, in that case, $\widehat{p_i(t_{j+1})Op_{i'}}(t_{j+1}) = \beta - 2\frac{\pi}{n} + \alpha$, which also equal to $\beta - 4\frac{\pi}{n} + \alpha + 2\frac{\pi}{n}$. From Remark 1, we know that $\beta = 4\frac{\pi}{n} - \alpha$. Hence,
       $$\widehat{p_i(t_{j+1})Op_{i'}}(t_{j+1}) = \beta - \beta + 2\frac{\pi}{n},$$ which is equal to $2\frac{\pi}{n}$.
   Note that (1) the trajectories of the robots do not cross between them, and (2) all the angles α (resp. β) increases up (resp. decrease down) to $\frac{2\pi}{n}$.
2. Assume that some robots, in the strict biangular circle, are not active at time t_j. In that case, there is only a subset of robots moving toward C' from t_j to t_{j+1}. Then, the robots form a quasi n-gon at time t_{j+1}—see Case (b) in Figure 6. Indeed at t_{j+1}, the robots are in a concentric configuration

where C_1 is C' and C_2 is the initial circle C (i.e the biangular circle at time t_j). Furthermore on C_1, the robots form a regular (k,n)-gon where $n - k$ represent the subset of robots remaining inactive at time t_j.

To show that, if the system eventually do not form a regular n-gon, we need to prove that it eventually forms a quasi n-gon. Following the above explanations, it remains to show that, in the above second case, the configuration is sliced into sectors at time t_{j+1} such that, in each sector, the missing robots on C_1 are located on C_2.

Lemma 5. *Using Procedure $<B{\rightsquigarrow}Q>$, if all the robots are in a strict biangular circle at time t_j, then the configuration is sliced into sectors at t_{j+1} when the n-gon is not formed.*

Proof. As already stated previously, the robots form a concentric configuration at time t_{j+1}. Moreover, at t_j, the robots are in a strict biangular circle such that $\alpha + \beta = \frac{4\pi}{n}$. Since the biangular circle is strict, without loss of generality, we can assume that $\alpha < \beta$ with $0 < \alpha < \frac{2\pi}{n}$ and $\frac{2\pi}{n} < \beta < \frac{4\pi}{n}$.

Assume, by contradiction, that there exists one robot r_i on C_2 located on the radius passing through any robot $r_{i'}$ on C_1 at t_{j+1}. This implies that at t_j, $\widehat{r_i O r_{i'}} = \frac{\pi}{n} - \frac{\alpha}{2}$ corresponding to the angle that $r_{i'}$ moved away from r_i on C' from t_j to t_{j+1}. Furthermore, at t_j, $r_{i'}$ is active and r_i is inactive. Note that $p_i(t_j)\widehat{O}p_{i'}(t_j)$ is either equal to α or β. Thus, either $\frac{\pi}{n} - \frac{\alpha}{2} = \alpha$ or $\frac{\pi}{n} - \frac{\alpha}{2} = \beta$. However, $\frac{\pi}{n} - \frac{\alpha}{2} < \frac{2\pi}{n}$, and $\frac{2\pi}{n} < \beta < \frac{4\pi}{n}$. Hence, $\frac{\pi}{n} - \frac{\alpha}{2} = \alpha$, and then $p_i(t_j)\widehat{O}p_{i'}(t_j) = \alpha$. By executing Procedure $<B \rightsquigarrow Q>$, $r_{i'}$ moves away from r_i with an angle $\frac{\pi}{n} - \frac{\alpha}{2}$, where $0 < \frac{\pi}{n} - \frac{\alpha}{2} < \frac{2\pi}{n}$. Since r_i is inactive we have $p_i(t_{j+1})\widehat{O}p_{i'}(t_{j+1}) = (\frac{\pi}{n} - \frac{\alpha}{2}) + \alpha$. Furthermore, Procedure $<B{\rightsquigarrow}Q>$ is called only when $n \geq 9$, and thus, we have $0 < (\frac{\pi}{n} - \frac{\alpha}{2}) + \alpha < \frac{2\pi}{9} + \frac{2\pi}{9} = \frac{4\pi}{9}$ and $0 < p_i(t_{j+1})\widehat{O}p_{i'}(t_{j+1}) < \frac{4\pi}{9}$. Thus, at t_{j+1}, r_i and $r_{i'}$ are not on the same radius. A contradiction. $\qquad\square$

Lemma 6. *Using Procedure $<B{\rightsquigarrow}Q>$, if all the robots form a strict biangular circle at time t_j, then in each sector, the missing robots on C_1 are located on C_2 at t_{j+1} when the n-gon is not formed.*

Proof. Clearly, when all the robots are active and move simultaneously by applying our method, the trajectories do not cross between them (see Figure 6). Assume by contradiction, that at time t_{j+1}, there exists any sector with one extra robot r. If all the robots have been active at time t_j, r would have crossed any other trajectory in order to form a regular n-gon. A contradiction. $\qquad\square$

The following lemma directly follows from the algorithm, Lemmas 5 and 6:

Lemma 7. *Procedure $<B \rightsquigarrow Q>$ is a deterministic algorithm transforming a biangular circle into either a regular n-gon or quasi n-gon in finite time.*

4   Concluding Remarks

In this paper, we studied the problem of forming a regular n-gon with a cohort of n semi-synchronous robots (CFP). We presented a new approach for this problem based on concentric circles formed by the robots. Combined with the solution in [11], our solution works with any number of robots n, except if $n = 4,6$ or 8. The main reasons that n must be different from 4, 6 or 8 comes from the fact that the robots may confuse in the recognition of the particular configurations if n is lower than 9. The CFP remains open for these three special cases. In a future work, we would like to investigate CFP in a weakest model such Corda.

Acknowledgements

We are grateful to Vincent Villain for the valuable discussions on the subject and to an anonymous reviewer who helped us improving the presentation of the paper.

References

1. Suzuki, I., Yamashita, M.: Agreement on a common x-y coordinate system by a group of mobile robots. Intelligent Robots: Sensing, Modeling and Planning (1996) 305–321
2. Sugihara, K., Suzuki, I.: Distributed motion coordination of multiple mobile robots. In: IEEE International Symosium on Intelligence Control. (1990) 138–143
3. Suzuki, I., Yamashita, M.: Distributed anonymous mobile robots - formation of geometric patterns. SIAM Journal of Computing **28(4)** (1999) 1347–1363
4. Flocchini, P., Prencipe, G., Santoro, N., Widmayer, P.: Hard tasks for weak robots: The role of common knowledge in pattern formation by autonomous mobile robots. In: 10th Annual International Symposium on Algorithms and Computation (ISAAC 99). (1999) 93–102
5. Prencipe, G.: Distributed Coordination of a Set of Autonomous Mobile Robots. PhD thesis, Dipartimento di Informatica, University of Pisa (2002)
6. Debest, X.A.: Remark about self-stabilizing systems. Communications of the ACM **38(2)** (1995) 115–117
7. Sugihara, K., Suzuki, I.: Distributed algorithms for formation of geometric patterns with many mobile robots. Journal of Robotic Systems **3(13)** (1996) 127–139
8. Defago, X., Konagaya, A.: Circle formation for oblivious anonymous mobile robots with no common sense of orientation. In: 2nd ACM International Annual Workshop on Principles of Mobile Computing (POMC 2002). (2002) 97–104
9. Chatzigiannakis, I., Markou, M., Nikoletseas, S.: Distributed circle formation for anonymous oblivious robots. In: 3rd Workshop on Efficient and Experimental Algorithms. (2004) 159–174
10. Samia, S., Défago, X., Katayama, T.: Convergence of a uniform circle formation algorithm for distributed autonomous mobile robots. In: Japan-Tunisia Workshop on Computer Systems and Information Technology (JT-CSIT 2004). (2004)
11. Katreniak, B.: Biangular circle formation by asynchronous mobile robots. In: 12th International Colloquium on Structural Information and Communication Complexity (SIROCCO 2005). (2005) 185–199
12. Dolev, S.: Self-Stabilization. The MIT Press (2000)

13. Dieudonné, Y., Petit, F.: Circle formation of weak robots and Lyndon words. Technical Report TR 2006-05, LaRIA, CNRS FRE 2733, University of Picardie Jules Verne, Amiens, France (2006) http://hal.ccsd.cnrs.fr/ccsd-00069724, submitted for publication.
14. Flocchini, P., Prencipe, G., Santoro, N.: Self-deployment algorithms for mobile sensors on a ring. In: 2nd International Workshop on Algorithmic Aspects of Wireless Sensor Networks (Algosensors 2006). (2006) To appear.

Self-stabilizing Device Drivers*

(Extended Abstract)

Shlomi Dolev[1] and Reuven Yagel[1,2]

[1] Department of Computer Science, Ben-Gurion University of the Negev,
Beer-Sheva, 84105, Israel
{dolev, yagel}@cs.bgu.ac.il
[2] Rafael Ltd. 3M, POB 2205, Haifa 31021, Israel

Abstract. This work presents approaches for designing the input-output device management components of self-stabilizing operating systems. As an example, we demonstrate the non-stability of the ATA standard protocol for storage devices. We state the requirements that an operating system and I/O devices should satisfy in order to become self-stabilizing. Then we suggest two solutions to satisfy these requirements. The first uses leases in order to guarantee progress from the I/O device side. The second assumes stabilization of the I/O device, and uses snapshots to perform consistency checks. By supplying an infrastructure for practical self-stabilizing systems, robust and dependable systems can be achieved.

Keywords: self-stabilizing systems, device driver failures, ATA interface standard.

1 Introduction

Device drivers are known to be a major cause of operating system failures [6,25,27]. This phenomena is often connected to a combination of reasons. First, drivers are usually loaded into the operating system kernel's address space and are running in privileged processor modes where an error has a greater effect on the total system behavior. Additionally, usually essential system parts are designed, built, verified and tested with extra care while drivers are many times brought from the outside. The following are techniques which are used to deal with these failures: (a) reducing the driver's access to system's resources [34,13], (b) containment of errors in realtime through kinds of virtualization [27,2], (c) using typed languages [13,28], and (d) static analysis of the drivers' code, and of their resource usage [4,30]. Applying such techniques helps improve the system's robustness, but the bottom line is that in systems running for a long period of time, errors (e.g., soft errors [17]) in device drivers accumulate and lead to undesired behavior.

---

* Partially supported by Rafael, Israeli Ministry of Science, Deutsche Telekom, Rita Altura Trust Chair in Computer Sciences and Lynn and William Frankel Center for Computer Sciences.

A.K. Datta and M. Gradinariu (Eds.): SSS 2006, LNCS 4280, pp. 276–289, 2006.

Device drivers are programs which are practically an essential part of any operating system. They serve as an adaption layer by managing the various operation and communication details of I/O devices. They also serve as a translation layer providing consistent and more abstract interface between other programs and the hardware device resources (and sometimes they also add extra services not provided by the hardware devices). Devices usually contain a controller which is the electronic part with which drivers communicate. The communication is carried out via the system bus, and is usually done through some standard protocols and interfaces e.g., ATA and SCSI for disk drives. In [23] it is stated that "a modern Seagate drive contains roughly 400,000 lines of code". In [34] it is noted that "modern disk controllers often have many megabytes of memory inside the controller". The complexity of today's I/O devices emphasize the need for robust device drivers.

In this work we suggest enhancing the robustness of device-drivers by designing them to be self-stabilizing. Generally, a system is *self-stabilizing* [8,9] if it can be started in any possible state and subsequently it converges to a desired behavior. A *state* of a system is an assignment of arbitrary values to the system's variables. Building a system, and specifically device drivers, in this way, ensures that errors will be contained autonomously by each driver, leading eventually to correct behavior of the whole system.

SELF-STABILIZING OPERATING SYSTEM (SOS). In order to have a full self-stabilizing system, the other system parts must also be self-stabilizing. This work uses building blocks from our previous work [10] where simple self-stabilizing process schedulers are presented, and from [11] where various memory management schemes are suggested. We also rely on [7], which addresses self-stabilization of the microprocessor. Thus, based on the idea of fair composition [9], once the microprocessor stabilizes and starts fetching and executing instructions, the system's kernel converges to a legal behavior, in which other programs are executed infinitely often to fulfill the system's goal.

RELATED WORK. Extensive theoretical research has been done towards self-stabilizing systems [8,9,31] and recovery-oriented/ autonomic-computing/ self-repair, e.g., [15,24,32]. Fault tolerance properties and robustness of operating systems (e.g., [27,22]) were also extensively studied.

As explained earlier, robustness of device drivers is of great importance in system design. It is stated in [6] and [21] that about 70% percent of operating system code is devoted to device drivers. It is stated in [25] that "In Windows XP, for example, device drivers cause 85% of reported failures". Moreover, in [6] it is claimed that for some cases in Linux "the error rate for drivers is almost seven times higher than the error rate for the rest of the kernel". Here we shortly survey various efforts in this field.

Device driver isolation and monitoring. The micro-kernel system architecture (pioneered in the Mach system [1]), suggests achieving minimal trusted computing base (TCB) by removing as much as possible from the kernel. For example, in the last version (3) of Minix [34] the drivers' access to system resources was reduced. This was achieved by factoring the common low level and privileged commands, such as access to I/O ports and interrupts, and moving most drivers parts to user space, where they communicate with the kernel through a simple messages mechanism (see [12] for another version).

Virtualization. A variation of this approach, lately suggested by many, is to run the original drivers of common operating systems, but to monitor their activity, and contain errors by different kinds of virtualization [27,2,20,21]. This method counts heavily on the robustness of the core kernel (also known as Virtual Machine Monitor), which we actually address in this work. In [14], [18] and [20] this is combined with an IO-MMU which adds hardware protection to I/O access. In [2] it is claimed that this method is not enough, and "in the case of more "sophisticated" statefull devices it may be in addition necessary to reset the device to a known state". In [26], a monitor which records the inputs sent to a driver by an application is added. In case of a failure a restart of the driver is carried out together with replaying the inputs.

Type safety and model checking. In Coyotos [28], the whole kernel including drivers, is written in a typed language as a stage towards achieving formal correctness. Static analysis of the drivers' code appears in [4]. They claim that kernel APIs are usually too complex so there is a great chance for coding bugs. They categorize bugs in order to find them automatically. This emphasizes the need for a good understanding of the protocols between drivers and the rest of the system. Many others (e.g., [6]) use code analysis to find kernel bugs in general.

Singularity is a recent ongoing research project [13] which combines many of the past system research advances, in order to achieve greater system dependability. In Singularity drivers are also treated as user programs so their state is separated from the rest of the system. Hardware resources are accessed only through messages, and when the system is compiled or started, there is a verification process carried out according to meta-data resource declarations. In [30], details concerning device drivers are provided. This project also relies on a typed language to restrict drivers abilities. To prevent malicious code behavior, runtime code changes are restricted by eliminating language features like reflection. On the other hand, all programs in Singularity run in privileged mode. These settings do not prevent a transient error from corrupting system execution (to quote [13] itself a "malicious driver can program a DMA capable device to overwrite any part of memory").

None of the above suggest a design for an operating system, or, in particular, device driver design and implementation that can automatically recover from an arbitrary state (that may be reached due to a combination of unexpected faults and sequence of unexpected inputs).

PAPER ORGANIZATION. In this paper we demonstrate how device drivers can be designed to be self-stabilizing. We start, in Section 2, by demonstrating how the current ATA specification for storage devices (such as hard disks) requires a behavior which can lead a system into undesirable combined states. Based on the definitions and settings presented in Section 3, we demonstrate in Section 4 how the design can be augmented to behave in a self-stabilizing way. We also sketch proofs of the correctness of the suggested solutions. Concluding remarks are given in Section 5.

2   A Non-self-stabilizing Driver Specification

The AT-Attachment protocol (standard draft version 8, also historically known as IDE), defines a parallel transport protocol between *host* systems and *device*s [33]. In the following we will first describe this protocol. Then we will show that the protocol defines interactions which can lead to non-stabilizing executions. Note that the standard defines only the *interface* between a host and a device. Therefore an implementation can add states and transitions to achieve stability, and still conform to this standard.

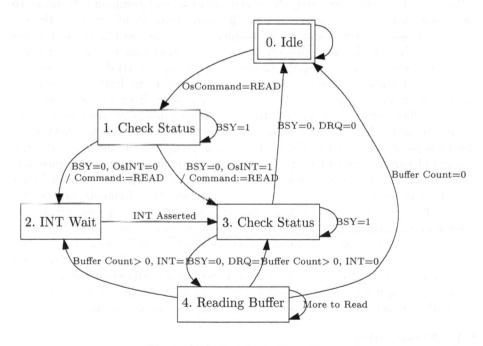

Fig. 1. ATA Host State Transitions

The communications between the host and the device is by means of input/output registers (shared memory model). There are control, command, status and data registers through which the host and the device communicate. Additionally, the device might signal the host through an interrupt line. The required behavior is defined with state diagrams describing states and transitions

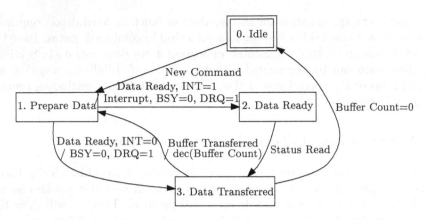

Fig. 2. ATA Device State Transitions

of both protocol parties. For the purpose of demonstrating the non-stability we follow the diagrams describing the execution of a read command. In order to carry out such a command the two parties move from an idle state to the executing command states and upon completion back to the idle state. Figures 41 and 43 in [33] describe the idle states of the host and the device respectively. Figures 47 and 48 describe the PIO (Programmed I/O) data-in command states, which transfer blocks of data from the device to the host, without using DMA (Direct Memory Access). We combine these four diagrams into two state machine diagrams each describing the possible executions of the host and the device, respectively. In general, upon a read request the host checks whether the device is ready (state #1 of Figure 1), it then configures the device, writes the command parameters and waits for response through an interrupt (state #2) or by repeatedly checking status (state #3). The device fills its transfer buffer with part of the requested data (state #1 of Figure 2) and signals the host for availability (states #2 and #3, by asserting the interrupt line or setting the data request (DRQ) status bit). The host then reads this data (host state #4) and the interaction continues until completion (buffer count reaches zero), when they both return to their idle state (states #0). For this demonstration we omit many technical details, e.g., selection of devices and media error handling. We show that even if we make the model simpler and also assume perfect operation of the device mechanics, the execution can still become erroneous.

2.1   Non-stability

The model above does not describe a behavior in which progress is achieved infinitely often. Even assuming correct behavior of each party, still the combined execution can enter states in which progress is not achieved infinitely often. Figure 3 presents the various combinations of states that the system can reach. The arrowed path demonstrates a possible correct execution which is cyclic and includes the combined idle state (marked "h0d0"). Possible non-stabilizing executions are described next:

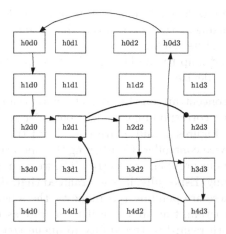

Fig. 3. Union State Transitions (h=host, d=device)

Deadlock. The upper dot-headed transition in Figure 3 demonstrates a scenario in which the execution reaches the combined host state #2 with device state #3. In host state #2, the host waits for an interrupt in order to transfer data. In the meantime, the device (say, due to a transient error) assumes that interrupts are disabled and waits in its state #3 for the host to read data from its buffer. From such a combination of states there is no defined progress.

Livelock. Another case is demonstrated in Figure 3 where the other dot-headed path causes to circle back to state "h2d1" without ever finishing the execution of the current command. This happens when the host is cycling between states #2 and #4, reading the device's buffer content, but the buffer counter never goes down to zero.

Another example is the host waiting for the device. It reads in the state register that it is busy, while the device is really non-busy. The standard also addresses some other scenarios. For example, if a command is issued by the host while the device is busy with a previous command, the device should immediately start executing the new command. However we require a design in which the system converges from any combined state.

3   System Model and Requirements

Settings. We divide the system into four parts: (a) The *operating system*, which contains *processes* (or programs) which can request I/O operations. The operating system contains a special program which schedules all the various processes, including part *b* which will now be described. (b) The *operating system device driver* (or OS *driver*) is the special program which handles the I/O requests and communicates with the device. (c) The device *controller* is the program executed by a specialized micro-processor (it usually resides inside the I/O device itself) which commands the I/O device to perform its task. (d) The (I/O) *device* is the actual peripheral machinery that carries out the commands, e.g., rotating the disk media under one of its reading head.

(a) and (b) together map to the host in the ATA specification while (c) and (d) are mapped to the device.

Assumptions. We concentrate on the correct behavior and interactions of one OS driver (b) and the corresponding device controller (c). Thus the state diagrams presented in Figures 1 and 2 are considered transitions made by the OS driver and the device controller. Concerning the operating system (a), using methods described in our previous works [10], [11], we assume that the operating system is self-stabilizing. Especially, it is guaranteed that, during the system execution, whenever there are pending I/O requests, the scheduler will eventually execute the driver program, thus allowing it to operate as required. Fair access between processes with regard to the ability to queue I/O requests is achieved either by assuming eventual correct behavior of the processes (we do not assume the Byzantine model) or by leasing the right to queue messages in ways that will guarantee fairness as done before by the memory manager (see [11]).

It is also assumed that the I/O device's micro-processor is self-stabilizing, which means that it keeps fetching and executing the device controller program. Methods to achieve such behavior are described in [7]. Additionally, the device mechanics (or other equivalences in other devices) always eventually respond to the device controller commands either by carrying them out or by reporting an error in case of say physical disabilities, e.g., bad sectors on the disk media.

The OS driver and the device controller communicate by writing in each others registers. It is assumed that every read/write operation is performed atomically and without errors.

Definitions. We describe briefly a set of definitions related to states and state transitions (see [10,11] for details concerning processor executions, interrupt and register settings, and additional requirements). A *state* of the operating system driver or the device controller is an assignment to its registers including the program counter resister. Each party is modeled by a program which specifies its behavior. It has a clock which triggers a *step* which is a state transition. The transition is done according to the current state (including input registers and the program counter). A *configuration* is a pair of states, the first of which is of the OS driver, and the second belongs to the device controller. An example of such a configuration is "h0d0" which appears in Figure 3 in which both parties are in their idle state. An *execution* is a sequence of alternating configurations and steps $E = (c_1, s_1, c_2, s_2, ...)$, such that configuration c_{i+1} is reached from configuration c_i by one step s_i taken by one of the parties. A configuration like "h0d0" is called a *safe configuration* since an execution that starts from this configuration carries out the task of executing I/O commands correctly.

Table 1 lists, for each protocol party, the various register roles used in the described read command.

Table 1. ATA Registers

Owner	Register	I/O	Role
OS driver	OsCommand	I	Command parameters written by OS
	OsINT	I	Interrupt Configuration written by OS
	INT Line	I	Interrupt line* asserted by device controller (*Not a register)
Device controller	Command	I	Command parameters written by OS driver
	INT	I	Interrupt status written by OS driver
	BSY	O	Controller working status read by OS driver
	DRQ	O	Data ready status read by OS driver
	Buffer Count	I/O	Data ready status written by OS driver and decremented by device controller

The Error Model. The OS driver and the device controller states, including their program counters, might become corrupted (assigned any possible value).

Requirements. We now define the requirements which should be satisfied in order for the described system to be self-stabilizing.

(r1) Liveness. Assuming that there is an infinite system execution, in which there are infinitely many I/O requests, the OS driver and the device controller are infinitely often exchanging requests and replies.

(r2) Safety. Eventually every I/O request is executed completely and correctly according to the ATA specification.   As explained, the result can be a success, e.g., data moved according to the command's parameters, or a failure due to bad parameters, some transient error (such as dust on the disk surface) or even non-transient device errors such as bad sectors.

A *self-stabilizing* OS *driver and device controller combination* ensures that every infinite execution of a system has a suffix in which both requirements hold.

4   Self-stabilizing Driver

The OS driver and the device controller can be viewed as a master and a slave working together according to the protocol to achieve their mission. Thus, the driver acting as a master can check that the slave is following, say the ATA protocol, correctly. We suggest two solutions. In the first solution the device controller is not required to be self-stabilizing, and the OS driver leases the device controller some (usually enough) time to complete its tasks. Then we relax the timing constrains by assuming that the device controller itself is also self-stabilizing. Therefore we only need to guarantee that the execution is carried out by both parties according to the protocol. This is achieved by the OS driver performing consistency checks according to its current state. Note that the device controller itself is working against the underlying device so an implementation of the controller-device protocol can use either the leasing or the consistency checks solutions for this level as well.

4.1   Leasing

In order to satisfy our requirements we suggest that the device controller should be augmented by a counter register which is used to implement a watchdog. The OS driver is able to write some value to this register, while the device hardware is lowering the register value towards zero, say in every clock tick. Additionally the OS driver is augmented with additional transitions which guarantee that in case the lease expires, which means that there is no progress from the device controller side, the OS driver resets the device controller's state and also moves to the idle state. Figure 4 describes the new OS driver transitions.

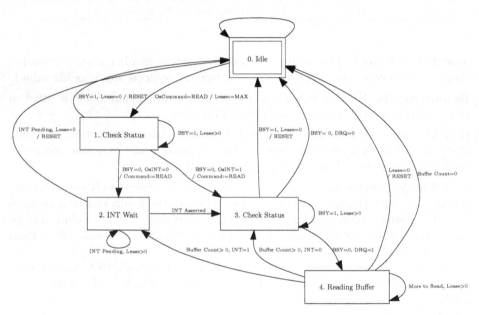

Fig. 4. A Leasing Host (OS Driver)

Next we prove the correctness of the leasing solution:

Lemma 1. *The OS driver reaches its idle state infinitely often.*

Sketch of proof: The OS driver always converges towards the idle state. This can be observed by examining the possible state transitions. We can see that in every state the OS driver can either move to a higher numbered state (modulo the number of states) or stay in the current state. The only exception to this rule is the move from state #4 to states #2 or #3 (depending on the interrupt status), but the number of such possible backward moves is bounded by the countdown of buffer reads, which is decreased towards zero every time such a back move is taken. So the OS driver is guaranteed either to proceed through the protocol stages and eventually reach the idle state, or else to get stuck in some state. In the latter case, since the OS driver stopped leaving the idle state, the only state where it updates the device leasing counter, this register will eventually reach zero causing the OS driver to perform a move to the idle state.   □

Lemma 2. *From any configuration a safe configuration is eventually reached.*

Sketch of proof: From Lemma 1, the OS driver reaches the idle state infinitely often. Usually according to the protocol design, the device controller will reach the idle state following the OS driver. Whenever the OS driver starts a new command it advances along the protocol stages waiting for the device controller to follow it as they carry out the I/O request together. Whenever a command is completed both parties proceed to the idle state, which is a safe configuration. Otherwise, the OS driver will eventually reset the device controller which will bring it to its idle state, and also will move to its idle state, thus again reaching a safe configuration ("h0d0"). Note that in case of successive commands the OS driver might wait in state #1 for the controller to finish the last command and join. Therefore the configurations "h1d3" and "h1d0" are safe configurations as well.   □

Corollary 1. *Since a safe configuration is reached from any state, liveness holds.*

Lemma 3. *Eventually safety holds.*

Sketch of proof: From Lemma 2, a safe configuration is eventually reached. From this configuration on the OS driver and the device controller fulfill requests according to the protocol specification.   □

Corollary 2. *Since in every infinite system execution, the liveness and safety requirements hold infinitely often, the OS driver and device controller combination is self-stabilizing.*

4.2   Consistency Check

Alternatively, if we can assume stabilization of the device controller, then it is suffices to guaranty that the device follows the OS driver while executing commands. The OS driver will be augmented with a consistency checker routine that checks consistency of both parties. The timing of the execution of this routine can be tuned to occur before each driver code execution, or periodically by means of a watchdog timer and a non-maskable interrupt as described in [10]. The routine freezes the OS driver and reads its program counter register. It also interrupts the device controller, which stops all activity and then reads a snapshot of the device controller's state. Then it ensures that the controller is in a proper state according to the driver stage of the protocol. In case of consistency violation, actions are taken e.g., resetting the controller.

For each (abstract) state of the diagrams presented by Figures 1 and 2, there can actually be a set of program counter values which fits that state. The programs of the OS driver and the device controller can be assembled in such a way that there is a simple function which maps every program counter value to its corresponding diagram state. We say that every diagram state is represented by a Program Counter Segment (PCS). This can be implemented for example in the Intel's IA32 architecture [16] by allocating a full code segment for each PCS (more details appear in a previous work [10]).

Table 2. Consistency Check Rules

OS Driver PCS	Device Controller Snapshots
0,1	PCS=0
	PCS=3
2	PCS=1, INT=1
	PCS=2, INT=1
3	PCS=1
	PCS=2, INT=1
	PCS=3, INT=0
4	PCS=3

Table 2 includes for every such OS driver PCS, the legal device controller PCS and other register values. For example, when the OS driver is waiting for an interrupt (state #2) the device controller must be in states #1 or #2 but not in state #3, where it is waiting for the driver forever. The interrupt status of the device controller must also be checked to ensure that the device controller will inform the OS driver upon completion. As to other registers, such as DRQ, there is no need to check consistency since the self-stabilization of the device controller guarantees that it will eventually (and in bounded time) set the required values needed for the execution to progress according to the protocol.

Lemma 4. *Eventually liveness holds.*

Sketch of proof: Similarly to Lemma 1 the OS driver advances along the protocol stages. In every state it can either advance to the next stage or wait for the device controller. Since we have the consistency checker assuring that the device controller is in a proper matching state, and since the device controller is self-stabilizing, eventually the device controller will perform the current stage, and the OS driver will advance to the next stage.   □

Lemma 5. *Eventually safety holds.*

Sketch of proof: Similar to the proof of Lemma 3.   □

Corollary 3. *Since in every infinite system execution the liveness and safety requirements hold infinitely often, the OS driver and the device controller combination is self-stabilizing.*

5   Concluding Remarks

Self-stabilization methods enhance the robustness of device drivers, and consequently of their including systems. We demonstrated the lack of such properties in one of the well known standard protocols. The two solutions that were proposed can be practically combined according to the level of stabilization that can be expected from various I/O devices. The snapshot of the I/O device, taken during a consistency check, can be enlarged if its stabilization ability is diminished. If not all the device producers can be relied upon, then one can have a fall back that uses leases and restarts to achieve self-stabilization. Prototype implementations can be found in [29]. Finally, we predict that provable self-stabilizing operating systems will be an essential part of every critical computing system in the near future.

References

1. M. Accetta, R. Baron, W. Bolosky, D. Golub, R. Rashid, A. Tevanian, M. Young. "MACH: A New Kernel Foundation for UNIX Development", *Proceedings of the USENIX Summer Conference*, Atlants, GA, 1986.
2. P. Barham, B. Dragovich, K. Fraser, S. Hand, A. Ho, I. Pratt. "Safe Hardware Access with the Xen Virtual Machine Monitor", *1st Workshop on Operating System and Architectural Support for On-Demand IT Infrastructure*, May 2004.
3. O. Brukman, S. Dolev, H. Kolodner. "Self-Stabilizing Autonomic Recoverer for Eventual Byzantine Software", *Proceedings of IEEE International Conference on Software-Science Technology & Engineering*, (SwSTE03), Israel, 2003.
4. T. Ball, S.K. Rajamani. "The SLAM Project: Debugging System Software via Static Analysis", *Proceedings of the 29th Symposium on Principles of Programming Languages (POPL 2002)*, Portland, OR, 200.
5. M. Castro, B. Liskov. "Proactive Recovery in a Byzantine-Fault-Tolerant System", *Proceedings of the Fourth Symposium on Operating Systems Design and Implementation*, pp. 273-288, San Diego, CA, October 2000.
6. A. Chou, J. Yang, B. Chelf, S. Hallem, D. Engler. "An empirical study of operating systems errors", *Proceedings of the 18th ACM Symposium on Operating Systems Principles (SOSP)*, 2001.
7. S. Dolev, Y. Haviv. "Self-Stabilizing Microprocessor: Analyzing and Overcoming Soft Errors", *IEEE Trans. on Computers 55(4)*, 2006. Also at: *17th International Conference on Architecture of Computing Systems (ARCS04)*, 2004.
8. E. W. Dijkstra. "Self-Stabilizing Systems in Spite of Distributed Control," *Communications of the ACM*, Vol. 17, No. 11, pp. 643-644, 1974.
9. S. Dolev. *Self-Stabilization*, The MIT Press, Cambridge, 2000.
10. S. Dolev, R. Yagel. "Toward Self-Stabilizing Operating Systems", *Proceedings of the 15th International Conference on Database and Expert Systems Applications, 2nd International Workshop on Self-Adaptive and Autonomic Computing Systems* (SAACS04,DEXA), pp. 684-688, Zaragoza, Spain, August 2004.
11. S. Dolev and R. Yagel. "Memory Management for Self-Stabilizing Operating Systems (Extended Abstract)". *Proceedings of the 7th Symposium on Self Stabilizing Systems*, Barcelona, October 2005.

12. K. T. Van Maren. "The Fluke Device Driver Framework", *Master's thesis*, The University of Utah, 1999.
13. G. C. Hunt, J. R. Larus, M. Abadi, M. Aiken, P. Barham, M. Fahndrich, C. Hawblitzel, O. Hodson, S. Levi, N. Murphy, B. Steensgaard, D. Tarditi, T. Wobber, B. Zill. "An Overview of the Singularity Project", *Microsoft Research Technical Report MSR-TR-2005-135*, Microsoft Corporation, Redmond, WA, October 2005.
14. H. J. Löeser, F. Mehnert, L. Reuther, M. Pohlack, A. Warg. "An I/O Architecture for Mikrokernel-Based Operating Systems", *Proceedings of the Sixth Symposium on Operating Systems Design and Implementation (OSDI)*, San Francisco, 2004
15. IBM. Autonomic computing initiative, http://www.research.ibm.com/autonomic, 2001.
16. Intel Corporation. "The IA-32 Intel Architecture Software Developer's Manual", http://developer.intel.com/design/pentium4 /documentation.htm, 2006.
17. M. Kistler, P. Shivakumar, L. Alvisi, D. Burger, and S. Keckler. "Modeling the effect of technology trends on the soft error rate of combinational logic". In *ICDSN*, volume 72 of *LNCS*, pages 216–226, 2002.
18. B. Leslie, G. Heiser. "Towards untrusted device drivers", *Technical Report UNSW-CSE-TR-0303, School of Computer Science and Engineering*, 2003.
19. L. Lamport, R. Shostak, and M. Pease. "The Byzantine Generals Problem", *ACM Trans. on Programming Languages and Systems*, Vol. 4, No. 3, pp. 382-401, 1982.
20. J. LeVasseur, V. Uhlig. "A Sledgehammer Approach to Reuse of Legacy Device Drivers", *Proceedings of the 11th ACM SIGOPS European Workshop*, Belgium, 2004.
21. J. LeVasseur, V. Uhlig, J. Stoess, S. Götz. "Unmodified Device Driver Reuse and Improved System Dependability via Virtual Machines", *Proceedings of the Sixth Symposium on Operating Systems Design and Implementation (OSDI)*, San Francisco, 2004
22. P. G. Neumann, R. S. Boyer, R. J. Feiertag, K. N. Levitt, L. Robinson. "A provably secure operating system: The system, its applications, and proofs", *Technical Report CSL-116, SRI International*, 1980.
23. V. Prabhakaran, L. N. Bairavasundaram, N. Agrawal, H. S. Gunawi, A. C. Arpaci-Dusseau, R. H. Arpaci-Dusseau. "IRON File Systems", *Proceedings of the 20th ACM Symposium on Operating Systems Principles (SOSP '05)* Brighton, UK, October 2005.
24. D. Patterson, A. Brown, P. Broadwell, G. Candea, M. Chen, J. Cutler, P. Enriquez, A. Fox, E. Kiciman, M. Merzbacher, D. Oppenheimer, N. Sastry, W. Tetzlaff, J. Traupman, N. Treuhaft. "Recovery Oriented Computing(ROC): Motivation, definition, techniques and case studies", UC Berkeley Computer Science Technical Report UCB/CSD-02-1175, Berkeley, CA, March 2002.
25. M. Swift. "Improving the Reliability of Commodity Operating Systems", *Ph.D. Dissertation*, University of Washongton, 2005.
26. M. Swift, M. Annamalai, B. N. Bershad, H. M. Levy. "Recovering Device Drivers", *Proceedings of the 6th ACM/USENIX Symposium on Operating Systems Design and Implementation (ODSI)*, San Francisco, 2004.
27. M. Swift, B. N. Bershad, H. M. Levy. "Improving the reliability of commodity operating systems", *Proceedings of the 19th ACM Symposium on Operating Systems Principles (SOSP)*, Bolton Landing, NY, October 2003.
28. J. Shapiro, M. S. Doerrie, E. Northup, S. Sridhar, M. Miller. "Towards a verified, general-purpose operating system kernel". Available at http://www.coyotos.org, 2005.

29. http://www.cs.bgu.ac.il/~yagel/sos
30. M. Spear, T. Roeder, O. Hodson, G. Hunt, S. Levi. "Solving the Starting Problem: Device Drivers as Self-Describing Artifacts", *Proceedings of EuroSys2006*. Leuven, Belgium, April 2006.
31. http://www.selfstabilization.org
32. Sun Microsystems, Inc. 'Predictive Self-Healing in the Solaris™ 10 Operating System", *White paper*, September 2004. http://www.sun.com/software/whitepapers /solaris10/self_healing.pdf.
33. InterNational Committee for Information Technology Standards, *T13 ATA Storage Interface - T13/1532D Vol. 2. Revision 4a (working drafts)*. http://www.t13.org/#Projects.
34. A. S. Tanenbaum, A. S. Woddhull. *Operating Systems Design and Implementation*, 3nd edition, (p. 225). Prentice Hall, New Jersey, 2006.

Secure Communication for RFIDs Proactive Information Security Within Computational Security*
(Extended Abstract)

Shlomi Dolev[1] and Marina Kopeetsky[2]

[1] Department of Computer Science, Ben-Gurion University of the Negev,
Beer-Sheva, 84105, Israel
dolev@cs.bgu.ac.il
[2] Department of Software Engineering, Sami-Shamoon College of Engineering,
Beer-Sheva, 84100, Israel
marinako@sce.ac.il

Abstract. We consider repeated communication sessions between a sender (e.g., Radio Frequency Identification, RFID, reader) and a receiver (RFID). A proactive information security scheme is proposed. The scheme is based on the assumption that the information exchanged during at least one of every n successive communication sessions is not exposed to an adversary. Then a computational secure scheme based on the information secure scheme is used to ensure that even in the case that the adversary listens to all the information exchanges, the communication between the sender and the receiver is secure. In particular, the scheme can be used in the domain of remote controls (e.g., for cars).

Keywords: authentication protocol, information security, computational security, RFID tags, pseudo-random numbers.

1 Introduction

RFID tag is a small microchip, supplemented with an antenna, that transmits a unique identifier in response to a query by a reading device. The RFID technology is designed for the unique identification of different kinds of objects. According to [9] RFID communication systems are composed of three major elements: (a) the RFID tag carries object identifying data; (b) the RFID reader interfaces with tags to read or write tag data; (c) the back-end database aggregates and utilizes tag data collected by readers.

RFID sender (or reader) broadcasts an RF signal to access data stored on tags that usually includes a unique identification number. RFID tags are designed as low cost devices that use cheap radio transmission media. Such tags

---

* Partially supported by Microsoft, IBM, NSF, Intel, Deutsche Telekom, Rita Altura Trust Chair in Computer Sciences, Intel, vaatat and Lynn and William Frankel Center for Computer Sciences.

A.K. Datta and M. Gradinariu (Eds.): SSS 2006, LNCS 4280, pp. 290–303, 2006.

have no internal source of power, nevertheless they receive their power from the reading devices. The range of the basic tags transmission is up to several meters. Possible applications of the RFID devices include: RFID-enabled banknotes, libraries, passports, pharmaceutical distribution of drugs, and organization of the automobile security system or any key-less entry system. Nevertheless, the wide deployment of RFID tags may cause new security and privacy protecting issues. RFID tags usually operate in insecure environment. The RFID reader privacy may be compromised by the adversary that extracts unencrypted data from the unprotected tags. RFID tags are limited devices that cannot support complicated cryptographic functions. Hence, there is nowadays an interest in achieving high security and privacy level for the RFID devices, without usage of computationally expensive encryption techniques.

The focus of our paper is the authentication protocol for the basic passive RFID tags. We present new proactive and cost effective information and computationally secure authentication protocols for RFIDs. The main scope is one sided authentication, where the receiver has to identify the sender. Such (non mutual) one sided authentication is useful in applications in which the sender may have other means to identify (that it is communicating with) the desired receiver (say by being geographically close to the receiver). We also exclude the possibility of man-in the-middle attacks, having similar applications in minds, where the sender may identify the existence of a man-in the-middle. Still, we conclude and suggest ways to cope with these limitations.

Background and related work. A brief introduction to RFID technology appears in [9] where potential security and privacy risks are described. Schemes for providing desired security properties in the unique setting of low-cost RFID devices are discussed in [9]. The authors of [9] depict several advantages of the RFID tags over traditional optical bar codes. Unlike the optical bar codes, RFID tags are able to read data automatically through non-conducting material at a rate of several hundred tags per second and from a distance of several meters. The authors state that low-cost smart RFID tags may become an efficient replacement for optical bar codes. The main security risks stated in that paper are the violations of "location privacy" and denial of service that disable the tags. With the RFID resource constraints in mind, the cryptography techniques proposed in developing the RFID security mechanisms are: (a) a simple access mechanism based on hardware-efficient one-way hash functions, low-cost traditional symmetric encryption schemes, randomizing tag responses based on random number generator; (b) integrating RFID systems with a key management infrastructure. Regardless of the mechanisms used for privacy and access control, management of tag keys is an important issue. The new challenge in the RFID system design is to provide access control and key management tools compatible with the tags cost constraints.

The research survey in [6] examines different approaches proposed by researches for providing privacy protection and integrity assurance in RFID systems. In order to define the notions of "secure" and "private" for RFID tags a formal model that characterizes the capabilities of potential adversaries is proposed. The author state that it is important to adapt RFID security models to cope with the weakness of the RFID devices. Few weak security models that reflect real threats and tag capabilities are discussed. A "minimalist" security model that serves low-cost tags is introduced in [7]. The basic model assumption is that the potential RFID adversary is necessarily weaker than the one in traditional cryptography. Besides, such an adversary comes into scanning range of a tag only periodically. The minimalist model aims to take into account the RFID adversary characteristics. Therefore, this model is not perfect, but it eliminates some of the standard cryptographic assumptions that may be not appropriate for the deployment in other security systems that are based on a more powerful adversary model. The author of [7] states that standard cryptographic functionality is not needed to achieve necessary security in RFID tags.

An adversary model adapted to RFID protocols is introduced in [1]. Many existing privacy protecting RFID protocols are examined for their *traceability*. *Traceability* is defined as the capability of the adversary to recognize a tag which the adversary has already seen, at another time or in another location [1]. The traceability is stated as a serious problem related to the privacy protection in the RFID systems. The paper concludes that in a realistic model, many protocols are not resistant to traceability.

The Newsletter of the RFID Society [4] proposes zero-knowledge proofs technology in solving the privacy issue for RFID. The main idea is to enhance RFID chips with additional cryptographic functions supporting zero knowledge identity proofs. This approach requires a large amount of memory and long computational time. Note that basic RFID tags are low-memory devices and are not capable to store and process large amount of data.

Existing techniques and secure protocols proposed for implementation in existing RFID systems are described next.

Inexpensive RFID tag known as Electronic Product Code (EPC) tag is proposed in [5] to protect against RFID tag cloning. Basic EPC tags do possess features geared toward privacy protection and access control mechanisms, notwithstanding they do not possess explicit authentication functionality. That is, EPC standards prescribe no mechanism for RFID-EPC readers to authenticate the validity of the tags they scan. The authors show how to construct tag-to-reader and reader-to-tag authentication protocols.

However, the security analysis of the basic EPC RFID tags is described in [2]. The authors present in detail the successful strategy for defeating the security of an RFID device known as Digital Signature Transponder (DST). The main conclusion of [2] is that basic EPC tags are no longer secure due to the tags weakness caused by the inadequate short key length of 40 bits. Note that it is possible to increase the computational security level by increasing the length of the key, still the resulting scheme will not be information secure but only computationally secure. Hence, it is of interest to design a proactive information secure scheme within computational secure scheme as we do in the sequel.

Our contribution. Our goal in this paper is to design new algorithms for providing authentication for the computationally limited basic RFID systems with small amount of storage capability.

We propose a new security protecting model that is information and computationally secure. The security power of the basic and combined authentication protocols is provided by maintaining at the sender and the receiver's sides square n-dimensional matrix B. The XOR of the appropriate columns elements is used as the secret key for performing the authentication procedure by the RFID. A row of the matrix B is replaced by a row with randomly chosen elements at any communication session.

The basic information secure protocol AP_1 is based on the the limited adversarial capabilities. The underlining assumption of this protocol is that the adversary is not listening in at least one of each n successive interactions between the sender and the receiver. In essence, this protocol follows the "minimalist" security model in [7]. The underlying assumption of AP_1 is that each communication session is atomic. We mean that the adversary cannot modify part of the communication in a session. The adversary may either listen to the communication during a session, or try to communicate (on behalf of the RFID sender) during an entire session. AP_1 is not resistant against active intruder-in the-middle attacks [10]. Compared with [7] our scheme also works when we do not know explicitly which session the adversary is not listening in. Moreover, the security failure in a certain session does not bear on successful implementation of the next sessions since our algorithms are proactive. The restriction imposed on the adversary is dropped in the combined proactive computational secure protocol AP_2 that operates successfully even if the adversary has gotten access to any number of successive interactions between the sender and the receiver. AP_2 protocol does not follow the "minimalist model" proposed in [7]. There are only (reasonable) computation limitations on the adversarial capabilities. AP_2 does not rely on atomic sessions and it is resistant against active intruder-in the-middle attacks [10]. The proactive combined computational secure protocol has several advantages.

Low computational cost combined with a very high security level. Our algorithms continuously use random numbers generator as a source for preserving the security level. Low computational power is required compared with the standard cryptographic techniques like stream and block ciphers.

Protocols' robustness. Our proactive computational secure protocol is not based on the refreshing procedure as suggested in [7]. The refreshing procedure in [7] provides the complete initialization of the protocol's secure parameters on the assumption that the adversary is not listening in the refreshing session. Moreover, the trusted party or RFID verifier in [7] accesses the RFID system on a periodic basis refreshing the system. Our model provides high computational security level by involving a trusted party only during initialization.

Security system reliability. AP_1 does not rely on information concerning the specific session among consecutive n sessions the adversary was listening in and the sessions in which the adversary was not present (as [7] assumes).

Functionality in the proactive mode. According to [3] proactive security provides a method for maintaining the overall security of a system, even when individual components are repeatedly broken into and controlled by an attacker. The automated recovery of the security protocol is provided in the proactive security model [3]. Any listening adversary's success and consequent protocol's security failure do not affect further functionality of the protocol. Recovery from a failure (assuming nonfatal effect of failures) is automatic. That is to say, assuming that no fatal damage is caused when the adversary reveals the clear text, the future communication security is established.

Possibility of proactive information security within computational security. Our second protocol AP_2 assumes that if the adversary was not listening in at least for a single session among n consecutive sessions between the RFID sender and the RFID receiver the proposed protocol automatically becomes information and computationally secure and, therefore the original security level is established.

We believe that our protocol is useful in several domains including remote keys, e.g., automobile security system.

Paper organization. The formal system description appears in Section 2. The basic information secure protocol AP_1 is introduced in Section 3. The combined computational secure protocol AP_2 is described in Section 4. The extended abstract is completed with conclusions and extensions. Proofs are only sketched in this extended abstract.

2   Security Model for RFID Tags

We consider the (RFID) sender and the (RFID) receiver denoted by S and R, respectively. The sender and the receiver communicate by sending and receiving messages according to their predefined programs, that form together a communication protocol. We denote the ith message sent by the sender and by the receiver as s_i and r_i, respectively. The sequence of alternating messages $M = s_1, r_1, s_2, r_2, \cdots$ sent during the course of the protocol execution can be divided into non overlapping subsequences, so that each subsequence $S_i = s_{i_k}, r_{i_k}$ is called *communication session*. The union of the communication sessions forms the entire sequence of messages M. Each S_i starts with a message sent by the sender and ends when the receiver decides to send a message $r_{i_k} = Open$ or $r_{i_k} = DoNotOpen$. Any message s_k sent by the RFID sender is defined as a key message. Actually, the message r_{i_k} represents a change in state of the receiver which corresponds to the sender password authentication as the one that can enter to use a resource.

We assume a *Byzantine adversary* denoted as A, that listens in to part or all of the sequence M and may try to send complete messages on behalf of the sender. The goal of the adversary is either making the receiver sending message $r = Open$ or driving the receiver into a state after which the receiver will not send the message $r = Open$ to the sender.

Given the features of the proposed model, we describe basic and combined authentication protocols. The first basic authentication protocol AP_1 is the proactive information secure protocol. The information security feature of this protocol is provided by the assumption that within any n consecutive communication sessions $S_{i_1} = s_{i_1}, r_{i_1}, \cdots S_{i_n} = s_{i_n}, r_{i_n}$ there is at least one message s_{i_k} sent by the RFID sender S which the adversary is not aware of. The strict limitation imposed on the adversary is lessened in the combined computational secure protocol AP_2. The security power of AP_1 and AP_2 protocols is based on random numbers generation and their updating at each communication session. AP_1 and AP_2 are introduced and analyzed in the next sections.

3   Proactive Information Secure Protocol

The proactive information secure protocol AP_1 is described in Figure 2. Here the matrix B is defined as a linked list data structure. Denote the space of the matrix's B elements by $\{a_{ij}, b_{ij}\}$. Here the sub-set $\{a_{ij}\}$ denote the elements of $B's$ granted to S and R respectively during the initialization procedure while the sub-set $\{b_{ij}\}$ consist of random numbers that update B matrix during the communication sessions. At the initialization stage S and R both get a unique square matrix $B = (a_{ij})$ so that $dim\,(B) = n$ (Figure 2, Protocols for RFID Sender and Receiver, lines 1-5). In order to perform the authentication procedure, S starts the communication session and passes to R the key message $s_1 = (X_1, b_1)$ (lines 6-9 in Figure 2, Protocol for RFID Sender). s_1 consists of the following pair: XOR of the nth column elements $X_1 = a_{1n} \oplus a_{2n} \oplus \ldots \oplus a_{nn}$ and randomly generated n-dimensional vector $b_1 = (b_{11}, b_{12}, \ldots, b_{1n})$.

After transmission of the first key message s_1, S and R, respectively, shift $B's$ rows below so that $b_1 = (b_{11}, b_{12}, \ldots, b_{1n})$ is treated as the first $B's$ row and the last row is deleted (lines 10-11 in Figure 2, Protocol for RFID Sender).

During the next authentication session S and R repeat the same procedure: S

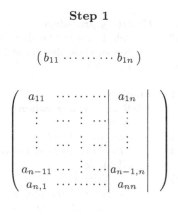

Step 1

$$(\,b_{11} \cdots\cdots\cdots b_{1n}\,)$$

$$\begin{pmatrix} a_{11} & \cdots\cdots\cdots & a_{1n} \\ \vdots & \cdots\ \vdots\ \cdots & \vdots \\ \vdots & \cdots\ \vdots\ \cdots & \vdots \\ a_{n-11} & \cdots\ \vdots\ \cdots & a_{n-1,n} \\ a_{n,1} & \cdots\cdots\cdots & a_{nn} \end{pmatrix}$$

Step 2

$$(\,b_{21} \cdots\cdots\cdots b_{2n}\,)$$

$$\begin{pmatrix} b_{11} & \cdots\cdots & b_{1n-1} & b_{1n} \\ \vdots & \cdots\ \vdots & \cdots & \vdots \\ \vdots & \cdots\ \vdots & \cdots & \vdots \\ a_{n-21} & \cdots\ \vdots & a_{n-2n-1} & a_{n-2n} \\ a_{n-11} & \cdots\cdots & a_{n-1n-1} & a_{n-1n} \end{pmatrix}$$

Fig. 1. Operation of Proactive Information Secure Protocol

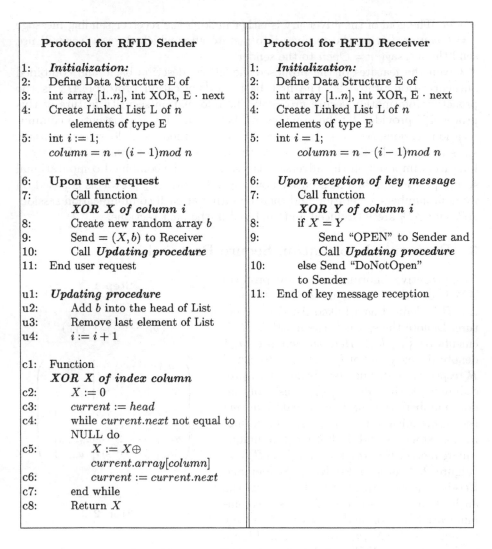

Protocol for RFID Sender	Protocol for RFID Receiver
1: *Initialization:*	1: *Initialization:*
2: Define Data Structure E of	2: Define Data Structure E of
3: int array [1..n], int XOR, E · next	3: int array [1..n], int XOR, E · next
4: Create Linked List L of n	4: Create Linked List L of n
elements of type E	elements of type E
5: int $i := 1$;	5: int $i = 1$;
$column = n - (i - 1)mod\ n$	$column = n - (i - 1)mod\ n$
6: **Upon user request**	6: **Upon reception of key message**
7: Call function	7: Call function
XOR X of column i	**XOR Y of column i**
8: Create new random array b	8: if $X = Y$
9: Send $= (X, b)$ to Receiver	9: Send "OPEN" to Sender and
10: Call **Updating procedure**	Call **Updating procedure**
11: End user request	10: else Send "DoNotOpen"
	to Sender
u1: *Updating procedure*	11: End of key message reception
u2: Add b into the head of List	
u3: Remove last element of List	
u4: $i := i + 1$	
c1: Function	
XOR X of index column	
c2: $X := 0$	
c3: $current := head$	
c4: while $current.next$ not equal to	
NULL do	
c5: $X := X \oplus$	
$current.array[column]$	
c6: $current := current.next$	
c7: end while	
c8: Return X	

Fig. 2. Proactive Information Secure Protocol

generates the new random n-dimensional vector $b_2 = (b_{21}, b_{22}, \ldots, b_{2n})$, calculates XOR of $(n - 1)$ $B's$ column elements $X_2 = b_{1n-1} \oplus a_{1n-1} \oplus \ldots \oplus a_{n-1n-1}$ and sends the newly generated key message $s_2 = (X_2, b_2)$ to R.

The authentication procedure is repeated continually scanning the matrix columns (one after the other) and changing the appropriate row. After each ith authentication success both S and R, respectively, shift the $B's$ rows below so that the last matrix' B row is deleted and the vector b_i occupies the first $B's$ row. Note that b_i has been previously randomly generated by S and has been sent to B in the message s_{j-1}. Updating procedure and calculation of XOR for the corresponding $B's$ column elements are described in Figure 2 (lines u1-u4 and c1-c8, respectively, Protocol for RFID Sender).

In order to confirm the correct authentication, the RFID receiver R executes the authentication procedure in the following manner: upon receiving the key message $s_i = (X_i, b_i)$ R verifies that X_i is the correct XOR of the appropriate $(n - (i-1)(mod(n)))^{th}$ column. If so, then R confirms the correct authentication, "transmits" to S the message $r_i = Open$ and updates the matrix B (lines 6-11 in Figure 2, Protocol for RFID Receiver). Otherwise, R "transmits" to S the message $r_i = DoNotOpen$ and does not update the matrix B.

Assume that during the course of executing AP_1 it holds that in any sequence of alternating messages $M = s_1, r_1, s_2, r_2, \ldots$ the following condition is satisfied: in any n-length sequence M of alternating messages between S and R there is at least a single message s_{j_k} not captured by the adversary. Assume that in order to break the security system of the RFID receiver, the adversary performs authentication procedure on behalf of the RFID sender. To do so in any S_j^{th} communication session the adversary has to forge the key message s_{j_i}, namely, to correctly guess the XOR of the corresponding $(n - (j_i - 1)(mod(n)))^{th}$ column elements of the basic matrix B.

Assume that $dim\,(B) = n$. Assume that the single unknown to the adversary key is n^{th} $B's$ column $(a_{1n}, a_{2n}, \ldots, a_{nn})$ and the appropriate row vector is $b_1 = (b_{11}, b_{12}, \ldots, b_{1n})$ that have been sent by S in the message $s_1 = (X_1, b_1)$ during the first communication session (Figure 1, Step 1).

After transmitting the first key message $s_1 = (X_1, b_1)$, $X_1 = (a_{1n} \oplus a_{2n} \oplus \ldots \oplus a_{nn})$, $b_1 = (b_{11}, b_{12}, \ldots, b_{1n})$ to the RFID receiver both S and R shift the rows of $B's$ according to the described above procedure.

Note that in the next trial S will send to R the XOR of the updated $(n-1)^{th}$ $B's$ column $X_2 = (b_{1n-1} \oplus a_{1n-1} \oplus \ldots \oplus a_{n-1n-1})$ and a new randomly generated vector $b_2 = (b_{2n}, b_{2n-1}, \ldots, b_{21})$ (Figure 1, Step 2).

Now matrix B differs from the previous one by the newly inserted first row and the appropriate deletion of the last row. The matrix B updating is done by S and R in each successful communication session.

The AP_1 authentication protocol is information theoretic secure. It means that the probability that the adversary will forge the key message and perform successfully the communication session on behalf of the RFID sender S, is negligible for long enough l, where l is the number of bits of the entry in the matrix B.

The following Theorem proves that the introduced protocol is information-theoretic secure.

Theorem 1. AP_1 protocol is theoretical information secure and proactive.

Proof sketch: The AP_1 information security feature is based on the fact that at any authentication step i the following conditions hold: (a) the RFID sender S and the RFID receiver R maintain the same matrix B; (b) S and R are synchronized in the sense that both S and R perform the authentication procedure using as a key the XOR of the same $n - (j-1)(mod(n))$ column; (c) the matrix

B shared by S and R contains at least one row unknown to the adversary. The proof is implemented by induction of session number i.

Basis of induction $i = 1$
As it has been mentioned above, the first key message $s_1 = (X_1, b_1)$ at the first communication session S_1 contains XOR of nth column elements $X_1 = a_{1n} \oplus a_{2n} \oplus \ldots \oplus a_{nn}$ that is unknown to the adversary. Evidently, S and R maintain the same matrix B that has been defined at the initialization stage when the adversary was not present.

S and R are synchronized because the first key message that S sends to R and R expects to receive is the XOR of the nth column elements.

Induction step
(a) For $i < n$ the B matrix in each communication session S_j among i communication sessions $S_1, \ldots, S_i$ contains at least one row unknown to the adversary. The induction assumption is correct due to the initialization procedure performed by S and R, respectively. In addition, for any $i \geq n$ the basic condition that for each ith communication session B contains a row unknown to the adversary also holds. It is based on the assumption that among any n successive communication sessions there is at least a single session that the adversary was not eavesdropping.

(b) Assume that during every $i < n$ communication session S and R maintain the same matrix B. Then the matrix B shared by S and R during the next $i, i \geq n$ communication session will differ from the previous one by appropriate inserting the new first random row and deleting the last one at the sender and receiver's side, respectively. For that reason, during any communication session, S and R share the same matrix.

(c) Finally, assume that during any $i < n$ communication session S and R agree on the same $B's$ column $n - (i - 1)(mod(n))$ that is the basis for constructing the key message. Then, at the next $i > n$ communication session the column number is reduced by $1 \ mod(n)$. As a result, the basis for constructing the key message at the sender and the receiver' sides, respectively, is the same $B's \ n - (i - 2)(mod(n))$ column.

The AP_1 proactive feature is proved in the following way. Assume that the adversary has gotten access to the whole matrix B. Assume that in the jth communication session S_j that follows this security failure, the adversary was not listening in to the message s_j sent by the RFID sender. In essence, during any of the following $(j + i)^{th}$ session, $i \geq 1$ the XOR of the appropriate $B's$ column elements contains at least a single number $b_{j+i,n-(j+i)+1} \in b_j$ that the adversary was not listening in. Here b_j is the unknown to the adversary random vector that has been sent by S in the secure message s_j. Therefore, the basic condition, that within n consecutive messages sent from S to R there is at least a single message unknown to the adversary, is restored. As a result, the AP_1 information security feature is regained.

Assume that the adversary tends to drive the RFID receiver to a deadlock state after which the sender will not be able to cause the receiver to send a message $r=Open$. In order to do so the adversary must corrupt the matrix B, say, by inserting a new row on behalf of the RFID sender. Nevertheless, the adversary will fail in this attempt because in order to insert a new raw in the matrix B the adversary has to authenticate himself or herself on behalf of the RFID sender. The message s_j that the adversary has to send to the receiver must include the XOR X_j of the appropriate column elements.   ∎

As a matter of fact, AP_1 has two parameters. The first parameter is matrix' B size n. The larger n is, the weaker is the assumption about the adversary. The price payed for large n is the additional memory usage in the restricted memory size of the RFID devices. The second secure parameter is the number of bits l of an entry in B. The longer are $B's$ elements, the smaller is the possibility for the adversary to guess the correct key.

Note that when the assumption concerning one session in each sequential session, in which the adversary does not listen in, is violated, then the adversary can drive the system into a deadlock by, say, replacing a row in the matrix B, unknown to the sender.

4   Combined Computational Secure Protocol

We now allow the adversary to listen to any session between the RFID sender S and the RFID receiver R. Our purpose is to enhance the basic proactive information secure protocol AP_1.

As in the AP_1 case, both S and R get in the initialization stage the initial n-dimensional square matrix B (Figure 3, lines 1-6, Protocols for RFID Sender and Receiver). In addition a certain predefined key word string keyword$[k]$ is granted to S and R, respectively.

During the first authentication session S executes the following encryption procedure: As in the case of the proactive information secure protocol, S calculates the XOR of the nth B's column $X_1 = a_{1n} \oplus a_{2n} \oplus \ldots \oplus a_{nn}$. New vector row $b_1 = (b_{11}, \ldots, b_{1n})$ is also created as in the proactive information secure protocol case. X_1 is used as a seed for the generation of the pseudo-random sequence $(c_{11}, \ldots, c_{1m})$ of length $m = n \cdot l + k$, where k is the keyword length [8]. See [8], Chapter 12 for possible choices of the generation mechanism of the pseudo-random numbers.

S creates a new vector row Y_1 that should be sent to R in the first authentication message. Y_1 is equal to XOR of the previously generated pseudorandom sequence $(c_{11}, \ldots, c_{1m})$ with vector b_1 concatenated with the keyword: $Y_1 = (c_{11}, \ldots, c_{1m}) \oplus (b_1 \| keyword[k])$ (Figure 3). Eventually, the secure information encapsulation is provided. The first key message sent from S to R during the first communication session is $s_1 = (Y_1)$ (Figure 3, Protocol for RFID Sender, lines 7-13).

Upon receiving the message $s_1 = Y_1$ R decrypts it by calculating $Y_1 \oplus (c_{11}, \ldots, c_{1m})$. If the decrypted suffix of the string is equal to the predefined string keyword$[k]$, then the RFID receiver R authenticates the RFID sender S and returns the message $r_1 = Open$ to the RFID sender S. The matrix B

Protocol for RFID Sender	Protocol for RFID Receiver
1: *Initialization:*	1: *Initialization:*
2: Define Data Structure E of	2: Define Data Structure E of
3: int array $[1..n]$, int XOR, E $\cdot$ next	3: int array $[1..n]$, int XOR, E $\cdot$ next
4: Create Linked List L of n elements of type E	4: Create Linked List L of n elements of type E
5: int $j := 1$, $column = n - (j-1)mod\ n$	5: int $j := 1$, $column = n - (j-1)mod\ n$
6: int keyword$[k]$	6: int keyword$[k]$
7: Upon user request	7: Upon key message reception
8: Call function **XOR X[column]**	8: Call function **XOR Z[column]**
9: Create new random array b	9: if $j = 1$ calculate $Y \oplus c[column]$ else calculate $Y \oplus c[column]$ $\oplus c[column-1]$
10: Create pseudo-random sequence $(c[column])$	
11: of length m if $j = 1$ from seed $X[column]$ else from seed $X[column]\oplus$ $X[column-1]$	10: if $Z[column] = X[column]$
	11: send "OPEN" to Sender and call **Updating procedure**
	12: else
	13: send "DoNotOpen" to Sender
12: $Y = (X\|b)XOR(c)$	14: End of key message reception
13: Send $s = Y$ to Receiver	
14: Call **Updating procedure**	
15: End user request	
u1: **Updating procedure**	
u2: Add b into the head of List	
u3: Remove last element of List	
u4: $j := j+1$	
c1: Function **XOR X[column]** of index *column*	
c2: $X[column] := 0$	
c3: *current := head*	
c4: while *current.next* not equal to NULL do	
c5: $X[column] := X[column]\oplus$ *current.array[column]*	
c6: *current := current.next*	
c7: end while	
c8: Return X	

Fig. 3. Proactive Computational Secure Protocol

updating is provided by the prefix of the decrypted string as in the basic information secure protocol. Otherwise, the message $r_1 = DoNotOpen$ is sent to S (Figure 3, lines 7-14, Protocol for RFID Receiver). Updating procedure and calculation of XOR for the corresponding $B's$ column elements is described in Figure 2 (lines u1-u4 and c1-c8 respectively, Protocol for RFID Sender).

During any j^{th} authentication session $S_j, j = 1, 2, \ldots$ the message s_j sent by S is as follows: $Y_j = (c_{j1}, \ldots, c_{jm}) \oplus (b_j \| keyword[k])$, where $c_j = (c_{j1}, \ldots, c_{jm})$ is the pseudo-random sequence generated by the seed $X_j \oplus X_{j-1}$. X_j is equal to XOR of $(n - (j - 1)(mod(n)))^{th}$ column elements, and b_j is a newly generated random vector that updates matrix B. X_{j-1} is the seed that has been used in the previous communication session S_{j-1}. It should be noted that the keyword and the one way function that generates the pseudo-random numbers can be known to the adversary. The computational security of the designed protocol AP_2 is provided by means of the random seed generation in each session. Moreover, the recursive reuse of the seed used in the previous communication session enhance the security of AP_2 where the adversary does not listen in.

As a matter of fact, the seed X_1 used in the first communication session S_1 is unknown to the adversary. The reason is that the adversary has not been present at the initialization stage. Therefore, the initial $B's$ elements are not available for the adversary. The seed updating is performed continuously in each communication session. Hence, the adversary does not get enough time to guess the secret seeds by observing the transmitted messages.

In essence, the encryption scheme is based on the message encapsulation by means of the One Time Pads techniques ([10]), whereas the pads are created by pseudo-random sequence using a randomly created seed defined by the update procedure of the matrix B. The following theorem proves the correctness of AP_2.

Theorem 2. The AP_2 protocol is proactive computationally secure protocol.

Proof sketch: Assume that the adversary is listening in all communication sessions $S_{i_1}, \ldots, S_{i_n}$ between S and R. Even though the one way function f that generates the pseudo-random sequence is available to the adversary, calculating its invert f^{-1} is computationally infeasible ([10]). Hence, correct prediction of the seed $X_{i_{n+1}}$ and the corresponding pseudo-random sequence $c_{i_{n+1}}$ for the next communication session $S_{i_{n+1}}$ that the adversary wishes to provide in order to break the security system, is computationally impossible.

The RFID receiver R confirms the sender S authentication at each jth communication session by revealing the keyword$[k]$ string from the received decrypted message s_i. If the decrypted keyword$[k]$ string is correct, then R accepts S as a correct authentication.

We now prove the proactive feature of AP_2. Assume that the adversary has successfully broken the security system and has gotten access to the whole matrix B. Hence, the adversary can correctly calculate the seeds that should be used in the following sessions. However, after the first session in which the adversary is not present, AP_2 satisfies the conditions of the information secure protocol AP_1. As a result, the information and computational security features are restored. ∎

The AP_2's parameters that define the pseudo-random sequence length are n, l is the number of bits of an entry in the matrix B, and the keyword length k.

5   Conclusions and Extensions

We presented a secure authentication protocol that is based on the assumption that among any n consecutive interactions between the RFID sender and the RFID receiver there is at least a single session in which the adversary was not listening in. This model is not perfect, nevertheless it takes into account the restricted capabilities of the real world RFID adversary. Actually, AP_1 provides information theoretic security guarantees.

The AP_2 protocol loosens the assumption of the RFID adversary's weakness. It provides computational security in a proactive manner. The computational security of AP_2 is provided by involving basic arithmetic operations and using small size memory. The larger are the values of the matrix' B elements, the larger is its $XOR\ X_j$ value and, consequently the generated pseudo-random sequence is closer to a real random sequence ([8]).

Note that one can use symmetric authentication scheme to obtain mutual authentication of the sender and the receiver. For example, we may double the number of columns in the matrices of the sender and the receiver and use the XOR of one column to authenticate the sender and the XOR of the next column to authenticate the receiver. Obviously, computational security "envelop" can be implemented for the symmetric version as well, resulting in a proactive computational secure symmetric scheme.

The AP_1 and AP_2 protocols can be used in the case of multiple RFID senders and a single RFID receiver. In order to provide secure communication the RFID receiver has to store different matrices and to share an unique matrix with each RFID sender. As a matter of fact, the limitation imposed on the number of RFID senders is only related to the limited storage capabilities of the RFID receiver. More details concerning the extensions above are deferred to the full version of the paper.

References

1. G. Avoine, "Radio Frequency Identification: Adversary Model and Attacks on Existing Protocols", Technical Report LASES-REPORT-2005-001, September 2005.
2. S. Bono, M. Green, A. Stubblefield, A. Juels, A. Rubin, M. Szydlo, "Security Analysis of a Cryptographically Enabled RFID Device",P. McDaniel, ed.,*USENIX Security 05*, pp. 1-16, 2005.
3. R. Canetti, Rosario Gennaro, A. Herzberg, D. Naor, "Proactive Security: Long-term Protection Against Break-ins", *RSA CryptoBytes*, No.1, Vol. 3, p.p. 1-8, 1997.
4. R. Goossens, F. Lambi, "RFID Society Newsletter", http://informationweek.com/ story/showArticle.jhtml?articleID=163101002, May, 2005.
5. A. Juels, "Strengthening EPC Tags Against Cloning", *ACM Workshop on Wireless Security*, pp.67-76, 2005.

6. A. Juels, "RFID Security and Privacy: A Research Survey", RSA Laboratories
   http://www.rsasecurity.com/rsalabs/node.asp?id=2937, Condensed version to appear in 2006 in the *IEEE Journal on Selected Areas in Communication*.
7. A. Juels, "Minimalist Cryptography for Low-Cost RFID Tags", RSA Laboratories
   http://www.rsasecurity.com/rsalabs/node.asp?id=2937. In C. Blundo, ed., Security of Communication Networks (SCN), 2004. To appear.
8. A. Menezes, P. van Oorschot, S. Vanstone, "Handbook of Applied Cryptography",
   CRC Press, 1-st edition, 1996.
9. S. E. Sarma, S. A. Weis, D. W. Engels, "Radio-Frequency Identification: Security
   Risks and Challenges", *RSA CryptoBytes*, No. 1, Vol. 6, 2003.
10. D. R. Stinson, *Cryptography. Theory and Practice*, CRC Press, 3-rd edition, 2006.

Fault Masking in Tri-redundant Systems

Mohamed G. Gouda[1], Jorge A. Cobb[2], and Chin-Tser Huang[3]

[1] Department of Computer Sciences
The University of Texas at Austin
gouda@cs.utexas.edu
[2] Department of Computer Science
The University of Texas at Dallas
cobb@utdallas.edu
[3] Department of Computer Science and Engineering
University of South Carolina at Columbia
huangct@cse.sc.edu

Abstract. A tri-redundant version of a system S is a system T that is specified from S as follows. First, system T has the same number of processes and the same topology as system S. Second, each variable x in a process in system S is replaced by three variables x, x', and x'' in the corresponding process in system T. Third, the actions in each process in system S are modified before they are added to the corresponding process in system T and some new actions are added to the corresponding process in system T. In this paper, we show that a tri-redundant version T of a system S has interesting stabilization and fault-masking properties. In particular, we show that if S is stabilizing, then T is also stabilizing. We also show that if T ever reaches stabilization, and then a "visible fault" occurs, then the effect of the fault is masked and the reached stabilization of T remains in effect.

1 Introduction

A system S is called P-stabilizing, where P is a boolean expression over the variables in S, iff the following two conditions hold. First, any computation of S, that starts at a state where P is false, reaches a state where P is true. Second, the execution of any action in system S that starts at a state where P is true, ends at a state where P is true. See for example [4,5,9].

The fact that a system S is P-stabilizing indicates that S is fault-tolerant to some degree. In particular, if a fault ever causes system S to reach a state where P is false, further executions of the actions in S causes S to return to a state where P is true. Moreover, once S reaches a state where P is true, P continues to be true at each subsequent state of S.

There are (at least) two research directions that can be followed in order to enhance the relationship between stabilization and fault-tolerance. The first research direction is called fault-containment and it has been explored in [7,8,10]. The second research direction is called fault-masking and it is the subject of the current paper. We compare these two research directions next.

A.K. Datta and M. Gradinariu (Eds.): SSS 2006, LNCS 4280, pp. 304–313, 2006.

Let S be a P-stabilizing system, and let F be a class of faults each of which can change the value of some variable in S. Assume that each fault f in F is assigned a "severity measure" $m(f)$. System S is called F-containing iff for each fault f in F, any computation of S, that starts at a state s_f, where s_f can be reached by applying fault f to a state where P is true, reaches a state where P is true after at most $O(m(f))$ transitions from the starting state s_f. In other words, F-containment ensures that the time that system S needs to recover from a fault f in F is proportional to some measure of the severity of fault f.

Let S be a P-stabilizing system, and let F be a class of faults each of which can change the value of some variable(s) in S. System S is called F-masking iff for each fault f in F, and for each variable x whose value is changed by fault f, any computation of S, that starts at a state s_f, where s_f can be reached by applying fault f to a state where P is true, has an execution of some action ac that restores the value of variable x to its value before f is applied, and moreover any action execution, that precedes the execution of ac in the computation, neither reads nor writes variable x. In other words, F-masking ensures that the application of any fault f in F has a limited effect on the action execution in system S.

In this paper, we describe a transformation that can transform any stabilizing system S to a "tri-redundant" version T such that T is both stabilizing and F-masking, where F is a rich class of faults called visible faults.

The concept of fault masking presented in this paper has somewhat similar objectives, if not the same technical details, as two earlier concepts: superstabilization and snap stabilization. A superstabilizing system [6] is a stabilizing system that dampens the effects of its own "topology changes" when they occur. This is accomplished by ensuring that the system satisfies a specified safety predicate from the instant when the topology of the system changes, causing the system to lose its stabilization, until the instant when the stabilization of the system is restored. A snap stabilizing system [3] is a stabilizing system that is guaranteed to always behave according to its specification regardless of how the state of the system is changed due to fault occurrence. Clearly, snap stabilization is a lofty goal. Unfortunately, many systems cannot be made snap stabilizing.

2   Stabilizing Systems

The *topology* of a system is a connected undirected graph, where each node represents one process in the system, and each edge between two nodes p and q indicates that processes p and q are neighbors in the system, and so each of the two processes can read the variables of the other process, as discussed below.

Each *process* in a system is specified by a finite set of variables and a finite set of actions. The values of each variable are taken from some bounded domain of values. Each action of a process p is of the form

$$\langle \text{guard} \rangle \rightarrow \langle \text{assignment} \rangle$$

where $\langle \text{guard} \rangle$ is a boolean expression over the variables of process p and the variables of all neighboring processes of p, and $\langle \text{assignment} \rangle$ is a sequence of assignment statements, each of which is of the form

$$x := \mathrm{E}(y, \ldots)$$

where x is a variable in process p, E is an expression of the same type as variable x, and y is a variable either in process p or in any neighboring process of p.

A *state* of a system S is specified by one value for each variable, taken from the domain of values of that variable, in each process in S.

A *transition* of a system S is a triple of the form

$$(s, ac, s')$$

where s and s' are two states of system S and ac is an action in some process in S such that the following two conditions hold.

    i. *Enablement:* The guard of action ac is true at state s.
    ii. *Execution:* Executing the assignment of action ac, when system S is in state s, yields system S in state s'.

A *computation* of a system S is a sequence of the form

$$(s_0, ac_0, s_1), (s_1, ac_1, s_2), \ldots$$

where each element $(s_i, ac_i, s_{(i+1)})$ is a transition of S such that the following two conditions hold.

    i. *Maximality:* Either the sequence is infinite or it is finite and its last element $(s_{(z-1)}, ac_{(z-1)}, s_z)$ is such that the guard of every action in system S is false at state s_z.
    ii. *Fairness:* If the sequence has an element $(s_i, ac_i, s_{(i+1)})$ and the guard of some action ac is true at state $s_{(i+1)}$, then the sequence has a later element $(s_k, ac_k, s_{(k+1)})$ where ac is ac_k or the guard of ac is false at state $s_{(k+1)}$.

A *predicate* P of a system S is a boolean expression over the variables in all processes in system S.

A predicate P of a system S is said to be *closed* in S iff for every transition (s, ac, s') of system S, if predicate P is true at state s, then P is true at state s'.

A system S is called *P-stabilizing* iff predicate P satisfies the following two conditions [1].

    i. *Closure:* Predicate P is closed in system S.
    ii. *Convergence:* Predicate P is true at a state in every computation of system S.

3   Systems with Tri-redundancy

In the previous section, we discussed how to specify a system S. Next, we describe how to specify a tri-redundant version T of any system S. The tri- redundant version T is specified from S as follows.

i. *Topology:* System S has the same number of processes and the same topology as system T. Thus, there is a natural one-to-one correspondence between the processes in S and those in T. For convenience, each process p in S has the same name as that of the corresponding process p in T.

ii. *Variables:* For each variable x in a process p in system S, there are three corresponding variables x, x', and x'' in the corresponding process p in system T. Each of the variables x, x', and x'' in system T is of the same type and has the same domain of values as variable x in system S. We refer to x in T as the original copy of variable x in S, and refer to x' and x'' in T as the shadow copies of x in S.

iii. *Actions:* For each action of the form $\langle \text{guard} \rangle \rightarrow \langle \text{assignment} \rangle$ in a process p in system S, there is a corresponding action of the form $\langle \text{guard}' \rangle \rightarrow \langle \text{assignment}' \rangle$ in the corresponding process p in system T such that the following three conditions hold.

 (a) First, each occurrence of a variable x in $\langle \text{guard} \rangle$ is replaced by an occurrence of the original copy of x, also called x, in $\langle \text{guard}' \rangle$.

 (b) Second, for each variable x that occurs in $\langle \text{guard} \rangle$ or in $\langle \text{assignment} \rangle$, add a conjunct of the form $(x = x' \land x' = x'')$ to $\langle \text{guard}' \rangle$.

 (c) Third, each statement of the form $x := \text{E}(y, \dots)$ in $\langle \text{assignment} \rangle$ is replaced by a statement of the form $(x, x', x'') := \text{E}(y, \dots)$ in $\langle \text{assignment}' \rangle$. The latter statement computes the value of expression E and then assigns the computed value to each of the three copies x, x', and x'' in T.

iv. *Additional Actions:* For each original copy x in a process p in system T, add an action of the following form to process p in T

$$x \neq x' \lor x' \neq x'' \;\rightarrow\; (x, x', x'') := \text{MJR}(x, x', x'')$$

where $\text{MJR}(x, x', x'')$ is the bit-wise majority function applied to the three variables x, x', and x''. This function is defined in some detail next.

Recall that each variable in a system has a bounded domain of values and that the three copies x, x', and x'' have the same (bounded) domain $D(x)$ of values. Thus, every value of each of the three copies x, x', and x'' can be represented by the same number, say r, of bits. The function $\text{MJR}(x, x', x'')$ computes a value in the same domain $D(x)$ of values, and so each value of $\text{MJR}(x, x', x'')$ can be represented by r bits.

The bits of $\text{MJR}(x, x', x'')$ can be computed from the bits of x, x', and x'' as follows. For every i in the range $0 \mathinner{..} (k-1)$, the i-th bit of $\text{MJR}(x, x', x'')$ is computed as the majority of three bits: the i-th bit of x, the i-th bit of x', and the i-th bit of x''.

4   Stabilization Theorem

In this section, we show that if a system S is stabilizing, then any tri-redundant version T of S is also stabilizing.

Theorem 1. (Stabilization of Tri-Redudant Systems).
*Let S be a P-stabilizing system, and T be a tri-redundant version of S. System
T is Q-stabilizing, where Q is the predicate*

$$P' \wedge (\textit{for every original copy of } x \textit{ in } T, x = x' \wedge x' = x'')$$

*and predicate P is syntactically identical to predicate P'. (Note that P is a
predicate of system S and P' is a predicate of system T. Thus, each occurrence
of x in P refers to a variable x in system S, and each occurrence of x in P'
refers to the original copy of x in system T.)*

Proof. The proof is divided into two parts. In the first part, we show that predicate Q is closed in system T, and in the second part, we show that Q is true at a state in every computation of system T.

First Part: Let (t, ac', t') be a transition of system T and assume that predicate Q is true at state t, we need to show that Q is true at state t'.

Because Q is true at t, we conclude that the predicate (for every original copy of x in T, $x = x' \wedge x' = x''$) is true at t. Thus, the guard $(x \neq x' \vee x' \neq x'')$ of each additional action in system T is false at t, and so ac' in the transition (t, ac', t') is not an additional action in system T. Rather, ac' is an action in system T that corresponds to an action ac in system S. The two actions ac and ac' are of the form

$$ac : \langle\text{guard}\rangle \rightarrow \langle\text{assignment}\rangle$$
$$ac' : \langle\text{guard}'\rangle \rightarrow \langle\text{assignment}'\rangle$$

where $\langle\text{guard}'\rangle$ is the predicate $\langle\text{guard}\rangle \wedge$ (for every variable x that occurs in ac, $x = x' \wedge x' = x''$), also, $\langle\text{assignment}\rangle$ and $\langle\text{assignment}'\rangle$ are identical except that each statement $x := \mathrm{E}(y, \dots)$ in $\langle\text{assignment}\rangle$ is replaced by the statement $(x, x', x'') := \mathrm{E}(y, \dots,)$ in $\langle\text{assignment}'\rangle$.

Let s and s' be the two states of system S that correspond to states t and t', respectively, of system T. It follows that the triple (s, ac, s') is a transition of system S. Moreover, because predicate Q is true at state t, we conclude that P is true at state s.

From the fact that system S is P-stabilizing (and so P is closed in system S), and the fact that triple (s, ac, s') is a transition of system S, and the fact that P is true at state s, it follows that P is true at state s'. Thus, both P' and Q are true at state s'.

Second Part: Let the sequence (t_0, ac_0, t_1), (t_1, ac_1, t_2), $\dots$ be a computation of system T. We need to show that predicate Q is true at some state in this computation.

Let x be an original copy in system T where the predicate $(x \neq x' \vee x' \neq x'')$ is true at the initial state t_0 of this computation. Then the guard of the additional action $x \neq x' \vee x' \neq x'' \rightarrow (x, x', x'') := \mathrm{MJR}(x, x', x'')$ in T is true at t_0. From the fairness condition of the computation, it follows that the predicate $(x = x' \wedge x' = x'')$ is true at a later state t_j in the computation. Moreover, because each action in system T either keeps the values of x, x', and x'' unchanged, or assigns each of them the same new value, the predicate $(x = x' \wedge x' = x'')$ remains true at each of the states that occur after t_j in the computation.

From the above discussion, the computation $(t_0, ac_0, t_1), (t_1, ac_1, t_2), \ldots$ has a suffix $(t_k, ac_k, t_{(k+1)}), (t_{(k+1)}, ac_{(k+1)}, t_{(k+2)}), \ldots$ where the predicate (for each original copy x in T, $x = x' \wedge x' = x''$) is true at each state t_k, $t_{(k+1)}$, $\ldots$ in this suffix. Along this suffix, the execution of system T mirrors that of system S. Because system S is P-stabilizing, predicate P' is true at some state t_z in this suffix. Therefore, predicate Q is true at the same state t_z in the computation.   □

5   Fault Masking Theorem

Let S be a P-stabilizing system and T be a tri-redundant version of S. From the stabilization theorem of tri-redundant systems (in the previous section), T is Q-stabilizing where Q is the predicate $(P' \wedge$ (for each original copy x in T, $x = x' \wedge x' = x''$)). In this section, we argue that if T is at a legitimate state, one where Q is true, and then some fault, from a rich class of faults called visible faults, occurs, then the effects of the fault are masked and the system quickly returns to a legitimate state, one where Q is true. We start by defining visible faults.

A fault f is visible iff it changes the values of some variables in system T such that the following two conditions hold:

  i. *Legitimacy:* Immediately before f occurs, system T is at a legitimate state where predicate Q is true. It follows that for every original copy x in T, $xa = xa' \wedge xa' = xa''$, where (xa, xa', xa'') is the value of (x, x', x'') immediately before f occurs.
  ii. *Transparency:* For every original copy x in T,

$$\text{MJR}(xa, xa', xa'') = \text{MJR}(xb, xb', xb''),$$

  where (xa, xa', xa'') is the value of (x, x', x'') immediately before f occurs and (xb, xb', xb'') is the value of (x, x', x'') immediately after f occurs.

Assume that a visible fault f occurs in system T, and also assume that f changes the value of some (x, x', x'') in T from (xa, xa', xa'') to (xb, xb', xb''). From the legitimacy condition of f, $xa = xa' \wedge xa' = xa''$. Thus, from the transparency condition of f and from the fact that f has changed the value of (x, x', x''), $xb \neq xb' \vee xb' \neq xb''$.

Let t be the state of system T immediately after f occurs. Then, the predicate $(x \neq x' \vee x' \neq x'')$ is true at state t. System T has two types of actions where the triple (x, x', x'') occurs: actions ac_0, ac_1, $\ldots$ that correspond to some actions, where x occurs, in system S and the added action ac:

$$ac \; : \; (x \neq x' \vee x' \neq x'') \rightarrow (x, x', x'') := \text{MJR}(x, x', x'')$$

The guard of each action ac_i in T has a conjunct $(x = x' \wedge x' = x'')$ and so none of these actions can be executed until after action ac is executed. From the transparency condition of f, executing action ac changes back the value of (x, x', x'') from (xb, xb', xb'') to (xa, xa', xa''). Thus, the effect of fault f on the triple, and ultimately on system T, is masked. This argument proves the following theorem.

Theorem 2. (Fault-Masking of Tri-Redundant Systems).
Let S be a P-stabilizing system and T be a tri-redundant version of S. System T is F-masking, where F is the class of visible faults.

6   A Tri-redundant Spanning Tree

As an example, consider a system S that consists of n processes $p[i : 0 .. n - 1]$. The processes in S maintain an outgoing spanning tree whose root is process $p[0]$. Each process $p[i]$ has a variable $ds[i]$ to store the smallest number of hops needed to go from $p[0]$ to $p[i]$. Also each process $p[i]$, other than process $p[0]$ has a variable $pr[i]$ to store index g of the parent $p[g]$ of $p[i]$. The processes in S can be specified as follows.

process $p[0]$

var $ds[0] : 0 .. n$

begin
                true $\rightarrow$ $ds[0] := 0$
end

process $p[i : 1 .. n - 1]$

var $ds[i]$ $: 0 .. n$
              $pr[i]$: index of parent of $p[i]$ in spanning tree

par g : index of an arbitrary neighbor of $p[i]$

begin
                $ds[i] \neq \min(n, ds[pr[i]] + 1)$ $\rightarrow$
                        $ds[i] := \min(n, ds[pr[i]] + 1)$

        $[]$ $ds[i] > ds[g] + 1$ $\rightarrow$
                        $ds[i] := ds[g] + 1;$
                        $pr[i] := g$
end

This system has been shown to be stabilizing [2]. Unfortunately the system is not F-masking for any reasonable class F of faults. Consider for example a fault that changes the value of $ds[0]$ in process $p[0]$ from 0 to 1. The first action in any neighboring process $p[g]$ can be executed and read the faulty value of $ds[0]$ before the correct value of $ds[0]$ is restored (by the action of process $p[0]$).

To achieve F-masking, for class F of visible faults, system S needs to be transformed to a tri-redundant version T. The processes in system T are specified as follows.

process $p[0]$

var $ds[0],\ ds'[0],\ ds''[0]\ :0\mathinner{\ldotp\ldotp}n$

begin
$$(ds[0] = ds'[0] \wedge ds'[0] = ds''[0])\ \rightarrow$$
$$(ds[0], ds'[0], ds''[0]) := 0$$

$\qquad\square\quad (ds[0] \neq ds'[0] \vee ds'[0] \neq ds''[0])\ \rightarrow$
$$(ds[0], ds'[0], ds''[0]) := \mathrm{MJR}(ds[0], ds'[0], ds''[0])$$
end

process $p[i : 1\mathinner{\ldotp\ldotp}n-1]$

var $ds[i],\ ds'[i],\ ds''[i]\ :\ 0\mathinner{\ldotp\ldotp}n$
$\qquad\quad pr[i],\ pr'[i],\ pr''[i]\ :$ index of parent of $p[i]$ in spanning tree

par g $\qquad\qquad\qquad\qquad:$ index of an arbitrary neighbor of $p[i]$

begin
$$ds[i] \neq \min(n, ds[pr[i]] + 1)\ \wedge$$
$$(ds[i] = ds'[i] \wedge ds'[i] = ds''[i])\ \wedge$$
$$(pr[i] = pr'[i] \wedge pr'[i] = pr''[i])\ \wedge$$
$$(ds[pr[i]] = ds'[pr[i]] \wedge ds'[pr[i]] = ds''[pr[i]])$$
$$\rightarrow$$
$$(ds[i], ds'[i], ds''[i]) := \min(n, ds[pr[i]] + 1)$$

$\qquad\square\quad ds[i] > ds[g] + 1 \wedge$
$$(ds[i] = ds'[i] \wedge ds'[i] = ds''[i])\ \wedge$$
$$(pr[i] = pr'[i] \wedge pr'[i] = pr''[i])\ \wedge$$
$$(ds[g] = ds'[g] \wedge ds'[g] = ds''[g])$$
$$\rightarrow$$

$$(ds[i], ds'[i], ds''[i]) := ds[g] + 1;$$
$$(pr[i], pr'[i], pr''[i]) := g$$

☐ $(ds[i] \neq ds'[i] \lor ds'[i] \neq ds''[i])$

$$\rightarrow$$

$$(ds[i], ds'[i], ds''[i]) := \text{MJR}(ds[i], ds'[i], ds''[i])$$

☐ $(pr[i] \neq pr'[i] \lor pr'[i] \neq pr''[i])$

$$\rightarrow$$

$$(pr[i], pr'[i], pr''[i]) := \text{MJR}(pr[i], pr'[i], pr''[i])$$

end

7 Concluding Remarks

In this paper, we described a transformation to transform any system S to a tri-redundant version T. We showed that if S is stabilizing then T is both stabilizing and F-masking for the class F of visible faults.

In our presentation, we assumed that system S is stabilizing under the assumption that the actions of S are executed one at a time. Nevertheless, the presentation can be extended in straightforward manner to the case where system S is stabilizing under the assumption that any subset of actions (at most one action from each process) in S are executed at a time. In this case, system T is stabilizing and F-masking under the same assumption that any subset of actions (at most one action from each process) in T are executed at a time.

In the above presentation, we assumed that the redundant version of any system S has "three" copies (x, x', x'') of every variable x in S. However, the only magic that is associated with this number "three" is that it is odd, and so when any fault occurs in the redundant system, the MJR function can always return a meaningful value. Therefore, the above presentation can be generalized in a straightforward manner such that the redundant version of a system has $(2 \cdot r + 1)$ copies of every variable in that system, where r is a positive integer.

In [11], Huang and Gouda have shown how to utilize two ideas, namely state checksums and tri-redundancy, to design a stabilizing token system that masks visible faults. Surprisingly, the theory of fault masking presented in the current paper is based solely on the idea of tri-redundancy. The question, of how to enrich this theory by injecting the idea of state checksums into it, seems interesting and enticing, but so far remains open.

Acknowledgment

The work of M. G. Gouda is supported in part by the National Science Foundation under Grant No. 0520250. The work of J. A. Cobb is supported in part by a UTD Project Emmitt startup grant. The work of C. T. Huang is supported in part by by the AFRL/DARPA under grant No. FA8750-04-2-0260. The authors would like to thank Professor Eunjin (EJ) Jung, at the University of Iowa, for her comments on an earlier version of this paper.

References

1. A. Arora and M. G. Gouda. Closure and convergence: A foundation of fault-tolerant computing. *IEEE Transactions on Software Engineering*, 19:1015–1027, November 1993.
2. N.-S. Chen, H.-P. Yu, and S.-T. Huang. A self-stabilizing algorithm for constructing spanning trees. *Inf. Process. Lett.*, 39(3):147–151, 1991.
3. A. Cournier, A. K. Datta, F. Petit, and V. Villain. Enabling Snap Stabilization. *Proceedings of the 23rd International Conference on Distributed Computing Systems (ICDCS-03)*, 2003.
4. E. W. Dijkstra. Self-stabilization in spite of distributed control. *ACM Communications*, 17:643–644, 1974.
5. S. Dolev. *Self-Stabilization*. MIT Press, 2000.
6. S. Dolev and T. Herman. Superstabilizing Protocols for Dynamic Distributed Systems. *Chicago Journal of Theoretical Computer Science*, Vol. 1997, Article 4, 1997.
7. S. Ghosh, A. Gupta, T. Herman, and S. Pemmaraju. Fault-containing self-stabilizing algorithms. In *Proceedings of 15th Annual ACM Symposium on Principles of Distributed Computing (PODC '96)*, pages 45–54, 1996.
8. S. Ghosh, A. Gupta, and S. Pemmaraju. A fault-containing self-stabilizing algorithm for spanning trees. *Journal of Computing Information*, 2:322–338, 1996.
9. T. Herman. A comprehensive bibliography on self-stabilization. *Chicago Journal of Theoretical Computer Science*, 1996.
10. T. Herman and S. Pemmaraju. Error-detecting codes and fault-containing self-stabilization. *Information Processing Letters*, 73:41–46, 2000.
11. C. T. Huang and M. G. Gouda. State Checksum and Its Role in System Stabilization. *Proceedings of the 4th International Workshop on Assurance in Distributed Systems and Networks (ADSN 2005)*, 2005.

Logarithmic Keying of Communication Networks

Mohamed G. Gouda[1], Sandeep S. Kulkarni[2], and Ehab S. Elmallah[3]

[1] University of Texas at Austin
gouda@cs.utexas.edu
[2] Michigan State University
sandeep@cse.msu.edu
[3] University of Alberta
ehab@cs.ualberta.ca

Abstract. Consider a communication network where each process needs to securely exchange messages with its neighboring processes. In this network, each sent message is encrypted using one or more symmetric keys that are shared only between two processes: the process that sends the message and the neighboring process that receives the message. A straightforward scheme for assigning symmetric keys to the different processes in such a network is to assign each process $O(d)$ keys, where d is the maximum number of neighbors of any process in the network. In this paper, we present a more efficient scheme for assigning symmetric keys to the different processes in a communication network. This scheme, which is referred to as logarithmic keying, assigns $O(\log d)$ symmetric keys to each process in the network. We show that logarithmic keying can be used in rich classes of communication networks that include star networks, acyclic networks, limited- cycle networks, and planar networks.

Keywords: Secure communications, symmetric keys, keying scheme.

1 Introduction

A communication network consists of processes and connecting channels such that for each pair of processes p and q, either there are no connecting channels between p and q, or there is a single two-way channel between p and q. Two processes in a communication network are called neighbors iff there is a two-way channel between the two processes in the network. Two neighboring processes can exchange messages over the two-way channel between them. A communication network is said to be of degree d iff the network has a process that has exactly d neighbors, and each process in the network has at most d neighbors.

Let p and q be two neighboring processes in a communication network and assume that both p and q know a symmetric key s and that no other process in the network knows s. In this case, each exchanged message between p and q can be encrypted using s before it is sent (by p or q) and can be decrypted using s after it is received (by q or p, respectively) in order to guarantee the confidentiality of the communication between p and q. This simple arrangement suggests that if a process p in a communication network has d neighbors, then p needs to store and use d symmetric keys in order to guarantee the confidentiality of its d communications with each one of its neighbors.

A.K. Datta and M. Gradinariu (Eds.): SSS 2006, LNCS 4280, pp. 314–323, 2006.

We refer to any keying scheme, where $O(d)$ symmetric keys are assigned to each process in a communication network whose degree is d, as a *linear keying* scheme.

As it happened, recently published results [1], [2], and [3] have shown that linear keying is not the most efficient scheme, for assigning symmetric keys to the processes in a communication network, in the case where the network is fully connected (i. e. where each two distinct processes in the network are neighbors). In [1], Gong and Wheeler described a keying scheme where $O(\sqrt{d})$ symmetric keys are assigned to each process in a fully connected communication network. In [2], Kulkarni, Gouda, and Arora described a variation of the scheme in [1], and showed that this scheme is optimal if each pair of distinct processes share no more than two symmetric keys. In [3], Aiyer, Alvisi, and Gouda described a keying scheme where $O(\log^2 d)$ symmetric keys are assigned to each process in a fully connected network. They also showed, using a probabilistic but non-constructive argument, that there exists a keying scheme where $O(\log d)$ symmetric keys are assigned to each process in a fully connected communication network. Note that all these results apply only communication networks that are fully connected. So far, there are no corresponding results to arbitrary communication networks; hence, this paper.

We refer to any keying scheme, where $O(\log d)$ symmetric keys are assigned to each process in a communication network, whose degree is d, as a *logarithmic keying* scheme.

In this paper, we describe logarithmic keying schemes for assigning symmetric keys to the processes in rich classes of communication networks, which include star networks, acyclic networks, cycle-limited networks, and planar networks.

2   Logarithmic Keying of Star Networks

Consider a *star* network where a process p needs to communicate securely with each of its d neighboring processes, $q.0, q.1, \cdots, q.(d-1)$. This requirement can be easily fulfilled by assigning d symmetric keys $s.0, s.1, \cdots, s.(d-1)$ to the network processes as follows. Each symmetric key $s.i$ is assigned only to the two processes p and $q.i$. Thus, the messages exchanged between p and $q.i$ can be encrypted using the symmetric key $s.i$ before they are sent, and they can be decrypted using $s.i$ after they are received.

This straightforward assignment of symmetric keys to processes requires that process p stores d symmetric keys, namely $s.0, s.1, \cdots, s.(d-1)$, and each other process $q.i$ stores one symmetric key, namely $s.i$. Next, we describe a more balanced assignment of symmetric keys to the processes in this star network. According to this assignment, process p needs to store only $(2 * \log d)$ symmetric keys, and each other process $q.i$ needs to store $(\log d)$ symmetric keys. We refer to this scheme of assigning symmetric keys to the processes in a star network as a *logarithmic keying* of the star network. (Throughout this paper, we adopt the convention that $\log x$ denotes the smallest integer whose value is at least $\log x$.)

The main idea of our logarithmic keying scheme is as follows. First, process p is assigned a set S of $(2 * \log d)$ symmetric keys. Second, each process $q.i$ is assigned a distinct subset $B.i$, that has $(\log d)$ symmetric keys, of set S. Later, if process p needs to send a secure message to process $q.i$, then p applies the bit-wise, exclusive-or operator to the keys in subset $B.i$ in order to compute a single symmetric key that is used to encrypt the message before p sends it to $q.i$. When process $q.i$ receives the encrypted message from process p, then $q.i$ applies the bit-wise, exclusive-or operator to the keys in subset $B.i$ in order to compute a single symmetric key that is used to decrypt the message after $q.i$ receives it from p. Similar procedure can be used to send an encrypted message from any process $q.i$ to process p.

The $(2 * \log d)$ symmetric keys in set S, assigned to process p, are named:

$$
\begin{array}{ll}
s.(0,0), & s.(0,1), \\
s.(1,0), & s.(1,1), \\
\cdots & \cdots \\
s.(\log d - 1, 0), & s.(\log d - 1, 1)
\end{array}
$$

In other words, these symmetric keys can be viewed as forming a two-dimensional matrix that has $(\log d)$ rows and two columns. We refer to this matrix as the S-matrix.

Next, we describe how to compute from set S a distinct subset $B.i$ of $(\log d)$ keys to be assigned to process $q.i$. Subset $B.i$ has exactly one key from each row in the S-matrix. Which of the two keys in the j-th row of the S-matrix is in subset $B.i$ depends on the j-th bit, $b.j$, in the bit representation of index i of process $q.i$ as follows.

if $b.j = 0$
then key $s.(j, 0)$ is in $B.i$
else key $s.(j, 1)$ is in $B.i$

Therefore, each process $q.i$ is assigned a subset $B.i$ that is defined as follows:

$$
B.i \;=\; \{\; s.(j, b.j) \mid 0 \le j < \log d \;\}
$$

where $b.0, b.1, \cdots, b.(\log d - 1)$ is the bit representation of index i.

As an example, we describe a logarithmic keying of a star network that has five processes $p, q.0, q.1, q.2, q.3$. In this case, $d = 4$ and the logarithmic keying assigns $(2 * \log 4) = 4$ symmetric keys to process p. These four keys are named as follows.

$$
\begin{array}{ll}
s.(0,0), & s.(0,1), \\
s.(1,0), & s.(1,1)
\end{array}
$$

The index, 0, of process $p.0$ can be represented by the two bits $b.0 = 0$ and $b.1 = 0$. Thus, $q.0$ is assigned the two keys $s.(0,0)$ and $s.(1,0)$. The index of process $q.1$ can be represented by the two bits $b.0 = 1$ and $b.1 = 0$. Thus, $q.1$ is assigned the two keys $s.(0,1)$ and $s.(1,0)$. The index of process $q.2$ can be represented by the two bits $b.0 = 0$ and $b.1 = 1$, and so $q.2$ is assigned the two keys $s.(0,0)$ and $s.(1,1)$. Finally, the index of process $q.3$ can be represented by the two bits $b.0 = 1$ and $b.1 = 1$, and so $q.3$ is assigned the two keys $s.(0,1)$ and $s.(1,1)$. Note that no two of the four processes $q.0$ through $q.3$ are assigned the same subset of symmetric keys.

If each process $q.i$ uses the symmetric keys in its subset $B.i$ merely to encrypt mcs-sages before sending them to p and to decrypt messages after receiving them from p, then $q.i$ does not need to keep the keys in $B.i$ as separate keys. Instead, process $q.i$

can apply the bit-wise exclusive-or operator to the keys in $B.i$ and end up with a single key. Process $q.i$ needs to store only this one key (instead of storing the log d keys in subset $B.i$) and uses it to encrypt messages before sending them to p and to decrypt messages after receiving them from p. However, as discussed in the next section, there are other uses for the keys in subset $B.i$ that require these keys to remain separate and not be combined into a single key. Henceforth, we assume that the keys in each subset are stored as separate keys.

We end this section by showing that the logarithmic keying of a star network (described above) is asymptotically optimal. Assume that there is another keying scheme of the star network where process p is assigned a set T that has $|T|$ symmetric keys. To achieve security, it is necessary (but not sufficient) that process p shares with each process $q.i$ a distinct nonempty subset of set T. Because set T has $2^{|T|} - 1$ distinct nonempty subsets, and there are d of the $q.i$ processes, we have

$$|T| \geq \log(d+1)$$

This implies that $|T|$ is of $O(\log d)$ which is the same size as that of set S in our logarithmic keying scheme.

3   Authenticated Broadcast in Star Networks

Consider the star network described in the previous section, and assume that symmetric keys are assigned to the processes in this network according to the logarithmic keying scheme discussed in the previous section. Thus process p is assigned $(2 * \log d)$ symmetric keys named

$$
\begin{array}{ll}
s.(0,0), & s.(0,1), \\
s.(1,0), & s.(1,1), \\
\cdots & \cdots \\
s.(\log d - 1, 0), & s.(\log d - 1, 1)
\end{array}
$$

Also each process $q.i$ is assigned the $(\log d)$ symmetric keys $s.(0, b.0), \cdots, s.(logd - 1, b.(logd - 1))$ where the bit string $b.0, b.1, \cdots, b.(logd - 1)$ is the bit representation of index i of process $q.i$.

Now assume that process p needs to broadcast a message m to all the processes $q.0, q.1, ..., q.(d-1)$, and it needs to attach to message m an "authentication code" so that when a process $q.i$ receives the message, process $q.i$ can verify that only process p could have sent this message, and accept the message. But how to design this authentication code?

Thanks to the logarithmic keying scheme that we adopted for this star network, the authentication code for any broadcast message m can have a logarithmic length. Specifically, the authentication code for message m consists of the following $(2*\log d)$ digests of m:

$$
\begin{array}{ll}
md.(0,0), & md.(0,1), \\
md.(1,0), & md.(1,1), \\
\cdots & \cdots \\
md.(\log d - 1, 0), & md.(\log d - 1, 1)
\end{array}
$$

Each digest $md.(x, y)$ is defined as $MD.(m|s.(x, y))$, where MD is a well known digest function, "$|$" is the concatenation operation, and $s.(x, y)$ is one of the symmetric keys assigned to process p by the logarithmic keying scheme.

Therefore, the format of the message that process p ends up broadcasting to each of the processes $q.0, q.1, ..., q.(d-1)$ is as follows.

$$(m, md.(0, 0), md.(0, 1), ..., md.(logd - 1, 1))$$

In other words, the broadcasted message consists of message m followed by $(2 * \log d)$ digests of m.

When a process $q.i$ receives a copy of the broadcasted message, $q.i$ computes $(\log d)$ digests of m using the symmetric keys in subset $B.i$. (Each digest $md.(x, y)$ is computed as $MD.(m|s.(x, y))$, where $s.(x, y)$ is a symmetric key in subset $B.i$.) If process $q.i$ detects that every one of its computed digests is present in the received message, $q.i$ concludes that the received message was sent by p and accepts m. Otherwise, $q.i$ concludes that the message was not sent by p and rejects it.

So far, we have presented a logarithmic keying scheme of star networks, and discussed how to take advantage of this scheme to encrypt and decrypt unicast messages, and to authenticate broadcast messages in any star network. In the next section, we extend this logarithmic keying scheme to a richer class of networks, called acyclic networks.

4   Logarithmic Keying of Acyclic Networks

The *topology* of a network is a connected undirected graph, where each node $p.j$ corresponds to a distinct process, also called $p.j$, in the network, and where each (undirected) edge connecting nodes $p.j$ and $p.k$ corresponds to a two-way channel that can be used in exchanging messages between the two corresponding processes $p.j$ and $p.k$ in the network.

(It follows from this definition that if a network topology has no edge between two nodes $p.j$ and $p.k$, then the two corresponding processes $p.j$ and $p.k$ cannot directly exchange messages in the network.)

A network is called a *star* iff the network topology consists of one center node and several peripheral nodes, and each peripheral node is connected only to the center node (by an edge).

A network is called *acyclic* iff the network topology is an acyclic undirected graph. Thus each star network is also acyclic, but not vice versa. In this section, we extend our logarithmic keying scheme for star networks to acyclic networks.

Consider an acyclic network that has n processes:

$$p.0, p.1, ..., p.(n-1)$$

Assume that the degree of this network is d. Therefore, we can use a straightforward edge coloring algorithm to assign an index in the range $0..d - 1$ to each (two-way) channel in the network such that the indices of any two channels incident at the same process are distinct.

Each process $p.j$ in this network is assigned $(2 * \log d)$ symmetric keys named

$$
\begin{array}{ll}
s.j.(0,0), & s.j.(0,1), \\
s.j.(1,0), & s.j.(1,1), \\
\cdots & \cdots \\
s.j.(\log d - 1, 0), & s.j.(\log d - 1, 1)
\end{array}
$$

Before we can describe how to compute the symmetric keys assigned to each process, we need first to describe how can a process use its assigned keys to encrypt and decrypt messages that this process exchanges with its neighboring processes.

Assume that a process $p.j$ needs to securely send a message m to a neighboring process $p.k$ via a channel whose index has the bit representation $b.0, b.1, ..., b.(\log d - 1)$. In this case, $p.j$ applies the bit-wise exclusive-or operator to the symmetric keys

$$
s.j.(0, b.0), s.j.(1, b.1), ..., s.j.(\log d - 1, b.(\log d - 1))
$$

and ends up with a single key that $p.j$ uses to encrypt each message m before sending it to $p.k$ via the channel. When process $p.k$ receives the encrypted message via the channel whose binary representation is $b.0, b.1, ..., b.(\log d - 1)$, then $p.k$ applies the bit-wise exclusive-or operator to the symmetric keys

$$
s.k.(0, b.0), s.k.(1, b.1), ..., s.k.(\log d - 1, b.(\log d - 1))
$$

and ends up with a single key that $p.k$ uses to decrypt the received message and obtain the original message m.

Clearly, the symmetric key that $p.j$ used to encrypt message m needs to be identical to the symmetric key that $p.k$ used to decrypt the received message. This can be achieved by requiring that the following $\log d$ equalities hold

$$
\begin{array}{ll}
s.j.(0, b.0) & = \quad s.k.(0, b.0), \\
s.j.(1, b.1) & = \quad s.k.(1, b.1), \\
\cdots & \\
s.j.(\log d - 1, b.(\log d - 1)) = & s.k.(\log d - 1, b.(\log d - 1))
\end{array}
$$

These $\log d$ equalities can be written more succinctly as the following condition.

For every i in the range $0..(\log d - 1)$, $s.j.(i, b.i) = s.k.(i, b.i)$

We refer to this condition as the *key consistency condition*.

The key consistency condition states that half the keys in a process $p.j$ are equal to the corresponding keys in a process $p.k$, provided that $p.j$ and $p.k$ are neighbors, i.e., they are connected by a two-way channel. Hence, in computing the symmetric keys in each process in an acyclic network, one needs to ensure that the keys in each pair of neighboring processes satisfy the key consistency condition.

An algorithm for computing the $(2*\log d)$ keys in each process in an acyclic network consists of the following two steps.

Step 0: choose any process $p.j$ in the network and randomly selects its $(2 * \log d)$ keys:
$s.j.(0,0), \cdots, s.j.(\log d - 1, 1)$

Step 1: while the network has two neighboring processes $p.j$ and $p.k$ such that
> a. the secrets in $p.j$ are already computed,
> b. the secrets in $p.k$ are not yet computed, and
> c. the connecting channel between $p.j$ and $p.k$ has an index whose bit
>   representation is $b.0, \cdots, b.(\log d - 1)$

do
for each i in the range $0..(\log d - 1)$, compute the i-th secrets in $p.k$ as follows
$s.k.(i, b.i) \quad := s.j.(i, b.i)$
$s.k.(i, 1 - b.i) := \text{any random value}$
od

Note that this algorithm is written under the reasonable assumption that the network is connected. It is straightforward to extend this algorithm to the general case where the network is partitioned into two or more components.

The $(2 * \log d)$ keys assigned to each process $p.j$ in an acyclic network can also be used by $p.j$ to compute the authentication code for any message m that $p.j$ needs to broadcast to all its neighboring processes. Specifically, the authentication code for message m consists of $(2 * \log d)$ digests, and each digest is of the form $MD.(m|s.j.(x, y))$ where MD is the message digest function, "$|$" is the concatenation operation, and $s.j.(x, y)$ is one of the symmetric keys assigned to process $p.j$ by logarithmic keying.

When a neighboring process $p.k$ receives a copy of the broadcast message (along with its authentication code) via a channel whose index has the binary representation $b.0, ..., b.(\log d - 1)$, then $p.k$ computes, for every i in the range $0..(\log d - 1)$, the message digest $MD.(m|s.k.(i, b.i))$ and checks whether this message digest is part of the authentication code of the received message. If every computed message digest is part of the authentication code of the received message m, then $p.k$ concludes correctly that message m is sent by $p.j$ and accepts m. Otherwise, $p.k$ rejects message m.

5   Logarithmic Keying of Limited-Cycle Networks

In this section and the next, we describe two methods for extending our logarithmic keying scheme for acyclic networks to networks with cycles. These two methods are called superimposition and decomposition.

In the *superimposition method*, we start with an acyclic network. We then observe that some of the keys that are assigned to the network processes using our logarithmic keying are *spare*, i. e. they are not used in encrypting or decrypting any message that is exchanged over any edge in the acyclic network. Thus, we superimpose new edges on the acyclic network to add cycles to it, and use the spare keys to encrypt and decrypt the messages that are exchanged over the superimposed edges.

In the *decomposition method*, we start with a network with cycles. We then partition this network into a small number of edge-disjoint acyclic subnetworks. Then, we use our logarithmic keying scheme, described in the previous section, to assign symmetric keys to each process in each acyclic subnetwork. The net effect is that each process is assigned $O(\log d)$ symmetric keys, where d is the degree of the original network with cycles. Thus, the resulting keying scheme is logarithmic.

In the remainder of this section, we show that the superimposition method can be used in the logarithmic keying of a special class of communication networks, called limited-cycle networks. (In the next section, we show that the decomposition method can be used in the logarithmic keying of a special class of networks, called planar networks.)

Consider an acyclic network whose degree is d, and without loss of generality, assume that d is at least 2. This network has at least two processes $p.j$ and $p.k$ such that the following two conditions hold. (For example, these two conditions hold for any two leaf processes in the network.)

1. Process $p.j$ has $a.j$ incident edges and
    $(\log d - \log a.j)$ is at least one.

2. Process $p.k$ has $a.k$ incident edges and
    $(\log d - \log a.k)$ is at least one.

As the network is acyclic, the network processes are assigned symmetric keys according to the logarithmic keying scheme described in the previous section. From Condition 1, at least one of the keys assigned to process $p.j$ is spare, i.e. this key is not used to encrypt or decrypt any message sent or received by process $p.j$ over any of its incident edges. Similarly, from Condition 2, at least one of the keys assigned to process $p.k$ is spare.

Let $s.j.(x.j, y.j)$ be a spare key assigned to $p.j$, and let $s.k.(x.k, y.k)$ be a spare key assigned to $p.k$. Because these two keys are spare, they are selected at random by the two-step algorithm in the previous section. Now, assume that these two keys are selected to be identical. In this case, a new edge can be superimposed between the two processes $p.j$ and $p.k$ in the acyclic network causing the network to have a cycle. For convenience, we refer to this superimposed edge as a *c-edge* in order to distinguish it from the edges in the original acyclic network, which we call *a-edges*.

As mentioned above, each a-edge has an index in the range $0..d - 1$. Now, we adopt the convention that the superimposed c-edge has two indices: one index $(x.j, y.j)$ is known only to process $p.j$, and the other index $(x.k, y.k)$ is known only to process $p.k$.

When process $p.j$ needs to send a message over the c-edge $(x.j, y.j)$ to process $p.k$, $p.j$ encrypts the message using its symmetric key $s.j.(x.j, y.j)$ before sending the message over the c-edge. When process $p.k$ receives the encrypted message over the c-edge $(x.k, y.k)$ from process $p.j$, $p.k$ decrypts the message the message using its symmetric key $s.k.(x.k, y.k)$ after receiving the message over the c-edge.

When process $p.j$ needs to broadcast a message m to all its neighbors, $p.j$ computes the authentication code of m using all the symmetric keys assigned to $p.j$, as described in the previous section. Then $p.j$ sends a copy of the message

$(m,$ authentication code of $m)$

over every edge incident at $p.j$, including the c-edge $(x.j, y.j)$. When process $p.k$ receives the broadcasted message over the c-edge $(x.k, y.k)$, $p.k$ computes the message digest $MD.(m|s.k.(x.k, y.k))$ and checks whether this digest is part of the authentication code in the received message. If so, $p.k$ accepts m. Otherwise, $p.k$ discards m.

So far, we discussed how to superimpose one (the first) c-edge on the original acyclic network to create one cycle in the network. In fact, many c-edges can be superimposed, sequentially one after the other, in order to create many cycles in the network. The only requirement needed to superimpose one more c-edge between two nodes in the network is that each of the two nodes satisfies the following condition.

$(\log d - \log a - c)$ is at least one

where d is the network degree, a is the numbers of a-edges that are currently incident at the node, and c is the number of c-edges that are currently incident at the node.

We are now ready to define the class of limited-cycle networks that can be logarithmically keyed using the above superimposition method. A *limited-cycle network* is one where each edge in its topology graph G can be classified as either an a-edge or c-edge such that the following two conditions hold.

1. The subgraph of G that consists of a-edges only is acyclic.

2. For each process p in G, $(\log d - \log a - c)$ is at least zero, where
    d is the network degree,
    a is the number of a-edges incident at p, and
    c is the number of c-edges incident at p.

6   Logarithmic Keying of Planar Networks

In this section, we utilize a decomposition method to extend our logarithmic keying scheme for acyclic networks to a scheme for planar networks, where a *planar network* is one whose topology is a planar graph.

It is well known, e.g. [4] and [6], that any planar graph G can be decomposed into at most three acyclic subgraphs, called *factors*, such that the following two conditions hold. First, every factor has the same nodes as the original graph G. Second, each edge in the original graph G appears in exactly one factor. It follows that the degree of each factor is at most the degree of the original graph G.

The decomposition method works as follows. Given a planar network G, whose degree is d, the keying scheme proceeds by decomposing the edges of G into k factors, where $0 \leq k \leq 3$. Each edge in G is then given an index (r, i), where r is an index of the factor that contains the edge, $0 \leq r < k$, and i is the index of the edge in factor r, $0 \leq i < d$. (Recall that any two edges that are incident to the same node in a factor are assigned distinct indices.) Hence, in the network G, if a node has two incident edges labeled (r, i) and (r', i), then these two edges must belong to two different factors (i.e., $r \neq r'$). The logarithmic keying scheme for acyclic graphs mentioned above is then applied independently to each of the k factors. As a result, each node is assigned k sets of keys, where each set has at most $(2 * \log d)$ keys. Since computing the key of any given edge in G can be deduced from the index of that edge, we conclude that $O(\log d)$ keys per process are sufficient for keying any planar network.

We note that this decomposition method can be equally applied to other classes of networks. For example, any graph with *treewidth* $\leq k$, for constant $k > 0$, can be decomposed into k acyclic factors, as discussed in [5] and [6]. Therefore, using the decomposition method, any bounded treewidth graph can be logarithmically keyed.

7   Concluding Remarks

In this paper, we described logarithmic keying schemes for assigning symmetric keys to the different processes in several classes of communication networks, which include acyclic networks, limited-cycle networks, and planar networks. We also described two methods, namely superimposition and decomposition, for extending logarithmic keying schemes of acyclic networks to networks with cycles.

Two open problems are suggested by the investigation described in this paper. The first problem is to design a logarithmic keying scheme that can be used in any fully connected communication network. The second problem is to design a logarithmic keying scheme that can be used in any communication network, regardless of the network topology. Note that the second open problem is a generalization of the first problem. But we believe that solving the first problem first will make the second problem easier to tackle.

Acknowledgment

The work of M. G. Gouda is supported in part by the National Science Foundation under Grant No. 0520250. The work of S. Kulkarni is supported in part by the National Science Foundation under Grant No. CCR-0092724. The work of E. S. Elmallah is supported by NSERC Canada.

References

[1] L. Gong and J. Wheeler. A Matrix Key-Distribution Scheme. *Journal of Cryptology: The Journal of the International Association for Cryptologic Research*. Vol. 2, No. 1, pp. 51-59, 1990.

[2] S. S. Kulkarni, M. G. Gouda, and A. Arora. *Computer Communications*. Vol. 29, pp. 200-215, 2006.

[3] A. S. Aiyer, L. Alvisi, and M. G. Gouda. Key Grids: A protocol Family for Assigning Symmetric Keys. Proceedings of the IEEE International Conference on Network Protocols (ICNP-06), 2006.

[4] B. Bollobás. *Modern Graph Theory*. Springer-Verlag, 1998.

[5] A. Brandstädt, V. B. Le, and J. Spinrad. *Graph Classes: A Survey*. SIAM Monographs on Discrete Mathematics and Applications, 1999.

[6] C. J. Colbourn. *The Combinatorics of Network Reliability*. Oxford University Press, 1987.

Safe Peer-to-Peer Self-downloading

Kajari Ghosh Dastidar[1,*], Ted Herman[1], and Colette Johnen[2,**]

[1] Department of Computer Science, University of Iowa
[2] LRI-CNRS, Université Paris-Sud 11, 91405 Orsay cedex, France

Abstract. Peer-to-peer applications share files between users them selves rather than downloading files from file servers. Self-downloading protocols have the property that eventually, every user downloads only from other users. This paper considers efficient ways of dividing files into segments so that users can exit the system as soon as file downloading is complete. One vulnerability of file sharing between peers is the possibility that files or segments could be counterfeit or corrupt. Protocols that are d-safe tolerate some number of instances of faulty segments in a file being downloaded, because each segment is downloaded d times before being uploadable. It is shown that d-safe self-downloading is possible for a sufficiently large arrival rate of users to the system. In addition, the paper presents upper and lower connectivity and sharing bounds for $d = 2$.

1 Introduction

File sharing is the most popular peer-to-peer application in the Internet. Much peer-to-peer research investigates problems of locating files and interesting overlay networks have been developed that make finding content efficient [2,5]. Most of these overlay networks assume a relatively stable population of peers. In the Internet, users join and leave peer-to-peer software systems frequently and the costs are mainly related to the bandwidth needed for downloading content and sharing files. File sharing between users, rather than downloading files from a few servers, can be a useful solution to the flash crowd phenomenon [1]. At present, the BitTorrent protocol [3] is the dominant protocol for peer-to-peer downloading of files (although estimates range widely, 10-15% is a conservative figure for the amount of Internet traffic due to BitTorrent [6,7]).

BitTorrent succeeds by splitting files into parts, allowing users to download different parts from different peers, and enforcing an incentive motivating users to share files. This incentive is important because peer-to-peer file sharing can be vulnerable to the problem of *freeloaders* (a freeloader is a user who downloads significantly more content than the user shares with other peers). Our research is motivated by the BitTorrent model. We investigate file sharing for some ideal assumptions about user arrival rates and download bandwidth, but also for the extreme case where users continuously download while in the system, yet exit the system immediately upon completing the download.

* Work supported by the National Science Foundation under Grant Number 0519907.
** This research was supported in part by FRAGILE, an aciSI "security and dependability" project.

A.K. Datta and M. Gradinariu (Eds.): SSS 2006, LNCS 4280, pp. 324–334, 2006.
© Springer-Verlag Berlin Heidelberg 2006

Related Work. Several studies have evaluated BitTorrent's performance (a survey is presented in [14] along with a brief explanation of how BitTorrent selects the download order of pieces). Some improvements to BitTorrent's policies are investigated in [9,14,13] (and [9] proposes a hybrid to bypass BitTorrent for the case of small files). Newer protocols [10,11,16] exploit dynamic properties of network connections and location-awareness to get better results than BitTorrent. The general problem of efficient and fast downloading predates the field of peer-to-peer research; it is known that more efficient downloading is achievable if files can be coded with some redundancy and content is mirrored or otherwise placed properly [8,12]. The downloading problem has been formalized as an optimization problem [15] and also as a game-theoretic problem [13].

Our paper builds on [4], which introduced the topic of deterministic strategies for self-downloading when users depart the system as soon as downloading is completed, yet users continuously download the desired content so long as they are present in the system. The questions raised and answered in [4] do not touch on the safety issue raised here. The main results of [4] are about various rates of user arrival and minimizing the number of connections needed for downloading.

Contributions. This paper introduces the notion of d-safety. Protocols that are d-safe detect and tolerate some number of instances of faulty segments in a file being downloaded. Each segment is downloaded d times from distinct sources before being uploadable. This safety property makes a protocol more robust to certain types of attack or failure by containing the effect of corrupt or counterfeit data. For instance, any user can retrieve the correct segment from $2x + 1$ copies by voting if there are at most x corrupt pieces. One of our strategies is shown to be optimal with respect to the number of connections needed to for self-downloading streams of users. An additional result shows how self-downloading can accommodate a slower user arrival rate than was previously known, though at the cost of more connections needed for downloading.

2   Application Model

For this paper, we suppose that there is one file F residing at some root location, and initially any user must get a file from this root location. Later, after some users have copied the file, or even parts of the file, a newly arriving user should be able to copy from other users rather than from the root location. The process of a user fetching a file or a portion of a file is called *downloading*; the process of a user providing a file or a portion of a file to another user is called *sharing*.

File F is divided into k *segments* of equal size and users download F's segments in some prescribed order. Let F_i denote the i-th segment of the file, $1 \leq i \leq k$. Operationally, a user entering the system first contacts the *tracking service*, which we assume to be aware of all users currently in the system, tracking the progress of each user and directing users on where to find segments (BitTorrent implements this using a tracking server [14]).

Let $\mathcal{H}$ denote a (possibly unbounded) history of all user downloads, which includes for each user the sequence of events (copying segments) while that user downloads. Events in $\mathcal{H}$ include the copying of segments from the root location as well as users copying segments from other users. A protocol for fetching segments and providing concurrent sharing of segments is called *self-downloading* if for every possible history $\mathcal{H}$, at most a constant number of events in $\mathcal{H}$ copy segments from the root location. Self-downloading protocols therefore have the property that eventually the root location is no longer required to disseminate the file.

Definition 1. *Within an execution of a downloading protocol, a user u is called d-safe if (a) u downloads F_i d times before leaving the system, (b) u does not download any segment F_i more than once from any other user, and (c) u does not share any segment F_i until u has first downloaded d copies of F_i.*

A self-downloading protocol is d-safe if there is a t such that every user joining after time t is d-safe. Notice that if $d > 1$, a user will download the same segment more than once; we use the term *piece* to distinguish between copies of segments. In a d-safe protocol, a user downloads $d \cdot k$ pieces (which constitute k segments).

Our intended application of d-safety is for robustness of downloading protocols to limited cases of transient faults or malicious users who share counterfeit pieces. With values of d greater than 2, voting can be used for tolerating $(d-1)/2$ bad pieces. Even for $d = 2$ a single malicious user will be detected and the counterfeit piece will not be propagated. The last sentence may imply that if a user cannot tell which of two pieces is corrupt, then self-downloading may not proceed. For instance, the user in such a case may need to get a segment from the root, or just quit the system. However, even if the self-downloading cannot proceed, no new user gets infected by copying and sharing a corrupt piece. So there is a safety value for $d = 2$ in any case.

An alternative to comparing or voting among d copies to achieve safety would be to use message digests. While detecting a corrupt segment may be possible using message digests, the timing of a self-downloading scheme is disrupted by the injection of a corrupt segment: the digest comparison completes only after the segment is retrieved, and refetching from another source delays sharing of that segment to others in a self-downloading stream of users. The delay incurred may include queries to the tracking server and to the root server, and such delay can cascade to affect many other users the self-downloading stream. Our self-downloading strategies are robust to limited injection of corrupt segments, that is, the self-downloading property is preserved, without any extra delay, even if some corrupt segments are encountered. The issue of message digests is discussed further in Section 5.

We assume that the time taken to download or share any piece is μ, and this is the same for all users. A user cannot download a piece p and concurrently share p to another user: copies can only be provided for completely downloaded pieces. We consider only serial download strategies for users, so no user is allowed to concurrently download two or more pieces (we remark in the conclusion that concurrent downloading is possible by applying parallel incarnations of our protocols). After a user downloads a piece, that user immediately begins downloading the next piece, so the total time to download all pieces is $d \cdot k\mu$.

Users arrive at times that are integral with respect to μ^{-1}. That is, we suppose user arrival times are normalized to the download rate. For convenient analysis, let $\mu = 1$ and call integer t_u the arrival time of user u. Users arriving earlier than t_u are called *seniors* to u, whereas users who arrive later than t_u are *juniors* to u; users other than u who arrive at time t_u are called *peers* of u. The protocols given in this paper suppose a fixed arrival rate λ. Arrival rate is measured in users per time unit, however the self-downloading strategies in this paper specify particular patterns of arrival. We denote by $\lambda = i/j$ that i users arrive in j time units. For example, if one user arrives at each of times $1, 3, 5, \ldots$, with no user arriving at an even-numbered time, then $\lambda = 1/2$; if four users arrive at time 1, none at times 2 and 3, another four at time 4, none at times 5 and 6, and so on, then $\lambda = 4/3$. Rate $\lambda = 4/3$ can also be realized by two users arriving at time 1, two at time 2, and none at time 3. For a self-downloading strategy specifying a particular pattern, say with $\lambda = 4/3$, a sustained[1] arrival rate of 1.3333 users per time unit can be coerced into the needed pattern by having some arriving users wait before commencing the self-downloading.

Two metrics of interest for a downloading protocol are the number of connections needed to download and the number of times that a user shares a segment. Let r be the number of times that a user can share a copy of a segment to another user: for example, if $r = 3$ then no user shares any particular segment with four or more users. For the root location, there is no restriction on the number of times that a segment could be shared, however for a self-downloading protocol, eventually the root no longer supplies copies for downloading. Let c be the number of network connections that a user has to make in order to download all pieces. We assume that copying any individual piece requires no more than one connection.

3   Safe Self-downloading

The results of this section show possibility and limits for d-safe downloading. Lemma 1's proof describes a protocol for d-safe downloading using $d \cdot k/2$ connections. As observed in [9,7], the BitTorrent protocol can suffer from high overhead when the number of connections is large[2]. Can the number of connections be reduced below $d \cdot k/2$ for d-safe downloading? Lemma 2 finds a lower bound of $c = 3$ for the case $d = 2$, and Lemma 4's proof shows an optimal construction using three connections for $d = 2$ and $k = 4$ (which is less than $2 \cdot 4/2$ connections), however the cost of this optimality is a higher user arrival rate.

Lemma 1. *For $\lambda = 1/1$, d-safe self-downloading is possible with $c = d \cdot k/2$ and $r = 2d$, with even $k > 2$ and $d \geq 2$.*

---

[1] Characteristics of the sustained rate would need to be further constained to achieve the pattern transformation; we consider this to be outside the scope of our study of self-downloading strategies.

[2] In fact, BitTorrent *suboptimizes* performance by allowing a user to have many connections to reduce downloading time, yet the overall effect of establishing many connections could actually reduce overall network performance (see [7]).

Proof. The construction for this proof has user u_i downloading $d \cdot k$ pieces, numbered by segment $(1,2,\ldots,k)$, according to the following pattern. Let i be the arrival time of user u_i. For even i, u_i downloads d copies of segment 1, then d copies of segment 2, and so on. For odd i, u_i downloads d copies of segment $1 + k/2$, then d copies of segment $2 + k/2$, and so on up to d copies of segment k; then u_i downloads d copies of segment 1, followed by downloading d copies of segment 2, and so on up to downloading d copies of segment $k/2$.

User u_i departs at time $i + d \cdot k$, immediately upon downloading the final piece. Observe that u_i is concurrent with $d \cdot k - 1$ seniors and $d \cdot k - 1$ juniors. In the time interval $[i, i + d \cdot k/2)$, there are $d \cdot k/2$ seniors concurrent to u_i, and half of these have the same download pattern as u_i (that is, $d \cdot k/4$ concurrent seniors have the same pattern). The first $d \cdot k/2$ pieces in u_i's pattern are therefore downloaded by u_i from these $d \cdot k/4 \geq d$ seniors having the same pattern: this supplies d independent copies of the first $k/2$ segments to u_i. The remaining $d \cdot k/2$ pieces in u_i's patterns are downloaded from its juniors and arguments symmetric to the case for seniors show that there are sufficient juniors with the other pattern (compared to u_i) to supply the needed pieces. This completes our examination of u_i's downloading, with the result that $d \cdot k/2$ connections suffice.

To evaluate r (other users connecting to u_i), we observe that the pattern of u_i's downloads is to copy only the first $k/2$ pieces, hence u_i only shares the first $k/2$ segments downloaded with others. These segments are shared with d juniors and d seniors, hence $r = 2d$.   ◻

Figure 1 illustrates the construction of Lemma 1's proof for $k = 4$ and $d = 2$. Each successive line is indented to show sequential arrival times. The figure focuses on one user u, represented by the line with all segment numbers circled. This user copies segments 1 and 2 from its seniors, and the lines representing these seniors have circles around the numbers of the pieces shared to u. Similarly, numbers circled in u's juniors are pieces shared to u. The lines in the figure without circled numbers represent users that copy segments from u. Note that the source of every piece copied is to the left of the target of the copy, reflecting that a segment can only be shared after it has been fully downloaded.

Lemma 2. *No 2-safe self-downloading protocol is possible for $c < 3$.*

Proof. Proof by contradiction. Suppose $c = 2$ (that $c = 1$ is impossible is shown in [4] even for a protocol that is not d-safe). The first and second piece that u downloads cannot come from a peer or junior because no segment can be shared until both copies are downloaded from independent sources; therefore, u connects to at least one senior user s. Notice that s cannot share all k segments that it downloads, because s exits the system as soon as the final segment is obtained. So, u can copy at most $k - 1$ pieces from s. This implies u copies at least one segment v from a user different from s, but because v has to be obtained from two different sources, u has to connect to two other users, hence $c \geq 3$.   ◻

Lemma 3. *No 2-safe self-downloading protocol is possible for $r < 3$.*

```
1 ① 2 ② 3   3   4   4
  3 3 4   4   1   1   2   2
    1 ① 2 ② 3   3   4   4
      3 3 4   4   1   1   2   2
        ① ① ② ② ③ ③ ④ ④
          3 ③ 4 ④ 1   1   2   2
            1 1 2   2   3   3   4   4
              3 ③ 4 ④ 1   1   2   2
                1 1 2   2   3   3   4   4
```

Fig. 1. Downloading two copies with four connections for $k = 4$

Proof. Because, eventually, users only download from other users and the arrival rate is equal to the rate of departure from the system, it follows that on average, users share as many pieces as they download. That observation implies that at least one user u shares at least $2k$ pieces. However, no user can share the final segment it downloads, which implies that u can share at most $k - 1$ segments. If $r = 2$, then user u shares $2k - 2$ pieces which contradicts the required sharing bound. ☐

The proof of Lemma 2 notes that u cannot copy the first two pieces from a peer or junior; the same observation holds of u's immediate senior, that is, u cannot copy its first two pieces from a user arriving at time $t_u - 1$. This observation partly motivates the construction for the following result.

Lemma 4. *For $\lambda = 24/2$, a 2-safe self-downloading protocol is possible with $r = 3$, $c = 3$, and $k = 4$.*

Proof. The proof is based on a particular user arrival schedule. The number of arrivals at time $2t + 1$ is 24, and at time $2t$ is zero. Each user downloads the pieces according to the following generic pattern $\langle i, i, j, j, k, l, k, l \rangle$ where $i \neq j \neq k \neq l$, called GP. A specific GP is completely defined by the values of i, j, and of k; thus there are $4! = 24$ specific downloading orders. A specific order of GP is denoted by $\langle i, j, k, l \rangle$. Users that start at the same time have distinct downloading orders; these downloading orders belong to GP. Clearly, every specific downloading order of GP is used by exactly one user starting at time $2t + 1$. All users that start at time 1 download their pieces from the root. User u that follows the pattern $\langle i, j, l, k \rangle$ and starts at time $2t + 1$ where $t > 0$ downloads its pieces following the schema:

- the 1st, 3rd, and 6th pieces are downloaded from the user that starts at time $2t - 1$ and follows the pattern $\langle i, j, k, l \rangle$.
- the 2nd, and 5th, pieces are downloaded from the user that starts at time $2t - 1$ and follows the pattern $\langle i, l, k, j \rangle$.
- the 4th, 7th and 8th pieces are downloaded from the user that starts at time $2t + 1$ and follows the pattern $\langle j, l, k, i \rangle$.

330   K.G. Dastidar, T. Herman, and C. Johnen

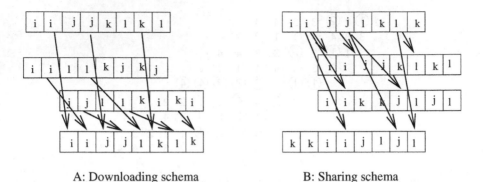

A: Downloading schema   B: Sharing schema

Fig. 2. Downloading and Sharing Schema

Figure 2.A presents the piece downloading for the user following the downloading order $\langle i,j,l,k \rangle$ at time $2t+1$ where $t > 0$. Notice the user needs to open only three network connections to download the 8 pieces thus $c = 3$. Each segment is downloaded two times from distinct users.

According figure 2.A, one may automatically compute from the downloading schema of a user u, the following downloading order $\langle i,j,l,k \rangle$. Figure 2.B presents this sharing schema. Notice that $r = 3$. A specific segment is shared after two copies of this segment have been downloaded by the user u from distinct sources.

Studying Figure 3, we establish that all users arriving at time $2t+3$ are able to download each segment two times from two distinct users arriving at time $2t+1$ or at time $2t+3$. For instance, from the users $\langle 1,2,3,4 \rangle$ and $\langle 1,4,3,2 \rangle$, arriving at time $2t+1$, 10 pieces are copied to provide 5 of the 6 first pieces to the user $\langle 1,2,4,3 \rangle$, and to the user $\langle 1,4,2,3 \rangle$ arriving at time $2t+3$. The other pieces are downloaded from users arriving at time $2t+3$: the user $\langle 1,2,4,3 \rangle$ gets these pieces from $\langle 2,4,3,1 \rangle$; the user $\langle 1,4,2,3 \rangle$ gets these pieces from $\langle 4,2,3,1 \rangle$. □

Observation 1. *In the protocol presented in the proof of lemma 4, 8 pieces are downloaded from a user. At any time slot, at most two pieces are simultaneously shared.*

Fault Tolerance Properties. The protocol of Lemma 4 tolerates some cases of corrupt pieces, as explained in following lemmas. In the following, we assume that an user is able to retrieve the correct value of a segment from two versions of this segment with at most one corrupt copy. Hence, u's segment is corrupt iff u has downloaded two corrupt versions of this segment or if u is byzantine.

Lemma 5. *Assume that at time $2t+1$, one user has a corrupt segment, and that no corruption will occur in the following step. No user arriving at time $2t+3$ has a corrupt segment.*

Proof. Let us name u the user that provides a corrupt segment. Any user u' that copies a corrupt piece from u copies an uncorrupt piece of the same segment from

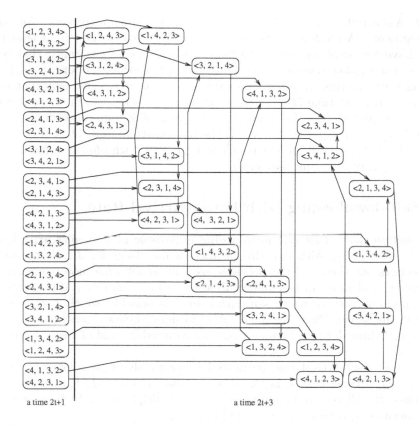

Fig. 3. Overview of downloading process for users arriving at the same time

another user. u' is able to retain a correct piece from the two copied versions if at least one of them is correct. Thus u' will keep the correct segment version. □

Lemma 6. *Assume that at time $2t+1$, at most two users have a corrupt segment and that no new corruption will be injected during the two following steps. Then at most 2 users arriving at time $2t + 3$ have a corrupt segment; no user arriving at time $2t + 5$ has a corrupt segment.*

Proof. Assume that the two users arriving at time $2t + 1$, who follow the downloading order $\langle i, -, l, - \rangle$, have a corrupt segment i. Only the two users arriving at time $2t + 3$ who follow the downloading order $\langle i, -, -, l \rangle$ (called $u1$ and $u2$) will have a corrupt segment i. Other users will not have a corrupt segment. No user copies the segment i from $u1$ and from $u2$. Thus, no user arriving at time $2t + 5$ has a corrupt version of segment i. In any other cases, no user arriving at time $2t + 3$ has a corrupt segment. □

Lemma 7. *Assume that at time $2t + 1$, at most five users have a corrupt piece, and that no corruption will occur in the three following steps. No user arriving at time $2t + 7$ has a corrupt segment.*

Proof. Assume that at time $2t + 7$, one user have a corrupt segment. We name this segment i. According to the proof of lemma 6, at time $2t + 5$, at least two users have a corrupt segment i. Suppose, without loss of generality, that both of these users follow some segment downloading pattern of the form $\langle i, -, j, - \rangle$. Having a user at time $2t + 7$ with a corrupt segment is possible only if at least 4 users arriving at time $2t + 3$ have a corrupt segment i: two of the four users follow some pattern $\langle i, -, k, - \rangle$ and the other ones follow some pattern $\langle i, -, l, - \rangle$ where $l \neq i \neq k$, $l \neq j \neq k$, and $k \neq l$. Having a corrupt segment at time $2t + 7$ is possible only if the 6 users arriving at time $2t + 1$ who follow some pattern $\langle i, -, -, - \rangle$ have a corrupt segment i. $\quad\square$

4   Self-downloading with Lower Arrival Rate

This section shows that self-downloading is possible at a smaller arrival rate than is given in [4]. Although this protocol is not d-safe for $d > 1$, the result here echoes one theme of the previous section: by allowing more connections, the user arrival rate can be smaller. Enabling a lower user arrival rate extends the domain of rates for which self-downloading is possible, which motivates the result of this section. However the result of Lemma 8 below shows this lower rate has a cost: three download connections are required instead of two connections per user.

The least user arrival rate permitted by protocols in [4] is obtained when users arrive at times $0, k/4, 2k/4, 3k/4, \ldots$, that is, $\lambda = 1/(k/4)$ (here, we have simplified the [4] results by supposing k is a multiple of 4). In that protocol, $c = 2$ because u_i copies from u_{i-2} and u_{i+1}.

Lemma 8. *Self-downloading is possible for $r = 2$, $c = 3$, $k \geq 3$, and k divisible by 3 with an arrival rate $\lambda = 1/(k/3)$.*

Proof. Supposing $\mu = 1$ to simplify the presentation, one new user arrives to the system at each time $i \cdot k/3$: users arrive at times $k/3, 2k/3, \ldots$, that is, $\lambda = 1/(k/3)$. Because $k \geq 3$, u_i is concurrent with two seniors u_{i-1} and u_{i-2} and two juniors. Because k is divisible by 3, we may consider u_i's downloading in three groups of $k/3$ segments. While it is downloading the first group, u_i is concurrent with both u_{i-1} and u_{i-2}; while downloading the second group, u_i is concurrent with one senior u_{i-1} and one junior u_{i+1}; while downloading the third group, u_i is concurrent with two juniors.

We now develop some constraints on where u_i can find segments to copy; these constraints will suggest the download pattern. Because u_i is not concurrent with any senior while it downloads its last group, u_i copies the third group from a junior, say u_{i+1}. The users in downloading protocols do not copy segments they already have, so we deduce that u_{i+1} does not copy from u_i the segments it shares to u_i: these segments u_{i+1} must copy from another senior, namely u_{i-1}. u_{i+1} cannot download the first two groups from u_{i-1}, for the simple reason that u_{i-1} departs the system after u_{i+1} downloads the first group.

These constraints suggest the following pattern. First, u_i downloads a group from u_{i-2}, then u_i downloads the second group from u_{i-1}, and the third group is downloaded from u_{i+1}.

To complete the proof, we show a pattern that satisfies this recurrent download schema for all u_i. Label the three groups a, b, c, which are pairwise disjoint with respect to the segments they contain. User u_i's pattern, for even i, is to download sequence $\langle a\ b\ c \rangle$; for odd i the pattern is $\langle c\ b\ a \rangle$. Notice that group b occupies the middle third of both patterns: each user u_i copies group b from its immediate senior u_{i-1}. Each user copies its final group from the first group of its immediate junior, and this explains why the successive patterns are reflections.   □

5   Conclusion

We showed the possibility of d-safe downloading and an optimal protocol for $d = 2$. The results given in this paper suggest that higher user arrival rates may enable self-downloading schemes with fewer connections per download. An intuition for this is that with larger arrival rates, the cohort of concurrent users can be larger, with a diversity of distinct downloading patterns.

We have limited the study here to serial downloading, that is, protocols where a user fetches only one piece of a file at any time. A natural question is how to treat the possibility of concurrent downloading for any user – a user will presumably download the file more quickly by parallel downloading. Our results can apply to parallel downloading by applying the scheme in parallel threads: first split the file into ℓ, equal-size parts, and then use a serial downloading scheme for each part.

Another direction is to consider self-downloading in the context of multiple files. If users request a set of files, then one could investigate different sets of files, which have significant intersection. Under what conditions can different sets enable self-downloading while allowing users to depart the system after completing the downloading (similar to the hypotheses of this paper)?

Finally, we return to the issue of message digests and how their availability could be exploited in our self-downloading schemes. As noted in Section 2, the timing of self-downloading is disrupted if a segment has to be refetched, triggered by message digest comparison that indicates corruption. An alternative interpretation of our self-downloading schemes is the following. In a d-safe self-downloading protocol, each segment is *potentially* downloaded d times. If the first copy is correct, as validated by a trusted message digest, then no subsequent copy of that segment is fetched. More generally, a d-safe protocol could thus tolerate up to $d - 1$ corrupt pieces, only refetching pieces until a correct copy is obtained. In any case, a user waits for the time it would take to download d copies of a segment before sharing that segment to other users. This wait is pessimistic, but guarantees the timing of the self-downloading strategy in spite of the injection of corrupt pieces.

References

1. S Adler. The slashdot effect, an analysis of three Internet publications. In *Linux Gazette*, Issue 38, March 1999.
2. J Aspnes, G Shah. Skip graphs. In *SODA 2003. Proceedings of the Fourteenth Annual ACM-SIAM Symposium on Discrete Algorithms*, pp. 284-393, 2003.
3. B Cohen. Incentives build robustness in BitTorrent. In *First Workshop on Economics of Peer-to-Peer Systems*, Berkeley, California, June, 2003. http://www.sims.berkeley.edu/research/conferences/p2pecon
4. T Herman and C Johnen. Strategies for peer-to-peer downloading. *Information Processing Letters*, 94(5):203-209, 2005.
5. C Wang, B Li. Peer-to-peer overlay networks: a survey. Technical Report, Department of Computer Science, HKUST, Feb. 2003.
6. P Sevcik. Peer-to-peer traffic: another internet myth is born. *Business Communication Review*, November 2005.
7. RX Cringely. Net neutered. *Electric Money*, Volume 7.25, June 22, 2006.
8. J Byers, M Luby, M Mitzenmacher. Accessing multiple mirror sites in parallel: using tornado codes to speed up downloads. In *Proceedings of the 18th Annual Joint Conference of the IEEE Computer and Communications Societies (INFOCOM99)*, pp. 275-284, 1999.
9. W Baohua, G Fedak, F Cappello. Scheduling independent tasks sharing large data distributed with BitTorrent. In *Proceedings of the 6th IEEE/ACM International Workshop on Grid Computing*, pp. 219-226, 2005.
10. R Sherwood, R Braud, B Bhattacharjee. Slurpie: a cooperative bulk data transfer protocol. In *Proceedings of the Twenty-third Annual Joint Conference of the IEEE Computer and Communications Societies (INFOCOM04)*, pp. 941-951, 2004.
11. S Sohail, CT Chou, SS Kanhere, S Jha. On large scale deployment of parallelized file transfer protocol. In *Proceedings of the 24th IEEE International Conference on Performance, Computing, and Communications (IPCCC05)*, pp. 225-232, 2005.
12. M Ciglan, O Habala, L Hluchy. Striped replication from multiple sites in the grid environment. In *Proceedings of Advances in Grid Computing (EGC05)*, LNCS 3470, pp. 778-785, 2005.
13. S Jun, M Ahamad. Incentives in BitTorrent induce free riding. In *Proceeding of the 2005 ACM SIGCOMM workshop on Economics of Peer-to-Peer Systems*, pp. 116-121, 2005.
14. G Wu, T Chiueh. How efficient is BitTorrent? In *Proceedings of SPIE Conference on Multimedia Computing and Networking*, Volume 6071, 2006.
15. D Bickson, D Dolev, Y Weiss. Efficient peer-to-peer content distribution. http://citeseer.ist.psu.edu/738516.html, 2006.
16. BG Chun, P Wu, H Weatherspoon, J Kubiatowicz. ChunkCast: an anycast service for large content distribution. In *Proceedings of the International Workshop on Peer-to-Peer Systems (IPTPS06)*, February 2006.

Best Paper: Stabilizing Clock Synchronization for Wireless Sensor Networks

Ted Herman* and Chen Zhang

Department of Computer Science, University of Iowa

Abstract. One of the simplest protocols for clock synchronization in wireless ad hoc and sensor networks is the converge-to-max protocol, which has the simple logic of adjusting each node's clock to be at least as large as any neighbor's. This paper examines the converge-to-max protocol, showing it to be stabilizing even when node clocks have skew, bounded domains, and dynamic communication links.

1 Introduction

Clock synchronization is an important service in wireless sensor networks. Because wireless sensor platforms have limited resources and some sensor applications need precise time measurements, traditional synchronization protocols may not be appropriate. Sensor hardware and communication should be fault tolerant and self-managing, and their low-cost construction tends to make faults more likely. A lightweight, self-stabilizing protocol for clock synchronization is thus well motivated for wireless sensor networks.

1.1 Protocol Designs

Quite a few clock protocols have been described in the literature for wireless sensor networks [3], with various assumptions about platform, application requirements, and fault tolerance. The following five design approaches (1)–(5) indicate the rich design space in this area. (1) *Leader-based* clock synchronization seeks to enslave all clocks to one leader clock. General examples of leader-based synchronization are GPS and NTP [9]. Within multihop wireless sensor networks, a fault tolerant (and conceptually self-stabilizing) protocol is to elect one node, say the node with smallest identifier, to be the leader and construct a spanning tree rooted at the leader [6,8]. Each node periodically transmits a timestamped beacon message, and each node except the root upon receiving a beacon copies the timestamp to its clock. (2) *Pulse-based* clock synchronization [2] has biological inspiration and could be promising for pulse-coded radio protocols (ultra wide-band, see [5]); this type of protocol is self-stabilizing [4], however the type of processing and encoding for the protocol is not well-suited to current sensor networks. Also, after all nodes have stabilized on pulse timing, an

---

* Work supported by the National Science Foundation under Grant Number 0519907.

A.K. Datta and M. Gradinariu (Eds.): SSS 2006, LNCS 4280, pp. 335–349, 2006.

additional protocol may be needed for agreement on a clock value. (3) *Reference-broadcast* synchronization was originally developed for single-hop wireless sensor networks with noisy timestamping. A repeatedly transmitted pulse signal is simultaneously recorded at all nodes, and subsequent conversation among the nodes results, *post facto*, in consensus times for the pulses. Statistical techniques overcome noise. In theory, reference-broadcast also applies to multihop networks distributively if multiple overlapping time zones are established, but significant memory and processing resource would be needed in practice. (4) *Averaging* is an intuitively appealing way to synchronize clocks. Each node periodically transmits a timestamped beacon, and a node adjusts its clock to be the average of its neighborhood (including its own clock). Unfortunately, this method has been shown to converge slowly [7]; it can also be difficult in practice to adjust beacon rates and define the neighborhood average for a node when messages are lost. (5) *Converge-to-max* clock protocols are perhaps the simplest distributed synchronization algorithms. Periodically, each node transmits a timestamped beacon. Upon receiving a beacon, if the timestamp of that beacon is greater than the node's global clock, then the node adjusts its clock to agree with the beacon. This protocol is the technique specified in IEEE 802.11 ad hoc networks [10,11,12]. Two advantages of (5) are that it is inherently monotonic (clocks only increase) and it can synchronize in networks with links that are too dynamic for method (1) to work; this latter advantage motivated the use of (5) in [1].

1.2   Contributions and Roadmap

This paper investigates method (5), called here the "converge to max" protocol. Section 2 presents the basic model, which is used in Section 3 to present the protocol. Section 3 also looks at questions of finite clock domain and fault containment.

The contribution of this research goes in two directions. We show how concepts of self-stabilization can be useful for a practical problem in sensor networks. In the other direction, the contribution to the field of self-stabilization is the choice of model: we advance the topic of real-time, stabilizing synchronization, which has not been widely investigated. The research takes into account practical model details like clock skew and bounded clock domain, discovering some interesting behaviors in the analysis.

2   Sensor Network

Protocol design is generally constrained by platform limitations and metrics, and knowledge of the platform is especially important for sensor networks with limited resource. This section gives an abridged presentation of platform and application considerations that motivate and define the computation model used to verify and analyze clock protocols.

For clock synchronization, there is considerable variability in application requirements. Sensor network applications need clocks to measure elapsed time, schedule wakeups, and compare time coordinates of sensor readings at different nodes. A protocol design should therefore relate clock readings at different nodes, e.g., there is a *synchrony bound* stating how far apart simultaneous clock readings can be at different nodes.

Sensor platforms do not have hardware clocks as such, instead providing counters with wakeup and rollover interrupts to the processor. The rate of counter incrementing deviates from real time; we assume in this paper that the rate for any particular node v is fixed at ρ_v, which is a value in the range $(1 - \kappa, 1 + \kappa)$ for some known manufacturing tolerance κ. Conceptually, ρ_v is the first derivative of the counter value with respect to time, and ρ_v is called skew: if $\rho_v > 1$, the node's counter increments faster than real time. The second derivative of the counter with respect to time is called *drift*.

The operating system encapsulates the counter by a software module called the *native clock*; the native clock, in turn, is encapsulated by a module called the *local clock* to extend the range (so that it can increment for a longer period without rollover); and one more layer of encapsulation creates the *global clock* module, which is the basic unit used in this paper. The global clock module offers two interfaces to the protocol designer, *read* and *adjust*. The goal of the designer is to invent a protocol so that nodes adjust their global clocks to satisfy a synchrony bound useful to applications. We denote by C_v the value that a global clock *read* operation returns at sensor node v.

Sensor nodes communicate by sending and receiving small-size messages on a single-frequency radio, and access to the shared wireless media is mediated by randomized media access control (MAC) delay. Any node transmission implicitly sends to all nodes within that node's vicinity, limited by radio range. The network topology is modeled as a graph (V, E) of connections with nodes as vertices and links between nodes where communication is possible. Let $|V| = n$ be the number of nodes. If unidirectional links are allowed, then the graph is directed and (x, y) is a directed link signifying that node x's transmissions may be received by node y. For bidirectional (x, y), call x and y *neighbors* in the network. The *static* model has bidirectional links and the graph is undirected and connected. The *dynamic* model allows links to be unidirectional and transient, motivated by networks where radio properties or node mobility varies the network connectivity. We suppose the graph is strongly connected in the dynamic model. For either model, let d_{xy} be the graph distance from x to y and let diam be the maximum distance between any pair of vertices.

Rather than proposing a detailed model of link behavior, we make the following assumption for an (x, y) link: if node x sends messages periodically, once every ϕ time units, then within Φ time units, y receives a message from x. This assumption allows us to treat (x, y) as a link that can be reliable within a given time period. Links do not queue more than one message: the issue of old messages arriving after new ones cannot arise in this model. For the dynamic model, we assume that the network is sufficiently connected such that diffusion completes within a time bound T. Suppose, for example, that node v has a message m to broadcast throughout the network. Node v periodically broadcasts m every ϕ

time units, and when any node w receives message m, then w periodically broadcasts m every ϕ time units. Each link guarantees delivery of m within time Φ, and network connectivity (which is a property of maximum graph diameter and the evolution of links) satisfies the property that every node receives m within T seconds of v's initial transmission of m.

Ideally, a synchronization protocol could use as a building block an instantaneous transfer of a clock reading to another node. Implementing (approximately) instantaneous transfer of timestamps using messages is nontrivial: though propagation delay is not significant, the latency of transferring a timestamp using a message includes other contributors: media access control (MAC) delay, routing and device driver processing overhead, and possibly nondeterministic scheduling of concurrent sensor tasks competing for processor time. For some networks, frequency distribution of these contributors is such that statistical techniques like linear regression or building profiles of upper and lower bounds provide adequate estimates for offset and skew between sender and receiver clocks [9,17,18,8,20]. Several sensor network platforms give programmer access to delays introduced at the MAC layer, or even the ability to timestamp almost precisely at the instant of message transmission; this is called the *sender timestamp* of the message. The same platforms can also record the clock at the instant of message reception, which is called the *receiver timestamp*. The pseudorandom MAC delay is the dominant component of the noise, so subtracting the receiver timestamp from the sender timestamp is a good approximation to the difference between sender and receiver clocks [19,8]. We assume MAC-layer adjustments to timestamps are used for our model.

The timestamp mechanism effectively transfers a global clock reading instantaneously between neighboring nodes. The layered implementation (global clock, local clock, native clock) compensates for delays in processing a message, however such compensation does not enable precise comparison of the clocks of sender and receiver, because the compensation is implemented by addition or subtraction in terms of the native clock, which includes skew. Thus if a message is timestamped by a clock synchronization protocol at some time t_0, transmitted at a later time t_1, then given a corresponding timestamp by the receiver at time t_2, and finally processed at the receiver at a later time t_3, the compensation for the delay $t_1 - t_0$ includes sender skew whereas compensation for delay $t_3 - t_2$ includes receiver skew. We assume that skews and delays are small enough so that the inaccuracy due to the skews (as well as the difference $t_2 - t_1$) are negligible: the difference between the timestamp at t_2 and the timestamp at t_0 is therefore taken to be the difference in offsets of the two clocks at the instant t_3.

3   Converge-to-Max

The technique (5), briefly explained in Section 1, is presented in more detail here, using *read* and *adjust* interfaces of the global clock and assuming timestamping of beacon messages. Each node executes the following thread concurrently with a sensor application:

event(timeout):
    read global clock & prepare beacon message m ;
    local-broadcast(m) to neighborhood ;
    schedule next timeout in ϕ seconds ;

We assume that the system's timeout mechanism is such that the above event eventually occurs every ϕ seconds, even for arbitrary initial state. To complete the protocol, there is an event to handle an incoming beacon.

event(receive beacon m):
    c = *read* global clock ;
    if $m.timestamp > c$ then
        adjust global clock by $+ (m.timestamp - c)$;

One should expect that such a simple protocol has a simple proof of correctness. This is the case if every node has zero skew and clocks are unbounded, and we sketch the argument here. A legitimate state is one where the global clocks of all nodes have the same value. The closure property holds for a legitimate state because every receive beacon event contains a timestamp equal to the node's global clock (recall that we assume a MAC timestamping mechanism that compensates for all message latencies), hence no global clocks are adjusted; since all clocks increment at the same rate, all global clocks remain equal. Convergence is also straightforward. In the initial state (or some time after the initial state if we consider arbitrary messages initially in queues and arbitrary timeout values), there is some maximum clock value at some set of nodes M. Invariantly, no global clock of a node in M adjusts (easily shown by contradiction) in the subsequent execution. Within time ϕ, each node v of M performs a local broadcast of a beacon. For a static network, within Φ time units after the local broadcast, each neighbor w of v receives and processes a beacon from v; if $w \notin M$, then w adjusts its global clock to be equal to v's. Hence w joins M, and $V \setminus M$ is a decreasing variant function to establish convergence to a legitimate state. The static network's convergence time is $O((\phi + \Phi) \cdot \text{diam})$. For a dynamic network, each node $w \notin M$ receives a beacon within time T after some node in m transmits a beacon, and convergence time is $O(\phi + T)$.

Defining a legitimate state, showing closure, and proving convergence are more difficult when clocks have skews. We introduce some definitions that help us with the analysis. A *clock history* is a projection of the system execution consisting of the global clock operations and protocol steps of the converge-to-max protocol. Let c_p^k denote the kth protocol operation by node p: c_p^k is either a *read* and beacon-transmit or a beacon reception and possible *adjust* of p's global clock. The clock history is a sequence of such operations. Each operation has an associated real time, and the clock history is ordered by time. For any c_p^k, we refer to its real time as $t(c_p^k)$ and its global clock value by c_p^k. Our convention when c_p^k is an *adjust* operation is to associate with c_p^k the global clock value resulting from the adjustment. The expression $c_p^k < c_q^j$ compares global clock values for two operations. Arguments about executions of a clock protocol may refer to operations in the clock history, or to points in real time; our convention for references to points in time is that operations are atomic (consuming no real time), and points in time are moments between operations.

The relation $c_p^k \prec c_q^j$ holds if c_p^k causally precedes c_q^j. In the static network model, we have a special case of $\prec$ for a chain of beacon transmissions and receptions. Let $c_p^k \prec_1 c_q^j$ hold if p and q are neighbors, c_p^k is a beacon transmission operation, and c_q^j is the first subsequent receive by q from p; by assumption c_q^j occurs no more than Φ time after c_p^k. Let $c_p^k \prec_2 c_q^j$ hold if there are c_r^i and $c_r^{i'}$ so that $c_p^k \prec_1 c_r^i$, $c_r^{i'} \prec_1 c_q^j$, and $c_r^{i'}$ is the first beacon transmission by r following the receive operation c_r^i. Notice that by our model assumptions, c_q^j occurs no more than $\phi + 2\Phi$ time after c_p^k, because r may wait at most ϕ time after reception for its next beacon transmission, and latency for a successful beacon transmission is at most Φ for both p and r. More generally, let $\prec_\ell$ be an ℓ-hop causal chain of beacon operations.

Corresponding to $\prec_\ell$, we define $\prec_{min}$ for the dynamic network model. Let $c_p^k \prec_{min} c_q^j$ hold iff k is the largest index such that $c_p^k \prec_{d_{pq}} c_q^j$. Let ρ_v denote the skew of node v, let ρ_{max} be the maximum skew of any node, and let ρ_{min} be the minimum skew in the network.

Lemma 1. *In the static network model, for distinct $p \neq q$, beacon transmission operation c_p^k and beacon reception c_q^j satisfying $c_p^k \prec_{d_{pq}} c_q^j$,*

$$c_q^j \;\geq\; max\left(c_q^j + t_{pq} \cdot \rho_q \,,\, c_p^k + t_{pq} \cdot \rho_{min}\right) \tag{1}$$

$$t_{pq} \;\leq\; d_{pq} \cdot (\Phi + \phi) \tag{2}$$

$$where \quad t_{pq} \;=\; t(c_q^j) - t(c_p^k)$$

Bound (1) holds also for the dynamic network model, if $c_p^k \prec_{min} c_q^j$.

Proof. To verify (1), observe that between the timestamp and beacon transmission c_p^k and c_q^j, it is possible that each hop in a path of length d_{pq} causes an increase to the global clock along the path, and the clock value at each hop in the path is affected by the skew of that node, which is at least ρ_{min}. Therefore the timestamp arriving at q, in the last hop along the path, is at least $c_p^k + (t(c_q^j) - t(c_p^k)) \cdot \rho_{min}$. Meanwhile during this clock propagation along the path, q's global clock increases by at least $(t(c_q^j) - t(c_p^k)) \cdot \rho_q$. The value of q's global clock c_q^j is bounded below by the minimum of these two quantities, which derives (1). The other cases to verify are global clock increases at q or the event in the path from p to q where a beacon's timestamp is no larger than the global clock at the recipient. For any of these cases, (1) is a conservative lower bound. To complete the proof, inequality (2) holds by induction on the path, considering the worst case for the time ϕ until the next beacon transmission (in fact, the bound could be sharpened because the delay for p's initial beacon transmission is zero rather than ϕ, by definition of $\prec_{d_{pq}}$). ❑

Lemma 2. *In the static network model, for distinct $p \neq q$ and any point in any execution, within a delay of at most $d_{pq} \cdot (\Phi + \phi)$ time, there occurs a beacon reception c_q^j satisfying $c_p^k \prec_{d_{pq}} c_q^j$ for some previous beacon transmission operation c_p^k in the execution.*

Proof. The lemma is a corollary of the proof of Lemma 1. $\square$

To quickly show the utility of Lemma 1, we show a case where it allows comparison of global clocks. Recall that C_v at a given state is the value that v would obtain from a *read* of the global clock at that state. Similarly, we let C_v at any real time instant denote the value that v would obtain should a *read* execute at that instant.

Lemma 3. *In the static network model, suppose there is an execution where p never adjusts its global clock. Then at any time at least $d_{pq}(\Phi + \phi)$ following the execution's start,*

$$C_q \;\geq\; C_p - d_{pq} \cdot (\Phi + \phi) \cdot 2(\rho_p - \rho_{min}) \qquad (3)$$

In the dynamic network model the bound is $C_q \geq C_p - T \cdot 2(\rho_p - \rho_{min})$.

Proof. After time $d_{pq}(\Phi + \phi)$, node q has executed some event c_q^j causally preceded by one of p's beacon transmissions c_p^k with a real time satisfying (2). Because p never adjusts its clock, at time $t(c_q^j)$ we know that

$$C_p \;=\; c_p^k + \big(t(c_q^j) - t(c_p^k)\big) \cdot \rho_p$$

which implies, at time $t(c_q^j)$,

$$c_p^k \;=\; C_p - \big(t(c_q^j) - t(c_p^k)\big) \cdot \rho_p$$

Therefore at time $t(c_q^j)$ we may substitute C_q for c_q^j and the equation for c_p^k above into (1) to obtain

$$
\begin{aligned}
C_q \;&\geq\; C_p - \big(t(c_q^j) - t(c_p^k)\big) \cdot \rho_p \;+\; \big(t(c_q^j - t(c_p^k)\big) \cdot \rho_{min} \\
&\geq\; C_p - \big(t(c_q^j) - t(c_p^k)\big) \cdot (\rho_p - \rho_{min})
\end{aligned}
$$

The worst case for this inequality occurs when the amount being subtracted from C_p is maximized, which by (1) results in

$$C_q \;\geq\; C_p - d_{pq} \cdot (\Phi + \phi) \cdot (\rho_p - \rho_{min}) \qquad (4)$$

This inequality verifies the lemma for those times when q receives a beacon along a minimum-length path from p to q; it remains to consider the value of C_q during the time interval between two beacon receive events c_q^j and $c_q^{j'}$. By Lemma 2, such a time interval's duration is at most $x \overset{def}{=} d_{pq} \cdot (\Phi + \phi)$, which implies C_q increases by at least $x\rho_q$ in the worst case, and C_p increases by at least $x\rho_p$. If $\rho_q \geq \rho_p$, then (4) continues to hold throughout the interval because the quantity added on the left-hand side is at least as large as the quantity added on the right-hand side. However if $\rho_q < \rho_p$, then to preserve the lower bound on C_q, we add the larger quantity, with factor ρ_p, on the left-hand side, and the smaller quantity on the right:

$$C_q + x\rho_p \;\geq\; C_p - x(\rho_p - \rho_{min}) + x\rho_q$$

This simplifies to

$$C_q \; \geq \; C_p \; - \; x(\rho_p - \rho_{min}) - x(\rho_p - \rho_q) \; = \; C_p \; - \; x \cdot (2\rho_p - \rho_{min} - \rho_q)$$

Therefore a looser inequality than (4) holds throughout the execution, namely (3). ❐

Suppose we apply Lemma 3 to the case where node p has the maximum global clock value in the system throughout the execution (and hence never adjusts its clock by beacon reception). For such a case, we have both upper and lower bounds on C_q, since $C_p \geq C_q$ by assumption and (3) provides a lower bound.

Lemma 4. *In the static network model, suppose there is an execution where p never adjusts its global clock and $C_p \geq C_r$ for any r throughout the execution. Then at any time at least $d_{pq}(\Phi + \phi)$ following the execution's start,*

$$C_p - C_q \;\; \leq \;\; \text{diam} \cdot (\Phi + \phi) \cdot 2(\rho_{max} - \rho_{min}) \tag{5}$$

In the dynamic network model the bound is $C_p - C_q \leq T \cdot 2(\rho_{max} - \rho_{min})$.

Proof. Taking the worst case on distance and skew, (3) reduces to (5). ❐

Inequality (5) provides a synchrony bound for applications. If the range of possible skews is known and a bound on the network diameter is given, and application-specific constants Φ and ϕ are established, the application programmer can derive a bound on the difference between clocks at different nodes.

3.1   Legitimate State

Self-stabilization is verified by showing closure of, and convergence to, a set of legitimate states. Previous observations suggest that a definition of legitimate state will imply one node has a global clock of maximum value in the system, and that clock does not adjust by any beacon reception operation. This turns out to be a simple obligation to satisfy. Let V_{max} be the set of nodes which have maximum skew:

$$v \in V_{max} \;\; \equiv \;\; (\forall w \in V : \; \rho_v \geq \rho_w)$$

Definition 1. *With respect to an execution E, let a network state σ be called consistent if every receive beacon operation c_q^j subsequent to σ has, for every $p \in V \setminus \{q\}$, some beacon transmission operation c_p^k in E satisfying $c_p^k \prec c_q^j$.*

Consistency is an invariant: any state following a consistent state is also consistent. Definition 1 can be extended to apply to an initial state of an execution E in the standard way: if some prefix A can be constructed so that Definition 1 holds for $A \cdot E$, and prefix A has a duration of at least $\text{diam} \cdot (\Phi + \phi)$ time for a static network or at least $T + \phi$ time for a dynamic network, then all states of E are defined to be consistent. An execution is called consistent if all its states are consistent under this extended notion of consistency.

Definition 2. *State σ is* legitimate *if it is consistent and at least one $v \in V_{max}$ satisfies $C_v \geq C_w$ for every $w \in V$.*

Closure and convergence are simple arguments, which we sketch as follows. For any $v \in V_{max}$ with maximal C_v, no beacon reception operation c_v^k will adjust the clock: this can be shown by contradiction, based on the assumption that C_v and ρ_v are maximal. This establishes the invariance of $v \in V_{max}$ having maximum clock values, which is all we need for closure. Convergence is likewise simple to argue. If $|V_{max}| = 1$, then C_v for $v \in V_{max}$ increases at a faster rate than any other clock in the system, so eventually it obtains a larger clock value than any other clock (even without adjustment). Similar reasoning applies to the case where $|V_{max}| > 1$.

3.2 "Pseudo" Legitimate Execution

Definition 2 may not be useful in practice because the convergence time is dependent on the difference in rates of skew. For example, consider p and q with $d_{pq} \approx diam$, ρ_q is the maximum skew, and ρ_p is the second largest skew in the network. From a state where C_p is the maximum global clock, it can be happen that a beacon transmission c_p^k causally precedes reception c_q^j, however the intermediate nodes along the path from p to q have minimum skews, so the global clock of q is only guaranteed to be at least $c_p^k + \rho_{min} \cdot (t(c_q^j) - t(c_p^k))$. Eventually, p overtakes q, but the rate of overtaking could be $\rho_p - \rho_q$, which might be a very small quantity. One would prefer a convergence result in terms of diam or T, which better relates to application assumptions. The following lemma provides a useful insight for this purpose.

Lemma 5. *Suppose there is a consistent execution E such that $C_p \geq C_r$ for all r holds continuously for some time interval of length t, but immediately after time t, there exists C_q such that $C_q > C_p$; then $\rho_q > \rho_p$.*

Proof. Consider q such that C_q is the first global clock to become larger than C_p. There are two cases for this event, either it is the result of an adjustment or it is due to the advancement of q's global clock at the rate ρ_q. Suppose C_q increases by adjustment ahead of C_p, by some reception operation c_q^j. Then the timestamp in the received message is larger than C_p, and this timestamp was created by some node r satisfying $C_r > C_p$; but this contradicts q having the first global clock to exceed C_p. If q's clock rate advances C_q ahead of C_p, then $\rho_q \leq \rho_p$ cannot hold, hence the lemma. ☐

In an execution whose states are all consistent, we say that node p is *demoted* at time t if C_p is the maximum clock at t, and $C_q > C_p$ for some node q immediately following time t.

Lemma 6. *In any consistent execution, there occur at most $n - 1$ demotions.*

Proof. Each demotion implies the existence of a node with larger skew than had the previous maximum clock-holder, by Lemma 5. The number of different skew values in the system is $|V| = n$, and the last global clock to become maximum would be one with maximum skew, which cannot be overtaken subsequently. ☐

Lemma 3 may not hold throughout an execution of consistent states subject to demotions, however a modified version of the lemma, useful as an ongoing synchrony bound, can be proved (we omit details). Lemma 6 clarifies the structured behavior of the converge-to-max protocol. It is "pseudo" stabilizing to a consistent state within time $\mathrm{diam} \cdot (\Phi + \phi)$ (or $T + \phi$ for the dynamic network), and the network experiences at most $n - 1$ epochs in which some node (perhaps joined by others) has the maximum clock value. During each epoch, Lemma 4 provides a synchrony bound after a delay of $\mathrm{diam} \cdot (\Phi + \phi)$ (we speculate that synchrony bounds can also be derived for transitions from one epoch to the next). Strictly speaking, execution is not pseudo-stabilizing in the sense of [13], because eventual convergence to a state satisfying Definition 2 is deterministic, whereas pseudo-stabilization [13] is based on nondeterministic selection. Nonetheless, we feel that pseudo-stabilization is an appropriate characterization of the behavior of Lemma 6, particularly when we consider that in practice, skews are not constant, and could nondeterministically fluctuate (one could also call this "provisional" stabilization, however we do not formally investigate any new definition here).

3.3 Finite Clocks

Practical computer clocks are based on counters with finite domains, whereas the protocol and verification in Section 3 supposes global clocks have no finite limit. The issue of infinite clocks is more important for self-stabilizing monotonic clock protocols, because a transient failure could move global clocks close to a finite limit value long before this otherwise would occur. Sensor network models motivate using a small domain for clocks because messages have small payloads (saving even a few bytes, or piggybacking to reduce the number of messages, can be useful).

A *bounded* global clock has domain $[0, L]$. The standard way to deal with the event of a bounded clock reaching maximum value L is rollover: $C_v + b \stackrel{def}{=} (C_v + b) \bmod (L + 1)$ for any b; this is also how the hardware counters behave. The event of a clock rollover from L to zero disrupts the converge-to-max protocol, since a large clock instantly becomes a small one. Two relevant techniques from the literature of self-stabilizing phase-clocks are (a) to redefine comparison of clock values in the clock protocol to behave modulo $L + 1$ [14], or (b) let the event of a clock reaching L initiate a system reset, after which all clocks begin from zero [15]. Neither of (a) nor (b) is directly applicable to the converge-to-max protocol because the model of phase clocks differs in key aspects from real-time clock behavior. Below, we adapt the theme of (a) in a modification of converge-to-max, but first we show a surprising result.

Lemma 7. *For bounded clocks with rollover in domain $[0, L]$, where in the static network model $L \gg \mathrm{diam} \cdot (\Phi + \phi)$ and $L \gg T$ in the dynamic network, the converge-to-max protocol is stabilizing.*

Proof. We examine three cases for an initial state. The first case is where no clock is near to rollover, and the behavior is the that of an unbounded clock for long enough for convergence. Let $R = \text{diam} \cdot (\Phi + \phi)/\rho_{max}$. The first case consists of states where $C_v < L - R$ for all nodes v. Here, no global clock advances to L in $\text{diam} \cdot (\Phi + \phi)$ time, which makes behavior with respect to convergence the same as an unbounded clock. Hence arguments of Section 3 are applicable.

The second case is where all clocks are near or just past rollover:

$$(\forall v \in V : C_v \geq L - R \vee C_v \leq R)$$

Call C_v *large* if $C_v \geq L - R$ and *small* if $C_v \leq R$. If no C_v is large, then the second case reduces to the first case. Our proof obligation is to show that any execution reduces to zero the number of large clocks. Let $C_{min} \stackrel{def}{=} \min\{C_v \mid C_v \geq L - R\}$. We claim that within $\text{diam} \cdot (\Phi + \phi)$ time, C_{min} reaches the point of rollover. In reaching this point, small clocks may copy values from large clocks, and some large clocks may roll over to become small. If $C_{min} = L$ and a beacon is transmitted with timestamp L, then either a rollover occurs in the message processing layers, or in the beacon processing, or immediate after beacon processing. Thus within $\text{diam} \cdot (\Phi + \phi)$ time, no clock is large.

The third case is an initial state σ_0 with at least one large clock, in $[L - R, L]$, and with at least one clock that is neither large nor small, in the range $(R, L - R)$. After $\text{diam} \cdot (\Phi + \phi)$ time, a state σ_1 occurs where each node has received a beacon that is causally preceded by a large clock beacon (we ignore trivial cases where all large clocks roll over before beacon transmission). It can thus occur that every clock is high or has rolled over, so that σ_1 is a state of the second case, which would complete the lemma. Therefore we suppose that in the execution reaching σ_1, large clock beacons roll over during propagation, and some C_p does not adjust to become large; in σ_1, nodes with maximum clock value did not have large clocks in σ_0. Again, if σ_1 is a state of the first case, the lemma holds. Therefore, suppose some C_p has increased to at least $L - R$, but not by adjustment, which implies σ_1 is a state of the third case. Another important observation concerning C_p's increase is that σ_0 had at least one clock in the range $(L - 2R, L - R)$, so that $\text{diam} \cdot (\Phi + \phi)$ time is enough for C_p to become large. Notice that all the large clocks of σ_0 roll over in the execution leading to σ_1. Let σ' be the first state for which C_p, not a large clock, becomes large. Although other clocks may be greater than C_p, they will all roll over in this execution and C_p will not adjust under their influence. By Lemma 3, in the $\text{diam} \cdot (\Phi + \phi)$ time after σ', C_p does not roll over and every other node receives a beacon causally preceded by a transmission of p's beacon. The result is a state fitting the second case. □

The proof of Lemma 7 shows that clock behavior can be chaotic when clocks roll over: for instance, a node with a large clock can become small, then adjust to a large value, then roll over again, all within a brief period. Strategy (a) avoids this by redefining clock comparison so that, for example, $L - \epsilon < \epsilon$ holds for small values of ϵ; in this way, comparison wraps around the domain $[0, L]$. To avoid pathological race conditions preventing convergence, a new reset mode is introduced to the algorithm. Each node p has a *reset clock* U_p in the range $[0, S]$, where $S = \text{diam} \cdot (\Phi + \phi) \cdot (1 + \kappa)$ (recall that $1 + \kappa$ is an upper bound on ρ_{max}). We suppose $S \ll L$. The reset clock U_p advances at the same rate ρ_p

as the global clock, until $U_p = S$, whereat the reset clock stops and an event is triggered. We explain below how the reset clock is used to coordinate a resetting of global clocks.

$$C_p \leq C_q \overset{def}{=} (\exists b: 0 \leq b \leq 2 \cdot S: C_q = (C_p + b) \bmod (L+1))$$
$$C_p \circlearrowleft C_q \overset{def}{=} \neg (C_p \leq C_q \vee C_q \leq C_p)$$

This redefinition of inequality is not a total order of clock values, and that fact motivates the definition of $\circlearrowleft$ to test for incomparable timestamps (see [14]). Beacon transmission for node p changes to the following.

    event(timeout):
        if $U_p < S$ then prepare beacon message m from U_p ;
        else prepare beacon message m from C_p ;
        local-broadcast(m) to neighborhood ;
        schedule next timeout in ϕ seconds ;

Beacons are thus of two types, either a normal beacon with a timestamp from a global clock or a beacon containing a reset clock. When node receives the latter type, the reset clock value is handled like a timestamp by lower layers so that MAC and other processing delays are added to the reset clock value (topping out, of course, at the maximum possible reset clock value S). Beacon processing at node p changes to:

    event(receive beacon m):
        if m contains reset clock value u then $U_p = \min(U_p, u)$;
        if $U_p = S$ and m contains a global clock value, then
            if $m.timestamp \circlearrowleft C_p$ then assign $U_p = 0$;
            else if $m.timestamp > C_p$ then
                adjust global clock C_p by $+ (m.timestamp - C_p)$;

Finally, this protocol handles the event of p's reset clock increasing to the maximum:

    event(reset clock U_p increases to S):
        adjust global clock C_p to be zero ;

A legitimate state for the strategy (a) protocol is a consistent state where all clocks are comparable and all reset clocks are at S, so that (3) holds; the synchrony bound (3) should be loosened for pseudo-stabilization (we omit details).

Lemma 8. *The strategy (a) clock protocol is stabilizing.*

Proof. If all reset clocks are S and all beacon receive operations find timestamps that are comparable to the receiver's global clock, then the behavior of the protocol is that same as for the converge-to-max protocol, using unbounded clocks. Moreover, in an execution where no node assigns $U_p = 0$ due to an incomparable timestamp detection, all reset clocks equal S within $O(S)$ time, because the minimum reset clock not equal to S increases (beacon processing does not lower the minimum). Now suppose we have an execution starting from a consistent state and consider the first node p to assign $U_p = 0$. At such an assignment, U_p is the smallest reset clock in the network. Within a diam $\cdot (\Phi + \phi)$-length time interval, every reset clock U_q satisfies $U_q < S$ (including U_p in the case that $\rho_p = \rho_{max}$, because even if p's reset clock runs faster than real time, the κ-bound in the definition of S assures that p will not reach S in this time interval). Following a state with all reset clocks below S, reset clocks advance to S and the global clocks restart from zero. Therefore the execution has a state where all global clocks are in the range $[0, S]$, no reset clock is below S, and subsequently no beacon receive operation detects an incomparable timestamp.   □

3.4 Fault Containment

The converge-to-max protocol's weakness with respect to transient faults is the span of its reaction to small perturbations. Even one global clock stricken by a fault that increases the clock value will propagate throughout the network before the system converges. The same can occur with traditional algorithms, such as leader-based clock synchronization, presumably with lower probability than for the fully distributed converge-to-max protocol. We suggest using single-fault containment to decrease the probability of such widespread contamination (generalization to k-fault containment is likely unrealistic given the limited space resource of sensor network platforms). Each node q can maintain a list of recent beacon value for its neighbors; a list item for neighbor p contain the difference between C_q and the corresponding timestamp of p's most recent beacon. In this way, q has the ability to estimate the value of C_p for any neighbor p.

We describe fault containment for node q upon receiving a beacon m from neighbor p. To begin, q estimates the set Q of global clock values for its neighborhood, including C_q itself, C_p from the timestamp of m, and estimates for the remaining neighbors from the list of recent beacon values. The next step of containment is for q to test Q for a single outlier: set Q has a single outlier if

$$(\exists x \in Q : (\forall y, z \in Q \setminus \{x\} : |y - z| \leq \xi_0) \wedge (\forall y \in Q \setminus \{x\} : |x - y| > \xi_1))$$

for appropriate constants ξ_0 and ξ_1. When there is a positive test for an outlier $x \in Q$, we have two cases, either $x = q$ or x represents some neighbor of q. If $x = q$, then node q can adopt a new global from beacon m; if $x \neq q$, then q can discard m because it is presumably faulty.

There are pitfalls in the fault containment described above. First, the notion of an outlier is ambiguous when a node q has only one neighbor: in this situation, fault containment should not be used. Second, fault containment could inhibit self-stabilization. For example, suppose a single link (p, q) joins two dense sub-networks, and nodes p and q find each other to be outliers while agreeing with many other neighbors. Here, discarding beacons prevents clock synchronization in the network. A practical remedy to this is to use the idea of a reset timer to limit the application of fault containment (see [16]), so that the heuristic of fault containment is used infrequently and the protocol falls back to self-stabilization if containment does not quickly repair the state.

4   Conclusion

The apparently simple converge-to-max protocol turns out not to be so simple when realistic factors of the sensor network model (skew, message delay, finite clock domain), and this is seen in the stabilization analysis. It is our opinion that real-time protocols, widely used in practice, should be further investigated with regard to stabilizing fault tolerance.

One reviewer of this paper commented on the presentation's lack of formality, finding amusement that we "get away with defining legitimate states operationally" (likely referring to Section 3.2). We agree that the structure of provisional stability during a sequence of demotions, can be further formalized. The results of Section 3.2 were motivated by observing the behavior of the converge-to-max protocol during experiments on a testbed of 35 MicaZ motes. Whereas previous papers [11,12] describe the protocol as synchronizing to the fastest clock, we sometimes observed that the property of being "fastest" changed over the course of several hours; we also observed cases where multiple "fastest" clocks occured. While these experimental results could be attributed to factors such as noise in the timestamping of messages and nonzero drift, we found that even in the model of this paper, there can occur periods of provisional stability. Users of sensor networks and application programmers care about the stability of properties relevant to application requirements, mainly in some synchrony bound on the difference between clocks at different nodes, and a bound relating elapsed time, as measured by clocks, to real time. Ultimately, one would like to formally relate characterizations of clock protocol stability (including demotions, bounded nonzero drift, and bounded noise in timestamping) to application requirements.

References

1. A Arora, P Dutta, S Bapat, V Kulathumani, H Zhang, V Naik, V Mittal, H Cao, M Demirbas, M Gouda, Y Choi, T Herman, S Kulkarni, U Arumugam, M Nesterenko, A Vora, M Miyashita. A line in the sand: a wireless sensor network for target detection, classification, and tracking. *Computer Networks* 46(5):605-634, 2004.
2. G Werner-Allen, G Tewari, A Patel, M Welsh, R Nagpal. Firefly-inspired sensor network synchronicity with realistic radio effects. Sensys'05, pp. 142-153, 2005.
3. B Sundararaman, U Buy, A Kshemkalyani. Clock synchronization for wireless sensor networks: a survey. *Ad Hoc Networks*, 3:281-323, 2005.
4. RE Mirollo, SH Strogatz. Synchronization of pulse-coupled biological oscillators. *SIAM Journal of Applied Mathematics* 50(6):1645-1662, 1990.
5. YW Hong, A Scaglione. Time synchronization and reach-back communications with pulse-coupled oscillators for UWB wireless ad hoc networks. In Proceedings of IEEE Conference on Ultra Wideband Systems and Technologies, pp. 190-194, 2003.

6. T Herman. Mote timesync implementation, 2003: http://tinyos.cvs. sourceforge.net/tinyos/tinyos-1.x/contrib/minitasks/02/osu/timesync/

7. Q Li, D Rus. Global clock synchronization in sensor networks. *IEEE Transactions on Computers*, 55(2):214-216, 2005.

8. M Maroti, B Kusy, G Simon, A Ledeczi. The flooding time synchronization protocol. In Proceedings of the Second ACM Conference on Embedded Networked Sensor Systems (SenSys'04), pp. 39-49, 2004.

9. DL Mills. The network time protocol. *IEEE Transactions on Communications*, pp. 1482-1493, 1991.

10. TH Lai, D Zhou. Efficient and scalable IEEE 802.11 ad hoc mode timing pattern formation function. In 17th International Conference on Advanced Information Networking and Applications, pp. 318-323, 2003.

11. TH Lia, D Zhou. A scalable and adaptive clock synchronization protocol in IEEE 802.11-based multihop ad hoc networks. In The 2nd IEEE International Conference on Mobile Adhoc and Sensor Systems, pp. 551-558, 2005.

12. P Rauschert, A Honarbacht, A Kummert. The predictive timer synchronization function - efficient network synchronization of MANETs. In Proceedings of the 7th IASTED International Conference on Signal and Image Processing (SIP'05), 2005.

13. JE Burns, MG Gouda, RE Miller. Stabilization and pseudo-stabilization. *Distributed Computing* 7:35-42, 1993.

14. JM Couvreur, N Francez, MG Gouda. Asynchronous unison. In *Proceedings of the 12th International Conference on Distributed Computing Systems (ICDCS'92)*, pp. 486-493, 1992.

15. A Arora and MG Gouda. Distributed reset. *IEEE Transactions on Computers* 43(9):1026-1038, 1994.

16. S Ghosh, A Gupta, T Herman, SV Pemmaraju. Fault-containing self-stabilizing algorithms. In *Proceedings of the Fifteenth Annual ACM Symposium on Principles of Distributed Computing (PODC'96)*, pp. 45-54, 1996.

17. M Lemmon, J Ganguly, L Xia. Model-based clock synchronization in networks with drifting clocks. In Proceedings of the 2000 Pacific Rim International Symposium on Dependable Computing, pp. 177-185, 2000.

18. JE Elson, L Girod, D Estrin. Fine-grained network time synchronization using reference broadcasts. The Fifth Symposium on Operating Systems Design and Implementation (OSDI02), pp. 147-163, 2002.

19. S Ganeriwal, R Kumar, MB Srivastava. Timing-sync protocol for sensor networks. In Proceedings of the First ACM Conference on Embedded Networked Sensor Systems (SenSys'03), pp. 138-149, 2003.

20. JP Sheu, CM Chao, CW Sun. A clock synchronization algorithm for multi-hop wireless ad hoc networks. In Proceedings of the 24th International Conference on Distributed Computing Systems (ICDCS'04). pp. 574-581, 2004.

Self-stabilizing Byzantine Digital Clock Synchronization

Ezra N. Hoch, Danny Dolev*, and Ariel Daliot

School of Engineering and Computer Science,
The Hebrew University of Jerusalem, Israel
{ezraho, dolev, adaliot}@cs.huji.ac.il

Abstract. We present a scheme that achieves self-stabilizing *Byzantine* digital clock synchronization assuming a "synchronous" system. This synchronicity is established by the assumption of a common "beat" delivered with a regularity in the order of the network message delay, thus enabling the nodes to execute in lock-step. The system can be subjected to severe transient failures with a permanent presence of *Byzantine* nodes. Our algorithm guarantees eventually synchronized digital clock counters, i.e. common increasing integer counters associated with each beat. We then show how to achieve regular clock synchronization, progressing at real-time rate and with high granularity, from the synchronized digital clock counters.

There is one previous self-stabilizing *Byzantine* clock synchronization algorithm, which also converges in linear time (relying on an underlying pulse mechanism), but it requires to execute and terminate *Byzantine* agreement in between consecutive pulses. Such a scheme, although it does not assume a synchronous system, cannot be easily transformed to a synchronous system in which the pulses (beats) are in the order of the message delay time apart. The only other digital clock synchronization algorithm operating in a similar synchronous model converges in expected exponential time. Our algorithm converges (deterministically) in linear time.

1   Introduction

Clock synchronization is a very fundamental task in distributed systems. The vast majority of distributed tasks require some sort of synchronization; and clock synchronization is a very straightforward and intuitive tool for supplying this. It thus makes sense to require an underlying clock synchronization mechanism to be highly fault-tolerant. A self-stabilizing algorithm seeks to attain synchronization once lost; a *Byzantine* algorithm assumes synchronization is never lost and focuses on containing the influence of the permanent presence of faulty nodes.

We consider a system in which the nodes execute in lock-step by regularly receiving a common "pulse" or "tick" or "beat". We will use the "beat" notation

---

* Part of the work was done while the author visited Cornell University. This research was supported in part by ISF, NSF, CCR, and AFSOR.

A.K. Datta and M. Gradinariu (Eds.): SSS 2006, LNCS 4280, pp. 350–362, 2006.

in order to stay clear of any confusion with "pulse synchronization" or "clock ticks". Should the beat interval be at least as long as the worst-case execution-time for terminating *Byzantine* agreement, then the system becomes, in a sense, similar to classic non-stabilizing systems, in which algorithms are initialized synchronously.[1] On the other hand, should the pulse interval length be in the order of the communication end-to-end delay, then the problem becomes agreeing on beat-counters or on "special" beats among the frequent common beats received.

The digital clock synchronization problem is to ensure that eventually all the correct nodes hold the same value of the beat counter (*digital clock*) and as long as enough nodes remain correct, they will continue to hold the same value and to increase it by one following each beat.

The mode of operation of the scheme proposed in this paper is to initialize at every beat *Byzantine* consensus on the digital clocks. Thus, after a number of beats (or *rounds*), which equals the bound for terminating *Byzantine* consensus, say Δ, all correct nodes have identical views on an agreed digital clock value of Δ rounds ago. Based on this global state, a decision is taken at every node how to adjust its local digital clock. At each beat, if the two most recently terminated consensus instances show consecutive digital clock values then the node increments its digital clock and initializes a new consensus instance on this updated digital clock value. If the digital clocks are not synchronized, the new consensus instance is initialized with the "zero" value. The algorithm converges within $3 \cdot \Delta$ rounds. We use "clock"and "digital clock" interchangeably.

Related work: We present a self-stabilizing *Byzantine* clock synchronization algorithm that assumes that common beats are received synchronously (simultaneously) and in the order of the message delay apart. The clocks progress at real-time rate. Thus, when the clocks are synchronized, in-spite of permanent *Byzantine* faults, the clocks may accurately estimate real-time.[2] Following transient failures, and with on-going *Byzantine* faults, the clocks will synchronize within a finite time and will progress at real-time rate, although the actual clock-reading values will not be directly correlated to real-time. Many applications utilizing the synchronization of clocks do not really require the exact real-time notion (see [12]). In such applications, agreeing on a common clock reading is sufficient as long as the clocks progress within a linear envelope of any real-time interval. Clock synchronization in a similar model has earlier been denoted as "digital clock synchronization" ([1,8,10,14]) or "synchronization of phase-clocks" ([11]), in which the goal is to agree on continuously incrementing counters associated with the beats. The convergence time in those papers is not linear, whereas in our solution it is linear.

The additional requirement of tolerating permanent *Byzantine* faults poses a special challenge for designing self-stabilizing distributed algorithms due to the capability of malicious nodes to hamper stabilization. This difficulty may be

---

[1] See [6] for such a self-stabilizing *Byzantine* clock synchronization algorithm, which executes on top of a self-stabilizing *Byzantine* pulse-synchronization primitive.

[2] All the arguments apply also to the case where there is a small bounded drift among correct clocks.

indicated by the remarkably few algorithms resilient to both fault models (see [3] for a short review). The digital clock synchronization algorithms in [9] are, to the best of our knowledge, the first self-stabilizing algorithms that are tolerant to *Byzantine* faults. The randomized algorithm, presented in [9], operating in the same model as in the current paper, converges in expected exponential time.

In [6] we have previously presented a self-stabilizing *Byzantine* clock synchronization algorithm, which converges in linear time and does not assume a synchronous system. That algorithm executes on top of a pulse synchronization primitive with intervals that allow to execute *Byzantine* agreement in between. The solution presented in the current paper only assumes that the (synchronously received) beats are on the order of the message delay apart and also converges in linear time. In [2] and [5] two pulse synchronization procedures are presented that do not assume any sort of prior synchronization such as common beats. One is biologically inspired and the other utilizes a self-stabilizing Byzantine agreement algorithm developed in [4]. Both these pulse synchronization algorithms are complicated and have complicated proofs, while the current solution is achieved in a relatively straightforward manner and its proofs are simpler. Due to the relative simplicity of the algorithm, formal verification methods, as were used in [13], can be used to increase the confidence in the correctness of the proposed algorithm. An additional advantage of the current solution is that it can be implemented without the use of local physical timers at the nodes.

2   Model

We consider a fully connected network of n nodes. All the nodes are assumed to have access to a "global beat system" that provides "beats" with regular intervals. The communication network and all the nodes may be subject to severe transient failures, which might eventually leave the system in an arbitrary state. The algorithm tolerates a permanent fraction, $f < \frac{n}{4}$, of faulty *Byzantine* nodes.

We say that a node is *Byzantine* if it does not follow the instructed algorithm and *non-Byzantine* otherwise. Thus, a node that has crashed or experiences some other fault that does not allow it to exactly follow the algorithm as instructed, is considered *Byzantine*, even if it does not behave maliciously. A non-*Byzantine* node will therefore be called *non-faulty*.

We assume that the network has bounded time on message delivery when it behaves coherently. Nodes are instructed to send their messages immediately after the delivery of a beat from the global beat system. We assume that message delivery and the processing involved can be completed between two consecutive global beats. More specifically, the time required for message delivery and message processing is called a *round*, and we assume that the time interval between global beats is greater than and in the order of such a round.

At times of transient failures there can be any number of concurrent *Byzantine* faulty nodes; the turnover rate between faulty and non-faulty behavior of the nodes can be arbitrarily large and the communication network may behave arbitrarily. Eventually the system behaves coherently again. At such a state a non-faulty node may find itself in an arbitrary state.

Definition 1. *The system is* coherent *if there are at most f Byzantine nodes, messages arrive and are processed at their non-faulty destinations between two consecutive beats.*

Since a non-faulty node may find itself in an arbitrary state, there should be some time of continues non-faulty operation before it can be considered correct.

Definition 2. *A non-faulty node is considered* correct *only if it remains non-faulty for Δ_{node} rounds during which the system is coherent.*[3]

Denote by $DigiClock_p(r)$ the value of the digital clock at node p at beat r. We say that the system is in a *synchronized_ state* if for all correct nodes the value of their *DigiClock* is identical.

Definition 3. The digital-clock synchronization problem

Convergence: *Starting from an arbitrary system state, the system reaches a synchronized_ state after a finite time.*

Closure: *If at beat r the system is in a synchronized_ state then for every r', $r' \geq r$,*
  1. *the system is in a synchronized_ state at beat r'; and*
  2. *$DigiClock(r') = (DigiClock(r) + r' - r) \mod overlap$,*[4] *at each correct node.*

Note that the algorithm parameters n, f, as well as the node's id are fixed constants and thus considered part of the incorruptible correct code. Thus we assume that non-faulty nodes do not hold arbitrary values of these constants.

2.1 The Byzantine Consensus Protocol

Our digital clock synchronization algorithm utilizes a *Byzantine* consensus protocol as a sub-routine. We will denote this protocol by $\mathcal{BC}$. We require the regular conditions of Consensus from $\mathcal{BC}$, in addition to one additional requirement. That is, in $\mathcal{BC}$ the following holds:

  1. Agreement: All non-faulty nodes terminate $\mathcal{BC}$ with the same output value.
  2. Validity: If all non-faulty nodes have the same initial value v, then the output value of all non-faulty nodes is v.
  3. Termination: All non-faulty nodes terminate $\mathcal{BC}$ within Δ rounds.
  4. Solidarity. If the non-faulty nodes agree on a value v, such that $v \neq \perp$ (where $\perp$ denotes a non-value), then there are at least $n - 2 \cdot f$ non-faulty nodes with initial value v.

---

[3] The assumed value of Δ_{node} in the current paper will be defined later.
[4] "overlap" is the wrap around of the variable $DigiClock$. All additions to $DigiClock$ in the rest of the paper are assumed to be (*mod overlap*).

Remark 1. Note that for $n > 4f$ the "solidarity" requirement implies that if the *Byzantine* consensus is started with at most $\frac{n}{2}$ non-faulty nodes with the same value, then all non-faulty nodes terminate with the value $\perp$.

As we commented above, since $\mathcal{BC}$ requires the nodes to maintain a consistent state throughout the protocol, a non-faulty node that has recently recovered from a transient fault cannot be considered correct. In the context of this paper, a non-faulty node is considered *correct* once it remains non-faulty for at least $\Delta_{node} = \Delta + 1$ and as long as it continues to be non-faulty.

In Appendix A we discuss how typical synchronous *Byzantine* consensus protocols can be used as such a $\mathcal{BC}$ protocol. The specific examples we discuss have two early stopping features: First, termination is achieved within $2f + 4$ of our rounds. If the number of actual *Byzantine* nodes is $f' \leq f$ then termination is within $2f' + 6$ rounds. Second, if all non-faulty nodes have the same initial value, then termination is within 4 rounds.

The symbol Δ denotes the bound on the number of rounds it takes $\mathcal{BC}$ to terminate at all correct nodes. That is, if $\mathcal{BC}$ has some early stopping feature, we still wait until Δ rounds pass. This means that the early stopping may improve the message complexity, but not the time complexity. By using the protocols in Appendix A, we can set $\Delta := 2f + 4$ rounds.

3   Digital Clock Synchronization Algorithm

The following digital clock synchronization algorithm tolerates up to $f < \frac{n}{4}$ concurrent *Byzantine* faults. We target for the digital clocks to be incremented by "1" every beat and we target at achieving synchronization of these digital clocks.

3.1   Intuition for the Algorithm

The idea behind our algorithm is that each node runs many simultaneous *Byzantine* consensus protocols. In each round of the algorithm it executes a single round in each of the *Byzantine* consensus protocols, but each *Byzantine* consensus protocol instance is executed with a different round number. That is, if $\mathcal{BC}$ takes Δ rounds to terminate, then the node runs Δ concurrent instances of it, where, for the first one it executes the first round, for the second it executes the second round, and in general for the ith $\mathcal{BC}$ protocol it executes the ith round. We index a $\mathcal{BC}$ protocol by the number of rounds passed from its invocation. When the Δth $\mathcal{BC}$ protocol is completed, a new instance of $\mathcal{BC}$ protocol is initiated. This mechanism, of executing concurrently Δ $\mathcal{BC}$ protocols, allows the non-faulty nodes to agree on the clock values as of Δ rounds ago. The nodes use the consistency of these values as of Δ rounds ago and the exchange of their current values to "tune" the future clock values.

3.2   Preliminaries

Given a *Byzantine* consensus protocol $\mathcal{BC}$, each node maintains the following variables and data structures:

Algorithm **Digital-SSByz-ClockSync**   /* executed at each beat */

1. for each $i \in \{1, .., \Delta\}$ do
   execute the ith round of the $Agree[i]$ BC protocol;
2. send value of $DigiClock$ to all nodes and store the received clocks of other nodes in $ClockVec$;
3. set the following:
   (a) $v :=$ the agreed value of $Agree[\Delta]$;
   (b) $DigiClock_{most} :=$ the value appearing at least $\lfloor \frac{n}{2} \rfloor + 1$ times in $ClockVec$, and 0 otherwise;
4. (a) if $(v = 0)$ or $(v = v_{prev} + 1)$ then
      $DigiClock := DigiClock_{most} + 1 \ (mod \ overlap)$;
   (b) else
      $DigiClock := 0$;
5. for each $i \in \{2, ..., \Delta\}$ do
   $Agree[i] := Agree[i-1]$;
6. initialize $Agree[1]$ by invoking $BC(DigiClock)$.
7. $v_{prev} := v$.

Fig. 1. The digital clock synchronization algorithm

1. $DigiClock$ holds the beat counter value at the node.
2. $ClockVec$ holds a vector containing the value of $DigiClock$ each node sent in the current round.
3. $DigiClock_{most}$ holds the value that appears at least $\frac{n}{2} + 1$ times in $ClockVec$, if one exists.
4. $Agree[i]$ is the memory space of the ith instance of BC protocol (the one initialized i rounds ago).
5. v holds the agreed value of the currently terminating BC.
6. v_{prev} holds the value of v one round ago.

Note that all the variables are reset or recomputed periodically, so even if a node begins with arbitrary values in its variables, it will acquire consistent values. The consistency of the variable values used for BC are taken care of within that protocol.

Figure 1 presents the digital clock synchronization algorithm.

Remark 2. The model allows for only one message to be sent from node p to p' within one round (between two consecutive beats). The digital clock synchronization algorithm in Figure 1 requires sending two sets of messages in each round. Observe that the set of messages sent in Step 2 is not dependent on the operations taking place in Step 1, therefore, all messages sent by the algorithm during each round can be sent right after the beat and will arrive and processed before the next beat, meeting the model's assumptions.

Note that a "simpler" solution, such as running consensus on the previous $DigiClock$, adding to it $\Delta + 1$ and setting it as the current $DigiClock$ would not work, because for some specific initial values of $DigiClock$ the *Byzantine* nodes can cause the non-faulty nodes to get "stuck" in an infinite loop of alternating values.

4   Lemmata and Proofs

All the lemmata, theorems, corollaries and definitions hold only as long as the system is coherent. We assume that all nodes may start in an arbitrary state, and that from some time on, no more than f of them are *Byzantine*. We will denote by $\mathcal{G}$ a group of nodes that behave according to the algorithm, and that are not subject to (for some pre-specified number of rounds) any new transient faults. If, $|\mathcal{G}| \geq n - f$ and remain non-faulty for a long enough period of time ($\Omega(\Delta)$ global beats), then the system will converge.

For simplifying the notations, the proof refers to some "external" round number. The nodes do not maintain it, it is only used for the proofs.

Definition 4. *We say that the system is* $\mathrm{CALM}(\alpha, \sigma)$, $\sigma > \alpha$, *if there is a set* $\mathcal{G}$, $|\mathcal{G}| = n - f$, *of nodes that are non-faulty during all rounds in the interval* $[\alpha, \sigma - 1]$.

The notation $\mathrm{CALM}(\alpha, \sigma \geq \beta)$ denotes that $\mathrm{CALM}(\alpha, \sigma)$ and $\sigma \geq \beta$. Specifically, the notation implies that the system was calm for at least β rounds. Notice that all nodes in $\mathcal{G}$ are considered correct when the system is $\mathrm{CALM}(\alpha, \sigma \geq \Delta)$.

Note that in typical self-stabilizing algorithms it is assumed that eventually all nodes behave correctly, and therefore there is no need to define $\mathrm{CALM}()$. In our context, since some nodes may never behave correctly, and additionally some nodes may recover and some may fail we need a sufficiently large subset of the nodes to behave correctly for sufficiently long time in order for the system to converge.

In the following lemmata, $\mathcal{G}$ refers to the set implied by $\mathrm{CALM}(\alpha, \sigma)$, without stating so specifically.

Lemma 1. *If the system is* $\mathrm{CALM}(\alpha, \sigma \geq \Delta + 1)$, *then for any round* β, $\beta \in [\alpha + \Delta + 1, \sigma]$, *all nodes in* $\mathcal{G}$ *have identical* v *values after executing Step 2 of Digital-SSByz-ClockSync.*

Proof. Irrespective of the initial states of the nodes in $\mathcal{G}$ at the beginning of round α (which is after the last transient fault in $\mathcal{G}$ occurred), the beats received from the global beat system will cause all nodes in $\mathcal{G}$ to perform the steps in synchrony. By the end of round α, all nodes in $\mathcal{G}$ reset $\mathcal{BC}$ protocol $Agree[1]$.

Note that at each round another $\mathcal{BC}$ protocol will be initialized and after Δ rounds from its initialization each such protocol returns the same value at all nodes in $\mathcal{G}$, since all of them are non-faulty and follow the protocol. Hence, After $\Delta + 1$ rounds, the values all nodes in $\mathcal{G}$ receive as outputs of $\mathcal{BC}$ protocols are identical. Therefore v is identical at all $g \in \mathcal{G}$, after executing Step 2 of that round.

Since this claim depends only on the last $\Delta + 1$ rounds being "calm", the claim will continue to hold as long as no node in $\mathcal{G}$ experiences a transient fault. Thus, this holds for any round β, $\alpha + \Delta \leq \beta \leq \sigma$.   □

Lemma 2. *If the system is* $\mathrm{CALM}(\alpha, \sigma \geq \Delta + 2)$, *then for any round* $\beta \in [\alpha + \Delta + 1, \sigma]$, *either all nodes in* $\mathcal{G}$ *perform Step 4.a, or all of them perform Step 4.b.*

Proof. By Lemma 1, after the completion of Step 2 of round $\alpha + \Delta + 1$ the value of v is the same at all nodes of $\mathcal{G}$, hence after an additional round the value of v_{prev} is the same at all nodes of $\mathcal{G}$. Since the decision whether to perform Step 4.a or Step 4.b depends only on the values of v, and v_{prev}, all nodes in $\mathcal{G}$ perform the same line (either 4.a or 4.b). Moreover, because this claim depends on the last $\Delta + 2$ rounds being "calm", the claim will continue to hold as long as no node in $\mathcal{G}$ is subject to a fault.   □

Denote $\Delta_1 := \Delta + 2$. All the following lemmata will assume the system is CALM(α, β), for rounds $\beta \geq \Delta_1$. Therefore, in all the following lemmata, we will assume that in each round β, all nodes in $\mathcal{G}$ perform the same Step 4.x (according to Lemma 2).

Lemma 3. *If the system is* CALM$(\alpha, \sigma \geq \Delta_1)$*, and if at the end of some $\beta \geq \alpha + \Delta_1 - 1$, all nodes in $\mathcal{G}$ have the same value of $DigiClock$, then at the end of any β', $\beta \leq \beta' \leq \sigma$, they will have the same value of $DigiClock$.*

Proof. Since we consider only $\beta \geq \alpha + \Delta_1 - 1$, by Lemma 2 all nodes in $\mathcal{G}$ perform the same Step 4.x. For round $\beta' = \beta + 1$, the value of $DigiClock$ can be changed at Lines 4.a or 4.b. If it was changed at 4.b then all nodes in $\mathcal{G}$ have the value 0 for $DigiClock$. If it was changed by Step 4.a, then because we assume that at round β all nodes in $\mathcal{G}$ have the same $DigiClock$ value, and because $|\mathcal{G}| = n - f \geq \lfloor \frac{n}{2} + 1 \rfloor$, the value of $DigiClock_{most}$ computed at round β' is the same for all nodes in $\mathcal{G}$, and therefore, executing Step 4.a will produce the same value for $DigiClock$ in round β' for all nodes in $\mathcal{G}$.

By induction, for any $\beta \leq \beta' \leq \sigma$, all nodes in $\mathcal{G}$ continue to agree on the value of $DigiClock$.   □

Denote $\Delta_2 := \Delta_1 + \Delta + 1$. All the following lemmata will assume the system is CALM(α, σ), for $\sigma \geq \Delta_2$.

Lemma 4. *If the system is* CALM$(\alpha, \sigma \geq \Delta_2)$*, then at the end of any round $\beta, \beta \in [\alpha + \Delta_2 - 1, \sigma]$, the value of $DigiClock$ at all nodes in $\mathcal{G}$ is the same.*

Proof. Consider any round $\beta' \in [\alpha + \Delta_1 - 1, \alpha + \Delta_1 + \Delta - 1]$. If at the end of β' all nodes in $\mathcal{G}$ hold the same $DigiClock$ value, then from Lemma 3 this condition holds for any $\beta, \beta \in [\alpha + \Delta_2 - 1, \sigma]$. Hence, we are left to consider the case where at the end of any such β' not all the nodes in $\mathcal{G}$ hold the same value of $DigiClock$. This implies that Step 4.b was not executed in any such round β'. Also, if Step 4.a was executed during any such round β', and there was some $DigiClock$ value that was the same at more than $\frac{n}{2}$ nodes in $\mathcal{G}$, then after the execution of Step 4.a, all nodes would have had the same $DigiClock$ value. Hence, we assume that for all β', only Step 4.a was executed, and that no more than $\frac{n}{2}$ from $\mathcal{G}$ had the same $DigiClock$ value.

Consider round $\beta'' = \alpha + \Delta_1 + \Delta$. The above argument implies that at round $\beta'' - \Delta$, Step 4.a was executed, and there were no more than $\frac{n}{2}$ nodes in $\mathcal{G}$ with the same $DigiClock$ value. Since $\frac{n}{2} < n - 2 \cdot f$, the "solidarity" requirement of

$\mathcal{BC}$ implies that the value entered into v at round β'' is $\perp$. Hence, at round β'' Step 4.b would be executed.

Therefore, during one of the rounds $\beta \in [\alpha + \Delta_1 - 1, \alpha + \Delta_1 + \Delta]$, all the nodes in $\mathcal{G}$ have the same value of $DigiClock$, and from Lemma 3 this condition holds for all rounds, until σ. $\qquad \square$

Remark 3. The requirement that $f < \frac{n}{4}$ stems from the proof above. That is because we require that $\frac{n}{2} < n-2 \cdot f$ (to be able to use the "solidarity" requirement of $\mathcal{BC}$). We note that this is the only place that the requirement $f < \frac{n}{4}$ appears, and that it is a question for future research whether this can be improved to the known lower bound of $f < \frac{n}{3}$.

Corollary 1. *If the system is* $\text{CALM}(\alpha, \sigma \geq \Delta_2)$, *then for every round* β, $\beta \in [\alpha + \Delta_2 - 1, \sigma - 1]$, *one of the following conditions holds:*

1. *The value of $DigiClock$ at the end of round $\beta + 1$ is "0" at all nodes in $\mathcal{G}$.*
2. *The value of $DigiClock$ at the end of round $\beta + 1$ is identical at all nodes in $\mathcal{G}$ and it is the value of $DigiClock$ at the end of round β plus "1".*

Lemma 5. *If the system is* $\text{CALM}(\alpha, \sigma \geq \Delta_2 + \Delta)$, *then for every round* $\beta \in [\alpha + \Delta_2 + \Delta - 1, \sigma]$, *Step 4.b is not executed.*

Proof. By Corollary 1, for all rounds β, $\beta \in [\alpha + \Delta_2 - 1, \sigma - 1]$ one of the two conditions of the $DigiClock$ values holds. Due to the "validity" property of $\mathcal{BC}$, after Δ rounds, the value entered into v is the same $DigiClock$ value that was at the nodes in $\mathcal{G}$, Δ rounds ago. Therefore, after Δ rounds, the above conditions hold on the value of v, v_{prev}. Hence, for any round β, $\beta \in [\alpha + \Delta_2 + \Delta - 1, \sigma]$ one of the conditions holds on v, v_{prev}. Since for both of these conditions, Step 4.a is executed, Step 4.b is never executed for such a round β. $\qquad \square$

Corollary 2. *If the system is* $\text{CALM}(\alpha, \sigma \geq \Delta_2 + \Delta)$, *then for every round* β, $\beta \in [\alpha + \Delta_2 + \Delta - 1, \sigma]$, *it holds that all nodes in $\mathcal{G}$ agree on the value of $DigiClock$ and increase it by "1" at the end of each round.*

Corollary 2 implies, in a sense, the convergence and closure properties of algorithm Digital-SSByz-ClockSync.

Theorem 1. *From an arbitrary state, once the system stays coherent and there are* $n - f$ *correct nodes that are non-faulty for* $3\Delta + 3$ *rounds, the Digital-SSByz-ClockSyncensures converges to a synchronized_ state. Moreover, as long as there are at least* $n - f$ *correct nodes at each round the closure property also holds.*

Proof. The conditions of the theorem implies that the system satisfies $\text{CALM}(\alpha, \sigma \geq \Delta_2 + \Delta)$. Consider the system at the end of round $\Delta_2 + \Delta$ and denote by $\bar{\mathcal{G}}$ a set of $n - f$ correct nodes implied by $\text{CALM}(\alpha, \sigma \geq \Delta_2 + \Delta)$. Consider all the Δ instances of $\mathcal{BC}$ in their memory. Denote by $\mathcal{BC}_i$ the instance of $\mathcal{BC}$ initialized i ($0 \leq i \leq \Delta - 1$) rounds ago. By Lemma 5, Step 4.b is not going to be executed (if the nodes in $\bar{\mathcal{G}}$ will continue to be non-faulty). Therefore, at the end of the current round,

1. the set of inputs to each $\mathcal{BC}_i$ contained at least $\lfloor \frac{n}{2} \rfloor + 1$ identical values from non-faulty nodes, when it was initialized (denote that value I_i);
2. for every i, $0 \leq i \leq \Delta - 1$, either $I_i = I_{i+1}$ or $I_i = 0$;
3. I_0 is the value that at least $\lfloor \frac{n}{2} \rfloor + 1$ non-faulty hold in their DigiClockat the end of the current round.

The first property holds because otherwise, by the "solidarity" property of $\mathcal{BC}$, the agreement in that $\mathcal{BC}$ will be on $\perp$ and Step 4.b will be executed. The second property holds because otherwise Step 4.b will be executed. The third property holds since this is the value they initialized the last $\mathcal{BC}$ with.

Observe, that each $\mathcal{BC}_i$ will terminate in $\Delta - i$ rounds with a consensus agreement on I_i, as long as there are $n - f$ non-faulty nodes that were non-faulty throughout its Δ rounds of execution. Thus, under such a condition, for that to happen some nodes from $\bar{\mathcal{G}}$ may fail and still the agreement will be reached. Therefore, Corollary 2 holds for each node that becomes correct, i.e., was non-faulty for Δ rounds, because it will compute the same values as all the already correct nodes.

By a simple induction we can prove that the three properties above will hold in any future round, as long as for each $\mathcal{BC}$ there are $n - f$ non-faulty nodes that executed it.

Thus, the three properties imply that the basic claim in Corollary 2 will continue to hold, which completes the proof of the convergence and closure properties of the system.   □

Note that if the system is stable and the actual number of *Byzantine* faults f' is less than f, then Theorem 1 implies that any non-faulty node that is not in $\mathcal{G}$ (there are no more than $f - f'$ such nodes) synchronizes with the *DigiClock* value of nodes in $\mathcal{G}$ after at most Δ global beats from its last transient fault.

5   Complexity Analysis

The clock synchronization algorithm presented above converges in $3 \cdot \Delta + 3$ rounds. That is, it converges in $\Omega(f)$ rounds (since $\Delta = 2 \cdot f + 4$ for our $\mathcal{BC}$ of choice).

Once the system converges, and there are at least $|\mathcal{G}| = n - f$ correct nodes, $\mathcal{BC}$ protocol will stop executing after 4 rounds for all nodes in $\mathcal{G}$ (due to the early stopping feature of $\mathcal{BC}$ we use). During each round of $\mathcal{BC}$, there are n^2 messages exchanged. Note that we execute Δ concurrent $\mathcal{BC}$ protocols; hence, over a period of Δ rounds, $\Delta \cdot 4 \cdot n^2$ messages. Therefore, the amortized message complexity per round is $O(n^2)$. Note that the early stopping of $\mathcal{BC}$ does **not** improve the convergence rate. It only improves the amortized message complexity.

6   Discussion

A Scheme for "Rotating Consensuses". Although the current work is presented as a digital clock synchronization algorithm, it actually surfaces a more general scheme for "rotating" *Byzantine* consensus instances, which allows all non-faulty nodes to have a global "snapshot" of the state that was several rounds ago. This mechanism is self-stabilizing and tolerates the permanent presence of *Byzantine* nodes. This mechanism ensures that all non-faulty nodes decide on their next step at the next round, based on the same information.

Our usage of consensus provides agreement on a global "snapshot" of some global state. By replacing each *Byzantine* consensus with n *Byzantine* agreements, this mechanism can provide a global "snapshot" of the states of all the nodes several rounds ago. That is, instead of agreeing on a single state for the entire system, we would agree on the local state of each node. Every time the agreement instances terminate the nodes may evaluate a predicate that can determine whether the past global state was legal. The nodes may then decide whether to reset the non-stabilizing algorithm accordingly.

The next subsection specifies some additional results which can be achieved using this scheme.

Additional Results. The digital clock synchronization algorithm presented here can be quickly transformed into a token circulation protocol in which the token is held in turn by any node for any pre-determined number of rounds and in a pre-determined order. The pre-determined variables are part of the required incorruptible code. E.g. if the token should be passed every k beats, then node p_i, $i = 1 + \frac{DigiClock}{k}$ mod n holds the token during rounds $[k \cdot (i-1) + 1, k \cdot i]$. Similarly, it can also produce synchronized pulses which can then be used to produce the self-stabilizing counterpart of general *Byzantine* protocols by using the scheme in [3]. These pulses can be produced by setting *overlap* to be the pulse cycle interval, and issuing a pulse each time $DigiClock = 0$.

Digital Clock vs. Clock Synchronization. In the described algorithm, the non-faulty nodes agree on a common integer value, which is regularly incremented by one. This integer value is considered "the synchronized (digital) clock value". Note that clock values estimating real-time or real-time rate can be achieved in two ways. The first one, is using the presented algorithm to create a new distributed pulse, with a large enough cycle, and using the algorithm presented in [6] to synchronize the clocks. The second, is to adjust the local clock of each node, according to the value of the common integer value, multiplied by the predetermined length of the beat interval.[5] This way, at each beat of the global beat system, the clocks of all the nodes are incremented at a rate estimating real-time.

Future Work. We consider three main points to be interesting for future research.

  – Can the tolerance of the algorithm be improved to support $f < \frac{n}{3}$?
  – Can the above mechanism be applied in a more general way, leading to a general stabilizer of *Byzantine* tolerant algorithms without using the scheme proposed in [3], which requires pulses that are sufficiently spaced apart?

---

[5] This value need also be defined as part of the incorruptible code of the nodes.

- What happens if the global beats are received at intervals that are less than the message delay, i.e. common clock beats. Is there an easy solution to achieve synchronized clocks? If yes, can it attain optimal precision like the current solution? If no, is the only option then to synchronize the clocks in a fashion similar to [2,5,6]? i.e. by executing an underlying distributed pulse primitive with pulses that are far enough apart in order to be able to terminate agreement in between. In that case, is there any advantage in having a common source of the clock ticks or is it simply a replacement for the local timers of the nodes?

References

1. A. Arora, S. Dolev, and M.G. Gouda, "*Maintaining digital clocks in step*", Parallel Processing Letters, 1:11-18, 1991.
2. A. Daliot and D. Dolev, "*Self-stabilizing Byzantine Pulse Synchronization* ", Technical Report TR2005-84, Schools of Engineering and Computer Science, The Hebrew University of Jerusalem, August 2005. A revised version appears in http://arxiv.org/abs/cs.DC/0608092
3. A. Daliot and D. Dolev, "*Self-stabilization of Byzantine Protocols*", Proc. of the 7th Symposium on Self-Stabilizing Systems (SSS'05 Barcelona), pp. 48-67, 2005.
4. A. Daliot and D. Dolev, "*Self-stabilizing Byzantine Agreement*", Proc. of Twenty-fifth ACM Symposium on Principles of Distributed Computing (PODC'06), Denver, Colorado, July 2006.
5. A. Daliot, D. Dolev and H. Parnas, "*Self-stabilizing Pulse Synchronization Inspired by Biological Pacemaker Networks*", Proc. of the 6th Symposium on Self-Stabilizing Systems (SSS'03 San-Francisco), pp. 32 48, 2003.
6. A. Daliot, D. Dolev and H. Parnas, "*Linear Time Byzantine Self-Stabilizing Clock Synchronization*", Proc. of 7th International Conference on Principles of Distributed Systems (OPODIS'03 La Martinique, France), December, 2003. A corrected version appears in http://arxiv.org/abs/cs.DC/0608096 .
7. D. Dolev, R. Reischuk, H. R. Strong, "*'Eventual' Is Earlier than 'Immediate*'", In Proceedings, 23nd Annual Symposium on Foundations of Computer Science, 196-203, Nov. 1982
8. S. Dolev, "*Possible and Impossible Self-Stabilizing Digital Clock Synchronization in General Graphs*", Journal of Real-Time Systems, no. 12(1), pp. 95-107, 1997.
9. S. Dolev, and J. L. Welch, "*Self-Stabilizing Clock Synchronization in the presence of Byzantine faults*", Journal of the ACM, Vol. 51, Issue 5, pp. 780 - 799, 2004.
10. S. Dolev and J. L. Welch, "*Wait-free clock synchronization*", Algorithmica, 18(4):486-511, 1997.
11. T. Herman, "*Phase clocks for transient fault repair*", IEEE Transactions on Parallel and Distributed Systems, 11(10):1048-1057, 2000.
12. B. Liskov, "*Practical Use of Synchronized Clocks in Distributed Systems*", Proceedings of 10th ACM Symposium on the Principles of Distributed Computing, 1991, pp. 1-9.
13. M. R. Malekpour, and R. Siminiceanu, "*Comments on the "Byzantine Self-Stabilizing Pulse Synchronization" Protocol: Counterexamples*", NASA/TM-2006-213951, February 2006.
14. M. Papatriantafilou, P. Tsigas, "*On Self-Stabilizing Wait-Free Clock Synchronization*", Parallel Processing Letters, 7(3), pages 321-328, 1997.
15. S. Toueg, K. J. Perry, T. K. Srikanth, "*Fast Distributed Agreement*", SIAM Journal on Computing, 16(3):445-457, June 1987.

A $\mathcal{BC}$ Protocol

A typical synchronous *Byzantine* agreement / consensus protocol runs in a fixed number of rounds (Δ) (for practical ones it is about $2f + 4$) rounds (or phases). If such a protocol will be invoked by at least $n - f$ non-faulty nodes, without having in their memory any residue of previous runs of the protocol, it will end up producing a consensus value at all non-faulty nodes. Therefore, it is enough to augment any such protocol with an initial action of resetting all variables used in the protocol when it is invoked.

Our results require that the non-faulty nodes execute a consensus protocol. All synchronous agreement protocols can be converted to consensus. The "Solidarity" requirement poses no problem, since in consensus protocols all nodes exchange values at the first round, and only a value that was sent by $n - f$ nodes (at least $n - 2f$ of them are non-faulty) will be a candidate value at the next phase. It requires setting the default value to $\perp$.

Specifically, the non-self-stabilizing protocols in [7,15] can be transformed to the required $\mathcal{BC}$ protocol. Similarly the self stabilizing protocol in [4] can be simplified to a synchronous protocol satisfying the required properties.

In the context of the current paper each node executes Δ copies of the modules, each copy is separated from the others, therefore, the messages of the non-faulty nodes are separated for each copy. Faulty nodes may behave arbitrarily. Notice that a node that just recovered from a transient fault invokes a clean copy of $\mathcal{BC}$ which it executes correctly, while the other copies may still be affected by the transient fault. Notice that after executing Line 5 of the digital clock synchronization algorithm Digital-SSByz-ClockSync a non-faulty node can distinguish between the Δ copies of $\mathcal{BC}$.

Distributed Edge Coloration for Bipartite Networks*

Shing-Tsaan Huang[1] and Chi-Hung Tzeng[2]

[1] National Central University, Chung-Li, Taiwan 32054
sthuang@csie.ncu.edu.tw
[2] National Tsing Hua University, Hsin-Chu, Taiwan 30013
clark@cs.nthu.edu.tw

Abstract. This paper develops a distributed algorithm to color the edges of a bipartite network in such a way that any two adjacent edges receive distinct colors. The algorithm has the self-stabilizing property. It works with an arbitrary initialization. Its execution model is assumed to be the central daemon, and its time complexity is $O(n^2 m)$ moves, where n and m are the number of nodes and the number of edges, respectively.

Keywords: Distributed system, Edge coloring, Fault-tolerance, Self-stabilization.

1 Introduction

This paper develops a distributed algorithm to color the edges of a bipartite network in such a way that any two adjacent edges receive distinct colors. The algorithm has the *self-stabilizing* property [1, 2]. That is, given any improper edge coloring, the system will automatically adjust that coloring into a proper one. Thus the system is *fault-tolerant* and can cope with *transient faults*.

Edge coloring is useful for many scheduling problems. For example, in the resource-sharing problem there are a set of nodes and a set of resources. If a node can access a certain resource, we then assign an edge between them and thus construct a bipartite network. The next thing is to compute a proper edge coloring for this network. After that, a node is allowed to access the resource when the index of the time slot matches the color of the edge between them. In this way, resource scheduling is done in advance and thus eliminating contention for resources. Similar applications can be found in [3, 4].

Edge-coloring bipartite graphs has been long investigated. In 1912, König found that every bipartite graph is Δ-edge-colorable [5], where Δ is the maximum degree of the graph. Such algorithms began to be widely developed in the late 1970s. In [6, 7], Gabow and Kariv used a divide-and-conquer technique called euler-split, which splits the input graph G into two edge-disjoint graphs and then colors them. In [8], Schrijver developed an $O(\Delta m)$ time perfect matching

---

* This research was supported in part by the National Science Council of the Republic of China under the Contract NSC94-2213-E008-001.

A.K. Datta and M. Gradinariu (Eds.): SSS 2006, LNCS 4280, pp. 363–377, 2006.

algorithm and combined it with euler-split to yield an $O(\Delta m)$ time edge coloring algorithm, where m is the number of edges. Cole et al. later improved the result of [8] by finding a perfect matching in $O(m)$ time and achieved an $O(m \log \Delta)$ time algorithm [9].

Surprisingly, in the field of distributed computing, few edge-coloring algorithms are known [4, 10, 11, 12, 13], because finding an optimal edge-coloring (namely, using the least number of colors) usually involves global operations, such as path augmentation. In addition, people sometimes prefer using more colors in order to make the proposed algorithm faster and easier to comprehend and implement [3, 11], or meet a more restricted fault-tolerant criteria, such as *Byzantine faults* [12, 13]. In [11], Panconesi and Srinivasan proposed a randomized algorithm that uses roughly $1.58\Delta + \log n$ colors and runs in $O(\log n)$ time In [10], they improved the result by using $(1 + \epsilon)\Delta$ colors, where $\epsilon > 0$ is a given constant, and speeding up the time complexity to $O(\log \log n)$ if Δ is sufficiently large. In [4], Herman et. al utilized [10] to derive a TDMA time slot assignment algorithm; they also use $(1 + \epsilon)\Delta$ colors. In [12], Sakurai et. al aimed at not only transient faults but also Byzantine faults and colored tree networks with $\Delta + 1$ colors in three rounds. This result was later improved by [13], which colors arbitrary anonymous networks with $2\Delta - 1$ colors.

In this paper, we propose the first self-stabilizing edge-coloring algorithm for bipartite networks and get an optimal edge coloring by using only Δ colors. The idea is to extend a partial edge coloring to a bigger one by the concept of *alternative chain*, an approach similar to path augmentation. We first demand each node to assign distinct colors to adjacent edges, and thus each edge receives two colors assigned by its endpoints. We say an edge is colored if the two colors are the same, and uncolored, otherwise. It is easy to see that the colored edges of the same color form a matching [14, 15, 16]. Our alternative chain mechanism guarantees that (1) the summation of the size of all the matchings is non-decreasing, and (2) eventually the size of some matching increases. In this way, all the edges are eventually colored properly.

The rest of the paper is organized as follows. Section 2 introduces the computation model and basic ideas. Section 3 presents the proposed algorithm. Sections 4 and 5 are the correctness proofs and time complexity analysis, respectively. Finally, section 6 concludes this paper.

2   The Computation Model and Basic Ideas

A *distributed system* can be represented by a graph $G = (V, E)$, where V is the set of nodes and E is the set of edges. Two nodes are *neighbors* if they are connected by an edge and can communicate with each other. In this paper, we concentrate on edge coloration for bipartite graphs. Edge coloration for G is to *properly color* the edges so that adjacent edges (i.e., edges incident to a common node) are of different colors. For the edge-coloring problem, the system is said to be in a *legitimate state* if and only if it has a proper edge coloring. Ideally, the system should be always in legitimate states, but due to arbitrary initialization or unexpected transient faults, the system might be in an *illegitimate state*. To cope with such situations, we propose a self-stabilizing edge-coloring algorithm so that (1) the system converges to a legitimate state regardless of any initial (possibly illegitimate) state in finite time, and (2) when it is in a legitimate state, it remains so henceforth [1, 2].

The proposed algorithm is described by a set of rules. Each rule has the format: *guard* → *action*, where the *guard* is a boolean function of the state of the node itself and the states of its neighbors and the *action* is a set of program statements. When the guard of a rule for a node is true, we say that the node is *privileged* and the rule is *enabled*. A privileged node can execute the *action* of an enabled rule.

Several nodes may be privileged simultaneously. We assume that there is a *central daemon*, which selects one privileged node to execute at a time [1]. When the selected node finishes the action, the daemon randomly selects another privileged node to execute, and so on. If the selected node has many enabled rules, it non-deterministically picks one to execute. We also assume that the central daemon is fair in the sense that a privileged node eventually has the chance to be selected, and an enabled rule eventually has the chance to be executed.

The proposed algorithm needs to deal with the symmetry problem. In order to break the symmetry, each node is assumed to have a unique ID with the range $[1..n]$, where n is the number of nodes. In this paper, we assume that all the nodes know the value of n.

Let Δ be the maximum degree of G. As already known in references [5] and [17], Δ colors are sufficient to properly color the edges. For the rest of the paper, the colors are numbered as $0, 1, 2 \ldots$, and $\Delta - 1$. In this paper, we assume that all the nodes know the value of Δ.

The color of an edge (x, y) is decided by nodes x and y. Let $C(y).x$ be the color assigned by node x and $C(x).y$ be the color assigned by node y. We say that edge (x, y) is colored if $C(y).x = C(x).y$ And Is Uncolored, Otherwise. That is, a colored edge has a consistent color and an uncolored edge has two colors on the two ends.

Let us deal with the simplest case first: there is only one edge being uncolored while all other edges are properly colored. As shown in Fig. 1, there is an alternative chain identified by the two colors of the uncolored edge. It is not hard to see that a cyclic alternative chain with one uncolored edge in it must be of odd size. However, for a bipartite network, every cycle must be of even size. Therefore, for bipartite networks, the existence of a cyclic alternative chain with one uncolored edge in it is impossible, and the alternative chain containing only one uncolored edge must be a linear one, as in Fig. 1. For the rest of the paper, we may simply use the term "chain" instead of "alternative chain".

According to the above discussion, we can have a simple algorithm, which considers only one uncolored edge with all others being properly colored. The idea is to shift the uncolored edge in a *constant* direction until it reaches an end of the chain. And then, it can be properly colored. The algorithm is as follows.

Each node x maintains two variables for each edge (x, y):

$C(y).x$: the color for edge (x, y) decided by node x with range $[0..\Delta - 1]$;

Fig. 1. An alternative chain with an uncolored edge

$T(y).x$: indicating the shifting direction on the chain with range $[0, 1, 2]$. The operations on this variable are assumed under module 3.

The rules for each node x:

S1: $C(y).x \neq C(x).y \wedge (T(y).x = T(x).y) \rightarrow T(y).x = T(x).y + 1$;

S2: $C(y).x \neq C(x).y \wedge (T(x).y = T(y).x + 1) \wedge (\exists z: C(z).x = C(x).y = C(x).z) \rightarrow \text{Switch}(C(z).x, C(y).x); T(z).x = T(x).z + 1$;

S3: $C(y).x \neq C(x).y \wedge \neg(\exists z : C(z).x = C(x).y) \rightarrow C(y).x = C(x).y$;

Rule S1 determines that the shifting direction is from node x to node y. Rule S2 shifts the uncolored edge from edge (y, x) to edge (x, z). Repeating the shifting, the uncolored edge will eventually reach the end of the chain, and then can be properly colored via rule S3.

However, there may be many chains in the network and they may interfere each other. Therefore, the problem is how to handle multiple uncolored edges, or, how to concurrently shift multiple uncolored edges so that eventually all uncolored edges can be properly colored.

3   The Algorithm

In concurrently shifting multiple uncolored edges, we shall face the problem that shifting an uncolored edge in a chain in a constant direction may not reach an end of the chain. This is because we may have a cyclic chain with even number of uncolored edges in the cycle. We may also face the problem of different chains interfering one another. We give an example in Fig. 2. In the illustration, subfigure (a) is a partial edge coloring and subfigures (b), (c) and (d) are the chains of color pair (0, 1), (0, 2) and (1, 2) respectively. It is easy to see that the cyclic chain of color pair (0, 1) contains even number of uncolored edges, which may be shifted in the same direction and in the same speed. Moreover, that chain may interfere the acyclic chain of color pair (1, 2) because they both contain a common edge of color 1.

To solve the interference problem, we use a locking mechanism with priorities assigned to different chains. And, to solve the multiple uncolored edges in a cyclic chain, we let the node with the maximum ID in the cycle be a turn-around point so that the shifting of each uncolored edge in the cycle changes the direction at the turn-around point, and in this way, two uncolored edges have the chance to meet each other to become colored ones.

Fig. 2. An example of multiple chains

When an uncolored edge shifts over an edge, we lock the edge and mark it with its color pair, denoted as LockPair. LockPairs have priorities. We define LockPair(C_1, C_2) $\geq$ LockPair(C_3, C_4) iff (min(C_1, C_2), max(C_1, C_2)) $\leq$ (min(C_3, C_4), max(C_3, C_4)) in lexicographic order. That is, when we want to compare the priorities for two LockPairs, we first sort the color pair for each of them and then compare the two sorted pairs in lexicographic order. For example, LockPair(2, 5) = LockPair(5, 2); LockPair(2, 5) > LockPair(6, 2). Moreover, we define any LockPair $\geq$ *nil*. When two chains interfere each other, we allow the higher-priority chain destroy a lock but not the other way around.

Finding the node with the maximum ID in a cyclic chain is not an easy task. Each shifting uncolored edge can memorize the maximum ID that it has encountered. However, due to arbitrary initialization, the maximum ID, which the shifting uncolored edge memorized, might not exist in the cycle. If this happens on each shifting uncolored edges, then they may continuously shift in the same direction. Here our solution is to use a counter to avoid shifting without an end.

The counter is reset to zero in two cases: (1) when the counter reaches its upper bound, which is defined to be n, or (2) the shifted uncolored edge visits a node with ID greater than the maximum ID that the shifting uncolored edge memorized.

The uncolored edge also turns around its shifting direction when the counter is reset. By this way, an uncolored edge may turn around its shifting direction several times before it reaches the node with the maximum ID in the cycle, just like a swing pendulum with increasing amplitude.

To sum up, node x maintains the following variables for each neighbor y:

$C(y).x$: the color assigned by node x on edge (x, y), $[0..\Delta - 1]$.

$L(y).x$: LockPair, the alternative pattern $([0..\Delta - 1], [0..\Delta - 1])$ or *nil* if unlocked.

$T(y).x$: the trace of the shifting direction, $[0, 1, 2]$, $2 \rightarrow 1 \rightarrow 0 \rightarrow 2$. All the operations on this variable are assumed under module 3. The arrow, such as $2 \rightarrow 1$, stands for the shifting direction for an edge (x, y). More precisely, if $C(y).x = C(x).y + 1$ holds, it implies that the latest uncolored edge is shifted in the direction from x to y along a chain. On the other hand, if $C(y).x = C(x).y$ holds, it implies that no uncolored edge has been shifted over the edge (x, y).

$K(y).x$: the counter, $[0..n]$, where n is the number of nodes.

$M(y).x$: the maximum node ID memorized by a shifting uncolored edge, $[1..n]$.

In addition, we define two functions $ID(x)$ and $FreeColor(x)$. $ID(x)$ returns the ID of node x. $FreeColor(x)$ returns a free color not appearing in $C(y).x$ for all neighbors y of x, or returns $\emptyset$, otherwise. According to the above discussion, we can write down our edge-coloring algorithm, listed below. A node x is privileged if one of the rules R0,..., R6 is evaluated to be true for an edge (x, y). For the sake of simplicity, we assume that R0 has a higher priority than the other rules, whereas R1,...,R6 have the same priority. In the rest of this paper, when we say that a node x executes a rule with respect to an edge (x, y), we mean that node x executes that rule to change the variables maintained on the edge (x, y) (and the variables on another edge (x, z), for rules R2 and R5).

R0: $\exists z : C(y).x = C(z).x \rightarrow C(y).x = FreeColor(x)$;

R1: $C(y).x \neq C(x).y \wedge (\forall z : C(z).x \neq C(x).y) \rightarrow C(y).x = C(x).y$;

R2: $C(y).x \neq C(x).y \wedge (\exists z : C(z).x = C(x).y \wedge C(z).x \neq C(x).z)$
$\rightarrow \text{Switch}(C(z).x, C(y).x)$;

R3: $C(y).x \neq C(x).y \wedge (\exists z: C(z).x = C(x).y = C(x).z) \wedge (T(y).x = T(x).y \vee$
$(T(y).x = T(x).y + 1 \wedge L(y).x \neq \text{LockPair}(C(y).x, C(x).y)))$
$\rightarrow T(y).x = T(x).y + 1; \ L(y).x = \text{LockPair}(C(y).x, C(x).y); \ K(y).x = 0;$
$M(y).x = ID(x);$
/*Initialize for shifting the uncolored edge in the chain.*/

R4: $C(y).x \neq C(x).y \wedge T(x).y = T(y).x+1 \wedge L(x).y = \text{LockPair}(C(y).x, C(x).y)$
$\wedge (K(x).y = n \vee M(x).y \leq ID(x)) \wedge (\exists z: C(z).x = C(x).y = C(x).z)$
$\rightarrow T(y).x = T(x).y + 1; \ L(y).x = \text{LockPair}(C(y).x, C(x).y); \ K(y).x = 0;$
$M(y).x = ID(x);$
/*Initialize for a turn-around.*/

R5: $C(y).x \neq C(x).y \wedge T(y).x = T(x).y-1 \wedge L(x).y = LockPair(C(y).x, C(x).y)$
$\wedge \neg(K(x).y = n \vee M(x).y \leq ID(x))$
$\wedge (\exists z : C(z).x = C(x).y = C(x).z \wedge L(x).y \geq L(z).x)$
$\rightarrow \text{Switch}(C(z).x, C(y).x); \ T(z).x = T(x).z + 1; \ L(y).x = L(x).y; \ L(z).x =$
$L(y).x; \ K(y).x = K(x).y + 1; \ K(z).x = K(y).x; \ M(y).x = M(x).y;$
$M(z).x = M(x).y;$

R6: $C(y).x = C(x).y \wedge L(y).x \neq nil \wedge$
$($
$\quad (T(y).x = T(x).y + 1 \wedge (L(y).x \neq L(x).y \vee K(y).x \neq K(x).y - 1)) \vee$
$\quad (T(y).x = T(x).y - 1 \wedge$
$\quad \quad \neg(\exists z : L(y).x = L(z).x = L(x).y \wedge T(z).x = T(x).z + 1 \wedge$
$\quad \quad \quad K(y).x = K(z).x = K(x).y + 1)) \vee$
$\quad (T(y).x = T(x).y)$
$)$
$\rightarrow L(y).x = nil;$

Due to arbitrary initialization, a node may assign the same color to two neighboring edges. Rule R0 is used to correct such a situation.

When an uncolored edge reaches the end of a chain, it can be properly colored. Rule R1 is used in that case.

When two uncolored edges (x, y) and (x, z) with $C(z).x = C(x).y$ meet, at least edge (x, y) can be properly colored. Rule R2 is used in that case.

Rule R3 is used to initialize the shifting direction and the LockPair mark of a chain; it also initializes the counter K and memorizes the maximum node ID.

As mentioned before, there are two cases, viz. $(K(x).y = n \lor M(x).y \leq ID(x))$, when the counter is reset to zero and the shifting direction changes at node x. Rule R4 initializes such a turning around.

Two chains may interfere each other, so Rule R5 is used to allow the higher-priority chain to destroy a lock by other chain but not the other way around.

A lock is legal only if it can be traced to an uncolored edge with a consistent trace direction, counter values, and LockPair. Rule R6 is used to unlock an illegal lock.

4 The Correctness Proof

The edge coloration stabilizes when all edges are properly colored and no lock is on any edge, i.e., P1: ($\forall$ node $x : \forall$ edges $(x, y), (x, z) : y \neq z : C(y).x \neq C(z).x$) $\land$ P2: ($\forall$ edge $(x, y) : C(y).x = C(x).y$) $\land$ P3: ($\forall$ edge $(x, y) : L(y).x = nil$). When it stabilizes, no node is privileged. That is, the algorithm is silent when it stabilizes.

It is obvious that by rule R0, P1: ($\forall$ node $x: \forall$ edges $(x, y), (x, z) : y \neq z : C(y).x \neq C(z).x$) will eventually be true. In the following we assume P1 is already true.

To prove the convergence of P2. ($\forall$ edge $(x, y) : C(y).x = C(x).y$), we define a bounded function $F = \sum_{0 \leq i < j < \Delta} |E_{i,j}|$, where $E_{i,j} = \{(x, y) \in E | (C(y).x = i \land C(x).y = j) \lor (C(y).x = j \land C(x).y = i)\}$ is the set of uncolored edges with color i on one end and color j on the other end. Intuitively, the value of F is equal to the number of uncolored edges.

Lemma 1. *After a node x executes R1 or R2, the bounded function F decreases by at least one.*

Proof. To prove this lemma, we check how R1 and R2 effect the bounded function F.

First, consider R1. Since rule R1 makes edge (x, y) become colored without generating any uncolored edge, F obviously decreases by one.

Now, consider R2. Since $C(y).x \neq C(x).y$ and $C(x).y = C(z).x \neq C(x).z$ hold before the node x executes R2, which switches $C(z).x$ and $C(y).x$, edge (x, y) becomes a colored edge and edge (x, z) may become colored or remain uncolored. That is, F decreases at least by one. $\square$

Lemma 2. *After a node x executes R3, R4, R5 and R6, the bounded function F remains the same.*

Proof. Because rules R3, R4 and R6 do not alter any edge's color, F does not change by the moves of those rules. On the other hand, because rule R5 simply transforms an uncolored edge (x, y) into a colored edge and another colored edge (x, z) into an uncolored edge, the number of uncolored edges is unchanged, or, F does not change.   □

Now, we are going to prove that certain nodes eventually execute rules R1 or R2. And then by lemmas 1 and 2, eventually F decreases to 0. To do so, we first show that illegal locks will be cleared. We then show that the node with the maximum ID in a chain becomes a turn-around point. Finally, we show that an uncolored edge eventually reaches the end of an acyclic chain so that the tail node of the chain can execute R1, and that two uncolored edges in a cyclic chain eventually coincide to a common node so that the common node can execute R2.

Lemma 3. *Let (x, y) be a colored edge such that $L(y).x \neq nil$. If all nodes with the same lock of value $L(y).x$ cannot execute R6, then there exists another uncolored edge (u, v) with $L(v).u = L(y).x$.*

Proof. To prove this lemma, we show that we can find a path $x = x_0, x_1, x_2, ..., x_\ell$ such that $L(x_{\ell-1}).x_\ell = L(y).x, K(x_{\ell-1}).x_\ell = K(y).x + \ell$, and edge $(x_{\ell-1}, x_\ell)$ is uncolored, where $\ell > 0$. And it suffices to prove this lemma by letting $u = x_\ell$ and $v = x_{\ell-1}$.

First, let us focus on node x. Since $L(y).x \neq nil$ and node x cannot execute R6, the condition $T(y).x \neq T(x).y$ must hold. Because the possible values for the variable T is 0, 1, or 2, we have two cases to consider.

Case (1) $T(y).x = T(x).y + 1$: Let $x_1 = y$. Since node x cannot execute R6 to set $L(x_1).x = nil$, we have $L(x_1).x = L(x).x_1$. By the statement of this lemma, node x_1 cannot execute R6 to set $L(x).x_1 = nil$ either. Combining the condition $T(x).x_1 = T(x_1).x - 1$, we can infer that node x_1 has a neighbor x_2 such that $L(x).x_1 = L(x_2).x_1, T(x_2).x_1 = T(x_1).x_2 + 1$ and $K(x).x_1 = K(x_2).x_1 = K(x_1).x + 1$. If the edge (x_1, x_2) is uncolored, the path x, x_1, x_2 is what we want to find. Otherwise we repeat the above argument to infer that node x_2 has a neighbor x_3 such that $L(x_2).x_1 = L(x_1).x_2 = L(x_3).x_2, T(x_3).x_2 = T(x_2).x_3 + 1$ and $K(x_1).x_2 = K(x_3).x_2 = K(x_2).x_1 + 1$. Again, we check whether the edge (x_2, x_3) is colored and decide whether to extend the path to another node x_4. The path finding thus proceeds in this way; each lock on the path is of the same value $L(y).x$ and the counter $K(x_{i-1}).x_i$ is one more than $K(x_{i-2}).x_{i-1}$ for each x_i on the path. The path finding must terminate; namely, we eventually find an uncolored edge $(x_{\ell-1}, x_\ell)$ with $L(x_{\ell-1}).x_\ell = L(y).x$. Otherwise we trace to an edge on which the counter variable K exceeds the value n, which is impossible because its range is $[0..n]$.

Case (2) $T(y).x = T(x).y - 1$: We skip the proof because this case is very similar to case (1), except for $x_1 \neq y$.

According to the above discussion, this lemma holds.   □

According to our design, a legal lock should be able to trace to an uncolored edge of the same color pair by the tracing procedure shown in the proof of lemma 3. More precisely, given a lock $L(y).x = LockPair(i, j)$, we can find a path from

Fig. 3. Given a legal lock $L(y).x = \text{LockPair}(1,2)$, we can trace to an uncolored edge $(u, v) \in E_{1,2}$ and all the locks on the tracing path are of the same value $L(y).x$

edge (x, y) to an uncolored edge $(u, v) \in E_{i,j}$ such that all the locks from $L(y).x$ to $L(v).u$ are of the same value, as the example shown in Fig. 3. If the uncolored edge (u, v) is colored by rules R1 or R2, then the locks are cleared by rule R6 in the order from $L(v).u$ to $L(y).x$, one after another. However, an arbitrary initial state may lead to a similar, yet different case: Given a lock $L(y).x = \text{LockPair}(i, j)$, we trace to an uncolored edge $(u, v) \notin E_{i,j}$. For such a case, node u can execute R3, R4, or R5 to set $L(v).u$ a value different from $\text{LockPair}(i, j)$. By Lemma 3, it also implies that all the locks on the tracing path are cleared by rule R6, one after another. Therefore, we have the following lemma:

Lemma 4. *Let (i, j) be a color pair such that (1) $i = j$ or (2) $i \neq j$ and $|E_{i,j}| = 0$. For an edge (x, y) with $L(y).x = \text{LockPair}(i, j)$, node x eventually can execute R6 to set $L(y).x = nil$.*

Now, we begin to prove that rules R1 and R2 are eventually executed if there are uncolored edges.

Lemma 5. *(Deadlock-free). Let (i, j) be the least color pair in lexicographic order such that $i \neq j$ and $|E_{i,j}| > 0$ and let (x, y) be an edge such that $(x, y) \in E_{i,j}$. If no node can execute R1 and R2, node x (or node y) can execute R3, R4, or R5.*

Proof. We prove this lemma by contradiction. Because node x cannot execute R1 nor R2, it has a neighbor z_1 such that $C(z_1).x = C(x).y = C(x).z_1$. Similarly, node y has a neighbor z_2 such that $C(z_2).y = C(y).x = C(y).z_2$. For the sake of simplicity, we assume that no higher-priority lock than $\text{LockPair}(i, j)$ exists, according to lemma 4; that implies that $\text{LockPair}(i, j) \geq L(z_1).x$ and $\text{LockPair}(i, j) \geq L(z_2).y$.

Now we begin to deduce the contradiction. Suppose that neither node x nor node y can execute R3, R4 or R5. According to the relation between $T(y).x$ and $T(x).y$, we have three cases to consider:

Case (1) $T(y).x = T(x).y$: It is easy to check that node x or node y can execute R3.

Case (2) $T(y).x = T(x).y - 1$: Since node y cannot execute R3 and the condition $C(z_2).y = C(y).x = C(y).z_2)$ is true, we have $L(x).y = \text{LockPair}(C(y).x, C(x).y) = \text{LockPair}(i, j) \geq L(z_1).x$. Now, focus on node x. Since it cannot execute R4 and the condition $C(y).x \neq C(x).y \wedge T(y).x = T(x).y - 1 \wedge L(x).y = \text{LockPair}(C(y).x, C(x).y) \wedge (z_1 : C(z_1).x = C(x).y = C(x).z_1)$ is true, we can infer that the condition $(K(x).y = n \vee M(x).y \leq ID(x))$ is false, or equivalently, $\neg(K(x).y = n \vee M(x).y \leq ID(x))$ is true. By these conditions, it is easy to check that node x can execute R5.

Case (3) $T(y).x = T(x).y + 1$: In this case, node y can execute R5; the proof can be easily got by switching the labels x with y and z_1 with z_2 in Case (2).

No matter which case is, either node x or node y can execute a rule, so contradiction occurs. □

Lemma 6. *Let (i, j) be the least color pair in lexicographic order such that $i \neq j$ and $|E_{i,j}| > 0$. After a node y executes R5 to shift an uncolored edge to (x, y), node x can execute one of R1, R2, R4 and R5.*

Proof. We prove this lemma by contradiction. Similar to lemma 5, we assume that LockPair(i, j) has the highest priority in the system.

Suppose that node x cannot execute any of R1, R2, R4 and R5 after node y executes R5. According to our design, after node y executes R5, we have $T(x).y = T(y).x + 1$ and $L(x).y = $ LockPair(i, j). Since node x cannot execute R1 nor R2, it has a neighbor z such that $C(z).x = C(x).y = C(x).z$. In addition, we have $L(x).y \geq L(z).x$ because $L(x).y = $ LockPair(i, j) has the highest priority. By these conditions and by the hypothesis that node x cannot execute R4 with respect to edge (x, y), we can infer that $(K(x).y = n \vee M(x).y \leq ID(x))$ is false. With these conditions, it is easy to see that node x can execute R5. It is a contradiction. □

As we mentioned in section 3, our idea of getting a proper edge coloring is to shift uncolored edges, so that the uncolored edges in an acyclic chain will reach the end of the chain and those in a cyclic chain will eventually coincide to a common node. The shifting direction is decided by rules R3 and R4, whereas the shifting is by rule R5. Recall that when a node x executes R3 or R4 with respect to an edge (x, y), its state is $M(y).x = ID(x) \wedge T(y).x = T(x).y + 1$ and the node x is said to be a turn-around point in the chain containing the edge (x, y). Also note that rules R3 and R4 do not change an edge's color while rule R5 not only shifts an uncolored edge but also copies the variable M, so the ID of the turn-around point is propagated each time an uncolored edge is shifted.

After the shifting direction is initialized, the uncolored edges are shifted in that direction. It is because each time a node y shifts an uncolored edge to an edge (x, y), it also sets $T(x).y = T(y).x + 1$, meaning that node y specifies the shifting direction for edge (x, y) in advance.

However, whether node x accepts that shifting direction depends on the condition $(K(x).y = n \vee M(x).y \leq ID(x))$. If this condition is false, then node x shifts the uncolored edge in that direction. But if this condition is true, node x executes R4, setting $M(y).x = ID(x)$ and $T(y).x = T(x).y + 1$ to become a turn-around point. As a consequence, node y executes R5 to shift the uncolored edge (x, y) in the opposite direction.

That's how an uncolored edge is shifted in a chain: the uncolored edge's shifting direction is changed whenever the counter variable K reaches the upper bound n or node ID is greater than the memorized maximum ID. Informally speaking, it is shifted in a chain like a swing pendulum, with increasing amplitude. If this uncolored edge lies in an acyclic chain, it eventually reaches the end of the chain and becomes colored because the tail node of the chain can execute R1. On the other hand, if it lies in a cyclic chain, it and another uncolored edge eventually coincide to a common node because they eventually have different shifting directions. When this happens, the common node can execute R2 to color these two edges.

Lemma 7. *Let (i, j) be the least color pair in lexicographic order such that $i \neq j$ and $|E_{i,j}| > 0$. For a chain of color pair (i, j) containing uncolored edges, eventually its turn-around point is the node with the maximum ID in the chain.*

Proof. To prove this lemma, we use extremity to show that the node with the maximum ID in the chain eventually executes R3 or R4 to become a turn-around point. For the sake of simplicity, we assume that no node can execute R1 or R2. In addition, by lemma 4, we assume that $\text{LockPair}(i, j)$ has the highest priority in the system. By these two assumptions, for any uncolored edge (x, y) in the chain, node x has a neighbor z such that $C(z).x = C(x).y = C(x).z \wedge \text{LockPair}(i, j) \geq L(z).x$; another endpoint node y has a similar property.

Now we begin to show that the node with the maximum ID becomes a turn-around point. According to the existence of a turn-around point or not, we have two cases to consider:

Case (1) there is no node yet regarded as the turn-around point: Because the chain is of the least color pair, by lemma 5, either one of the endpoints of an uncolored edge executes R3 or R4 to become a turn-around point, or the uncolored edge keeps being shifted in the chain. In the former case, some node becomes a turn-around point and we can then consider Case (2), so we focus on the later case. Because rule R5 not only shifts an uncolored edge but also increments counter variables K, eventually the counter variable $K(x).y$ for certain edge (x, y) in the chain reaches the upper bound n, after node y shifts an uncolored edge to (y, x). Then it is easy to check that node x can execute R4 to become a turn-around point, and we can consider Case (2).

Case (2) the turn-around point is not the node with the maximum ID: Let u be that turn-around point and let (u, v) be an edge in the chain such that $T(v).u = T(u).v + 1$. Moreover, let x denote the node closest to node u in the chain along the direction $u \rightarrow v$ such that $ID(x) > ID(u)$. We show that node x will replace node u as a turn-around point.

Because node u is a turn-around point and $T(v).u = T(u).v + 1$, an uncolored edge is shifted along edges $(u, v) \rightarrow ... \rightarrow (z, y) \rightarrow (y, x)$ in the chain. After node x's neighbor y executes R5 to shift an uncolored edge from (z, y) to (y, x), we have $C(x).y \neq C(y).x$, $T(x).y = T(y).x + 1$, $L(x).y = LockPair(C(y).x, C(x).y)$, and $M(x).y = ID(u)$. By these conditions and by $ID(x) > ID(u)$, node x can execute R4 to become a turn-around point and to set $T(y).x = T(x).y + 1$ and $K(y).x = 0$. As a result, the uncolored edge (y, x) is shifted back: $(y, x) \rightarrow (z, y) \rightarrow ... \rightarrow (u, v)$.

Now, consider the moment after node v shifts the uncolored edge back to edge (u, v). According to lemma 6, node u can execute one of the rules R1, R2, R4 and R5. However, we have already assumed that no node can execute R1 and R2. Moreover, it is impossible for node u to execute R4 because $K(u).v$, whose value is the distance between nodes v and x in the chain, is less than n and because $M(u).v = ID(x) > ID(u)$. Thus the only rule for node u to execute is R5. And after node u executes R5, we have $M(v).u \neq ID(u)$, meaning that node u no longer serves as a turn-around point.

Since Case (1) implies that eventually there is a turn-around point and since Case (2) implies that eventually the node with the maximum ID becomes a turn-around point, this lemma holds.   □

Lemma 8. *Eventually the bounded function F decreases to 0.*

Proof. Consider a chain of color pair (i, j) containing uncolored edges, where (i, j) is the least color pair in lexicographic order such that $i \neq j$ and $|E_{i,j}| > 0$. To prove this lemma, we show that certain node in such a chain eventually executes R1 or R2 so that F decreases, according to lemma 1. By lemma 7, we assume that the turn-around point is the node with the maximum ID in this chain.

Since a chain has two forms, one is acyclic and the other is cyclic, we have two cases to consider:

Case (1) The chain is acyclic: According to our design, an uncolored edge is shifted in the direction from the turn-around point to the end of the chain. When it does, the tail node of the chain can execute R1 to color the uncolored edge properly.

Case (2) The chain is cyclic: It is easy to see that the number of uncolored edges in the chain is even because the network is bipartite. For those uncolored edges, they eventually have different directions due to the existence of the turn-around point. In other words, two uncolored edges eventually coincide to a common node. When this happens, that common node can execute R2 to color the two uncolored edges.

For either case, certain node in the chain can execute R1 or R2. Since lemmas 1 and 2 imply that F is a monotonically decreasing function (if the predicate P1 holds) and since lemma 1 implies that F does decrease when a node executes R1 or R2, the bounded function F eventually decreases to 0 by repeating the argument that certain node eventually executes R1 or R2. Thus this lemma holds.   □

Theorem 1. *Eventually the system stabilizes.*

Proof. To prove this theorem, we show that after the predicate P1 holds, eventually P2 and P3 hold.

Given any initial state, it is easy to see that P1 eventually holds by rule R0. After P1 holds, according to lemma 8, the bounded function $F = \sum_{0 \leq i < j < \Delta} |E_{i,j}|$ eventually decreases to 0. It implies P2, since there is no uncolored edge.

Now, we show that P3 eventually holds after P2 holds. Let (x, y) be an edge such that $L(y).x \neq nil$. According to the contrapositive part of lemma 3, certain lock of the value $L(y).x$ can be set to nil if there is no uncolored edge (u, v) with $L(v).u = L(y).x$. Since P2 implies that no uncolored edge exists, certain such a lock, and eventually all such locks, will be set to nil. By that time, the predicate P3 holds.   □

5 Time Complexity Analysis

In this section, we show that the time complexity is $O(n^2 m)$ moves, where a move corresponds to an execution of a rule. It is easy to see that a node executes R0 with respect to an edge at most once, so there are $O(m)$ moves of R0. It is also easy to see that, when there is a proper edge coloring, a node executes R6 with respect to an edge at most once, and thus there are only $O(m)$ moves after getting a proper coloring. Therefore, the time for getting a proper coloring dominates the time complexity, since its trivial lower bound is $\Omega(m)$ moves. And our goal is to show that getting a proper edge coloring takes $O(n^2 m)$ moves under the assumption that the predicate P1 holds.

First of all, we explain that the time complexity can be got without considering the interference between the chains. Note that two chains interference with each other only when they share (at least) a colored edge, as shown in Fig. 2. Therefore, let's consider two chains that have uncolored edges and can interfere with each other. Let (C_0, C_1) and (C_1, C_2) be the color pairs identify these two chains, respectively, and assume that e is their common edge, which is of color C_1. Without loss of generality, we further assume that an uncolored edge of color pair (C_0, C_1) is shifted to e. Focus on the moment after that shift. It is easy to see that $e \in E_{C_0, C_1}$ so e is no longer a part of the chain of color pair (C_1, C_2). As a consequence, the chain of color pair (C_1, C_2) is divided into two new chains. If the new chain contains uncolored edges, then they are shifted as usual. On the other hand, if it contains no uncolored edge, then all the locks of the value LockPair(C_1, C_2) in this chain are cleared. Note that only the moves of lock-clearance are caused by the interference between the two chains. They are not redaundant moves, because normally they will be executed after coloring the uncolored edges in the original chain; i.e., they are just executed ahead of schedule.

Lemma 9. *For a chain of color pair (i, j) containing uncolored edges, it takes at most $O(n^2)$ moves to make the node with the maximum ID in the chain become a turn-around point, where (i, j), $i \neq j$, is the least color pair in lexicographic order such that $|E_{i,j}| > 0$.*

Proof. Similarly to lemma 7, we prove this lemma by showing that (1) it takes $O(n)$ moves for certain node to become a turn-around point and then (2) it takes $O(n^2)$ moves for the node with the maximum ID to become a turn-around point.

Consider a chain with no node yet regarded as the turn-around point. We use extremity to show that certain node can become a turn-around point in $O(n)$ moves. Since a node can become a turn-around point if it executes R3 or R4, the worst case is that no node executes these two rules, meaning that an uncolored edge is continuously shifted in the chain. Because each shifting, through rule R5, increments the counter variables K, within n moves of R5 certain counter variable $K(x).y$ is equal to n when node y shifts an uncolored edge to an edge (y, x). After that, node x cannot execute R5 to shift the uncolored edge (y, x) because $K(x).y = n$ holds; instead, it executes R4 and thus becomes a turn-around point.

Now, we show that the node with the maximum ID in the chain becomes a turn-around point in $O(n^2)$ moves. This can be easily seen. As mentioned in lemma 7, an uncolored edge is shifted in a chain like a swing pendulum with increasing amplitude. It takes at most n swings for the uncolored edge to reach the node with the greater ID in the chain. And for each swing, it takes at most n moves. Therefore, the node with the maximum ID in the chain becomes a turn-around point in $O(n^2)$ moves.

According to the above discussion, the node with the maximum ID becomes a turn-around point in $O(n^2)$ moves, so this lemma holds.   □

Lemma 10. *For a chain of color pair (i, j) containing uncolored edges, some node in the chain executes R1 or R2 in $O(n^2)$ moves, where (i, j), $i \neq j$, is the least color pair in lexicographic order such that $|E_{i,j}| > 0$.*

Proof. By lemma 9, it takes $O(n^2)$ moves for the node with the maximum ID in the chain to become a turn-around point. Then, in another $O(n)$ moves of R5, some node executes R1 if the chain is acyclic, or some node executes R2 if the chain is cyclic, as shown in lemma 8. This suffices to prove this lemma.   □

Lemma 11. *The bounded function F decreases to 0 in $O(n^2 m)$ moves.*

Proof. It is a direct consequence of lemmas 1, 2 and 10, since the value of F is bounded by m.   □

Theorem 2. *The system stabilizes in $O(n^2 m)$ moves.*

Proof. It is a direct consequence of lemma 11, based on the reason mentioned at the beginning of this section.   □

6   Concluding Remarks

We have presented a distributed algorithm to color the edges of bipartite networks. The algorithm can be started with an arbitrary initialization of the variables because the algorithm has the self-stabilizing property.

There are three main ingredients in the algorithm. In a serial algorithm, one can easily maintain the color of an edge no matter it is colored or not. However, in a distributed environment, the color of an edge must be agreed by the two nodes connected by the edge. The way we assign the color on either side of an edge and decide the color of the edge is new. Locking mechanism is also an important ingredient of the algorithm. Finally, the way to make two shifted uncolored edges in a cyclic chain meet is another important new idea.

The last idea has potential applications in self-stabilizing systems. Tokens are widely used in self-stabilizing systems. Multiple tokens circulation in a cycle is usually considered incorrect. If the cycle is embedded in a network and no one knows the maximum node ID in the cycle, then the turning around mechanism proposed in the algorithm can be adopted to maintain only one token circulating in the cycle.

References

1. Dijkstra, E.W.: Self-stabilizing systems in spite of distributed control. Communications of the ACM **17** (1974) 643–644
2. Dolev, S.: Self-stabilization. MIT Press (2000)
3. Durand, D., Jain, R., Tseytlin, D.: Parallel I/O scheduling using randomized, distributed edge coloring algorithms. Journal of parallel and distributed computing **63** (2003) 611–618
4. Herman, T., Pirwani, I., Pemmaraju, S.: Oriented edge colorings and link scheduling in sensor networks. In: International Conference on communication Software and Middleware. (2006) 1–6
5. König, D.: Über graphen und ihre anwendung auf determinententheorie und mengenlehre. Math. Ann **77** (1916) 453–465
6. Gabow, H.N., Kariv, O.: Algorithms for edge coloring bipartite graphs. In: Conference of the 10th annual ACM symposium on theory of computing. (1978) 184–192
7. Gabow, H.N., Kariv, O.: Algorithms for edge coloring bipartite graphs and multigraphs. SIAM Journal on Computing **11**(1) (1982) 117–129
8. Schrijver, A.: Bipartite edge coloring in $O(\Delta m)$ time. SIAM Journal on Computing **28** (1999) 841–846
9. Cole, R., Ost, K., Schirra, S.: Edge-coloring bipartite multigraphs in $O(E \log D)$ time. Combinatorica **21**(1) (2001) 5–12
10. Grable, D., Panconesi, A.: Nearly optimal distributed edge-coloring in $O(\log \log n)$ rounds. RSA **10**(3) (1997) 385–405
11. Panconesi, A., Srinivasan, A.: Fast randomized algorithms for distributed edge coloring. SIAM Journal on Computing. **26**(2) (1992) 350–368
12. Sakurai, Y., Ooshita, F., Masuzawa, T.: A self-stabilizing link-coloring protocol resilient to byzantine faults in tree networks. In: OPODIS. (2004) 283–298
13. Masuzawa, T., Tixeuil, S.: A self-stabilizing link coloring algorithm resilient to unbounded byzantine faults in arbitrary networks. Technical report, Laboratoire de Recherche en Informatique (2005)
14. Chattopadhyay, S., Higham, L., Seyffarth, K.: Dynamic and self-stabilizing distributed matching. In: ACM symposium on principles of distributed computing. (2002) 290–297
15. Hsu, S.C., Huang, S.T.: A self-stabilizing algorithm for maximal matching. Information processing letters **24** (1992) 77–81
16. Karaata, M.H., Saleh, K.A.: A distributed self-stabilizing algorithm for finding maximum matching. Computer systems science and engineering **3** (2000) 175–180
17. Rizzi, R.: Konig's edge coloring theorem without augmenting paths. Journal of graph theory **29** (1998) 87

A Dependable Intrusion Detection Architecture Based on Agreement Services*

Michel Hurfin[1], Jean-Pierre Le Narzul[2], Frédéric Majorczyk[3], Ludovic Mé[3], Ayda Saidane[3], Eric Totel[3], and Frédéric Tronel[4]

[1] INRIA Rennes / IRISA – Campus de Beaulieu, 35042 Rennes cedex – France
Michel.Hurfin@irisa.fr
[2] GET ENST Bretagne – Campus de Rennes, 35512 Cesson-Sévigné – France
Jean-Pierre.LeNarzul@enst-bretagne.fr
[3] Supélec, équipe SSIR EA 4039 – Campus de Rennes,
35511 Cesson-Sévigné – France
Surname.Name@supelec.fr
[4] University of Rennes / IRISA – Campus de Beaulieu– 35042 Rennes cedex – France
Frederic.Tronel@irisa.fr

Abstract. In this paper, we show that the use of diversified COTS servers allows to detect intrusions corresponding to unknown attacks. We present an architecture that ensures both confidentiality and integrity at the COTS server level and we extend it to enhance availability. Replication techniques implemented on top of agreement services are used to avoid any single point of failure. On the one hand we assume that COTS servers are complex softwares that contain some vulnerabilities and thus may exhibit arbitrary behaviors. While on the other hand other basic components of the proposed architecture are simple enough to be exhaustively verified. That's why we assume that they can only suffer from crash failures. The whole system is assumed to be asynchronous and furthermore messages can be lost. In the particular case of Web servers connected to databases, we identify the properties that have to be maintained and the alarms that have to be raised. We describe in details how the different replicated levels interact together and, for each level, we precise the reasons that have led us to use a particular agreement service. Performance evaluations are conducted to measure the quality of service of the Intrusion Detection System (quantity of false positives and lack of false negatives) and the additional cost induced by the mechanisms used to ensure the availability of this secure architecture.

Keywords: Intrusion detection, dependability, diversity, COTS, agreement protocols.

1 Introduction

In the context of computer security, the strategies carried out to ensure the confidentiality and the integrity of a system often have a major drawback: they do

---

* This work is supported by the ACI-SI DADDi Project funded by the French ministry of research.

A.K. Datta and M. Gradinariu (Eds.): SSS 2006, LNCS 4280, pp. 378–394, 2006.

not include some specific mechanisms to ensure its availability in the event of accidental or intentional faults. Hence, the system is sensible to crashes/attacks as it can be interrupted temporarily or permanently when such failures occur.

Due to their high complexity, COTS servers have bugs and vulnerabilities that can be exploited by a remote attacker. Within the DADDi project (Dependable Anomaly Detection with Diagnosis), we have designed a first architecture [1] which provides an IDS (Intrusion Detection System) component in charge of detecting intrusions in an information system by comparing the outputs delivered by several diverse servers. In this approach, the idea is to take advantage of the existing software and hardware diversity in a way quite similar to the "n-version programming" strategy. As the COTS servers have been designed and developed independently, they do not exhibit the same vulnerabilities. Moreover, if the n different softwares (that provide the same functionalities) are neither running on the same operating system, nor on the same hardware, one can expect that a request carrying a malicious payload will exploit a vulnerability exhibited by at most one COTS server and will have no impact on the others.

In case of an attack, the aforementioned solution guarantees confidentiality. A confidential information (according to the COTS confidentiality policy) can appear in at most one of the generated responses. Hence, it can be filtered by simple comparison of the generated responses. An attack against integrity may also be detected if the response returned by a server carries enough information to identify all the modifications of the internal server state induced by the execution of the corresponding request. Moreover, this IDS has a nice property: it can detect new attacks whose signatures are not already known.

However, this basic architecture ([1]) exhibits a single point of failure. The availability of the IDS is not ensured. In order to enhance the dependability of this component, we propose now a solution in which classical mechanisms used in the domain of safety (such as replication and agreement services) are combined to the new techniques used in the context of intrusion detection that have been described above (diversity-based approaches). Comparatively to [1], the main contribution of this paper is to provide the design and evaluation of an architecture where both availability and security issues are addressed.

The paper is structured as follows. In Section 2 we briefly describe how to benefit from the software and hardware diversity to detect intrusions. The basic architecture, described in Section 2.1, allows to tolerate attacks against confidentiality and some attacks against integrity. As this architecture does not ensure availability, we identify the extensions required to ensure that the provided services operate without noticeable interruption. Replication of the IDS is presented in Section 2.2. The choice of both the replication scheme (active or passive) and the level of replication n depends on the failure model that has been adopted. We outline two particular failure models (the byzantine failure model and the crash failure model) that are well suited in the context of our study. We argue in favor of the following motivated choice: while byzantine failures will be considered within the set of diversified COTS servers, a crash failure model will be adopted within the group of replicated IDS. In Section 3, we discuss some related works. Section 4 is dedicated to the description of the EDEN [2,3] group communication toolkit. In this section, we outline the fact that the key component of EDEN (namely, a consensus protocol) matches all the assumptions we made regarding the failure models. Section 5 addresses a more specific problem, namely, how to ensure simultaneously availability, confidentiality and integrity in the particular case of web servers connected to databases. We complete the proposed architecture by identifying four types of replicated entities. Then we identify the agreement primitives that have to be used and describe how these primitives are called at different stages of the execution of an HTTP request. In Section 6, we provide some experimental results. Our aim on the one hand is to evaluate the quality of service of the proposed detection mechanism and, on the other hand, the cost induced by the use of replication mechanisms implemented on top of agreement services such as an atomic broadcast service. Finally, Section 7 concludes this paper.

2   Overview of a Generic Intrusion Detection Architecture

2.1   A Basic Architecture to Ensure Confidentiality

The architecture proposed in [1], shown on Figure 1, is clearly inspired by the classical architecture of the "n-version programming" technique used to mask software design faults. Here, our goal is to provide a way to detect intrusions that could affect a COTS server. The basic architecture is composed of three different components: a proxy, an IDS, and a set of servers.

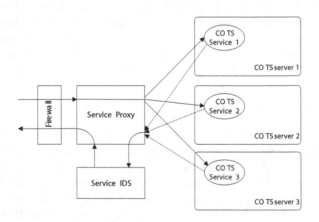

Fig. 1. Basic architecture

The role of the proxy is to handle the client's requests. It forwards the request received from a client to the COTS servers and later forwards the response received from the IDS to this client. It ensures that the COTS servers receive the same sequence of requests and thus evolve consistently. It is the sole part of the architecture directly accessible by the clients. The IDS is in charge of comparing the responses returned by the COTS servers. To select the response that has to be sent back to the client, it uses a majority voting algorithm. If it detects some differences among the responses, it raises an alarm. A set of COTS servers constitutes the core of the architecture: they provide the services requested by the client. All these servers offer the same services but they are diverse in terms of application software, operating system and hardware. This helps reducing the probability of a common-mode failure as it is also the case in the "n-version programming" technique. In the context of our studies, the vulnerabilities of the COTS servers are supposed to be different. If we assume that a malicious payload contained in a request cannot take advantage of two different vulnerabilities, then an intrusion may occur in only one COTS server at a time. In this case, because the other COTS servers are not exhibiting the same vulnerability, they are not affected by this attack and they all provide a same response that is supposed to be different from the response provided by the corrupted COTS server. A majority voting algorithm implemented within the IDS allows to detect the intrusion and to tolerate it.

In the architecture shown on Fig. 1, we use three COTS servers. It allows to tolerate one intrusion on one server without modifying the security properties of the whole architecture. It provides also a way to identify the failed server with a simple comparison algorithm: this would not have been possible on a two-versions architecture without additional mechanisms (e.g., server diagnostic). Once an intrusion has occurred, this architecture with three COTS servers cannot tolerate another intrusion before the reconfiguration of the compromised server has been completed. Of course it is possible to use more than three servers in order to tolerate more intrusions before performing a reconfiguration. Let's note that the reconfiguration can be made periodically or as soon as an intrusion is detected.

This architecture was applied to the particular case of Web servers. In Section 6, we provide some results that allow to measure the quality of service offered by such an IDS mechanism. More experimental results can be found in [1].

2.2   Enhancing Availability of a Basic Architecture

The solution described in Section 2.1 relies on existing software diversity to ensure confidentiality. Yet, as the proposed architecture is based on a single proxy/IDS couple, failures that affect this couple cannot be masked. To enhance availability, a classical solution consists in replicating the proxy/IDS couple. All the replicas of the proxy/IDS couple form a group whose composition may evolve dynamically and is controlled by a group membership service [4]. New replicas can be added by the administrator to enhance the resilience of the architecture. Replicas can be withdrawn from the group due to an administrative decision or because their crash has been detected.

Even if the code of the proxy/IDS couple is quite simple (in particular, it does not analyze the content of the requests issued by clients), one cannot preclude that some replicas will behave maliciously. For example, due to a buffer overflow attack, a replica of the proxy/IDS could deviate from its specification. This kind of faulty behavior is well-known and called byzantine behavior [5] in the literature. In that case, an active replication scheme of the proxy/IDS couple has to be chosen to resist to such faults. Different solutions have been proposed to provide group communication protocols and output voting protocols in the presence of malicious faults [6,7]. All these solutions require an high replication degree: at least $n > 3f$ replicas, where f is the maximal number of faulty replicas, have to be executed concurrently. As all the replicas execute the same code and react to the same external solicitations, a single attack can affect all of them. Hence, the assumption that at most $f < n/3$ replicas can be malicious is a strong assumption that is difficult to guarantee. As long as the risk of malicious behaviors is not totally eradicated, relying on the fact that attacks will just succeed on a limited number of replicas is not a realistic assumption. For this very reason, we believe that byzantine faults have to be addressed at the server level (thanks to diversity) but not necessarily at the proxy/IDS level. Using high-level programming languages with safe memory management combined with formal verification techniques could allow to reduce the risk of a malicious behavior to a very low probability. In that case, less expensive solutions can be adopted. This is the position we adopt in this paper. We assume that a replica of the proxy/IDS couple behaves always according to its specification but may stop prematurely at any time (fail/stop failure model). In this failure model, the set of processes is partitionned into two subsets: the correct processes and the faulty processes. A faulty process is a process that will eventually fail. Conversely, a correct process is a process that never fails. This failure model is consistent with the assumption that an intrusion occurs in only one COTS server at a time. Indeed, [8] shows that there are very few common mode failures in a pool of COTS database servers and a study of the vulnerabilities of IIS and Apache [9] exhibits the same property. As COTS servers are not affected by the same vulnerabilities, our architecture allows to detect intrusions and to tolerate them. This is true for any kind of intrusion and we do not have to make any assumption about what the attacker can or cannot do.

Nevertheless, if an attack has no impact on the behavior of the replicas, it may (1) arbitrarily slow down processes and (2) affect the communication network. This precisely characterizes a purely asynchronous system: there is no bound neither on relative speed of processes nor on transfer delays of messages. However, we assume that this model is augmented with unreliable failure detectors [10]: it allows to solve agreement problems. We also consider *fair-lossy* communication links: if a message is sent infinitely often to a correct receiver, then it is received infinitely often by that receiver.

3   Related Work

Delta-4 [11] was an European ESPRIT project ended in 1992. It focuses on building dependable secure and robust replicated systems that can tolerate both value faults and crashes. The Delta-4 architecture provides fault-tolerance by replication in an open distributed processing environment (where clients are external to the server group). Both active and passive replication schemes [12] are implemented using a group communication sub-system that is structured as a layered architecture and built on top of an atomic multicast protocol [13]. Replication services are used to implement mechanisms that aim at masking intrusions [14]: replicas of a server collaborate to agree on the response that will be provided to the client. Assuming that a majority of the replicas generates correct and identical responses, a valid response is provided to the client even when an intruder has successfully corrupted some replicas. Similarly to the approach adopted in this paper, the replicated security services offered in Delta-4 rely on agreement services. However, assumptions regarding the environment are different. Delta-4 assumes a synchronous communication network.

The DIT (Dependable Intrusion Tolerance) architecture [15,16] was developed in the context of the OASIS program (Organically Assured and Survivable Information Systems) of the DARPA. The goal was to develop Internet servers able to provide continuously a correct service despite the presence of attacks. The DIT architecture is based on the principles of redundancy and diversification. Redundancy is used to increase system availability and diversification is used to increase independence between the redundant sub-systems from the attacker point of view. The design was funded on the two following assumptions. Firstly, intrusions can succeed only on a limited number of components at the same time. Secondly, all non-faulty and non-compromised servers are deterministic (they generate the same response to a given request). The DIT architecture is composed of redundant tolerance proxies that mediate requests to a redundant bank of application servers which implement the application-specific functionalities needed to fulfill the client requests. The architecture includes a diversified set of detection mechanisms chosen for their complementarity. They propose the use of an adaptive redundancy level that is defined according to the alert level in the system in order to make an optimal compromise between security and performance. The proposed architecture is quite similar to the one described in this paper. Yet, we focus on asynchronous systems and we use in our performance evaluation a library of agreement components that do not rely on any strong timing assumptions.

In [17], researchers from the University of Texas at Austin present an architecture for byzantine fault tolerant state machine replication. In this work, several levels of replication are distinguished. Agreement services that tolerate byzantine failures [6] are used to coordinate the activities of the replicas. The system is supposed to be asynchronous and messages can be lost. Our work differs from this one on two points. Firstly, we consider that some components follow a crash failure model while others (the COTS servers in particular) can exhibit arbitrary behavior. Secondly, we are also interested in evaluating the quality of service of the proposed IDS: in practice, a difference between the responses generated by some Web servers does not imply that an attack has really occurred (existence of false positives).

4   The Eden Group Communication Toolkit

In Section 2.2, we expressed the need for availability of the proxy/IDS couple. To fullfill this requirement, replication is a classical solution. However, due to the considered asynchronous model, it can be difficult to implement correctly. To circumvent this difficulty, we have recourse to the commonly used group communication paradigm. We use a group communication toolkit, called EDEN, which has been designed for the particular fail/stop failure model.

More precisely, EDEN [3,2] is a library of agreement components used to implement group communication services in an asynchronous distributed system prone to fail/stop failures. As it will be stated later, group membership and atomic broadcast are the two main services required in the proposed architecture. In the EDEN toolkit, these services are provided using a consensus building block [18]. The design of this key component took as a starting point the Chandra-Toueg $\Diamond S$ algorithm [10]. The protocol is based on the rotating coordinator paradigm. A sequence of rounds is executed. Each round is managed by a coordinator that tries to converge to the decision value. Thanks to a sliding window mechanism [19], each process can be involved simultaneously in up to n consecutive rounds (rather than in a single round as it is the case in most $\Diamond S$ protocols). As each round has a fixed duration, the proposed solution allows to tolerate the lost of consensus messages without requiring a strong synchronization between the different local clocks. A failure detector is used to withdraw crashed processes from the group. To limit the occurrences of erroneous suspicion, long timeouts are used; this has no impact on the performance of the consensus protocol that does not use any information provided by the failure detector. Moreover, a process remains within the group as long as it is not suspected by a majority of the group members. Again, the aim is to avoid a useless and dangerous crumbling of the group when some communication links become temporarily very slow. This conservative strategy is not risky as long as a majority of the members of the group are still alive. When this assumption is satisfied, crashes, messages losses (fair-lossy assumption) and messages delays do not prevent the consensus protocol to satisfy its safety properties (this protocol is indulgent).

5   Case Study: Enhancing Integrity for Web Servers

In Section 2, we have proposed and discussed an architecture for intrusion detection whose availability has been improved. This solution guarantees confidentiality of data managed by the COTS servers. Indeed, even in case of an attack that would reveal confidential information, the COTS servers diversity ensures that only a minority of servers got corrupted. Hence, the majority voting algorithm implemented in the proxy/IDS would filter such information.

Although, as stated in the introduction, ensuring the integrity of these data is not an intrinsic property of this solution. To address this problem, we need additional assumptions about the particular COTS servers that are deployed.

Our choice is to focus on a particular case study, namely a Web server that delivers dynamic content. This technology traditionally implements the storage of this content in a database backend that receives read/write operations issued by the Web server. This latter executes scripts written in an interpreted language (such as PHP) that can query the database backend. These scripts are in charge of translating the SQL replies into HTML/XML code.

An interesting property of this technology resides in the fact that the whole internal state of the COTS servers is located in the database backend. Furthermore, any change to the internal state is carried out by the means of SQL queries. We take advantage of this property in order to ensure integrity of the data. To that purpose, we introduce a second set of proxies located between the Web servers and the database whose goal is to compare the SQL queries submitted by the diverse Web servers to the database. Indeed, unexpected SQL queries issued by a corrupted Web server can threaten data integrity. Using a majority voting algorithm to compare queries submitted to the database allows to detect and mask any attempt to data integrity.

We have identified several prerequisites that must be satisfied in order to improve the dependability of the system : (1) availability of the SQL backend must be guaranteed (2) SQL queries that are transmitted to the SQL backend must not have been generated by a Web server under attack. To ensure these two properties, we have chosen to replicate the SQL backend. In order to simplify the architecture, we use the same replication degree for the SQL servers as for the Web servers. Note that we do not assume that the different SQL servers are functionally diversified, even if with small changes, our architecture would be able to take advantage of such a diversification to detect and mask attacks targeted at the SQL backend itself.

In this section we first briefly describe the proposed architecture and introduce a model that allows us to formally describe the expected properties we want to guarantee and also the kind of attacks we detect. Secondly, we describe the path followed by an HTTP request submitted by a client up to the point it reaches the Web servers. Finally, we depict the path followed by SQL queries induced by a given HTTP request.

5.1   Models and Notations

The proposed solution relies on four distinct groups of entities, called WSP_i, WS_i, DBP_i and DB_i, whose respective roles are explained later. For sake of simplicity we assume that the replication degree is the same at each level. This replication degree is denoted n. Assuming that $1 \leq i \leq n$, the following notations are used to identified these different entities: (1) WSP_i denotes the ith proxy that receives HTTP requests; (2) WS_i denotes the ith diversified Web server. By design, each WS_i is equipped with a wrapper in charge of interacting with the $WSPs$ (its role will be detailed in Section 5.2); (3) DBP_i denotes the ith proxy that acts as an intermediary between the Web servers and their associated databases; (4) DB_i denotes the ith database. By design, DB_i interacts only with its corresponding DBP_i proxy and conversely.

HTTP requests addressed by external clients are ordered by the group of WSPs. The unique sequence that is obtained is called the history $\mathcal{H}$ of HTTP requests. By definition, the request that appears at position x is denoted h_x and thus $\mathcal{H} = h_1.h_2.\cdots h_x\cdots$.

The response generated by a server WS_i, in reply to the request h_x is denoted $r_{x,i}$. If WS_i generates no response (consequently to a crash failure or an attack), $r_{x,i}$ is assumed to be equal to $\perp$.

During the execution of an HTTP request h_x by a server WS_i, a sequence of SQL requests denoted $S_{x,i}$ is generated. Of course this sequence is empty when the execution of h_x does not require access to the database. By definition, $length(x, i)$ is equal to the number of SQL requests generated during the execution of h_x by WS_i. The sequence $S_{x,i}$ is equal to $s_{x,i}^1.s_{x,i}^2.\cdots.s_{x,i}^{length(x,i)}$.

We now define the concept of legality for a SQL query. A query s is legal if (1) it has been produced by a majority of Web servers and (2) its rank is the same in all the sequences of queries produced by these servers. More formally:

Definition 1. *A SQL query s is said to be legal if and only if $\exists x$ such that $h_x \in \mathcal{H}$, $\exists \mathcal{I}$, a subset of indexes in $[1, n]$ such that $\mid \mathcal{I} \mid > n/2$, $\exists u$ such that $\forall i \in \mathcal{I}, u \leq length(x, i)$ and $s = s_{x,i}^u \in S_{x,i}$.*

By definition, a legal SQL query s does not depend on the Web servers that produced it (at least a majority of them). Hence, it is uniquely determined by (1) the index x of its associated HTTP request and (2) its rank into the sequence of SQL queries induced by h_x. So, we will note $s = s_{x,\_}^u$. By definition, when no attack occurs all the SQL requests are legal even in a system prone to failure.

The proposed architecture implements an IDS that guarantees the confidentiality and the integrity of the data managed by the Web servers. When an attack against confidentiality or integrity is detected, the IDS raises an alarm. This happens when one of the three scenarios occurs:

- $\exists h_x, \exists i, \exists j$ such that $(r_{x,i} \neq \perp) \wedge (r_{x,j} \neq \perp) \wedge (r_{x,i} \neq r_{x,j})$
  An attack has occurred since two servers have provided different responses to the same HTTP request.
- $\exists h_x, \exists i$ such that $(r_{x,i} = \perp)$
  An attack or a failure has occurred since a server does not reply.
- $\exists h_x, \exists i, \exists u$ such that $u \leq length(x, i)$ and $s_{x,i}^u \in S_{x,i}$ such that $s_{x,i}^u$ is not legal.
  An illegal SQL query is detected which is the signature of an attack against integrity.

In the rest of this section, we describe in a more detailed manner the path of a request within the system. Each request follows a path composed of two parts. The first part of its journey within the system is mandatory and deals with its processing by the Web servers (we call this part the HTTP path). The second part is optional and is related to the potential SQL requests induced by the HTTP request (we call this part the SQL path).

5.2   HTTP Path of a Request

Leader Election. Each request to be submitted to the system is only addressed to the leader of the group of Web proxies $WSPs$. This leader is elected by a group leader election that is part of the underlying GCS (Group Communication System) called EDEN and described in Section 4. The leader election algorithm has the following property: it maintains the previous leader in its role if it does belong to the new view in order to minimize the perturbation of external clients. Otherwise a new leader is deterministically chosen among the set of proxies WSP that compose the new view. Note that due to the inherent asynchrony of the system, the situation where at a given time multiple proxies may have installed discordant views is still possible. However, all agreement protocols implemented by the GCS (membership protocol, atomic broadcast, etc.) are based on a consensus protocol. This protocol requires that all decisions to be taken, must have been approved by a majority of processes. Hence only the last view to be installed, and its associated leader can be promoted by a majority of proxies at a given time. This property precludes old leader (when it exists) to process any request. To sum up, at any given time, only one leader is supported by at least a majority of proxies and its role is to process requests sent by external clients. Hence all the requests must be addressed to the leader. This problem can be tackled by several mechanisms. We have chosen to use a virtual IP address which is automatically associated to the current leader. When a new view is installed, its leader will start an ARP cache update protocol whose goal is to associated its MAC address with the virtual IP address. Once this protocol has completed, layer 2 network equipment (such as Ethernet switch) will automatically deliver to the leader, all messages addressed to the virtual IP.

We now describe the fate of a request during the part of the path associated to its processing by Web servers. We first describe what happens when no failure occurs. Then we will detail the different possible scenarios in case of a leader failure.

When the Leader Does Not Fail. When the leader receives a request h_x, it broadcasts it within the group of proxies WSP using an atomic broadcast service. Hence, a unique order among concurrent requests is established by this service, so all the Web server replicas WS_i will process these requests in the same order. When no attack occurs the global state of the replicas is maintained consistent. We cannot ensure this property when the system suffers from an attack, since local states of a minority of Web servers and/or associated databases can be corrupted and diverged. But as explained in section 2.1, we are able to detect attacks, hence we can mask them.

Once a request h_x has been delivered by atomic broadcast service to the leader, this latter broadcasts it to the set of Web servers WS. In fact, what really happens is more convoluted than this simple schema, but we will detail this later when we will discuss failure scenarios. For now, we can assume that a regular HTTP request is opened with each of the Web server. This request makes its own progress within each copy WS_i. The leader collects sufficiently many replies $r_{x,i}$, so that at least a majority of them are equal. It is by assumption ensured to succeed since we assume that there is only a minority of failures. By comparing these replies, intrusion alarms can be raised as explained in section 5.1. A unique reply is transmitted back to the client. Once the connection with the client is closed, the leader informs others replicas that the last atomically delivered HTTP request has been processed, and that it can be discarded from their log. To sum up, the set of proxies WSP is building a totally ordered sequence of HTTP requests that can be submitted to the set of servers. By detecting inconsistency in the set of replies $r_{x,i}$ associated with a given HTTP request h_x, they can detect and mask attacks targeted at the Web servers.

In Case of a Proxy Failure. During the processing of a request, failures can occur. This can happen at several different places in time and space. Consequences on the fate of a request are quite different depending on the component that fails and when it occurs. First of all, a failure that concerns a Web proxy that is not a leader is invisible to the outside world since it only triggers the installation of a new view. As explained earlier, we guarantee that the leader remains the same as long as possible such as to minimize the disturbance of external clients. Hence now, we only focus on failures that may affect the leader. Note that any failure of the leader that occurs during the processing of a client request will affect the related TCP connection in two possible ways: a timeout or a connection reset. Anyway, the end user will be notified by its browser that an error has occurred. We assume that he will perform a reload operation. However, we want to guarantee that this operation is safe. To that purpose, we assume that an operation which modifies the database is uniquely identified by the means of its request content (either through its URL that includes an unique identifier, or by cookies included in the body of the request). This will help proxies to detect requests which have been partially processed (i.e that have suffered of broken connections during a leader failure) by the use of a replay detection cache that logs requests until it is safe to garbage collect them.

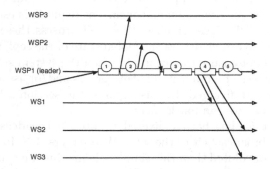

Fig. 2. Critical points in the processing of an HTTP request by the leader

If we analyze the leader behavior, several critical points where failures can occur can be identified : (1) before the leader has initiated the atomic broadcast, (2) during or after the call to the atomic broadcast service but before the delivery operation has occurred, (3) after the delivery operation, (4) during the broadcast of the request to the Web servers WS, (5) after this broadcast. This is depicted by Figure 2.

Case (1) is the most benign since the leader has not started processing the request. Hence, the client will eventually be notified of a TCP timeout error. It can safely reissue its request. In the meantime, a new leader will have been elected, and be willing to process it.

Case (2). The atomicity property of the operation guarantees that all or none of the proxies will deliver it. If they all deliver it, a future replay of the request can be detected and the client can be informed of the returned value. Otherwise, it is naturally safe for the client to replay its request.

Case (3) is similar to the previous case, but the processing of the request has goes further, and we are sure that the request will be delivered to all other proxies. Hence the detection replay cache will have to play its role if the leader fails after this point.

Case (4) is handled by a dedicated mechanism. Recall that we previously stated that once the leader has delivered the query by atomic broadcast, it will initiate a broadcast of the HTTP request to all the Web servers. We stated that it was doing so, by opening as many TCP connections as the number of WS servers. This strategy, if employed, would lead to problematic situations in case of a leader failure during this broadcast phase (broken TCP connections with a Web server). To solve this issue we have introduced a set of dedicated wrappers located on Web servers machines (one wrapper per Web server). Each wrapper has in charge the receipt of a HTTP request, and its transmission to the Web server. It supports broken connection that could arise from a failed leader, and it also avoids duplicate transmission of a HTTP request that can happened after the election of a new leader. Indeed, when a new leader is elected, it starts its activity by replaying the latest HTTP requests which have not been acknowledged by the previous leader. To sum up the role of a wrapper is to mask the potential failure of a proxy leader.

Case (5) is handled similarly to case (4). The new elected leader will interact with wrappers by replaying not acknowledged HTTP requests.

5.3   SQL Path of a Request

In this section, we describe the way we have chosen to deal with SQL queries that can be generated by HTTP requests. Each SQL server DB_i receives its SQL queries from a dedicated proxy PDB_i. This set of proxies forms a replicated group PDB for the underlying group communication system. Contrarily to the first replicated group of proxies, we have chosen here an active replication schema. The goal of this set of proxies is to build a unique order among the set of queries that are submitted to the SQL backend.

To that purpose, we need to give the SQL proxies the ability (1) to link a SQL query $s^v_{x,i} \in S_{x,i}$ with its associated HTTP request h_x (2) to be able to retrieve the index v of the query $s^v_{x,i}$ in the sequence $S_{x,i}$. This can only be achieved at the Web server level. To achieve this goal, we have written a dedicated library as a replacement for the SQL library loaded by the script language interpret (PHP) used by the Web servers. This library can retrieve the index x of the associated HTTP request being processed (by the use of information hidden in a cookie) and it can also enumerate the SQL queries that belongs to the same HTTP request. However, as we will see later, this piece of information is not sufficient to ensure the detection of certain attacks. That's why the total number of SQL queries associated with the previous SQL query h_{x-1} is also logged by our library. This number denoted $length(x-1,i)$ is equal to $\mid S_{x-1,i} \mid$.

The couple $(s^v_{x,i}, length(x-1,i))$ is broadcast by the library to the group DBP of SQL proxies for each SQL query to be executed. Each proxy DBP_i is in charge of building a totally ordered sequence of SQL queries. This sequence must preserve some important properties:

1. It contains only legal SQL queries.
2. Legal SQL queries are totally ordered using the total order relation $<$ defined by: $s_1 = s^u_{x,\_} < s_2 = s^v_{y,\_}$ if and only if $x < y \vee (x = y \wedge u < v)$.

Ensuring the first property. To ensure the first property each database proxy submits only SQL queries that have been received from a majority of Web servers and whose contents are identical. By definition, this is a non-blocking operation for legal queries. A non legal query $s^u_{x,j}$ associated with an HTTP request h_x will be detected by a proxy server DBP_i according to the following rules : (i) its content differs from the contents of the majority of queries received. It can be discarded and an alarm can be raised. (ii) The query is surnumerous. The detection of such a case might be delayed until the arrival of the next HTTP request that generates SQL queries. To simplify the discussion[1], assume it is h_{x+1}. Since h_{x+1} generates at least one SQL query, this one will be sent to DBP_i along with a counter $length(x,\_)$. This counter $length(x,\_)$ will be strictly smaller than the rank u associated with the surnumerous query $s^u_{x,j}$. An alarm can be raised. (iii) A query can be missing. This case can happen on a Web server that is under attack. This may be detected either (a) by the first set of proxies WSP that should detect differences in the replies of the corresponding HTTP request (due to the fact that the missing SQL reply may induce a different reply to the HTTP request from the corrupted server) or (b) by the inconsistency of the counters associated with the next HTTP request that generates SQL queries (similarly to rule (ii)).

Ensuring the second property. The second property which could be qualified of a FIFO order is implemented by the use of counters carried by the SQL queries. It ensures that the state of each database is maintained consistent, since they will execute the same set of queries in the same order.

---

[1] An HTTP request can generate no SQL query. In that case, SQL proxies will not be able to detect that the last SQL query was surnumerous.

Dealing with the response to an SQL query. The reply value of the database to a SQL query is simply transmitted by a SQL proxy to its associated Web server. However, note that a database proxy can already have submitted a SQL query to its associated database even before the Web server has initiated the corresponding SQL query. This desynchronization can be due to either the asynchrony assumption, or to a successful attack on the Web server. This problem is solved by logging the results of SQL queries that have been anticipatory sent to the database. It is sufficient to replay the results when the Web server will issue the corresponding requests.

6   Experimental Results

The performance of the proposed solution can be analyzed according to two metrics. First we analyze the quality of service of the IDS itself. Then we consider the cost induced by the replication. The proposed solution has an impact on the time required to execute a single request.

6.1   Quality of Service Offered by the IDS

The basic architecture presented in Section 2 was applied to Web servers and the results were presented in [1].

In summary, in the test carried out, the architecture was composed of three servers: an Apache server running on MacOS-X, a thttpd server running on Linux, and an IIS 5.0 running on Windows. They contained a copy of the Supelec institute Web site. They were configured so as to generate a minimum of differences in their respective outputs. The three servers were fed with the requests logged during one month (it represents more than 800.000 requests).

During the tests, we observed the alerts emitted by the IDS. Only 0.016% of the HTTP requests generated an alert. In one month, the administrator must thus analyze 150 alerts, that means about 5 alerts a day. We observed that only four first alert types were false positives (22% of the alerts). These results show that the IDS generates very few false alarms (false positives), and did not miss any intrusion (no false negatives). This is quite a good result, and it demonstrates the quality of the approach proposed.

6.2   Atomic Broadcast Performances

Let us now consider the mechanisms used to increase the availability of the system. As each HTTP request involves the use of the atomic broadcast service, its cost must be carefully evaluated. Moreover, since HTTP requests are sequentially executed, the throughput of the service can be severely degraded. This drawback is not specific to our solution [17]. In Figures 3 and 4, we aim at identifying some of the parameters that may impact the cost of the atomic broadcast service. Figure 3 gives the mean request delivering duration for a fixed arrival frequency of external requests (one request every 400ms). We sample this measure for a varying number of processes and different consensus round durations. Figure 3 clearly shows that the number of processes in the group (as long

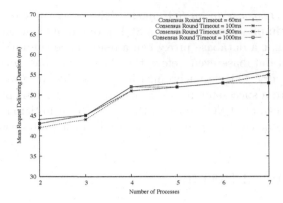

Fig. 3. Mean request delivering duration (for fixed arrival frequency of requests = 400ms

as it remains in a reasonable range) only slightly influences the overall performance of the atomic broadcast service. In this experiment, the arrival frequency of external requests is rather low (one request every 400ms). In this case, the consensus round duration is of limited influence. This parameter is of major influence only when a failure occurs. Indeed, the rotating coordinator paradigm induces a penalty each time a round is coordinated by the failed process.

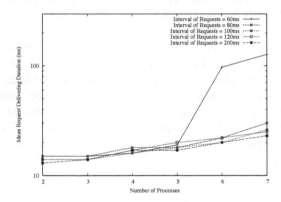

Fig. 4. Mean request delivering duration for different requests interval (consensus round timeout = 1000ms)

In Figure 4, we consider a fixed value for the duration of the round (1000 ms) and we sample the mean delivering duration for various arrival frequencies of the external requests and a varying number of processes. Figure 4 shows that when the arrival frequency of requests reaches a critical value, the mean request delivering duration increases significantly. However, this happens only when the number of processes is larger than 6. Recall that when there are 5 processes in the group, we can tolerate up to 2 failed processes (that is a reasonable assumption for the considered application).

7   Conclusion

In this paper, we have presented a dependable intrusion detection architecture. We started from a basic architecture that implements an intrusion detection system (IDS) based on the functional diversification of a set of COTS servers. This architecture is characterized by the fact that (1) it can detect previously unknown attacks (2) it ensures the confidentiality policy enforced by the set of non corrupted COTS servers. However, this architecture suffers from a single point of failure. Indeed, if the proxy/IDS fails, the whole system is down. To improve the availability of this architecture, we have employed a traditional solution from the dependability domain: the replication of the proxy/IDS. Thanks to this technique, we can tolerate up to a minority of failures among the set of replicated proxy/IDS. We have argued in favor of a fail-stop failure model in the case of the proxy/IDS, instead of the arbitrary failure model.

An inherent drawback of this architecture is that it is unable to ensure integrity of data manipulated by the COTS servers. This problem cannot be fixed by a generic solution without any assumption about the application to be deployed. Hence, we have focused on the particular case of a Web server for dynamic content (stored into a database backend). We have proposed a solution that in addition to ensuring confidentiality of data, also guarantees integrity of data stored in the database backend with respect to the integrity policy enforced by the Web servers. Replication of the different services in this architecture is made possible through the use of a group communication system called EDEN that offers basic services such as atomic broadcast and membership.

Finally, we have conducted a series of tests to evaluate the relevance of our solution along two axes. Firstly, we have shown that diversification of COTS servers can improve the detection of attacks with respect to false positives. Secondly we have shown that the cost of the atomic broadcast service is reasonable enough to be used in real applications where dependability is a key requirement.

References

1. Totel, E., Majorczyk, F., Mé, L.: COTS diversity based intrusion detection and application to web servers. In: Proceedings of 8th International Symposium on Recent Advances in Intrusion Detection (RAID '2005), Seattle, WA (2005) 43–62
2. Tronel, F.: Applications des problèmes d'accord à la tolérance aux défaillances dans les systèmes distribués asynchrones. PhD thesis, Université de Rennes (2003)
3. Greve, F.G.P.: Réponses efficaces au besoin d'accord dans un groupe. PhD thesis, Université de Rennes I (2002)
4. Powell, D.: Group communication. Communications of the ACM **39**(4) (1996) 50–53
5. Lamport, L., Shostak, R., Pease, M.: The byzantine generals problem. ACM Transactions on Programming Languages Systems **4**(3) (1982) 382–401
6. Castro, M., Liskov, B.: Practical byzantine fault tolerance. In: OSDI: Symposium on Operating Systems Design and Implementation, USENIX Association, Co-sponsored by IEEE TCOS and ACM SIGOPS (1999)

7. Reiter, M.K.: The Rampart toolkit for building high-integrity services. In: Selected Papers from the International Workshop on Theory and Practice in Distributed Systems, London, UK, Springer-Verlag (1995) 99–110
8. Gashi, I., Popov, P., Stankovic, V., Strigini, L.: On Designing Dependable Services with Diverse Off-The-Shelf SQL Servers. Springer (2004)
9. Wang, R., Wang, F., Byrd, G.: Design and implementation of acceptance monitor for building scalable intrusion tolerant system. In: Proceedings of the 10th International Conference on Computer Communications and Networks. (2001)
10. Chandra, T., Toueg, S.: Unreliable failure detectors for reliable distributed systems. Journal of ACM **43**(2) (1996) 225–267
11. Powell, D.: Delta-4: A Generic Architecture for Dependable Distributed Computing. Springer (1992)
12. Speirs, N., Barrett, P.: Using passive replicates in delta-4 to provide dependable distributed computing. In: Proceedings of the Nineteenth International Symposium on Fault-Tolerant Computing, IEEE (1989)
13. Powell, D., Bonn, G., Seaton, D., Verissimo, P., Waeselynck, F.: The delta-4 approach to dependability in open distributed computing systems. In: Proceedings of Twenty-Fifth International Symposium on Fault-Tolerant Computing, IEEE (1995) 56
14. Deswarte, Y., Blain, L., Fabre, J.C.: Intrusion tolerance in distributed computing systems. In: Proceedings of the IEEE Symposium on Research in Security and Privacy. (1991) 110–122
15. Saidane, A., Deswarte, Y., Nicomette, V.: An intrusion tolerant architecture for dynamic content internet servers. In Liu, P., Pal, P., eds.: Proceedings of the 2003 ACM Workshop on Survivable and Self-Regenerative Systems (SSRS-03), Fairfax, VA, ACM Press (2003) 110–114
16. Valdes, A., Almgren, M., Cheung, S., Deswarte, Y., Dutertre, B., Levy, J., Saidi, H., Stavridou, V., Uribe, T.: An adaptative intrusion-tolerant server architecture. In: Proceedings of the 10th International Workshop on Security Protocols, Springer (2003) 158–178
17. Yin, J., Martin, J.P., Venkataramani, A., Alvisi, L., Dahlin, M.: Separating agreement from execution for byzantine fault tolerant services. In: Proceedings of the 19th ACM Symp. on Operating Systems Principles (SOSP-2003). (2003)
18. Hurfin, M., Macêdo, R., Raynal, M., Tronel, F.: A generic framework to solve agreement problems. In: Proc. of the 19th IEEE Symposium on Reliable Distributed Systems (SRDS'99), Lausanne, Switzerland (1999) 56–65
19. Hurfin, M., Mostéfaoui, A., Raynal, M., Macêdo, R.A.: A consensus protocol based on a weak failure detector and a sliding round window. In: 20th Symposium on Reliable Distributed Systems (SRDS 2001). (2001) 120–129

Stabilizing Health Monitoring
for Wireless Sensor Networks

William Leal, Sandip Bapat, Taewoo Kwon, Pihui Wei, and Anish Arora*

Department of Computer Science and Engineering
The Ohio State University, Columbus, OH 43210
{leal, bapat, kwonta, weip, anish}@cse.ohio-state.edu

Abstract. Wireless sensor networks (WSNs) comprised of low-cost devices tend to be unreliable, with failures a common phenomenon. Being able to accurately observe the network health status — of nodes of each type and links of each type — is essential to properly configure applications on WSN fabrics and to interpret the information collected from them.

In this paper we study accurate network health monitoring in WSNs. Specifically, we reconsider the well-known problem of message-passing rooted spanning tree construction and its use in PIF (propagation of information with feedback) for the case of a WSN. We present a stabilizing protocol, Chowkidar, that is initiated upon demand; that is, it does not involve ongoing maintenance, and it terminates with accurate results, including detection of failure and restart during the monitoring process. Our protocol is distinguished from others in two important ways. Given the resource constraints of WSNs, it is message-efficient in that it uses only a few messages per node. And it tolerates ongoing node and link failure and node restart, in contrast to requiring that faults stop during convergence.

We have implemented the protocol as part of enabling a network health status service that is tightly integrated with a remotely accessible wireless sensor network testbed, Kansei, at The Ohio State University. We report on experimental results.

1 Introduction

Wireless sensor networks (WSNs) are inherently unreliable. When WSN nodes, generally built from low cost components, are deployed in large numbers, failures happen fairly often. Monitoring the health of nodes and interfaces of deployed WSNs is thus a core requirement for application managers. Similarly, WSN testbed users have a particular need for accurate information about the health of the testbed. In running an experiment, it is easy to confuse a failed node with a problem in the experiment itself. Experiments use controlled fault injection that simulates node, interface and other failures, so the actual failure

* This work was supported in part by NSF grants NSF-NETS/NOSS-0520222 and NSF-HDCCSR-0341703, and by DARPA contract OSU-RF #F33615-01-C-1901.

A.K. Datta and M. Gradinariu (Eds.): SSS 2006, LNCS 4280, pp. 395–410, 2006.

of a node or interface will give misleading results. Hence having an accurate view of the network before and after an experiment is important in interpreting results. In addition, the administrator of a testbed needs to know which nodes have failed so that they can be restarted or repaired.

In WSN deployments, monitoring is typically done using exfiltration on multi-hop radio paths that are unreliable and exhibit complex dynamics. Although WSN testbeds generally use reliable, high-speed back channels for experiment configuration and data retrieval that can be exploited to improve the efficiency and accuracy of monitoring, these channels may not always be available due to failures or policy issues such as interference with ongoing experiments. Thus, in either situation, a monitor cannot assume a persistent structure for its status collection, which motivates the need for a tolerant solution.

A simple way to gather health information for any WSN is to use the standard pattern of propagation of information with feedback (PIF). However, for our purposes, the PIF must have certain properties. First, it must give accurate, total results or else indicate that a problem occurred: node and interface failures can (and do) happen at any time, including during the running of the protocol itself; this can result in dramatically inaccurate results if, for example, a tree is formed but a node close to the root fails before feedback completes. Even if the node does not fail, its wireless link to its parent could become unreliable due to complex WSN link dynamics or channel interference, resulting in loss of information from that node. These scenarios could result in a partial report where the entire subtree dominated by that node is regarded as inaccessible when in fact an alternative reliable path to those nodes might exist. In such cases, partial PIFs would yield information that is, from the perspective of the users, potentially worse than no information.

Second, the protocol should be fast. We wish to run it between experiments on a testbed so it should not take long. Third, the protocol must be frugal in its use of communication resources since it shares the network with other user programs and might run on battery-based nodes. For the same reason, the protocol should run on demand and should terminate, not using resources when network information is not being collected. This precludes approaches that perform automatic tree repair when nodes or links fail or restart.

Since WSNs can be heterogeneous there can be many paths from the root to a node. A path that uses Ethernet will usually be more reliable than one that uses radio, for instance. Hence we prefer least-cost paths, where the cost of a link is a reflection of its reliability or other factors such as bandwidth. Thus, for instance, we can avoid low bandwidth multi-hop radio paths that could have higher bit error rates or be more prone to message interference unless they are the only way to reach certain nodes.

Designing for heterogeneity means that our approach is easily extended to new kinds of devices and networks. We are, for example, in the process of incorporating new motes that use new interfaces into our implementation.

Outline of our Chowkidar protocol.[1] Existing PIF-style approaches do not satisfy the above requirements. They either assume that faults have stopped to assure termination, or else they run continuously, often using using substantial resources when a fault occurs. By making judicious use of time, we present a simple, efficient protocol that produces in one shot a tree structure such that, in the presence of continuous faults, a subsequent PIF will either succeed or will indicate that a fault has rendered the tree defective. In this latter case, the tree can be rebuilt and a new PIF run.

Faults can cause a link or node to fail and a node to restart; in this latter case, local variables are reset and a restart message is broadcast that can be forwarded to the root[2]. Faults do not affect other variables.

Key to our approach is the tree-building protocol that includes a handshake between a node and its potential parent. When X receives a wave broadcast from Y with higher session number, it asks Y to become its parent. Y records X as a child and sends an acknowledgement. If the acknowledgement fails then X does not adopt Y as parent. In a subsequent PIF, Y expects to hear from X and when it doesn't, it knows there is a tree fault that requires a rebuild. We accomplish formation of least-cost paths by phasing the delivery of the wave messages: on links with lower cost, the messages are delivered earlier than on links with higher cost. A node that is connected to a neighbor on multiple networks will receive the message on the preferred network first. If faults do not occur during handshaking then the tree will be least-cost.

If node or link failures do not happen during the tree formation, the result is a tree with bidirectional edges: each child knows its parent and each parent knows its children; when a PIF is run on the tree, each parent waits on its children to report before it reports to its own parent and, if it fails to hear from a child in a timely fashion, it initiates a failure message to the root. As noted, the handshake process lets us handle failures that occur during the acknowledgement sequence. If a node fails to receive the acknowledgement from the proposed parent then it does not join the tree but waits for another wave message from another neighbor. As shown in Fig. 1, this means that it is possible for a *false parent* to incorrectly claim a node as child. In the figure, node A is the root and nodes B and C have joined the tree. In Fig. 1(b) to Fig. 1(d), a wave message reaches node D and it notifies B that it proposes adopting it as parent, so B includes D in its child set. However, a failure just after that causes the link to fail, so D does not join the tree. In Fig. 1(e) to Fig. 1(g), a wave message arrives from C and D joins with C as parent. Note now that both B and C claim D as a child. In a subsequent PIF, D will give feedback to C but not to B. When B fails to hear from D, it will respond with an error message to the root.

When tree formation or PIF is complete, the protocol is quiescent, so there is no ongoing message traffic unless a node restarts. In the absence of failures, a total of three messages per node are required for tree formation: one for the

---

[1] Chowkidar in the Hindi language stands for a watchman.

[2] Links can restart silently; detecting a restart efficiently is an issue we do not deal with here.

wave, two for the parent acknowledgement. For a PIF, two messages per node are required: one to propagate the token and one to propagate the feedback. If failures occur during the parent acknowledgement process, additional messages are required as a node attempts to confirm with subsequent potential parents. However, this occurs only if a failure happens after the wave message is sent but before the acknowledgement arrives.

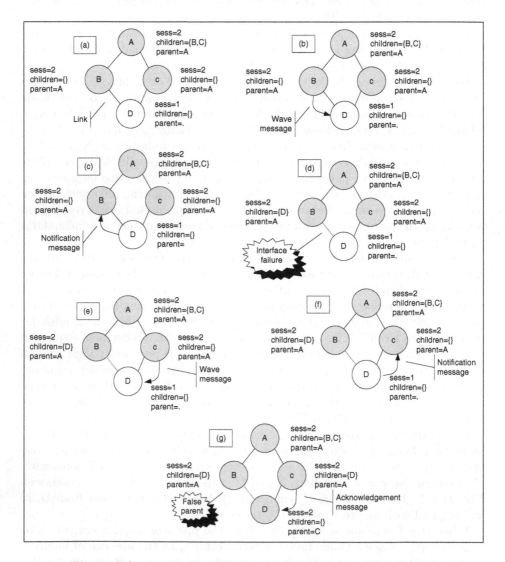

Fig. 1. Tolerating Failures During Acknowledgement: False Parents

Contributions. Our principal contribution is the message-passing terminating spanning tree protocol of Chowkidar that tolerates on-going faults. The structure is produced in such a way that a subsequent PIF will either succeed or will report that the structure is not a spanning tree.

Further, we analyze the protocol in the context of a formal network model, and offer experimental validation of the protocol performance via an implementation on a heterogenous WSN testbed, Kansei, comprising hundreds of Motes (of multiple types, specifically XSMs and TMoteSkys), Stargates, and PCs. The latter is necessary in part for validating that the performance in a real network (with associated complex dynamics) is consistent with that predicted by the analysis. It is also necessary for enabling a health monitoring service that is a crucial and tightly integrated component of Kansei.

Organization of the paper. The rest of the paper is organized is follows. We discuss related work in Section 2. The Chowkidar tree and PIF protocols are in Section 3. We give experimental results in Section 4 and present concluding remarks in Section 5. Appendices in the extended technical report version [1] contain the correctness proof for the tree protocol, a photo of the Kansei testbed, and screenshots for an implementation of Chowkidar.

2   Related Work

Efficient PIF with ongoing faults. The notion of a self-stabilizing PIF has been well-studied in distributed computing as it is an enabler for many other tasks such as distributed reset, global snapshot, termination detection, and others; see [2] for an overview of non-stabilizing, self-stabilizing and snap-stabilizing PIF protocols; in fact, our protocol is snap-stabilizing, completing in zero rounds. However, existing protocols that terminate do not tolerate ongoing faults, and those that do are not terminating.

[3] presents a PIF in the form of distributed reset. It is tolerant to ongoing faults, returning either a correct completion or an error indicating a tree failure. However, the protocol is not terminating since the tree structure is checked periodically and repair occurs when a problem is detected. [4] and [5] give terminating tree construction protocols but they make the standard stabilization assumption that faults have stopped.

Network health monitoring. A variety of monitoring facilities have been developed for testbeds and for deployed WSNs, but all those we are aware of fall short of our needs. Experiments are assumed to run on homogeneous devices; existing support tools do not handle the network heterogeneity of testbeds. Tools do not distinguish between the health of a node and the health of its links. For some, the reliability is too low to be useful and for others, there is a dependency on the communication structure of the application.

Traditional networks such as the Internet use standard protocols such as SNMP [6] for monitoring network devices and identifying faults. However, SNMP assumes the IP routing layer in its operation and is therefore dependent on the fault-tolerance of IP to be able to reach the monitored devices; this is not sufficient for a WSN with non-IP networks such as mote radio. Other monitors like Sympathy [7] only handle radio networks and do not admit heterogeneity.

Similarly, Motelab [8], Tutornet [9] and Orbit [10] provide users with a ping-based status for each device, indicating whether it is reachable or not. However, simply detecting that a device is unresponsive on a given network is not sufficient since it does not support heterogeneous networks and does not distinguish network and link faults.

The Sensor Network Management System (SNMS) [11] supports monitoring of WSNs by providing its own network stack that includes routing. SNMS allows administrators to remotely query network devices and learn their status. However, SNMS does not deal with heterogeneous networks, and studies such as [12] show that reliability of SNMS does not suffice to provide accurate fault status.

Sympathy [7] is designed for fault detection at a central base station in a data collection application in which nodes periodically send data to the base. Sympathy thus exploits knowledge of a specific application's traffic pattern to define certain fault metrics. A similar approach is used in [13] where the fault management system exploits the continuous data traffic flow in the network to piggy-back health information and uses route update messages to trace failed nodes. The dependency on an application makes these inappropriate for our purposes since monitoring is conducted only when an application is running.

3   Tree Construction and PIF for WSN Health Monitoring

In this section, we present our protocol for tree construction and for PIF. A client using the protocol would first execute the tree construction and when that terminates, execute the PIF. If the PIF returns an error then the tree must be rebuilt and the PIF rerun. If not, the tree that has been formed can be used again for the next PIF. For efficiency, the tree construction can be combined with an initial feedback from the leaves.

Communication Model. For purposes of design and analysis, we assume that links are bidirectional and reliable. Both assumptions need to be justified. In WSNs, unidirectional links may occur since a node might hear from a distant neighbor but messages sent in the other direction, for a variety of reasons, may not be received. In our tree construction protocol, a node must both send and receive on a selected link before it joins the tree, so a unidirectional link would be ignored or regarded as failed, and another parent/link candidate, if any, would be attempted. In any case, unidirectional links can be handled by estimating link quality or using topological information so that a node only accepts messages from near neighbors; however, link quality estimation usually requires exchanging several messages, which our protocol does not support, so estimation would have to be provided by a separate service.

To simplify our model we assume that links are reliable if they have not failed due to an interface fault. In reality, radio-based links tend to be unreliable due to contention for the channel. The problem can be mitigated by using low power and randomized transmission times, but the results of a PIF collection will be at best probabilistic. Alternatively, a TDMA-based scheme can be used to give deterministic communication, but TDMA itself comes with an overhead cost unless it is already provided for some other purpose.

Fault Model. We assume a base station as a fixed root that is not affected by faults. This assumption is justified in our application since a base station is relatively reliable. Failure of the base station is obvious to users, and it has to be repaired or replaced for correct network operation. The session number that is used to initiate tree construction is stored by the base station and is assumed to be reliable. For convenience we assume that session numbers are unbounded, but since the base is reliable, an integer with a sufficiently large bound suffices.

Faults can cause node or link to failure or node restart; as mentioned earlier, we do not consider link restart, which is postponed to future work. Node restart is clean in that the session number and other protocol control variables are re-initialized; it is detectable by the node so that when it happens, it broadcasts a "restart" message that is passed to the root.

Notation and Semantics. We use guarded commands with interleaving semantics for specifying the protocol. Parameters j and k range over nodes; i ranges over links. Among commands with true guards, one is chosen and is atomically executed. Communication actions are synchronous: after a node sends a message to X, X executes the corresponding receive before any other action of X and before any other node sends to X. Environment actions can interleave send-receive pairs, might or might not be executed when enabled, and execute at most finitely often.

We use Gouda's AP notation for timeouts, which are represented by global state predicates. In the case of the child-parent acknowledgement sequence during tree construction (T5 of Fig. 2), for instance, the timeout can be implemented by setting a time to wait for an acknowledgement after notification has been sent. Termination of each protocol can be given via a timeout predicate that negates the conjunction of the guards.

Timing Assumptions. We use delayed delivery of wave messages to construct a least-cost tree, implemented by an underlying broadcast service that delays actual broadcast until a specified time. In our implementation we have the following delays: Ethernet, 0s; serial link between Stargates and XSMs, 0s; XSM radio, 5s, where higher delay corresponds to higher link cost. From the base station to a given XSM X_0 there can be many potential paths, including B-E-SG_0-S-X_0 and B-E-SG_1-S-X_1-R-X_0, where B is base, SG is a Stargate, X is an XSM, E is Ethernet, S is serial link and R is radio. The first path costs 0s and the second 5s, so the first is preferred. Delayed delivery means that the wave via the serial link arrives at X_0 before the wave via the radio, so SG_0 will be selected as X_0's parent.

We assume that internal processing in nodes takes zero time and that links have associated timing values, including the delay enforced by the broadcast primitive. This lets us associate an upper bound on the time to wait before concluding that a timeout is satisfied.

Constants, Variables and Messages. We describe the constants, node variables, environment variables and message types. **Constants.** lktype is a constant set of link types for a given node corresponding to interface types. id is the identifier for a node; we assume that nodes have unique identities. **Node Vars for Both Protocols.** sess is an unbounded integer session number, initially 0. **Node Vars for Tree Construction.** parent is the (node id, interface) pair for a parent, initially (-1,-1) for unassigned. children is a set of of (node id, interface) pairs of children, initially $\emptyset$. busy ensures only one handshake at a time, initially false. tk, ti, tsess, initially -1, -1, 0, resp., store parent candidate information during handshake. newtree is true if a new tree should be formed, initially true. **Node Vars for PIF.** pphase is a Boolean that is true during the propagation phase, initially false. pchldcnt is a bounded integer that counts the number of children heard from during feedback. **Environment Vars.** up is an array of Booleans indexed by node ids that indicates whether the node is up or not. link is an array of Booleans indexed by node id pairs and link type that indicates whether the link is up or not; this is symmetric wrt nodes. **Message Types.** Each message begins with a message type. 'wave' is for tree wave messages. 'notify' is for a child to notify a potential parent in tree construction. 'ack' is for the parent to acknowledge the child in tree construction. 'token' is the propagation message for PIF. 'fb' is the feedback message for PIF. 'err' is the error message for the PIF when the structure is found to not be a tree. 'restart' is issued by a node that restarts.

Tree Construction Protocol. The Chowkidar protocol for tree construction is given in Fig. 2. After action T1a initiates a new wave in response to the need for a new tree, the normal sequence is as follows: a node gets a wave message from a neighbor in T2 over some interface and enqueues it; the queue stores other alternatives in case faults prevent the sender of the first wave message from being adopted as a parent. T3 removes a wave message and, if it has a higher session number, tries to adopt the sender as parent by sending it a notification. The parent receives the notification in T4, adds the node as a new child, and returns an acknowledgement to the child. The child receives the acknowledgement in T1b and propagates the wave. Note that the broadcast service ensures that wave messages are delivered in order of link cost.

Node and link faults may occur concurrently with the protocol. If a node or link fails before the wave reaches it then this is the same as failing before the protocol begins. If a node or interface used in the tree fails after the wave has passed, this is the same as failing after the protocol terminates and will be detected by a subsequent PIF since that node will fail to respond to its parent.

Now consider failures concurrent with the wave boundary. Suppose node Y broadcasts via action T1a or T1b, but before delivery, neighbor X or the link fails. This is the same as failure before the protocol begins and X will not be included in the tree. Suppose X sends notification to Y via T3 but Y or the link fails before receipt. This is the same as failing before the protocol starts. Suppose Y receives a notification from X in T4 but the link fails before X receives the acknowledgement. Then Y adopts X as a child but X does not learn this; T5 will cause a timeout and X will solicit a new parent. Since Y has falsely recorded X as a child, in a subsequent PIF will detect that X does not respond to Y. Similarly, if Y receives a notification from X but X fails before receiving the acknowledgement, X will not be responsive in the subsequent PIF.

Node restarts are clean and would normally be benign. However, if X starts a handshake with Y1, then fails and restarts, it can start a new handshake with Y2, perhaps in a later session, and either acknowledgement could arrive first. To handle this, T1b will accept an acknowledgement only from the node/link it notified last.

```
T1a  (id=Base∧newtree) → // begin new tree
     sess:=sess+1; parent:=(-1,-1); newtree:=false;
     ∀pi : (pi ∈ lktype) : broadcast ('wave',sess) on pi
       atTime tdeliv[pi];
     children:=∅; busy:=false;
T1b  rcv ('ack') from k on i → // join parent & echo wave
     if (k=tk ∧ i=ti)
       sess:=tsess; parent:=(tk,ti);
       ∀pi : (pi ∈ lktype) : broadcast ('wave',sess) on pi
         atTime tdeliv[pi];
       children:=∅; busy:=false; fi
T2   rcv ('wave',xsess) from k on i → // enqueue waves
     enqueue (k,i,xsess);
T3   ¬busy ∧ queue≠ ⟨⟩ → // begin handshake
     (tk,ti,tsess):=dequeue();
     if (tsess>sess)
       send ('notify') to tk on ti; busy:=true; fi
T4   rcv ('notify') from k on i → // acknowledge
     send ('ack') to k on i;
     children:=children ∪ (k,i);
T5   timeout (busy ∧ (¬up.tk ∨ ¬link.id.tk.ti)) →
     busy:=false;
```

Fig. 2. Tree Construction Protocol

The protocol tolerates simultaneous sessions. In the absence of faults, the protocol will form a spanning tree over the highest session number among non-tree nodes that were up when the wave was propagated by a neighbor. In the presence of faults that affect the tree structure, either the fault happens before the wave or else the structure contains nodes with nonresponsive children. As we have seen, a node listed as a child can be nonresponsive if it or its tree interface is down, or if it has identified a different parent. In this case, a subsequent PIF will detect the fact and initiate a new tree construction.

In the protocol, wave messages are delivered in order according to cost of the links. Hence the spanning tree formed is least-cost unless while handshaking with node Y, the link fails before X's notification is sent, causing X to attempt another parent which, if available, might result in a path that is not least-cost. The only active nodes are those that are at the wave boundary. Timeouts guarantee that wave progresses until it is extinguished, so the protocol terminates. Since we have assumptions about delivery and link times, we can calculate an upper bound on the time required to terminate. Proofs are in the extended technical version [1].

```
P1  (id=Base) ∧ (start new PIF) ∧ ¬newtree → //new PIF
    sess:=sess+1;
    ∀pk,pi : (pk,pi) ∈ children : send ('token',sess)
      to pk on pi;
    pphase:=true; pchldcnt:=0;
P2  rcv ('token',psess) from k on i → //propagate or respond
    if (psess > sess)
      sess:=psess;
      if (children≠ ∅)
        ∀pk,pi : (pk,pi) ∈ children : send ('token',sess)
          to pk on pi;
        pphase:=true; pchldcnt:=0;
      else
        send ('fb',sess) to parent.node on parent.link;
        pphase:=false; fi fi
P3  rcv (fb,psess) from k on i → //forward responses
    if (psess=sess)
      pchldcnt:=pchldcnt+1;
      if (pchldcnt=|children|)
        if (id≠Base) send ('fb',sess) to parent.node
            on parent.link; fi
        pphase:=false; fi fi
P4  timeout pphase ∧ (k,i)∈children ∧ (¬up.k ∨ ¬link.id.k.i ∨
        parent.k≠(j,i)) → //timeout unresponsive child
    if (id=Base) newtree:=true;
    else send ('err') to parent.node on parent.link; fi
    pphase:=false;
P5  rcv ('err') from k on i → //send error to Base
    if (id=Base) newtree:=true;
    else send ('err') to parent.node on parent.link; fi
```

Fig. 3. PIF Protocol

PIF Protocol. The Chowkidar PIF protocol is shown in Fig. 3. For WSN health monitoring, PIF should return appropriate health information or assessment of other predicates but this is an orthogonal issue.

P1 blocks if a tree fault has been detected and should be initiated only when the tree protocol has terminated. A token is initiated on the tree in the form of a message with a new sequence number. In P2, interior nodes forward the token to their children while leaf nodes begin the feedback response. In P3, a node that receives feedback from a child increments a counter; when all children have responded, it sends its feedback response to its parent. In P4, a node waiting on a child's response times out if it is unresponsive. This creates a message that is propagated up the tree by P5.

Implementation of timeout P4 can be based on the longest possible path in the network. An initial PIF can refine the timeouts based on a node's distance from its leaves to get tighter values.

A PIF execution terminates within some bounded time and, if the structure from the root is a spanning tree, then it completes with a report of success and otherwise with a report of failure. If a restart message is received by a node before it has completed feedback then the tree is not spanning; by our synchronous communication assumptions, the restart message will reach the root before the feedback message, triggering the creation of a new tree.

```
E1  id≠Base ∧ up → up:=false; //fail a node
E2  link.id.k.i → link.id.k.i,link.k.id.i:=false,false;
        //fail a link
E3  ¬up → //restart a failed node
    up:=true;
    (reset all variables)
    ∀pi : (pi∈lktype) : broadcast ('restart') on pi
        delivery now;
R1  rcv ('restart') from k on i → //send restart msg up tree
    if (id=Base) newtree:=true;
    else send ('restart') to parent.node on parent.link;
        if (k=tk) busy:=false; fi fi
```

Fig. 4. Environment and Restart Actions

Environment Actions. The environment-related actions are shown in Fig. 4. E1 causes a node to fail. E2 causes a link to fail. E3 causes a node to restart; a restart message is broadcast on all available interfaces.

If R1 receives a restart message, it resets the tree construction busy flag in case the restarted node had been involved in a handshake. To ensure correctness of collection, the message is forwarded towards the root so that a new tree can be formed. Consider the following cases. Suppose the restart message is received by a node with a tree path to the root that stays up sufficiently long. Then the message will arrive at the root. Suppose the receiving node's tree path has a failed node or interface closer to the root. Then a subsequent PIF will detect the problem and when the ensuing tree is formed, the restarted node will be included. Suppose the node is partitioned from tree nodes but there is a newly-restarted neighbor that is not. Then its reset message will trigger a tree rebuild that includes both. Otherwise the node is not reachable by any path of up nodes/links and would not be included the spanning tree even if it were rebuilt.

4   Experimental Results

At Ohio State, we have developed Kansei, a rich hardware-software platform for high-fidelity WSN experimentation, testing, and validation [14]. Its hardware platform couples a generic platform array with multiple domain sensing and communication arrays. The generic platform array consists of a stationary component that can be operated in real-time and via the Internet. It has several hundred static nodes that reside on an off-floor deck composed of 35 bench modules. The two main sensor node platforms in the stationary array, mounted below the deck, are XSM and TMoteSky motes and Stargates. Each XSM has a 4 MHz CPU, 4KB RAM and a low-power single channel 38.4kbps radio. Its sensors and actuators include photocell, PIR, temperature, magnetometer, microphone, GPS, and buzzers. Each TMoteSky is an 802.15.4 compliant device with a 250kbps radio, 8 MHz CPU and 10KB RAM. Each Stargate has a 400MHz Intel PXA255 CPU and a daughter-card with interfaces to the XSM and the TMoteSky and various other interfaces such as RS-232, Ethernet, USB and 802.11(b). The generic platform array also includes mobile sensor nodes that move on the deck above the static array.

We implemented and experimented with Chowkidar for stabilizing tree construction and PIF in Kansei. The implementation for this heterogenous network spans a PC-based Kansei server, Stargates running Linux and motes running TinyOS [15]. It uses Ethernet, 802.11b wireless, mote radio and Stargate-mote serial links for tree construction and data collection. Recall that our protocol uses different delays on different links to construct a least-cost path tree. According to Kansei policies, based on link characteristics such as reliability, available bandwidth, potential interference, etc., we assign a link delay of 0s on Ethernet and Stargate-XSM serial links, which are reliable, have high bandwidth and low interference effects; a 5s delay on XSM radio links, which have less bandwidth and more interference and a 10s delay on 802.11b links. 802.11b links are highest cost since we have only a single channel available and Chowkidar could interfere with concurrent experiments.

Our analysis and proofs assume that links are reliable and bidirectional. However, in reality, broadcast links such as wireless radio and even Ethernet suffer from transient message losses. Indeed, a naive implementation of Chowkidar where child-parent handshakes were initiated immediately upon receiving a wave message led to message implosion on these shared channels and loss of messages in the network due to contention. This network unreliability due to concurrent message transmission by all nodes was in fact so high that it affected not only the performance but also the correctness of our protocol since it resulted in an incomplete tree being constructed in several runs.

To avoid message implosion on shared channels, our implementation introduced a simple application-level backoff mechanism. Coarse-grained tuning of backoffs enabled us to obtain correct performance for our protocol implementation in that a tree spanning all correct nodes was constructed, albeit with increased execution time.

Table 1. Effect of faults on protocol performance for a 25 node network using a 2.5s backoff

Percentage of failed Stargates	0%	8%	20%	40%
Average time for tree construction	1.2s	8.7s	9.9s	10.5s
Percentage of failed runs	0%	0%	10%	30%

Table 1 shows the results of the first series of experiments performed on a 25 node network using a 2.5 second backoff on wireless links for congestion avoidance. We first ran our algorithm without introducing any failures. As expected, our algorithm always constructed a least-cost spanning tree using only Ethernet and serial links in very short time. We then injected failures by randomly stopping multiple Stargate nodes, which forced more and more wireless links to be used in tree construction. As the data shows, as the number of injected faults increases, not only does the average tree construction time increase, but in the worst case shown here, where 40% of the Stargates were failed, even correctness was affected in some runs due to excessive message loss. Fortunately, the degradation in performance is gradual and sublinear, so we can select a suitable backoff period based on the expected worst case failures in the network.

Table 2. Linear scaling of backoff with network size for 40% Stargate failures

Number of network nodes	25	25	50	50
Maximum backoff for radio	2.5s	5s	5s	10s
Percentage of failed runs	30%	0%	25%	0%

We validate this assertion in Table 2 in which we measure the minimum backoff period at which 100% of the runs are successful even in the worst failure case considered in Table 1, i.e. 40% failed Stargates for networks with different sizes. As seen from the data, using a 5 second backoff guarantees correct execution when up to 10 out of 25 (40%) nodes fail; however the same backoff does not guarantee correct execution if the network size is doubled to 50 nodes with the same failure rate. Nevertheless, as expected, with a linear scaling of the backoff period to 10 seconds, we observe correct protocol execution.

We thus conclude from our experiments that in WSNs, unreliability of message transmission affects both protocol correctness and performance and hence should be given careful consideration. However, as demonstrated by our experiments, using a simple backoff mechanism is sufficient to achieve correctness at the expense of increased completion time. Our assumption of reliable, bidirectional links can therefore be reasonably realized even in real network deployments.

An alternate means of obtaining reliable links and guaranteeing protocol correctness is to instrument reliability at the messaging layer either through MAC-level retransmissions or by replacing the CSMA based wireless MAC protocols with TDMA. In future work, we intend to evaluate the cost-benefit tradeoffs of these approaches by comparing their performance with that of the best performance that can be obtained using application-level tuning.

5   Conclusions

We have developed a WSN monitoring protocol that is extensible, has good energy dynamics, and gives accurate results in the presence of ongoing faults. We have given a theoretical model of the protocol and evaluated it against realistic assumptions, so our validation is based not only on analysis but also on experimentation with the Kansei WSN testbed. In the protocol, predicates about network control state can be evaluated locally and consolidated in-network to reduce message traffic; and further evaluation can take place at the base station.

For future work, we will focus on a variety of issues. At present, health monitoring in Kansei is an independent service. Users can view the network health status, but it is not used by Kansei's scheduler. We plan to integrate monitoring so that experiments are run only on nodes known to be good.

Monitoring is presently done only on nodes not running any application. Monitoring concurrently with a running application is desirable, but one would have to deal with the issue of interference between the application and the monitoring. This could be in part a policy issue for a network—an application may request that monitoring of a certain sort not be run concurrently, say on motes—and partly a research issue in case there is a way to exploit the semantics of an application for monitoring while still offering correctness guarantees.

A node interface has two parts, a transmitter and a receiver. Evaluating the receiver locally is easy; but a neighbor is needed to evaluate the transmitter. Broadcasts may be heard by many neighbors and if they all report it, there is excessive redundancy. Hence, we will study how to compress such information. There may additionally be other predicates that involve a node's neighbors, but those neighbors could be in different subtrees, so the structure of the spanning tree could work against us. We will study ways to ameliorate this problem.

Link quality is an important predicate for monitoring. This requires the exchange of several predicates before an evaluation can be made. Over time, if experiments or monitoring are run sufficiently often, link quality status can be assessed; or an estimation algorithm can be run periodically. This can provide information to users, and can also feedback into the monitoring protocol itself: a node can dynamically adjust link cost to build a better tree.

We are interested in the quality of sensors on nodes. The problem is difficult for several reasons. First, sometimes ground truth is not available, so there is no absolute reference point for evaluating the readings [16]. Second, an understanding of the physical model is critical, especially when comparing the readings from nearby sensors. Third, an understanding of the effect of hardware and other environmental faults is important.

As scale increases, the issue of bidirectional link reliability becomes increasingly critical. We need to evaluate whether interference-detection CSMA approaches combined with appropriate timings give us sufficiently accurate results or whether a deterministic scheme such as TDMA is necessary.

DAGs have been proposed as more suited to sensor networks than trees [17], and we plan to investigate this option.

References

1. W. Leal, S. Bapat, T. Kwon, P. Wei, and A. Arora. Stabilizing health monitoring for wireless sensor networks. Technical Report OSU-CISRC-6/06-TR62, Department of Computer Science and Engineering, The Ohio State University, 2006.
2. A. Cournier, A. K. Datta, F. Petit, and V. Villain. Enabling snap-stabilization. In *Proceedings of ICDCS 2003*, 2003.
3. S. Kulkarni and A. Arora. Multitolerance in distributed reset. *Chicago Journal of Computer Science*, 4, 1998.
4. B. Awerbuch, B. Patt-Shamir, and G. Varghese. Self-stabilization by local checking and correction (extended abstract). In *Proceedings of 32nd Annual IEEE Symposium on Foundations of Computer Science*, pages 268–277, 1991.
5. A. Cournier, F. S. Devismes, and V. Villain. Snap-stabilizing PIF and useless computations. In *Proceedings of 12th International Conference on Parallel and Distributed Systems - Volume 1 (ICPADS'06)*, pages 39–48, 2006.
6. IETF. RFC 1157. www.ietf.org/rfc/rfc1157.txt.
7. N. Ramanathan et al. Sympathy for the sensor network debugger. In *SenSys '05: 3rd Intl. Conf. on Embedded networked sensor systems*, pages 255–267, 2005.
8. G. Werner-Allen, P. Swieskowski, and M. Welsh. MoteLab: A Wireless Sensor Network Testbed. In *4th Intl Conf on Information Processing in Sensor Networks*, 2005.
9. Embedded Networks Laboratory, USC. Tutornet: A Tiered Wireless Sensor Network Testbed. http://enl.usc.edu/projects/tutornet/index.html.
10. D. Raychaudhuri et al. Overview of the ORBIT Radio Grid Testbed for Evaluation of Next-Generation Wireless Network Protocols. In *IEEE Wireless Communications and Networking Conference (WCNC)*, 2005.
11. G. Tolle and D. Culler. Design of an Application-Cooperative Management System for Wireless Sensor Networks. In *Proceedings of the EWSN'04*, 2004.
12. S. Bapat, V. Kulathumani, and A. Arora. Analyzing the Yield of ExScal, a Large-Scale Wireless Sensor Network Experiment. In *13th IEEE Intl. Conf. on Network Protocols (ICNP)*, pages 53–62, 2005.
13. J. Staddon, D. Balfanz, and G. Durfee. Efficient tracing of failed nodes in sensor networks. In *WSNA '02: Proceedings of the 1st ACM international workshop on Wireless sensor networks and applications*, pages 122–130, 2002.
14. A. Arora, E. Ertin, R. Ramnath, M. Nesterenko, and W. Leal. Kansei: A high-fidelity sensing testbed. *IEEE Internet Computing*, 10(2):35–47, March/April 2006.

15. J. Hill et al. System architecture directions for networked sensors. In *Architectural Support for Programming Languages and Operating Systems*, pages 93–104, 2000.

16. N. Ramanathan et al. Rapid deployment with confidence: Calibration and fault detection in environmental sensor networks. Technical Report CENS 62, Center for Embedded Network Systems, UCLA, 2006.

17. S. Nath et al. Synopsis diffusion for robust aggregation in sensor networks. In *2nd Intl. Conf. on Embedded Networked Sensor Systems*, pages 205–262, 2004.

A Byzantine-Fault Tolerant Self-stabilizing Protocol for Distributed Clock Synchronization Systems

Mahyar R. Malekpour

NASA Langley Research Center Hampton, VA 23681, USA
m.r.malekpour@larc.nasa.gov

Abstract. Embedded distributed systems have become an integral part of safety-critical computing applications, necessitating system designs that incorporate fault tolerant clock synchronization in order to achieve ultra-reliable assurance levels. Many efficient clock synchronization protocols do not, however, address Byzantine failures, and most protocols that do tolerate Byzantine failures do not self-stabilize. Of the Byzantine self-stabilizing clock synchronization algorithms that exist in the literature, they are based on either unjustifiably strong assumptions about initial synchrony of the nodes or on the existence of a common pulse at the nodes. The Byzantine self-stabilizing clock synchronization protocol presented here does not rely on any assumptions about the initial state of the clocks. Furthermore, there is neither a central clock nor an externally generated pulse system. The proposed protocol converges deterministically, is scalable, and self-stabilizes in a short amount of time. The convergence time is linear with respect to the self-stabilization period. Proofs of the correctness of the protocol as well as the results of formal verification efforts are reported.

Keywords: Byzantine, fault tolerant, self-stabilization, clock synchronization, distributed, protocol, algorithm, model checking, verification.

1 Introduction

Synchronization and coordination algorithms are part of distributed computer systems. Clock synchronization algorithms are essential for managing the use of resources and controlling communication in a distributed system. Also, a fundamental criterion in the design of a robust distributed system is to provide the capability of tolerating and potentially recovering from failures that are not predictable in advance. Overcoming such failures is most suitably addressed by tolerating Byzantine faults [1]. A Byzantine-fault model encompasses all unexpected failures, including transient ones, within the limitations of the maximum number of faults at a given time. Driscoll et al. [2] addressed the frequency of occurrences of Byzantine faults in practice and the necessity to tolerate Byzantine faults in ultra-reliable distributed systems. A distributed system tolerating as many as F Byzantine faults requires a network size of more than $3F$

A.K. Datta and M. Gradinariu (Eds.): SSS 2006, LNCS 4280, pp. 411–427, 2006.

nodes. Lamport et al. [1, 3] were the first to present the problem and show that Byzantine agreement cannot be achieved for fewer than $3F + 1$ nodes. Dolev et al. [4] proved that at least $3F + 1$ nodes are necessary for clock synchronization in the presence of F Byzantine faults.

A distributed system is defined to be self-stabilizing if, from an arbitrary state and in the presence of bounded number of Byzantine faults, it is guaranteed to reach a legitimate state in a finite amount of time and remain in a legitimate state as long as the number of Byzantine faults are within a specific bound. A legitimate state is a state where all good clocks in the system are synchronized within a given precision bound. Therefore, a self-stabilizing system is able to start in a random state and recover from transient failures after the faults dissipate. The concept of self-stabilizing distributed computation was first presented in a classic paper by Dijkstra [5]. In that paper, he speculated whether it would be possible for a set of machines to stabilize their collective behavior in spite of unknown initial conditions and distributed control. The idea was that the system should be able to converge to a legitimate state within a bounded amount of time, by itself, and without external intervention.

This paper addresses the problem of synchronizing clocks in a distributed system in the presence of Byzantine faults. There are many algorithms that address permanent faults [6], where the issue of transient failures is either ignored or inadequately addressed. There are many efficient Byzantine clock synchronization algorithms that are based on assumptions on initial synchrony of the nodes [6, 7] or existence of a common pulse at the nodes, e.g. the first protocol in [8]. There are many clock synchronization algorithms that are based on randomization and, therefore, are non-deterministic, e.g. the second protocol in [8]. Some clock synchronization algorithms have provisions for initialization and/or reintegration [7, 9]. However, solving these special cases is insufficient to make the algorithm self-stabilizing. A self-stabilizing algorithm encompasses these special scenarios without having to address them separately. The main challenges associated with self-stabilization are the complexity of the design and the proof of correctness of the protocol. Another difficulty is achieving efficient convergence time for the proposed self-stabilizing protocol.

Other recent developments in this area are the algorithms developed by Daliot et al [10, 11]. The algorithm in [11] is called the Byzantine self-stabilization pulse synchronization (BSS-Pulse-Synch) protocol. A flaw in BSS-Pulse-Synch protocol was found and documented in [12]. The biologically inspired Pulse Synchronization protocol in [10] has claims of self-stabilization, but no mechanized[1] proofs are provided.

In this paper a rapid Byzantine self-stabilizing clock synchronization protocol is presented that self-stabilizes from any state, tolerates bursts of transient failures, and deterministically converges within a linear convergence time with respect to the self-stabilization period. Upon self-stabilization, all good clocks

---

[1] A mechanized proof is a formal verification via either a theorem prover or model checker.

proceed synchronously. This protocol has been the subject of rigorous verification efforts that support the claim of correctness.

2   Topology

The underlying topology considered here is a network of K nodes that communicate by exchanging messages through a set of communication channels. The communication channels are assumed to connect a set of source nodes to a set of destination nodes such that the source of a given message is distinctly identifiable from other sources of messages. This system of K nodes can tolerate a maximum of F Byzantine faulty nodes, where $K \geq 3F + 1$. Therefore, the minimum number of good nodes in the system, G, is given by $G = K - F$ and thus $G \geq (2F + 1)$ nodes. Let K_G represent the set of good nodes. The nodes communicate with each other by exchanging broadcast messages. Broadcast of a message to all other nodes is realized by transmitting the message to all other nodes at the same time. The source of a message is assumed to be uniquely identifiable. The communication network does not guarantee any order of arrival of a transmitted message at the receiving nodes. To paraphrase Kopetz [13], a consistent delivery order of a set of messages does not necessarily reflect the temporal or causal order of the events. Each node is driven by an independent local physical oscillator. The oscillators of good nodes have a known bounded drift rate, $1 >> \rho \geq 0$, with respect to real time. Each node has two logical time clocks, *Local_Timer* and *State_Timer*, which locally keep track of the passage of time as indicated by the physical oscillator. In the context of this report, all references to clock synchronization and self-stabilization of the system are with respect to the *State_Timer* and the *Local_Timer* of the nodes. There is neither a central clock nor an externally generated global pulse. The communication channels and the nodes can behave arbitrarily, provided that eventually the system adheres to the system assumptions (see Section 3.5).

The latency of interdependent communications between the nodes is expressed in terms of the minimum event-response delay, D, and network imprecision, d. These parameters are described with the help of Figure 1. In Figure 1, a message transmitted by node N_i at real time t_0 is expected to arrive at all destination nodes N_j, be processed, and subsequent messages generated by N_j within the time interval of $[t_0 + D, t_0 + D + d]$ for all $N_j \in K_G$. Communication between independently clocked nodes is inherently imprecise. The network imprecision, d, is the maximum time difference between all good receivers, N_j, of a message from N_i with respect to real time. The imprecision is due to the drift of the clocks with respect to real time, jitter, discretization error, and slight variations in the communication delay due to various causes such as temperature effects and differences in the lengths of the physical communication medium. These two parameters are assumed to be bounded such that $D \geq 1$ and $d \geq 0$ and both have values with units of real time nominal tick. For the remainder of this report, all references to time are with respect to the nominal tick and are simply referred to as clock ticks.

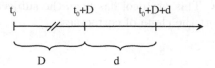

Fig. 1. Event-response delay, D, and network imprecision, d

3   Protocol Description

The self-stabilization problem has two facets. First, it is inherently **event-driven** and, second, it is **time-driven**. Most attempts at solving the self-stabilization problems have focused only on the event-driven aspect of this problem. Additionally, all efforts toward solving this problem must recognize that the system undergoes two distinct phases, un-stabilized and stabilized, and that once stabilized, the system state needs to be preserved. The protocol presented here properly merges the *time* and *event* driven aspects of this problem in order to self-stabilize the system in a gradual and yet timely manner. Furthermore, this protocol is based on the concept of a continual vigilance of state of the system in order to maintain and guarantee its stabilized status, and a continual reaffirmation of nodes by declaring their internal status. Finally, initialization and/or reintegration are not treated as special cases. These scenarios are regarded as inherent part of this self-stabilizing protocol.

The self-stabilization events are captured at a node via a selection function that is based on received valid messages from other nodes. When such an event occurs, it is said that a node has **accepted** or an **accept event** has occurred. When the system is stabilized, it is said to be in the **steady state**.

In order to achieve self-stabilization, the nodes communicate by exchanging two self-stabilization messages labeled **Resync** and **Affirm**. The *Resync* message reflects the time-driven aspect of this self-stabilization protocol, while the *Affirm* message reflects the event-driven aspect of it. The *Resync* message is transmitted when a node realizes that the system is no longer stabilized or as a result of a resynchronization timeout. The *Affirm* message is transmitted periodically and at specific intervals primarily in response to a legitimate self-stabilization *accept event* at the node. The *Affirm* message either indicates that the node is in the transition process to another state in its attempt toward synchronization, or reaffirms that the node will remain synchronized. The timing diagram of transmissions of a good node during the *steady state* is depicted in Figure 2, where *Resync* messages are represented as R and *Affirm* messages are represented as A. As depicted, the expected sequence of messages transmitted by a good node is a *Resync* message followed by a number of *Affirm* messages, i.e. $RAAA \ldots AAARAA$.

The time difference between the interdependent consecutive events is expressed in terms of the minimum event-response delay, D, and network imprecision, d. As a result, the approach presented here is expressed as a self-stabilization

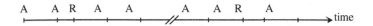

Fig. 2. Timing diagram of transmissions of a good node during the *steady state*

of the system as a function of the expected time separation between the consecutive *Affirm* messages, Δ_{AA}. To guarantee that a message from a good node is received by all other good nodes before a subsequent message is transmitted, Δ_{AA} is constrained such that $\Delta_{AA} \geq (D + d)$. Unless stated otherwise, all time dependent parameters of this protocol are measured locally and expressed as functions of Δ_{AA}. In the *steady state*, N_i receives one *Affirm* message from every good node between any two consecutive *Affirm* messages it transmits. Since the messages may arrive at any time after the transmission of an *Affirm* message, the *accept event* can occur at any time prior to the transmission of the next *Affirm* message.

Three **fundamental parameters** characterize the self-stabilization protocol presented here, namely K, D, and d. The bound on the number of faulty nodes, F, the number of good nodes, G, and the remaining parameters that are subsequently enumerated are **derived parameters** and are based on these three fundamental parameters. Furthermore, except for K, F, and G which are integer numbers, all other parameters are real numbers. In particular, Δ_{AA} is used as a threshold value for monitoring of proper timing of incoming and outgoing *Affirm* messages. The derived parameters $T_A = G$ - 1 and $T_R = F + 1$ are used as thresholds in conjunction with the *Affirm* and *Resync* messages, respectively.

3.1   The Monitor

The transmitted messages to be delivered to the destination nodes are deposited on communication channels. To closely observe the behavior of other nodes, a node employs $(K$-1$)$ *monitors*, one *monitor* for each source of incoming messages as shown in Figure 3.

A node neither uses nor monitors its own messages. The distributed observation of other nodes localizes error detection of incoming messages to their corresponding *monitors*, and allows for modularization and distribution of the self-stabilization protocol process within a node. A *monitor* keeps track of the activities of its corresponding source node. A *monitor* detects proper sequence and timeliness of the received messages from its corresponding source node. A *monitor* reads, evaluates, time stamps, validates, and stores only the last message it receives from that node. Additionally, a *monitor* ascertains the health condition of its corresponding source node by keeping track of the current state of that node. As K increases so does the number of *monitors* instantiated in each node. Although similar modules have been used in engineering practice and, conceptually, by others in theoretical work, as far as the author is aware this is the first use of the *monitors* as an integral part of a self-stabilization protocol.

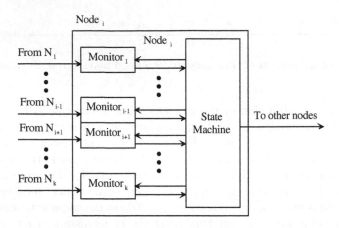

Fig. 3. The ith node, N_i, with its *monitors* and state machine

3.2   The State Machine

The assessment results of the monitored nodes are utilized by the node in the self-stabilization process. The node consists of a state machine and a set of $(K\text{-}1)$ *monitors*. The state machine has two states, **Restore** state (T) and **Maintain** state (M), that reflect the current state of the node in the system as shown in Figure 4. The state machine describes the behavior of the node, N_i, utilizing assessment results from its *monitors*, $M_1.. \ M_{i-1}, \ M_{i+1}.. \ M_K$ as shown in Figure 3, where M_j is the *monitor* for the corresponding node N_j. In addition to the behavior of its corresponding source node, a *monitor*'s internal status is influenced by the current state of the node's state machine. In a master-slave fashion, when the state machine transitions to another state it directs the *monitors* to update their internal status.

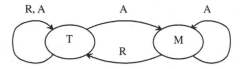

Fig. 4. The node state machine

The **transitory conditions** enable the node to migrate to the *Maintain* state and are defined as:

1. The node is in the *Restore* state,
2. At least $2F$ *accept events* in as many Δ_{AA} intervals have occurred after the node entered the *Restore* state,
3. No *valid Resync* messages are received for the last *accept event*.

The **transitory delay** is the length of time a node stays in the *Restore* state. The minimum required duration for the *transitory delay* is $2F\Delta_{AA}$ after the node enters the *Restore* state. The maximum duration of the *transitory delay* is dependent on the number of additional *valid Resync* messages received. Validity of received messages is defined in Section 3.3. When the system is stabilized, the maximum delay is a result of receiving *valid Resync* messages from all faulty nodes. Since there are at most F faulty nodes present, during the *steady state* operation the duration of the *transitory delay* is bounded by $[2F\Delta_{AA}, 3F\Delta_{AA}]$.

A node in either of the *Restore* or *Maintain* state periodically transmits an *Affirm* message every Δ_{AA}. When in the *Restore* state, it either will meet the *transitory conditions* and transition to the *Maintain* state, or will remain in the *Restore* state for the duration of the self-stabilization period until it times out and transmits a *Resync* message. When in the *Maintain* state, a node either will remain in the *Maintain* state for the duration of the self-stabilization period until it times out, or will unexpectedly transition to the *Restore* state because T_R other nodes have transitioned out of the *Maintain* state. At the transition, the node transmits a *Resync* message.

The self-stabilization period is defined as the maximum time interval (during the *steady state*) that a good node engages in the self-stabilization process. In this protocol the self-stabilization period depends on the current state of the node. Specifically, the self-stabilization period for the *Restore* state is represented by P_T and the self-stabilization period for the *Maintain* state is represented by P_M. P_T and P_M are expressed in terms of Δ_{AA}. Although a *Resync* message is transmitted immediately after the node realizes that it is no longer stabilized, an *Affirm* message is transmitted once every Δ_{AA}.

A node keeps track of time by incrementing a logical time clock, *State_Timer*, once every Δ_{AA}. After the *State_Timer* reaches P_T or P_M, depending on the current state of the node, the node experiences a timeout, transmits a new *Resync* message, resets the *State_Timer*, transitions to the *Restore* state, and attempts to resynchronize with other nodes. If the node was in the *Restore* state it remains in that state after the timeout. The current value of this timer reflects the duration of the current state of the node. It also provides insight in assessing the state of the system in the self-stabilization process. In addition to the *State_Timer*, the node maintains the logical time clock *Local_Timer*. The *Local_Timer* is incremented once every Δ_{AA} and is reset only when the node has transitioned to the *Maintain* state and remained in that state for at least $\lceil \Delta_{Precision} \rceil$, where $\Delta_{Precision}$ is the maximum guaranteed self-stabilization precision. The *Local_Timer* is intended to be used by higher level protocols and is used in assessing the state of the system in the self-stabilization process.

The *monitor*'s status reflects its perception of its corresponding source node. In particular, a *monitor* keeps track of the incoming messages from its corresponding source and ensures that only *valid* messages are stored. This protocol is expected to be used as the fundamental mechanism in bringing and maintaining a system within a known synchronization bound. This protocol neither maintains a history of past behavior of the nodes nor does it attempt to classify the nodes into good and faulty ones. All such determination about the health status of the nodes in the system is assumed to be done by higher level mechanisms.

3.3 Message Sequence

An **expected sequence** is defined as a stream of *Affirm* messages enclosed by two *Resync* messages where all received messages arrive within their expected arrival times. The time interval between the last two *Resync* messages is represented by Δ_{RR}. As described earlier, starting from the last transmission of the *Resync* message consecutive *Affirm* messages are transmitted at Δ_{AA} intervals. At the receiving nodes, the following definitions hold:

- A message (*Resync* or *Affirm*) from a given source is **valid** if it is the first message from that source.
- An *Affirm* message from a given source is **early** if it arrives earlier than $(\Delta_{AA} - d)$ of its previous *valid* message (*Resync* or *Affirm*).
- A *Resync* message from a given source is **early** if it arrives earlier than $\Delta_{RR,min}$ of its previous *valid Resync* message.
- An *Affirm* message from a given source is **valid** if it is not *early*.
- A *Resync* message from a given source is **valid** if it is not *early*.

The protocol works when the received messages do not violate their timing requirements. However, in addition to inspecting the timing requirements, examining the *expected sequence* of the received messages provides stronger error detection at the nodes.

3.4 Protocol Functions

Two functions, *InvalidAffirm()* and *InvalidResync()*, are used by the *monitors*. The *InvalidAffirm()* function determines whether or not a received *Affirm* message is *valid*. The *InvalidResync()* function determines if a received *Resync* message is *valid*. When either of these functions returns a true value, it is indicative of an unexpected behavior by the corresponding source node.

The *Accept()* function is used by the state machine of the node in conjunction with the threshold value $T_A = G - 1$. When at least T_A *valid* messages (*Resync* or *Affirm*) have been received, this function returns a true value indicating that an *accept event* has occurred and such event has also taken place in at least F other good nodes. When a node accepts, it consumes all *valid* messages used in the accept process by the corresponding function. Consumption of a message is the process by which a *monitor* is informed that its stored message, if it existed and was *valid*, has been utilized by the state machine.

The *Retry()* function is used by the state machine of the node with the threshold value $T_R = F + 1$. This function determines if at least T_R other nodes have transitioned out of the *Maintain* state. A node, via its *monitors*, keeps track of the current state of other nodes. When at least T_R *valid Resync* messages from as many nodes have been received, this function returns a true value indicating that at least one good node has transitioned to the *Restore* state. This function is used to transition from the *Maintain* state to the *Restore* state.

The *TransitoryConditionsMet()* function is used by the state machine of the node to determine proper timing of the transition from the *Restore* state to the *Maintain* state. This function keeps track of the *accept events*, by incrementing the *Accept_Event_Counter*, to determine if at least $2F$ *accept events* in as many Δ_{AA} intervals have occurred. It returns a true value when the *transitory conditions* (Section 3.2) are met.

The *TimeOutRestore()* function uses P_T as a boundary value and asserts a timeout condition when the value of the *State_Timer* has reached P_T. Such timeout triggers the node to reengage in another round of self-stabilization process. This function is used when the node is in the *Restore* state.

The *TimeOutMaintain()* function uses P_M as a boundary value and asserts a timeout condition when the value of the *State_Timer* has reached P_M. Such timeout triggers the node to reengage in another round of synchronization. This function is used when the node is in the *Maintain* state.

In addition to the above functions, the state machine utilizes the *TimeOutAcceptEvent()* function. This function is used to regulate the transmission time of the next *Affirm* message. This function maintains a *DeltaAA_Timer* by incrementing it once per local clock tick and once it reaches the transmission time of the next *Affirm* message, Δ_{AA}, it returns a true value. In the advent of such timeout, the node transmits an *Affirm* message.

3.5   System Assumptions

1. The source of the transient faults has dissipated.
2. All good nodes actively participate in the self-stabilization process and execute the protocol.
3. At most F of the nodes are faulty.
4. The source of a message is distinctly identifiable by the receivers from other sources of messages.
5. A message sent by a good node will be received and processed by all other good nodes within Δ_{AA}, where $\Delta_{AA} \geq (D + d)$.
6. The initial values of the state and all variables of a node can be set to any arbitrary value within their corresponding range. In an implementation, it is expected that some local capabilities exist to enforce type consistency of all variables.

3.6   The Self-stabilizing Clock Synchronization Problem

To simplify the presentation of this protocol, it is assumed that all time references are with respect to a real time t_0 when the *system assumptions* are satisfied and the system operates within the *system assumptions*. Let

- C be the maximum convergence time,
- $\Delta_{Local\_Timer}(t)$, for real time t, the maximum time difference of the *Local_Timers* of any two good nodes N_i and N_j, and
- $\Delta_{Precision}$ the maximum guaranteed self-stabilization precision between the *Local_Timer*'s of any two good nodes N_i and N_j in the presence of a maximum of F faulty nodes, $\forall\ N_i,\ N_j \in K_G$.

Convergence: From any state, the system converges to a self-stabilized state after a finite amount of time.

1. $N_i,\ N_j \in K_G,\ \Delta_{Local\_Timer}(C) \le \Delta_{Precision}$.
2. $\forall\ N_i,\ N_j \in K_G$, at C, N_i perceives N_j as being in the *Maintain* state.

Closure: When all good nodes have converged to a given self-stabilization precision, $\Delta_{Precision}$, at time C, the system shall remain within the self-stabilization precision $\Delta_{Precision}$ for $t \ge C$, for real time t.

$\forall\ N_i,\ N_j \in K_G,\ t \ge C,\ \Delta_{Local\_Timer}(t) \le \Delta_{Precision}$,

where, $C = (2P_T + P_M)\,\Delta_{AA}$,

$$
\begin{aligned}
\Delta_{Local\_Timer}(t) = \min(&\max(Local\_Timer_i, Local\_Timer_j) - \\
&\min(Local\_Timer_i, Local\_Timer_j), \\
&\max(Local\_Timer_i - \lceil \Delta_{Precision} \rceil, Local\_Timer_j - \lceil \Delta_{Precision} \rceil) - \\
&\min(Local\_Timer_i - \lceil \Delta_{Precision} \rceil, Local\_Timer_j - \lceil \Delta_{Precision} \rceil)),
\end{aligned}
$$

where,

$(Local\_Timer - \lceil \Delta_{Precision} \rceil)$ is the $\lceil \Delta_{Precision} \rceil^{th}$ previous value of the *Local_Timer*,

$\Delta_{Precision} = (3F - 1)\,\Delta_{AA} - D + \Delta_{Drift}$,

and the amount of drift from the initial precision is given by

$\Delta_{Drift} = ((1+\rho) - 1/(1+\rho))\,P_M\,\Delta_{AA}$.

4   The Byzantine-Fault Tolerant Self-stabilizing Protocol for Distributed Clock Synchronization Systems

The presented protocol is described in Figure 5 and consists of a state machine and a set of *monitors* which execute once every local oscillator tick.

Semantics of the pseudo-code:

- Indentation is used to show a block of sequential statements.
- ',' is used to separate sequential statements.
- '.' is used to end a statement.
- '.,' is used to mark the end of a statement and at the same time to separate it from other sequential statements.

Monitor:
case (incoming message from the corresponding node)
{ Resync:
if *InvalidResync()* then
    Invalidate the message
else
    Validate and store the message,
    Set state status of the source.
	Affirm:
	if *InvalidAffirm()* then
	    Invalidate the message
	else
	    Validate and store the message.
	Other:
	    Do nothing.
	
	} // case

Node: case (state of the node)
{ Restore:
if *TimeOutRestore()* then
    Transmit *Resync* message,
    Reset *State_Timer*,
    Reset *DeltaAA_Timer*,
    Reset *Accept_Event_Counter*,
    Stay in *Restore* state,
 	
elsif *TimeOutAcceptEvent()* then
    Transmit *Affirm* message,
    Reset *DeltaAA_Timer*,
    if *Accept()* then
        Consume *valid* messages,
        Clear state status of the sources,
        Increment *Accept_Event_Counter*,
        if *TransitoryConditionsMet()* then
            Reset *State_Timer*,
            Go to *Maintain* state,
        else
            Stay in *Restore* state.
    else
        Stay in *Restore* state.,
else
    Stay in *Restore* state.
	Maintain:
	if *TimeOutMaintain()* or *Retry()* then
	    Transmit *Resync* message,
	    Reset *State_Timer*,
	    Reset *DeltaAA_Timer*,
	    Reset *Accept_Event_Counter*,
	    Go to *Restore* state,
	
	elsif *TimeOutAcceptEvent()* then
	    if *Accept()* then
	        Consume *valid* messages.,
	        if $(State\_Timer = \lceil \Delta_{Precision} \rceil)$
	            Reset *Local_Timer*.,
	        Transmit *Affirm* message,
	        Reset *DeltaAA_Timer*,
	        Stay in *Maintain* state,
	
	else
	    Stay in *Maintain* state.
	} // case

Fig. 5. The self-stabilization protocol

5 Proof of the Protocol

The approach for the proof is to show that a system of $K \geq 3F + 1$ nodes converges from any condition to a state where all good nodes are in the *Maintain* state. This system is then shown to remain within the timing bounds of the self-stabilization precision of $\Delta_{Precision}$. A sketch of the proof of the protocol is presented here. Details of the proof are documented in [14].

Assumptions: All good nodes are active and the system operates within the *system assumptions*. In this proof, unless otherwise stated in the Lemmas and Theorems, no other assumptions are made about the system.

A node behaves **properly** if it executes the protocol.

Theorem. ResyncWithinP_T –*A good node remaining in the Restore state transmits a Resync message within at most P_T Δ_{AA} clock ticks.*

Lemma. DeltaRRmin – *The shortest time interval between any two consecutive Resync messages from a good node is $2F\Delta_{AA} + 1$ clock ticks.*

Theorem. RestoreToMaintain – *A good node in the Restore state will always transition to the Maintain state.*

From Theorem *RestoreToMaintain*, the maximum possible *transitory delay* for a node in the *Restore* state is $8F\Delta_{AA}$. However, in order to allow the node to transition to the *Maintain* state at the next Δ_{AA}, it has to be prevented from timing out. Therefore, the required minimum period, $P_{T,min}$ is constrained to be $P_{T,min} = (8F+2)\,\Delta_{AA}$. Although P_T can be any value larger than $P_{T,min}$, it follows from Theorem *RestoreToMaintain* that it cannot exceed that minimum value. Also, in order to expedite the self-stabilization process, the convergence time has to be minimized. Thus, P_T is constrained to $P_{T,min}$. The self-stabilization period for the *Maintain* state, P_M, is typically much larger than P_T. Thus, P_M is constrained to be $P_M \geq P_T$.

Corollary. RestoreToMaintainWithin2P_T – *A good node in the Restore state will always transition to the Maintain state within $2P_T$.*

All good nodes validate an *Affirm* message from a good node if the minimum arrival time requirement for that message is not violated. By Lemma *DeltaR-Rmin*, consecutive *Resync* messages from a good node are always more than $\Delta_{RR,min}$ apart. Therefore, after a random start-up, it takes more than $\Delta_{RR,min}$ clock ticks for *Resync* messages from a good node to be accepted by all other good nodes. If a node is in the *Restore* state, from Theorem *ResyncWithinP_T*, it will either time out and transmit a *Resync* message within P_T or from Theorem *RestoreToMaintain* and Corollary *RestoreToMaintainWithin2P_T*, it will transition to the *Maintain* state within $2P_T$. Therefore, for the proof of this protocol, and for the following lemmas and theorems, the state of the system is considered after $2P_T\,\Delta_{AA}$ clock ticks from a random start. At this point, the system is in one of the following three states and all messages from the good nodes meet their timing requirements at the receiving good nodes.

1. **None** of the good nodes are in the *Maintain* state
2. **All** good nodes are in the *Maintain* state
3. **Some** of the good nodes are in the *Maintain* state

Theorem. ConvergeNoneMaintain – A system of $K \geq 3F + 1$ nodes, where none of the good nodes are in the Maintain state and have not met the transitory conditions, will always converge.

The **self-stabilization precision**, $\Delta_{Precision}$, is the maximum time difference between the *Local_Timer*'s of any two good nodes when the system is stabilized. It is, therefore, the guaranteed precision of the protocol. From Theorem *ConvergeNoneMaintain*, the initial precision after the resynchronization is determined to be $\Delta_{LMEM} = (3F - 1) \Delta_{AA} - D$. After the initial synchrony and due to the drift rate of the oscillators, *Local_Timers* of the good nodes will deviate from the initial precision. Therefore, the guaranteed self-stabilization precision, $\Delta_{Precision}$, after elapsed time of $P_M \Delta_{AA}$ clock ticks, is bounded by, $\Delta_{Precision} = \Delta_{LMEM} + \Delta_{Drift}$, where the amount of drift from the initial precision is given by $\Delta_{Drift} = ((1+\rho) - 1/(1+\rho)) P_M \Delta_{AA}$. The factors $(1+\rho)$ and $1/(1+\rho)$ are, respectively, associated with the slowest and fastest nodes in the system. Therefore, $\Delta_{Precision} = (3F - 1) \Delta_{AA} - D + \Delta_{Drift}$.

Corollary. MutuallyStabilized – *All good nodes mutually perceive each other as being in the Maintain state.*

Theorem. ConvergeAllMaintain – *A system of $K \geq 3F + 1$ nodes, where all good nodes are in the Maintain state, will always converge.*

Theorem. ConvergeSomeMaintain – *A system of $K \geq 3F + 1$ nodes, where some of the good nodes are in the Maintain state will always converge.*

Theorem. ClosureAllMaintain – *A system of $K \geq 3F + 1$ nodes, where all good nodes have converged such that all good nodes are mutually stabilized with each other (in other words, all good nodes are in the Maintain state where $\Delta_{Local\_Timer}(t) \leq \Delta_{Precision}$), shall remain within the self-stabilization precision $\Delta_{Precision}$.*

Corollary. StateTimerLessThanPrecision – *In a stabilized system and during the re-stabilization process, the maximum value of the State_Timer is always less than the self-stabilization precision $\Delta_{Precision}$.*

Therefore, the *Local_Timer* can be reset at any point where *State_Timer* is greater than or equal to the precision. In order to expedite the self-stabilization process, *Local_Timer* is reset when *State_Timer* reaches the next integer value greater than $\Delta_{Precision}$, i.e. $\lceil \Delta_{Precision} \rceil$.

Theorem. LocalTimerWithinPrecision – *The difference of Local_Timers of all good nodes in a stabilized system of $K \geq 3F + 1$ nodes will always be within the self-stabilization precision, i.e. $\Delta_{Local\_Timer}(t) \leq \Delta_{Precision}$.*

Theorem. StabilizeFromAnyState – *A system of $K \geq 3F + 1$ nodes self-stabilizes from any random state after a finite amount of time.*

Proof – The proof of this theorem consists of proving the convergence and closure properties as defined in the Self-Stabilizing Clock Synchronization Problem section.

Convergence – *From any state, the system converges to a self-stabilized state after a finite amount of time.*
1. $N_i, N_j \in K_G$, $\Delta_{Local\_Timer}(C) \leq \Delta_{Precision}$.
2. $\forall\, N_i, N_j \in K_G$, at C, N_i perceives N_j as being in the Maintain state.

Proof – The proof is done in the following four parts:

Convergence – *None of the good nodes are in the Maintain state.*

Proof – It follows from Theorems *ConvergeNoneMaintain* and *ClosureAllMaintain* that such system always self-stabilizes.

Convergence – *All good nodes are in the Maintain state.*

Proof – It follows from Theorems *ConvergeNoneMaintain*, *ConvergeAllMaintain* and *ClosureAllMaintain* that such system always self-stabilizes.

Convergence – *Some of the good nodes are in the Maintain state.*

Proof – It follows from Theorems *ConvergeNoneMaintain*, *ConvergeAllMaintain*, *ConvergeSomeMaintain*, and *ClosureAllMaintain* that such system always self-stabilizes.

Mutually Stabilized –$\forall\, N_i, N_j \in K_G$, *at C, N_i perceives N_j as being in the Maintain state.*

Proof – It follows from Corollary *MutuallyStabilized* that all good nodes mutually perceive each other to be in the *Maintain* state.

Closure – *When all good nodes have converged such that $\Delta_{Local\_Timer}(C) \leq \Delta_{Precision}$, at time C, the system shall remain within the self-stabilization precision $\Delta_{Precision}$ for $t \geq C$, for real time t.*

$$\forall\, N_i, N_j \in K_G, \, t \geq C, \, \Delta_{Local\_Timer}(t) \leq \Delta_{Precision}.$$

Proof – It follows from Theorems *ClosureAllMaintain* and *LocalTimerWithin-Precision* that such system always remains stabilized and $\Delta_{Local\_Timer}(t) \leq \Delta_{Precision}$ for $t \geq C$. $\diamond$

This protocol neither maintains a history of past behavior of the nodes nor does it attempt to classify the nodes into good and faulty ones. Since this protocol self-stabilizes from any state, initialization and/or reintegration are not treated as special cases. Therefore, a reintegrating node will always be admitted to participate in the self-stabilization process as soon as it becomes active. Continual transmission of the *Affirm* messages by the good nodes expedites the reintegration process.

Theorem. ConvergeTime – A system of $K \geq 3F + 1$ nodes converges from any random state to a self-stabilized state within $C = (2P_T + P_M) \, \Delta_{AA}$ clock ticks.

If $P_M = P_T$, then $C = 3P_M$, but since typically $P_M \gg P_T$, therefore, C can be approximated to $C \cong P_M$. Therefore, the convergence time of this protocol is a linear function of the P_M.

6   Achieving Tighter Precision

Since the self-stabilization messages are communicated at Δ_{AA} intervals, if Δ_{AA}, and hence $\Delta_{Precision}$, are larger than the desired precision, the system is said to be **Coarsely Synchronized**. Otherwise, the system is said to be **Finely Synchronized**. If the granularity provided by the self-stabilization precision is coarser than desired, a higher synchronization precision can be achieved in a two step process. First, a system from any initial state has to be *Coarsely Synchronized* and guaranteed that the system remains *Coarsely Synchronized* and operates within a known precision, $\Delta_{Precision}$. The second step, in conjunction with the *Coarse Synchronization* protocol, is to utilize a proven protocol that is based on the initial synchrony assumptions to achieve optimum precision of the synchronized system. The *Coarse Synchronization* protocol initiates the start of the *Fine Synchronization* protocol if a tighter precision of the system is desired. The *Coarse* protocol maintains self-stabilization of the system while the *Fine Synchronization* protocol increases the precision of the system.

7   Conclusions

In this paper, a rapid Byzantine self-stabilizing clock synchronization protocol is presented that self-stabilizes from any state. It tolerates bursts of transient failures, and deterministically converges with a linear convergence time with respect to the self-stabilization period. Upon self-stabilization, all good clocks proceed synchronously. This protocol has been the subject of a rigorous verification effort. A 4-node system consisting of 3 good nodes and one Byzantine faulty node has been proven correct using model checking. The proposed protocol explores the *timing* and *event* driven facets of the self-stabilization problem. The protocol employs *monitors* to closely observe the activities of the nodes in the system. All timing measures of variables are based on the node's local clock and thus no central clock or externally generated pulse is used. The proposed protocol is scalable with respect to the *fundamental parameters*, K, D, and d. The self-stabilization precision $\Delta_{Precision}$, $\Delta_{Local\_Timer}(t)$, and self-stabilization periods P_T and P_M are functions of K, D and d. The convergence time is a linear function of P_T and P_M and deterministic. Therefore, although there is no theoretical upper bound on the maximum values for the *fundamental parameters*, implementation of this protocol may introduce some practical limitations on the maximum value of these parameters and the choice of topology. Since only two self-stabilization messages, namely *Resync* and *Affirm* messages, are required for the proper operation of this protocol, a single bit suffices to represent both messages. Therefore, for a data message w bits wide, the self-stabilization overhead will be $1/w$ per transmission.

A sketch of proof of this protocol has been presented in this paper. This protocol is expected to be used as the fundamental mechanism in bringing and maintaining a system within bounded synchrony. Integration of a higher level mechanism with this protocol needs to be further studied. Furthermore, if a higher level secondary protocol is non-self-stabilizing, it is conjectured that it can be made self-stabilizing when used in conjunction with the protocol presented here. We have started formalizing the integration process of other protocols with this protocol in order to achieve tighter synchronization. We are also planning to implement this protocol in hardware and characterize it in a representative adverse environment.

References

1. L Lamport, R Shostak, and M Pease, *The Byzantine General Problem*, ACM Transactions on Programming Languages and Systems, 4(3), pp. 382-401, July 1982.
2. K Driscoll, B Hall, H Sivencronam, and P Zumsteg, *Byzantine Fault Tolerance, from Theory to Reality: Computer Safety, Reliability, and Security*, Publisher: Springer-Verlag Heidelberg, ISBN: 3-540-20126-2, Volume 2788 / 2003, October 2003, pp. 235 – 248
3. L Lamport and P M Melliar-Smith, *Synchronizing clocks in the presence of faults*, J. ACM, vol. 32, no. 1, pp. 52-78, 1985.
4. D Dolev, J Y Halpern, and R Strong, *On the Possibility and Impossibility of Achieving Clock Synchronization*, proceedings of the 16th Annual ACM STOC (Washington D.C., Apr.). ACM, New York, 1984, pp. 504-511. (Also appear in J. Comput. Syst. Sci.)
5. B W Dijkstra, *Self stabilizing systems in spite of distributed control*, Commun. ACM 17,643-644m 1974.
6. T K Srikanth and S Toueg, *Optimal Clock Synchronization*, proceedings of the Fourth Annual ACM Symposium on Principles of Distributed Computing, 1985, pp. 71-86.
7. J L Welch and N Lynch, *A New Fault-Tolerant Algorithm for Clock Synchronization*, Information and Computation volume 77, no. 1, April 1988, pp.1-36.
8. S Dolev and J L Welch, *Self-Stabilizing Clock Synchronization in the Presence of Byzantine Faults*, Journal of the ACM, Vol.51, Np. 5, September 2004, pp. 780-799.

9. D. Dolev, J. Y. Halpern, B. Simons, and R. Strong, *Dynamic Fault-Tolerant Clock Synchronization*, J. ACM, Vol. 42, No.1, 1995.
10. A Daliot, D Dolev, and H Parnas, *Self-Stabilizing Pulse Synchronization Inspired by Biological Pacemaker Networks*, Proceedings of the Sixth Symposium on Self-Stabilizing Systems, DSN SSS '03, San Francisco, June 2003.
11. A Daliot, D Dolev, and H Parnas, *Linear Time Byzantine Self-Stabilizing Clock Synchronization*, Proceedings of 7th International Conference on Principles of Distributed Systems (OPODIS-2003), La Martinique, France, December 2003.
12. M R Malekpour and R Siminiceanu, *Comments on the "Byzantine Self-Stabilizing Pulse Synchronization" Protocol: Counterexamples*, NASA/TM-2006-213951, Feb 2006, pp. 7.
13. H Kopetz, *Real-Time Systems, Design Principles for Distributed Embedded Applications*, Kluwar Academic Publishers, ISBN 0-7923-9894-7, 1997.
14. M R Malekpour, *A Byzantine-Fault Tolerant Self-Stabilizing Protocol for Distributed Clock Synchronization Systems*, NASA/TM-2006-214322, August 2006, pp. 37.

A Memory Efficient Self-stabilizing Algorithm
for Maximal k-Packing

Fredrik Manne and Morten Mjelde

Department of Informatics, University in Bergen, Norway
{fredrik.manne, mortenm}@ii.uib.no

Abstract. The k-packing problem asks for a subset S of the nodes in a graph such that the distance between any pair of nodes in S is greater than k. This problem has applications to placing facilities in a network.

In the current paper we present a self-stabilizing algorithm for computing a maximal k-packing in a general graph. Our algorithm uses a constant number of variables per node. This improves the memory requirement compared to the previous most memory efficient algorithm [9] which used k variables per node. In addition the presented algorithm is very short and simple.

Keywords: self-stabilizing algorithms, k-packing.

1 Introduction

Facility location problems in a network involve distributing a set of resources such that the entire network is covered. Depending on the objective these can either be minimization problems where one wants to use as few resources as possible while covering the graph or maximization problems where one wants to distribute as many resources as possible under some constraint. There exists a number of such problems and they have been extensively studied in the literature of sequential algorithms [1,10,12,13].

In this paper we present a self-stabilizing distributed algorithm for one such problem, namely the k-packing problem. This involves selecting a set S of nodes such that the length of the shortest path between any pair of nodes $(v, w) \in S$ is greater than k (a 1-packing is better known as an independent set). The set S is referred to as black nodes while the remaining nodes are referred to as white. A maximum k-packing implies that S is the set with largest cardinality, and finding this is NP-hard on a general graph [6]. The simpler problem of computing a maximal k-packing (i.e. no superset of S is also a legal solution) can easily be solved by a sequential greedy algorithm in linear time.

Previous work on developing self-stabilizing algorithms for the k-packing problem has resulted in several different algorithms. Gairing et al. gave an algorithm that computed a maximal 2-packing on a general graph [5]. This algorithm used an exponential number of moves and a constant number of variables per node. Goddard et al. subsequently developed a self-stabilizing algorithm for solving maximal k-packing on a general graph [9]. This algorithm used an exponential number of

A.K. Datta and M. Gradinariu (Eds.): SSS 2006, LNCS 4280, pp. 428–439, 2006.

moves, and k variables per node. In a recent paper Goddard et al. also presented a self-stabilizing algorithm for the same problem that runs in $n^{O(\log k)}$ moves [8]. However, this algorithm requires that each node stores information about the graph within a radius of k from itself, thus substantially increasing the memory requirements. We also note that there exists a self-stabilizing algorithm for computing a maximum k-packing on a tree graph with a moves complexity of $O(n^3)$ [11].

From the above exposition it follows that there is a trade off between the number of moves and the amount of memory used on each node when designing self-stabilizing algorithms for computing a maximal k-packing on a general graph. In fact, if one first computed a spanning tree in the graph, a task which is considerable simpler than computing a maximal k-packing [7], one could copy the structure of the entire graph into each node in a polynomial number of moves [2] and then solve the maximal k-packing problem by a local deterministic sequential algorithm on each node. The same approach could also be used to compute a maximum k-packing (although this would require an exponential local running time on every node).

In this paper we fill in one part in this trade off between moves complexity and memory usage. We present an algorithm that computes a maximal k-packing for a general graph using only a constant number of variables per node, each of which hold at most $O(\log n)$ bits. However, the moves complexity of the algorithm is still exponential. In addition to using less memory than other algorithms for this problem the algorithm itself is very short, and thus easy to understand and implement.

Limiting the amount of memory is an important factor in many applications such as in sensor networks where the computational units are small and rely on battery power to operate.

The rest of this paper is organized as follows. In Section 2 we present some background on self-stabilizing algorithms. In Section 3 we present our algorithm and show that any stable solution produced by it is also a legal solution and that it will stabilize in a finite amount of time. Finally, we conclude in Section 4.

2   The Self-stabilizing Paradigm

Self-stabilizing algorithms are a variant of distributed systems first introduced by Dijkstra in 1974 [3]. However, the significance of the work was not immediately recognized, and serious work did not begin until the late 1980's. One of the most important properties of any self-stabilizing algorithm is its ability to recover from any transient errors that occurs, and even changes in the graph itself. This ability makes self-stabilizing algorithms extremely fault tolerant.

A self-stabilizing algorithm does not assume the existence of a central leader. Instead, all nodes in the graph are considered equals, and each of them has the same copy of the algorithm. Each node maintains a set of variables that together make up the nodes *local state*. The union of all local states is the graphs *global state*. In the normal self-stabilizing model any node has knowledge only of its own and its neighbors' local states. The algorithm itself is comprised of a set of rules. These are typically written in the form:

Rule i
  if $p(v)$
  then M

The function $p(v)$ is called the *predicate*, and M is called the *move*. The predicate takes the node v as a parameter, and becomes true or false based on v's local state and the local state of its neighbors. The move M will change one or more of v's local variables. If the predicate is true the rule is called *privileged*, and only then can it execute its corresponding move. For cases where there are more than one privileged rule in the graph, the self-stabilizing model assumes the existence of a *central daemon* that determines which rules will be permitted to make its move. Various self-stabilizing algorithms employ different daemons, and for the current algorithm we assume an adversarial daemon (as opposed to a fair or random daemon). Regardless of the type of daemon used any self-stabilizing algorithm has to guarantee to reach a solution in a finite number of moves independent of the starting configuration. This is called to *stabilize* and implies that no node in the graph has a privileged rule. For further reading on self-stabilizing algorithms, see [4].

For our algorithm we assume the existence of an undirected graph $G = (V, E)$ where V is the set of nodes and E the set of edges. We further assume that each node has a unique ID, and that these IDs can be ordered. The ID of a node v is denoted by ID_v. The set of nodes $N(v)$ is the open neighborhood of v, and contains all the neighbors of v.

3   The Algorithm

In the following we present and analyze our new algorithm. It is based on each node determining the distance to its two nearest black nodes (possibly including itself). Based on this information a node can then determine if it should be black or white.

3.1   The Local Variables

As mentioned in Section 2, each node in a self-stabilizing algorithm maintains a set of local variables that make up the nodes local state. In our algorithm, each node $v \in V$ has two pairs of variables: (p_v, b_v) and (p'_v, b'_v). The intention is that p_v denotes the shortest distance (i.e. number of edges) to v's closest black node y and with $b_v = ID_y$. The pair (p'_v, b'_v) gives the same information about v's second closest black node (assuming it exists). The range of p_v is $[0, \infty]$ while the range of p'_v is $[1, \infty]$. It then follows that in a stable configuration the black nodes are identified by having p-values equal to 0 and p'-values larger than k.

In the case where a node has more than one black node at a minimum distance from it we say that the black node with the smallest ID-value is the closest one. Thus the term "closest black node" will always be well defined.

As we will explain in further detail later, the purpose of the (p', b') values is for every black node in the graph to gain knowledge of its closest black node other than itself.

3.2 Definitions and Notations

Based on the local variables of each node we now give some definitions and notations that we will be using. This is done to make the ensuing presentation clearer and also more compact.

Two adjacent nodes v and w where $b_v = b_w$ and $p_v = p_w + 1$ belong to the same *domain* and we say that w is a *predecessor* of v in the domain. A node v that does not have a predecessor is a *leader* of the domain. The domain relation is transitive and thus each domain is a connected component of the graph. We will also say that adjacent nodes v and w where either $b'_v = b_w$ and $p'_v = p_w + 1$ or $b'_v = b'_w$ and $p'_v = p'_w + 1$ belong to the same domain. Thus a node can belong to two domains at the same time depending on if we are looking at the (p_v, b_v) or (p'_v, b'_v) values.

A domain U is *proper* if v is a leader of U and there exists a node w such that $b_v = ID_w$. Note that w does not have to be part of U for U to be proper. A domain that is not proper is *improper*.

We define the set T_v for a node v as being the pair (p_v, b_v) and (p'_v, b'_v). We further define the set T_M for some set of nodes M as $\cup_{v \in M} T_v$.

3.3 The Algorithm

The algorithm consists of one function and one rule. These are as follows:

support(v)
$\quad (\alpha, \beta) = \min\{(\gamma, \delta) \in T_{N(v)} : \delta \neq ID_v\}$
$\quad (\alpha', \beta') = \min\{(\gamma, \delta) \in T_{N(v)} : \delta \neq ID_v, \delta \neq \beta\}$

$\quad$ **if** $(\alpha \geq k) \vee (p_v = 0 \wedge \beta > ID_v)$
$\quad\quad$ return $(0, ID_v, \alpha + 1, \beta)$
$\quad$ **else**
$\quad\quad$ return $(\alpha + 1, \beta, \alpha' + 1, \beta')$

Rule 1
$\quad$ **if** $(p_v, b_v, p'_v, b'_v) \neq$ support(v)
$\quad$ **then** set $(p_v, b_v, p'_v, b'_v) =$ support(v)

The purpose of the support function is to return the correct (p, b) and (p', b') values for a node v based on the local state of v and its neighbors. The function starts by selecting a pair (α, β) from $T_{N(v)}$ such that α is as small as possible while $\beta \neq ID_v$. In the case of a tie a pair with the smallest β value is selected. Next the function selects a pair (α', β') in the same manner as above only with the added constraint that $\beta' \neq \beta$. In both of the above cases, if no valid pair can be found in $T_{N(v)}$ the pair (∞, ∞) will be used.

Based on the selected values the function will now determine if v should be black or not. With the assumption that (α, β) represents the distance to the closest black node (other than v itself) it follows that either if $\alpha \geq k$ or if $p_v = 0$ (indicating that v is at present black) and the closest black node has higher ID

than v ($\beta > ID_v$) then v can become (or remain) black. In the case where the above condition was met, the function returns $(0, ID_v, \alpha + 1, \beta)$, where the first pair of values indicates that v should be black and the second pair gives the distance and ID of the closest black other than v itself.

If v should not be black then it should become (or remain) white. All it has to do in this case is to gather data about its two closest black nodes. Thus the function returns $(\alpha + 1, \beta, \alpha' + 1, \beta')$.

Rule 1 is the only rule in the algorithm. It simply determines if one or more of the values returned by the support function does not correspond to the node's current values. If this is the case, the node is privileged for a move that corrects them.

3.4   Correct Stabilization

We now show that the algorithm, when stable, has solved the maximal k-packing problem. To do so we first show that in a stable configuration the values of p and p' will be set to the distance of the nearest and second nearest black node respectively.

We again remind the reader that in the case where a node v has more than one black node at minimum distance we will break ties by defining that which ever has the smallest ID is the one closest to v. Note that this is consistent with how the support function operates.

Lemma 1. *Let (p_v, b_v) be the local values for a node $v \in V$ in a stable configuration. Then there exists a black node y such that y is the closest black node to v of distance p_v from v and such that $ID_y = b_v$.*

> *Proof.* Note first that we cannot have a node v with $p_v > k$ in a stable configuration.
>
> The proof of the claim is by induction on the value of p_v. If $p_v = 0$ then v is black, and must have $b_v = ID_v$ in a stable configuration. Assume therefore that the claim is true for every $w \in V$ where $p_w < l, 1 < l \leq k$, and let $v \in V$ be a node such that $p_v = l$. Then by the construction of the support function there must exist a node $u \in N(v)$ such that $p_u = p_v - 1 = l - 1$ and $b_v = b_u$. From the induction claim it follows that there exists a black node y such that $b_u = ID_y$ where y is the closest black node at a distance $l - 1$ from u. We therefore have that there exists a path of length l between v and the black node y where $b_v = ID_y$.
>
> If there was to exist a path from a black node x to v of length less than l or of length l but with $ID_x < b_v$, then again by the induction hypothesis there must exist a node $z \in N(v)$ such that either $p_z + 1 < p_v$ or $p_z + 1 = p_v$ and $b_z < b_v$. In both of these cases v would be privileged for a move. □

Corollary 1. *In a stable configuration, the maximum distance from any node to a black node is at most k.*

Proof. Consider a white node v in a stable solution that has minimum distance $> k$ to the nearest black node. By Lemma 1 it then follows that every $w \in N(v)$ has $p_w \geq k$ in which case the support function will return 0 for p_v thus contradicting the assumption that the configuration is stable.   □

We now need to show that we cannot have two black nodes in a stable configuration that are closer to each other than k. To do so we first show that the value of p'_v will be set to the distance to the second closest black node of a node v.

Lemma 2. *Let (p'_v, b'_v) be the local values for some node $v \in V$ in a stable configuration containing at least two black nodes. Then there exists a black node y such that y is the second closest black node to v of distance p'_v from v and such that $ID_y = b'_v$.*

Proof. Note first that by the construction of the support function each node that has $0 < p'_v < \infty$ in a stable configuration must have a neighbor w where either $(p_w+1, b_w) = (p'_v, b'_v)$ and $b_w \neq b_v$ or where $(p'_w+1, b'_w) = (p'_v, b'_v)$ and $b_w = b_v$. Thus starting from v there exists a path along decreasing p or p' values such that the b-value is unchanged. If the path makes use of a p-value then since the p-values do not depend on the p'-values, the path will lead to a black node. This must eventually happen since a value of $p' = 1$ must have been obtained from a black neighbor. Thus it follows that if $p'_v = l$ then there exists a path of length l from v to a black node y such that $b'_v = ID_y$. It now remains to show that this path is the shortest path from v to a black node different from b_v.

Let v be a node with $b_v = ID_x$ in a stable configuration such that among the nodes with b-value set to ID_x, v has the shortest distance l to a black node y where $y \neq x$. Let $y = w_0, w_1, \ldots, w_{l-1}, v$ be the nodes on this path. Then y must be the closest black node to each w_i, $1 \leq i < l$, and by Lemma 1 we must have $p_{w_i} = i$ and $b_{w_i} = ID_y$. The support function applied to v then has the opportunity to return the pair $(l, b_{w_{l-1}} = ID_y)$ for (p'_v, b'_v). If it does not do so then this would indicate that there exists a black node different from x that is closer to v than y is. This is a contradiction and the result follows.

Assume by induction that p'_v and b'_v are set correctly for every node with both $b_v = ID_x$ and with shortest distance r, $r \geq l$, to a black node other than x. Let v now be a node with shortest distance $r + 1$ to a black node y other than x. Then if the shortest path from v to y does not pass through any node with b-value set to x the same argument as above shows that we must have $p'_v = r + 1$ and $b'_v = ID_y$. If the shortest path $y = w_0, w_1, \ldots, w_r, v$ does pass through at least one node with $b_{w_i} = ID_x$ then we must have $b_{w_r} = ID_x$. This follows since as soon as the shortest path from v to y leaves the x-domain it will not re-enter it. Thus by induction we have $p'_{w_r} = r$ and $b'_{w_r} = ID_y$ and in a stable configuration we must have $p'_v = r + 1$ and $b'_v = ID_y$.   □

Note that if there is only one black node y in G then each node v will have $b_v = y$ and the pair (p'_v, b'_v) will be set to (∞, ∞).

From Lemmas 1 and 2 it follows that in a stable configuration any white node v has p_v equal to the distance to the nearest black node while any black node w has p'_w equal to the distance to the nearest black node other than itself. Thus if x and y are the two closest black nodes and with $ID_x < ID_y$ and distance l from each other where $l \leq k$ then in a stable configuration we will have $p'_y = l$ and $b'_y \leq ID_y$. But with this configuration y cannot keep $p_y = 0$ and is privileged for a move. Thus we have the following result.

Lemma 3. *In a stable configuration there does not exist a pair of black nodes where the minimum distance between them is less than or equal to k.*

Putting all of this together it is now straightforward to show that a stable solution is also a maximal k-packing.

Theorem 1. *A stable configuration is a maximal k-packing.*

Proof. From Lemma 3 it follows that in a stable configuration there cannot exist black nodes within distance k of each other. Further from Corollary 1 we know that there cannot exist a non-privileged white node with distance greater than or equal to k to every black node in the graph. Thus it follows that a stable configuration is a maximal k-packing. □

3.5 Convergence

Now that we have shown that once the algorithm stabilizes it has reached a valid solution we proceed to show that the algorithm will do so in a finite amount of steps. To reduce the complexity of the presentation we will assume that the algorithm in each move either updates (p_v, b_v) or (p'_v, b'_v) (and not both). While this is not entirely keeping with how Rule 1 functions, making this assumption does not affect the correctness of the analysis. Consider that once the support function for a node v has returned, updating the two pairs (p_v, b_v) and (p'_v, b'_v) can be regarded as two separate moves where one has no bearing on the other.

Starting with (p_v, b_v) we first divide the execution of Rule 1 into three different cases depending on the outcome of the move. These three cases are as follows:

Black move. A node is said to make a *black move* if after the move it has changed its color from white to black.

Decremental move. A node v is said to make a *d-move* if it has changed p_v to $\bar{p}_v$ and b_v to $\bar{b}_v$ such that either $\bar{p}_v < p_v$ or $\bar{b}_v < b_v \wedge \bar{p}_v = p_v$.

Incremental move. A node v is said to make an *i-move* if it has changed p_v to $\bar{p}_v$ and b_v to $\bar{b}_v$ such that either $\bar{p}_v > p_v$ or $\bar{b}_v > b_v \wedge \bar{p}_v = p_v$.

Note that we label a move by the first condition in increasing order that evaluates to true. For example, a node makes a black move if it has become black, even if the move also qualified as a d-move. We note that both the d- and i-moves can be defined for the (p', b')-values. It is then straightforward to see that the three different types of moves cover every possible move that the algorithm can make. In the following we will first reason that we cannot have an infinite sequence of d- and i-moves when only applied to the (p, b)-values.

To be able to reason about what causes a node to make a move we note that a locally stable node v can only become privileged and make a new move if one of its neighbors x first makes a move. If this is the first move among the neighbors of v that causes v to become privileged we will say that the move made by x *initiated* the subsequent move by v. With this definition we can now show the following result.

Lemma 4. *A d-move cannot initiate an i-move.*

Proof. Consider a locally stable node v with values p_v and b_v. Then if v is white there must exist a node $w \in N(v)$ such that $p_w + 1 = p_v$ and $b_w = b_v$. If v is to make an i-move there cannot exist any node $u \in N(v)$ with either $p_u < p_v - 1$ or with $p_u = p_v - 1$ and $b_u \leq b_v$. In the case where w does not make a move this is not true. Also, if w makes a d-move then w must decrease either its p-value or b-value (or both). In either case the condition for v to make an i-move is not satisfied.

If v is a locally stable black node then it will only make an i-move if some neighbor w has $p_w < k$ and $b_w < ID_v$. But if this is not the case prior to when w makes an i-move it will not be true after the move. □

From Lemma 4 it follows that in a sequence of moves by the nodes of G that consists entirely of d- and i-moves one can analyze the number of i-moves independently from the d-moves. We will do this in the following, but first we show how many consecutive d-moves there can be.

Lemma 5. *The number of consecutive d-moves is at most $O(n^2 k)$.*

Proof. After a node has executed its initial move (which might be a d-move) it will have a p-value in the range $[0, k]$. Thus it follows that a node can at most decrement its p-value k times before it has to make an i-move. In addition a node can decrease its b-value while keeping its p-value fixed. Each node in the graph can at most give rise to one unique b-value. In addition there might be n additional b-values in the graph due to the initial values. Thus for a fixed p-value a node might decrease its b-value at most $2n$ times. This gives a total of at most $2nk$ d-moves per node. □

Next, we analyze the i-moves and show that any sequence consisting entirely of i-moves must stabilize.

Lemma 6. *There cannot be an infinite sequence of i-moves.*

Proof. Let $\beta_1, \beta_2, \ldots, \beta_l$, $1 \leq l \leq 2n$, be an increasing sequence containing the set of distinct b-values that are used during the execution of the algorithm. This contains the values given by the IDs of the nodes as well as any initial b-values.

Define a vector $A = [a_{(0,\beta_1)}, a_{(0,\beta_2)}, \ldots, a_{(0,\beta_l)}, a_{(1,\beta_1)}, a_{(1,\beta_2)}, \ldots, a_{(1,\beta_l)}, \ldots, a_{(k,\beta_1)}, a_{(k,\beta_2)}, \ldots, a_{(k,\beta_l)}]$ where entry $a_{(i,\beta_j)}$ is the number of nodes in the graph at any one time with p-value equal to i and b-value equal to β_j that are privileged for an i-move. Note that only a node v with $0 \leq p_v < k$ can be privileged for an i-move, thus every node that is privileged for an i-move is represented in A and the sum of the elements in A is always bounded by n. We will now show that if an i-move changes A to A' then $A > A'$ where the comparison is done by viewing each vector as a number consisting of at most $2(k+1)n$ digits.

Consider a node v that makes an i-move and let p_v, b_v be the associated values of v before the move. Then the value in position (p_v, b_v) of A will be reduced by one and since v will not be privileged for a new i-move immediately after this move v will not directly cause any other entry in A to change. In addition, any node $w \in N(v)$ that had v as its only neighboring node with either $p_v < p_w - 1$ or with $p_v = p_w - 1$ and $b_v \leq b_w$ before the move and where either $p_v > p_w - 1$ or $p_v = p_w - 1$ and $b_v > b_w$ is true after the move has now become privileged for an i-move. If this is the case the entry $a_{(p_w, b_w)}$ will increase by one for each such node w. But since the initial value of p_v is less than p_w it follows that $A > A'$. To see that any consecutive sequence of i-moves must terminate after a finite number of moves it is sufficient to note that we cannot have negative numbers in A and that the sum of the entries in A is always bounded by n. $\square$

The immediate bound obtained from the proof of Lemma 6 is fairly pessimistic as there are an exponential number of distinct configurations of the A vector used in the proof. Still, together with Lemmas 4 and 5 it shows that any sequence of d-moves and i-moves must stabilize. The only time where the (p', b') values might affect the (p, b) values is when making a black node privileged to perform an i-move. But then the node ceases to be black and as long as we don't allow for any black nodes this can at most happen once for each node.

To see that the i- and d-moves on the (p', b') values also must stabilize it is sufficient to note that for fixed (p, b) values the i- and d-moves on (p', b') behaves in the same way as on the (p, b) values. Thus it follows that between each set of i- and d-moves on the (p, b) values we can at most have a finite number of i- and d-moves on the (p', b') values. Thus we have the following result.

Lemma 7. *Any sequence of i- and d-moves applied to both the (p, b) and (p', b') values is bounded.*

It now remains to incorporate the black moves into the analysis. We do this with in the following.

Lemma 8. *There cannot be an infinite sequence of black moves.*

Proof. Any black node v at the start of the algorithm where $b_v \neq ID_v$ will be corrected by the first move v makes and thus there can at most be n such moves. Thus for the rest of the analysis we assume that $b_v = ID_v$ for every black node.

Similar to in the proof of Lemma 6 we define the vector $A = [a_{(1,\beta_1)},$ $a_{(1,\beta_2)}, \ldots, a_{(1,\beta_l)}, a_{(2,\beta_1)}, a_{(2,\beta_2)}, \ldots, a_{(2,\beta_l)}, \ldots, a_{(k,\beta_1)}, a_{(k,\beta_2)}, \ldots, a_{(k,\beta_l)}]$ where entry $a_{(j,\beta_i)}$ is the number of nodes in the graph at any one time with p-value equal to j and b-value equal to β_i that are privileged for an i-move on the (p,b) values. Again, we also assume that the different values of β_i span all possible values (at most $2n$) and that $\beta_i < \beta_{i+1}$.

It is then clear that only a domain where β_i corresponds to the ID_v of some $v \in V$ can contain a black node as a leader and there can only be one such black node at a time (apart from at start up).

Let v be the node with lowest ID among the nodes in G. Then $a_{(0,ID_v)}$ is the leftmost position in A that can correspond to a black node. If v is black it can only become white due to a node $w \in N(v)$ with values such that either $p_w < k$ and $b_w < b_v$ or that $p'_w < k$ and $b'_w < b_v$ (in which case $b_w = b_v$). Denote the one of b_w and b'_w that caused this to happen by b''_w and let U be the domain containing b''_w. Since v had the lowest ID among the nodes in G it follows that U is improper, and must have a leader u whose b-value does not equal the ID of any node.

For v to become black again the value of p_w must increase to at least k. This cannot happen until u makes an i-move and increases its p-value. Thus between each time v becomes black some node belonging to an improper domain must make an i-move. It follows from the proof of Lemma 6 that this can only happen a finite number of times.

Now assuming that the r nodes with lowest IDs, $r \geq 1$, can only change between white and black a finite number of times we will show that this implies that the node v with the $(r+1)$st smallest ID also only can change between white and black a finite number of times.

Let R denote the set of domains with lower IDs than v. Then using the same argument as above it follows that between each time v changes from black to white some node in R must have executed an i-move. We know that each such move will cause $A < A'$ and that any d-moves will not change any value of A. Thus between each time some domain in R executes a black move v can only perform a finite number of black moves. Since by assumption each proper domain in R can only execute a finite number of black moves the result follows.   □

Combining the results from lemmas 5 through 8 we now have our main result.

Theorem 2. *Algorithm* **Rule 1** *will stabilize in a finite number of moves.*

4 Conclusion

We have presented a very simple self-stabilizing algorithm that solves the k-packing problem. In doing so it only uses a constant number of variables per node. The main mechanism for solving the problem is a method for a black node to compute the distance to its nearest black node other than itself. We believe that this mechanism can be used in designing self-stabilizing algorithms for other problems that also involves some k-distance property. This is something we intend to study further in the future.

We do not believe that this idea can be extended to an anonymous network, since a white node v would not be able to distinguish between black nodes that are not in $N(v)$.

Still, the main open question is to better understand the trade off between memory usage and moves complexity in self-stabilizing algorithms. There are currently few hardness results in terms of moves complexity in the literature on self-stabilizing algorithms and even if some self-stabilizing algorithms require an exponential number of moves there is still room for ranking these like one is currently seeing in the field of exact sequential algorithms.

References

1. C. BERGE, *Theory of Graphs and its Applications*, no. 2 in Collection Universitaire de Mathematiques, Dunod, Paris, 1958.
2. J. BLAIR AND F. MANNE, *Efficient self-stabilzing algorithms for tree networks*, in Proceedings of ICDS 2003, The 23rd IEEE International Conference on Distributed Computing Systems, 2003, pp. 20–26.
3. E. W. DIJKSTRA, *Self-stabilizing systems in spite of distributed control*, CACM, 17 (1974), pp. 643–644.
4. S. DOLEV, *Self-stabilization*, MIT press, 2000.
5. M. GAIRING, R. M. GEIST, S. T. HEDETNIEMI, AND P. KRISTIANSEN, *A self-stabilizing algorithm for maximal 2-packing*, Nordic J. Comput., 11 (2004), pp. 1–11.
6. M. R. GAREY AND D. S. JOHNSON, *Computers and Intractability*, W. H. Freeman and Co., 1978.
7. F. GÄRTNER, *A survey of self-stabilizing spanning-tree algorithms*, Tech. Report IC/2003/38, Swiss Federal Institute of Technology, 2003.
8. W. GODDARD, S. HEDETNIEMI, D. JACOBS, AND V. TREVISAN, *Distance-k information in self-stabilizing algorithms*, in Proceedings of SIROCCO 2006, 2006. To appear.
9. W. GODDARD, S. T. HEDETNIEMI, D. P. JACOBS, AND P. K. SRIMANI, *Self-stabilizing global optimization algorithms for large network graphs*, Int. J. Dist. Sensor Networks, 1 (2005), pp. 329 – 344.
10. M. A. HENNING, *Distance domination in graphs*, in Domination in Graphs: Advanced Topics, T. W. Haynes, S. T. Hedetniemi, and P. J. Slater, eds., Marcel Dekker, New York, 1998, pp. 321–349.

11. M. MJELDE, *k-packing and k-domination on tree graphs*, master's thesis, Department of Informatics, University of Bergen, Norway, 2004.
12. O. ORE, *Theory of Graphs*, no. 38 in American Mathematical Society Publications, AMS, Providence, 1962.
13. P. J. SLATER, *R-domination in graphs*, J. Assoc. Comput. Mach., 23 (1976), pp. 446–450.

Bounding the Impact of Unbounded Attacks in Stabilization

Toshimitsu Masuzawa[1,*] and Sébastien Tixeuil[2,**]

[1] Osaka University, Japan
masuzawa@ist.osaka-u.ac.jp
[2] LRI-CNRS UMR 8623 & INRIA Grand Large, France
tixeuil@lri.fr

Abstract. As a new challenge of containing the unbounded influence of Byzantine processes in self-stabilizing protocols, this paper introduces a novel concept of *strong stabilization*. The strong stabilization relaxes the requirement of *strict stabilization* so that processes beyond the containment radius are allowed to be disturbed by Byzantine processes, but only a limited number of times. A self-stabilizing protocol is (t, c, f)-strongly stabilizing if any process more than c hops away from any Byzantine process is disturbed at most t times in a distributed system with at most f Byzantine processes. Here c denotes the *containment radius* and t denotes the *containment times*.

The possibility and the effectiveness of the strong stabilization is demonstrated using *tree orientation*. It is known that the tree orientation has no strictly stabilizing protocol with a constant containment radius. This paper first shows that the problem has no constant bound of the containment radius in a tree with two Byzantine processes even when we allow processes beyond the containment radius to be disturbed any finite number of times. Then we consider the case of a single Byzantine process and present a $(1, 0, 1)$-strongly stabilizing protocol, which achieves optimality in both containment radius and times.

1   Introduction

Self-stabilization [5] is one of the most effective and promising paradigms for fault-tolerant distributed computing [6]. A self-stabilizing protocol can achieve its desired behavior eventually regardless of the initial configuration (*i.e.*, global state). This implies that a self-stabilizing protocol is resilient to any number and any type of transient faults since it converges to its desired behavior from any configuration resulting from transient faults. However the convergence to the

* This work is supported in part by MEXT: The 21st Century Center of Excellence Program, JSPS: Grant-in-Aid for Scientific Research ((B)15300017), MEXT: Grant-in-Aid for Scientific Research on Priority Areas (16092215) and MIC: Strategic Information and Communications R&D Promotion Programme (SCOPE).
** This author is supported in part by the FRAGILE and SOGEA projects of the ACI "Sécurité et Informatique" of the French Ministry of Research. Part of this work was done while visiting Osaka University.

A.K. Datta and M. Gradinariu (Eds.): SSS 2006, LNCS 4280, pp. 440–453, 2006.
© Springer-Verlag Berlin Heidelberg 2006

desired behavior is guaranteed only under the assumption that no further fault occurs during convergence.

There exist several researches on self-stabilizing protocols that are also resilient to permanent and intermittent faults [1,2,3,7,8,9,10,11,12,13]. Most of those consider only crash faults, and guarantee that each non faulty process achieves its intended behavior regardless of the initial configuration. Nesterenko and Arora [11] provided solutions that are self-stabilizing and tolerate an unbounded number of Byzantine faults. The main difficulty in this setting is caused by arbitrary and unbounded state changes of Byzantine processes: processes around the Byzantine processes may change their states in response to the state changes of the Byzantine processes, and processes next to those processes may also change their states. This implies that the influence of Byzantine processes could spread to the whole system, preventing every process from conforming to its specification forever. Nesterenko and Arora [11] introduced the concept of *strict stabilization*: strictly stabilizing protocols manage to contain the influence of Byzantine processes within nearby processes, while remaining processes eventually exhibit expected behavior. The measure for evaluating the containment quality is the *containment radius*, which is the maximum distance between a Byzantine process and a process affected by this Byzantine process. They also propose strictly stabilizing protocols for the vertex coloring problem and the dining philosophers problem. The containment radius is one for the vertex coloring problem and two for the dining philosophers problem. Following their work, strictly stabilizing protocols for the link-coloring problem are presented for rooted trees in [12] and for arbitrary anonymous networks in [9]. These protocols achieve containment radius of two and containment radius of one, respectively.

Limitations of the strict stabilization are also investigated in [11]. The authors introduce the class of r-restrictive problems for which the containment radius cannot be less than r, and shows that there is no constant bound of the containment radius for the problem of routing.

Our Contribution: In this paper, to circumvent the aforementioned limitations of strict stabilization, we consider a new way of containing the unbounded influence of Byzantine processes in self-stabilizing protocols. In more details, we discuss the possibility of containment concerning the number of times that correct processes are disturbed by Byzantine ones. The strict stabilization requires that processes beyond the containment radius eventually achieve their desired behavior and are never disturbed by Byzantine processes afterwards. We relax this requirement in the following sense: we allow these correct processes beyond the containment radius to be disturbed by Byzantine processes, but only a limited number of times.

The most important contribution of this paper is to present new possibilities of containing the influence of unbounded Byzantine behaviors. We define the notion of *strong stabilization* as the novel form of the containment and introduce *containment times* to quantify the quality of the containment. The notion of strong stabilization is weaker than the strict stabilization but is stronger than the classical notion of self-stabilization (i.e. every strongly stabilizing protocol is self-stabilizing, but not necessarily strictly stabilizing). While strict stabilization aims to tolerate an unbounded number of Byzantine processes, we explicitly specify the number of Byzantine processes to be tolerated. A self-stabilizing protocol is (t, c, f)-strongly stabilizing if any process more than c hops away from any Byzantine process is disturbed at most t times in a distributed system with at most f Byzantine processes. Here c denotes the containment radius and t denotes the containment times.

To demonstrate the possibility and effectiveness of our notion of strong stabilization, we consider *tree orientation*. It is shown in [11] that there is no strictly stabilizing protocol with a constant containment radius for this problem. The impossibility result can be extended even when the number of Byzantine processes is upper bounded (by one). In this paper, we first show that the problem has no constant bound for the containment radius in a tree with two Byzantine processes even when we allow processes beyond the containment radius to be disturbed a finite number of times. Then we consider the case of a single Byzantine process and present a $(1, 0, 1)$-strongly stabilizing protocol: every correct process eventually executes its desired behavior and is disturbed by the Byzantine process at most once. This implies the protocol attains the containment radius of zero and the containment times of one: both are trivially optimal.

2   Preliminaries

2.1   Distributed System

A *distributed system* $S = (P, L)$ consists of a set $P = \{v_1, v_2, \ldots, v_n\}$ of processes and a set L of bidirectional communication links (simply called links). A link is an unordered pair of distinct processes. A distributed system S can be regarded as a graph whose vertex set is P and whose link set is L, so we use graph terminology to describe a distributed system S.

Processes u and v are called *neighbors* if $(u, v) \in L$. The set of neighbors of a process v is denoted by N_v, and its cardinality (the *degree* of v) is denoted by $\Delta_v (= |N_v|)$. The degree Δ of a distributed system $S = (P, L)$ is defined as $\Delta = \max\{\Delta_v \mid v \in P\}$. We do not assume existence of a unique identifier for each process. Instead we assume each process can distinguish its neighbors from each other by locally arranging them in some arbitrary order: the k-th neighbor of a process v is denoted by $N_v(k)$ $(1 \leq k \leq \Delta_v)$.

In this paper, we consider only *tree systems*, i.e. distributed systems containing no cycles. We assume that all processes in a tree system are identical and thus no process is distinguished as a root.

Processes can communicate with their neighbors through link registers. For each pair of neighboring processes u and v, there are two link registers $r_{u,v}$ and $r_{v,u}$. Message transmission from u to v is realized as follows: u writes a message to link register $r_{u,v}$ and then v reads it from $r_{u,v}$. The link register $r_{u,v}$ is called an *output register* of u and is called an *input register* of v. The set of all output (resp. input) registers of u is denoted by Out_u (resp. In_u), i.e. $Out_u = \{r_{u,v} \mid v \in N_u\}$ and $In_u = \{r_{v,u} \mid v \in N_u\}$.

The variables that are maintained by processes denote process states. Similarly, the values of the variables stored in each link register denote the state of the registers. A process may take actions during the execution of the system. An action is simply a function that is executed in an atomic manner by the process.

A global state of a distributed system is called a *configuration* and is specified by a product of states of all processes and all link registers. We define C to be the set of all possible configurations of a distributed system S. For a process set $R \subseteq P$ and two configurations ρ and ρ', we denote $\rho \overset{R}{\mapsto} \rho'$ when ρ changes to ρ' by executing an action of each process in R simultaneously. Notice that ρ and ρ' can be different only in the states of processes in R and the states of their output registers.

A *schedule* of a distributed system is an infinite sequence of process sets. Let $Q = R^1, R^2, \ldots$ be a schedule, where $R^i \subseteq P$ holds for each i ($i \geq 1$). An infinite sequence of configurations $e = \rho_0, \rho_1, \ldots$ is called an *execution* from an initial configuration ρ_0 by a schedule Q, if e satisfies $\rho_{i-1} \overset{R^i}{\mapsto} \rho_i$ for each i ($i \geq 1$). Process actions are executed atomically, and we also assume that a *distributed daemon* schedules the actions of processes, i.e. any subset of processes can simultaneously execute their actions.

The set of all possible executions from $\rho_0 \in C$ is denoted by E_{ρ_0}. The set of all possible executions is denoted by E, that is, $E = \bigcup_{\rho \in C} E_\rho$. We consider *asynchronous* distributed systems where we can make no assumption on schedules except that any schedule is *weakly fair*: every process is contained in infinite number of subsets appearing in any schedule.

In this paper, we consider (permanent) *Byzantine faults*: a Byzantine process (i.e. a Byzantine-faulty process) can make arbitrary behavior independently from its actions. If v is a Byzantine process, v can repeatedly change its variables and its output registers arbitrarily.

In asynchronous distributed systems, time is usually measured by *asynchronous rounds* (simply called *rounds*). Let $e - \rho_0, \rho_1, \ldots$ be an execution by a schedule $Q = R^1, R^2, \ldots$. The first round of e is defined to be the minimum prefix of e, $e' = \rho_0, \rho_1, \ldots, \rho_k$, such that $\bigcup_{i=1}^k R^i = P$. Round t ($t \geq 2$) is defined recursively, by applying the above definition of the first round to $e'' = \rho_k, \rho_{k+1}, \ldots$. Intuitively, every process has a chance to update its state in every round.

2.2   Self-stabilizing Protocol Resilient to Byzantine Faults

Tree orientation considered in this paper is a so-called *static problem*, i.e. it requires the system to find a static solution. For example, the spanning-tree construction problem is a static problem, while the mutual exclusion problem is not. Some static problems can be defined by a *specification predicate* (shortly, specification), $spec(v)$, for each process v: a configuration is a desired one (with a solution) if every process satisfies $spec(v)$. A specification $spec(v)$ is a boolean expression on variables of P_v ($\subseteq P$) where P_v is the set of processes whose variables appear in $spec(v)$. The variables appearing in the specification are called *output variables* (shortly, *O-variables*). In what follows, we consider a static problem defined by specification $spec(v)$.

A *self-stabilizing protocol* is a protocol that eventually reaches a *legitimate configuration*, where $spec(v)$ holds at every process v, regardless of the initial configuration. Once it reaches a legitimate configuration, every process never changes its O-variables and always satisfies $spec(v)$. From this definition, a self-stabilizing protocol can tolerate any number and any type of transient faults. However, when (permanent) Byzantine processes exist, Byzantine processes may not satisfy $spec(v)$. In addition, correct processes near the Byzantine processes can be influenced and may be unable to satisfy $spec(v)$. Nesterenko and Arora [11] define a *strictly stabilizing protocol* as a self-stabilizing protocol resilient to unbounded number of Byzantine processes.

Definition 1 ((c, f)-containment). *A configuration ρ is (c, f)-contained for specification spec if, given at most f Byzantine processes, in any execution starting from ρ, every process v more than c hops away from any Byzantine process always satisfies $spec(v)$ and never changes its O-variables.*

The parameter c of Definition 1 refers to the *containment radius* defined in [11]. The parameter f refers explicitly to the number of Byzantine processes, while [11] dealt with unbounded number of Byzantine faults (that is $f \in \{0 \ldots n\}$).

Definition 2 ((c, f)-strict stabilization). *A protocol is (c, f)-strictly stabilizing for specification spec if, given at most f Byzantine processes, any computation $e = \rho_0, \rho_1, \ldots$ contains a configuration ρ_i that is (c, f)-contained for spec.*

An important limitation of the model of [11] is the notion of *r-restrictive* specifications. Intuitively, a specification is *r*-restrictive if it prevents combinations of states that belong to two processes u and v that are at least r hops away. An important consequence related to Byzantine tolerance is that the containment radius of protocols solving those specifications is at least r. For some problems, such as the tree orientation we consider in this paper, r can not be bounded to a constant. As a result, there can not exist a strictly stabilizing protocol for this problem.

To circumvent the impossibility result, we define a weaker notion than the strict stabilization. Here, the containment radius is not constant, i.e. there may exist processes outside the containment radius that invalidate the specification predicate, due to Byzantine actions. However, the impact of Byzantine triggered action is limited in times: the set of Byzantine processes may only impact processes outside the containment radius a bounded number of times, even if Byzantine processes execute an infinite number of actions.

Definition 3 ((t, c, f)-time containment). *A configuration ρ is (t, c, f)-time contained for specification spec if, given at most f Byzantine processes, in any execution starting from ρ, every process v more than c hops away from any Byzantine process executes at most t actions that change its O-variables, and eventually always satisfies $spec(v)$ and never changes its O-variables.*

Note that a (t, c, f)-time contained configuration is a (c, f)-contained configuration when $t = 0$. The (t, c, f)-time containment guarantees that every process outside the containment radius is disturbed at most t times by Byzantine processes. In the remaining of the paper, t denotes the *containment times* of the configuration.

Definition 4 (((t, c, f)-strong stabilization). *A protocol is (t, c, f)-strongly stabilizing for specification spec if, given at most f Byzantine processes, any computation $e = \rho_0, \rho_1, \ldots$ contains a configuration ρ_i that is (t, c, f)-time contained for spec.*

A strongly stabilizing protocol is weaker than a strictly stabilizing one (as processes outside the containment radius may take incorrect actions due to Byzantine influence), but stronger than a classical self-stabilizing protocol (that may never meet their specification in the presence of Byzantine processes).

The parameters t and c are introduced to quantify the strength of fault containment, we do not require each process to know the values of the parameters. Actually, the protocol proposed in this paper assumes no knowledge on the parameters.

2.3 Discussion

There exists an analogy between the respective powers of (c, f)-strict stabilization and (t, c, f)-strong stabilization for the one hand, and self-stabilization and pseudo-stabilization for the other hand.

A *pseudo-stabilizing* protocol (defined in [4]) guarantees that every execution has a suffix that matches the specification, but it could never reach a legitimate configuration from which any possible execution matches the specification. In other words, a pseudo-stabilizing protocol can continue to behave satisfying the specification, but with having possibility of invalidating the specification in future. A particular schedule can prevent a pseudo-stabilizing protocol from reaching a legitimate configuration for arbitrarily long time, but cannot prevent it from executing its desired behavior for arbitrarily long time. Thus, a pseudo-stabilizing protocol is useful since desired behavior is eventually reached.

Similarly, every execution of a (t, c, f)-strongly stabilizing protocol has a suffix such that every process outside the containment radius executes its desired behavior. But (t, c, f)-strongly stabilizing protocol could never reach a configuration after which Byzantine processes cannot disturb the processes outside the containment radius: every processes outside the containment radius can continue to execute its desired behavior, but with having possibility that it could be disturbed at most t times by Byzantine processes in future. A notable but subtle difference is that the invalidation of the specification is caused only by the effect of Byzantine processes in a (t, c, f)-strongly stabilizing protocol, while the invalidation can be caused by a scheduler in a pseudo-stabilizing protocol.

3 Tree Orientation

Informally, *tree orientation* consists in transforming a tree system (with no root) into a rooted tree system. Each process v has an O-variable $prnt_v$ to designate a neighbor as its parent. Since processes have no identifiers, $prnt_v$ actually stores k ($\in \{1, 2, \ldots, \Delta_v\}$) to designate its k-th neighbor as its parent. But for simplicity, we use $prnt_v = k$ and $prnt_v = u$ (where u is the k-th neighbor of v) interchangeably.

The goal of tree orientation is to set $prnt_v$ of every process v to form a rooted tree. However, it is impossible to choose a single process as the root because of impossibility of symmetry breaking. Thus, instead of a single root process, a single *root link* is determined as the root: link (u, v) is the root link when processes u and v designate each other as their parents (Fig. 1(a)). From any process w, the root link can be reached by following the neighbors designated by the variables $prnt$.

When a tree system S has a Byzantine process (say w), w can prevent communication between subtrees of $S - \{w\}$[1]. Thus, we have to allow each of the subtrees to form a rooted tree system independently. We define the specification predicate $spec(v)$ of the tree orientation as follows.

$$spec(v) : \forall u \ (\in N_v)[(prnt_v = u) \vee (prnt_u = v) \vee (u \text{ is Byzantine faulty})].$$

When every correct process v satisfies $spec(v)$, the configuration is called a *legitimate configuration*.

Figure 1 shows examples of legitimate configurations (a) with no Byzantine process and (b) with a single Byzantine process w. The arrow attached to each process points the neighbor designated as its parent. Notice that, from Fig. 1(b), subtrees consisting of correct processes are classified into two categories: one is the case of forming a rooted tree with a root link in the subtree (T_1 in Fig. 1(b)), and the other is the case of forming a rooted tree with a root process, where the root process is a neighbor of a Byzantine process and designates the Byzantine process as its parent (T_2 in Fig. 1(b)).

Tree orientation seems to be a very simple task. Actually, for tree orientation in a fault-free systems, we can design a self-stabilizing protocol that chooses a link incident to a center process[2] as the root link: in case that the system has a single center, the center can choose a link incident to it, and in case that the system has two neighboring centers, the link between the centers become the root link. However, tree orientation becomes impossible if we have Byzantine processes. By the impossibility results of [11], we can show that tree orientation has no $(o(n), 1)$-strictly stabilizing protocol; i.e. the Byzantine influence cannot be contained in the sense of "strict stabilization", even if only a single Byzantine process is allowed.

An interesting question is whether the Byzantine influence can be contained in a weaker sense of "strong stabilization". The following theorem gives a negative answer to the question: if we have two Byzantine processes, bounding the

---

[1] For a process subset P' ($\subseteq P$), $S - P'$ denotes a distributed system obtained by removing processes in P' and their incident links.

[2] A process v is a center when v has the minimum eccentricity where eccentricity is the largest distance to a leaf. It is known that a tree has a single center or two neighboring centers.

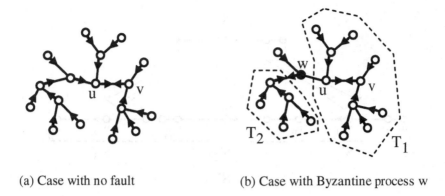

(a) Case with no fault   (b) Case with Byzantine process w

Fig. 1. Tree orientation

contamination times is impossible. We prove the impossibility for more restricted schedules, called the *central daemon*, which disallows two or more processes to make actions at the same time. Notice that impossibility results under the central daemon are stronger than those under the distributed daemon.

Theorem 1. *Even under the central daemon, there exists no deterministic $(t, o(n), 2)$-strongly stabilizing protocol for tree orientation where t is any (finite) integer and n is the number of processes.*

Proof. Let $S = (P, L)$ be a chain (or a special case of a tree system) of n processes: $P = \{v_1, v_2, \ldots, v_n\}$ and $L = \{(v_i, v_{i+1}) \mid 1 \leq i \leq n-1\}$.

For purpose of contradiction, assume that there exists a $(t, o(n), 2)$-strongly stabilizing protocol A for some integer t. In the following, we show, for S with Byzantine processes v_1 and v_n, that A has an execution where a center process $w - v_{\lceil n/2 \rceil}$ changes $prnt_w$ infinitely often. Since w is outside the containment radius $o(n)$, this contradicts the assumption that A is a $(t, o(n), 2)$-strongly stabilizing protocol.

It remains to construct an execution e where $prnt_w$ changes infinitely often. In S with Byzantine processes v_1 and v_n, A eventually reaches a configuration ρ_1 where w satisfies $spec(w)$. This execution to ρ_1 constitutes the prefix of e.

To construct e after ρ_1, consider another chain $S' = (P', L')$ of $3n$ processes and an execution of A on S', where let $P' = \{u_1, u_2, \ldots, u_{3n}\}$ and $L = \{(u_i, u_{i+1}) \mid 1 \leq i \leq 3n-1\}$. We consider the initial configuration ρ'_1 of S' that is obtained by concatenating three copies (say S'_1, S'_2 and S'_3) of S in ρ_1 where only the central copy S'_2 is reversed right-and-left (Fig. 2). The center process w is copied to $w'_1 = u_{\lceil n/2 \rceil}, w'_2 = u_{2n+1-\lceil n/2 \rceil}$ and $w'_3 = u_{2n+\lceil n/2 \rceil}$, but only $prnt_{w'_2}$ designates the neighbor in the different direction from $prnt_{w'_1}$ and $prnt_{w'_3}$. From the configuration ρ'_1, protocol A eventually reaches a legitimate configuration ρ''_1 of S' when S' has no Byzantine process. In the execution from ρ'_1 to ρ''_1, at least one $prnt$ variable of w'_1, w'_2 and w'_3 has to change. Assume w'_i changes $prnt_{w'_i}$.

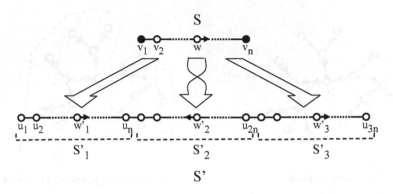

Fig. 2. Construction of S' from three copies of S

Now, we construct the execution e on S after ρ_1. Since v_1 and v_n are Byzantine processes in S, v_1 and v_n can simulate behavior of the end processes of S'_i i.e. $u_{(i-1)n+1}$ and u_{in}), and thus, S can behave in the same way as S'_i (containing w'_i) does from ρ'_1 to ρ''_1. The execution constitutes the second part of e, where $prnt_w$ changes at least once. Let the resulting configuration be ρ_2 (that coincides with the configuration of S'_i in ρ''_i), and construct the initial configuration ρ'_2 of S' from ρ_2 in the same way. By repeating the argument, we can construct the execution e of A on S where $prnt_w$ changes infinitely often.   □

4   A Strongly-Stabilizing Tree Orientation for a Single Byzantine Process

4.1   Protocol *ss-TO*

In the previous section, we proved that there is no strongly stabilizing protocol for tree orientation if two Byzantine processes exist. In this section, we consider the case with only a single Byzantine process and present a $(1, 0, 1)$-strongly stabilizing tree orientation protocol *ss-TO*: every correct process v eventually satisfies $spec(v)$ and is disturbed by the Byzantine process at most once. Note that we consider the distributed daemon for this possibility result.

In a fault-free tree system, orientation can be easily achieved by finding a center process. A simple strategy for finding the center process is that each process v informs each neighbor u of the maximum distance to a leaf from u through v. The distances are found and become fixed from smaller ones. When a tree system contains a single Byzantine process, however, this strategy cannot prevent perturbation caused by wrong distances the Byzantine process provides: by reporting longer and shorter distances than the correct one alternatively, the Byzantine process can repeatedly pull the chosen center closer and push it farther.

constants of process v
     Δ_v = the degree of v;
     N_v = the set of neighbors of v;
variables of process v
     $prnt_v$: a neighbor of v; // $prnt_v = u$ if u is a parent of v.
     $level_v$: integer;
variables in shared register $r_{v,u}$
     $r\text{-}prnt_{v,u}$: boolean; // $prnt_{v,u} = true$ iff u is a parent of v.
     $r\text{-}level_{v,u}$: integer; // the value of $level_v$
predicates
     $pred_1 : \exists u \in N_v[r\text{-}level_{u,v} > level_v]$
     $pred_2 : \exists u \in N_v - \{prnt_v\}[(r\text{-}level_{u,v} = level_v) \wedge (r\text{-}prnt_{u,v} = false)]$
atomic actions // represented in form of guarded actions
     GA1 : $pred_1 \longrightarrow$
             $prnt_v := u; \; level_v := r\text{-}level_{u,v};$
             $(r_{v,prnt_v}\text{-}prnt, r_{v,prnt_v}\text{-}level) := (true, level_v);$
             for each $r \; (\in Out_v - \{r_{v,prnt_v}\})$ **do** $(r\text{-}prnt, r\text{-}level) := (false, level_v);$
     GA2 : $\neg pred_1 \wedge pred_2 \longrightarrow$
             $prnt_v := u; \; level_v := level_v + 1;$
             $(r_{v,prnt_v}\text{-}prnt, r_{v,prnt_v}\text{-}level) := (true, level_v);$
             for each $r \; (\in Out_v - \{r_{v,prnt_v}\})$ **do** $(r\text{-}prnt, r\text{-}level) := (false, level_v);$

Fig. 3. Protocol $ss\text{-}TO$ (actions of process v)

The key idea of protocol $ss\text{-}TO$ to circumvent the perturbation is to restrict the Byzantine influence to one-sided effect: the Byzantine process can pull the chosen root link closer but cannot push it farther. This can be achieved using a non-decreasing variable $level_v$.

Protocol $ss\text{-}TO$ is presented in Fig. 3. For simplicity, we regard constant N_v as denoting the neighbors of v and regard variable $prnt_v$ as storing a parent of v. Notice that they should be actually implemented using the ordinal numbers of neighbors that v locally assigns.

4.2   Legitimate Configurations of $ss\text{-}TO$

We refine legitimate configurations of protocol $ss\text{-}TO$ and show their properties. First we consider the fault-free case.

Definition 5 (legitimate configurations $LC0$). *In a fault-free tree, a configuration is* legitimate *if* (a) $spec(v)$ *holds for every process* v *and* (b) $level_u = level_v$ *holds for any processes* u *and* v. *The set of all legitimate configurations in a fault-free tree is denoted by $LC0$.*

The following lemma obviously holds from protocol $ss\text{-}TO$.

Lemma 1. *In a fault-free tree, once protocol $ss\text{-}TO$ reaches a configuration ρ ($\in LC0$), it remains at ρ. (No further action can be executed from ρ.)*

For the case with a single Byzantine process, legitimate configurations are refined as follows.

Definition 6 (legitimate configurations $LC1$). *Let z be the single Byzantine process in a tree system. A configuration is* legitimate *if every subtree (or connected component) of S-$\{z\}$ satisfies either the following (C1) or (C2).*

(C1) (a) $spec(u)$ *holds for every correct process u,* (b) $prnt_v = z$ *holds for the neighbor v of z, and* (c) $level_w \geq level_x$ *holds for any neighboring correct processes w and x where w is nearer than x to z.*

(C2) (d) $spec(u)$ *holds for every correct process u, and* (e) $level_v = level_w$ *holds for any correct processes v and w.*

The set of all legitimate configurations for a single Byzantine process is denoted by $LC1$.

When every subtree of S-$\{z\}$ satisfies (C1), the configuration is said to be strictly legitimate.

For strictly legitimate configurations, the following lemma holds.

Lemma 2. *Once protocol ss-TO reaches a strictly legitimate configuration ρ, it remains in strictly legitimate ones and no correct process u changes $prnt_u$ afterwards. That is, any strictly legitimate configuration is $(0, 1)$-contained.*

Proof. Consider any execution e starting from a strictly legitimate configuration ρ. If no correct process u changes $prnt_u$ in e, it is clear that every configuration of e is strictly legitimate. We show that $prnt_u$ never changes in e.

For contradiction, assume that a correct process y changes $prnt_y$ first among all correct processes. Let z be the Byzantine process. In ρ, $prnt_x = w$ holds for any neighboring correct processes w and x where w is nearer than x to z. From condition (c), y cannot be x satisfying $prnt_x = w$ for a correct process w. Thus, y is a neighbor of z, where $prnt_y = z$ holds from the condition (b). Process y changes $prnt_y$ from z to p ($\neq z$) only when $level_p > level_y$ holds. But this never holds in any execution starting from ρ. Thus, a contradiction. □

Notice that a correct process u may change $level_u$ even after a strictly legitimate configuration. When the Byzantine process z increments $level_z$ infinitely often, every process u may also increment $level_u$ infinitely often.

Lemma 3. *Any configuration ρ in $LC1$ is $(1, 0, 1)$-time contained. In any subtree satisfying the condition (C1) at ρ, no correct process u changes $prnt_u$ after ρ. In any subtree satisfying the condition (C2) at ρ, no correct process u changes $prnt_u$ in some execution starting from ρ. But, once some process u in the subtree changes $prnt_u$ after ρ, the subtree reaches a configuration satisfying (C1) in $O(n')$ rounds where n' is the number of processes in the subtree.*

Proof. Consider any execution e starting from ρ. By the same discussion as the proof of Lemma 2, we can show that any subtree satisfying (C1) at ρ always satisfies the condition and no correct process u in the subtree changes $prnt_u$ afterwards.

Consider a subtree satisfying (C2) at ρ and let y be the neighbor of the Byzantine process z in the subtree. It is clear that no process u in the subtree changes $prnt_u$ or $level_u$ unless y executes $prnt_y := z$ in e. When $prnt_y := z$ is executed, $level_y$ becomes larger than $level_u$ of any other process u in the subtree. It is clear that the subtree satisfies (C1) in $O(n')$ rounds, and that each process u changes $prnt_u$ at most once during the execution.   □

4.3 Convergence of *ss-TO*

We first show convergence of protocol *ss-TO* to legitimate configurations in fault-free case.

Lemma 4. *In a fault-free tree system, protocol ss-TO reaches a legitimate configuration of LC0 from any initial configuration in $O(n)$ rounds.*

Proof. For lack of space, we prove only the convergence to a legitimate configuration and do not prove the round complexity.

Let u be any leaf process and v be its only neighbor. After v executes its action, $level_v \geq level_u$ holds. Process u can execute only Action **GA1** since $prnt_u = v$ always holds. Thus, after some configuration ρ_1, $prnt_u = v$ and $level_v \geq level_u$ always hold for any leaf u and its neighbor v. Also, once $level_v = level_u$ holds, $level_u$ never changes unless $level_v$ increments.

Now, consider a tree $S^1 = S - Leaf(S)$ where $Leaf(S)$ is the set of all leaves in S. Let u be any leaf process of S^1 and v be its only neighbor in S^1. Since any other neighbor w ($\neq v$) of u in S is a leaf of S, $prnt_w = u$ and $level_u \geq level_w$ always hold after ρ_1. It follows that u never executes $prnt_u := w$ after ρ_1. This implies that either (i) $prnt_u = w$ always holds for some w ($\neq v$) after ρ_1 or (ii) $prnt_u = v$ always holds after some configuration that may appear after ρ_1. Notice that $level_u$ never changes after ρ_1 in case (i). In case (ii), $level_u$ may increase but $level_v \geq level_u$ always holds after some configuration.

In case that (i) *holds for some leaf u of S^1*: After v executes its action, $level_v \geq level_u$ always holds. From the fact that u never changes $prnt_u$ or $level_u$, eventually $level_v = level_u$ and $prnt_v = u$ always hold. Since $level_u$ never changes after ρ_1, eventually $level_v$ becomes constant. Similarly, for every neighbor x ($\neq u$) of v, we can show that eventually $level_x = level_v$ and $prnt_x = v$ always hold. By repeating the argument, we can show that *ss-TO* reaches a legitimate configuration in $LC0$.

In case that (ii) *holds for every leaf u of S^1*: Consider a tree $S^2 = S - (Leaf(S) \cup Leaf(S^1))$. By similar discussion to that for S^1, we can show, for any leaf process u of S^2 and its only neighbor v in S^2, that eventually either (i) $prnt_u = w$ always holds for some w ($\neq v$) or (ii) $prnt_u = v$ always holds.

By repeating the above argument until S^j becomes empty, we can show that eventually $prnt_u$ of every process u becomes constant and $spec(u)$ holds. Therefore, *ss-TO* eventually reaches a legitimate configuration in $LC0$.   □

Now, we consider the case with a single Byzantine process.

Lemma 5. *In a tree system with a single Byzantine process, protocol ss-TO reaches a legitimate configuration of LC1 from any initial configuration in $O(n)$ rounds.*

Proof. We only show the outline of the convergence proof.

Let z be the Byzantine faulty process and $S' = (P', L')$ be any subtree (or connected component) of $S - \{z\}$. Let y be the neighbor of z in S'.

Eventually every leaf process u in S' (except for y if it is a leaf) always satisfies $prnt_u = v$ and $level_v \geq level_u$ where v is the only neighbor of u.

Now consider $S^1 = S - (Leaf(S) - \{y\})$. Let u be any leaf process of S^1 (except for y if it is a leaf) and v be its only neighbor in S^1. By similar discussion to that in proof of Lemma 4, we can show that eventually either (i) $prnt_u = w$ always holds for some w ($\neq v$), or (ii) $prnt_u = v$ always holds.

In case that (i) *holds for some leaf u of S^1:* Process u never changes $prnt_u$ or increments $level_u$. This implies that eventually the variables $level$ of all processes in S' have the same value and remain unchanged. In such a configuration, the variables $prnt$ of all processes form a rooted tree with a root link: the configuration is in $LC1$.

In case that (ii) *holds for every leaf u in S^1:* We consider $S^2 = S - ((Leaf(S) \cup Leaf(S^1)) - \{y\})$ and repeat the same argument. Consequently, we can show that protocol *ss-TO* eventually reaches a legitimate configuration in $LC1$.   □

The following main theorem is obtained from Lemmas 1, 2, 3, 4 and 5.

Theorem 2. *Protocol ss-TO is a* $(1,0,1)$*-strongly stabilizing tree-orientation protocol. The protocol reaches a legitimate configuration of* $LC0 \cup LC1$ *from any initial configuration in* $O(n)$ *rounds. The protocol may move from a legitimate configuration to an illegitimate one because of the influence of the Byzantine process, but it can stay in illegitimate configurations during* $O(n)$ *rounds (that are not necessarily consecutive) in the whole execution.*

5   Conclusions

We introduced *strong stabilization* and *containment times* as novel notions for containing the unbounded influence of Byzantine behavior. The strong stabilization is weaker than strict stabilization, but is stronger than classical self-stabilization. We demonstrated the possibility and effectiveness of the strong stabilization using the tree orientation as an example: the problem, even assuming a single Byzantine process, is unsolvable in the context of strict stabilization, but it is solvable in the context of strong stabilization. In addition, our strongly stabilizing solution is optimal for all considered criteria: it achieves tolerance to the maximum possible number of Byzantine processes, with a containment radius of zero and a containment times of 1. Thus, the strong stabilization sheds new light to self-stabilizing protocols resilient to transient and permanent faults.

One of our future works is to investigate the sufficient and necessary conditions for problems to admit a (t, c, f)-strongly stabilizing solution.

References

1. E. Anagnostou and V. Hadzilacos. Tolerating transient and permanent failures. In *Proceedings of the 7th International Workshop on Distributed Algorithms (LNCS 725)*, pages 174–188, 1993.
2. J. Beauquier and S. Kekkonen-Moneta. Fault-tolerance and self-stabilization: impossibility results and solutions using self-stabiling failure detectors. *International Journal of Systems Science*, 28(11):1177–1187, 1997.
3. J. Beauquier and S. Kekkonen-Moneta. On ftss-solvable distributed problems. In *Proceedings of the 6th Annual ACM Symposium on Principles of Distributed Computing*, page 290, 1997.
4. J. E. Burns, M. G. Gouda, and R. E. Miller. Stabilization and pseudo-stabilization. *Distributed Computing*, 7(1):35–42, 1993.
5. E. W. Dijkstra. Self-stabilizing systems in spite of distributed control. *Communications of the Association of the Computing Machinery*, 17:643–644, 1974.
6. S. Dolev. *Self-Stabilization*. MIT Press, 2000.
7. A. S. Gopal and K. J. Perry. Unifying self-stabilization and fault-tolerance. In *Proceedings of the 12th Annual ACM Symposium on Principles of Distributed Computing*, pages 195–206, 1993.
8. T. Masuzawa. A fault-tolerant and self-stabilizing protocol for the topology problem. In *Proceedings of the 2nd Workshop on Self-Stabilizing Systems*, pages 1.1–1.15, 1995.
9. T. Masuzawa and S. Tixeuil. A self-stabilizing link-coloring protocol resilient to unbounded byzantine faults in arbitrary networks. In *Proceedings of the 9th International Conference on Principles of Distributed Systems (OPODIS 2005)*, pages 283–298, 2005.
10. H. Matsui, M. Inoue, T. Masuzawa, and H. Fujiwara. Fault-tolerant and self-stabilizing protocols using an unreliable failure detector (in Japanese). *IEICE Transactions on Information and Systems*, E83-D(10):1831–1840, 2000.
11. M. Nesterenko and A. Arora. Tolerance to unbounded byzantine faults. In *Proceedings of 21st IEEE Symposium on Reliable Distributed Systems*, pages 22–29, 2002.
12. Y. Sakurai, F. Ooshita, and T. Masuzawa. A self-stabilizing link-coloring protocol resilient to byzantine faults in tree networks. In *Proceedings of the 8th International Conference on Principles of Distributed Systems*, pages 196–206, 2004.
13. S. Ukena, Y. Katayama, T. Masuzawa, and H. Fujiwara. A self-stabilizing spanning tree protocol that tolerates non-quiescent permanent faults (in Japanese). *IEICE Transaction*, J85-D-I(11):1007–1014, 2002.

On Bootstrapping Topology Knowledge
in Anonymous Networks

Toshimitsu Masuzawa[1,*] and Sébastien Tixeuil[2,**]

[1] Osaka University, Japan
masuzawa@ist.osaka-u.ac.jp
[2] LRI-CNRS UMR 8623 & INRIA Grand Large, France
tixeuil@lri.fr

Abstract. In this paper, we quantify the amount of "practical" information (*i.e.* views obtained from the neighbors, colors attributed to the nodes and links) to obtain "theoretical" information (*i.e.* the local topology of the network up to distance k) in anonymous networks. In more details, we show that a coloring at distance $2k + 1$ is necessary and sufficient to obtain the local topology at distance k that includes outgoing links. This bound drops to $2k$ when outgoing links are not needed. A second contribution of this paper deals with color bootstrapping (from which local topology can be obtained using the aforementioned mechanisms). On the negative side, we show that *(i)* with a distributed daemon, it is impossible to achieve deterministic color bootstrap, even if the whole network topology can be instantaneously obtained, and *(ii)* with a central daemon, it is impossible to achieve distance m when instantaneous topology knowledge is limited to $m - 1$. On the positive side, we show that *(i)* under the k-central daemon, deterministic self-stabilizing bootstrap of colors up to distance k is possible provided that k-local topology can be instantaneously obtained, and *(ii)* under the distributed daemon, probabilistic self-stabilizing bootstrap is possible for any range.

1 Introduction

Topology update is an essential problem in distributed computing (*e.g.* see [14]). It has direct applicability in practical systems. For example, link-state based routing protocols such as OSPF use topology discovery mechanisms to compute the routing tables. Recently, the problem came to the fore with the introduction of ad hoc wireless sensor networks, such as Berkeley mote network [9], where topology discovery is essential for routing decisions.

* This author is supported in part by MEXT: The 21st Century Center of Excellence Program, JSPS: Grant-in-Aid for Scientific Research ((B)15300017), MEXT: Grant-in-Aid for Scientific Research on Priority Areas (16092215) and MIC: Strategic Information and Communications R&D Promotion Programme (SCOPE).
** This author is supported in part by the FRAGILE and SOGEA projects of the ACI "Sécurité et Informatique" of the French Ministry of Research. Part of this work was done while visiting Osaka University.

A.K. Datta and M. Gradinariu (Eds.): SSS 2006, LNCS 4280, pp. 454–468, 2006.

Self-stabilization is now considered to be the most general technique to design a system to tolerate arbitrary transient faults. A self-stabilizing system guarantees that starting from an arbitrary state, the system converges to a legal configuration in a finite number of steps and remains in a legal state until another fault occurs (see also [4]). Intuitively, a self-stabilizing topology update algorithm guarantees that, even if the system is started from a global state where the topology information is erroneous, then within a finite number of steps, correct topology information is maintained at every node.

In this paper, we investigate the problem of distributed topology update in an arbitrary anonymous network. Each node is only aware of its neighboring peers and it needs to learn the topology of the network up to some finite distance k. "Bootstrapping" topology knowledge refers to the fact that each node is required to construct topology at distance k with only topology knowledge distance $k-1$. While this task can be performed in identifier based networks (where each node has a unique identifier) [5], no solution exists in *anonymous* networks, where nodes have no identifier whatsoever. While most modern networks have identifiers for nodes in the network (*e.g.* the address of the network card), it is also likely (with the advent of very hydrogenous systems including RFIDs, computers, smartphones) that there are identifiers clashes (either unintentional due to conflicting addressing schemes, or intentional due to *e.g.* a reconfiguration of the network card). An algorithm that is able to perform in anonymous networks will also behave correctly in a network with identifiers, but the converse is not true.

While most distributed algorithms dealing with topology information are self-stabilizing [5,3,10], they only deal with networks where nodes have unique identifiers. In the context of anonymous networks, self-stabilizing solutions are either run on networks where topology information is known (ring, tree, etc), or consider problems that can be solved without topology information [2]. For classical algorithms, [13] provides a classification of problems according to how much asymmetry is initially provided in the system (*e.g.* a unique leader vs. a set of k leaders). Also, [15] study the feasibility of leader election when the processor identity numbers are not distinct, and use techniques based on (infinite) colored views obtained from the neighbors as well as global knowledge (the size of the network) and a synchronous setting.

Our contribution. In this paper, we quantify the amount of "practical" information (*i.e.* views obtained from the neighbors, colors attributed to the nodes and links) to obtain "theoretical" information (*i.e.* the local topology of the network up to distance k) in anonymous networks. In more details, we show that a coloring at distance $2k+1$ is necessary and sufficient to obtain the local topology at distance k that includes outgoing links. This bound drops to $2k$ when outgoing links are not needed. A second contribution of this paper deals with color bootstrapping (from which local topology can be obtained using the aforementioned mechanisms). On the negative side, we show that *(i)* with a distributed daemon, it is impossible to achieve deterministic color bootstrap, even if the whole network topology can be instantaneously obtained, and *(ii)* with a central daemon, it is impossible to achieve distance m when instantaneous topology knowledge is limited to $m - 1$. On the positive side, we show that *(i)* under the k-central dae-mon, deterministic bootstrap of colors up to distance k is possible provided that k-local topology can be instantaneously obtained, and *(ii)* under the distributed daemon, probabilistic bootstrap is possible for any range.

2   Model

Distributed systems. A *distributed system* $S = (P, L)$ consists of a set $P = \{v_1, v_2, \ldots, v_n\}$ of processes and a set L of bidirectional communication links (simply called links). A link is an unordered pair of distinct processes. A dis-tributed system S can be regarded as a graph whose vertex set is P and whose link set is L, so we use some graph terminology to describe a distributed system S. The *girth* of a graph is the length of a shortest (simple) cycle in the graph; and the *circumference*, the length of a longest (simple) cycle. The girth and cir-cumference of an acyclic graph are defined to be infinity (∞). The *k-th power* G^k of a graph G is a supergraph formed by adding an edge between all pairs of vertices of G with distance at most k.

Processes u and v are called *neighbors* if $(u, v) \in L$. The set of neighbors of a process v is denoted by N_v, and its cardinality (the *degree* of v) is denoted by $\Delta_v (= |N_v|)$. The degree Δ of a distributed system $S = (P, L)$ is defined as $\Delta = \max\{\Delta_v \mid v \in P\}$. We do not assume existence of a unique identifier of each process. Instead we assume each process can distinguish its neighbors from each other by locally arranging them in some arbitrary order: the k-th neighbor of a process v is denoted by $N_v(k)$ $(1 \leq k \leq \Delta_v)$.

Processes can communicate with theirs neighbors through link registers. For each pair of neighboring processes u and v, there are two link registers $r_{u,v}$ and $r_{v,u}$. Message transmission from u to v is realized as follows: u writes a message to link register $r_{u,v}$ and then v reads it from $r_{u,v}$. The link register $r_{u,v}$ is called an *output register* of u and is called an *input register* of v. The set of all output (resp. input) registers of u is denoted by Out_u (resp. In_u), *i.e.*, $Out_u = \{r_{u,v} \mid v \in N_u\}$ and $In_u = \{r_{v,u} \mid v \in N_u\}$. The variables that are maintained by processes denote their states. Similarly, the values of the variables stored in each register denote the state of these registers. The algorithm executed by each processor is described by a finite set of guarded actions of the form $\langle \text{guard} \rangle \longrightarrow \langle \text{statement} \rangle$. Each guard of process p is a boolean expression involving the variables of p and its input registers. When there is no explicit register communication described in the algorithm, it is implicitly assumed that the state of the process is copied in each output register after the execution of any action.

A global state of a distributed system is called a *configuration* and is specified by a product of states of all processes. We define C to be the set of all possi-ble configurations of a distributed system S. For a process set $R \subseteq P$ and two configurations ρ and ρ', we denote $\rho \overset{R}{\mapsto} \rho'$ when ρ changes to ρ' by executing an action of each process in R simultaneously. A *schedule* of a distributed sys-tem is an infinite sequence of process sets. Let $Q = R^1, R^2, \ldots$ be a schedule, where $R^i \subseteq P$ holds for each i $(i \geq 1)$. An infinite sequence of configurations

$e = \rho_0, \rho_1, \ldots$ is called an *execution* from an initial configuration ρ_0 by a schedule Q, if e satisfies $\rho_{i-1} \overset{R^i}{\mapsto} \rho_i$ for each i $(i \geq 1)$.

Process actions are executed atomically, and we consider in this paper three kinds of scheduling possibilities:

1. the *distributed daemon* schedules the actions of processes, in such a way that any subset of processes can simultaneously execute their actions,
2. the *central daemon* schedules the actions of processes such that exactly one process executes its actions at a given time,
3. the *k-central daemon* schedules the actions of processes such that no two processes that are k hops away or less execute their actions at the same time.

Of course, the central scheduler is a special case of the k-central scheduler, which in turn is a special case of the distributed scheduler. The most realistic scheduler is the distributed scheduler but the other two can be emulated using a mutual exclusion protocol (for the central scheduler) or a k-local mutual exclusion protocol (for the k-central scheduler), with an additional overhead.

The set of all possible executions from $\rho_0 \in C$ is denoted by E_{ρ_0}. The set of all possible executions is denoted by E, that is, $E = \bigcup_{\rho \in C} E_\rho$. We consider *asynchronous* distributed systems where we can make no assumption on schedules except that any schedule is *weakly fair*: every process is contained in infinite number of subsets appearing in any schedule.

In this context, a protocol is self-stabilizing for some specification $\mathcal{S}$ if there exists a global predicate P on configurations, such that the two following conditions are satisfied: *(i)* any execution starting from a configuration satisfying P satisfies the problem $\mathcal{S}$ (correctness), and *(ii)*, any computation reaches a configuration that satisfies P (convergence). In this paper, we also consider probabilistic protocols, for which the convergence is only achieved with probability 1 (see [1] for more details).

Local view and topology. We now define notions that are centric in this paper, and related to local views and local topology.

Definition 1 (Local Topology). *The local topology at distance k of a node p is the subgraph T_p^k of the communication graph G that contains nodes and edges of G up to distance k from p[1].*

A slightly different definition of local topology is given by Peleg in [12]:

Definition 2 (P-Local Topology). *The P-local topology at distance k of a node p is the subgraph $P\text{-}T_p^k$ of the communication graph G that contains nodes of G up to distance k from p and edges of G up to distance $k-1$ from p.*

---

[1] The distance from a node (say p) to an edge (say $e = (q,r)$) is defined as $\min\{dist(p,q), dist(p,r)\}$.

The significant difference between the local topology and the P-local topology at distance k is that the former requires to recognize exactly the links between processes at distance k but the latter does not.

Definition 3 (Local View). *The local view at distance 0 of a node p is the set V_p^0 of locally labeled edges that are adjacent to p. The local view at distance 1 of a node p is a tree V_p^1 of height 1 rooted at p that contains one leaf V_q^0 for every neighbor q of p. The local view at distance k of a node p is a tree V_p^k of height k that contains one local view V_q^{k-1} as subtree of p for each neighbor q of p.*

Informally, the local view is the knowledge about the network that a node can collect by getting information from its neighbors. In contrast, the local topology is the exact knowledge.

It is obvious that the (P-)local topology coincides with the local view when the (P-)local topology is acyclic. Thus, the following two observations hold.

Observation 1. *Let k be a strictly positive integer. In any network of girth $2k + 2$ or more, $T_p^k \subset V_p^k$ holds for any process p.*

Observation 2. *Let k be a strictly positive integer. In any network of girth $2k + 1$ or more, $P\text{-}T_p^k \subset V_p^k$ holds for any process p.*

3   Local View vs. Local Topology

In this section, we show that there exists a relation between views (resp. P-views) and local topology. In more details, when sufficient node or link coloring is provided, it is possible to construct the local topology from the local view (resp. P-view).

Definition 4 (k-local Node Coloring). *A coloring of the nodes is k-local, if any two nodes that are at distance at most k from each other have different colors.*

Definition 5 (k-local Link Coloring). *A coloring of the links is k-local, if any two links that are at distance at most k from each other have different colors.*

Observation 3. *To provide k-local node coloring (resp. k-local link coloring), at least $\min(n, k+1)$ (resp. $\min(m, k+1)$) colors are required, where n (resp. m) is the number of nodes (resp. links) in the network.*

The first two lemmas (Lemmas 1 and 2) show that when cycles are sufficiently small (or sufficiently large), there is no problem to identify the local topology from the local view (resp. P-view).

Lemma 1 (Girth upper bound). *Given a local view at distance k for each process, it is possible to construct a local (resp. P-local) topology at distance k at every node for any network of girth $2k + 2$ (resp. $2k + 1$) or more.*

Proof. The lemma immediately follows from Observations 1 and 2.

Lemma 2 (Circumference lower bound). *Given a local view at distance k for each process, a node or a link coloring at distance $2k$, it is possible to construct a local (resp. P-local) topology at distance k at every node for any network of circumference at most $2k$.*

Proof. In all cycles that can appear in such networks, all nodes (resp. links) have different colors. Now, consider the view V_p^k of a particular node p. If all nodes (resp. links) in V_p^k have different colors, then no cycle of size $2k$ or less can be compatible with this view (this implies that there is no cycle in the local topology at distance k). Now, if there is a node whose view presents twice (or more) the same node (resp. link), this means that this node belongs to a cycle. In this case, the node (resp. link) in the local topology is obtained by merging the two nodes (resp.links) in the view. Since it is possible to identify all cycles of length at most $2k$, using either a node or a link coloring at distance $2k$, it is possible to obtain the local topology at distance k using the view at distance k, for every node in the network.

The next two lemmas (Lemmas 3 and 4) prove that the previously obtained bound for topology identification from local view (resp. P-view for Corollaries 1 and 2) are tight.

Lemma 3 (Even cycles lower bound). *Given a local view at distance k for each process, a node coloring at distance $2k - 1$, a link coloring at distance $2k - 1$, there exists a network with an even cycle of size $2k$ where it is impossible to construct a local topology at distance k for every node p.*

Proof. Consider a $2k$ sized ring network where processes (numbered for the purpose of this proof from p_1 to p_{2k}) up to distance $2k - 1$ apart have different colors, and links (numbered for the purpose of this proof from l_1 to l_{2k}) up to distance $2k - 1$ apart have different colors. As there are from Observation 3 at least $2k$ available node colors and at least $2k$ available link colors, each node and each link has a unique color in this network.

Now suppose that there exists one process p in this ring that is able to construct the local topology at distance k. In the $2k$ sized ring, the local topology at distance k includes the full ring. So, there exists a j such that p_j is able to construct the full $2k$ ring. This is exemplified as Figure 1.*b* for the particular case of $k = 3$. Then, consider a $4k$ sized ring where processes (numbered from p_1' to p_{4k}') and links (numbered from l_1' to l_{4k}') are colored as follows:

– for any i in $\{1 \ldots 2k\}$, p_i' and p_{2k+i}' are colored as p_i,
– for any i in $\{1 \ldots 2k\}$, l_i' and l_{2k+i}' are colored as l_i,

This is exemplified as Figure 1.*a* for the particular case of $k = 3$. This new $4k$ sized ring is also $2k - 1$-local node and link colored. We can show for any i in $\{1 \ldots 2k\}$ that p_i' and p_{2k+i}' in the $4k$ sized ring can behave exactly in the same way as p_i in the $2k$ sized ring. This implies that p'_j and p'_{2k+j} construct the full $2k$ ring, which is incorrect.

Then, consider the complementary case, where p'_j is able to correctly construct the local topology at distance k in the $4k$ sized ring. Since p_j in the $2k$ sized ring can behave exactly in the same way as p'_j in the $4k$ sized ring. This implies that p_j constructs a local topology at distance k which is a tree, which is incorrect.

So, every processor is unable to construct a local topology at distance k in either of the two networks.

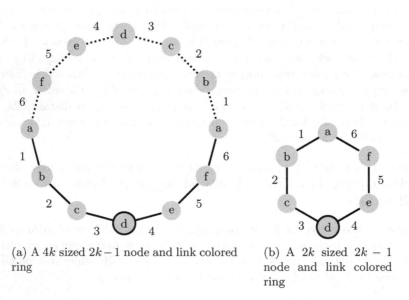

(a) A $4k$ sized $2k-1$ node and link colored ring

(b) A $2k$ sized $2k-1$ node and link colored ring

Fig. 1. Example with $k = 3$ and even cycle of size $2k$

Since the P-local topology of each process is same as the local topology in networks considered in the above proof, a similar impossibility result holds for the P-local topology.

Corollary 1. *Given a local view at distance k for each process, a node coloring at distance $2k - 1$, a link coloring at distance $2k - 1$, there exists a network with an even cycle of size $2k$ where it is impossible to construct a P-local topology at distance k for every node p.*

The length $2k$ is tight since P-$T_p^k = V_p^k$ holds for any process p if the network has no cycle of length $2k$ or less (see Observation 2).

Lemma 4 (Odd cycles lower bound). *Given a local view at distance k for each process, a node coloring at distance $2k$, a link coloring at distance $2k$, there exists a network with an odd cycle of size $2k+1$ where it is impossible to construct a local topology at distance k for any node p.*

Proof. Consider a $2k + 1$ sized ring network where processes (numbered for the purpose of this proof from p_1 to p_{2k+1}) up to distance $2k$ apart have different colors, and links (numbered for the purpose of this proof from l_1 to l_{2k+1}) up to distance $2k$ apart have different colors. As there are from Observation 3 at least $2k + 1$ available node colors and at least $2k + 1$ available link colors, each node and each link has a unique color in this network.

Now suppose that there exists one process p in this ring that is able to construct the local topology at distance k. In the $2k+1$ sized ring, the local topology at distance k includes the full ring. So, there exists a j such that p_j is able to construct the full $2k + 1$ ring. This is exemplified as Figure 2.b for the particular case of $k = 3$.

Then, consider a $4k + 2$ sized ring where processes (numbered from p'_1 to p'_{4k+2}) and links (numbered from l'_1 to l'_{4k+2}) are colored as follows:

- for any i in $\{1 \dots 2k + 1\}$, p'_i and p'_{2k+i+1} are colored as p_i,
- for any i in $\{1 \dots 2k + 1\}$, l'_i and l'_{2k+i+1} are colored as l_i,

This is exemplified as Figure 2.a for the particular case of $k = 3$. This new $4k + 2$ sized ring is also $2k$-local node and link colored. We can show for any i in $\{1 \dots 2k + 1\}$ that p'_i and p'_{2k+i+1} in the $4k + 2$ sized ring can behave exactly in the same way as p_i in the $2k + 1$ sized ring. This implies that p'_j and p'_{2k+j+1} construct the full $2k + 1$ ring, which is incorrect.

Then, consider the complementary case, where p'_j is able to correctly construct the local topology at distance k in the $4k + 2$ sized ring. Since p_j in the $2k + 1$ sized ring can behave exactly in the same way as p'_j in the $4k + 2$ sized ring. This implies that p_j constructs a local topology at distance k which is a tree, which is incorrect.

So, every processor is unable to construct a local topology at distance k in either of the two networks.

Notice that the similar impossibility result does not hold for the P-local topology. Actually, from Observation 2), the P-local topology and the local view of distance k coincide, and thus, can be obtained from each other.

From the above lemma, we can immediately obtain the following corollary:

Corollary 2. *Given a local view at distance k for each process, a node (resp. link) coloring at distance $2k$, it is possible to construct a P-local topology at distance k at every node for any graph that has no cycle of size $2k$.*

We now present the main result of the section.

Theorem 1. *Given a local view at distance k for each process, a node coloring at distance $2k + 1$ (resp. $2k$) or a link coloring at distance $2k + 1$ (resp. $2k$), it is possible to construct a local (resp. P-local) topology at distance k for every node. The bounds on the coloring distance are tight.*

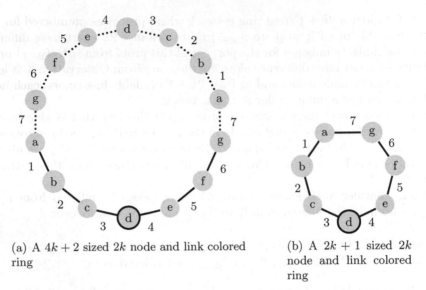

(a) A $4k + 2$ sized $2k$ node and link colored ring

(b) A $2k + 1$ sized $2k$ node and link colored ring

Fig. 2. Example with $k = 3$ and odd cycle of size $2k + 1$

Proof. Assume that we wish to obtain the local topology at distance k. Now, this local topology is a subgraph of the global graph G. The cycles of size $2k + 2$ or more cause no problem to the topology discovery from the proof of Lemma 1. Similarly, the cycles of size $2k$ or less cause no problem either from the proof of Lemma 2. The tightness of the bounds is presented in Lemmas 3 and 4. The results for the P-view result from Corollaries 1 and 2.

4   Bootstrapping Topology Knowledge

In this section, we discuss the possibility to bootstrap topology knowledge in anonymous networks. Bootstrapping topology knowledge is the process of learning local topology at distance $k + 1$ assuming local topology at distance k is known. As proved in Section 3, this is tantamount to requiring that node or link coloring can be bootstrapped, *i.e.* being able to compute a node (link, respectively) coloring at distance $k + 1$ given a node (link respectively) coloring at distance k.

On the negative side, Theorems 2 and 3 show that *(i)* with a distributed daemon, it is impossible to achieve deterministic color bootstrap, even if the whole network topology can be instantaneously obtained, and *(ii)* with a central daemon, it is impossible to achieve distance m when instantaneous topology knowledge is limited to $m - 1$.

Theorem 2 (Deterministic Bootstrap with Distributed Daemon). *Given a m-local node and link coloring, the ability for each process to instantaneously get a colored topology of the whole network, and a distributed daemon, it is impossible* *to get either a node coloring at distance $m+1$ or a link coloring at distance $m+1$ with a deterministic algorithm.*

Proof. The proof for the node coloring at distance $m+1$ is implied by the proof of Theorem 5.4 in [13]. The basic argument is to consider a ring of size $m \times l$, where the node colors repeat along the cycle in the same order. If the schedule is synchronous (which can occur with a distributed scheduler), all nodes that were in the same state had the same view of the system. Since their code is deterministic, they all reach the same new state. This is true for all nodes, so we do not get more asymmetry in the network, and $m+1$ colors can not be generated.

Now, for the case of $m+1$-local link coloring. We simply consider the fact that the color of a link is determined by the state of its two incident processes. From the previous argument, pairs of processes (p_j, p_{m+j+1}), for $j \in \{1 \ldots m+1\}$, remain in the same state infinitely often, so pairs of pairs of processes $((p_j, p_{m+j+1}), (p_{j+1}, p_{m+j+2}))$, for $j \in \{1 \ldots m+1\}$ remain in the same state. As a result, the colors of links l_j and l_{m+j+1} remains the same forever, so a $m+1$ local link coloring is never achieved.

Theorem 3 (Deterministic Bootstrap with Central Daemon). *Let k and m be two integers such that $m \geq k \geq 2$. Given a m-local node and link coloring, the ability of each process to instantaneously get a colored local topology at distance k, and a central daemon, it is impossible to get either a node coloring at distance $m+1$ or a link coloring at distance $m+1$ with a deterministic algorithm.*

Proof. Consider a $2m+2$ sized ring whose processes are numbered from p_1 to p_{2m+2} and whose links are numbered from l_1 to l_{2m+2}, with l_i corresponding to the link between p_i and p_{i+1} (if $i < 2m+2$) or p_1 (if $i = 2m+2$). Since a m-local node and link coloring is assumed, we have $m+1$ possible colors for both nodes and links. We consider that for every $i \in \{1 \ldots m+1\}$, processes p_i and p_{m+i+1} share the same color, and that links l_i and l_{m+i+1} share the same color. This case is exemplified in Figure 3 when $m = k = 5$.

As a result, for any $k \leq m$, p_i and p_{m+i+1} share the same local topology at distance k. Now, the central scheduler indefinitely activates the processes as follows:

– for $j \in \{1..m+1\}$, p_j then p_{m+j+1} are successively activated.

Now consider a starting configuration where all pairs of processes (p_j, p_{m+j+1}), for $j \in \{1 \ldots m+1\}$, are in the same state. Then, after all processes have been activated exactly once by the central scheduler, all pairs of processes (p_j, p_{m+j+1}), for $j \in \{1 \ldots m+1\}$ are *still* in the same state, because they run a deterministic algorithm that is fed with the same input. Also, this process may repeat so that all pairs of processes (p_j, p_{m+j+1}), for $j \in \{1 \ldots m+1\}$ remain in the same state forever. As a result, no symmetry breaking at distance more than m can occur, and nodes at distance $m+1$ from each other keep the same color, so a $m+1$-local node coloring is never achieved.

Now, for the case of $m + 1$-local link coloring. We simply consider the fact that the color of a link is determined by the state of its two incident processes. From the previous argument, pairs of processes (p_j, p_{m+j+1}), for $j \in \{1 \ldots m + 1\}$, remain in the same state infinitely often, so pairs of pairs of processes $((p_j, p_{m+j+1}), (p_{j+1}, p_{m+j+2}))$, for $j \in \{1 \ldots m + 1\}$ remain in the same state. As a result, the colors of links l_j and l_{m+j+1} remains the same forever, so a $m + 1$ local link coloring is never achieved.

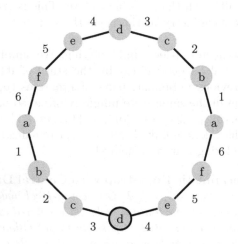

Fig. 3. Example with $m=5$

On the positive side, Theorems 4 and 5 show that *(i)* under the k-central daemon, deterministic bootstrap of colors up to distance k is possible provided that k-local topology can be instantaneously obtained, and *(ii)* under the distributed daemon, probabilistic bootstrap is possible for any range.

Theorem 4 (Deterministic Self-stabilizing Bootstrap with k-Central Daemon). *Let k, m be two integers such that $k > m \geq 2$. Given a m-local node and link coloring, the ability of each process to instantaneously get a colored local topology at distance k, and a central daemon, there exists a deterministic self-stabilizing algorithm that permits to get a $m+1$ local node and link coloring.*

Proof. In fact, we prove that knowing the local topology at distance k permits to node and link color the network so that the coloring is k-local. Each process p knows the local topology at distance k, so each process p is able to construct the graph G^k. By the k-local central daemon hypothesis, no two neighbors in G^k are activated at the same time. Then each process executes *e.g.* Algorithm [7] (that performs under the 1-local central daemon) to node color G^k. Of course, a 1-local node coloring of G^k is a k-local node coloring in G.

For the case of k-local link coloring, each process executes *e.g.* algorithm [11] to edge color G^k (that requires a 1-local central daemon). By the k-local central daemon hypothesis, no two neighbors in G^k are activated at the same time. Of course, a 1-local edge coloring of G^k is a k-local edge coloring in G.

Theorem 5 (Probabilistic Self-stabilizing Bootstrap with Distributed Daemon). *Let k, m be two integers such that $k > m \geq 2$. Given a m-local node and link coloring, the ability of each process to get a colored local view at distance k, and a distributed daemon, there exists a probabilistic self-stabilizing algorithm that permits to get a $m + 1$ local node and link coloring.*

Proof. The proof is by providing such a self-stabilizing probabilistic algorithm. The core components of this protocol are described as Algorithms 4.1, 4.2, and 4.3.

The first component is described as Algorithm 4.1, and essentially propagates local variables of each node to neighboring nodes up to distance k. This algorithm only assumes that a node is able to locally distinguish its neighbors, so that it can update parts of its own view accordingly to updates provided by its neighbors. This scheme is essentially the same as the one used in [5] (with the notable exception that here node do not have unique identifiers) and [2], which were proved to be self-stabilizing. So, Algorithm 4.1 is able to produce a view at distance k, for any arbitrary k, in a self-stabilizing way.

Since a view at distance k for a limited set of variables can be achieved using Algorithm 4.1, Algorithm 4.2 is run in parallel (using the fair composition of [6]) to node color the network up to distance k. The algorithm is quite similar to the neighborhood coloring of [8], with the notable exception that here the local topology is not known, and the local view is used instead. Informally, the algorithm runs as follows: each node checks whether its color conflicts with another color visible in its view at distance k (excluding itself). If a conflict is found, the node randomly draws a new color, in the set of available colors (*i.e.* the set of colors that do not appear in its view at distance k).

Of course, it is still possible that a node actually detects a conflict with itself if it gets a view at distance k in a cycle of size exactly k. To resolve this issue, a node p detecting a conflict uses a *probe* mechanism. The node p first extracts the path (using local labeling on edges stored in its view) towards and backwards the conflicting node. Then p draws a big random number, stores it in a $probe_p$ variable, and sends the random number along the path. When the random variable arrives at the destination q, q checks whether its last calculated $probe_q$ matches the received one. If no, a "fail" response is sent using the backward path. If yes, a "success" response is sent using the backward path. Now, when p receives a "fail" response, it randomly chooses a new color, as in the original algorithm. If p receives a "success", it draws a new random number and sends a new probe. As there is a strictly positive probability that two different nodes draw different probe numbers, eventually every node changes its color only when it implies a conflict with a different node. As a conflict in the view implies a conflict in the topology, the same proof argument as in [8] can be applied here. As a result, Algorithm 4.2 provides coloring at distance k, for any arbitrary k.

Algorithm 4.3 assumes that a node coloring at distance 1 is achieved, and provides a distance 1 link coloring of the same graph. Distance 1 node coloring is used to define *domination* between neighboring nodes as follows: the node whose color is larger dominates the other node. In the link coloring protocol, the dominating node is responsible for setting the color of a particular edge (since the network is node colored, such a dominator always exists). The algorithm then runs as follows. First, each node collects in a shared variable *report* the colors of adjacent edges (Rule $\mathcal{R}_1$). Second, a node p detecting a conflict between an edge it dominates (to another node j) and either:

Algorithm 4.1. View construction (distance k)

---

variables:
   V_p^k: view of p at distance k
   $// V_p^{k-1}|j$ *denotes the part of* V_p^k *related to neighbor* j
   $// V_p^0$ *denotes the monitored variable of* p
actions::
   $\exists k > 0, \exists j \in N_p, V_j^{k-1} \neq V_p^{k-1}|j$
   $\rightarrow V_p^{k-1}|j := V_j^{k-1}$

Algorithm 4.2. Probabilistic node coloring (distance k)

---

variables:
   c_p: color of node p (in domain Γ)
functions:
   $colors(V)$: returns the set of colors contained in view V
   $random(S)$: returns a random element of set S
actions::
   $\exists j \in \cup_{i \in N_p} V_p^k|i, c_j = c_p$
   $\rightarrow cc_p := random\left(\Gamma \setminus colors(\cup_{i \in N_p} V_p^k|i)\right)$

Algorithm 4.3. Probabilistic link coloring (distance 1)

---

variables:
   $l_{p \rightarrow j}$: color of link (p, j), with $c_p > c_j$ (in domain Γ')
   $report_p$: multiset of colors
functions:
   $conflict(M, l)$: returns true if color l is present more than once in color multiset M
actions::
   $\mathcal{R}_1 :: report_p \neq \left(\cup_{k \in N_p, c_p > c_k} l_{p \rightarrow k}\right) \cup \left(\cup_{k' \in N_p, c_{k'} < c_p} l_{k' \rightarrow p}\right)$
   $\rightarrow report_p := \left(\cup_{k \in N_p, c_p > c_k} l_{p \rightarrow k}\right) \cup \left(\cup_{k' \in N_p, c_{k'} < c_p} l_{k' \rightarrow p}\right)$
   $\mathcal{R}_2 :: \exists j \in N_p, conflict(report_p, l_{p \rightarrow j})$
   $\rightarrow l_{p \rightarrow j} := random(\Gamma' \setminus \{report_p \cup report_j\})$
   $\mathcal{R}_3 :: \exists j \in N_p, conflict(report_j, l_{p \rightarrow j})$
   $\rightarrow l_{p \rightarrow j} := random(\Gamma' \setminus \{report_p \cup report_j\})$

---

1. another adjacent edge of p (Rule $\mathcal{R}_2$), or
2. another adjacent edge of j (Rule $\mathcal{R}_3$)

randomly chooses a new color for this particular link it dominates among the set of available link colors. Self-stabilization of the protocol can be proved as follows. Assume there is a conflict of link colors (without loss of generality, assume that those links are (k, i) and (i, j)), then two cases may occur:

1. i dominates both k and j, then i randomly chooses a new color for one of the links, and the conflict disappear,
2. k dominates i but i dominates j, then either k (by Rule $\mathcal{R}_3$), i (by Rule $\mathcal{R}_2$), or both randomly choose a new color. In the first two cases, the conflict is solved. In the last case, there is a strictly positive probability that the conflict is solved (if k and i draw different colors).
3. i is dominated by both k and j, then either k (by Rule $\mathcal{R}_3$), j (by Rule $\mathcal{R}_3$), or both randomly choose a new color. In the first two cases, the conflict is solved. In the last case, there is a strictly positive probability that the conflict is solved (if k and j draw different colors).

So at each step, there is at least a positive constant probability to reduce the number of conflicting colors for links. As a result, Algorithm 4.3 is a probabilistic self-stabilizing algorithm for distance 1 link coloring assuming distance 1 node coloring.

We now construct the probabilistic self-stabilizing algorithm for distance k link coloring. First, we execute distance $2k + 1$ node coloring, which by Theorem 1 results in constructing the topology at distance k. After stabilization of this protocol, nodes are aware of G^k. The distance 1 probabilistic link coloring algorithm we just presented in run in parallel on G^k, resulting in a link coloring of G^k. Now, a distance 1 link coloring of G^k is a distance k link coloring of G. Hence the claimed result.

5 Conclusion

We provided evidence that graph coloring (either node or link) is related to topology knowledge as $2k + 1$ coloring is necessary and sufficient for topology knowledge up to distance k (if outgoing edges are necessary). Also, we proved that deterministic algorithms are of no practical help for coloring at distance k, as they require hypothesis that are either unrealistic (topology knowledge at distance k, which is strictly stronger than distance k coloring, the output of the algorithm), or have no known solutions in anonymous networks (k-central scheduler). The probabilistic solution we provided practically solves the whole problem: the network is anonymous, topology is not known, and the scheduling daemon is distributed. The distance one probabilistic self-stabilizing link coloring that we presented as a part of the solution may be of particular interest, as it is the first self-stabilizing solution to this problem that performs under the distributed scheduler (this problem is impossible to solve with a deterministic self-stabilizing algorithm).

468 T. Masuzawa and S. Tixeuil

References

1. Joffroy Beauquier, Maria Gradinariu, and Colette Johnen. Memory space requirements for self-stabilizing leader election protocols. In *PODC*, pages 199–207, 1999.
2. Paolo Boldi and Sebastiano Vigna. Universal dynamic synchronous self-stabilization. *Distributed Computing*, 15(3):137–153, 2002.
3. Sylvie Delaët and Sébastien Tixeuil. Tolerating transient and intermittent failures. *Journal of Parallel and Distributed Computing*, 62(5):961–981, May 2002.
4. S. Dolev. *Self-stabilization*. MIT Press, March 2000.
5. Shlomi Dolev and Ted Herman. Superstabilizing protocols for dynamic distributed systems. *Chicago J. Theor. Comput. Sci.*, 1997, 1997.
6. Mohamed G. Gouda and Ted Herman. Adaptive programming. *IEEE Trans. Software Eng.*, 17(9):911–921, 1991.
7. Maria Gradinariu and Sébastien Tixeuil. Self-stabilizing vertex coloring of arbitrary graphs. In *International Conference on Principles of Distributed Systems (OPODIS'2000)*, pages 55–70, Paris, France, December 2000.
8. Ted Herman and Sébastien Tixeuil. A distributed tdma slot assignment algorithm for wireless sensor networks. In *Proceedings of the First Workshop on Algorithmic Aspects of Wireless Sensor Networks (AlgoSensors'2004)*, number 3121 in Lecture Notes in Computer Science, pages 45–58, Turku, Finland, July 2004. Springer-Verlag.
9. Jason L. Hill and David E. Culler. Mica: A wireless platform for deeply embedded networks. *IEEE Micro*, 22(6):12–24, 2002.
10. T Masuzawa. A fault-tolerant and self-stabilizing protocol for the topology problem. In *Proceedings of the Second Workshop on Self-Stabilizing Systems*, pages 1.1–1.15, 1995.
11. Toshimitsu Masuzawa and Sébastien Tixeuil. A self-stabilizing link coloring algorithm resilient to unbounded byzantine faults in arbitrary networks. In *Proceedings of OPODIS 2005*, Lecture Notes in Computer Science, page to appear, Pisa, Italy, December 2005. Springer-Verlag.
12. David Peleg. *Distributed Computing: A Locality-Sensitive Approach*. SIAM, Philadelphia, PA, 2000.
13. Naoshi Sakamoto. Structure of initial conditions for distributed algorithms. *IEICE Transactions on Information and Systems*, E83-D(12):2029–2038, December 2000.
14. J.M. Spinelli and R.G. Gallager. Event driven topology broadcast without sequence numbers. *IEEE Transactions on Communications*, 37:468–474, 1989.
15. Masafumi Yamashita and Tsunehiko Kameda. Leader election problem on networks in which processor identity numbers are not distinct. *IEEE Trans. Parallel Distrib. Syst.*, 10(9):878–887, 1999.

Self-adaptive Disk Arrays

Jehan-François Pâris[1,*], Thomas J.E. Schwarz[2], and Darrell D.E. Long [3,*]

[1] Dept. of Computer Science, University of Houston
Houston, TX 77204-3010
paris@cs.uh.edu
[2] Dept. of Computer Engineering, Santa Clara University
Santa Clara, CA 95053
tjschwarz@scu.edu
[3] Dept. of Computer Science, University of California
Santa Cruz, CA 95064
darrell@cs.ucsc.edu

Abstract. We present a disk array organization that adapts itself to successive disk failures. When all disks are operational, all data are mirrored on two disks. Whenever a disk fails, the array reorganizes itself, by selecting a disk containing redundant data and replacing these data by their exclusive or (XOR) with the other copy of the data contained on the disk that failed. This will protect the array against any single disk failure until the failed disk gets replaced and the array can revert to its original condition. Hence data will remain protected against the successive failures of up to one half of the original number of disks, provided that no critical disk failure happens while the array is reorganizing itself. As a result, our scheme achieves the same access times as a mirrored organization under normal operational conditions while having a much lower likelihood of loosing data under abnormal conditions. In addition it tolerates much longer repair times than mirrored disk arrays.

Keywords: fault-tolerant systems, storage systems, repairable systems, k-out-of-n systems.

1 Introduction

Today's disks have mean time to failures of more than ten years, which means that a given disk has a less than ten percent probability of failing during any given year of its useful lifetime. While this reliability level is acceptable for all the applications that only require the storage of a few hundreds of gigabytes of non-critical information over relatively short time intervals, it does not satisfy the needs of applications having to store terabytes of data over many years.

Backups have been the traditional way of protecting data against equipment failures. Unfortunately, they suffer from several important limitations. First, they do not scale well; indeed the amount of time required to make a copy of a large data set

---

[*] Supported in part by the National Science Foundation under award CCR-0204358.

A.K. Datta and M. Gradinariu (Eds.): SSS 2006, LNCS 4280, pp. 469–483, 2006.

can exceed the interval between daily backups. Second, the process is not as trustworthy as it should be due to both human error and the frailty of most recording media. Finally, backup technologies are subject to technical obsolescence, which means that saved data risk becoming unreadable after only ten to twenty years. A much better solution is to introduce redundancy into our storage systems

The two primary ways of introducing that redundancy are mirroring and *m*-out-of-*n* codes. Both techniques have their advantages and disadvantages. Mirroring offers the two main advantages of reducing read access times and having a reasonable update overhead. Identifying failed disks can always be done by detecting which replicas have become unavailable. On the other hand, *m*-out-of-*n* codes provide much higher data survivability. Consider, for instance, the case of a small disk array consisting of eight disks. A mirrored organization that maintains two copies of each file on separate disks would protect data against all single disk failures and most double disk failures. A simultaneous failure of three disks would have a bigger impact as it would result in data loss in 43 percent of the cases. This is much worse than an optimal 4-out-of-8 code that protects data in the presence of up to four arbitrary disk failures. In fact, this is such an improbable event that erasure codes that tolerate more than two simultaneous failures are never used in actual storage systems.

We propose a self-adaptive disk array organization that combines most of advantages of mirroring and erasure coding. As long as most disks are operational, it will provide the same read and write access times as a mirrored organization. Whenever a disk fails, it will reorganize itself and quickly return to a state where data are again protected against a single failure. As a result, data will remain protected against the consecutive failures of up to one half of the original number of disks, provided that no critical disk failure happens while the array is reorganizing itself. This is a rather unlikely event as the reorganization process will normally take less than a few hours.

The remainder of this paper is organized as follows. Section 2 will introduce our self-adaptive disk array organizations. Section 3 will compare the mean times to data loss (MTTDL) achieved by self-adaptive arrays with those achieved by mirrored disk arrays. Section 4 will review previous work and Section 5 will have our conclusions.

2 Our Approach

Consider the small disk array displayed on Fig. 1. It consists of four pairs of disks with data replicated on each pair of disks. For instance, disks A_1 and A_2 contain the same data set A. Assume now that disk B_1 fails. As a result, only one remaining copy of data set B remains and the array will become vulnerable to a failure of disk B_2. Waiting for the replacement of disk B_1 is not an attractive option as the process make take several days. To adapt itself to the failure, the array will immediately locate a disk containing data that are replicated elsewhere, say, disk A_1, and replace its contents by the exclusive or (XOR) of data sets A and B thus making the array immune to a single disk failure. Fig. 2 displays the outcome of that reconfiguration.

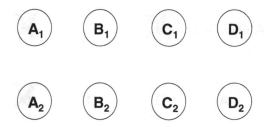

Fig. 1. A small disk array consisting of four pairs of disks with data replicated on each pair of disks

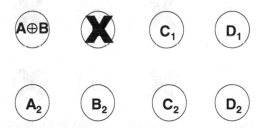

Fig. 2. The same disk array after disk B_1 has failed and the array is reconfigured

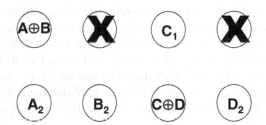

Fig. 3. The same disk array after disk D_1 has failed and the array is reconfigured

The array can again tolerate any single disk failure. The sole drawback of the process is that accesses to data sets A and B will now be slightly slower. In particular, updates to these two data sets will be significantly slower as each update will now require one additional read operation. This condition is only temporary as the array will revert to its original condition as soon as the failed disk is replaced.

Consider now what would happen if a second disk failed, say, disk D_1, before disk B_1 was repaired. This second failure would remove one of the two copies of data set D and make the array vulnerable to a failure of disk D_2. To return to a safer state, the array will locate a disk containing data that are replicated elsewhere, say, disk C_2, and replace its contents by the exclusive or (XOR) of data sets C and D. Fig. 3 displays the outcome of this reorganization.

Under most circumstances, the two failing disks will be replaced before a third failure could occur. Delays in the repair process and accelerated disk failures resulting

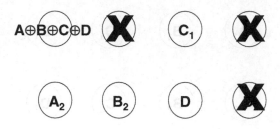

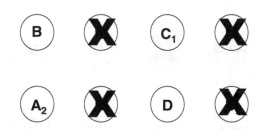

Fig. 4. The same disk array after disk D_2 has failed

Fig. 5. The same disk array after disk B_2 has failed

from environmental conditions could however produce the occurrence of a third disk failure before disks B_1 and D_1 are replaced. Let us assume that disk D_2 fails this time. Observe that this failure destroys the last copy of data set D. The fastest way to reconstitute this data set is to send the contents of disk C_1 to the disk that now contains $C \oplus D$ and to XOR the contents of these two disks *in situ*. While doing that, the array will also send the old contents of the parity disk, that is, $C \oplus D$, to the disk that contains $A \oplus B$ in order to obtain there $A \oplus B \oplus C \oplus D$. As seen on Fig. 4, the disk array now consists of four disks holding data and one parity disk.

Let us now consider for the sake of completeness the rather improbable case of a fourth disk failure occurring before any of the three failed disks can be replaced. Assume that disk B_2 fails this time. As Fig. 5 indicates, the sole option left is to reconstitute the contents of the failed disk by XORing the contents of the parity disk $(A \oplus B \oplus C \oplus D)$ with those of disks A_2, C_1 and D and store these contents on the former parity disk. This would keep all four data sets available but would leave all of them vulnerable to a single disk failure.

In its essence, our proposal is to let the array adapt itself to the temporary loss of disks by switching to more compact data representations and selecting when possible a configuration that protects the data against a single disk failure. That process will involve introducing parity disks, merging them and sometimes using them to reconstitute lost data.

Figs. 6 and 7 give a more formal description of our scheme. The first algorithm describes how the array reacts to the loss of a data disk. Two main cases have to be considered, depending on whether the contents of the failed disk D can be found on

Assumptions:
   disk D is failed data disk

Algorithm:
   begin
      find disk E having same contents as disk D
      if found **then**
         find a disk F whose contents are replicated on another disk G
         if found **then**
            replace contents (F) by contents (E) XOR contents(F)
         else
            find parity disk Z whose contents are XORed contents of fewest
            data disks
            if found **then**
               replace contents (Z) by contents (E) XOR contents(Z)
            else
               do nothing
            endif
         endif
      else
         find sufficient set S of disks to reconstitute contents (D)
         if found **then**
            reconstitute contents (D) on a parity disk X in S
            replace parity disk X
         else
            declare failure
         endif
      endif
   end

Fig. 6. Replacing a failed data disk

another disk E. When this is the case, the array will protect the contents of disk E against of a failure of that disk by storing on some disk F the XOR of the contents of E and the contents of one or more disks. To select this disk F, the array will first search for disks whose contents are replicated on some other disk. If it cannot find one, it will then select the parity disk Z whose contents are the XORed contents of the fewest data disks. The second case is somewhat more complex. When the contents of the failed disk D cannot be found on another disk, the array will attempt to find a sufficient set S of disks to reconstitute the contents of the lost disk. If this set exists, it will reconstitute the contents of the lost data disk D on a parity disk X in S. Once this is done, the array will try to remedy the loss of the parity data on disk X by calling the second algorithm.

Our second algorithm describes how the array reacts to the loss of a parity disk X. This loss can either be the direct result of a disk failure or a side-effect of the recovery of the contents of a data disk D. In either case, the array checks first if it can reconstitute the contents of the failed parity disk X. This will be normally possible unless the array has experienced two simultaneous disk failures. If the contents of X

Assumptions:
disk X is failed parity disk

Algorithm:
   begin
        find sufficient set S of disks to reconstitute contents(X)
        if found **then**
            find a disk F whose contents are mirrored on another disk G
            if found **then**
                replace contents (F) by contents (E) XOR contents (F)
            else
                find parity disk Z whose contents are XORed contents of fewest
                data disks
                if found **then**
                    replace contents (Z) by contents(Z) XOR contents(X)
                else
                    do nothing
                endif
        else
            declare failure
        endif
   end

Fig. 7. Replacing a failed parity disk

can be reconstituted, the array will try to XOR them with the contents of a data disk that was replicated elsewhere. If no such data disk exists, the array will XOR the reconstituted contents of X with the contents of the parity disk Z whose contents are the XORed contents of the fewest data disks.

Space considerations prevent us from discussing in detail how the array will handle disk repairs. In essence, it will attempt to return to its original configuration, first by splitting the parity disks whose contents are the XORed contents of the largest number of parity disks then by replacing the remaining parity disks by pairs of data disks. A more interesting issue is how the self-adapting array would react to the loss of a disk involved in a reconfiguration step. Let us return to our previous example and consider what would happen if disk B_2 failed after disk B_1 failed but before the contents of disk A_1 could be completely replaced by the XOR of the contents of disks A_1 and B_2. Assuming that we do this replacement track by track, disk A_1 would be left in a state where it would contain some of its original tracks and some tracks containing the XOR of the corresponding tracks of disks A_1 and B_2. This means that some but not all the contents of disk B_2 would be recoverable and that some but not all contents of disk A_1 would have become vulnerable to a single disk failure.

3 Reliability Analysis

Self-adaptive disk arrays occupy a place between mirrored disk organizations and organizations using erasure coding. As long as most disks are operational, they provide the same read and write access times as static mirrored organizations. In addition, they are more resilient to disk failures. We propose to evaluate this resilience and to compare it with that of mirrored disk organizations.

Estimating the reliability of a storage system means estimating the probability R(t) that the system will operate correctly over the time interval [0, t] given that it operated correctly at time $t = 0$. Computing that function requires solving a system of linear differential equations, a task that becomes quickly unmanageable as the complexity of the system grows. A simpler option is to focus on the mean time to data loss (MTTDL) of the storage system. This is the approach we will take here.

Our system model consists of a disk array with independent failure modes for each disk. When a disk fails, a repair process is immediately initiated for that disk. Should several disks fail, the repair process will be performed in parallel on those disks. We assume that disk failures are independent events exponentially distributed with rate λ, and that repairs are exponentially distributed with rate μ.

The MTTDL for data replicated on two disks is [9]

$$MTTDL = \frac{3\lambda + \mu}{2\lambda^2}$$

and the corresponding failure rate L is

$$L = \frac{2\lambda^2}{3\lambda + \mu}.$$

Consider an array consisting of n disks with all data replicated on exactly two disks. Since each pair of disk fails in an independent fashion, the global failure rate $L(n)$ of the array will be $n/2$ times the failure rate L of a single pair of disks

$$L(n) = \frac{n}{2} L = \frac{n\lambda^2}{3\lambda + \mu}$$

and the global mean time to data loss $MTTDL(n)$ will be

$$MTTDL(n) = \frac{1}{L(n)} = \frac{3\lambda + \mu}{n\lambda^2}.$$

Fig. 8 shows the state transition diagram for a very small self-adaptive array consisting of two pairs of disks with each pair storing two identical replicas of the same data set. Assume that disks A_1 and A_2 contain identical copies of data set A while disks B_1 and B_2 store identical copies of data set B. State <2, 2> represents the normal state of the array when its four disks are all operational. A failure of any of these disks, say disk A_1 would bring the array to state <2, 1>. This state is a less than desirable state because the array has now a single copy of data set A on disk A_2. Hence a failure of that disk would result in a data loss.

To return to a more resilient state, the array will immediately start replacing the contents of either disk B_1 or disk B_2 with the XOR of data sets A and B, thus bringing the system from state <2, 1> to state <1, 1, X>. We assume that the duration of this self-adaptive process will be exponentially distributed with rate κ.

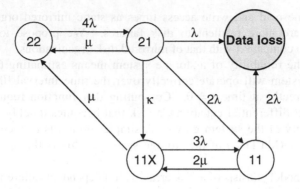

Fig. 8. State transition diagram for a self-adaptive disk array consisting of two pairs of mirrored disks

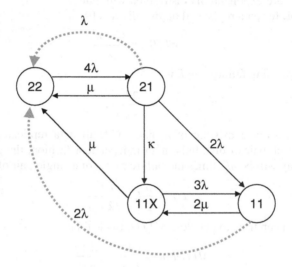

Fig. 9. Modified state transition diagram for the same disk array. The two dotted gray arcs returning the array to state <2, 2> represent data losses.

Once this reorganization is completed, the array will have single copies of both data sets A and B on two of the three surviving disks as well as their XOR on the third disk. A failure of either of the two redundant disks present in state <2, 1> or a failure of any of the three disks in state <1, 1, X> would leave the array in state <1, 1>, incapable of tolerating any additional disk failure.

Recovery transitions correspond to the repair of one of the disks that failed. They would bring the array first from state <1, 1> to state <1, 1, X> and then from state <1, 1, X> to state <2, 2>. A third recovery transition would bring the array from state <2, 1> to state <2, 2>. It corresponds to situations where the failed disk was replaced before the self-adaptive process can be completed.

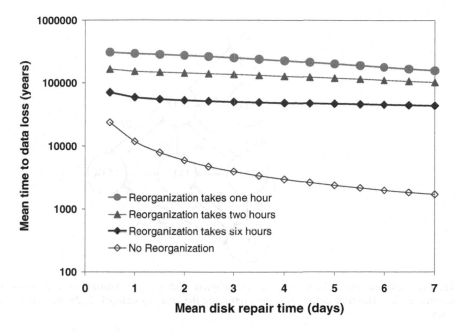

Fig. 10. Mean times to data loss achieved by a self-adaptive disk array consisting of two pairs of mirrored disks

Since data losses are essentially irrecoverable, the state corresponding to such a loss is an absorbing state. Hence a steady state analysis of the array would provide no insight on its performance.

Let us now consider the state transition diagram displayed in Fig. 9. It has the same states and the same transitions as that of Fig. 8 but for the two transitions leading to a data loss, which are now redirected to state <2, 2>. This diagram represents what would happen if the array went through continuous cycles during which it would first operate correctly then lose its data and get instantly repaired and reloaded with new data [7]. The corresponding system of equations is

$$4\lambda p_{22} = \mu(p_{21} + p_{11X}) + \lambda p_{21} + 2\lambda p_{11}$$
$$(3\lambda + \mu + \kappa)p_{21} = 4\lambda p_{22}$$
$$(3\lambda + \mu)p_{11X} = \kappa p_{21}, +2\mu p_{11}$$
$$(2\lambda + 2\mu)p_{11} = 3\lambda p_{11X} + 2\lambda p_{21}$$
(1)

together with the condition that $p_{22} + p_{21} + p_{11X} + p_{11} = 1$, where p_{ij} represents the steady-state probability of the system being in state <i, j>. In addition, the rate at which the array will fail before returning to its normal state is

$$L = \lambda p_{21} + 2\lambda p_{11}$$

Solving system (1), we obtain

$$L = \frac{4\lambda^2(9\lambda^2 + 3\kappa\lambda + 3\lambda\mu + \mu^2)}{33\lambda^3 + 13\kappa\lambda^2 + 5\kappa\lambda\mu + 8\lambda\mu^2 + \kappa\mu^2 + \mu^3}.$$

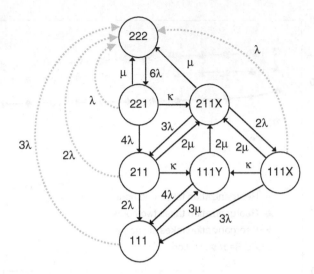

Fig. 11. State transition diagram for a self-adaptive disk array consisting of three pairs of mirrored disks. The four dotted gray arcs returning the array to state <2, 2, 2> represent data losses.

The mean time to data loss of our disk array (MTTDL) is then

$$MTTDL = \frac{1}{L} = \frac{33\lambda^3 + 13\kappa\lambda^2 + 5\kappa\lambda\mu + 8\lambda\mu^2 + \kappa\mu^2 + \mu^3}{4\lambda^2(9\lambda^2 + 3\kappa\lambda + 3\lambda\mu + \mu^2)}.$$

Fig. 10 displays on a logarithmic scale the MTTDLs achieved by the self–adaptive array for selected values of κ and repair times varying between half a day and seven days. We assumed that the disk failure rate λ was one failure every one hundred thousand hours, that is, slightly less than one failure every eleven years and conservative relative to the values quoted by disk manufacturers. Disk repair times are expressed in days and MTTDLs expressed in years.

Fig. 11 displays the state transition diagram for a self-adaptive disk array consisting of three pairs of mirrored disks. Assume that disks A_1 and A_2 contain identical copies of data set A, disks B_1 and B_2 store identical copies of data set B and disks C_1 and C_2 have identical copies of data set C. State <2, 2, 2> represents the normal state of the array when its six disks are all operational. A failure of any of these six disks, say disk A_1, would leave the system in state <2, 2, 1>. This state is a less than desirable state as the array is left with only one copy of data set A. To return to a more resilient state, the array will immediately start replacing the contents of one of the four redundant disks, say, disks B_1, with the XOR of data sets A and B, thus bringing the system from state <2, 2, 1> to state <2, 1, 1, X> with the XOR of data sets A and B on disk B_1. Failure of a second disk would bring the array to either state <2, 1, 1> or state <1, 1, 1, X>. Both states are less than desirable states, as they leave the array vulnerable to a single disk failure. To return to a more resilient state, the array will bring itself to state <1, 1, 1, Y>, having a single copy of each data set on separate disks and their XOR $(A \oplus B \oplus C)$ on disk Y.

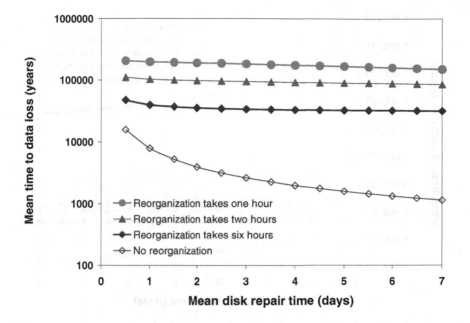

Fig. 12. Mean times to data loss achieved by a self-adaptive disk array consisting of three pairs of mirrored disks

Finally, a failure of any of these four disks would bring the array from state <1, 1, 1, Y> to state <1, 1, 1>, having survived three successive data losses and being unable to tolerate a fourth disk failure. Less desirable outcomes would result from the failure of the critical disk in state <2, 2, 1> and <1, 1, 1, X> or from the failure of either of the two critical disks in state <2, 1, 1>. All these failures would result in permanent data loss. As in Fig. 9, all failure transitions that result in a data loss are represented by dotted gray arcs returning to the normal state of the array.

Using the same techniques as in our previous model, we can compute the steady-state probabilities of the system of being in any of its seven possible states and derive from them the rate L at which the array will fail before returning to its normal state

$$L = \lambda p_{221} + 2\lambda p_{211} + \lambda p_{111X} + 3\lambda p_{111}$$

and its MTTDL

$$MTTDL = \frac{1}{L} = \frac{1}{\lambda p_{221} + 2\lambda p_{211} + \lambda p_{111X} + 3\lambda p_{111}}$$

The outcome of these computations is a quotient of polynomials that is too large to be displayed. We refer instead the reader to Fig. 12, which displays on a semi-logarithmic scale the MTTDLs achieved by the self-adaptive array for selected values of κ and repair times varying between half a day and seven days.

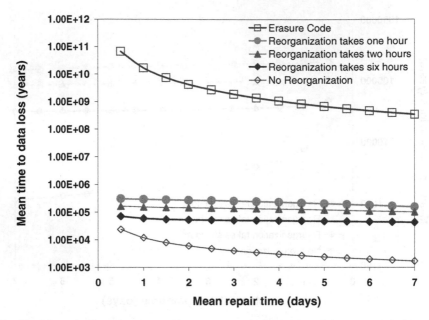

Fig. 13. Mean times to data loss achieved by (a) a self-adaptive disk array consisting of two pairs of mirrored disks and (b) a 2-out-of-4 erasure code

Let us now see how our technique compares with erasure coding. Rather than storing our data on two pairs of mirrored disks, we could use a 2-out-of-4 erasure code that would tolerate the simultaneous loss of two disks. We can easily derive the MTTDLs achieved by these erasure codes by observing they correspond to the limit case when the reorganization rate κ goes to infinity. Hence, we would have

$$MTTDL_{2-\text{out}-\text{of}-4} = \lim_{\kappa \to \infty} \frac{33\lambda^3 + 13\kappa\lambda^2 + 5\kappa\lambda\mu + 8\lambda\mu^2 + \kappa\mu^2 + \mu^3}{4\lambda^2(9\lambda^2 + 3\kappa\lambda + 3\lambda\mu + \mu^2)}$$

$$= \frac{13\lambda^2 + 5\lambda\mu + \mu^2}{12\lambda^3}.$$

Fig. 13 compares the MTTDLs achieved by a 2-out-of-4 erasure code, a pair of self-adaptive mirrored disks and a pair of conventional mirrored drives. As we can see, the 2-of-out-4 erasure code achieves much higher MTTDLs than a self-adaptive disk array with four disks. These excellent results need however to be qualified in two important ways. First, all our analyses have assumed that disk failures were the only causes of data losses. We did not consider other types of system malfunctions such as media errors, human errors, power failures, fires, floods and other acts of God. As we consider solutions minimizing the impact of disk failures, these other malfunctions will quickly become the main cause of data losses. Second, 2-out-of-4 erasure codes will result in much costlier write accesses that mirroring or even conventional RAID level 5.

We can make four main observations from our results. First, our self-adaptive array provides much better MTTDLs than a static array that makes no attempt at reconfiguring itself after disk failures. The improvements vary between a minimum of 200 percent and a maximum of almost 13,000 percent depending on the disk repair rate and the array reorganization rate, with the best results achieved for a combination of a slow disk repair rate and a fast array reconfiguration rate. This is a very significant result as we have only considered arrays consisting of two and three pairs of mirrored drives. Larger self-adaptive disk arrays should perform even better as they can perform many more corrective actions to protect their data after successive disk failures.

Second, these benefits remain evident even when the reconfiguration process takes six hours. Since the reconfiguration process normally consists of reading the whole contents of a disk and XORing these contents with the contents of a second disk, this is clearly an upper bound. In reality we expect most reconfiguration tasks to take between one and two hours depending on the disk bandwidths and capacities.

Third, the MTTDLs achieved by our self-adaptive organization remain nearly constant over a wide range of disk repair times. This is a significant advantage because fast repair times require maintaining a local pool of spare disks and having maintenance personnel on call 24 hours a day. Since our self-adaptive organization tolerates repair times of up to one week, if not more, it will be cheaper and easier to maintain than a static mirrored disk organization with the same number of disks.

Finally, erasure codes ought to be seriously considered whenever we want to provide the highest level of protection to data that are very unlikely to be ever updated.

4 Previous Work

The idea of creating additional copies of important data in order to increase their chances of survival is likely to be as old as the use of symbolic data representations by mankind and could well have preceded the discovery of writing. Erasure coding appeared first in RAID organizations as $(n-1)$-out-of-n codes [3, 4, 6, 8, 9]. RAID level 6 organizations use $(n-2)$-out-of-n codes to protect data against double disk failures [1].

The HP AutoRAID [11] automatically and transparently manages migration of data blocks between a replicated storage class and a RAID level 5 storage class as access patterns change. This system differs from our proposal in several important aspects. First, its objective is different from ours. AutoRAID attempts to save disk space without compromising system performance by storing data that are frequently accessed in a replicated organization while relegating inactive data to a RAID level 5 organization. As a result, data migrations between the two organizations are normally caused by changes in data access patterns rather than by disk failures. Self-adaptive disk arrays only reconfigure themselves in response to disk failures and repairs. Second, AutoRAID actually migrates data between its two storage classes while self-adaptive disk arrays keeps most data sets in place. Finally, the sizes of the transfer units are quite different. A self-adaptive disk array manages its resources at the disk level. The transfer units managed by AutoRAID are *physical extent groups* (PEGs) consisting of at least three *physical extents* (PEXes) whose typical size is a megabyte. Consequently, AutoRAID requires a complex addressing structure to locate these

PEGs while a self-adaptive array must only keep track of what happened to the contents of its original disks. Assuming that we have n data sets replicated on $2n$ disks, the actual locations of data sets and their parities can be stored in $2n^2$ bits. In addition, this information is fairly static as it is only updated after a disk failure or a disk repair.

Another form of adaptation to disk failure is *sparing*. Adding a spare disk to a disk array provides the replacement disk for the first failure. Distributed sparing [10] gains performance benefits in the initial state and degrades to normal performance after the first disk failure.

5 Conclusions

We have presented a disk array organization that adapts itself to successive disk failures. When all disks are operational, all data are replicated on two disks. Whenever a disk fails, the array will immediately reorganize itself and adopt a new configuration that will protect all data against any single disk failure until the failed disk gets replaced and the array can revert to its original condition. Hence data will remain protected against the successive failures of up to one half of the original number of disks, provided that no critical disk failure happens while the array is reorganizing itself. As a result, our scheme achieves the same access times as a mirrored disk organization under normal operational conditions while having a much lower likelihood of loosing data under abnormal conditions. Furthermore, the MTTDLs achieved by our self-adaptive organization remain nearly constant over a wide range of disk repair times.

More work is still needed to investigate larger disk arrays. As the number of possible reconfiguration steps increases with the size of the array, simulation will become an increasingly attractive alternative to Markov models. We also plan to investigate self-adaptive strategies for disk arrays where some data are more critical than other and thus deserve a higher level of protection. This is the case for archival storage systems implementing chunking to reduce their storage requirements. Chunk-based compression, or chunking, partitions files into variable-size chunks in order to identify identical contents that are shared by several files [5]. Chunking can significantly reduce the storage requirements of archival file systems. Unfortunately, it also makes the archive more vulnerable to the loss of chunks that are shared by many files. As a result, these chunks require a higher level or protection than chunks that are only present in a single file [2].

References

1. Burkhard, W. and J. Menon: Disk Array Storage System Reliability. Proc. 23rd International Symposium on Fault-Tolerant Computing (FTCS-23), pp. 432-441, 1993.
2. Bhagwat, D., K. Pollack, D. D. E. Long, E. L. Miller, T. J. Schwarz and J.-F. Pâris: Providing High Reliability in a Minimum Redundancy Archival Storage System. Proc. 14th International Symposium on Modeling, Analysis and Simulation of Computer and Telecommunication Systems, to appear, Sep. 2006.

3. Chen, P. M., E. K. Lee, G. A. Gibson, R. Katz, and D. Patterson: RAID, High-Performance, Reliable Secondary Storage. ACM Computing Surveys, Vol. 26, No. 2, pp. 145–185, 1994.
4. Ganger, G., B. Worthington, R. Hou, Y. Patt: Disk arrays: High-performance, high-reliability storage subsystems. IEEE Computer vol. 27(3), p. 30–36. 1994.
5. Muthitacharoen, A., B. Chen, and D. Mazieres: A Low-Bandwidth Network File System. Proc. 18th Symposium on Operating Systems Principles, pp. 174-187, 2001.
6. Patterson, D. A., G. A. Gibson, and R. H. Katz: A Case For Redundant Arrays Of Inexpensive Disks (RAID). Proc. SIGMOD 1988 International Conference on Data Management, pp. 109–116, June 1988.
7. Pâris, J.-F., T. J. E. Schwarz and D. D. E. Long: Evaluating the Reliability of Storage Systems. Technical Report UH-CS-06-08, Department of Computer Science, University of Houston, June 2006.
8. Schwarz, T. J. E., and W. A. Burkhard: RAID Organization and Performance. Proc. 12th International Conference on Distributed Computing Systems, pp. 318–325, June 1992.
9. Schulze, M., G. Gibson, R. Katz and D. Patterson: How Reliable is a RAID? Proc. Spring COMPCON '89 Conference, pp. 118–123, March 1989.
10. Thomasian, A. and J. Menon: RAID 5 Performance with Distributed Sparing. IEEE Transactions on Parallel and Distributed Systems, Vol. 8(6), pp. 640–657, June 1997.
11. J. Wilkes, R. Golding, C. Stealin, C. and T. Sullivan: The HP AutoRAID hierarchical storage system. ACM Transactions on Computer Systems, Vol. 14(1), pp. 1–29, Feb. 1996.

Using Eventually Consistent Compasses to Gather Oblivious Mobile Robots with Limited Visibility*

Samia Souissi[1], Xavier Défago[1], and Masafumi Yamashita[2]

[1] School of Information Science
Japan Advanced Institute of Science and Technology (JAIST)
{ssouissi, defago}@jaist.ac.jp
[2] Department of Computer Science and Communication Engineering,
Kyushu University, Fukuoka, Japan
mak@csce.kyushu-u.ac.jp

Abstract. Reaching agreement between a set of mobile robots is one of the most fundamental issues in distributed robotic systems. This problem is often illustrated by the gathering problem, where the robots must self-organize and meet at some (not predetermined) location, without a global coordinate system. While being very simple to express, this problem has the advantage of retaining the inherent difficulty of agreement, namely the question of breaking symmetry between robots. In previous works, it was proved that gathering is solvable in asynchronous model with oblivious robots and limited visibility, as long as the robots share the knowledge of some direction, as provided by a compass. However, the problem has no solution in the semi-synchronous model when robots do not share a compass and cannot detect multiplicity.

In this paper, we define a model in which compasses may be unreliable, and study the solvability of gathering oblivious mobile robots with limited visibility in a semi-synchronous model. In particular, we give an algorithm that solves the problem in finite time in a system where compasses are unstable for some arbitrary long periods, provided that they stabilize eventually. In addition, our algorithm is self-stabilizing.

1 Introduction

The problem of reaching agreement among robots has attracted considerable attention within the last few years. However, most of the algorithmic results we are aware of do not consider cases when sensors are unreliable. In particular, the models under which the majority of the problems are studied rely on the assumption that compasses provide perfect information. However, these components are frequently prone to failures, and are sensitive to magnetic interference. In this paper, we revise the practical significance of this assumption. We thus, define a model in which compasses are unreliable, and we study the solvability of the gathering problem in the face of instability of the compasses for some

---

* Work supported by MEXT Grant-in-Aid for Young Scientists (A) (Nr. 18680007).

A.K. Datta and M. Gradinariu (Eds.): SSS 2006, LNCS 4280, pp. 484–500, 2006.

arbitrary periods, with the guarantee that they stabilize eventually. However, the time when the stabilization occurs is unknown to the robots. Moreover, we consider that the robots have limited visibility and they are oblivious (i.e., stateless). Since the problem is solvable with perfect compasses, one might argue that the problem would be easy, since eventually the compasses show the correct direction, and hence, the problem has almost the same complexity as in the case of a perfect compass. However, this is not true, as the robots do not know when the stabilization time will occur. Therefore, the algorithm designed for the case must guarantee that the robots do not lose sight of each other when their compasses are inconsistent (safety condition), and when their compasses eventually become consistent, the algorithm should allow the robots to progress and gather at a single point in a finite number of steps (liveness condition). This is where the difficulty of the problem arises, as one algorithm that can be designed satisfying, for instance, the safety condition will not let the robots progress when their compasses eventually stabilize, and vice versa. In this paper, in particular, we study the solvability of the gathering problem relying on eventually consistent compasses in the Suzuki and Yamashita model [1] (called ATOM), referred to as a semi-synchronous model, by providing a deterministic solution to the problem. Our algorithm is guaranteed to recover from any arbitrary configuration when the compasses of the robots eventually stabilize. We can argue that our algorithm is intrinsically self-stabilizing[1] [1] and offers protection against any number of transient failures in the compasses. Moreover, we show that our algorithm proposed for the Suzuki and Yamashita model solves the problem in the fully asynchronous model (called CORDA), for up to three robots.

Related Work. Despite its apparent simplicity, the problem of gathering robots at a single point is surprisingly difficult, and has been studied extensively in the literature, in different models and under several assumptions. In fact, several factors render this problem difficult to solve [4,5,6,7,1]. In particular, in these studies, the problem has been solved only by making some additional assumptions regarding the capabilities of the robots.

Earlier study of the gathering problem includes the work of Suzuki and Yamashita [1]. In their model,[2] they proposed an algorithm to solve the gathering problem deterministically for three or more robots in the case where robots have unlimited visibility and they are oblivious. In the same model, Ando et al. [8] have proposed an algorithm to address the gathering problem in systems wherein robots have limited visibility. Their algorithm converges toward a solution to the problem, but it does not solve it within a finite time.

In the CORDA model [9], Cieliebak et al. [5] proposed a deterministic gathering algorithm for systems in which robots have unlimited visibility. Among other things, the algorithm requires that robots be able to detect multiple robots

---

[1] Self-stabilization is the property of a system which, starting in an arbitrary state, always converges toward a desired behavior [2,3].

[2] The model of Suzuki and Yamashita [1] assumes that activations (look, compute, move) occur atomically, resulting in a form of implicit synchronization. The model is called *semi-synchronous* model for this reason.

located at a single point. In the same model, Flocchini et al. [6] proposed a deterministic gathering algorithm in the limited visibility setting. However, their algorithm requires that robots share a compass which provides perfect information. Later, Prencipe [7] proved that, in both ATOM or CORDA, it is impossible to solve the gathering problem deterministically without additional assumption, such as (1) non-oblivious robots, (2) multiplicity detection, or (3) compasses. Other studies of gathering have been devoted to providing solutions to eventually *converge* to a point [10]. The gathering problem has been also studied in the presence of faulty robots by Agmon and Peleg [11], both in synchronous and asynchronous settings. In particular, they proposed an algorithm that tolerates one crash-faulty robot in a system of three or more robots, and show the impossibility of tolerating Byzantine[3] robots. Défago et al. [12] strengthen this impossibility by showing that it still holds in stronger models. They also show the existence of randomized solutions for systems with Byzantine-prone robots.

Contribution. The main contribution of this paper is to consider an important agreement problem (gathering) in the face of eventually consistent compasses. In particular, we study the solvability of the gathering problem deterministically in oblivious and limited visibility settings in the ATOM model, and we provide a solution to the problem. The proposed solution guarantees that the robots gather at a single point in finite time, if their compasses provide correct output after some unknown period of instability, during which our algorithm can tolerate any number of transient failures of the compasses. In addition, we show that our algorithm proposed for the ATOM model can solve the gathering of a maximum of three robots in the CORDA model when compasses are eventually consistent.

Structure. The remainder of this paper is organized as follows. Section 2 describes the system model and introduces definitions used in the paper. In Sect. 3, we define different classes of compasses. In Sect. 4, we discuss the solvability of the gathering problem deterministically in the limited visibility and oblivious settings. In Sect. 5, we describe our algorithm, and in Sect. 6, we prove its correctness. Finally, Sect. 7 concludes the paper.

2   System Model and Definitions

2.1   System Model

In this paper, we consider the system model of Suzuki and Yamashita [1], which is defined as follows. The system consists of a set of autonomous mobile robots roaming on a two-dimensional plane. Each robot is modeled and viewed as a point in the plane and equipped with sensors to observe the positions of the other robots. In particular, each robot is able to sense its surroundings, perform computations on the sensed data, and move toward the computed destination.

---

[3] A robot is said to be Byzantine if it executes arbitrary steps that are not in accordance with its local algorithm.

This behavior constitutes its cycle of sensing, computing, moving and being inactive. The sequence *Look-Compute-Move-Wait* is called the *cycle* of a robot.

The robots are *anonymous*, in the sense that they can not be distinguished by their appearance, and they do not have any kinds of identifiers that can be used during the computation. In addition, there is no direct means of communication among them. Hence, the only way for robots to acquire information is by observing each other's positions. In this paper, we further make the following assumptions. First, we assume that the robots have *limited visibility*, in the sense that each robot can sense only up to a distance $VR > 0$ from it. In other words, each robot can see only the robots which are within its visibility radius VR. We assume that all the robots have the same visibility radius. Second, we assume that the robots are *oblivious* (i.e., stateless), which implies that they are unable to remember past actions and observations, and thus, their computations can not be based on previous observations. Finally, we assume that the robots are unable to detect the presence of multiple robots at a single point.

In the ATOM model, time is represented as an infinite sequence of discrete time instants $t_0, t_1, t_2, \ldots$, during which each robot can be either *active* or *inactive*. When a robot becomes active, it observes the environment, computes a new location, and moves. In particular, the robots execute their activity cycle (observe-compute-move) atomically. Thus, a robot observes other robots only when a cycle begins (i.e., when they are stationary). The cycle of a robot is finite, and the activation of robots is determined by an activation schedule, which is unpredictable and unknown to the robots. At each time instant, a subset of the robots become active, with the guarantees that: (1) every robot becomes active at infinitely many time instants, (2) at least one robot is active during each time instant,[4] and (3) the time between two consecutive activations is finite.

In every single activation, the distance that robot r can travel in a cycle is bounded by $\sigma_r > 0$. Specifically, if the destination point computed at a given cycle by robot r is farther than σ_r, then the algorithm returns a point of at most σ_r. This distance may be different between two robots.

In the ATOM model, each robot uses its own local x-y coordinate system which includes: an origin, a unit distance, and the directions/orientation of the two x and y axes. However, the robots have no knowledge of the coordinate systems of the other robots, nor of a global coordinate system.

2.2   The CORDA Model

The CORDA model [9] is similar to the ATOM model except for the total absence of synchrony between the actions of the robots. In particular, in the CORDA model, the amount of time spent in observation, computation, movement and inaction is finite but, otherwise unpredictable. Consequently, each robot executes its computation cycle as follows: a robot is initially in a *waiting* state (*Wait*).

---

[4] As the duration of the interval between two time instants is by no means fixed, the second condition incurs no loss of generality. It is only required for convenience.

Asynchronously and independently from the other robots, it *observes* the environment (*Look*) by taking a snapshot of the positions of the robots. Then, it *computes* a destination point based on the observed positions (*Compute*). Finally, the robot moves toward its destination (*Move*), and the move can end anywhere before the destination point. The robots can be partitioned into sets depending on their state at a given time t: $\mathbb{W}(t)$ and $\mathbb{L}(t)$ are the sets of all robots that are respectively in state *Wait* and *Look* at time t. $\mathbb{C}(t)$ is the set of all robots in the state *Compute* at time t; the subset $\mathbb{C}_{\varnothing}(t)$ contains the robots whose computation results in executing a *null move*. Finally, $\mathbb{M}(t)$ is the set of all the robots that are executing a movement at time t; the subset $\mathbb{M}_{\varnothing}(t)$ contains the robots executing a *null move*.

In this model, the cycle of a robot is finite. In addition, there is the following assumption related to the distance traveled by a robot in one cycle.

Assumption 1. *It is assumed that the distance traveled by a robot r in a move is not infinite. Furthermore, it is not infinitesimally small: there exists a constant $\Delta_r > 0$, such that, if the target point is closer than Δ_r, r will reach it; otherwise, r will move toward it by at least Δ_r.*

2.3   Notations and Geometric Properties

We denote by $\mathcal{U} = \{r_1, \cdots, r_n\}$ the set of all robots in the system. Given some robot r, $r(t)$ is the position of r at time t. The circle $\mathcal{C}_r(t)$, centered at r with radius VR denotes the visibility range of r at time t. $\mathcal{R}_r(t)$ is the region enclosed by $\mathcal{C}_r(t)$. The parameter t is omitted whenever clear from context.

Let A and B be two points, with $\overline{AB}$, we will indicate the segment starting at A and terminating at B, and $dist(A, B)$ is the length of such a segment. By $(\overline{AB})$, we denote the line passing through points A and B.

$\mathcal{C}(o, R)(t)$, denotes the circle centered at o, and with radius R at time t. Let θ be a central angle with endpoints A and B are located on the circumference of $\mathcal{C}$, then $\triangleleft(AoB)$, denotes the circular sector at the central angle θ. Finally, we denote by $\mathcal{C}(\overline{AB})$, the circle with diameter $\overline{AB}$.

Given a region $\mathcal{X}$, we denote by $|\mathcal{X}|$, the number of robots in that region at time t. S is a set of robots, $|S|$ indicates the number of robots in the set S.

Finally, given three distinct points A, B, and C, we denote by $\triangle(A, B, C)$, the triangle that they define, and $\widehat{BAC}$, the angle that A forms with B and C.

We now introduce important observations used later in the paper.

Observation 1. *Every internal chord of a triangle has a length less than the longest side of the triangle.*

Observation 2. *In an obtuse triangle, the side opposite the obtuse angle (angle greater than $\frac{\pi}{2}$ and less than π) is the longest side in the triangle.*

Observation 3. *Every internal chord of a circle has a length less than or equal to the diameter. That is the distance between any two points that belong to a circle is less than or equal to the diameter.*

2.4   Definitions

We now introduce definitions and a lemma due to Flocchini et al. [6].

Definition 1 (Distance graph). *Let* $G(0) = (N, E(0))$ *indicates the initial distance graph of the robots, whose node set* N *is the set of input robots, and* $\forall r, s \in N$, $(r, s) \in E(0)$ *if and only if* r *and* s *are at a distance no greater than the visibility radius* VR.

Lemma 1. *If the initial distance graph* $G(0)$ *is disconnected, the gathering problem is unsolvable.*

Definition 2 (Mutual visibility). *In the CORDA model, two robots* r *and* r' *are* mutually visible *at time* t, *if both robots include each other in their computations. Formally,* r *and* r' *are mutually visible at time* t *if and only if both conditions hold:*
1. $0 < dist(r, r') \leq VR$,
2. $r, r' \in \mathbb{L}(t) \cup \mathbb{C}_{\varnothing}(t) \cup \mathbb{M}_{\varnothing}(t) \cup \mathbb{W}(t)$.

Note that mutual visibility does not include robots with the same location.

3   Definition of Compasses

Definition 3 (Compass). *A compass is a function of time and robots. The function outputs a north direction for some robot* r *at time* t. *By* $compass_r(t)$, *we denote the north direction of the compass of robot* r *at time* t.

3.1   Perfect Compass

With a *perfect compass*, the robots always agree on the same north direction. In other words, the robots agree on the directions and orientations of both x and y axes at any time t. Formally, the robots on the system share a *perfect compass* if and only if the *agreement* and *invariance* properties are satisfied:

Definition 4 (Perfect compass). *A perfect compass is defined as follows:*
1. *Agreement:* $\forall r, r' \in \mathcal{U}, \forall t, compass_r(t) = compass_{r'}(t)$
2. *Invariance:* $\forall r \in \mathcal{U}, \forall t, t', compass_r(t) = compass_r(t')$

3.2   Eventually Consistent Compass

With an *eventually consistent compass*, there exists a time after which all the robots agree on the same north direction. The agreement holds after some time *GST* (Global Stabilization Time) unknown to the robots. In other words, it is only guaranteed that the agreement on the north direction will hold, but the time for which the agreement holds is unknown to the robots. More precisely, an eventually consistent compass has the following properties: (1) The north direction of a robot's compass can change with time. (2) At a given time, the compasses of any two robots may disagree. (3) There exists some time GST after which, the compasses of all the robots agree for a sufficiently long period. Yet, the robots do not know when the time GST will occur.

Formally, the robots on the system share an *eventually consistent compass* if and only if the *eventual agreement* and *eventual invariance* properties hold:

Definition 5 (Eventually consistent compass). *An* eventually consistent compass *is defined as follows:*

1. *Eventual agreement:* $\exists GST, \forall r, r' \in \mathcal{U}, \forall t \geq GST, compass_r(t) = compass_{r'}(t)$
2. *Eventual invariance:* $\forall r \in \mathcal{U}, \forall t, t' \geq GST, compass_r(t) = compass_r(t')$

Table 1. Solvability of the gathering problem deterministically with oblivious robots and limited visibility for $n \geq 2$ with no multiplicity detection

	Compasses		
Model	Perfect	Eventually consistent	None
Asynchronous (CORDA)	Solvable (proved in [6])	Impossible for $n > 4$ (Conjecture)	Impossible (proved in [7])
Semi-synchronous (ATOM)	Solvable (Deduct. from [6])	Solvable (Sect. 5)	Impossible (proved in [1] for $n = 2$) (proved in [7] for $n \geq 2$)

4   Solvability of the Gathering Problem

In this section, we discuss the solvability of the gathering problem *deterministically* in both ATOM and CORDA models in the case of oblivious and limited visibility settings, where robots cannot detect multiplicity. Flocchini et al. [6] proved that the gathering problem is solvable deterministically when robots share perfect compasses by providing a solution to the problem. It is easy to see that the gathering problem is also solvable in the ATOM model, when robots are equipped with perfect compasses, since all the possible executions in the ATOM model are a subset of the possible executions in the CORDA model.

In the Suzuki and Yamashita model [1] (ATOM), the authors showed that there is no oblivious algorithm for solving the gathering problem for the case of two robots. At a more general level, Prencipe [7] showed that in both ATOM and CORDA models, without a compass and without multiplicity detection, there exists no deterministic oblivious algorithm that solves the gathering problem in finite time for $n \geq 2$ robots. Table 1 summarizes these results.

In this paper, we focus on the solvability of gathering using eventually consistent compasses in limited visibility and oblivious settings. In particular, we show that gathering is solvable deterministically in the ATOM model relying on eventually consistent compasses, by providing a solution to the problem (Sect. 5).

Then, we show that our algorithm proposed for the ATOM model solves the problem in the CORDA model for a maximum of three robots, and we conjecture that in general, it is impossible to solve the gathering problem in a finite time in the CORDA model, for a set of robots greater than 4 with eventually consistent compasses.

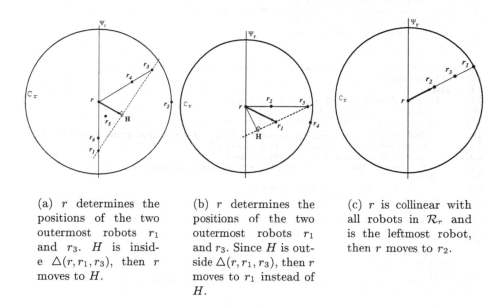

(a) r determines the positions of the two outermost robots r_1 and r_3. H is inside $\triangle(r, r_1, r_3)$, then r moves to H.

(b) r determines the positions of the two outermost robots r_1 and r_3. Since H is outside $\triangle(r, r_1, r_3)$, then r moves to r_1 instead of H.

(c) r is collinear with all robots in $\mathcal{R}_r$ and is the leftmost robot, then r moves to r_2.

Fig. 1. Principle of the algorithm

5 Gathering with Eventually Consistent Compasses

In this section, we present a deterministic algorithm for solving the gathering problem in the ATOM model, where robots are oblivious, they have limited visibility, and they are equipped with eventually consistent compasses.

5.1 Description

The idea of the algorithm is to solve the problem by achieving the following two sub-goals at every time instant t:

1. Robots that are visible at time t must remain visible at time $t + 1$, in spite of the inconsistencies in their compasses;
2. Robots located on the leftmost side at time t move toward the visible ones on their right side at time $t + 1$, and eventually gather at the rightmost and bottommost robot in the system after GST.

The gathering algorithm is depicted in Algorithm 1, where the functions Activation_Step($\mathcal{R}_r$, $compass_r$), Do_nothing(), and Move_to($Goal$) are as follows:

492   S. Souissi, X. Défago, and M. Yamashita

Algorithm 1. Gathering with Eventually Consistent Compasses

1: Activation_Step($\mathcal{R}_r$, $compass_r$)
2: **if** ($|\mathcal{R}_r| = 1$) **then** {*Gathering terminated; r sees only itself.*}
3:     Do_nothing();
4: **else**
5:     $\Psi_r :=$ vertical axis passing through robot r according to $compass_r$;
6:     $\Phi_r :=$ perpendicular to Ψ_r passing by r;
7:     $Left_r :=$ any robot in $\mathcal{R}_r$ to the left of Ψ_r, but not on Ψ_r;
8:     $Top_r :=$ any robot in $\mathcal{R}_r$ above Φ_r;
9:     $Bottom_r :=$ any robot in $\mathcal{R}_r$ below Φ_r;
10:    $\Psi_r^+ := Top_r \cap \Psi_r$;
11:    $\Psi_r^- := Bottom_r \cap \Psi_r$;
12:    **if** ($|Left_r| > 0 \vee |\Psi_r^+| > 0$) **then** {*r sees robots on its left side or on Ψ_r^+.*}
13:        Do_nothing();
14:    **else**
15:        **if** (r is collinear with all robots in $\mathcal{R}_r$) **then**
16:            $Goal :=$ nearest robot to r;
17:        **else** {*r computes two outermost robots s_1 and s_2.*}
18:            $\widehat{ArB}$: biggest central angle of $\mathcal{C}_r$ with endpoints A and B that includes robots in $\mathcal{R}_r$;
19:            $s_1 :=$ farthest robot from r on the segment $\overline{rA}$;
20:            $s_2 :=$ farthest robot from r on the segment $\overline{rB}$;
21:            $H :=$ foot of the height of the triangle $\triangle(r, s_1, s_2)$ starting from r;
22:        **end if**
23:        $s :=$ nearest robot to r among s_1 and s_2;
24:        **if** ($H \in \triangle(r, s_1, s_2)$) **then**
25:            $Goal := H$;
26:        **else** {*H is outside the triangle $\triangle(r, s_1, s_2)$.*}
27:            $Goal := s$;
28:        **end if**
29:        Move_to($Goal$);
30:    **end if**
31: **end if**

---

the function Activation_Step($\mathcal{R}_r$, $compass_r$) is executed by robot r when it becomes active, and it takes as input the parameters visibility region $\mathcal{R}_r$ and $compass_r$ of robot r. The function Do_nothing() is executed by r when it stays still. Finally, the function Move_to($Goal$) terminates the computation of robot r and moves it toward $Goal$.

Before we proceed to the description of the algorithm in more detail, we further introduce the following notations. Let Ψ_r be the vertical axis passing through robot r according to its compass at time t. Ψ_r is collocated with the north direction indicated by the compass of r at time t. We denote by $Left_r(t)$ and $Right_r(t)$, the regions respectively, to the left and to the right of Ψ_r excluding Ψ_r. Let also Φ_r, be the perpendicular axis to Ψ_r passing by r. Then, we denote $Top_r(t)$ and $Bottom_r(t)$ as the regions respectively, above and below Φ_r excluding Φ_r. When no ambiguity arises, we shall omit the temporal indication. Finally, Ψ_r^+ and Ψ_r^- denote the intersections of Top_r and Ψ_r, and of $Bottom_r$ and Ψ_r, respectively.

Algorithm 1 is described informally as follows. First, at every time instant t where some robot r becomes active, r queries its compass, considers all the robots in its visibility region $\mathcal{R}_r(t)$, and then decides its movement as follows:

– If r sees robots on its left side $Left_r$, or on Ψ_r^+ (above it on Ψ_r), then, r does not move (line 13).

- If r is collinear with all robots in $\mathcal{R}_r(t)$ (see Fig. 1(c)), then r moves linearly to the nearest robot. In this case, r must be the topmost or leftmost robot in the line (line 16).

- If r sees robots on its right side $Right_r$ or on $Right_r$ and some robots on Ψ_r^-, then r computes the two robots furthest away from it (we call them *outermost robots*). The two outermost robots are the robots that form the biggest sector with r in its circle of visibility $\mathcal{C}_r$ that contains all robots visible to r. In other words, they are the two robots that form the biggest central angle in $\mathcal{C}_r$. When there are more than one pair of such robots, then the robots with maximum distance from r is selected (e.g., r_1 and r_3 in Fig. 1(a)). Thus, the two outermost robots are the two robots that form the biggest central angle with r and are at the greatest distance from r. Afterwards, r computes the height of the triangle that it forms with the two outermost robots s_1 and s_2, and having a base segment $\overline{s_1 s_2}$. Let H be the foot of a perpendicular starting at r. Then, r moves to H if H is inside the triangle $\triangle(r, s_1, s_2)$ (see Fig. 1(a)). Otherwise, if H is outside $\triangle(r, s_1, s_2)$, then r moves to the closest robot to it among s_1 and s_2 (see Fig. 1(b)).

6   Correctness

We prove the correctness of our algorithm in two steps. In the first step, we show that the connectivity of the distance graph is preserved before and after GST. That is, the robots that are initially visible remain always visible during the entire execution of the algorithm. In a second step, we show that all the robots will gather at one point in a finite number of steps after GST. Before proceeding, let us recall an important lemma proved by Flocchini et al. [6]; if the initial *distance graph* is disconnected, the gathering problem is unsolvable. Hence, throughout we will always assume that the initial distance graph is connected.

6.1   Preserved Connectivity

We now prove that the connectivity of the distance graph is preserved during the entire execution of the algorithm. Recall that the compasses of the robots may be inconsistent, including the robots that are located at the same location. From the algorithm, trivially, we derive the following lemma:

Lemma 2. *Let r_1 and r_2 be the two outermost robots for some robot r, and $\widehat{ArB}$, the central angle whose sides pass by r_1 and r_2, and with endpoints A and B located on the circumference of $\mathcal{C}_r$. Let G be the destination of r. Then, $G \in \sphericalangle(ArB)$.*

Lemma 3. *Let robot r be active at time t, and $Left_r = \emptyset$ and $\Psi_r^+ = \emptyset$ (i.e., no robots are to its left, or on Ψ_r^+). Let r_1 and r_2 be its two outermost robots, and $\widehat{ArB}$, the central angle whose sides pass by r_1 and r_2, and with endpoints A and B located on the circumference of $\mathcal{C}_r$. Let also G be the destination of r. Then, for all point p in $\sphericalangle(ArB)$, we have $dist(p, G) < VR$.*

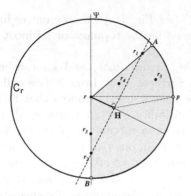 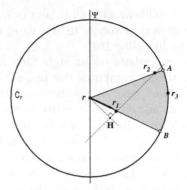

(a) Case where H is inside the triangle $\triangle(r, r_1, r_2)$ that r forms with the two outermost robots r_1 and r_2

(b) Case where H is outside the triangle $\triangle(r, r_1, r_2)$ that r forms with the two outermost robots r_1 and r_2

Fig. 2. The destination of r is within distance VR from all robots in $\sphericalangle(ArB)$

Proof (Lemma 3). Let H be the foot of the height of the triangle $\triangle(r, r_1, r_2)$ starting at r, and G be the destination of r.

By the algorithm, $G = H$ if $H \in \triangle(r, r_1, r_2)$; otherwise $G = r_1$ or $G = r_2$. Then, two cases follow, depending on whether H is inside or outside the triangle $\triangle(r, r_1, r_2)$:

1. *H belongs to $\triangle(r, r_1, r_2)$* (see Fig. 2(a)).
   Consider the triangle $\triangle(r, r_1, H)$, by Lemma 1, for every point p in triangle $\triangle(r, r_1, H)$, we have $dist(p, H) < dist(r, r_1) \leq VR$. Similarly, $\forall p \in \triangle(r, r_2, H)$, $dist(p, H) < dist(r, r_2) \leq VR$. Consider now the subregion $\mathbf{P}(r_1, r_2, A, B)$ of the circular sector $\sphericalangle(ArB)$ delimited by r_1, r_2, A, and B, then $\forall p \in \mathbf{P}(r_1, r_2, A, B)$, the triangle that p forms with r and H is an obtuse triangle at H since $\widehat{rHr_1} = 90°$. Consequently, by Lemma 2, $\forall p \in \sphericalangle(ArB)$, $dist(p, H) < dist(p, r) \leq VR$. Hence, $\forall p \in \sphericalangle(ArB)$, $dist(p, G) < VR$.

2. *H does not belong to $\triangle(r, r_1, r_2)$* (see Fig. 2(b)).
   In this case, $G = r_1$ (nearest to r among r_1 and r_2). Since H is outside the triangle $\triangle(r, r_1, r_2)$, then $\triangle(r, r_1, r_2)$ is an obtuse triangle at r_1. By Lemma 2, the segment $\overline{rr_2}$ is the longest side of the triangle. Thus, $\forall p \in \triangle(r, r_1, r_2)$, $dist(p, r_1) < dist(r, r_2) \leq VR$. Consider now the subregion $\mathbf{P}(r_1, r_2, A, B)$ of the circular sector $\sphericalangle(ArB)$ excluding the point B, then $\forall p \in \mathbf{P}(r_1, r_2, A, B)$, the triangle that forms p with r and r_1 is an obtuse triangle at r_1, since $\widehat{rr_1r_2} > 90°$. Consequently, by Lemma 2, $\forall p \in \mathbf{P}(r_1, r_2, A, B)$, $dist(r_1, p) < dist(r, p) \leq VR$. Let us now consider the point B, by hypothesis, $dist(r, B) = VR$ and $r_1 \in \overline{rB}$, then $dist(r_1, B) < VR$. Consequently, $\forall p \in \sphericalangle(ArB)$, $dist(r_1, p) < VR$. Hence, for all point p in $\sphericalangle(ArB)$, we have $dist(p, G) < VR$.

In both cases, $\forall p \in \sphericalangle(ArB)$, $dist(p, G) < VR$. This completes the proof. ☐

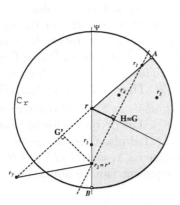
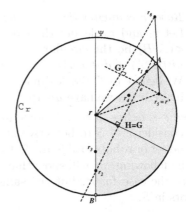

(a) r' has the robots r and r_7 as outermost robots, and computes G' as destination. Then, $dist(G, G') < dist(r, r') \leq VR$

(b) r' has the robots r and r_8 as outermost robots, and computes G' as destination. Then, $dist(G, G') \leq dist(r, e) \leq VR$

Fig. 3. The destination of r is within distance VR from all robots in $\sphericalangle(ArB)$

Lemma 4. *Let S be the set of robots visible to r at some time t. Then, at any time $t' > t$, r is at a distance of at most VR from all robots in S.*

Proof (Lemma 4). The proof consists of showing that the destination of r, and the destination of any robot in S at time $t+1$, will not bring them to a distance greater than VR from each other. Trivially, the case of two robots holds, since one robot must move toward the other one. Thus, in the following, we assume that the number of robots in S is greater than one. Let robot r be active at time t. We distinguish the following cases depending on the movement of r and whether the robots in S are active or not:

1. *Robot r is active at time t; all robots in S are inactive at time t.*
   We distinguish the following cases depending on the movement of robot r.

   (a) *Robot r executes a null move.*
   If r has robots on $Left_r$ or Ψ_r^+ then it does not move. In addition, by hypothesis, $\forall s \in S$, s is inactive at time t. This means that at time $t+1$, r remains at the original distance from all robots in S, which is by hypothesis less than or equal to VR.

   (b) *Robot r is collinear with all robots in S.*
   Two possibilities follow: (1) Robot r can be in case a. above (i.e., it executes a null move), so the lemma holds for case 1. (2) robot r can be the leftmost or topmost robot, then it performs a real move. Let r_1 be the robot farthest away from r on the line. By hypothesis, $dist(r, r_1) \leq VR$ and by the algorithm, r moves on the segment $\overline{rr_1}$. Thus, at time $t+1$, r gets closer in distance to all robots in S.

(c) *Robot r computes the positions of the two outermost robots.*
   Let r_1 and r_2 denote the two outermost robots of r at time t, and let $\sphericalangle(ArB)$ be the circular sector enclosing all the robots in S such that $dist(r, A) = dist(r, B) = VR$, and $r_1 \in \overline{rA}$ and $r_2 \in \overline{rB}$ (see Fig. 2(a)). We denote by G the destination of r. Then, by Lemma 3, for every point p in $\sphericalangle(ArB)$, we have $dist(p, G) < VR$. Thus, $\forall r_i \in S$, $dist(r_i, G) < VR$.

2. *Robot r is active at time t; some or all robots in S are also* active *at time t.*
   We consider $r' \in S$ to be active at time t. Let G' be its destination, and S' be the set of robots visible to r' at time t. Let also G be the destination of r. In the following, we will show that at time $t + 1$, $dist(G, G') \leq VR$. We only prove the case for r', but the same argument can be applied to the other robots in S.

   (a) *Robot r executes a* null *move; Robot r' executes a* null *move.*
      By hypothesis, $dist(r, r') \leq VR$, thus the case holds trivially.
   (b) *Robot r executes a null move; Robot r' is collinear with all robots in S'.*
      This case is similar to case 1.*b* above, since r stays still at time t.
   (c) *Robot r executes a null move; Robot r' computes the positions of its two outermost robots.*
      This case holds by case 1.*c* above, since r stays still at time t.
   (d) *Robot r is collinear with all robots in S; Robot r' computes the positions of its two outermost robots.*
      Let $\sphericalangle(A'r'B')$ be the circular sector of robot r' at time t. By Lemma 2, $G' \in \sphericalangle(A'r'B')$. In addition, $r \in \sphericalangle(A'r'B')$, and by the algorithm, $G \in \overline{rr'}$ (r moves on $\overline{rr'}$). Consequently, $G \in \sphericalangle(A'r'B')$, and by Lemma 3, the proof holds for this case.
   (e) *Robot r computes the positions of its two outermost robots; Robot r' computes the positions of its two outermost robots.*
      Depending where robot r' is located in the circular sector $\sphericalangle(ArB)$, and where its visible robots (other than robot r) are located, its destination G' can either be within $\sphericalangle(ArB)$ or outside it. We thus, distinguish the following cases:

   – The destination G' of r' belongs to $\sphericalangle(ArB)$ (r can be an outermost robot of r' or not): In all cases where $G' \in \sphericalangle(ArB)$, by Lemma 3, $\forall p \in \sphericalangle(ArB)$, $dist(p, G) < VR$. Therefore, $dist(G', G) < VR$. This completes the proof for this case.
   – The destination G' of r' does not belong to $\sphericalangle(ArB)$ (r can be an outermost robot of r' or not):
      Let r_1 and r_2 denote the two outermost robots of r at time t. In this case, we assume that the destination G of r is the foot of the perpendicular to the segment $\overline{r_1r_2}$ starting from r. The case when the destination of r is the location of one of its two outermost robots can be adapted easily. We assume the same for the destination G' of r' (i.e., G' is the foot of the perpendicular to the segment defined by its two outermost robots).
      (a) $\exists s \in S'$ such that s does not belong to $\sphericalangle(ArB)$; and r' is one of the outermost robots of r (see Fig. 3(a)).

In this case, assume that r' is the robot r_2, and its two outermost robots are r and r_7. We will show that $dist(G, G') \leq VR$. Consider the circle $\mathcal{C}(\overline{rr'})$ with diameter $\overline{rr'}$, we have $G \in \mathcal{C}(\overline{rr'})$ because $\widehat{rGr'}$ is a right angle by construction (see Algorithm 1). Similarly, $G' \in \mathcal{C}(\overline{rr'})$. Consequently, by Lemma 3, $dist(G, G') \leq dist(r, r') \leq VR$.

(b) $\exists s \in S'$ such that s does not belong to $\triangleleft(ArB)$; and r' is not an outermost robot for r (see Fig. 3(b)).

In this case, assume that r' is the robot r_5, and its two outermost robots are r and r_8. We will show that $dist(G, G') \leq VR$. Let $e = (\overline{r'G'}) \cap \overline{r_1 r_2}$. Consider the circle $\mathcal{C}(\overline{re})$ with diameter $\overline{re}$, we have $G \in \mathcal{C}(\overline{re})$ because $\widehat{rGr_1}$ is a right angle by construction. Similarly, $G' \in \mathcal{C}(\overline{re})$. Consequently, by Lemma 3, $dist(G, G') \leq dist(r, e) \leq VR$. This completes the proof.

In all cases, r remains within distance VR from all robots in S at time $t + 1$, and the rest follows by induction. □

From Lemma 4, we conclude that:

Theorem 1. *Algorithm 1 preserves the connectivity of the distance graph.*

6.2 Termination of the Algorithm

In this section, we show that Algorithm 1 solves the gathering problem deterministically. Thus, in the following, we consider the system after time GST has been reached. Thus, all robots agree on the direction of their compasses.

Lemma 5. *In any collinear configuration of robots, all robots will gather in a finite time at the rightmost or bottommost robot.*

Proof (Lemma 5). In a configuration where robots are collinear, there exists two cases; either all the robots are located on the same vertical axis Ψ or they are collinear, but not on the same Ψ. Consider the first case, where all robots are located on the same Ψ. By assumption, the activation schedule is fair. Then, whenever the topmost robot becomes active, it will move to the nearest one below it. Since, the cycle of a robot is finite, and the number of robots is finite, then recursively, all robots in Ψ will gather at the bottommost robot in finite time. Similarly, in the second case, the leftmost robot will reach the nearest one to its right in a finite time. Thus, by using the same arguments, all robots will gather at the rightmost robot in a finite time, and the lemma holds. □

Lemma 6. *In any configuration with three or more robots, all robots will gather in a finite time at the rightmost and bottommost robot.*

Proof (Lemma 6). We recall that the robots reach the time GST. The proof is a simple adaptation of the proof of the Flocchini et al [6] algorithm.

Let Ψ_{left} be the leftmost vertical axis that passes by the leftmost robot (one or many robots) at time t. Let also Ψ_{right} be the rightmost vertical axis that passes by the rightmost robot at time t. Let D be the horizontal distance between Ψ_{left} and Ψ_{right}. If $D = 0$, this means that all the robots in the system are located on the same vertical axis. Then, by Lemma 5, they will gather at the bottommost robot in a finite time.

We now consider the case when $D \neq 0$. Assume by contradiction that some robots never reach Ψ_{right}. This means that there are some axes that will not be passed by all the robots that were to their left at the beginning of the algorithm: we call them *limit axes*. Let Ψ be the leftmost such axis. Let $\mathbb{A}$ be the sets of robots, initially to the left of Ψ, that will become arbitrarily close to Ψ but never reach it. Let $\mathbb{B}$ be the sets of robots, initially to the left of Ψ, that will pass Ψ within finite time. Finally, let $\mathbb{C}$ be the sets of robots, initially to the left of Ψ, that will reach Ψ without ever moving to its right.

First observe that since the robots reach the time GST, they only can move to the right. Second, if some robot r leaves its vertical axis Ψ_r, then by Assumption 1, it will progress toward Ψ_{right} by some distance $d > 0$, with $d = \delta_r \sin\beta_r$, where $\delta_r \neq 0$ is the distance between r and its target on the right, and $0 < \beta_r \leq 90°$ is a non null angle that r forms with Ψ_r and its destination. Let $\beta > 0$ be the minimal angle that some robot can form with its vertical axis and its destination to the right, and δ be the minimal distance traveled by any robot toward its target.

Let t' be a time when all robots in $\mathbb{B}$ have passed Ψ, and those in $\mathbb{C}$ have reached Ψ. That is at time t', the only robots to the left of Ψ are those in $\mathbb{A}$.

Consider first the case when $\mathbb{A} = \emptyset$. In this case, by Lemma 5, after a finite number of moves, one of the robots in $\mathbb{C}$ will leave Ψ. A contradiction.

Now we assume that $\mathbb{A} \neq \emptyset$. Consider a vertical axis Ψ' to the left of Ψ, at distance $d' < \delta \sin\beta$ from Ψ. Since Ψ is the leftmost limit axis, each $r \in \mathbb{A}$ will be to the right of Ψ' within finite time. Observe that, once on the right of Ψ', r must stop at least once, since by definition, it does not reach Ψ. Let $t'' > t'$ be a time when all robots in $\mathbb{A}$ have stopped at least once to the right of Ψ'. Let also Ψ'' be an axis between Ψ' and Ψ, such that at time t'' no robot in $\mathbb{A}$ is to its right. Since Ψ'' is not a limit axis, the robots of $\mathbb{A}$ will pass Ψ'' within finite time. Since at time t'' there are no robots between Ψ'' and Ψ, the first robot $r \in \mathbb{A}$ that passes Ψ'' must have as destination a point to the right of Ψ or on Ψ. According to the Algorithm, r will move on a straight line at an angle β', with $\beta \leq \beta' \leq 90°$; such a line intersects Ψ at a point H. Since this move by r is started from a point S to the right of Ψ', then $dist(S, H) < \frac{d'}{\sin\beta'} < \frac{\sin\beta}{\sin\beta'} \cdot \delta \leq \delta$. Thus, in this move r will reach Ψ. A contradiction. Consequently, no limit axis Ψ exists, and all robots reach the rightmost axis Ψ_{right} in finite time.   □

Lemma 7. *Under Algorithm 1, all the configurations in which all the robots gather at one point are stable.*

Proof (Lemma 7). Assume that at some time t, all the robots gather at one point. In such a configuration, none of the robots see other robots in their visibility regions. Thus, by the algorithm, none of the robots will ever move. Consequently, such a configuration is stable by the algorithm.   □

Theorem 2. *Under Algorithm 1, all robots gather at one point in finite time.*

Proof (Theorem 2). By Lemma 5 and Lemma 6, any configuration of robots is transformed to the gathering in a finite time. Moreover, by Lemma 7, the gathering configuration is stable. This completes the proof. □

From Theorem 1 and Theorem 2, it follows that:

Theorem 3. *In a system, with n anonymous, oblivious mobile robots, with limited visibility, and eventually consistent compasses, the gathering problem is solvable deterministically in the ATOM model.*

Theorem 4. *Algorithm 1 solves the gathering problem deterministically for at most three robots in the CORDA model, assuming eventually consistent compasses in oblivious and limited visibility settings.*

The proof, straightforward, is omitted here.

7 Conclusion

In this paper, we took a new look at the gathering of a group of oblivious mobile robots with limited visibility and no multiplicity detection. In particular, we studied the solvability of gathering when robots are equipped with unreliable compasses, and found that gathering can nevertheless be solved in finite time with such compasses in the semi-synchronous model ATOM. The main benefit of our approach is its practical value. In particular, eventually consistent compasses allow the algorithm to tolerate transient faults, and also gives the algorithm the nice property of self-stabilization.

We have also shown that our algorithm proposed for the ATOM model solves the gathering for a maximum of three robots in the CORDA model, when robots are equipped with eventually consistent compasses. Thus, we can argue that *eventually consistent compasses* have the same computational power as a *perfect compass* for solving the gathering problem for a maximum of three robots.

Finally, we conjecture that gathering has no deterministic solution for four or more in the asynchronous model (CORDA) with eventually consistent compasses. This means that there is an inherent trade-off between the synchrony of the system and the reliability of sensors. Currently, we are investigating this issue. The results of this paper raise also new and interesting research questions. For instance, we are also studying the solvability of gathering under another class of unreliable compasses, namely, compasses with permanent bounded errors (i.e., *imprecise compass*).

Acknowledgments

We are especially grateful to Hirotaka Ono, Matthias Wiesmann and Rami Yared for their insightful comments regarding this work.

References

1. Suzuki, I., Yamashita, M.: Distributed anonymous mobile robots: Formation of geometric patterns. SIAM Journal of Computing **28**(4) (1999) 1347–1363
2. Dolev, S.: Self-Stabilization. MIT Press (2000)
3. Schneider, M.: Self-stabilization. ACM Computing Surveys **25**(1) (1993) 45–67
4. Cieliebak, M.: Gathering non-oblivious mobile robots. In: Proc. 6th Latin American Symp. on Theoretical Informatics (LATIN'04). (2004) 577–588
5. Cieliebak, M., Flocchini, P., Prencipe, G., Santoro, N.: Solving the robots gathering problem. In: Proc. Intl. Colloquium on Automata, Languages and Programming (ICALP'03). (2003) 1181–1196
6. Flocchini, P., Prencipe, G., Santoro, N., Widmayer, P.: Gathering of asynchronous robots with limited visibility. Theor. Comput. Sci. **337**(1–3) (2005) 147–168
7. Prencipe, G.: On the feasibility of gathering by autonomous mobile robots. In: Proc. Colloquium on Structural Information and Communication Complexity (SIROCCO'05). (2005) 246–261
8. Ando, H., Oasa, Y., Suzuki, I., Yamashita, M.: Distributed memoryless point convergence algorithm for mobile robots with limited visibility. IEEE Trans. on Robotics and Automation **15**(5) (1999) 818–828
9. Prencipe, G.: CORDA: Distributed coordination of a set of autonomous mobile robots. In: Proc. ERSADS'01, Bertinoro, Italy (2001) 185–190
10. Cohen, R., Peleg, D.: Robot convergence via center-of-gravity algorithms. In: Proc. Colloquium on Structural Information and Communication Complexity (SIROCCO'04). Number 3104 in LNCS (2004) 79–88
11. Agmon, N., Peleg, D.: Fault-tolerant gathering algorithms for autonomous mobile robots. In: Proc. 15th Annual ACM-SIAM Symp. on Discrete Algorithms (SODA'04), Philadelphia, PA, USA (2004) 1070–1078
12. Défago, X., Gradinariu, M., Messika, S., Raipin-Parvédy, P.: Fault-tolerant and self-stabilizing mobile robots gathering. In Dolev, S., ed.: Proc. 20th Intl. Symp. on Distributed Computing (DISC'06). LNCS (2006)

Self-stabilizing Asynchronous Phase Synchronization in General Graphs*

Chi-Hung Tzeng[1], Jehn-Ruey Jiang[2], and Shing-Tsaan Huang[2]

[1] National Tsing Hua University, Hsinchu, Taiwan 30013
clark@cs.nthu.edu.tw
[2] National Central University, Chungli, Taiwan 32054
jrjiang@csie.ncu.edu.tw,
sthuang@csie.ncu.edu.tw

Abstract. The phase synchronization problem requires each node to infinitely transfer from one phase to the next one under the restriction that at most two consecutive phases can appear among all nodes. In this paper, we propose a self-stabilizing algorithm under the parallel execution model to solve this problem for semi-uniform systems of general graph topologies. The proposed algorithm is memory-efficient; its space complexity per node is $O(\log \Delta + \log K)$ bits, where Δ is the maximum degree of the system and $K > 1$ is the number of phases.

Keywords: Distributed system, Fault tolerance, Phase Synchronization, Self-Stabilization, Spanning tree.

1 Introduction

This paper proposes a self-stabilizing phase synchronization algorithm for asynchronous systems of general graph topologies. A system may be disordered due to unexpected transient faults. We can make the system resilient to such faults by the concept of *self-stabilization*, introduced by Dijkstra [1]. A system is said to be self-stabilizing if it has the following two properties: (1) *Convergence*: Starting from any initial configuration (possibly illegal), the system can converge to a legal one in finite time. (2) *Closure*: Once the system is in a legal configuration, it remains so henceforth. When a self-stabilizing system encounters transient faults, it can be thought as in an arbitrary initial configuration. With the convergence property, it can reach a legal configuration; with the closure property, it can then function correctly henceforth.

The proposed algorithm makes each node go through a cyclic sequence of K phases: phase 0, phase 1,..., phase $K-1$, phase 0, phase 1, ... The phases of all nodes must satisfy the following criterion:

Criterion 1 (Phase Synchronization)

– No node can proceed to phase $k+1$ (mod K) until all nodes are in phase k.

---

* This research was supported in part by the National Science Council of the Republic of China under the Contract NSC 92-2213-E-008-029.

A.K. Datta and M. Gradinariu (Eds.): SSS 2006, LNCS 4280, pp. 501–515, 2006.

- When all nodes are in phase k, each node eventually proceeds to phase $k+1$ (mod K).

The above phase synchronization criterion follows that discussed in [2]. Since the nodes in the system make moves in *asynchronous mode*, each time when we observe the phases of all the nodes, the phase may not be identical, but should be no more than one apart. (There is another kind of phase synchronization which demands that the phases of two adjacent nodes differ by at most 1. For interested readers, see [3, 4, 5].) However, in illegitimate states caused either by transient faults or by arbitrary initialization, the phases of the nodes may be more than one apart.

The phase synchronization algorithm builds a synchronous environment over asynchronous one. Thus, applications developing for a synchronous environment can be executed on an asynchronous environments.

There are many self-stabilizing phase synchronization algorithms proposed in the literature [2, 6, 7, 8, 9, 10, 11, 12, 13]. The algorithms in [2, 6, 7, 8, 9] are for the asynchronous environment; the others, the synchronous environment. Since we focus on the asynchronous environment in this paper, we only introduce the former algorithms below. The algorithm in [2] is designed for uniform complete graphs. (If all nodes have identical behavior, the system is said to be *uniform*.) It demands a node to proceed to a proper phase by examining all others' phases. The algorithm in [6] is for non-uniform rings. It uses the concept of token circulation: a node with a token can proceed to the next phase. The algorithm in [7] devoted to rooted tree networks and classifies nodes into the root node, internal nodes and leaf nodes. The root initiates a new phase whenever it detects the end of the last phase, whereas any other node just copies that phase. The algorithm in [8] is for uniform rings of odd size. It also uses token circulation to carry out the synchronizer: a node receiving a token copies the sender's phase and increments the token's counter by one. When the counter value is equal to the number of nodes in the system, the token owner resets the counter, then proceeds to the next phase and sends out the token. The algorithm in [9] is for uniform rings of any size. It views a ring as a set of segments whose heads can move from one node to another and make the number of segments decrease to one. Therefore, it works by allowing only the head to change its phase.

The proposed algorithm is semi-uniform; i.e., all system nodes, except a special node, have identical behavior. The basic idea of the algorithm is to utilize token circulation to construct a spanning tree and then to achieve phase synchronization. After the construction of the spanning tree, the tree root can initiate a phase and then sends a token containing the phase number to all its children. On receiving the token, a node just follows the phase and then again forwards the token to all its children. The token bounces at leaf nodes; that is, on receiving the token, leaf nodes just send it back to parents. Furthermore, a node sends the bounced token to its parent if all its children have done so. In this manner, the token circulates in the root-to-leaf and then the leaf-to-root directions. The root can initiate a new phase when it receives bounced tokens from all its children. The new phase then proceeds properly, and so do all phases. Note that the proposed algorithm is not just a combination [14] of a tree construction algorithm, such as those in [15], and a phase synchronization algorithm for the tree network, such as that in [7]. Instead, we use the the token circulation concept to achieve spanning tree construction and phase synchronization simultaneously. That is, by the time the tree is constructed, the system immediately meets the criterion of phase synchronization.

The proposed algorithm has the advantage of memory efficiency; its space complexity per node is $O(\log \Delta + \log K)$ bits, where Δ is the maximum degree of the system and $K > 1$ is the number of phases (we note that nodes need not to know what the value of Δ is). As we will show later, it works without depending on any system parameter, such as the number of nodes [2, 6, 9, 8], or on any property of the system topology, such as the diameter [5], the cyclomatic characteristic [3], and the length of the longest simple cycle [4]. Another advantage of the algorithm is that it operates correctly in the parallel model, which is more general than the serial model adopted by the algorithm in [8].

The rest of the paper is organized as follows. Section 2 presents the system model and some terms used throughout this paper. Section 3 shows the proposed algorithm and its correctness proofs. Finally, section 5 concludes this paper.

2 The System Model

We model the system by a connected, undirected, n-node graph $G = (V, E)$ where V is the set of nodes and E is the set of edges representing the links between a pair of nodes. Two nodes i and j are said to be neighbors if $(i, j) \in E$. Each node keeps a set of variables, to which it can write its own state and from which it can read the neighbors' states. Throughout this paper, we use the notation $VAR.i$ to denote the variable VAR maintained by node i.

The behavior of a node is defined by a set of rules of the form "$guard \rightarrow action$", where $guard$ is a boolean formula while $action$ is a set of program statements instructing how to update the values of the variables. Once a node evaluates the guard part of one rule to be true, we say that the node is *privileged* and the rule is *enabled*. The privileged node can execute the action part of the enabled rule; we say that it executes a rule. In this paper, we assume that the system is *semi-uniform*; namely, each node except the special node r has the same set of rules.

We use the term *configuration* to refer to a vector of all nodes' states for representing the system status. Given a configuration c and its successor c', the transition from c to c' is called a *computation step*, denoted by $c \rightarrow c'$. During $c \rightarrow c'$, one or more privileged nodes in the configuration c concurrently execute rules and each of them executes exactly one rule. After executing the rules, the system enters the configuration c' and the next computation step starts. In this paper, we assume a system running under the *parallel model*. That is, we assume a *daemon* selecting an arbitrary non-empty subset of privileged nodes to execute rules during every computation step.

The computation of the system can be expressed by a series of configurations $(c_0, c_1, \ldots)$, where c_0 is an arbitrary initial configuration and each $c_k \to c_{k+1}$ is a computation step. We use $c_k \rightsquigarrow c_{k+m}$ to denote m consecutive computation steps, where $m > 0$ and $k \geq 0$. Given a configuration, its successor may not be unique, depending on how the daemon selects privileged nodes. A self-stabilizing system must guarantee that it eventually reaches a legal configuration c_ℓ from any possible initial configuration c_0; that is, $c_0 \rightsquigarrow c_\ell$, where ℓ is a finite integer. This requirement is called *convergence*. Another requirement of self-stabilization is called *closure*: Given a legal configuration, its successor is also legal.

For the sake of simplicity, we use *round* instead of computation step to explain how the system converges to a legal configuration. Starting from a configuration c_k, a round is the least consecutive computation steps $c_k \rightsquigarrow c_{k+m}$ such that every privileged node in c_k has executed one or more rules when the system is in c_{k+m}. The first round starts from c_0, and its ending configuration is the beginning of the second round, ..., and so on. By this definition, the time complexity is the number of rounds converging to the first legal configuration in the worst case.

3 The Algorithm

In this section, we develop a phase synchronization algorithm for semi-uniform systems under the parallel execution model. Our idea is to construct a spanning tree rooted at the special node r. The node r is responsible for initiating a new phase when it detects the end of the last phase. Any other node simply copies the phase of its parent; thus the new phase is propagated in a top-down manner and eventually all nodes proceed to the new phase.

To realize the above idea, we define a conceptual object called token circulating along tree edges only. (An edge is an tree edge if one of the endpoints is the other's parent.) There are two types of tokens: *forward tokens* and *backward tokens*. Forward tokens travel the tree from the root to the leaf nodes, while backward tokens travel reversely. During traveling, forward tokens help (1) propagate the current phase, and (2) construct the spanning tree. On the other hand, backward tokens help the root node to know when to initiate a new phase, but they don't have actual effects on tree construction.

The proposed algorithm is developed on the basis of token circulation mechanism adapted from [16], which is originally designed for a static tree rooted at r. Fig. 1 shows the three rules of the token circulation mechanism, in which $P.i$ is the parent of node i and $Child.i = \{j | P.j = i\}$ stands for the set of i's children nodes. In addition to the pointer variable P, every node keeps two scalar variables D and C. The variable D stands for the token's direction and its value is either B (Backward) or F (Forward). The variable C stands for the node's color and its value is 0, 1, or 2. Throughout this paper, the arithmetic operations on C are assumed to be under modulo 3 and such predicates as $(\forall j \in Child.r : D.j = B \land C.j = C.r)$ are assumed to be true if $Child.r = \emptyset$. A token is assumed to have the same color as its owner. A non-r node i is said to own a forward token if $(D.i = B) \land (D.P.i = F) \land (C.i \neq C.P.i)$, and it is said to

---

Variables:
P: Parent pointer
$D \in \{F, B\}$
$C \in \{0, 1, 2\}$

For the root node r, $P.r = r$ and $D.r = F$.
R0: $(\forall j \in Child.r : D.j = B \wedge C.j = C.r) \rightarrow C.r = C.r + 1;$

For $i \neq r$:
R1: $(D.i = F) \wedge (\forall j \in Child.i : D.j = B \wedge C.j = C.i) \rightarrow D.i = B;$
R2: $(P.i \neq nil) \wedge (D.i = B) \wedge (D.P.i = F) \wedge (C.i \neq C.P.i) \rightarrow D.i = F; C.i = C.P.i;$

Fig. 1. The token circulation for a static tree rooted at r

receive a backward token from its child j if $(D.i = F) \wedge (D.j = B) \wedge (C.i = C.j)$. For the root node r, the definition of receiving a backward token is the same as that of a non-r node. However, the node r is assumed to have a forward token once it receives backward tokens from all of its children.

Consider the following *perfect state*: $\forall i \neq r : (C.i = C.r) \wedge (D.i = B) \wedge (D.r = F)$, in which only r has a forward token. From the perfect state, tokens circulate the tree as follows: By executing R0, the root node r changes its color to $C.r + 1$, and propagates a forward token with this color to each of its children. When a non-r node receives a forward token, it executes R2 to copy the parent's color and passes one forward token with the new color to each of its children. When a leaf node receives a forward token, it will execute R2 and then R1. The forward token thus becomes a backward token and travels back to the root. When a non-r node receives backward tokens from all of its children, it merges those tokens into one and passes the backward token to its parent by executing R1. Once the node r receives backward tokens from all of its children, a period of token circulation is assumed to be finished and the system enters another perfect state. Afterwards, the root node will initiate a new token circulation. Note that during the time of the token circulation, the colors of nodes are either $C.r$ or $C.r - 1$. Therefore, the color variable C can be viewed as a kind of phase variable and Fig. 1 is actually a 3-phase synchronizer.

Because the network topology in this paper is a general graph instead of a tree, we define that the root node r always points to itself and that any other node points to its neighbor or nil. When a node points to nil, it means that this node has no parent node. By this setting, the system has three kinds of connected components: *R-tree*, *O-tree* and *Nil-tree*. The R-tree is the tree rooted at the node r; an O-tree contains a cycle and branches pointing to the cycle; a Nil-tree is a tree rooted at a node pointing to nil. A Nil-tree of single node is especially called an *isolated node*. We show an example in Fig. 2, in which r is labeled 0 and the arrows represent parent pointers. The set $\{0, 1\}^*$ (the symbol * stands for the inclusion of the attached arrow edges) is the R-tree; $\{2, 3\}^*$ and $\{4, 5, 6, 7, 8, 9, 10, 11\}^*$ are two O-trees in which $\{8, 9, 10\}^*$ and $\{11\}^*$ are branches;

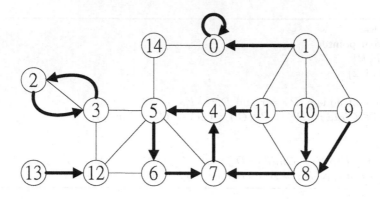

Fig. 2. An example of connected components

{12, 13}* is a Nil-tree; node 14 is an isolated node. Note that the labels in Fig. 2 are only used for illustration since our algorithms don't rely on node IDs.

As shown in [16], when we apply the token circulation mechanism in Fig. 1 to a tree network, such as the R-tree, the system eventually reaches the perfect state from any arbitrary initial state and then tokens circulate the system infinitely often. However, when we apply the mechanism to an O-tree or a Nil-tree, there will be no token eventually. This is because there is no root node r generating and propagating tokens in O-trees/Nil-trees. In terms of phases, nodes in the R-tree keep changing their phases, whereas no node in O-trees/Nil-trees can change its phase. As it will be shown later, this asymmetric property is useful to determine whether a node is in the R-tree.

Below, we start to develop the rules for constructing a spanning tree. The basic idea is to break O-trees to be Nil-trees and then to be isolated nodes, and isolated nodes then join the R-tree. Our solution requires a node to know whether its neighbor has a forward token or not, so the range of the variable D is extended to be $\{FT, F\}$ for the root node r and to be $\{FT, F, B\}$ for every non-r node. When $D.i = FT$ holds, it means that i is owning a token of the direction "Forward". Before passing a forward token, a node first sets $D = FT$ and renews its color. Afterwards, the node sets $D = F$ and the token is sent out. Due to this setting, $\mathbb{R}0$ is divided into two rules (a) and (b):

(a) $(D.r = F) \wedge (\forall j \in Child.r : D.j = B \wedge C.j = C.r) \rightarrow D.r = FT; C.r = C.r + 1;$
(b) $(D.r = FT) \rightarrow D.r = F;$

Since the variable P of a non-r node i may point to nil, rule $\mathbb{R}1$ becomes rule (c) by adding the condition $(P.i \neq nil)$ into the guard part. On the other hand, $\mathbb{R}2$ becomes two rules (d) and (e) as $\mathbb{R}0$ does.

(c) $(P.i \neq nil) \wedge (D.i = F) \wedge (\forall j \in Child.i : D.j = B \wedge C.j = C.i) \rightarrow D.i = B;$
(d) $(P.i \neq nil) \wedge (D.i = B) \wedge (D.P.i = F) \wedge (C.i \neq C.P.i) \rightarrow D.i = FT; C.i = C.P.i;$
(e) $(D.i = FT) \rightarrow D.i = F;$

Now, we explain how to use forward tokens to break O-trees. As we mentioned above, during the token circulation with color $C.r$ in the R-tree, the colors of nodes should be either $C.r$ or $C.r - 1$. Also recall the asymmetric property that there is always a token in the R-tree, whereas there will be no token in O-trees eventually. Thus, if a node i detects that one of its neighbors j owns a forward token of color $C.i + 2$, then i is aware that j is in the R-tree and itself is in an O-tree/Nil-tree. For such a case, node i should set $P.i = nil$ to break the O-tree/Nil-tree. Let $N.i$ denote the set of i's neighbors. We thus have the following rule:

(f) $(P.i \neq nil) \wedge (\exists j \in N.i : D.j = FT \wedge C.j = C.i + 2) \rightarrow P.i = nil$;

By rule (f), an O-tree is broken to be a Nil-tree. The next thing is to break the Nil-tree to be isolated nodes. This task is easy to achieve because a Nil-tree can collapse in a top-down manner without the help of tokens:

(g) $(P.i \neq nil) \wedge (P.P.i = nil) \rightarrow P.i = nil$;

The last step is to make isolated nodes join the R-tree with the help of forward tokens:

(h) $(P.i = nil) \wedge (Child.i = \emptyset) \wedge (\exists j \in N.i : D.j = FT \wedge P.j \neq nil) \rightarrow P.i = j$;

Below, we discuss the issues caused by an adversary daemon. Let j be a node not in the R-tree such that j and r are neighbors. When j evaluates the guard of rule (f) to be true, r must also evaluate the guard of rule (b) to be true at the same time. If r takes a move earlier than j does, j's privilege vanishes. An adversary daemon can make this always happen to prevent j from executing rule (f). Therefore, we must modify (b) to demand node r to wait until j takes a move.

(b*) $(D.r = FT) \wedge (\forall j \in N.i : C.j \neq C.r + 1) \rightarrow D.r = F$;

Similarly, rule (e) should be modified to be (e*):

(e*) $(D.i = FT) \wedge (\forall j \in N.i : C.j \neq C.i + 1) \rightarrow D.i = F$;

A Nil-tree root node i with $(D.i = FT)$ should reset $D.i$ unconditionally. Thus rule (e*) is modified to be rule (e**):

(e**) $(D.i = FT) \wedge ((\forall j \in N.i : C.j \neq C.i + 1) \vee (P.i = nil)) \rightarrow D.i = F$;

The last issue is to guarantee no disturbance in token circulation even when isolated nodes join the R-tree. Therefore, rule (h) should be further modified: When i sets $P.i = j$, it also sets $D.i = B$ and $C.i = C.j$, as if i has already received a token of color $C.j$ in this period of token circulation.

(h*) $(P.i = nil) \wedge (Child.i = \emptyset) \wedge (\exists j \in N.i : D.j = FT \wedge P.j \neq nil) \rightarrow P.i = j; D.i = B; C.i = C.j$;

The above rules are sufficient to build a spanning tree as well as a 3-phase synchronizer by the variable C. To extend the rules to be a K-phase synchronizer, each node maintain another variable $H \in \{0, 1, ..., K - 1\}, K > 1$ to keep track of its phase. We add $H.r = H.r + 1 \mod K$ to the action part of rule (a) and add $H.i = H.P.i$ to that of rules (d) and (h*). The guard parts of all the rules remain unchanged. That is, a node updates its phase variable H whenever it changes its color. For this reason, the system satisfies criterion 1 as soon as the spanning tree is constructed.

All the rules mentioned above constitute our algorithm, which is listed in Fig. 3. The root node r has two rules (a) and (b*), corresponding to R0 and R1 respectively. For non-r nodes, the rules (f) and (g) are combined into one rule R5, so it has five rules: R2 to R6. We assume that each rule has a priority and a rule with a smaller number has a higher priority. As readers can check, the memory space is quite low and is independent of system size. Each node keeps a pointer variable P, a phase variable H, and two scalar variables of totally 6 (resp., 9) states for the node r (resp., for a non-r node.) Let Δ denote the maximum degree of the graph; the variable P requires $O(\log \Delta)$ bits. Combining the number bits for the variables H, D, and C, the space complexity per node is $O(\log \Delta + \log K)$.

Variables:
P: parent pointer
$C \in \{0, 1, 2\}$ // for color
$D \in \{FT, F, B\}$ // for direction
$H \in \{0, 1, .., K - 1\}$ // for phase

For the root node r: $P.r = r$ and $D.r \in \{FT, F\}$
R0: $(D.r = F) \wedge (\forall j \in Child.r : D.j = B \wedge C.j = C.r)$
$\to D.r = FT; C.r = C.r + 1; H.r = H.r + 1;$
R1: $(D.r = FT) \wedge (\forall j \in N.r : C.j \neq C.r + 1) \to D.r = F;$

For $i \neq r$:
R2: $(P.i \neq nil) \wedge (D.i = F) \wedge (\forall j \in Child.i : D.j = B \wedge C.j = C.i) \to D.i = B;$
R3: $(P.i \neq nil) \wedge (D.i = B) \wedge (D.P.i = F) \wedge (C.i \neq C.P.i)$
$\to D.i = FT; C.i = C.P.i; H.i = H.P.i;$
R4: $(D.i = FT) \wedge ((\forall j \in N.i : C.j \neq C.i + 1) \vee (P.i = nil)) \to D.i = F;$
R5: $(P.i \neq nil) \wedge ((\exists j \in N.i : D.j = FT \wedge C.j = C.i + 2) \vee (P.P.i = nil))$
$\to P.i = nil;$
R6: $(P.i = nil) \wedge (Child.i = \emptyset) \wedge (\exists j \in N.i : D.j = FT \wedge P.j \neq nil)$
$\to P.i = j; D.i = B; C.i = C.j; H.i = H.j;$

Fig. 3. The proposed algorithm

4 Correctness and Time Complexity Analysis

In this section, we show that the system stabilizes in $O(n^2)$ rounds, regardless of any arbitrary initial configuration. Let $n = |V|$ denote the number of nodes in the system; we first define the legal configuration as below.

Definition 1. *(Legitimate Configuration)*
A configuration is legitimate if it satisfies the following three conditions:
(1) $\forall i \neq r : (C.i = C.r) \wedge (D.i = B)$.
(2) $D.r = F$.
(3) the number of nodes in the R-tree is n.
Furthermore, any configuration that arises from the one satisfying (1), (2) and
(3) by the completion of one or more moves is also a legal configuration.

Before showing that the system eventually reaches a legal configuration, we must guarantee that at least one node is privileged for any arbitrary configuration. In other words, the system is never deadlocked.

Lemma 1. *For any configuration, at least one node is privileged.*

Proof. We prove this lemma by contradiction. Assume that no node is privileged. According to the value of the variable D, there are two cases to be considered: Case (1) every node has either $D = B$ or $D = F$:

Let $h(i) \geq 1$ be the height of a node i in the R-tree. We first use induction on $h(i)$ to show that every non-r node i in the R-tree has $D.i = B$. (Basis) Since a leaf node i ($h(i) = 1$) cannot execute R2, we have $D.i = B$. (Hypothesis) $D.j = B$ for any non-r node j with $h(j) < \lambda$. (Induction) Let i be a non-r node with $h(i) = \lambda$ and j be a child of i. We have $D.j = B$ by the hypothesis. Assume that $D.i = F$. If $C.j \neq C.i$ for some node j, then j can execute R3. If $C.j = C.i$ for any node j, node i can execute R2. Since no rule is enabled, the case of $D.i = F$ does not occur and we have $D.i = B$, as desired.

For the root node r, $D.r = F$ holds because the range of $D.r$ doesn't contain B. Since r cannot execute R0, it has a child j such that $C.j \neq C.r$, by which the node j can execute R3 due to $(P.j \neq nil) \wedge (D.j = B) \wedge (D.P.j = F) \wedge (C.j \neq C.P.j)$. Contradiction occurs.

Case (2) some node i has $D.i = FT$:

Because node i cannot execute R4, we have $P.i \neq nil$ and i has a neighbor j with $C.j = C.i + 1$. We have two sub-cases to consider: (i) $P.j \neq nil$: j can execute R5 because $(D.i = FT) \wedge (C.i = C.j - 1 = C.j + 2)$. (ii) $P.j = nil$: Since j cannot execute R6, we have $Child.j \neq \emptyset$. Node j's child k can execute R5 because $(P.k \neq nil) \wedge (P.P.k = P.j = nil)$. We get a contradiction for each sub-case.

Below, we begin to prove the convergence property. We first define tokens as follows:

Definition 2. *(Forward Token)*
The root node r is said to own a forward token iff
   $(D.r = F \wedge (\forall j \in Child.r : D.j = B \wedge C.r = C.j)) \vee (D.r = FT)$,
whereas a non-r node is said to own a forward token iff
   $(P.i \neq nil) \wedge ((D.i = B \wedge D.P.i = F \wedge C.i \neq C.P.i) \vee D.i = FT)$.

Definition 3. *(Backward Token)*
A non-leaf node i is said to receive a backward token from its child j iff
$$(D.i = F) \wedge (D.j = B) \wedge (C.i = C.j),$$
whereas a non-isolated leaf node i is said to have a backward token iff
$$(D.i = F).$$

Our ultimate goal is to show that eventually there is a fixed spanning tree. To do this, we first prove some properties of tokens in lemmas 2, 3, 4, and 5. By these lemmas, we can infer the property of tokens in O-trees, Nil-trees, and the R-tree, as shown in lemmas 6, 7 and 8, respectively. Finally, lemmas 9 and 10 show how the system converge to the legal configuration.

Lemma 2. *In fixed components(R-tree, O-trees, or Nil-trees), a non-r node does not receive contiguous forward and contiguous backward tokens.*

Proof. We first show that a non-r node i never receives contiguous forward tokens. By definition, when node i owns a forward token, either $D.i = B$ or $D.i = FT$ holds and it can execute R3 and then R4 (in case of $D.i = B$), or simply execute R4 (in case of $D.i = FT$) to pass the token to its children. After the token passing, its status is $D.i = F$. Before owning a forward token again, node i has to execute R2 so that the value of $D.i$ becomes B from F. Since the guard of R2 implies the possession of (at least) a backward token, it means that node i must own (at least) a backward token before getting a forward token again. That is, node i never receives contiguous forward tokens.

Based on the same strategy, we can also prove that node i never receives contiguous backward tokens, so this proof is skipped.

Lemma 3. *Once a forward token meets a backward token, one of them disappears.*

Proof. Consider two nodes i and j, $P.j = i$ and $P.i \neq nil$, such that j can execute R2 and i can execute R0 (if $i = r$) or R3 (if $i \neq r$). By definition, node j has a backward token, whereas node i has a forward token. We prove this lemma by checking how many tokens are left after the node pass the tokens.

Because the tokens meet by node i or node j or both executing the rules, we have the following three cases to consider:
Case (1) Only j passes the backward token by executing R2:
For this case, node j is of $D.j = B$ so the backward token disappears. On the other hand, node i still holds the forward token.
Case (2) Only i passes the forward token by executing R0 and R1 (or R3 and R4):
For this case, node i is of $D.i = F$ so the forward token disappears. On the other hand, node j still holds the backward token.
Case (3) Both i and j pass tokens:
After j executes R2 and i executes R0 and then R1 (or R3 and then R4), we have $D.j = B$, $D.i = F$ and $C.i = C.P.i$. According to the relation between $C.i$ and $C.j$, we have two sub-cases to consider: (i) $C.i = C.j$: Node i has

$(D.j = B) \wedge (D.i = F) \wedge (C.i = C.j)$, so it has a backward token coming from j. On the other hand, node j does not own the forward token. (ii) $C.i \neq C.j$: In this case, node j has $(D.j = B) \wedge (D.P.j = F) \wedge (C.j \neq C.P.j)$ so it has a forward token. On the other hand, node i does not receive the backward token coming from j.

Because either the forward token or the backward token disappears in each case, this lemma holds.

For normal token circulation, tokens bounce between the root node r and leaf nodes. That is, a backward token should become a forward token when it arrives the node r, whereas a forward token should become a backward token when it arrives a leaf node. However, in the beginning a token may change its direction at an internal node because of the unpredictable initial configuration. And we say that an internal node i performs an *illegal forward (resp., backward) token reverse* if it receives a forward (resp., backward) token but sends out a backward (resp., forward) token. In terms of rules, if node i perform an illegal forward token reverse, it executes R3, R4, and R2 consecutively. (Note that node i can execute R2 right after executing R4, but in normal situations it cannot do so.) Similarly, if node i perform an illegal backward token reverse, it executes R2, R3 and R4 consecutively.

Lemma 4. *Eventually no internal node can perform illegal forward or backward token reverse.*

Proof. To prove this lemma, we show that an internal node i can perform at most one illegal reverse of a forward token and of a backward token respectively.

Consider the case that node i performing an illegal forward token reverse. By definition, it executes R3, R4 and R2 consecutively. After executing the three rules, node i has $(D.i = B) \wedge (\forall j \in Child.i : C.j = C.i \wedge D.j = B)$. Let j be a child of i. The next time i receives a forward token, node i has $C.i \neq C.P.i$. After i executes R3 and R4 to pass the forward token, the condition $C.j \neq C.i$ holds so it cannot execute R2 immediately. That is, node i cannot reverse the forward token.

Now, consider the case that node i performing an illegal backward token reverse. Similarly, it means that node i executes R2, R3 and R4 consecutively. After executing the three rules, node i has $(D.i = F) \wedge (D.P.i = F) \wedge (C.i = C.P.i)$. The next time i owns a backward token and executes R2, it cannot execute R3 immediately because $C.i = C.P.i$ holds. That is, node i cannot reverse the backward token.

According the proof of lemma 4, an illegal token reverse never occurs at a node having executed R2, R3, and R4, or never occurs at a node having received a token. By the fact that a token transfer from a node to the next one in $O(1)$ rounds, we have the following lemma:

Lemma 5. *After $O(n^2)$ rounds, no internal node can perform illegal forward or backward token reverse.*

Proof. We call a node an illegal bouncing point if it is an internal node that can perform an illegal token reverse. Similarly, we call a node a bouncing point if it is the root node r, a leaf node, or an illegal bouncing point. To prove this lemma, we show that no illegal bouncing point exists in $O(n^2)$ rounds. For the sake of simplicity, we assume that no token disappears.

Because tokens travel along tree edges only and they swing between bouncing points, in $O(n)$ rounds a token reaches a bouncing point. If that bouncing point is an internal node, according to lemma 4, the node no longer serve as a bouncing point. That is, every $O(n)$ rounds a token eliminates an illegal bouncing point, or arrives either the root node or a leaf node. Because there may be $O(n)$ illegal bouncing points in the initial configuration, it takes $O(n) \times O(n) = O(n^2)$ rounds to get rid of all of them, as desired.

In the following three lemmas, we show the behavior of tokens in O-trees, Nil-trees, and the R-tree, respectively.

Lemma 6. *After $O(n^2)$ rounds, there will be no token in O-trees.*

Proof. To prove this lemma, we show that, for any O-tree, tokens in the branches go into the cycle in $O(n)$ rounds and then disappear in $O(n^2)$ rounds. With the help of lemma 5, we assume that no illegal token reverse would occur.

First, focus on the tokens in the O-tree branches. In such components, a forward token becomes a backward when it arrives a leaf node and the backward token either goes into the O-tree cycle or disappears. The time complexity for this is $O(n)$ rounds, including $O(n)$ rounds for a forward token to become a backward token and another $O(n)$ rounds for the backward token to go into the cycle.

Now, consider the tokens in the O-tree cycle. According to lemma 3, the number of tokens decreases when two tokens of different directions meet; hence eventually the tokens in the cycle are of the same direction, either forward or backward. The time complexity for this is $O(n) \times O(n) = O(n^2)$ rounds because there may be $O(n)$ tokens in the cycle and two tokens of different types meet in $O(n)$ rounds. Afterwards, these survival tokens disappear in $O(n)$ rounds, since a node never continuously receive tokens of the same direction, according to lemma 2. In summary, all the tokens in the O-tree cycle disappear in $O(n^2)$ rounds, as desired.

Lemma 7. *After $O(n)$ rounds, there will be no token in Nil-trees.*

Proof. By definition, an isolated has no token. Therefore, we prove this lemma by showing that any Nil-tree becomes a set of isolated nodes in $O(n)$ rounds.

According to R5, a child of a Nil-tree root can point to nil, so the Nil-tree's height decreases by one every $O(1)$ rounds. Combining the fact that the tree height is $O(n)$, the Nil-tree becomes a set of isolated nodes in $O(n)$ rounds.

Below, we show that the R-tree eventually reaches the *perfect state*; viz. $D.r = F$ and any non-r node i in the R-tree has $(C.i = C.r) \wedge (D.i = B)$.

Lemma 8. *After $O(n^2)$ rounds, the R-tree reaches the perfect state.*

Proof. To prove this lemma, we first show that in $O(n^2)$ rounds only one token exists in each tree path from a leaf node to the root node r. Afterwards, the R-tree enters the perfect state in $O(n)$ rounds. Similar to lemma 6, we assume that no illegal token reverse would occur.

Consider a tree path from a leaf node to the root node r. By the proof of lemma 1, there is at least one token in this path. Let the number of tokens in this path be $O(n)$. Because the tokens bounce between the root node and the leaf node, they meet one another in $O(n)$ rounds. By lemma 3, it means that the number of tokens decreases by one every $O(n)$ rounds, or, equivalently, decreases to one in $O(n) \times O(n) = O(n^2)$ rounds. If the last survival token is forward, it reaches the leaf node in $O(n)$ rounds and becomes a backward token traveling back to the root node.

Now we consider the configuration in which there is exactly one backward token in any tree path from a leaf node to the root node. For a non-r node i receiving all of the backward tokens from its children, it executes R2 to pass the merged backward token to its parent. After the execution, node i has $D.i = B \wedge C.j = C.i \wedge D.j = B$, where $j \in Child.i$. Since every $O(1)$ rounds a backward token moves from the node of height k to the node of height $k+1$, the root node receives backward tokens from all the children in $O(n)$ rounds. By that time, the root node is of $D.r = F$ and any non-r node i in the R-tree is of $D.i = B \wedge C.i = C.P.i = C.r$. That is, the R-tree is in the perfect state.

According to the above proof, the R-tree enters the perfect state in $O(n^2)$ rounds.

Lemma 9. *Once the R-tree reaches the perfect state and there is no token in O-trees/Nil-trees, the number of nodes in the R-tree is monotonically increasing.*

Proof. To prove this lemma, we show that a node i in the R-tree does not execute R5 to depart from the R-tree. Let j be a neighbor of i. Our attempt is to show that $C.j \neq C.i - 2$ holds when $D.j = FT$ holds. This node j must be in the R-tree; otherwise $D.j = FT$ cannot hold since there is no token in O-trees/Nil-trees. Below, we consider a token circulation in the R-tree, observe how the color C changes, and prove the desired property: $C.j \neq C.j - 2$.

Let's consider a token circulation starting from the perfect state, in which every node has the same color $C.r = \alpha - 1$. During this token circulation, the root node r executes exactly two rules R0 and R1, and any other R-tree node executes exactly three rules R2, R3, and R4. Because a node changes its color to be α only when it executes R0 or R3, and because these two rules set $D = FT$ as well, the condition $C.j = \alpha$ must hold when $D.j = FT$ holds. For node i, its color is either $C.i = \alpha$ or $C.i = \alpha - 1$. It is easy to check that $C.j \neq C.i - 2$, as desired.

Lemma 10. *Once the R-tree reaches the perfect state and there is no token in O-trees/Nil-trees, the R-tree spans all the nodes in $O(n^2)$ rounds.*

Proof. Let i and j be two adjacent nodes such that j is in the R-tree, while i is not. We can prove this lemma by showing that node i joins the R-tree in $O(n)$ rounds.

Consider the token circulations in the R-tree. During a token circulation propagating color 0, node j is of $D.j = FT$ and $C.j = 0$ at some time by executing R0 (if $j = r$) or R3 (if $j \neq r$). Similarly, during the token circulations propagating color 1 and color 2, node j is of $(D.j = FT) \wedge (C.j = 1)$ and $(D.j = FT) \wedge (C.j = 2)$ at some point, respectively. Because node i has no token and thus cannot change $C.i$, the condition $(D.j = FT) \wedge (C.j = C.i + 2)$ holds at some time within three consecutive token circulations. Since each token circulation finishes in $O(n)$ rounds, this condition holds within $3 * O(n)$ rounds. The next step is to prove that node i points to node j within $O(1)$ rounds when this condition holds.

By the components where i locates, there are three cases to consider:
Case (1) i is an isolated node:
Node i executes R6 to set $P.i = j$ to join the R-tree.
Case (2) i is in an O-tree:
Node i executes R5 to set $P.i = nil$ and becomes a Nil-tree root. Then its children, if any, execute R5 so node i becomes an isolated node. The remaining proof of this case is similar to that of Case (1).
Case (3) i is in a Nil-tree containing more than one node:
The proof of this case is similar to that of Case (2).

The actions in all the three cases take $O(1)$ rounds, so node i becomes a part of the R-tree in $O(1)$ rounds when $(D.j = FT) \wedge (C.j = C.i + 2)$ holds. Because this condition holds in $O(n)$ rounds, the number of nodes in the R-tree increases by one every $O(n)$ rounds, until the R-tree spans all the nodes. Thus the overall time complexity is $O(n) \times O(n) = O(n^2)$ rounds.

Theorem 1. *The system enters legal configurations in $O(n^2)$ rounds. (convergence)*

Proof. This is a direct consequence of lemmas 5, 6, 7, 8, 9 and 10.

Theorem 2. *Once the system is in a legal configuration, it remains so henceforth. (closure)*

Proof. Note that criteria (1) and (2) in definition 1 are the conditions of perfect states. Therefore, this theorem is a direct consequence of lemma 9.

5   Conclusion

We propose a self-stabilizing algorithm for the phase synchronization problem for asynchronous systems of general graph topologies. The algorithm runs under the parallel model and constructs a spanning tree rooted at the unique special node r that is responsible for initiating a new phase. To the best of our knowledge, it is the first such algorithm for general graphs. Its another advantage is the low space complexity: $O(\log \Delta + \log K)$ bits per node, where Δ is the maximum degree of the graph and $K > 1$ is the number of phases. Moreover, it can be refined to be a spanning tree construction algorithm and a 3-phase synchronizer by removing the phase variable H.

In our algorithm, we assume a semi-uniform system. This assumption is for constructing a spanning tree in a deterministic way, but it may be unnecessary for a phase synchronizer. Therefore, it is an open problem of how to develop a deterministic, memory-efficient phase synchronizer for uniform systems.

References

1. Dijkstra, E.W.: Self-stabilizing systems in spite of distributed control. Communications of the ACM **17**(11) (1974) 643–644
2. Kulkarni, S., Arora, A.: Multitolerant barrier synchronization. Information Processing Letters **64**(1) (1997) 29–36
3. Boulinier, C., Petit, F., Villain, V.: Synchronous vs. asynchronous unison. In: Self-Stabilizing Systems. (2005) 18–32
4. Gouda, M.G., Haddix, F.F.: The alternator. In: WSS. (1999) 48–53
5. Awerbuch, B., Kutten, S., Mansour, Y., Patt-Shamir, B., Varghese, G.: Time optimal self-stabilizing synchronization. In: ACM Symposium on Theory of Computing. (1993) 652–661
6. Kulkarni, S., Arora, A.: Fine-grain multitolerant barrier synchronization. Technical report, Technical Report OSU-CISRC TR34, Ohio State University (1997)
7. Alima, L.O., Beauquier, J., Datta, A.K., Tixeuil, S.: Self-stabilization with global rooted synchronizers. In: Proceedings of the 18th International Conference on Distributed Computing Systems. (1998) 102–109
8. Huang, S.T., Liu, T.J.: Phase synchronization on asynchronous uniform rings with odd size. IEEE Transactions on Parallel and Distributed System **12**(6) (2001) 638–652
9. Huang, S.T., Liu, T.J., Hung, S.S.: Asynchronous phase synchronization in uniform unidirectional rings. IEEE Transactions on Parallel and Distributed System **15**(4) (2004) 378–384
10. Arora, A., Dolev, S., Gouda, M.G.: Maintaining digital clocks in step. Parallel Processing Letters **1** (1991) 11–18
11. Dolev, S.: Possible and impossible self-stabilizing digital clock synchronization in general graphs. Real-Time Systems **12**(1) (1997) 95–107
12. Gouda, M.G., Herman, T.: Stabilizing unison. Information Processing Letters **35** (1990) 171–175
13. Huang, S.T., Liu, T.J.: Self-stabilizing 2^m-clock for unidirectional rings of odd size. Distributed Computing **12** (1999) 41–46
14. Arora, A., Gouda, M.: Distributed reset. IEEE Transactions on Computers **43**(9) (1994) 1026–1038
15. Gärtner, F.C.: A Survey of Self-Stabilizing Spanning-Tree Construction Algorithms. Technical report, Swiss Federal Institution of Technology (2003)
16. Kruijer, H.S.M.: Self-stabilization(in spite of distributed control) in tree-structured systems. Information Processing Letters **8**(2) (1979) 91–95

Composition of Fault-Containing Protocols Based on Recovery Waiting Fault-Containing Composition Framework

Yukiko Yamauchi[1], Sayaka Kamei[2], Fukuhito Ooshita[1], Yoshiaki Katayama[3], Hirotsugu Kakugawa[1], and Toshimitsu Masuzawa[1]

[1] Graduate School of Information Science and Technology, Osaka University
[2] Department of Information Systems Faculty of Environmental and Information Studies, Tottori University of Environmental Studies
[3] Graduate School of Computer Science and Engineering, Nagoya Institute of Technology
{y-yamaut, f-oosita, kakugawa, masuzawa}@ist.osaka-u.ac.jp,
s-kamei@kankyo-u.ac.jp,
katayama@nitech.ac.jp

Abstract. Self-stabilizing protocols provide autonomous recovery from finite number of transient faults. Fault-containing self-stabilizing protocols promise not only self-stabilization but also quick recovery from and small effect of a small number of faults. However, existing composition techniques of self-stabilizing protocols (e.g. fair composition) cannot preserve the fault-containment property when composing fault-containing protocols. In this paper, we present *Recovery Waiting Fault-containing Composition (RWFC)* framework that preserves the fault-containment property of the composed protocol. We show an example of fault-containing composition of a minimum spanning tree protocol on arbitrary weighted graphs and a median finding protocol on trees via *RWFC*.

Keywords: Fault-containment, Self-stabilization, Composition, Minimum Spanning Tree, Median.

1 Introduction

A self-stabilizing protocol[1] converges to a legitimate configuration regardless of the arbitrary initial configuration. This property provides autonomous adaptability against any number and any type of faults. In practice, the adaptability to small scale faults is important because catastrophic faults rarely occur. However, self-stabilization does not promise efficient recovery from small scale of faults and sometimes the effect of small number of faults spreads over the entire network.

A fault-containing self-stabilizing protocol[6][7][8] is a self-stabilizing protocol which contains the effect of faults and promises rapid recovery for a small number of faults. The motivation of fault-containment is that the time and effect should

A.K. Datta and M. Gradinariu (Eds.): SSS 2006, LNCS 4280, pp. 516–532, 2006.

depend on the scale of the faults. The scale of faults is measured by the number of corrupted processes. When the states of f processes are corrupted at a legitimate configuration, we call the obtained configuration as an f-faulty configuration. Many fault-containing protocols bound the time to recover and the number of processes affected by the faults with polynomial in f or some constant[6][14][15].

Executing two different self-stabilizing protocols in parallel is known as fair composition[10][11]. Fair composition composes two self-stabilizing protocols such that a protocol (called an upper protocol) utilizes (as its input) the output of the other (called a base protocol), and guarantees self-stabilization of the obtained protocol. This composition provides a protocol, whose input is the input to the base protocol and whose output is the output of the upper protocol, and extends the scope of the upper protocol. However, a fair composition does not preserve fault-containment when composing two fault-containing protocols. This is because the upper protocol does not wait for the recovery of the base protocol by fair composition. Then the effect of faults may spread by some processes changing their local states of upper protocol according to the incorrect output of the base protocol. When the base protocol recovers, the number of such contaminated processes may become larger than the number that the upper protocol guarantees fault-containment and the upper protocol cannot recover in its bounded recovery time.

The framework for composing fault-containing protocols preserving fault containment is important both theoretically and practically. In this paper, we present a simple framework for such compositions. Our strategy is to prevent the execution of the upper protocol until the base protocol recovers. Our framework suggests the possibility of an uniform framework for fault-containing composition, however the proposed framework currently put several assumptions on protocols. So, we examine the sufficient conditions for the proposed framework. As a case study, we show composition of a fault-containing minimum spanning tree protocol on arbitrary graphs and a fault-containing median finding protocol on tree graphs, which yields a fault-containing minimum spanning tree and median finding protocol on arbitrary graphs.

Related work. Self-stabilization was first introduced by Dijkstra[1]. Since then, many self-stabilizing protocols have been designed for many problems e.g. spanning tree construction[2][3], leader election[4] and token circulation[5].

Fault-containing self-stabilizing protocols were presented by Ghosh et al. [6][7][8]. Many fault-containing protocols can be obtained by adding the property of fault-containment to self-stabilizing protocols. Katayama et al. proposed a 1-fault-containing minimum spanning tree protocol in [14] from a self-stabilizing minimum spanning tree protocol[13]. There are other fault-containing protocols obtained in the same way[6][15]. Ghosh et al. introduced fault-containment using priority scheduler in [9]. Priority scheduler provides a weak priority rule which makes the recovery of faulty process precedent the actions of non-faulty processes. There exists such fault-containing protocols obtained by composing multiple layer of protocols where each protocol is not fault-containing by itself[17][18].

Kutten et al. proposed time-adaptive self-stabilization in [20]. Time adaptability guarantees the recovery time is polynomial in the number of faults.

Composition of self-stabilizing protocols is expected to ease the design and to extend usability. A fair composition of self-stabilizing protocols was introduced by [10][11]. Beauquier et al. introduced a cross-over composition in [16] which uses the base protocol as a filter to the execution of the upper protocol and improves the adaptability to scheduler. Dolev et al. proposed parallel composition in [21], which accelerate the stabilization by executing self-stabilizing protocols in parallel. However a composition of fault-containing protocols has not been proposed and we first present such a composition.

Contribution. In this paper we present a framework for a fault-containing composition which guarantees that the obtained protocol is also fault-containing. Our strategy is to stop the upper protocol till the base protocol recovers. This framework can be applied to a subclass of fault-containing protocols but the constraint seems to be reasonable. We then show a fault-containing composition of a minimum spanning tree protocol[14] and a median finding protocol on the obtained tree based on [12].

2 Preliminary

2.1 Network and Processes

A system is a network which is represented by an undirected graph $G = (V, E)$ where the vertex set V is a set of processes and the edge set E is a set of bidirectional communication links. Each process has a unique identity. Process p is a neighbor of process q iff there exists a communication link between p and q, which is denoted by (p, q). A set of neighbors of p is denoted by N_p. Let $N_p^1 = N_p$ and for $i \geq 2$, $N_p^i = N_p^{i-1} \cup \bigcup_{q \in N_p^{i-1}} N_q \setminus \{p\}$. N_p^i represents the set of processes within distance i from process p.

Each process p owns local variables, and the values of local variables of p define the local state of p. A configuration of a system is represented by a tuple of local states of all processes.

Process p can communicate directly with process $q \in N_p$ by reading the local variables of q. Each process changes its state by updating its local variables by execution of a protocol. We define *step* as a computation at a single processor. When c_1 and c_2 are two configurations of the system, such that c_2 is reached from c_1 by a single step a, we use notation $c_1 \xrightarrow{a} c_2$. An *execution* $\epsilon = \langle c_1, a_1, c_2, a_2, \ldots \rangle$ is an alternating sequence of configurations and steps such that $c_{i-1} \xrightarrow{a_{i-1}} c_i$.

2.2 Self-stabilization

A distributed protocol P computes an output defined by the input. The input (output) is represented by the conjunction of input (output, respectively) variables at each process. P cannot change input variables during the execution.

A self-stabilizing protocol autonomously reaches a legitimate configuration. We assume that the legitimate configuration is uniquely determined by the input.

Definition 1. *Self-stabilization*
A distributed protocol P is self-stabilizing iff it reaches a legitimate configuration starting from any arbitrary initial configuration and once it reaches a legitimate configuration it remains in legitimate configurations under any execution of P.

A fault we assume in this paper is a transient fault i.e. corruption of local states. A self-stabilizing protocol autonomously recovers from a finite number of arbitrary transient faults.

2.3   Fault-Containment

We consider a configuration resulting from occurrence of faults at a legitimate configuration. We assume that no input variables are corrupted by the faults.

Definition 2. *f-faulty configuration of P*
An f-faulty configuration is a configuration that is obtained from a legitimate configuration of P by corrupting the local variables except input variables of f processes.

We call a process whose local state is different from the legitimate configuration as *faulty*, and otherwise *non-faulty*. A self-stabilizing protocol is *f-fault-containing* iff it reaches a legitimate configuration from any f'-faulty configuration ($f' \leq f$) with a bounded contamination number and bounded recovery time. *Contamination number* is the maximum (worst) number of processes that change their variables during the recovery. *Recovery time* is the maximum (worst) time to reach a legitimate configuration.

Definition 3. *f-fault-containment*
A self-stabilizing protocol P is f-fault-containing iff its recovery time is bounded by a polynomial in f and contamination number is bounded by a polynomial in f starting from f'-faulty configuration for any $f' \leq f$.

An f-fault-containing self-stabilizing protocol autonomously reaches a legitimate configuration from f'-faulty configuration ($f' \leq f$) in a polynomial time in f, and the effect of faults is bounded by a polynomial in f e.g. f, f^2 (not $|V|$). We simply denote a f-fault-containing self-stabilizing protocol as f-fault containing protocol. In this paper we consider a subclass of f-fault containing protocols P that have the following properties.

Input and output. Local variables of P are classified into three classes: input, output and inner. Each process p computes the values of inner variables and output variables by the input, inner and output variables of p and all its neighbors.

Recovery. During the recovery from any f'-faulty configuration ($f' \leq f$), faulty processes can change their output and inner variables while non-faulty processes can change only their inner variables.

Problem. Protocol P solves a problem Π iff $\forall p \in V : \neg incons_p(P)$, where $incons_p(P)$ is a predicate on input and output variables of p and all its neighbors. We say a process p is inconsistent iff $incons_p(P)$ is true. Starting from any f'-faulty configuration, until output variables of a faulty process p recover, there exists at least one process q in $N_p^k \cup \{p\}$ in every configuration, such that $incons_q(P)$ is true. The value of k is defined by protocol P and we call this k as *inconsistency range*. We call a process p which has recovered from f'-faulty configuration and $incons_q(P)$ is false at all $q \in N_p^k \cup \{p\}$ as *recovered process* and otherwise *non-recovery process*.

Non-reactive protocol. No process makes a move in a legitimate configuration.

Legitimate configuration. The input to P defines a unique legitimate configuration of P, which means that the set of faulty processes is unique in an f-faulty configuration and that P always recovers a unique configuration. The legitimate configuration of P is defined by conjunction of local states of each process, that is, a configuration is legitimate iff $\forall p \in V : L_p(P)$. $L_p(P)$ is a predicate on input, inner and output variables of p and all $q \in N_p$, and it is defined as $L_p(P) = \neg incons_p(P) \wedge \ell_p(P)$. The predicate $\ell_p(P)$ is a predicate on input and inner variables of p and its neighbors, and it defines the values of inner variables in a legitimate configuration.

Guarded commands. A protocol at each process p is a set of guarded commands of the form $G \to A$, where G is a guard which is a boolean function of local states of p and its neighbors, and A is an action to update p's state when G is true. We say a guard G is *enabled* when it is true. To distinguish the actions that change output variables from those that change inner variables, we classify guarded commands into the following two types without loss of generality.

- **type1:** $can\_move_p(P) \to$ (update output variables)
- **type2:** (inner variables at p need updated) $\to$ (update inner variables)

Predicate $can\_move_p(P)$ consists of predicate $incons_p(P)$ and some predicates on states of p and its neighbors. It eventually becomes true at each faulty process during the recovery from f'-faulty configuration and triggers a recovery action.

Performance measures of a fault-containing are as follows.

- **Stabilization time** is the worst number of steps to reach a legitimate configuration from an arbitrary initial configuration.
- **Recovery time** is the worst number of steps to reach a legitimate configuration from any f'-faulty configuration $(f' \leq f)$.
- **Output contamination number** is the worst number of processes that change their output variables during the recovery from any f'-faulty configuration $(f' \leq f)$.
- **Contamination number** is the worst number of processes that change their inner or output variables during the recovery from any f'-faulty configuration $(f' \leq f)$.

The fault-containing composition is a composition of two fault-containing protocols P_1 and P_2 and the composition keeps fault-containment. Note that the input to P_2 can be corrupted because they are the output of P_1. The maximum number of faults that a fault-containing protocol P_i guarantees fault-containment is denoted by f_i.

Definition 4. *fault-containing composition*
Let P_1 be an f_1-fault-containing protocol and P_2 be an f_2-fault-containing protocol. Consider a composition of P_1 and P_2 denoted by $(P_1 * P_2)$, such that the input variables of P_2 are the output variables of P_1 and the output variables of the composed protocol is the output variables of P_2. The composed protocol $(P_1 * P_2)$ is fault-containing composition iff it is $f_{1,2}$-fault-containing for some $0 < f_{1,2} \le f_1, f_2$.

3   Fault-Containing Composition

Executing two self-stabilizing protocols in parallel, which is introduced as fair composition by [10][11], promises that the composed protocol is self-stabilizing. However, a fair composition of fault-containing protocols cannot preserve the property of fault-containment. Let P_1 and P_2 are fault-containing protocols such that the output of P_1 is input to P_2. Consider a fair-composition of P_1 and P_2. The input to P_2 may be corrupted at a faulty process p because the input variables of P_2 at p are output variables of P_1. The difficulty is that the number of processes that change their output can be greater than the number of faults and the faulty processes may change their output variables repeatedly. P_2 cannot adapt to this spacial and temporal dynamics of the input and cannot guarantee fault containment.

3.1   Framework for Fault-Containing Composition

We present *Recovery Waiting Fault-containing Composition (RWFC)* framework for a fault-containing composition. Our strategy is to stop the execution of P_2 until P_1 stabilizes. After P_1 reaches its unique legitimate configuration from f'-faulty configuration($f' \le f_{1,2}$), there are at most f' processes whose inner and output variables of P_2 are corrupted. Then P_2 regards the configuration as f'-faulty configuration and takes advantage of its fault-containment property.

For P_2 to wait until P_1 stabilizes, a process p should check if it is a neighbor of a faulty process of P_1 when it has an enabled guard of P_2, because p's guards refer to the output variables of P_1 at $q \in N_p \cup \{p\}$ However p cannot determine whether it is a neighbor of a faulty process of P_1 by simply observing the variables of neighbors. It is possible that variables of P_1 at p and all its neighbors are corrupted and happen to be consistent for p, that is, local view may be the same as the one at a legitimate configuration.

Let $k_1(k_2)$ be the inconsistency range of $P_1(P_2$, respectively). We prevent p to execute P_2 by checking $incons_q$ of $q \in N_p^{k_1+1}$. To simplify our logic, we assume there exists a communication mechanism that allows each process p to check the value of $incons_q(P_1)$ for any $q \in N_p^{k_1+1}$ immediately, since our focus is not on a communication mechanism but on a fault-containing composition. We call this mechanism $IC(k_1 + 1)$.

Definition 5. *($IC(k_1 + 1)$)*
The system has a communication mechanism $IC(k_1 + 1)$ that allows a process $p \in V$ to check $incons_q(P_1)$ of any process $q \in N_p^{k_1+1}$ immediately.

Figure 1 shows the $(P_1 * P_2)$ via $RWFC$ at process p. For each $i \in \{1, 2\}$, $G_p(P_i)$ is the disjunction of all guards of protocol P_i at p, and $A_p(P_i)$ is the corresponding action of $G_p(P_i)$ at p. By S1, p executes P_1 whenever there is an enabled guard of P_1. By $S2$, p executes P_2 when p is not a neighbor of any faulty process of P_1.

$$
\begin{aligned}
&\text{S1}: G_p(P_1) \quad \rightarrow \quad A_p(P_1) \\
&\text{S2}: G_p(P_2) \wedge \forall q \in N_p^{k_1+1} \cup \{p\} : \neg incons_q(P_1) \quad \rightarrow \quad A_p(P_2)
\end{aligned}
$$

Fig. 1. $(P_1 * P_2)$ via $RWFC$

We define the output variables of $(P_1 * P_2)$ is the output variables of P_2. A legitimate configuration of $(P_1 * P_2)$, is defined as $\forall p \in V : L_p((P_1 * P_2))$ where $L_p(P_1 * P_2) = L_p(P_1) \wedge L_p(P_2)$, since in a legitimate configuration of a fault-containing protocol, all of its variables stabilizes.

3.2 Correctness

In this section, we present the proof that $(P_1 * P_2)$ via $RWFC$ is a $f_{1,2}$-fault-containing composition for $f_{1,2} = \min\{f_1, f_2\}$.

Lemma 1. *(Self-stabilization of $(P_1 * P_2)$)*
Starting from an arbitrary initial configuration, $(P_1 * P_2)$ via RWFC eventually converges to a legitimate configuration.

Proof. If P_1 is in an illegitimate configuration, there is at least one process p that has an enabled guard. Eventually p executes P_1 by S1 and P_1 eventually stabilizes. During the recovery of P_1, P_2 may be executed, but it has no influence on P_1's recovery. Then if P_2 is still in an illegitimate configuration, there is at least one process q that has an enabled guard. Since P_1 has stabilized, q eventually executes P_2 by S2. Then P_2 eventually stabilizes.   □

We show fault-containment of $(P_1 * P_2)$.

Lemma 2. *(Recovery of output variables of P_1)*
Starting from any f'-faulty configuration where $f' \leq f_{1,2}$, output variables of P_1 at each faulty process p eventually recover, that is, $incons_q(P_1)$ is false at any process q in $N_p^{k_1} \cup \{p\}$. During the recovery, each p and all its neighbors do not execute P_2.

Proof. Process p and its neighbors execute P_1 by S1, and p eventually recovers to the state which satisfies $\neg incons_p(P_1)$. Since the input to P_1 defines a unique legitimate configuration, p recovers to a unique state defined by the input to P_1. Sice $incons_r(P_1)$ is true at least one process r in $N_p^{k_1} \cup \{p\}$ until output variables at p recover, p and its neighbors do not execute P_2 by S2 until output variables of P_1 at p recover.   □

Lemma 3. *(Recovery of inner variables of P_1)*
Starting from any f'-faulty configuration where $f' \leq f_{1,2}$, after output variables of P_1 at each faulty process p recover, in which $incons_p(P_1)$ is false for any process $p \in V$, P_1 eventually reaches a legitimate configuration. During the recovery, no process changes its output variables of P_1.

Proof. After output variables at each faulty process p recover, if $\ell_p(P_1)$ is false, p fixes its inner variables by S1. If other correct processes need to execute P_1, they can execute P_1 by S1. By our assumption **Recovery**, correct processes changes only their inner variables during the recovery. So, they just fix their inner variables by S1. Eventually p satisfies $L_p(P_1)$. During this recovery, p does not change output variables. □

Lemma 4. *(Recovery of P_2)*
Starting from any f'-configuration, after the output variables of P_1 recovers, P_2 eventually reaches a legitimate configuration.

Proof. While there exists a process q where $incons_q(P_1)$ is true in $N_p^{k_1+1} \cup \{p\}$, p cannot execute P_2 by S1. Eventually by Lemma 2 configuration reaches the one in which there is no such process in $N_p^{k_1+1} \cup \{p\}$ for each process p. Then each process p starts to execute P_2 by S2. By Lemma 2, the output variables of P_1 are the values uniquely defined by the input to P_1, since consistent values of output variables at each process r are defined by $\neg incons_r(P_1)$. And Lemma 2 guarantees P_2 does not execute according to incorrect input. Then, P_2 eventually reaches a legitimate configuration by P_2 which is uniquely defined by the unique legitimate configuration of P_1.

Although it is possible that inner variables of P_1 change their values during this recovery of P_2, their recovery does not disturb the recovery of P_2 by Lemma 3. □

We have the following assumption on the communication mechanism $IC(k_1 + 1)$.

Assumption 1. *The communication mechanism $IC(k_1 + 1)$ of the system slows down the protocols on the system at the rate of α_{k_1+1} and causes state change at processes in $N_p^{\beta_{k_1+1}}$ for any $p \in V$ to communicate $q \in N_p^{k_1+1}$.*

We simply denote α_{k_1+1} as α and β_{k_1+1} as β. We denote the performance measures of f_i-fault-containing protocol P_i for each $i \in \{1, 2\}$ as follows.

- Stabilization time : ts_i
- Recovery time : tr_i
- Output contamination number : c_i
- Contamination number : c_i'

Lemma 5. *(Metrics of fault-containment)*
The maximum number of faults that $(P_1 * P_2)$ via RWFC framework promises fault-containment is $f_{1,2} = \min\{f_1, f_2\}$. The output contamination number is c_2, the contamination number is $\max\{c_1', d^\beta c_2'\}$ and the recovery time is $(tr_1 + \alpha \, tr_2)$, where the maximum degree of G is d.

Proof. Since $(P_1 * P_2)$ executes P_1 and P_2 in the coordinated order, each protocol executes its own recovery actions. So the maximum number of faults that both protocols recover in a fault-containing fashion is $\min\{f_1, f_2\}$. The output contamination number is c_2, because the output of $(P_1 * P_2)$ is the output variables of P_2. S2 makes a process p with an enabled guard of P_2 to determine $incons_q(P_1)$ of all $q \in N_p^{k_1+1} \cup \{p\}$ and the underlying communication mechanism $IC(k_1 + 1)$ causes state change of a process $r \in N_p^\beta$. The contamination number of P_2 is now $\beta c_2'$. P_1 does not need such communication and its contamination number is still c_1'. So, $RWFC$'s contamination number is $\max\{c_1', \beta c_2'\}$.

The recovery time is at most the sum of the two protocols, since those processes which has recovered locally executes P_2 before P_1 recovers. However $IC(k_1 + 1)$ slows down the execution of P_2 and the recovery time is $(tr_1 + \alpha\, tr_2)$.   □

Theorem 1. $(P_1 * P_2)$ *via RWFC gives a fault-containing composition* $(P_1 * P_2)$.

From Lemma 1 $\sim$ 5, $(P_1 * P_2)$ via $RWFC$ is $f_{1,2}$-fault containing.   □

3.3   Multilayer Fault-Containing Composition

$RWFC$ framework is able to compose more than three fault-containing protocols. We define the interface of $(P_1 * P_2)$ via $RWFC$ as follows.

- $incons(P_1 * P_2) = incons(P_1) \vee incons(P_2)$
- $can\_move(P_1 * P_2) = can\_move(P_1) \vee can\_move(P_2)$.

Let $P_1, P_2, \ldots, P_j$ be fault-containing protocols and we will consider a composition where the input to P_i is output variables of P_{i-1}. The multilayer fault-containing composition is obtained in this way : $((\ldots((P_1 * P_2) * P_3)\ldots) * P_j)$.

4   Fault-Containing Composition of Median Finding and Minimum Spanning Tree Construction

In this section we present a fault-containing composition of 1-fault-containing minimum spanning tree constructing protocol MST[14] and 1-fault-containing median finding protocol MF.

4.1 $(MST * MF)$ Via $RWFC$

A 1-fault-containing minimum spanning tree protocol MST for a weighted graph $G = (V, E, W)$ was proposed by Katayama et al.[14]. The detail of this protocol is shown in appendix.

A self-stabilizing median finding protocol SMF was proposed by Bruell et al.[12]. A median of a tree $T = (V, E)$ is a process with a minimum weight where a weight of a process $p \in V$ is the sum of the distance from p to q, for each $q \in V$. We propose a 1-fault-containing version of this protocol MF, and the detail is also shown in appendix.

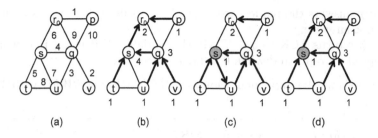

Fig. 2. Median Finding on Minimum Spanning Tree

$$S1 : G_p(MST) \quad \rightarrow \quad A_p(MST)$$
$$S2 : G_p(MF) \wedge \forall q \in N_p \cup \{p\} : \neg incons_q(MST) \quad \rightarrow \quad A_p(MF)$$

Fig. 3. $(MST * MF)$ via $RWFC$ with $IC(2)$

The $(MST * MF)$ via $RWFC$ is shown in Figure 2. Fault-containing composition of MST and MF gives a 1-fault-containing median finding protocol on an arbitrary graph.

Figure 2(c) shows an 1-faulty configuration of $(MST * MF)$. Processes r_0, q, s, and u are not allowed to execute MF because $incons(MST)$ is enabled at q and s. Eventually s changes its route to the root process to a correct value and becomes recovered process of MST as shown in Figure 2(d). After that $can\_move(MF)$ is true at s and s changes its output variable of MF. The output contamination number of $(MST * MF)$ is just 1 and recovery time is $O(d^3)$ where d represents the maximum degree of G.

4.2 Communication Mechanism $WIC(1)$

In this section we show an implementation of communication mechanism $IC(2)$ for $(MST * MF)$ via $RWFC$ on a model in which each process can read the variables of its direct neighbors. Though we assume $IC(2)$ for $(MST * MF)$ via $RWFC$, the implementation does not guarantee immediate communication and not always transit current information and our implementation $WIC(1)$ is weak on this point. In addition, though communication mechanism should be fault-containing, we show that $WIC(1)$ can be implemented by the *question and answer* technique in [19] without developing a new fault-containing communication mechanism. The proof for $(MST * MF)$ via $RWFC$ with $WIC(1)$ is shown in appendix.

In $WIC(1)$, each process p asks $incons_q(MST)$ to all $q \in N_p$. This implementation uses the following variables at each process p.

- $q_{p,q}$: p requests $incons_q(P_1)$ to $q \in N_p$ via this. When $q_{p,q}$ is 0, it means p is not requesting and when 1, p is requesting.

- $a_{p,q}$: p answers the request from $q \in N_p$ via this. When $a_{p,q}$ is $\perp$, it means p is not answering.
- $r_{p,q}$: p returns ACK to $q \in N_p$ via this variable. When $r_{p,q}$ is 1, it means p accepted q's reply and when 0 p has not accepted.

Figure 4 shows the implementation for $(MST*MF)$ via $RWFC$ with $WIC(1)$.

S1-1 : $G_p(\boldsymbol{MST})$ $\rightarrow$ execute **MST**
S2-1 : $G_p(\boldsymbol{MF}) \wedge \forall q \in N_p : a_{q,p} = false$
$\quad\quad \rightarrow$ execute **MF**, for each $q \in N_p$ do $r_{p,q} = 1$
S2-2 : $G_p(\boldsymbol{MF}) \wedge \exists q \in N_p : q_{p,q} \neq 1$
$\quad\quad \rightarrow$ for each $q \in N_p$ do if $q_{p,q} \neq 1$ then $q_{p,q} = 1, r_{p,q} = 0$
S2-3 : $\exists q \in N_p : (q_{q,p} = 1 \wedge a_{p,q} \neq incons_p(\boldsymbol{MST}))$
$\quad\quad \rightarrow$ for each $q \in N_p$ do if $(q_{q,p} = 1 \wedge a_{p,q} \neq incons_p(\boldsymbol{MST}))$
$\quad\quad\quad\quad$ then $a_{p,q} = incons_p(\boldsymbol{MST})$
S2-4 : $\neg G_p(\boldsymbol{MF}) \wedge \exists q \in N_p : q_{p,q} \neq 0$
$\quad\quad \rightarrow$ for each $q \in N_p$ do if $q_{p,q} \neq 0$ then $q_{p,q} = 0$
S2-5 : $\exists q \in N_p : (q_{p,q} = 0 \vee r_{p,q} = 1)$
$\quad\quad \rightarrow$ for each $q \in N_p$ do if $(q_{p,q} = 0 \vee r_{p,q} = 1)$ then $a_{p,q} = \perp$
S2-6 : $\forall q \in N_p : a_{q,p} \neq \perp \wedge \exists q \in N_p : a_{q,p} = true$ $\rightarrow$ $r_{p,q} = 1$
S2-7 : $\exists q \in N_p : (a_{q,p} = \perp \wedge r_{p,q} = 1)$ $\rightarrow$ $r_{p,q} = 0$

Fig. 4. $(MST*MF)$ via $RWFC$ with $WIC(1)$

5   Conclusion

We show $RWFC$ framework which guarantees fault-containment for a composed protocol. Our strategy to fault-containing composition $(P_1 * P_2)$ is to stop the execution of P_2 until P_1 recovers. This concept is very simple but provides significant improvement on fault-containment. Furthermore, this framework helps designing new fault-containing protocols, and we can easily built new protocols on top of other protocols. We assumed underlying communication mechanism for $RWFC$ which may have influence on the performance of obtained protocol. As an example of fault-containing composition via $RWFC$, we show a composition of a minimum spanning tree protocol on an arbitrary weighted graph and a median finding protocol on a tree, which provides median finding of the underlying minimum spanning tree on arbitrary weighted graph. The performance of obtained protocol is affected by the underlying communication mechanism at the rate of d where d is a maximum degree of a graph. Though the example is simple, it shows the possibility of fault-containing composition via $RWFC$ of more complicated protocols.

$RWFC$ framework depends on the underlying communication mechanism $IC(k)$, which must be fault-containing. We show a weak implementation $WIC(1)$ is sufficient to $(MST * MF)$ via $RWFC$. In the same way, we can substitute for a weaker implementation of $IC(k)$ depending on protocols.

Future work. *RWFC* is depend on several assumptions on the source protocols of the composition e.g. an unique legitimate configuration and output contamination number. It is necessary to relax the assumptions on them to extend the generality of our framework and extend the application of fault-containing composition. For example, we assumed that only the faulty processes change their output variables during the recovery from f-faulty configuration. However, it is difficult for each process to determine whether it is faulty or non-faulty and a non-faulty process may change its output variables. So it is necessary to consider a framework for fault-containing protocols whose recoveries are more complicated and there may be other keys to check the configuration of each protocol to control the execution of the others.

Acknowledgments. This work is supported in part by MEXT: "The 21st Century Center of Excellence Program", JSPS: Grant-in-Aid for Scientific Research ((B)15300017 and (B)17300020), MEXT: Grant-in-Aid for Scientific Research on Priority Areas (16092215), MEXT: Grand-in-Aid for Young Scientists ((B)18700059), MIC: Strategic Information, Communications R&D Promotion Programme (SCOPE), and Ookawa Foundation Research Grant.

References

1. E. W. Dijkstra. Self-stabilizing system in spite of distributed control. Communications of the ACM, 17(11), pp.643–644. (1974)
2. S. Dolev, A. Israeli and S. Moran. Self-stabilization of dynamic systems assuming only read/write atomicity. In Proceedings of the 9th Annual ACM Symposium on Principles of Distributed Computing, pp.103–118. (1990)
3. N. S. Chen, H. P. Yu and S. T. Huang. A self-stabilizing algorithm for constructing a spanning tree. Information Processing Letters, Vol.39, pp.147–151. (1991)
4. X. Lin and S. Ghosh. Maxima finding in a ring. In Proceedings of the 28th Annual Allerton Conference on Computers, Communication and Control, pp.662–671. (1991)
5. S. T. Huang and N. S. Chen. Self-stabilizing depth-first token circulation on networks. Distributed Computing, Vol.7(1). pp.61–66. (1993)
6. S. Ghosh and A. Gupta. An exercise in fault-containment: Self-stabilizing leader election. Information Processing Letters, Vol.59, pp.281–288. (1996)
7. S. Ghosh and A. Gupta. A fault-containing self-stabilizing spanning tree algorithm. Journal of Computing and Information, Vol.2, No.1, pp.322–338. (1996)
8. S. Ghosh, A. Gupta, T. Herman and S. V. Pemmaraju. Fault-containing self-stabilizing algorithms. In Proceedings of 15th Annual ACM Symposium on Principles of Distributed Computing, pp.45–54. (1996)
9. S. Ghosh and X. He. Fault-containing self-stabilization using priority scheduling. Information Processing Letters, Vol.73, pp.145–151. (2000)
10. S. Dolev, A. Israeli and S. Moran. Self-stabilization of dynamic systems. In Proceedings of the MCC Workshop on Self-Stabilizing Systems, MCC Technical Report No. STP-379-89. (1989)
11. S. Dolev, A. Israeli and S. Moran. Self-stabilization of dynamic systems assuming only read/write atomicity. Distributed Computing, 7:pp.3–16. (1993)

12. S. C. Bruell, S. Ghosh, M. H. Karaata, S. V. Pemmaraju. Self-Stabilizing Algorithms for Finding Centers and Medians of Trees. SIAM Journal on Computing, Vol. 29, pp.600–614. (1999)
13. K. Kotani, Y. Katayama, T. Masuzawa and N. Tokura. A self-stabilizing algorithm for constructing a minimum weight spanning tree. Technical Report of IEICE (In Japanese), Vol.92, No.52.pp.37–44. (1992)
14. Y. Katayama and T. Masuzawa. A fault-containing self-stabilizing protocol for constructing a minimum spanning tree. Transactions of the IEICE (In Japanese), D-I, Vol.J-84-D-I, No. 9, pp.1307–1317. (2001.3)
15. S. Ghosh, A. Gupta and S. V. Pemmaraju. Fault-containing network protocols. In Proceedings of the ACM Symposium on Applied Computing, pp.431–437. (1997)
16. J. Beauquier, M. Gradinariu and C. Johnen. Cross-Over composition - Enforcement of fairness under unfair adversary. In Proceedings of 5th Workshop on Self-Stabilizing Systems, pp.19–34. (2001)
17. Y. Azar, S. Kutten and B Patt-Shamir. Distributed Error Confinement. In Proceedings of 22nd Annual ACM Symposium on Principles of Distributed Computing, pp.33–42. (2003)
18. A. Arora and H. Zhang. LSRP: Local Stabilization in Shortest Path Routing. In Proceedings of International Conference of Dependable Systems and Networks, pp.139–148. (2003)
19. S. Ghosh and A. Gupta. An exercise in fault-containment: Self-stabilizing leader election. Information Processing Letters, Vol. 59, pp.281–288. (1996)
20. S. Kutten and B. Patt-Shamir. Time-Adaptive Self Stabilization. In Proceedings of 16th Annual ACM Symposium on Principles of Distributed Computing, pp.149–158. (1997)
21. S. Dolev and T. Herman. Parallel Composition of Stabilizing Algorithms. In Proceedings of Fourth Workshop on Self-Stabilizing Systems, pp.25–32. (1999)

Appendix

6 Minimum Spanning Tree Protocol

Katayama et al.[14] proposed 1-fault-containing minimum spanning tree protocol MST. Let a graph $G = (V, E, W)$ is a weighted graph, whose number of processes is n and whose communication links have unique weights. The weight of a link (p, q) is denoted by $w(p, q)$. The minimum spanning tree of G is a set of $(n - 1)$ edges of minimum total weight which form a spanning tree of the graph.

Model. Each communication link of G has a unique wight and each process knows the weights of the connected communication links as input variables.

Non-fault-containing version. MST is based on self-stabilizing minimum spanning tree constructing protocol $SMST$ proposed in [13]. We first introduce the sketch of $SMST$.

$SMST$ is based on that a minimum spanning tree can be constructed by applying the following operation repeatedly to an arbitrary spanning tree :

> Consist a new spanning tree by adding a new link which is not the spanning tree link to the existing spanning tree and deleting the maximum weighted link from the closed path.

Each process p owns an output variables and functions as follows.

- Variables
  - $mypath_p$: the output variable that represents the path from r_0 to p denoted by an alternating sequence of identity of a process and a weight of a communication link starting with r_0 :
  $$\langle r_0, w(r_0, s), s, w(s, t), \ldots, o, w(o, p), p \rangle$$
- Functions
  - $parent(mypath_p)$ returns the process preceding p in $mypath_p$. If the size of $mypath_p$ is smaller than two, it returns $\emptyset$.
  - $ischild(mypath_p, mypath_q)$ returns true iff there exists w and ID such that $mypath_p$ is obtained by adding w and ID to $mypath_q$.

MST converges to a configuration where each process p keeps a correct path from r_0 on the minimum spanning tree.

Fault-containing version. MST controls the execution of $SMST$ so that starting from 1-faulty configuration only the faulty process executes the $SMST$.

We say a process p is *consistent* iff the following predicate $cons(p)$ holds.

$$cons(p) = \forall q \in N_p : \{ ischild(mypath_q, mypath_p) \vee ischild(mypath_p, mypath_q)$$
$$\vee (maxl(mypath_p, mypath_q, w(i,j)) = w(i,j)) \}$$

The function $maxl(mypath_p, mypath_q, w)$ returns the maximum weight of a closed path, which contains a link l, in a graph of $mypath_p$, $mypath_q$ and l with weight w, which is between the end of them. If there is no such closed path, it returns 0.

MST defines the following predicates Q_1, Q_2, Q_3 and Q_4.

- Q_1 is true when there exists $mypath' \neq mypath_p$ such that $mypath'$ is the correct path from r_0 on the minimum spanning tree.
- Q_2 is true when there exists just one process $q \in N_p$ such that p can become consistent by q changing $mypath_q$.
- Q_3 is true when there exists more than two processes in N_p (denoted by P') such that Q_1 is true at any $q \in P'$ and a process $r \in P'$ can resolve the inconsistency of other processes in P' by changing $mypath_r$.
- Q_4 is true when p is a leaf process and Q_1 is true at p's parent process s and p can be consistent by s changing $mypath_s$.

In 1-faulty configuration, a faulty process p and its neighbors whose parent is p may be inconsistent and a process where $\{ (Q_1 \wedge Q_4) \vee Q_2 \vee Q_3 \}$ is true is a neighbor of a faulty process and should not execute $SMST$.

Each process should communicate with N_p^2 to determine its predicates. MST consists of the implementation of N_p^2 communication mechanism and tree maintenance mechanism. The N_p^2 communication mechanism is implemented by *question and answer* technique similar to [19]. The N_p^2 communication mechanism and the tree maintenance mechanism of Figure 5 are executed in parallel.

$$\neg cons(p) \wedge \neg Q_0 \wedge ((\neg Q_1 \vee \neg Q_4) \wedge \neg Q_2 \wedge \neg Q_3) \quad \rightarrow \quad \textbf{execute} \quad \textbf{\textit{SMST}}$$

Fig. 5. Fault-containing Minimum Spanning Tree Protocol *MST*

The legitimate configuration of *MST* is the following.

$$\forall p \in V : \big[cons(p) \wedge (\textit{local variables for communication mechanism stabilize}) \big]$$

The predicates that we assumed on a fault-containing protocol are as follows.

- $\ell_p(MST) = \forall q \in N_p : \{ q_{pq} = a_{pq} = \perp \}$
- $incons_p(MST) = \neg cons(p)$
- $can\_move_p(MST) = \neg cons(p) \wedge \neg Q_0 \wedge ((\neg Q_1 \vee \neg Q_4) \wedge \neg Q_2 \wedge \neg Q_3)$

7   Median Finding Protocol

We propose 1-fault-containing median finding protocol *MF* based on the self-stabilizing median finding protocol *SMF* proposed by Bruell et al.[12] Consider a tree $T = (V, E)$ where the vertex set V is a set of processes and the edge set E is a set of communication links. A weight of a process p is a sum of the distances from p to $\forall q \in V$. A *median* of T is a process with the minimum weight.

Model. A tree T was given to the protocol as an input variable which represents the parent on T at each process.

Non-fault-containing version. To construct fault-containing version *MF*, we first consider the self-stabilizing median finding protocol *SMF*[13].

Each process p owns an output variable s_p and a function $S(\{s_1, s_2, \ldots, s_j\})$ which returns the sum of $s_1, s_2, \ldots, s_j$ excluding one of the maximum items. A legitimate configuration of *SMF* is defined as follows:

$$\forall p \in V : s_p = S(\{ s_r \mid r \in N_p \}) + 1$$

The self-stabilizing version *SMF* is shown in Figure 6. A process whose s value is greater than or equal to that of all neighbor processes is the medians of T. It is possible that there are more than one medians in T.

$$s_p \neq S(\{ s_r \mid r \in N_p \}) + 1 \quad \rightarrow \quad s_p := S(\{ s_r \mid r \in N_p \}) + 1$$

Fig. 6. Self-stabilizing Median Finding Protocol *SMF*[12]

Fault-containing version. We say a process p is *consistent* iff $s_p = S(\{ s_r \mid r \in N_p \}) + 1$ and else *inconsistent*. In 1-faulty configuration, a faulty process p is inconsistent, and if every such p fixes s_p, MF recovers to a legitimate configuration. Although $r \in N_p$ may be inconsistent, r cannot resolve inconsistency, p must execute SMF and r should not execute SMF.

To implement this idea, we use additional variables and functions at each process p.

- Inner variables
  - $q_{p,r}$: p proposes new value of s_p to $r \in N_p$ via this. When $q_{p,r}$ is 0, it means p is not proposing a new value.
  - $a_{p,r}$: the answer for the proposal of $r \in N_p$. The value of $a_{p,r}$ is $\perp$ when p is not answering, and 0 when it agrees the proposed value $q_{q,r}$ and 1 when it disagrees.
- Function
  - $F(p, r, q_{r,p})$ is 0 if the proposal $q_{r,p}$ by $r \in N_p$ resolves inconsistency of p, and otherwise it is $S(\{s_t \mid t \in N_p\}) + 1$.
- Predicate
  - $can\_stabilize_p = \{s_p = S(\{s_r \mid r \in N_p\}) + 1\}$
  - $single\_fault_p$: this predicate is evaluated when p gets answers to its proposal from all its neighbors. This predicate is true iff there exists just one neighbor r whose $a_{r,p} \neq 0$ and r's proposal resolves p's inconsistency.

The legitimate configuration of MF is defined as follows :

$$\forall p \in V : \{s_p = S(\{s_r \mid r \in N_p\}) + 1\} \wedge \{\forall r \in N_p : (q_{p,r} = 0 \wedge a_{p,r} = \perp)\}$$

The predicates that we assumed are as follows:

- $\ell_p(MF) = \{\forall r \in N_p : (q_{p,r} = 0 \wedge a_{p,r} = \perp)\}$
- $incons_p(MF) = \{s_p \neq S(\{s_r \mid r \in N_p\}) + 1\}$
- $can\_move_p = [can\_stabilize_p \wedge \{\forall r \in N_p : q_{p,r} = S(\{s_t \mid t \in N_p\}) + 1\} \wedge \{\forall r \in N_p : a_{r,p} \neq \perp\}] \wedge [\{\forall r \in N_p : a_{r,p} = 0\} \vee \neg single\_fault_p]$

The correctness proof of fault-containing version is omitted due to the space restriction.

8   Correctness of $(MST * MF)$ Via $RWFC$ with $WIC(1)$

In this section we show the sketch of the proof of the correctness of $(MST * MF)$ via RWFC with $WIC(1)$ shown in Figure 4.

Lemma 6. *Starting from any initial configuration, $(MST * MF)$ via RWFC with $WIC(1)$ eventually converges to a legitimate configuration.*

To show the fault containment property, we need to show the following lemma for MST.

Lemma 7. *A process p such that $incons_p(MST)$ is false in a 1-faulty configuration does not change $incons_p(MST)$ to true during the recovery.*

$S_{1a} : can\_move_p \quad \rightarrow \quad \textbf{execute } \textbf{\textit{SMF}}$

$S_{2a} : incons_p \wedge \left\{ \exists q \in N_p : \left(q_{p,q} = 0 \wedge a_{q,p} = \perp \right) \right\}$

$\quad \rightarrow \quad \textbf{for each} \quad q \in N_p \textbf{ do if} \quad \left(q_{p,q} = 0 \wedge a_{q,p} = \perp \right)$

$\qquad \textbf{then} \quad q_{p,q} = S(\{ s_r \mid r \in N_p \}) + 1$

$S_{2b} : \exists q \in N_p : \left(q_{q,p} \neq 0 \wedge a_{p,q} \neq F(p,q,q_{q,p}) \right)$

$\quad \rightarrow \quad \textbf{for each} \quad q \in N_p \textbf{ do if} \quad \left(q_{q,p} \neq 0 \wedge a_{p,q} \neq F(p,q,q_{q,p}) \right)$

$\qquad \textbf{then} \quad a_{p,q} = F(p,q,q_{q,p})$

$S_{2c} : \left\{ \exists q \in N_p : q_{p,q} \neq S(\{ s_r \mid r \in N_p \}) + 1 \right\} \vee$

$\qquad \left\{ \neg incons_p \wedge \left\{ \exists q \in N_p : q_{p,q} \neq 0 \right\} \right\}$

$\quad \rightarrow \quad \textbf{for each} \quad q \in N_p \textbf{ do if} \quad q_{p,q} \neq 0 \textbf{ then} \quad q_{p,q} = 0$

$S_{2d} : \exists q \in N_p : \left(q_{q,p} = 0 \wedge a_{p,q} \neq \perp \right)$

$\quad \rightarrow \quad \textbf{for each} \quad q \in N_p \textbf{ do if} \quad \left(q_{q,p} = 0 \wedge a_{p,q} \neq \perp \right) \textbf{ then} \quad a_{p,q} = \perp$

Fig. 7. Fault-containing Median Finding Protocol *MF*

Now we return to the proof of fault-containment of communication $(MST * MF)$ via *RWFC* with *WIC(1)*.

Lemma 8. *Starting from 1-faulty configuration, a process p such that $a_{q,p} = false$ for any process $q \in N_p$ is not a neighbor of a non-recovery process of MST.*

Lemma 9. *Starting from any 1-faulty configuration, MF recovers to a legitimate configuration in $O(d^3)$ time.*

Then we obtain the following theorem.

Theorem 2. *Fault-containing composition $(MST * MF)$ via RWFC with WIC(1) is 1-fault-containing protocol and the recovery time of the obtained protocol is $O(d^3)$, where d is the maximum degree of the graph.*

Energy-Efficient and Non-interactive Self-certification in MANETs*

Jeong Hyun Yi

Networking Technology Lab
Samsung Advanced Institute of Technology
jeong.yi@samsung.com

Abstract. Mobile ad hoc networks (MANETs) have many well-known applications in military settings as well as in emergency and rescue operations. However, lack of infrastructure and lack of centralized control make MANETs inherently insecure, and therefore specialized security services are needed for their deployment. *Self-certification* is an essential and fundamental security service in MANETs. It is needed to securely cope with dynamic membership and topology and to bootstrap other important security primitives and services without the assistance of any centralized trusted authority. An ideal protocol must involve minimal interaction among the MANET nodes, since connectivity can be unstable. Also, since MANETs are often composed of weak or resource-limited devices, self-certification protocol must be efficient in terms of computation and communication. Unfortunately, previously proposed protocols are far from being ideal.

In this paper, we propose fully non-interactive self-certification protocol based on bi-variate polynomial secret sharing and threshold BLS signature techniques. In contrast with prior work, our techniques do not require any interaction and do not involve any costly reliable broadcast communication among MANET nodes. We thoroughly analyze our proposal and show that it compares favorably to previous mechanisms.

Keywords: Security protocol, self-configuration, threshold cryptography, authentication, key management.

1 Introduction

Unlike cellular networks whose infrastructure includes base stations or access points, routers and switches that are fixed and wired together, mobile ad hoc networks (MANETs) are infrastructure-less and the mobile nodes act as wireless routers. Lack of infrastructure and lack of centralized control, coupled with a dynamic network topology, results in vulnerabilities that do not exist in wired networks, and therefore specialized security services are needed for their deployment.

Self-certification is a fundamental security service in MANETs; it is required to ascertain membership eligibility and to bootstrap other important security services, such as secure routing and secure group communication.

---

* This work has been done while at UC Irvine.

A.K. Datta and M. Gradinariu (Eds.): SSS 2006, LNCS 4280, pp. 533–547, 2006.

Node authentication in MANETs cannot be performed centrally. Since, requiring constant presence (availability) of a central fixed entity is not realistic for many types of MANETs. First, such an entity is a single point of failure. Second, it represents an attractive and high-payoff target for attacks. Third, topology changes due to mobility and node outages may cause the central entity to be unreachable and thus unable to perform its duties in the parts of a MANET not connected to it. This motivates us to investigate self-configurable authentication techniques that function in a distributed or decentralized manner. Since our emphasis is on security, the natural technology to consider is threshold cryptography.

Two features of MANETs make self-certification a very challenging problem. *First*, MANET devices often have very weak computational facilities and battery power. *Second*, MANET nodes usually function in an asynchronous (on/off) manner, often becoming temporarily unavailable. Therefore, an ideal solution must be efficient in terms of both computation and communication[1]. It must also involve minimal (ideally, *none* at all) interaction among the nodes of the network which requires synchronous communications.

A number of self-certification techniques have been proposed in recent years [2,3,4,5,6,7]. Most are based on (t, n) threshold cryptography and allow any set of t-out-of-n nodes (called sponsors) to admit a new node by issuing to it: 1) a share of a network secret (to be used in future admissions), and 2) a membership token (used for authentication and secure communication). Unfortunately, all previous schemes are far from ideal. They are **heavily interactive** among the sponsors. This severely limits their practicality.

Contributions: We present fully non-interactive self-certification protocol based on bi-variate polynomial secret sharing and threshold BLS signature techniques. In contrast with prior work, our techniques do not require any interaction and do not involve any costly reliable broadcast communication among MANET nodes. We thoroughly analyze our proposal and show that it compares favorably to previous mechanisms.

Organization: The rest of the paper is organized as follows: we first review prior work in Section 2. Some cryptographic backgrounds are introduced in Section 3, followed by the system model in Section 4. We then describe, in Section 5, the proposed self-certification mechanism called NISC. Finally, the detailed performance results, analysis and comparison are presented in Section 6.

2 Related Work

We now review relevant prior work for robust self-certification in MANETs. Kong, et al. [2,8] proposed a set of self-certification protocols for providing ubiquitous and robust security services for MANETs. The security of their protocols relies upon a specific variant of the proactive threshold RSA signature scheme.

---

[1] Communication is directly related to the consumption of battery power in MANET devices [1].

Unfortunately, this scheme is neither robust [5] (i.e., it can not tolerate malicious nodes) nor secure [9]. Narasimha, et al. [5] proposed similar protocols based on threshold DSA [10]. While provably secure, the solution is quite inefficient since it is at least heavily interactive among sponsoring nodes. In [7], Saxena, et al. proposed the self-certification protocol that uses uni-variate polynomial secret sharing [11] and threshold BLS [12] for certificate issuance. Although this scheme is non-interactive when issuing a certificate for new node, its secret share issuance still requires interaction due to the Lagrange interpolation of uni-variate secret sharing. In the rest of the paper we compare our proposed scheme with this protocol and refer to it as *Interactive Self-Certification* or ISC.

The self-certification technique developed in this paper is completely non-interactive in a certificate issuance as well as secret share acquisition. It uses secret sharing based on so-called bi-variate polynomials which have been employed for related purposes in the literature [13,14,15]. In particular, [16] presents a key pre-distribution scheme for sensor networks using bi-variate polynomials [15] *in the presence of a centralized authority*. The protocol we propose is fully distributed and allows nodes in a MANET to readily and efficiently share pairwise secret keys without any centralized support. [17] presents node admission protocol based on bivariate polynomials targeted only for short-lived MANETs, not for long-lived ones. The proposed scheme works for both short- and long-lived MANETs.

3   Preliminaries

3.1   Notation

Notation used in the rest of paper is summarized in Table 1.

3.2   Threshold Secret Sharing

In this section, we present Shamir's secret sharing scheme [11] which is based on uni-variate polynomial interpolation. We will refer to it as TSS. To distribute shares of a secret x among n entities, a trusted dealer TD chooses a polynomial $f(z)$ over $\mathbb{Z}_q$ of degree $(t-1)$: $f(z) = \sum_{i=0}^{t-1} a_i z^i \pmod{q}$ where the constant term a_0 is set to the network secret x; $f(0) = a_0 = x$. TD computes each entity's share x_i such that $x_i = f(id_i)$, where id_i is an identifier of entity P_i, and securely transfers x_i to P_i. Note that after distributing at least t secret shares, the dealer is no longer required.

Then, any set of t entities who have their shares can recover the secret using the Lagrange interpolation formula: $f(z) = \sum_{i=1}^{t} x_i \, \lambda_i(z) \pmod{q}$, where $\lambda_i(z) = \prod_{j=1, j \neq i}^{t} \frac{z - id_j}{id_i - id_j} \pmod{q}$. Since $f(0) = x$, the shared secret may be expressed as: $x = f(0) = \sum_{i=1}^{t} x_i \, \lambda_i(0) \pmod{q}$ Thus, the secret x can be recovered only if at least t shares are combined. In other words, no coalition of less than t entities yields any information about x.

Table 1. Notation

P_i	network node i
id_i	identity for P_i
t	admission threshold
n	total number of network nodes
$\mathbb{G}$	cyclic group in finite fields
$\mathbb{G}_1, \mathbb{G}_2$	cyclic GDH groups of order q
$\mathbb{P}$	generator of group $\mathbb{G}_1$
$\hat{e}$	bilinear map s.t. $\hat{e} : \mathbb{G}_1 \times \mathbb{G}_1 \to \mathbb{G}_2$
H	hash function such as SHA-1 or MD5
H_1	special hash function s.t. $H_1 : \{0,1\}^* \to \mathbb{G}_1^*$
x_i	secret share of P_i
$x_i^{(j)}$	partial share for P_i by P_j
T_i	membership token for P_i
PK_i	temporary public key of P_i
$S_i(m)$	P_i's signature on message m
$K_{i,j}$	pairwise key between P_i and P_j
$E_{K_{i,j}}$	encryption with $K_{i,j}$

3.3 BLS Signature Scheme

Boneh, et al. [18] proposed a short signature scheme that works in a EC-GDH group $\mathbb{G}$ of order q and a generator $\mathbb{P}$. In brief, the scheme operates as follows:

- **Key Generation.** Pick random $x \in \mathbb{Z}_q^*$ and compute $\mathbb{Q} = x\mathbb{P}$. x is the private key and $\mathbb{Q}$ is the corresponding public key.
- **Signing.** To sign a message m, compute $\sigma = xH_1(m)$, where H_1 is a special hash function that maps binary strings onto points in $\mathbb{G}_1$. σ is the signature on m.
- **Verification.** Given ($\mathbb{P}$, $\mathbb{Q}$, m, σ), check if $\hat{e}(\mathbb{Q}, H_1(m)) = \hat{e}(\mathbb{P}, \sigma)$.

4   System Model

The basic operations in our self-certification protocol involve only a set of secret share holders. A admission threshold (t) is an important system parameter that needs to be carefully tuned. A protocol is composed of the following steps:

1. *Bootstrapping:* The network is initialized by either a trusted dealer or a set of founding nodes. The dealer or founding nodes initialize the network by choosing a network secret key, and computing and publishing the corresponding public parameters [19]. The network secret is shared among the founding node(s) and the share possessed by each node is referred to as its *secret share.*
2. *Self-Certification:* A prospective node P_{n+1} who wishes to join the network must be issued 1) its secret share for participating in future admission and 2) a membership token for authentication and secure communication. Figure 1

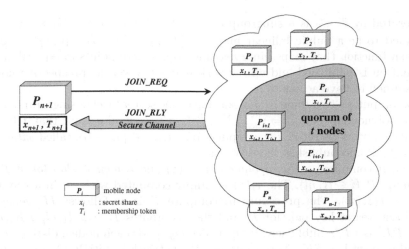

Fig. 1. System Model

gives a high-level view of self-certification protocol. Note that, depending on the underlying cryptographic technique, this step may involve multiple rounds and/or co-ordination among the nodes who commit to P_{n+1}.

3. *Pairwise Key Establishment:* The purpose of pairwise key agreement between nodes is to enable the use of secure channels for communicating secret shares during the self-certification process above. Therefore, pairwise key establishment between a new node and each of the current nodes is also required. Apart from self-certification, this functionality can also be applied to achieve secure routing (e.g., in MANETs).

5   Non-interactive Self-certification

In this section, we now describe new self-certification technique for MANETs. By coupling the bi-variate polynomial based secret share issuance technique with the non-interactive threshold BLS signature [12], we obtain a fully non-interactive self-certification protocol. We call the protocol *Non-Interactive Self-Certification* or NISC.

5.1   Bootstrapping

The network can be initialized by either a single node called a trusted dealer, denoted by *TD*, or a set of nodes in distributed way. For the sake of simplicity, we describe only a centralized method in this section[2]. The set-up first involves the following: elliptic curve parameters $(p, \mathbb{F}_p, a, b, \mathbb{P}, q)$ are chosen, the curve being represented by a equation: $y^2 = x^3 + ax + b$. $\mathbb{G}_1$ is set to be a group of order

---

[2] In case of decentralized method, a set of t or more founding nodes agree on a random bi-variate polynomial $f(z, y)$ using the JSS protocol [20].

q generated by $\mathbb{P}$, $\mathbb{G}_2$ is a subgroup of $\mathbb{F}_{p^2}^*$ of order q, and $\hat{e} : \mathbb{G}_1 \times \mathbb{G}_1 \to \mathbb{G}_2$ is defined to be a public bilinear mapping [21,22]. Also, $H_1 : \{0,1\}^* \to \mathbb{G}_1$ is the hash function that maps binary strings to non-zero points in $\mathbb{G}_1$. All of this information is published and all network nodes (as well as prospective nodes) are assumed to have access to it.

TD computes a two-dimensional sharing of the secret by choosing a random bivariate polynomial: $f(z,y) = \sum_{\alpha=0}^{t-1} \sum_{\beta=0}^{t-1} f_{\alpha\beta} z^\alpha y^\beta \pmod{q}$ such that $f(0,0) = x$, for the network secret x. TD computes $W_{\alpha\beta}$ ($\alpha, \beta \in [0, t-1]$), called *witnesses*: $W_{\alpha\beta} = f_{\alpha\beta}\mathbb{P}$ and publishes these $W_{\alpha\beta}$-s.

Then, it computes a *share-polynomial* $x_i(z)$ and a *membership token* T_i for each node P_i ($i \in [1, n]$). The $x_i(z)$ is simply computed with id_i in a way that $x_i(z) = f(z, id_i)$. The procedure to compute T_i is as follows: TD generates public and secret key pair for P_i and then computes $T_i = xH_1(id_i, PK_i, etc.)$ where PK_i is a P_i's public key. It then *securely* sends each node a distinct $x_i(z)$, T_i, and a secret key SK_i. Note that once the network is initialized, TD securely erase the network secret x and all secret coefficients $f_{\alpha\beta}$ of the polynomial. After that, TD is no longer needed.

5.2 Self-certification

To join the network, P_{n+1} must collect at least t partial shares of the polynomial and partial membership tokens from the current nodes, respectively. Figure 2 shows the protocol message flow for the self-certification process.

Step 1 (JOIN_REQ). P_{n+1} broadcasts:

$$P_{n+1} \qquad \xrightarrow{\quad m=\{id_{n+1}, PK_{n+1}, etc.\},\ S_{n+1}(m) \quad} \qquad \{P_1, \cdots, P_n\}$$

Step 2 (JOIN_RLY). Each P_i ($i \in [1, t']$) where $t \le t' \le n$:
- computes its partial secret share $x_i(id_{n+1}) = f(id_{n+1}, id_i)$,
- computes partial membership token $T_{n+1}^{(i)} = x_i H_1(m)$
- encrypts $x_i(id_{n+1})$ and $T_{n+1}^{(i)}$.

$$P_{n+1} \qquad \xleftarrow{\quad m'=\{id_i, PK_i, E_{K_{i,n+1}}\{x_i(id_{n+1})\}, T_{n+1}^{(i)}\},\ S_i(m') \quad} \qquad \{P_1, \cdots, P_{t'}\}$$

Step 3. P_{n+1}:
- selects any t out of t' partial shares and constructs its share-polynomial $x_{n+1}(z)$ using Gaussian elimination,
- computes the membership token $T_{n+1} = \sum_{j=1}^{t} T_{n+1}^{(j)} \lambda_j(0)$.

Fig. 2. NISC Protocol

1. A prospective node P_{n+1} broadcasts signed JOIN_REQ message m which contains its public key PK_{n+1} and identity id_{n+1} in order to prove the knowledge of the corresponding private key[3].

2. After verifying the signature on the JOIN_REQ message, each receiving node (P_i) willing to admit P_{n+1} computes a *partial share* $x_i(id_{n+1})$ using its own *share-polynomial* such that $x_i(id_{n+1}) = f(id_{n+1}, id_i)$. P_i also issues a membership token for P_{n+1} via the threshold BLS signing protocol (refer to Section 3.3). It computes the partial membership token $T_{n+1}^{(i)}$ on the request message m such that $T_{n+1}^{(i)} = x_i H_1(m)$ where $x_i = x_i(0)$. (Note that $T_{n+1}^{(i)}$ is computed without Lagrange coefficient $\lambda_i(0)$ which means that the signing does not require any interaction among t sponsoring nodes.)

   Each sponsor P_i then replies to P_{n+1} with a JOIN_RLY message. Each message is signed by the sender and contains encrypted $x_i(id_{n+1})$ and partial membership token $T_{n+1}^{(j)}$ along with the respective values of id_i and PK_i. The encryption key $K_{i,n+1}$ is computed using the technique described in Section 5.3.

   To compute their partial shares, sponsors do not need to be aware of each other, and, thus, no interaction is needed. This is in contrast with ISC, where each sponsor needs to be aware of all other sponsors in order to compute the Lagrange coefficient $\lambda_i(id_{n+1})$ in partial share issuance [7].

   We note that, in ISC, since $\lambda_j(id_{n+1})$-s are publicly known, P_{n+1} can derive P_i's secret share x_i from partial share $x_i\lambda_j(id_{n+1})$. This is prevented using the *random shuffling* technique proposed in [24] by adding extra random value R_{ij} to each share. These R_{ij}-s are securely shared between sponsors P_i and P_j and sum up to zero by construction. Due to the random shuffling procedure, ISC protocol becomes heavily interactive among the t sponsoring nodes – it requires $O(t^2)$ point-to-point messages as well as extremely expensive $O(t)$ reliable broadcast messages [25]. All this makes it impractical for most MANET settings.

3. Upon receiving t' ($\geq t$) JOIN_RLY messages, P_{n+1} selects *any* t of them and computes its own share-polynomial $x_{n+1}(z)$ and membership token T_{n+1}. First, the share-polynomial is constructed using standard Gaussian elimination [26]. Let us denote the share-polynomial $x_{n+1}(z)$ reconstructed by P_{n+1} as $\sum_{\alpha=0}^{t-1} A_\alpha z^\alpha$. Since $x_i(id_{n+1}) = x_{n+1}(id_i)$ due to the symmetry, the selected t partial shares $\{x_{n+1}(id_1), \cdots, x_{n+1}(id_t)\}$ can be represented as

$$A_0 + A_1 id_1 + A_2 id_1{}^2 + \cdots + A_{t-1} id_1{}^{t-1} = x_{n+1}(id_1)$$
$$A_0 + A_1 id_2 + A_2 id_2{}^2 + \cdots + A_{t-1} id_2{}^{t-1} = x_{n+1}(id_2)$$
$$\vdots$$
$$A_0 + A_1 id_t + A_2 id_t{}^2 + \cdots + A_{t-1} id_t{}^{t-1} = x_{n+1}(id_t).$$

---

[3] We note that it is necessary to include timestamps, nonces and protocol message identifiers in order to secure the protocol against *replay* attacks [23]. However, we omit these values to keep our description simple.

Thus, the problem of interpolating $x_{n+1}(z)$ using t $x_i(id_{n+1})$-s is equivalent to the problem of computing the matrix A such that $XA = B$:

$$\begin{bmatrix} (id_1)^0 & (id_1)^1 & \cdots & (id_1)^{t-1} \\ (id_2)^0 & (id_2)^1 & \cdots & (id_2)^{t-1} \\ & & \vdots & \\ (id_t)^0 & (id_t)^1 & \cdots & (id_t)^{t-1} \end{bmatrix} \begin{bmatrix} A_0 \\ A_1 \\ \vdots \\ A_{t-1} \end{bmatrix} = \begin{bmatrix} x_{n+1}(id_1) \\ x_{n+1}(id_2) \\ \vdots \\ x_{n+1}(id_t) \end{bmatrix}$$

The above system of linear equations yields a unique solution since the id_i values are distinct and the matrix $X = [x_{ij}]$, where $x_{ij} = (id_i)^{j-1}$ for all $i, j \in [0, t]$, is invertible. In order to validate the acquired share-polynomial $x_{n+1}(z)$, P_{n+1} must perform the verifiability procedure: $A_\alpha = \sum_{\beta=0}^{t-1} f_{\alpha\beta}(id_{n+1})^\beta$ for $\alpha \in [0, t-1]$. Using the public witness values $W_{\alpha\beta} = f_{\alpha\beta}\mathbb{P}$, the polynomial can be verified: $A_\alpha\mathbb{P} = \sum_{\beta=0}^{t-1} (id_{n+1})^\beta W_{\alpha\beta}$ for $\alpha \in [0, , t-1]$. Note that the right-hand side in the equation can be pre-computed by P_{n+1} prior to starting the process.

If the verification fails, P_{n+1} must trace the faulty share providers by performing the traceability procedure. This involves verifying the validity of each partial share $x_i(id_{n+1}) = f(id_{n+1}, id_i)$ by checking: $x_i(id_{n+1})\mathbb{P} = \sum_{\alpha=0}^{t-1} \sum_{\beta=0}^{t-1} (id_{n+1})^\alpha (id_i)^\beta W_{\alpha\beta}$. Similar to share verification, we note that $\sum_{\alpha=0}^{t-1} (id_{n+1})^\alpha W_{\alpha\beta}$ in the equation can be pre-computed since $W_{\alpha\beta}$-s and id_{n+1} are known to P_{n+1} in advance.

Next, P_{n+1} also computes the threshold signature to construct its own membership token by simply multiplying the appropriate Lagrange coefficient with each partial signature and simply adding them, i.e., $T_{n+1} = \sum_{j=1}^{t} T_{n+1}^{(j)}\lambda_j(0) = \sum_{j=1}^{t} (x_j\lambda_j(0))H_1(m) = xH_1(m)$. Similar to the share verifying and tracing as above, P_{n+1} verifies the acquired signature, and if required can trace the malicious signer(s). The membership token T_{n+1} is verified by checking $\hat{e}(\mathbb{P}, T_{n+1}) = \hat{e}(\mathbb{Q}, H_1(m))$ where $\mathbb{Q} = x\mathbb{P}$. In case the verification of T_{n+1} fails, P_{n+1} can trace sponsors that sent invalid partial token(s) as $\hat{e}(\mathbb{P}, T_{n+1}^{(j)}) = \hat{e}(\sum_{\beta=0}^{t-1} (id_i)^\beta W_{0\beta}, H_1(m))$.

5.3   Pairwise Key Establishment

Once every node has its share-polynomial, pairwise key establishment is the same as in [15] and [16]. Any pair of nodes P_i and P_j can establish shared keys as follows: P_i uses its share-polynomial $f(z, id_i)$ to compute K_{ij} such that $K_{ij} = f(id_j, id_i)$. Similarly, P_j uses its share-polynomial $f(z, id_j)$ to compute K_{ji} such that $K_{ji} = f(id_i, id_j)$. Since $f(z, y)$ is a symmetric polynomial, $K_{ij} = K_{ji}$. Thus, P_i and P_j now have a shared key that can be used for secure communication.

The security of above procedure is unconditional, i.e., not based on any assumption. Refer to [15] for details regarding the security arguments of this pairwise key establishment.

6   Performance Analysis

In this section we discuss the implementation of ISC and NISC and compare them in terms of self-certification, traceability and pair-wise key establishment costs. We also summarize and compare some salient features in Table 2. As expected, NISC significantly outperforms ISC in our overall evaluation.

Table 2. Feature Comparison

Key Features	ISC	NISC
DoS Resistance (traceability)	Yes	Yes
Interaction among Sponsors Required	Yes	No
Random Shuffling Required	Yes	No
Reliable Broadcast Required	Yes	No

6.1   Complexity Analysis and Comparison

We summarize computation and communication complexities in Table 3. More specifically, for self-certification, NISC requires each sponsoring node P_i to perform $O(t)$ scalar-point-multiplication ($\mathcal{M}$) operations in ECC and the joining node P_{n+1} to perform only two Tate pairing ($\mathcal{P}$) operations in ECC. On the other hand, ISC requires each P_i to perform $O(t^2)$ $\mathcal{M}$ operations, and P_{n+1} to perform two $\mathcal{P}$ operations. For traceability, both the schemes require $O(t^2)$ $\mathcal{M}$-s and $O(t)$ $\mathcal{P}$-s with pre-computation. NISC is significantly more efficient than ISC for computing pairwise keys, since the former requires only $O(t)$ 160-bit modular multiplications, while the latter needs $O(t)$ $\mathcal{M}$ ECC operations. Note that, pairwise key establishment is a very frequent operation in a MANET, thus, its efficiency is extremely important.

As far as overall communication costs[4], NISC consumes $O(t \log q)$ and $O(t \log p)$ bits, while bandwidth consumption in ISC is $O(t^2 \log q)$ plus $O(t \log p)$ bits due to the interactive random shuffling procedure.

6.2   Experimental Setups

ISC and NISC protocols have been implemented over the popular OpenSSL library [27] and MIRACL [28] (optimized using Comba method). We now describe the experimental testbeds for measuring the performance of our proposed protocol. We ran experiments in a *real* wireless MANET environment and also measured energy costs for each scheme with power measuring system below.

Wireless Mobile Ad Hoc Networks. We used five laptop computers for our wireless experimental set-up: four laptop computers with Pentium-3 800 MHz

---

[4] We assume that the identity and the public key are $\log q$ bits long and $\log p$ bits long, respectively.

Table 3. Cost Comparison

Category			ISC	NISC
Computation	Self-Certification	$\mathcal{M}$	$t^2 + 2t + 1$	$3t$
		$\mathcal{P}$	2	2
	Traceability	$\mathcal{M}$	$2t^2 + 3t$	$2t^2 + 3t$
		$\mathcal{P}$	$2t$	$2t$
	Key Establishment	$\mathcal{M}$	t	0
		$\mathcal{P}$	0	0
Communication	Round	broadcast	1	1
		unicast	$t^2 + 2t$	t
	Bandwidth	$\log q$-bit	$2t^2 + 2t$	$3t$
		$\log p$-bit	$3t$	$3t$

$\mathcal{M}$: scalar-point-multiplication in ECC, $\mathcal{P}$: Tate pairing operation in ECC

CPU and 256 MB memory and one laptop computer with Mobile Pentium 1.8 GHz CPU and 512 MB memory. Each machine is configured with 802.11b in ad-hoc mode and runs the Optimized Link State Routing protocol (OLSR) [29]. Each machine runs Linux kernel 2.4.

Power Measurement Systems. To measure consumption of battery power, we configured the following equipment, as shown in Figure 3. The test machine was an iPAQ (model H5555) running Linux (Familiar-0.7.2). The CPU on the iPAQ is a 400 MHz Intel XScale with 48MB of flash memory and 128MB of SDRAM. In order to obtain accurate power measurements, we removed the battery from the iPAQ during the experiment and placed a resistor in series with power supply. We used a National Instruments PCI DAQ (Data AcQuisition) board to sample the voltage drops across the resistor to calculate the current at 1000 samples per second.

6.3   Test Methodology

Parameter Selection. To perform fair comparisons, we consider the following parameters. The size of the parameter q was set to be 160-bit and p to be 1024-bit. For more details, we used the elliptic curve E defined by the equation: $y^2 = x^3 + 1$ over $\mathbb{F}_p$ with $p > 3$ a prime satisfying $p = 2 \ (mod) \ 3$ and q being a prime factor[5] of $p + 1$. The parameter p is a 512-bit prime in order to make sure that the security of pairing $\hat{e}$ is equivalent to the security as in finite field of 1024 bits[6]. The measurements were performed with different threshold values

---

[5] By Euler's theorem, q must divide $\#E(\mathbb{F}_p)$. For the curve $y^2 = x^3 + 1$, $\#E(\mathbb{F}_p) = p + 1$.

[6] The $\mathbb{G}_1$ is a subgroup of points generated by $\mathbb{P}$ such that $\mathbb{P} \in E(\mathbb{F}_p)$. The $\mathbb{G}_2$ is a subgroup of $\mathbb{F}_{p^2}^*$ of order q. The bilinear map $\hat{e} : \mathbb{G}_1 \times \mathbb{G}_1 \to \mathbb{G}_2$ is the well-known Tate pairing. Computing discrete log in $\mathbb{F}_{p^2}$ is sufficient for computing discrete log in $\mathbb{G}_1$. Therefore, for proper security of discrete log in $\mathbb{F}_{p^2}$ the prime p should be at least 512-bits long (so that the group size is at least 1024-bits long).

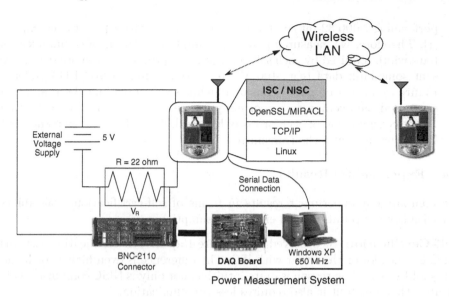

Fig. 3. Power Measurement Testbed

t from 1 to 9. We used 1024-bit RSA signature algorithm with the fixed public exponent $65537(= 2^{16} + 1)$ for protocol message authentication. All experiments were repeated $1,000$ times for each measurement in order to get fairly accurate average results.

Test Cases. We measured the respective costs of self-certification, traceability, pairwise key establishment, and energy consumption.

1. **Self-Certification.** To measure the self-certification cost, four laptops with same computing power were used as current nodes and the high-end laptop was used as the joining/new node. In this experiment, each node (except the joining node) was emulated by a daemon and each machine was running up to three daemons. We then measured total processing time between sending of JOIN_REQ by the prospective node and receiving (plus verification) of acquired secret shares. The measurement results thus include the average computation time of the basic operations as well as communication costs, such as packet en/decoding time, network delay, etc.
2. **Traceability.** We measured the computation time for tracing partial shares that are received during the self-configuration protocol. We measured this cost using pre-computed values as much as possible.
3. **Pairwise Key Establishment.** We measured the processing time for a node to compute a pairwise key on the high-end laptop. Note that no communication is involved in this measurement.
4. **Energy Consumption.** This experiment is quite tricky to measure fairly. It is meaningless to measure energy consumption with all the test cases above. However, it is well known that, in many small devices such as low-end MANET nodes or sensors, sending a single bit is roughly equivalent to

performing 1,000 32-bit computations in terms of batter power consumption [1]. Therefore, we measured power consumption in terms of communication bandwidth required by each self-configuration protocol. For more details, we sent some bulk data (e.g., 100 Mbytes) from a single iPAQ PDA (refer to Figure 3), measured power consumed while sending out this data, and then computed the average power consumption per bit. After that, we calculated power consumption of each protocol by multiplying this measurement result by the bit length of the transmitted data.

6.4   Experimental Results

We compare our experiment results in terms of self-certification, traceability, pairwise key computation, and energy consumption.

Self-Certification. As observed from Figure 4(a), the self-certification cost with NISC is much lower than that with ISC. The difference is even higher for higher threshold values. The reason is quite intuitive: not only is NISC computationally cheaper than ISC, but it also requires less communication.

Traceability. Figure 4(b) displays traceability costs for the two protocols. Even in the worst case, NISC is as good as ISC for performing the (very infrequent) operation of tracing malicious nodes.

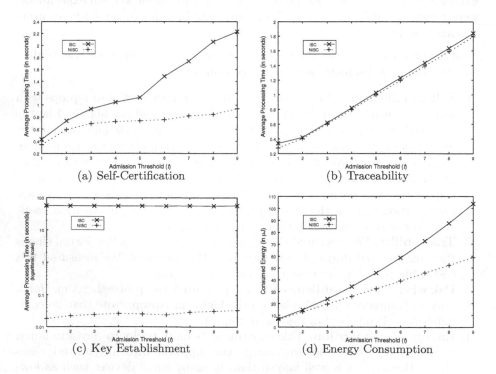

(a) Self-Certification

(b) Traceability

(c) Key Establishment

(d) Energy Consumption

Fig. 4. Experimental Results

Pairwise Key Establishment. Figure 4(c) shows that NISC is significantly more efficient than ISC for computing pairwise keys. This result was actually expected because in NISC the pairwise key computation requires only $O(t)$ multiplications where the modular size is 160 bits. In contrast, ISC requires $O(t)$ exponentiations with a modular size of 1024 bits as well as $O(t)$ multiplications with 160-bit modulus.

Energy Consumption. Energy consumption results for self-certification operation are plotted in Figure 4(d). These results in Figure 4(d) clearly illustrate that NISC is much more energy-efficient than ISC.

7   Conclusion

In this paper, we proposed NISC, a fully non-interactive self-certification protocol by novel combination of bi-variate polynomial secret sharing and threshold BLS signature scheme. We demonstrated from theoretical and experimental evaluation that NISC is more efficient than previous mechanism, based on uni-variate polynomial secret sharing and threshold BLS signature, in terms of computation, communication, and energy consumption.

Acknowledgments

We are in debt to Nitesh Saxena and Gene Tsudik for making this work possible and their insightful comments on it. We would like to thank the anonymous reviewers for their valuable suggestions.

References

1. Barr, K., Asanovic, K.: Energy Aware Lossless Data Compression. In: ACM International Conference on Mobile Systems, Applications, and Services. (2003) 231–244
2. Kong, J., Zerfos, P., Luo, H., Lu, S., Zhang, L.: Providing Robust and Ubiquitous Security Support for MANET. In: IEEE International Conference on Network Protocols. (2001) 251–260
3. Kong, J., Luo, H., Xu, K., Gu, D.L., Gerla, M., Lu, S.: Adaptive Security for Multi-level Ad-hoc Networks. In: Wiley Journal of Wireless Communications and Mobile Computing. Volume 2. (2002) 533–547
4. Luo, H., Zerfos, P., Kong, J., Lu, S., Zhang, L.: Self-securing Ad Hoc Wireless Networks. In: IEEE Symposium on Computers and Communications. (2002) 567–574
5. Narasimha, M., Tsudik, G., Yi, J.H.: On the Utility of Distributed Cryptography in P2P and MANETs: The Case of Membership Control. In: IEEE International Conference on Network Protocols. (2003) 336–345
6. Saxena, N., Tsudik, G., Yi, J.H.: Admission Control in Peer-to-Peer: Design and Performance Evaluation. In: ACM Workshop on Security of Ad Hoc and Sensor Networks. (2003) 104–114

7. Saxena, N., Tsudik, G., Yi, J.H.: Identity-based Access Control for Ad-Hoc Groups. In: International Conference on Information Security and Cryptology. Volume 3506 of LNCS. (2004) 362–379

8. Luo, H., Kong, J., Zerfos, P., Lu, S., Zhang, L.: URSA: Ubiquitous and Robust Access Control for Mobile Ad Hoc Networks. In: IEEE/ACM Transactions on Networking. Volume 12. (2004) 1049–1063

9. Jarecki, S., Saxena, N., Yi, J.H.: An Attack on the Proactive RSA Signature Scheme in the URSA Ad Hoc Network Access Control Protocol. In: ACM Workshop on Security of Ad Hoc and Sensor Networks. (2004) 1–9

10. Gennaro, R., Jarecki, S., Krawczyk, H., Rabin, T.: Robust Threshold DSS Signatures. In: CRYPTO'96. Volume 1070 of LNCS. (1996) 354–371

11. Shamir, A.: How to Share a Secret. In: Communications of the ACM. Volume 22. (1979) 612–613

12. Boldyreva, A.: Efficient Threshold Signatures, Multisignatures and Blind Signatures based on the Gap-Diffie-Hellman-Group Signature Scheme. In: International Workshop on Practice and Theory in Public Key Cryptography. Volume 2567 of LNCS. (2003) 31–46

13. Ben-Or, M., Goldwasser, S., Wigderson, A.: Completeness Theorems for Non-Cryptographic Fault-Tolerant Distributed Computation. In: ACM Symposium on the Theory of Computing. (1988) 1–10

14. Naor, M., Pinkas, B., Reingold, O.: Distibuted Pseudo-Random Functions and KDCs. In: EUROCRYPT'99. Volume 1592 of LNCS. (1999) 327–346

15. Blundo, C., Santis, A.D., Herzberg, A., Kutten, S., Vaccaro, U., Yung, M.: Perfectly-Secure Key Distribution for Dynamic Conferences. In: CRYPTO'92. Volume 740 of LNCS. (1999) 471–48

16. Liu, D., Ning, P.: Establishing Pairwise Keys in Distributed Sensor Networks. In: ACM Conference on Computers and Communication Security. (2003) 52–61

17. Saxena, N., Tsudik, G., Yi, J.H.: Efficient Node Admission for Short-lived Mobile Ad Hoc Networks. In: IEEE International Conference on Network Protocols. (2005) 269–278

18. Boneh, D., Lynn, B., Shacham, H.: Short Signatures from the Weil Pairing. In: ASIACRYPT'01. Volume 2248 of LNCS. (2001) 514–532

19. Kim, Y., Mazzocchi, D., Tsudik, G.: Admission Control in Peer Groups. In: IEEE International Symposium on Network Computing and Applications. (2003) 131–139

20. Gennaro, R., Jarecki, S., Krawczyk, H., Rabin, T.: Secure Distributed Key Generation for Discrete-Log Based Cryptosystems. In: EUROCRYPT'99. Volume 1592 of LNCS. (1999) 295–310

21. Boneh, D., Franklin, M.: Identity-based Encryption from the Weil Pairing. In: CRYPTO'01. Volume 2139 of LNCS. (2001) 213–229

22. Frey, G., Müller, M., Rück, H.G.: The Tate Pairing and the Discrete Logarithm Applied to Elliptic Curve Cryptosystems. In: IEEE Transactions on Information Theory. Volume 45. (1999) 1717–1719

23. Menezes, A.J., van Oorschot, P.C., Vanstone, S.A.: Handbook of Applied Cryptography. CRC Press (1997) ISBN 0-8493-8523-7.

24. Herzberg, A., Jarecki, S., Krawczyk, H., Yung, M.: Proactive Secret Sharing, Or How To Cope With Perpetual Leakage. In: CRYPTO'95. Volume 963 of LNCS. (1995) 339–352

25. Bracha, G.: An Asynchronous $\lfloor (n-1)/3 \rfloor$-resilient Consensus Protocol. In: ACM Symposium on Priniciples of Distributed Computing. (1984) 154–162
26. Press, W.H., Flannery, B.P., Teukolsky, S.A., Vetterling, W.T.: Numerical Recipes in C : The Art of Scientific Computing. Cambridge University Press (1992) ISBN 0-521-43108-5.
27. OpenSSL Project: (http://www.openssl.org)
28. MIRACL Library: (http://indigo.ie/ mscott)
29. OLSR Protocol: (http://menetou.inria.fr/olsr)

Self-adaptive Worms and Countermeasures

Wei Yu[1], Nan Zhang[2], and Wei Zhao[1]

[1] Department of Computer Science
Texas A&M University, College Station, TX 77843-3112
{weiyu, zhao}@cs.tamu.edu
[2] Department of Computer Science and Engineering
University of Texas at Arlington, Arlington, TX 76019-0015
nzhang@cse.uta.edu

Abstract. In this paper, we address issues related to defending against wide-spreading worms on the Internet. We study a new class of worms called the self-adaptive worms. These worms dynamically adapt their propagation patterns to defensive countermeasures, in order to avoid or postpone detection, and to eventually infect more computers. We show that existing worm detection schemes cannot effectively defend against these self-adaptive worms. To counteract these worms, we introduce a game-theoretic formulation to model the interaction between worm propagator and defender. We show that the effective integration of multiple defensive schemes (e.g., worm detection, forensics analysis) is critical for defending against self-adaptive worms. We propose different combinations of defensive schemes for different kinds of self-adaptive worms, and evaluate the performance of defensive schemes based on real-world traffic traces.

Keywords: Worm, Game theory.

1 Introduction

In this paper, we address issues related to defending against wide-spreading worms on the Internet. Worm is a malicious software program that propagates itself on the Internet to infect other computers (by remotely exploiting vulnerabilities in these computers). The ultimate goal of a worm is to infect as many computers as possible, such that the worm propagator can remotely control these infected computers and use them as resources to launch other attacks[1] [1], which may bring significant damage to the Internet [2].

Due to the substantial damage caused by wide-spreading worms, there has been extensive work on the modeling of worms and the design of defensive countermeasures. Most existing work makes a tacit assumption that a worm will always propagate itself at the highest possible speed. Nonetheless, some recently evolved worms contradict this assumption by intentionally reducing their propagation speed to avoid detection. For example, the "Atak" worm [3] and "self-stopping" worm [4] attempt to avoid detection by hibernating (i.e., stop propagating themselves) periodically. If a worm can successfully avoid detection, it can eventually infect more computers, and bring more damage to the Internet.

---

[1] A common example is distributed denial-of-service (DDoS) attack.

A.K. Datta and M. Gradinariu (Eds.): SSS 2006, LNCS 4280, pp. 548–562, 2006.

In order to model the threats from such worms, we introduce a new class of worms called *self-adaptive worms*. These worms dynamically adapt their propagation patterns to defensive countermeasures, with the objective to avoid or postpone detection, and to eventually infect more computers. Our contributions in this paper are two-fold:

- *Self-adaptive Worm Modeling:* We introduce a formal model of self-adaptive worm, and classify such worm into two categories, namely *static self-adaptive worm* and *dynamic self-adaptive worm*, respectively, based on the propagation growth rate of worm (i.e., the percentage of maximum propagation speed that a worm actually uses to propagate itself). Static self-adaptive worms propagate themselves with constant propagation growth rate. Dynamic self-adaptive worms vary their propagation growth rate over time.
- *Defensive Countermeasures and Game Theoretic Analysis:* We show that the integration of multiple defensive schemes can be used to effectively defend against self-adaptive worms. In particular, we consider three kinds of defensive schemes in this paper: the traditional threshold detection scheme [5],[6], the forensic traceback scheme [7],[8], and the spectrum-based detection scheme, which is first introduced in this paper. We show that the integration of first two schemes can be used to defend against static self-adaptive worms, while defending against dynamic self-adaptive worms requires the integration of all three schemes. Table 1 shows a summary of the results in this paper. In order to analyze the performance of defensive countermeasures, we introduce a game-theoretic formulation of the system, which models the dynamic interaction between the self-adaptive worms and the defensive countermeasures.

Table 1. Performance of Countermeasure Schemes

	VT	VT+TB	VT + TB+SA
Traditional worm	Effective	Effective	Effective
Static self-adaptive worm		Effective	Effective
Dynamic self-adaptive worm			Effective

VT: Threshold scheme
TB: Trace-back scheme
SA: Spectrum analysis scheme

To the best of our knowledge, this paper is the first to formally address worms that dynamically adapt their propagation pattern to defensive countermeasures. This paper is also the first to introduce an effective integration of different defensive schemes (including both worm detection and forensic analysis), and to use game-theoretic formulation to model the dynamic interaction between the worm propagator and the defensive countermeasure.

The rest of the paper is organized as follows. We briefly review the background and some related work in Section 2. In Section 3, we present the formulation and classification of self-adaptive worms, and demonstrate that existing detection schemes are not effective on defending against such worms. In Section 4, we introduce a game-theoretic formulation of the system that models the dynamic interaction between self-adaptive worms and defensive countermeasures. We present the defensive countermeasures against static self-adaptive worms and dynamic ones in Section 5 and Section 6, respectively. We evaluate the performance of our defensive countermeasures on real-world traffic traces in Section 7, and conclude the paper with some final remarks in Section 8.

2 Background and Related Work

In this section, we first introduce the basic propagation mechanisms of worms. Then, we briefly review some existing defensive countermeasure schemes.

2.1 Worm Propagation

Worm propagation on the Internet is an iterative process. Generally speaking, the propagation of a worm starts with a computer called the worm propagator. The worm propagator identifies vulnerable computers on the Internet, remotely exploits the vulnerability to obtain access to these computers, and then infect the computers. Once a computer is infected by the worm, the computer also starts propagating the worm to other computers on the Internet.

As we can see, in order to propagate itself on the Internet, a worm must be capable of identifying vulnerable computers that it can infect. Given the complicated Internet topology and the diversified nature of the vulnerability of computers, such identification can be hardly optimal in practice. A commonly used identification mechanism is Pure Random Scan (*PRS*) approach [9]. Based on this approach, a worm-infected computer continuously scans *random* IP addresses to identify vulnerable computers. Besides the PRS approach, there has also been work that allows a worm to carry a pre-determined "hit-list", which contains a list of (possibly) vulnerable computers [10]. Note that the number of computers in the hit-list is limited by the size of the worm. Thus, the hit-list may not be able to support the wide propagation of a worm. Since we focus on wide-spreading worm in this paper, we do not consider such propagation mechanism in our system.

2.2 Defensive Countermeasures

In order to reduce the damage brought by worms, there are two kinds of defensive schemes that have been proposed. One is the worm detection, which focuses on the detection of propagating worms on the Internet. Once a propagating worm is detected, many actions can be done to stop or slow down worm propagation. For example, patches can be released to fix the vulnerability, worm scan traffic can be throttled, and infected computer can be quarantined [9],[11].

The other scheme is forensic analysis, which aims to identify the original worm propagator. Once the worm propagator is found, law enforcement can punish the propagator. If successfully deployed, this scheme can prevent worm attacker from launching the attack. We briefly review previous work on these two kinds of defensive countermeasures respectively as follows.

Worm Detection. Many detection mechanisms have been proposed [12], [13]. A common worm detection mechanism requires one control center and numerous distributed monitors on the Internet [14],[15]. The distributed monitors can be honeypots [16] and Internet sinks [15], and are located at hosts, gateways, and border routers of local networks. These monitors passively record abnormal scan traffic (e.g., connection attempts to unavailable IP address and/or restricted service ports), and periodically transmit the logs to the control center, which processes such log files and determines if there is a worm propagating on the monitored network.

As we can see, the control center relies on the collected scan traffic data to determine whether there is an on-going propagation of wide-spreading worm. Most existing worm detection mechanisms measure the average volume of abnormal scan traffic, and generate an alert if the volume exceeds a predetermined threshold [6]. We call these mechanisms as mean-threshold mechanisms. Some other schemes measure the variance [5] or trend [17] of abnormal scan traffic.

Forensic Analysis. The objective of forensic analysis is to identify the worm propagator accountable for the malicious acts [7], [8]. Most existing work uses a random walk scheme to identify the origin of worm propagation [7], [8]. In order to enable forensic analysis, the defender must be capable of analyzing audit data on attack reconstruction (i.e., analyzing the structure of worm propagation to determine the attack origin). There have been many real cases where the worm propagator was traced back, arrested, and prosecuted based on electronic evidence [18].

3   Self-adaptive Worms

In this section, we introduce self-adaptive worms that adapt their propagation patterns based on the defensive countermeasure in order to avoid or postpone detection. We first introduce the propagation growth rate of a worm. Based on the growth rate, we define self-adaptive worms and classify them into two categories: static self-adaptive worms and dynamic self-adaptive worms.

3.1   Propagation Growth Rate

Recall that during worm propagation, a worm first scans the network to identify vulnerable computers, and then infects the identified vulnerable computers. Previous work tacitly assumes that all worms scan the network with the maximum possible speed (i.e., scan as many computers as possible in every single time slot). Based on this assumption, previous work detects worm by monitoring the number of illegal scans in a single time slot, and then issues an alert when the number exceeds a predetermined threshold [5], [6].

While the assumption is intuitive as the ultimate goal of a worm is to infect as many computers as possible, we find that a worm can actually avoid or postpone detection (by the defensive countermeasure) if the worm reduces the number of scans in a single time slot. With the avoided (or postponed) detection, the worm can eventually infect more computers.

Let S be the maximum number of scans a worm host (i.e., an infected computer) can perform in a single time slot. We use *propagation growth rate* p to denote the percentage of such maximum speed that a worm propagator actually uses to propagate a worm. That is, the number of scans a worm host actually performs in a single time slot is $p \cdot S$. Apparently, the worms studied in previous work have $p = 1$, as previous work assumes that a worm always scans computers on the Internet at the maximum speed.

We now briefly show the propagation pattern of a worm with $p < 1$. Let N be the number of vulnerable computers on the Internet. Let $f(t)$ be the number of computers the worm has infected at time t. Note that $f(0) = 1$. Recall that S is the maximum number of scans a worm host can perform in a single time slot. Let $\beta = S/V$, where V is the total number of IP addresses on the Internet. We have

$$\frac{df(t)}{dt} = \beta \cdot f(t) \cdot p \cdot [N - f(t)], \tag{1}$$

where $df(t)/dt$ is the number of computers newly infected at time t. Note that $df(t)/dt$ is statistically in proportion to the number of illegal scans detected by the detection system. When the mean-threshold detection scheme is used, the system will issue an alert when $f(t) \cdot p \geq T_R$, where T_R is the detection threshold. As we can see, when $f(t) < N/2$, the smaller p is, the larger $f(t)$ is at the moment when the worm is detected. That is, a worm can (eventually) infect more computers by reducing p.

Figure 1 shows the number of computers that a Pure Random Scan (PRS) worm can eventually infect when the mean-threshold and variance-threshold detection mechanisms [6],[5] are used, respectively. In the figure, we assume that the number of vulnerable computers on the Internet is 350,000. We show the cases where the propagation growth rate changes from 0.03 to 1. As we can see, a worm can actually infect more computers when p is smaller.

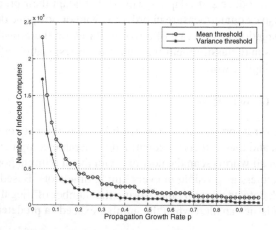

Fig. 1. Number of Infected Computers vs. Propagation growth rate

Note that the propagation growth rate is not necessarily constant during worm propagation. In many cases, the worm propagator may deliberately change p during propagation in order to avoid or postpone detection. In this paper, we consider the cases where p

changes over time t. That is, the worm records the time it starts propagating. By counting the time passed since the beginning of the propagation, each infected computer can accurately estimate the number of infected computers as well as the number of scans sent by such computers. As such, the worm can control the number of scans (to avoid detection) by changing the propagation growth rate p over time t.

3.2 Classification of Self-adaptive Worms

We define *self-adaptive worms* as worms with propagation growth rate not always equal to 1. Suppose t_D is the time when a worm is detected. Formally speaking, a worm is self-adaptive if and only if there exists time t_0 which satisfies

- $0 < t_0 < t_D$, and
- the propagation growth rate of the worm at time t_0: $p(t_0) < 1$.

Recall that a worm can arbitrarily change its propagation growth rate p over time t. In this paper, we classify self-adaptive worms into two categories, namely static self-adaptive worms and dynamic self-adaptive worms, respectively, based on the change of propagation growth rate.

- Static self-adaptive worms are self-adaptive worms that have constant $p(t)$. That is, for all $t_0, t_1 < t_D$ with $t_0 \neq t_1$, there is $p(t_0) = p(t_1) < 1$.
- Dynamic self-adaptive worms are self-adaptive worms that have variant $p(t)$ over time t. That is, there must exist $t_0, t_1 < t_D$ with $t_0 \neq t_1$, such that $p(t_0) \neq p(t_1)$.

Table 2 depicts our classification of worms. As we can see, a self-adaptive worm is either static or dynamic. In particular, the "Atak" worm [3] and the "self-stopping" worm [4] mentioned in Section 1 are special cases of dynamic self-adaptive worms, as their propagation growth rates are changing between 0 and 1 over time.

Table 2. Classification of Wide-Spreading Worms

Options	Description
$p(t) = 1$	Traditional worm
$0 < p(t) = c < 1$	Static self-adaptive worm
$p(t)$ varies over time	Dynamic self-adaptive worm

4 System Model with Self-adaptive Worms

As we can see, a self-adaptive worm can adapt its propagation growth rate to the defensive countermeasure, in order to avoid or postpone detection. In order to model the interaction between the two parties (i.e., worm propagator and defender), we introduce a game-theoretic formulation of the system. We first present the objective and strategies of each party. Then we show the game-theoretic model of the interaction between the two parties.

4.1 Basic Notions

Recall that we suppose there are N vulnerable computers on the Internet. Also recall that $\beta = S/V$, where S is the number of scans a worm host can perform within a single time slot, and V is the total number of IP addresses on the Internet.

Recall that a worm propagator intends to infect as many computers as possible. Note that it does not make much sense for a worm to propagate for an infinite amount of time. Therefore, we assume that the objective of a worm propagator is to infect as many computers as possible by a pre-determined time t_E, given the moment that the worm starts propagating as time 0. When a worm detection mechanism (e.g., threshold detection scheme in Section 2.2) is employed, we use t_D to denote the time when the worm is detected. Apparently, the detection scheme is only effective when $0 \leq t_D < t_E$.

When a trace-back scheme is in place, we assume that the original worm propagator can be tracked back if and only if at time $\max(0, t_D - t_B)$, the number of infected computers is less than or equal to m. That is, the trace-back scheme can trace back up to t_B amount of time based on the network trace, and is capable of identifying the worm propagator from m computers based on more comprehensive analysis on the log files related to the m computers.

4.2 Parties

There are two parties in the system: the worm propagator and the defender. The worm propagator has two objectives. One is to maximize the number of infected computers. The other is to avoid being traced back and punished for its malicious actions. Different worm propagators may have different priorities on these two objectives. Nonetheless, it is commonly believed that most worm propagators on the Internet consider the penalty of being traced back to be substantially more than the benefits they may receive from the worm propagation [7],[8]. Thus, we assume that a worm propagator will *not* propagate the worm if it knows that it will be traced back with probability more than P_R. In this paper, for the sake of simplicity, we assume that $P_R = 50\%$.

Formally speaking, the objective of the worm propagator is to maximize U_A, which satisfies

$$U_A = \begin{cases} 0, & \text{if traced back with probability of more than 50\%;} \\ f(\min\{t_E, t_D\}), & \text{otherwise.} \end{cases} \quad (2)$$

Recall that t_E is the maximum propagation time of the worm, and t_D is the time when the worm is detected. We refer to U_A as the *utility function* of the worm propagator.

The defender also has two objectives. One is to minimize the number of infected computers. The other is to minimize the probability that a detection alarm is falsely triggered when there is no worm propagation on the Internet. In our system model, we assume that the worm propagator must ensure the *false alarm rate* Λ (i.e., the probability that a false worm alarm is triggered when the system is not under worm attack) to be lower than a predetermined threshold δ.

Formally speaking, the objective of the defender is to maximize

$$U_D = \begin{cases} -\infty, & \text{if } \Lambda > \delta; \\ -U_A, & \text{otherwise.} \end{cases} \quad (3)$$

We refer to U_D as the utility function of the defender.

4.3 Strategies

We now present the strategies of the two parties in the system. The strategy of the worm propagator is to determine the propagation growth rate p. Recall that as we mentioned in Section 3, the worm propagator can choose either to use a constant propagation growth rate p or to vary p over time t.

The strategy of the defender is to determine the defensive countermeasures. Recall that as we mentioned in Section 2.2, we consider two kinds of defensive countermeasures: worm detection and forensic analysis schemes (i.e., trace-back). As such, the defender needs to determine the threshold T_R for the detection scheme and the (maximum) trace-back time t_B for the forensics analysis scheme. Since the trace-back time is commonly determined by the traffic volume of the network as well as the computational power of the defensive system, we assume that the defender cannot change t_B. Thus, in our system model, the strategy of the defender is to determine the detection threshold T_R.

4.4 Game Formulation

We formulate the system as a two-player non-cooperative game. The worm propagator and the defender are the two players in the game. The game is non-cooperative because the two players are in opposition and are unlikely to make any binding agreement when choosing their strategies. As in many security studies, we make an conservative assumption that the worm propagator has full knowledge of the strategy taken by the defender. Nonetheless, the defender has no knowledge about the strategy of the worm propagator. We assume that both players are rational, in that each player always chooses the strategy that maximizes its utility function.

5 Defense Against Static Self-adaptive Worms

In this section, we consider systems with traditional worms (with $p = 1$) and static self-adaptive worms (with constant $p \in (0,1)$). Recall that the worm propagator can be traced back if and only if at time $\max(0, t_D - t_B)$, the number of infected computers is less than or equal to m. Also recall that the worm propagator will not propagate a worm if it knows that it will be traced back with probability of more than 50%. We have the following theorem [19].

Theorem 1. *Let T_R be the minimum detection threshold to satisfy the requirement on false alarm rate $\Lambda \leq \delta$ (recall that δ is the threshold defined in Section 4.2). The propagator of a static self-adaptive worm will not propagate the worm if*

$$t_B \geq t_E \left(1 - \frac{1}{\log T_R} \log \frac{mN}{N - m} \right) \approx t_E \left(1 - \frac{\log m}{\log T_R} \right). \tag{4}$$

When t_B does not satisfy the above condition, the worm propagator will choose p that satisfies

$$f(t_E) \cdot p = T_R. \tag{5}$$

Recall that in order to achieve a smaller false alarm rate, we have to set a larger T_R. As we can see from (5) (note that $f(t_E)$ is a monotonically increasing function of p), the larger T_R is, the larger p will be, and the more computers a worm can eventually infect. Thus, in order to achieve a smaller false alarm rate, we have to afford a larger number of infected computers.

6   Defense Against Dynamic Self-adaptive Worms

In this section, we consider systems with dynamic self-adaptive worms. That is, the worm propagator can change the propagation growth rate p over time t, to better adapt to the defensive countermeasure and avoid detection and trace-back. We first show that the combination of threshold scheme and trace-back scheme no longer works with the presence of dynamic self-adaptive worms. After that, we introduce a new defensive scheme called *spectrum detection scheme*. We show that the combination of all three schemes can effectively defend against dynamic self-adaptive worms.

6.1   Performance of Threshold and Trace-Back Schemes

We now show that in order for the combination of threshold detection scheme and trace-back scheme to effectively defend against dynamic self-adaptive worms, the trace-back time must be nearly equal to the predetermined worm propagation deadline t_E. Since such a long trace-back time is hard, if not impossible, to realize in practical systems, the combination of threshold detection scheme and trace-back scheme cannot defend against dynamic self-adaptive worms effectively. We have the following theorem [19].

Theorem 2. *The propagator of a dynamic self-adaptive worm will not propagate the worm if and only if $t_B \geq t_E - \log m/\beta \approx t_E$.*

Apparently, the threshold detection scheme is no longer effective with the presence of dynamic self-adaptive worms. In order to effectively defend against dynamic self-adaptive worms, we have to prevent the worm from fast propagating itself at the initial stage of worm propagation. This is the motivation for us to propose the spectrum-based detection scheme presented below.

6.2   Spectrum-Based Detection Scheme

In the following, we introduce a spectrum-based detection scheme. This method has been widely used to distinguish signal from noise [20]. Thus, the basic idea of spectrum-based detection scheme is to detect a dynamic self-adaptive worm by distinguishing the worm attack traffic (as signal) from the background traffic (as noise).

Recall from Section 2.2 that, the worm detection system features a control center that collects reports from monitors distributed on the Internet. To conduct the spectrum analysis, we consider a detection sliding window W_d which includes $q(>1)$ continuous sampling windows (each of size W_s). Hence, within a sliding window W_d, there are q detection samples denoted by $(X(i-q-1), X(i-q-2), \ldots, X(i))$ recorded at time

i, where $X(i-j-1)$ ($j \in (1,q)$) is the $j-th$ data from time periods $i-j-1$ to $i-j$. The workflow of spectrum-based scheme includes following three steps:

1) Data Filter. We use a low-pass filter, e.g., weighted moving average filter [21], to filter high frequency terms in data series, e.g., $(X(i-q-1), X(i-q-2), \ldots, X(i))$. The output of digital filter becomes $(X'(i-q-1), X'(i-q-2), \ldots, X'(i))$.

2) Obtain Power Spectral Density (PSD) and Spectral Flatness Measure (SFM). We calculate autocorrelation of $X'(t)$ (output of previous step) as

$$R_{X'}(L) = E[X'(t)X'(t+L)]. \tag{6}$$

In (6), $R_{X'}(L)$ is the correlation of worm detection data in an interval L. If a fast growth or recurring behavior exists, a *Fourier* transform of the autocorrelation function of $R_{X'}(L)$ can reveal such behaviors. Using the *Discrete Fourier Transform (DFT)*, we derive the *PSD* function as follows,

$$\sum_{n=0}^{N-1} (R_{X'}[L]) \cdot e^{-j2\pi K \cdot n/N}, \tag{7}$$

where $K = 0, 1, \ldots, N-1$.

In order to distinguish worm attack traffic and non-worm traffic, we use *SFM* as the detection feature, which is defined as the ratio of the geometric mean to the arithmetic mean of the *PSD* coefficients [21]. It can be expressed as,

$$SFM = \frac{[\prod_{k=1}^{N} S(f_k)]^{\frac{1}{N}}}{\frac{1}{N}\sum_{k=1}^{N} S(f_k)}, \tag{8}$$

where $S(f_k)$ is the kth *PSD* coefficient for the *PSD* obtained from the results in (7). *SFM* is a well-known measure for discriminating frequencies in applications such as voice frame detection in speech recognition [20]. Low values of *SFM* imply concentration of data at narrow spectrum ranges.

3) Detection. With the *SFM* as the detection feature, we apply following simple detection rule. If the *SFM* value is smaller than a T_M (predetermined threshold value for *SFM*), then a worm detection is flagged. The value of threshold T_M is fittingly set based on the popular knowledge of PDF of *SFM* values that correspond to the background traffic. Based on the *PDF* of *SFM* values of background traffic, we set a T_M to obtain a reasonable detection rate and false alarm rate. The effectiveness of spectrum-based scheme can be justified based on the fact that the worm propagates faster in the early stage, and thus the *PSD* of low frequency bands is much higher than other frequency bands. Please refer to [19] for the detailed analysis.

6.3 Performance of Threshold, Trace-Back, and Spectrum-Based Detection Schemes

With the spectrum-based detection scheme, we have the following result. Suppose that the spectrum-based detection scheme can successfully detect a worm with more than 50% probability at time $t_S(p)$ if the worm propagates with p from time 0 to time $t_S(p)$.

Recall that the number of infected computers by a static self-adaptive worm with p at time t is

$$f(t) = \frac{Ne^{\beta \cdot p \cdot t}}{e^{\beta \cdot p \cdot t} + N}. \tag{9}$$

Apparently, the optimal strategy for the worm propagator is to follow the greedy strategy, which is to choose the largest p possible (i.e., without being detected) before the number of infected computers reaches m. After that, the only purpose of the worm propagator is to maximize the number of infected computers. Note that if worm propagator chooses p below a certain (very low) level, other human-scale countermeasures (e.g., signature-based virus detection, machine quarantine) may become effective to disrupt the propagation.

When the adversary chooses this optimal strategy, the number of computers infected by a dynamic self-adaptive worm at time t satisfies

$$f(t) \leq \int_{p_0}^{1} \frac{Ne^{\beta \cdot p \cdot dt_S(p)}}{e^{\beta \cdot p \cdot dt_S(p)} + \frac{N - f(t_S(p - dp))}{f(t_S(p - dp))}}. \tag{10}$$

where p_0 is the maximum value that satisfies $t_S(p_0) \geq t$.

As we can see, (10) is hard to solve. Nonetheless, we can estimate an upper bound on $f(t)$ by sampling several discrete values of p. For example, when $0 \leq t \leq t_S(0.5)$, there is

$$f(t) \leq \frac{Ne^{\beta \cdot t_S(1)}}{e^{\beta \cdot t_S(1)} + N} + \frac{Ne^{0.75 \cdot \beta \cdot t_S(0.75)}}{e^{0.75 \cdot \beta \cdot t_S(0.75)} + \frac{N - f(t_S(1))}{f(t_S(1))}} + \frac{Ne^{0.5 \cdot \beta \cdot t_S(0.5)}}{e^{0.5 \cdot \beta \cdot t_S(0.5)} + \frac{N - f(t_S(0.75))}{f(t_S(0.75))}}. \tag{11}$$

where $f(t_S(1))$ and $f(t_S(0.75))$ can be estimated by the first and second item of (11), respectively.

By solving (11), we can derive an upper bound on the value of $f(t)$. In the same manner, we can derive a lower bound on minimum value of t_A such that $f(t_A \geq m)$. Let such lower bound be $\tilde{t}_A$. Apparently, the worm propagator will not propagate the worm if $\tilde{t}_A + t_B \geq t_E$.

7   Performance Evaluation

In this section, we present the experimental results of our system based on real-world trace data. In particular, we evaluate the performance of our defensive countermeasures with the presence of self-adaptive worms.

7.1   Evaluation Methodology

Evaluation Metrics. As we mentioned in Section 4.2, all worm detection mechanisms have to make a tradeoff between worm detection accuracy and false alarm. In the experiments, we require the false alarm rate to be less than or equal to 0.1%. Based on this requirement, we measure the performance of worm detection by the *maximum infection ratio*, which is defined as the ratio of the number of infected computers to the total number of vulnerable computers at the moment when the worm is successfully detected. Recall that all evaluation schemes are in Table 1.

Experiment Setup. We used the real world DShield logs provided by SANs Institute which include the detail traces from 01/01/2005 to 01/15/2005 [2]. The traces used in our experiments contain log files which have over 80 million scan records and total size exceeds 80 GB [22]. We developed the tool to parse the data and provide the data input for our experiment. The input data has the format in terms of the number of scans for particular port in a given time window, i.e., 5 min, 20 min, etc. With the 15 days trace serving as real-world scan traffic (e.g., port 8080), we add the simulated worm attack traffic by using the parameters $p(t)$ defined in Section 3.

In our experiment, we set the total number of vulnerable computers on the Internet as $350,000$ which as described earlier. Using the unit of the scan rate S as number of scans per unit, we set different scan rates for each of the infected computers The scan rate (≥ 0) is predetermined assuming a normal distribution $N(S_m, S_\sigma^2)$ with S_m and $S_\sigma^2 \in (20, 70)$, similar to the way described in [17]. We set trace-back parameters: $m = 250$, 500 and $T_B \in [3000, 8000]$ units. The detection sampling window W_s is set to 5 units and the detection sliding window W_d is set to be incremental from 128 units to 255 units. We choose detection sampling window to be short enough and detection sliding window to be long enough to provide enough sampling and detection accuracy.

7.2 Performance of Detection Schemes

We evaluate the performance of detection schemes on static self-adaptive and dynamic self-adaptive worms, respectively. Recall that in all experiments, the false alarm rate is no more than 0.1%.

We first compare the performance of our approach with that of the previous approaches when static self-adaptive worm exists in the system. In particular, we perform the experiments when $p = 0.05$, 0.1, and 0.2. For previous approaches, we use the threshold detection scheme in [6] as the example. Note that volume variance-based scheme in [5] shows the similar results. Recall that in order to defend against static self-adaptive worms, we use a combination of threshold scheme and trace back scheme (*VT+TB* in short). Thus, the performance of our approach also depends on the maximum trace-back time that the system can afford. We evaluate the performance of our scheme with different amount of trace-back time: $[3000, 7000]$ units. The result is shown in Figure 2. As we can see, our scheme can achieve a much less maximum infection ratio than previous schemes (e.g., VT only). That is, our scheme can defend against static self-adaptive worm more effectively.

For dynamic self-adaptive worms, it is impossible to enumerate all possible functions of p with time t. We evaluate the performance of our integrated scheme (*VT+TB+SA* in short) based on the Nash equilibrium of the game. Note that the Nash equilibrium represents a state whether neither the worm propagator nor the defender can benefit by unitarily changing its strategy. Therefore, the Nash equilibrium contains the strategy that a rational worm propagator will choose to propagate the worm. We thus measure the performance of worm detection by the maximum infection ratio when both the worm propagator and the defender use the strategies defined by the Nash equilibrium.

[2] The authors would like to thank SANs Internet Storm Center (ISC) for providing us valuable detailed traces [14].

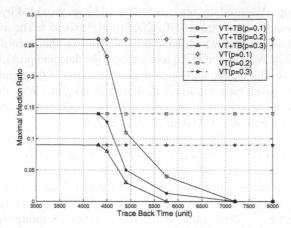

Fig. 2. Performance of countermeasures on static self-adaptive worm

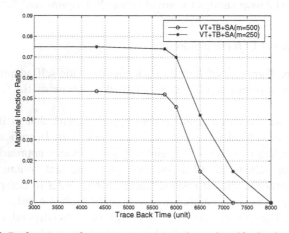

Fig. 3. Performance of countermeasures on dynamic self-adaptive worm

The results are shown in Figure 3. As we can see from the figure, our scheme can successfully bound the maximum infection ratio to 0.052 (when $m = 500$) and 0.073 (when $m = 250$).

8   Final Remarks

In this paper, we study a new class of worms called the self-adaptive worms, which adapt their propagation pattern to defensive countermeasures in order to avoid or postpone detection. Based on the degree of control on the propagation growth rate, we classify self-adaptive worms into two categories: static self-adaptive worms and dynamic ones. Since existing worm detection schemes are not sufficient to defend against these self-adaptive worms, we propose new defensive countermeasures in order to counter self-adaptive worms. We first introduce a game-theoretic formulation to model the dynamic interaction between the worm propagator and the defender. We show that an effective integration of multiple defensive schemes is critical for defending against self-adaptive worms. We present three schemes: traditional threshold detection scheme, trace-back scheme, and spectrum-based detection scheme. We show that the combination of the first two schemes can be used to defend against static self-adaptive worms while the combination of all three schemes can effectively defend against dynamic self-adaptive worms.

Acknowledgments. This work was supported in part by the National Science Foundation under Contracts 0081761, 0324988, 0329181, by the Defense Advanced Research Projects Agency under Contract F30602-99-1-0531, and by Texas A&M University under its Telecommunication and Information Task Force Program. Any opinions, findings, conclusions, and/or recommendations expressed in this material, either expressed or implied, are those of the authors and do not necessarily reflect the views of the sponsors listed above.

References

1. US-Cert: W32/MyDoom.B Virus. http://www.us-cert.gov/cas/techalerts/TA04-028A.html
2. Moore, D., Shannon, C., Brown, J.: Code-red: a case study on the spread and victims of an internet worm. Proceedings of the 2-th Internet Measurement Workshop (IMW), Marseille, France, November 2002.
3. Zdnet: Smart worm lies low to evade detection. http://news.zdnet.co.uk/internet/security/0,39020375,39160285,00.html
4. Voelker, G. M, Ma, J., Savage, S.: Self-stopping worms. Proceedings of the ACM Workshop on Rapid Malcode (WORM), Washington D.C, November 2005.
5. Wu, J., Vangala, S., Gao, L. X.:An effective architecture and algorithm for detecting worms with various scan techniques. Proceedings of the 11-th IEEE Network and Distributed System Security Symposium (NDSS), San Diego, CA, Febrary 2004.
6. Venkataraman, S., Song, D., Gibbons, P., Blum, A.: New streaming algorithms for superspreader detection. Proceedings of the 12-th IEEE Network and Distributed Systems Security Symposium (NDSS), San Diego, CA, Febrary 2005.
7. Sekar, V., Xie, Y., Maltz, D., Reiter, M., Zhang, H.: Toward a framework for internet forensic analysis. Proceeding of the 3-th Workshop on Hot Topics in Networks (HotNets-III), San Diego, CA, November 2004.
8. Xie, Y., Sekar, V., Maltz, D. A., Reiter, M. K., Zhang, H.: Worm origin identification using random moonwalks. Proceeding of the IEEE Symposium on Security and Privacy, Oakland, CA, May 2005.
9. Chen, Z. S. , Gao, L.X., Kwiat, K.: Modeling the spread of active worms. Proceedings of the IEEE Conference on Computer Communications (INFOCOM), San Francisco, CA, March 2003.
10. Staniford, S., Paxson, V., Weaver, N.: How to own the internet in your spare time. Proceedings of the 11-th USENIX Security Symposium, San Francisco, CA, August 2002.
11. Staniford, S.: Containment of scanning worms in enterprise networks. Journal of Computer Security, 2003.

12. Jung, J., Paxson, V., Berger, A. W., Balakrishnan H.: Fast portscan detection using sequential hypothesis testing. Proceedings of the 25-th IEEE Symposium on Security and Privacy, Oakland, CA, May 2004.
13. Kim, H., Karp, B.: Autograph: Toward automated, distributed worm signature detection. Proceedings of the 13-th USENIX Security Symposium, San Diego, CA, August 2004.
14. SANS: Internet Storm Center. http://isc.sans.org/
15. Yegneswaran, V., Barford, P., Plonka, D.: On the design and utility of internet sinks for network abuse monitoring. Proceeding of Symposium on Recent Advances in Intrusion Detection (RAID), Pittsburgh, PA, September 2003.
16. Spitzner, L.: Know Your Enemy: Honeynets, Honeynet Project. http://project.honeynet.org/papers/honeynet
17. Zou, C., Gong, W. B., Towsley, D., Gao, L. X.: Monitoring and early detection for internet worms. Proceedings of the 10-th ACM Conference on Computer and Communication Security (CCS), Washington DC, October 2003.
18. Sanders, T.: Turk and Moroccan arrested for Zotob worm author caught within two weeks. http://www.vnunet.com/vnunet/news/2141584/turk-moroccan-arrested-zotob
19. Yu, W., Zhang, N., Zhao, W.: Self-adaptive worm and countermeasures. Technical Report 2006-8-2, Computer Science Dept., Texas A&M Univ., August 2006.
20. Allen, R. L., Mills, D. W.: Signal Analysis: Time, Frequency, Scale, and Structure. Wiley and Sons, 2004.
21. Jayant, N. S., Noll, P.: Digital Coding of Waveforms. Prentice-Hall, 1984.
22. DShield.org: Distributed Intrusion Detection System. http://www.dshield.org/

Brief Announcement: Self-healing Algorithms for Reconfigurable Networks

Iching Boman, Jared Saia*, Chaouki T. Abdallah, and Edl Schamiloglu

University of New Mexico, Albuquerque, NM 87131, USA
saia@cs.unm.edu

Abstract. We present an algorithm to self-heal reconfigurable networks. This algorithm reconfigures the network during an attack to protect two critical invariants. First, it insures that the network remains connected. Second, it insures that no node increases its degree by more than $O(\log n)$. We prove that our algorithm can successfully maintain these invariants even for large networks under massive attack by a computationally unbounded adversary.

1 Motivation and Model

Many modern networks, such as peer-to-peer, are *reconfigurable* in the sense that their topology can change dynamically. We design self-healing algorithms that specifically exploit the reconfigurable nature of these networks. In contrast to many previous results, our algorithms: **provide more protection**: for example, we can guarantee that *all* nodes in the network stay connected instead of just almost all of the nodes; and **conserve resources**: for example, our algorithms devote no resources to defending the network until the time when an attack occurs.

Model: We assume an initially connected network over n nodes where every node knows not only its neighbors in the network but also the neighbors of its neighbors i.e. neighbor-of-neighbor (NoN) information. In particular, for all nodes x,y and z such that x is a neighbor of y and y is a neighbor of z, x knows z. We further assume that there is an *omniscient and computationally unbounded* adversary that is attacking the network. This adversary knows the network topology and our algorithms, and has the ability to delete carefully selected nodes from the network. However, we assume the adversary is constrained in that in any time step it can only delete a small number of nodes from the network. We further assume that after the adversary deletes some node x from the network, that the neighbors of x become aware of this deletion and that they have a small amount of time to react.

When a node x is deleted, we allow the neighbors of x to react to this deletion by adding some set of edges amongst themselves. We constrain these edges to only be between nodes which were previously neighbors of x. This is to ensure that, as much as possible, edges are added which respect locality information

---

* Contact author.

A.K. Datta and M. Gradinariu (Eds.): SSS 2006, LNCS 4280, pp. 563–565, 2006.

in the underlying network. We assume that there is very limited time to react to deletion of x before the adversary deletes another node. Thus, the algorithm for deciding which edges to add between the neighbors of x must be fast and localized.

2   Our Results

Our main results are summarized in the following two theorems. The theorems are proven in the full version of this paper (available at http://www.cs.unm.edu/~saia/sss06.pdf). We also include below a centralized version of the *Line* algorithm that is used to prove Theorem 1. We omit the discussion of how to make the algorithm distributed due to space limitations.

Theorem 1. *There exists an algorithm, which we call the* Line *algorithm with the following properties:*

- *Insures that the network is always connected*
- *Increases the degree of any vertex by at most* $\log_2 n$ *where* n *is the number of vertices in the network before attack*
- *Is* locality aware *in the sense that it adds edges only between nodes that have just had a neighbor deleted.*

Theorem 2. *Any locality aware algorithm that insures network connectivity can be forced to increase a node's degree by at least* $\log_3 n$.

2.1   The Line Algorithm

We first define several variables to aid with the description of our algorithm. For a fixed time step we define the following:

Line Algorithm:
Initialize each vertex v to have weight $w(v) = 1$ before the first timestep. Then, for each timestep:

- Let G, G' be the graphs at a fixed timestep as defined above, and let x be the node deleted by the adversary at the timestep.
- Let $N^*(x)$ be a maximal set of neighbors of x that are unconnected in $G - x$.

1. Let v_1, v_2 be vertices in $N^*(x)$ with maximal $W(*, x)$ values, i.e. $W(v_1, x) \geq W(v_2, x)$ and $\forall j \in N^*(x)$ s.t. $v_j \neq v_1$, $W(v_2, x) \geq W(v_j, x)$
2. $w(v_1) \leftarrow w(v_1) + w(x)$.
3. Add edges to connect the vertices in $N^*(x)$ in a line, L, such that $v1$ and $v2$ are the endpoints of L.

Fig. 1. The Line Algorithm

- Let $G(V, E)$ be the actual network at the given time step
- Let E' be the edges that have been added by the algorithm up to that time step. (note $E' \subseteq E$).
- Let $G' = (V, E')$. (We note, without proof here, that G' is a forest)
- Let each vertex v have a weight, $w(v)$.
- Let $T(v, x)$ be the tree in $G' - x$ that contains v.
- For vertices v and x, let $W(v, x) = \sum_{v' \in T(v,x)} w(v')$

Brief Announcement: Distributed Synthesis of Fault-Tolerance*

Borzoo Bonakdarpour, Sandeep S. Kulkarni, and Fuad Abujarad

Department of Computer Science and Engineering, Michigan State University
East Lansing, MI 48824, USA
{borzoo, sandeep, abujarad}@cse.msu.edu
http://www.cse.msu.edu/~{borzoo, sandeep, abujarad}

1 Introduction

Synthesis algorithms usually suffer from two factors of time and space complexity. In order to overcome the time complexity problem, several approaches have been proposed in the literature to incrementally *add* properties to existing verified programs (e.g., [1]). In order to overcome the space explosion problem, recently, an increasing interest in parallel and distributed techniques has emerged in the model checking community (e.g., [2, 3]). Such techniques parallelize the state space of a given model over a network or cluster of workstations and run a distributed model checking algorithm over the parallelized state space. On the other hand, the space explosion problem is still unaddressed in the context of automated program synthesis.

With this motivation, we concentrate on the problem of designing distributed algorithms for automated program synthesis. More specifically, we parallelize two synthesis algorithms (from [1]) for adding two levels of fault-tolerance, namely failsafe and masking, to existing fault-intolerant programs. We assume that programs are in the high atomicity model, where all processes can read and write all the program variables in one atomic step.

2 Algorithm Sketches

In this paper, we only focus on designing a distributed algorithm that runs over a distributed state space. In particular, we assume that parallelization of state space is already done using one of the known enumerative techniques in the literature. Precisely, we use the parallelization technique proposed by Garavel, Mateescu, and Smarandache [2] with some modifications tailored for the purpose of synthesis rather than model checking. Although there exist more efficient ways for parallel construction of state space (e.g., using abstract interpretation), we cannot trivially use them as a means for synthesizing programs. This is due to the fact that in synthesis (unlike model checking), we usually require full information about the system being synthesized, as we need to manipulate a program by removing or adding computations. Thus, we conservatively choose to develop distributed algorithms that run over a detailed parallelized explicit state space.

* This work was partially sponsored by NSF CAREER CCR-0092724, DARPA Grant OSURS01-C-1901, ONR Grant N00014-01-1-0744, NSF grant EIA-0130724, and a grant from Michigan State University.

A.K. Datta and M. Gradinariu (Eds.): SSS 2006, LNCS 4280, pp. 566–567, 2006.

Distributed Synthesis of Failsafe Fault-Tolerance. The essence of adding failsafe fault-tolerance consists of three parts: (1) a smallest fixpoint calculation for identifying the set of states from where safety may be violated, (2) a largest fixpoint calculation for computing the invariant of the failsafe program, and (3) emptiness checking of the synthesized program (to declare failure). Our distributed algorithm consists of a set of processes each running on one machine across the network. Each process consists of two threads, namely, Distributed_Add_failsafe and MessageHandler. Briefly, the thread Distributed_Add_failsafe is in charge of initiating local fixpoint calculations and synchronizing with other processes across the network. The thread MessageHandler is responsible for handling messages sent by other processes and invoking appropriate procedures. These messages inform a process whether a local state belongs to a global state predicate. For instance, if (1) a state s_0 is stored in machine i, (2) a state s_1 is stored in machine j, (3) there exists a fault transition (s_0, s_1), and (4) safety may be violated from s_1, then j sends a message to i indicating that s_0 belongs to a global state predicate from where safety of the program may be violated.

Distributed Synthesis of Masking Fault-Tolerance. Similar to the distributed addition of failsafe fault-tolerance, our algorithm for adding masking fault-tolerance consists of two threads. For adding masking fault-tolerance, we first generate a failsafe program and then add recovery paths from each state in the fault-span (the set states reachable by both program and fault transitions) to a state in the invariant (a state predicate which captures the normal behavior of the program). To this end, we identify two types of recovery paths: (1) recovery paths consist of only local program transitions, and (2) recovery paths consist of both local program transitions as well as cross transitions (transitions whose source and target states reside in different machines). In particular, we identify layers of states in the local fault-span corresponding to the number of steps of recovery paths. Since we require that recovery to the invariant must happen in a bounded number of steps, we identify the mentioned layers of states such that recovery transitions form no cycles in the fault-span. In other words, we construct a distributed tree whose leaves are states in the invariant in a distributed bottom-up fashion.

Implementation and performance. Since our synthesis algorithms are multithreaded and one of the threads are expected to be mostly busy with local computations, the computation time complexity is expected to be evenly distributed across the network. We plan to implement the distributed algorithms as an extension of our tool FTSyn, which is currently capable of synthesizing fault-tolerant programs using a single machine.

References

1. S. S. Kulkarni and A. Arora. Automating the addition of fault-tolerance. In *Formal Techniques in Real-Time and Fault-Tolerant Systems (FTRTFT)*, pages 82–93, 2000.
2. H. Garavel, R. Mateescu, and I. Smarandache. Parallel state space construction for model-checking. In *8th International SPIN Workshop on Model Checking of Software*, pages 217–234, 2001.
3. M. Leucker, R. Somla, and M. Weber. Parallel model checking for LTL, CTL*, and L_2^{μ}. In *International Workshop on Parallel and Distributed Model Checking (PDMC)*, 2003.

Brief Announcement: Exploration and Mitigation of Deafness Problems in Directional Antennas Based Wireless Ad-Hoc Networks

Kai Chen, Fan Jiang, and Zongyao Tang

Department of Computer Science, University of Science and Technology of China
Hefei, Anhui 230027, China
ckg@mail.ustc.edu.cn, fjiang@ustc.edu.cn, zytang@mail.ustc.edu.cn

1 Introduction

A switched antenna system can provide transmission or reception in any desired direction by an array of directional antennas. Directional antennas have tremendous potential for improving the performance of wireless ad hoc networks[1]. While offering higher spatial reuse and larger transmission range, they also pose new challenges. Deafness is one of such problems, which arises when a transmitter fails to communicate to its intended receiver either because the receiver is beamforming towards a different direction[2]. As we have identified, generally, there might be three kinds of deafness problems. First, deafness-I happens when the intended receiver is a transmitter or receiver engaged in an ongoing transmission. Second, deafness-II occurs when the intended receiver lies in the area covered by an ongoing transmission and hence becomes deaf to the transmitter. Third, unlike the former two kinds of deafness which occur because RTSs cannot be heard by the intended receivers, deafness-III arises when the receiver has actually received RTS but cannot reply CTS, because it is aware of that this CTS will interfere with an ongoing transmission nearby. If left unaddressed, deafness problems not only severely degrade the performance at MAC layer but also considerably influence the upper-layer protocols, which would probably offset the benefits of directional antennas.

2 The Proposed Methods

In practice, it is hard to completely resolve all kinds of deafness problems. However, we can elaborate some strategies to mitigate their severe impacts. To mitigate deafness-I, we propose to incorporate *start to send* (STS) frame and *deafness allocation vector* (DAV)[3]. STS has the same structure as RTS or CTS, aiming at informing the neighboring nodes of both sender and receiver of the imminent transmission, and DAV is used to record the deaf nodes in its neighborhood. Only after the RTS-CTS handshake is completed and the medium is reserved in corresponding directions, will both sender and receiver simultaneously send rotary STS, respectively, to inform their neighboring nodes of this imminent transmission. When receiving STS packets, each node in the vicinity will update

A.K. Datta and M. Gradinariu (Eds.): SSS 2006, LNCS 4280, pp. 568–569, 2006.

its DAV accordingly. To mitigate deafness-II, we suggest that the beam whose *directional network allocation vector* (DNAV) is set by RTS should be compulsorily blocked from receiving to avoid idle-reception[3]. To mitigate deafness-III, we propose to estimate the destination status (EDS)[3] before sending RTS, in other words, the transmitter must make sure that its intended receiver can reply back CTS without causing any collision to other ongoing transmission.

3 Simulation

We compare the performance of the proposed deafness mitigation methods (DM-MAC) with DMAC, circular-DMAC, and omni-directional 802.11 DCF. Fig.1(a, b) show the aggregate throughput of all the protocols with 4, 8 antenna beams, respectively. Strikingly, DM-MAC outperforms all other protocols. This is because DM-MAC has effective deafness avoidance strategies like STS, compulsory block, and EDS. Specifically, DM-MAC uses rotary STS to inform the neighborhood about the imminent transmission, differentiates deafness from collision by DAV, and suggests the beam be partially locked for deafness. However, other protocols have no such strategies, and are prone to get affected by deafness. Omnidirectional 802.11 performs smoothly in all scenarios because it has no deafness or sweeping delay. Furthermore, when the number of antenna beams increases from 4 to 8 (Fig.1(a to b)), we can see that DM-MAC achieves better performance by increased spatial reuse. Fig.1(c, d) show the average delay comparison. It is visible that DM-MAC has the lowest latency. Although using rotary STS frames may increase the overhead to some extent, we can infer that the delay consumed on rotation of STS could be eventually compensated by the improved throughput due to the effective deafness mitigation. Circular-DMAC and DMAC have high delay since deafness has not been well addressed therein.

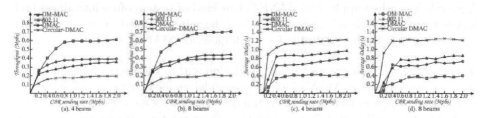

Fig. 1. Aggregate throughput and end-to-end delay comparison. (20 nodes are randomly distributed in a 300*300 meters square area).

References

1. R. Ramanathan, J. Redi, et.al, "Ad-hoc Networking with Directional Antennas: A Complete System Solution," IEEE J.SAC, vol. 23, no. 3, pp. 496-506, 2005.
2. R. R. Choudhury and N. H. Vaidya, "Deafness: A MAC Problem in Ad Hoc Networks when using Directional Antennas," in Proc. of IEEE ICNP, Oct, 2004.
3. K. Chen and F. Jiang, "Addressing Deafness Problems in Wireless Ad-hoc Networks with Directional Antennas," Technical report, USTC, Jun, 2006.

Brief Announcement: A Synthetic Public Key Management Scheme for Large-Scale MANET*

Pan Dong, Pei-dong Zhu, and Xi-cheng Lu

School of Computer, National University of Defense Technology,
Changsha, Hunan province, China
{pandong, pdzhu, xclu}@nudt.edu.cn**

Abstract. We introduce a new MANET structure model - party model - for the large scale MANET environment. For the party model MANET, we propose a new synthetic public key management scheme which applies web-of-trust and hierarchical trust simultaneously. The web-of-trust is used to design high efficient authentication between two nodes from the same party, and the frequent cooperation and communication inside a party can help to improve the security of authentication. In order to prevent falsification attack in remote authentication, we apply the hierarchical trust to establish CA in each party and use CA's certificate as the trust intermediary. In the whole, our scheme can get a good tradeoff among security, overhead and flexibility.

Problem Description. In our view, there are two trust models to build key management (KM): hierarchical trust and web-of-trust. KM based on web-of-trust can be self-organized easily, and has good robustness. However, this kind of system has some drawbacks in the trust base and is vulnerable to the falsification attack. By contrast, a hierarchical trust system has better reliability and security. Nevertheless, when applied in MANET, this kind of system often introduces high authentication overhead, and is difficult to be self-organized by nodes. So both kinds of system are not suitable for the large-scale MANET.

Party model. From the viewpoint of relation within the users and their nodes, we propose a universal MANET structure model, named party model. A party is a group of members who have the common tasks, interests or goals, and a large-scale MANET will contain a lot of parties. Trust relations inside (or among) the practical human parties will be considered in our new KM design.

Synthetic Public Key Management. There are two modes for the authentication in the party model: authentication in the same party (we call it intra-party authentication) and authenticating a node from different party (we call it remote authentication).

---

* This work was supported by the National Basic Research Program (No.2005CB321801), NSFC (No. 60573136) and High-Tech Research and Development Program (No. 2005AA121570).
** A full version of this paper is available by sending an email to pandong@nudt.edu.cn.

A.K. Datta and M. Gradinariu (Eds.): SSS 2006, LNCS 4280, pp. 570–571, 2006.

We adopt web-of-trust to the intra-party authentication. In the initial phase of network's formation, users (nodes) join different parties according to their tasks or interests, and each party has a unique party ID (PID). Nodes of a party assign each of themselves a member ID (MID) coded form 0 to $N_{PID} - 1$ in a distributed way, where N_{PID} is the (maximum) members' number of party PID. Every node creates its public/private key pair by itself. Then every node issues certificates for some selected nodes in the same party by using the way as follows:

for (counter =0; counter$\leq \lfloor N_{PID}/\sigma \rfloor$; counter++)
computes w=(i+1+$\sigma \times$ counter) and then issue certificate for w;

where i is the MID of issuer, and σ is a fix integer named issuing interval.

The special manner of certificate issuing is very advantageous to intra-party authentication. We give an algorithm that can compute several certificate chain paths (CCP) from verifier's key to the target key. Multiple authentication paths can help to effectively redeem the security defect of web-of-trust system. Our intra-party authentication does not need a node to maintain a local certificate repository, so it reduces corresponding cost and is very efficient.

When a node u requires executing a remote authentication (to v in another party), u pays more attention to the reliability of authentication process because he may feel unfamiliar to participants (from another party). We build the authentication on both the party trust and intra-party authentication foundation by the following five steps.

- Firstly, every party creates its CA by using threshold cryptosystem. Each CA consists of some nodes trusted by most nodes of their party.
- Secondly, party trusts are established by CAs issuing certificates for each other.
- Thirdly, u queries whether his CA (CA_1) has issued valid certificate (ξ) for the CA of v (CA_2). If the reply is negative, u abandons the authentication. Otherwise, u requests CA_2 to certificate v's public key.
- Fourthly, CA_2 summons its t (threshold) server nodes to authenticate v's public key in intra-party mode. If their results are all consistent success, these server nodes issue a certificate (ε) for v's public key.
- Fifthly, v transmits ε to u. After that u verifies CA_2's public key by CA_1's public key, then verifies v's public key by CA_2's public key.

In fact, trust between CAs acts as trust intermediary between nodes from different parties, and this measure strengthen security of remote authentication. Though the remote authentication is rather more complex, this kind of authentications accounts for a few proportions of total. So our scheme can get a good tradeoff among security, overhead and flexibility.

Brief Announcement: Termination Detection in an Asynchronous Distributed System with Crash-Recovery Failures

Felix C. Freiling[1], Matthias Majuntke[2], and Neeraj Mittal[3]

[1] University of Mannheim, D-68131 Mannheim, Germany
[2] RWTH Aachen University, D-52056 Aachen, Germany
[3] The University of Texas at Dallas, Richardson, TX 75083, USA

1 Termination Detection

In practice, it cannot easily be detected whether a computation running in a distributed system has terminated or not. Thus, suitable observing algorithms are required to solve this problem of *termination detection*.

A termination detection algorithm involves a computation of its own and the computation it observes without interfering it. Additionally, it satisfies two properties: (1) it should never announce termination unless the underlying computation has in fact terminated. (2) If the underlying computation has terminated, the termination detection algorithm should eventually announce termination.

For the definition of *termination*, the states of processes are mapped to just two distinct states: active and passive. An active process still actively participates in the computation while a passive process does not participate anymore unless it is activated by an active process. In message-passing systems, which we also assume here, activation can only be done by receiving a message. A widely accepted definition of termination is that (1) all processes are passive and (2) all channels are empty.

Related Work. Many algorithms for termination detection have been proposed in the literature (see the overview by Matocha and Camp [1]). Most of them assume a perfect environment in which no faults happen. There is relatively little work on fault-tolerant termination detection (e.g. [2,3]). All this work assumes the crash-stop failure model meaning that the only failures which may occur are crash faults where processes simply stop executing steps.

2 Problems in the Crash-Recovery Model

In this paper we revisit the termination detection problem in the more severe crash-recovery failure model. Roughly speaking, in the crash-recovery model, processes are allowed to crash just like in the crash-stop model but they are also allowed to restart their execution later. We are unaware, however, of any termination detection algorithm for the crash-recovery model.

A.K. Datta and M. Gradinariu (Eds.): SSS 2006, LNCS 4280, pp. 572–573, 2006.
© Springer-Verlag Berlin Heidelberg 2006

Solving the termination detection problem in the crash-recovery model is not an easy task. First of all, it is not clear what a sensible definition of termination is in the crash-recovery model. On the one hand, the classical (fault-free) definition of termination as mentioned above is clearly not suitable: If an active process crashes, there is always the possibility that it recovers later but there is no guarantee that it actually will recover. So an algorithm is in the dilemma to either making a false detection of termination or to possibly waiting infinitely long. On the other hand, the definition used in the crash-stop model is also not suitable: An algorithm might announce termination prematurely if an active process which was crashed recovers again. As a strict generalization, we introduce the definition of *robust-restricted termination*: (1) all alive and temporarily crashed processes have to be passive and (2) all the channels towards such processes have to be empty. Only crashed processes that will never recover, need not to be taken into account here.

Second, detecting robust-restricted termination in a crash-recovery system — even equipped with failure detectors — proves to be impossible to solve. Termination detection can be reduced to the problem of implementing a failure detector which is able to predict the future — of course not being feasible. Thus, we introduce the notion of *stabilizing* termination detection in which false termination detection announcements are allowed and may be revoked a finite number of times. The restriction to the *stabilizing* crash-recovery model in which all processes eventually either stay up or stay down (that is, the crash-recovery model eventually behaves like the crash-stop model) is also necessary. We present an algorithm for solving the stabilizing termination detection problem in the stabilizing crash-recovery model that uses a failure detector which is strictly weaker than the perfect failure detector [4]. The main idea of the algorithm is that every process logs the messages it sends and receives. By exchanging this information every process knows which messages it still has to expect. When a passive process does not expect any messages — its incoming channels are empty — it proposes to announce termination using a broadcast primitive. Termination is actually announced, if all live processes agree on announcing termination.

In summary, the results give insight into the additional complexities induced by the crash-recovery model in contrast to the crash-stop model.

References

1. Matocha, J., Camp, T.: A Taxonomy of Distributed Termination Detection Algorithms. J. Syst.Softw. **43**(3) (1998) 207–221
2. Wu, L.F., Lai, T.H., Tseng, Y.C.: Consensus and Termination Detection in the Presence of Faulty Processes. In: ICPADS, Hsinchu, Taiwan (1992) 267–274
3. Mittal, N., Freiling, F., Venkatesan, S., Penso, L.D.: Efficient Reduction for Wait-Free Termination Detection in a Crash-Prone Distributed System. In: DISC, Cracow, Poland (2005) 93–107
4. Majuntke, M.: Termination Detection in Systems Where Processes May Crash and Recover. Diploma Thesis, RWTH Aachen University (2006) https://pi1.informatik.uni-mannheim.de:8443/pub/research/theses/diplomarbeit-2006-majuntke.pdf.

Brief Announcement: Self-stabilizing Spanning Tree Algorithm for Large Scale Systems*

Thomas Herault, Pierre Lemarinier, Olivier Peres,
Laurence Pilard, and Joffroy Beauquier

LRI bat 490,
Universite Paris-Sud
91405 Orsay Cedex,
France
{herault, lemarini, peres, pilard, jb}@lri.fr

Abstract. We introduce a self-stabilizing algorithm that builds and maintains a spanning tree topology on any large scale system. We assume that the existing topology is a complete graph and that nodes may arrive or leave at any time. To cope with the large number of processes of a grid or a peer to peer system, we limit the memory usage of each process to a small constant number of variables, combining this with previous results concerning failure detectors and resource discovery.

Keywords: Distributed Algorithm, Large Scale Systems, Self-Stabilization, Spanning Tree Construction, Failure Detectors.

1 Introduction

Peer to peer networks and grids are emerging large scale systems that gather thousands of nodes. These networks usually rely on IP to communicate: each node has a unique address used by other nodes to communicate with it and every node can communicate with every other node provided it knows its address. In such a system, it is not practical or even not possible for any one node to know the whole list of its neighbors because of its size and also because of the occurrence of failures.

Classical distributed applications, however, need a notion of neighborhood. In a large scale systems, it is generally given by an overlay network built by a specific algorithm. To account for this, we propose to abstract out these requirements using theoretical devices that have to be implemented in a system-specific way.

An algorithm for such a system also needs to tolerate failures. We demonstrated how to use self-stabilization [2] in order to build a bounded-degree spanning tree [3]. We claim that self-stabilization is appropriate for the purpose of building an overlay network because it allows the system to recover from any perturbation affecting either a link or a local variable. It then verifies its specification until the next failure.

---

* This work is partially funded by the PCRI/INRIA Futurs - Project Grand-Large and ACI Grid (French incentive).

A.K. Datta and M. Gradinariu (Eds.): SSS 2006, LNCS 4280, pp. 574–575, 2006.

2 Contributions

We introduce [3] a self-stabilizing algorithm that builds a bounded-degree spanning tree over a virtual complete graph. The nodes only store the identifiers of their neighbors and only rely on the devices provided by our model to establish and maintain the overlay network. Each node only has a constant number of local variables.

Our first contribution is a new model for distributed algorithms. The main advantage that we claim for it is that it allows to run distributed algorithms in real-world large scale systems. To achieve this, we abandon the notion of a system-provided, automatically updated neighbor list found in most existing works and replace it with two theoretical devices: an oracle for resource discovery and a failure detector to deal with possible identifiers of stopped (crashed) processes.

The oracle, when queried, replies with a valid process identifier which may, or not, be that of a process in the system. For our spanning tree algorithm, the only requirement is to give the identifier of the highest process an infinite number of times over any infinite number of queries.

The failure detector follows Chandra and Toueg's definition [1]. We proved that in our case, we need a $\diamond\mathcal{P}$ detector, i.e. one that is eventually perfect.

Our second contribution is the algorithm itself. Each process has δ neighbor fields, where δ is a user-provided integer constant. The algorithm is given [3] as a set of guarded rules that eliminate inconsistent configurations, build the tree and maintain it. We provide a formal proof of its correctness.

To guarantee that the tree is correctly built, the algorithm enforces a global invariant: each process only accepts as a child a process whose identifier is lower than its own identifier. Only the roots attempt to connect the topology, thus only them query their oracles, which allows to design an efficient implementation. Eventually there is a single root, so only one process queries its oracle. Finally, when the system is converged, the algorithm only induces a very low overhead.

We implemented the algorithm and the two devices on which it depends and measured its performances on the Grid Explorer high-performance experimental cluster, comparing several approaches in places where the specification leaves room for choices. This allowed us to show that the system displays the expected scalability.

References

1. T. D. Chandra and S. Toueg. Unreliable failure detectors for reliable distributed systems. *Journal of the ACM*, 43, March 1996.
2. E. Dijkstra. Self stabilizing systems in spite of distributed control. *Communications of the Association of the Computing Machinery*, 17(11):643–644, 1974.
3. T. Herault, P. Lemarinier, O. Peres, L. Pilard, and J. Beauquier. Self-stabilizing spanning tree algorithm for large scale systems. Technical Report 1457, LRI, 2006.

Brief Announcement: Chasing the Weakest System Model for Implementing Ω and Consensus

Martin Hutle[1,3], Dahlia Malkhi[2], Ulrich Schmid[3], and Lidong Zhou[2]

[1] Ecole Polytechnique Fédérale de Lausanne (EPFL)
[2] Microsoft Research
[3] Vienna University of Technology, Embedded Computing Systems Group 182-2

The chase for the weakest system model that allows to solve consensus has long been an active branch of research in distributed algorithms. To circumvent the FLP impossibility in asynchronous systems, many models in between synchrony and asynchrony have been proposed over the years. Of specific interest is the chase for the weakest system model that allows the implementation of an eventual leader oracle Ω, and thus also enables consensus to be solved.

Recently, Aguilera et al. [ADGFT04] and Malkhi et al. [MOZ05] presented two system models which are weaker than all previously proposed models where Ω can be implemented. The former model assumes unicast steps and at least one correct process with f outgoing eventually timely links. The latter assumes broadcast steps and at least one correct process with f bidirectional but moving eventually timely links. Consequently, those models are incomparable.

Our main result in the full paper [HMSZ05:TR] shows that Ω can be implemented in a system with at least one process with f outgoing moving eventually timely links, assuming either unicast or broadcast steps. Our construction seems to solve consensus (via Ω) in the weakest system model known so far.

Definition 1 (The weak model $\mathcal{S}_{f*}^{\rightarrow}$). *Informally, a $\diamond$moving-f-source is a correct process that, eventually, if it sends a message to all other processes at time t, at least f of these messages are timely. Our system $\mathcal{S}_{f*}^{\rightarrow}$ assumes the existence of at least one $\diamond$moving-f-source. All other links can be totally asynchronous.*

Theorem 1. *It is possible to implement Ω in system $\mathcal{S}_{f*}^{\rightarrow}$.*

We also provide matching lower bounds for the communication complexity in this model, which are based on an interesting "stabilization property" of infinite runs. Those results reveal a price to be paid for the relaxation of synchrony properties, compared, e.g., with the last algorithm in Aguilera et al. [ADGFT04] where only f links are required to carry messages forever. Thus, these results indicate an interesting tradeoff between synchrony assumptions and communication complexity.

Theorem 2. *For all $n > f + 1 \geq 2$, in a system $\mathcal{S}_{f*}^{\rightarrow}$ with reliable links and n processes where up to f processes may crash, any implementation of Ω requires at least $\frac{nf}{2}$ links to carry messages forever in some run. This holds even when every process is a perpetual moving-f-source, and δ is known.*

A.K. Datta and M. Gradinariu (Eds.): SSS 2006, LNCS 4280, pp. 576–577, 2006.
© Springer-Verlag Berlin Heidelberg 2006

In the full paper [HMSZ05:TR] we give an algorithm that matches the $\Omega(nf)$ lower bound, i.e., where only $O(nf)$ links carry messages forever.

The Algorithm for $\mathcal{S}_{f*}^{\rightarrow}$. We now provide an informal description of the main ingredients of our solution. The algorithm bears similarities to the algorithm of [ADGFT04], with the following important distinctions: It introduces suspicion sequence-numbers, and the agreement on suspicions is done on a per-sequence-number basis.

The algorithm works as follows: Every process p periodically sends ALIVE messages with increasing sequence numbers (seq_p) to all. Every receiver process q maintains a receiver-sequence number $(rseq_q)$, and expects to receive an ALIVE message with a sequence number matching $rseq_q$ from every other process p within a timeout period. A timer is used for terminating the wait; both $rseq_q$ and the timeout value are incremented when the timer expires.

Every receiver process q maintains an array $counter_q[p]$, which essentially contains the number of suspicions of sender p encountered at q so far: The sender p is suspected at q if q is notified of the fact that at least $n - f$ receivers experienced a timeout for the same sequence number s. This notification is done via SUSPECT messages, which are sent to all by any receiver process that experienced a timeout for sender p with sequence number s. In addition, counter values are piggybacked onto ALIVE messages. If a larger counter value for process p is observed in any ALIVE message, $counter_q[p]$ adopts this value. The process $p = \ell$ with minimal counter value in $counter_q[p]$ (or the minimal process id in case of several such entries) is elected as q's leader.

Informally, the correctness of the algorithm follows from the following reasoning: At the time the $\diamond$moving-f-source becomes a moving-f-source, at least f outgoing links of the source p carry timely messages at any time. Thus, eventually, it is impossible that the quorum of $n - f$ SUSPECT messages is reached for p for any sequence number. Note that this even holds true if some of the f timely receiver processes have crashed. Consequently, all processes stop increasing the counter for process p, whereas the counter of every crashed sender process keeps increasing forever since every receiver obviously experiences a timeout here. Since the counter values are continuously exchanged via the content of the ALIVE messages, eventually all processes reach agreement upon all counters that have stopped increasing. Hence, locally electing the process with minimal counter indeed leads to a correct implementation of Ω.

References

[ADGFT04] Aguilera, M.K., Delporte-Gallet, C., Fauconnier, H., Toueg, S.: Communication-efficient leader election and consensus with limited link synchrony. In: Proc. PODC 04, ACM Press (2004) 328–337

[MOZ05] Malkhi, D., Oprea, F., Zhou, L.: Ω meets paxos: Leader election and stability without eventual timely links. In: Proc. DISC 05, Springer-Verlag (2005)

[HMSZ05:TR] Hutle, M., Malkhi, D., Schmid, U., Zhou, L.: Chasing the weakest system model for implementing omega and consensus. Research Report 74/2005, Technische Universität Wien, Institut für Technische Informatik, Treitlstr. 1-3/182-2, 1040 Vienna, Austria (2005)

Brief Announcement: Wait-Free Dining for Eventual Weak Exclusion

Scott M. Pike, Yantao Song, and Kaustav Ghoshal

Texas A&M University, Department of Computer Science
College Station, TX 77843-3112, USA
{pike, syt, kghoshal}@tamu.edu

Abstract. We present the first wait-free solution to dining philosophers under eventual weak exclusion in partially synchronous environments subject to crash faults. Potential applications include distributed daemon refinement for self-stabilizing algorithms.

Problem Statement. We consider the generalized dining philosophers problem [4,5] in environments subject to permanent crash faults, and explore its solvability in asynchronous message-passing systems augmented with unreliable failure detectors [2]. Dining is a fundamental model of static resource allocation, where distributed processes require periodic access to a fixed subset of mutually exclusive shared resources. Processes with overlapping resource requirements are connected as neighbors in a general conflict graph. Each diner is either *thinking*, *hungry*, or *eating*. These states correspond to three basic phases of computation: executing independently, requesting resources, and utilizing shared resources in a critical section, respectively. The traditional safety and progress specification for dining is that (1) No two live neighbors eat simultaneously (weak exclusion), and (2) Every correct hungry process eventually eats.

Application. Stabilizing algorithms withstand transient faults by automatically converging from any configuration to a closed set of safe states. Such algorithms are often easier to design under interleaving semantics, whereby at most one process is activated by a central daemon to take a step at any given time. In practice, stabilizing algorithms need to execute correctly under parallel semantics as well. This is often achieved via automatic model conversions, whereby an underlying distributed daemon schedules consistent sets of processes to take steps concurrently. Many existing transformations [1,6] use dining algorithms to implement such daemons. Such approaches have considered daemons that tolerate transient faults (such as data corruption), but they have not addressed the need for wait-free scheduling guarantees in the presence of process crashes.

Fundamental Limitations. For many classic dining solutions, a single crash fault can precipitate global starvation, whereby correct hungry diners never eat again. Choy and Singh [3] proved that dining under weak exclusion is unsolvable in asynchronous systems; the starvation neighborhood can be isolated, but processes within two hops of any crashed node can still starve. Pike and Sivilotti [7] strengthened this result for partial synchrony by showing that dining was still

A.K. Datta and M. Gradinariu (Eds.): SSS 2006, LNCS 4280, pp. 578–579, 2006.

unsolvable when using an eventually perfect failure detector $\Diamond \mathcal{P}$ from the classic Chandra-Toueg hierarchy [2]. The starvation neighborhood can be isolated further using $\Diamond \mathcal{P}$, but immediate neighbors of crashed nodes will still starve.

Significance. The unsolvability of dining under weak exclusion is problematic for proving the convergence of stabilizing algorithms. A necessary assumption for convergence is that correct nodes take infinitely many steps. If distributed daemons can stave nodes after crash faults, however, this assumption can be violated. As such, convergence requires wait-free daemons to guarantee that no correct process starves, regardless of how many processes crash. There are two apparent avenues to wait-freedom: (1) use stronger oracles, or (2) examine weaker exclusion models. The former is tantamount to greater synchrony, which limits applicability to real systems. As such, our work examines the latter.

Primary Results. We consider dining under a more permissive model called *eventual weak exclusion* ($\Diamond \mathcal{WX}$). This exclusion model requires that *for each run, there exists a time after which no two live neighbors eat simultaneously*. The time to convergence may be unknown, and it can vary from run to run. Still, $\Diamond \mathcal{WX}$ is a sufficiently powerful scheduling primitive for systems where resources can be recovered from crashed processes, and/or where sharing violations precipitate only transient faults. Our primary result constructs a wait-free dining algorithm for $\Diamond \mathcal{WX}$ using the oracle $\Diamond \mathcal{P}$. The advantage of wait-freedom comes at the cost of finitely many scheduling errors which may precipitate transient faults. After the final scheduling mistake of any run, the stabilizing protocol may have reached an arbitrary configuration. By convergence, however, the application will eventually recover to a safe state and continue execution thereafter without further errors by the underlying daemon. The full report can be found in [8].

References

1. J. Beauquier, A.K. Datta, M. Gradinariu, and F. Magniette. Self-Stabilizing Local Mutual Exclusion and Daemon Refinement. *Chicago J. Theor. Comput. Sci*, 2002.
2. T.D. Chandra and S. Toueg. Unreliable failure detectors for reliable distributed systems. *Journal of the ACM*, 43(2):225–267, 1996.
3. M. Choy and A.K. Singh. Localizing Failures in Distributed Synchronization. *IEEE Transactions on Parallel and Distribruted Systems (TPDS)*, 7(7):705–716, 1996.
4. E.W. Dijkstra. Hierarchical ordering of sequential processes. *Acta Informatica*, 1(2):115–138, Oct 1971. Reprinted in *Operating Systems Techniques*, C.A.R. Hoare and R.H. Perrot, Eds., pp. 72–93, Academic Press, 1972. Appeared also as EWD310.
5. N. Lynch. Fast allocation of nearby resources in a distributed system. In *Proceedings of the 12th ACM Symposium on Theory of Computing (STOC)*, pp. 70–81, 1980.
6. M. Nesterenko and A. Arora. Stabilization-Preserving Atomicity Refinement. *Journal of Parallel and Distributed Computing*, 62(5):766–791, May 2002.
7. S.M. Pike and P.A.G. Sivilotti. Dining Philosophers with Crash Locality 1. In *Proceedings of the 24th IEEE International Conference on Distributed Computing Systems (ICDCS)*, pp. 22–29. IEEE, 2004.
8. S.M. Pike, Y. Song, and K. Ghoshal. Wait-Free Dining under Eventual Weak Exclusion. Tech Report 2006-5-1, Texas A&M University, May 2006. Available at: http://www.cs.tamu.edu/academics/tr/tamu-cs-tr-2006-5-1

Brief Announcement: An Efficient and Self-stabilizing Link Formation Algorithm

Jun Kiniwa and Kensaku Kikuta

University of Hyogo, Japan
{kiniwa@econ, kikuta@biz}.u-hyogo.ac.jp

1 Introduction

We propose a self-stabilizing link formation algorithm based on a cooperative network formation game. An underlying network $G = (V, E)$ consists of n processors represented by nodes $V = \{1, 2, \ldots, n\}$, and communication links represented by edges $E = \{ij \mid i, j \in V\}$. An agent network $L = (A, E_L)$, where $A = V$ and $E_L \subseteq E$, is defined on G. Let δ_i be a benefit that agent i provides others, and c_{ij} a cost of linking i with j that agent i incurs. We assume a *state-reading model*, a fair *distributed daemon*, and a *token circulation* for formation/severance of links.

Let $d_{ij} = \alpha \cdot \delta_j - c_{ij}$ ($\alpha > 0$) and $D_{ij} = d_{ij} + d_{ji}$. We assume $D_{ij} + \delta_i + \delta_j > 0$ for every edge $ij \in E$. Let $C(i) = \{j \mid i, j\text{-path} \subseteq E_L \text{ exists}\}$ be a component of agents to which $i \in A$ belongs, and $CN(i) = \{j \mid ij \in E_L\}$ a set of directly linked agents. We define the *payoff* $Y_i(L)$ of agent i as $Y_i(L) = \sum_{k \in C(i)} \delta_k + \sum_{j \in CN(i)} (\alpha \cdot \delta_j - c_{ij})$. We say that network L is *efficient* if $v(L') \leq v(L)$ for any $L' = (A, E_{L'})$, where $v(L) = \sum_{i \in A} Y_i(L)$ and $E_{L'} \subseteq E$. A network L is *pairwise stable with transfers*[2] if

1. for all $ij \in E_L$, $Y_i(L - ij) + Y_j(L - ij) \leq Y_i(L) + Y_j(L)$, and
2. for all $ij \notin E_L$, $Y_i(L) + Y_j(L) \geq Y_i(L + ij) + Y_j(L + ij)$.

2 Algorithm

A *multiple MVI (minimal value inheritance)-BFS tree with FE (a forbidden edge)*, motivated by [1], is a set of r-rooted BFS trees for every $r \in A$ such that a pointer to r is forbidden (indicated by $forbid_r$) and the minimal D_{uv} is inherited in each path from the root. Let $CNF(i) = \{j \mid ij \in (E_L \setminus \text{a forbidden edge})\}$. Let p be a parent of i in an r-rooted tree if it satisfies $\min_{p \in CNF(i)} (dist_p^r, minD_p^r, e)$, where $dist_p^r$ is the distance from r to p, $minD_p^r$ is the minimal D_{uv} value for some $uv \in r, p$-path, and $e = \min\{u, v\}$. Similar to e, let $e_0 = \min\{i, j\}$ for D_{ij}. We say that i, j-path is a *positive path* if $D_{uv} \geq 0$ for every link uv in the path. Otherwise, i, j-path is a *negative path*. Let $Negative(i) = \{j \in CN(i) \mid D_{ij} < 0\}$. We represent $Incorrect(X) \Rightarrow X := B$ instead of $X \neq B \Rightarrow X := B$.

A.K. Datta and M. Gradinariu (Eds.): SSS 2006, LNCS 4280, pp. 580–581, 2006.

$$Incorrect(tree_i[i]) \Rightarrow tree_i[i] := (0, \infty, \bot, \bot)$$

$$\forall t \in Negative(i) : forbid_i \neq t \Rightarrow forbid_i := \exists u \in Negative(i)$$

$$\exists r \in A\backslash i : Incorrect(tree_i[r]) \Rightarrow tree_i[r] := (dist_i^r, minD_i^r, e, p)$$

$$\exists j \notin CN(i) : (0 \leq D_{ij}) \vee ((minD_j^i, e) \prec (D_{ij}, e_0)) \Rightarrow CN(i) := CN(i) \cup j$$

$$forbid_i = j : (D_{ij} < 0) \wedge ((D_{ij}, e_0) \prec (minD_j^i, e)) \Rightarrow CN(i) := CN(i)\backslash j$$

$$forbid_i = j : (D_{ij} < 0) \wedge (tree_j[i].p \neq i) \Rightarrow forbid_i := next(forbid_i)$$

3   Our Claims

Lemma 1. *Let $S_i = \sum_{k \in C(i)} \delta_k$. By the rule of pairwise stable with transfers, there are three cases whether or not each link is formed: (1) any link $ij \in E_L$ is severed if $D_{ij} < -(S_i + S_j)$, (2) critical link $ij \notin E_L$ is formed but noncritical link $ij \in E_L$ is severed if $-(S_i + S_j) \leq D_{ij} < 0$, and (3) any link $ij \notin E_L$ is formed if $0 \leq D_{ij}$.*   □

Lemma 2. *The multiple MVI-BFS tree with FE is constructed after $2 \cdot diam_L$ rounds, where $diam_L$ is the diameter of L.*   □

Lemma 3. *An efficient network L is connected and contains (1) every positive link, and (2) critical, negative links with non-minimal cost in each semicircle (i.e., a path without linking end nodes).*   □

Theorem 1. *Our algorithm restores an efficient network L in $O(\Delta n)$ rounds for the maximum degree Δ. The memory size required by each processor is bounded by $O(n \log(n + \delta))$ bits, where $\delta = \max_{i \in A} \delta_i$.*   □

4   Conclusion

We focused on the network formation game from the view point of self-stabilization. We showed that the dynamic game can be applied to convergence in decentralized settings.

References

1. S.Dolev, Self-Stabilizing Routing and Related Protocols, *Journal of Parallel and Distributed Computing*, vol.42, pp.122–127, 1997.
2. M.O.Jackson, A Survey of Models of Network Formation: Stability and Efficiency, *Chapter 1 in Group Formation in Economics; Networks, Clubs and Coalitions*, edited by G.Demange and M.Wooders, Cambridge University Press, 2004.

Brief Announcement: Analyzing the Interactions of Self-propagating Codes in Multi-hop Networks

Sapon Tanachaiwiwat and Ahmed Helmy

University of Southern California, Los Angeles CA 90037, USA
{tanachai, helmy}@usc.edu

Abstract. "War of the worms" is a war between opposing computer worms, creating complex worm interactions. We propose a new Worm Interaction Model focusing on random-scan worm interactions. We validate our worm interaction model using extensive ns-2 simulations. This study provides the first work to characterize and investigate multiple worm interactions of random-scan worms in multi-hop networks. The main finding of this study is that maximum number of infected hosts can be drastically affected by the type of interaction.

1   Worm Interaction Model

Since the Morris worm incident in 1988, worms have been a major threat to Internet users. In addition, more and more worms carry destructive payload enabling them to perform denial-of-service attacks, steal username/password or hijack victims' files. Network worms such as Slammer, Witty, and Code Red [4] aggressively scan and infect vulnerable machines. Basic operation of a worm is to find susceptible nodes to infect and the main goal of attackers is to have their worms infect the largest amount of hosts in the least amount of time, and if possible, remain undetected by antivirus or intrusion detection systems; however, recently the goal of attackers, has been expanded to eliminate opposing worms. Thus we want to investigate the worm propagation behavior caused by this and other types of interactions. Several worm propagation models have been proposed [2] but those worm propagation models have not considered the interaction among different worm types where interaction is the scenarios in which one worm terminating and/or patching other worm [3]. We aim to build a fundamental worm propagation model that captures worm interaction as a key factor. Understanding of worm interaction will help us effectively design fully distributed and automated security response mechanism.

In our model, number of infected hosts of one worm type affects number of infected hosts of others. Because the constant removal rate in basic SIR model [1] cannot directly portray such interactions, our model builds upon and extends beyond the conventional epidemic model to accommodate the notion of interaction reflecting dynamic removal rate. Our model assumes no change of total host population and multiple types of worms share the same susceptible hosts. We further assume that human security responses to worm incidents are much slower than the rates at which worms interact between each other.

A.K. Datta and M. Gradinariu (Eds.): SSS 2006, LNCS 4280, pp. 582–583, 2006.

2   Our Contributions

Worm interaction can be categorized as one-sided or two-sided interaction. One-sided interaction means one worm type terminating and/or patching other worm type. Two-sided interaction means two worm types terminating and/or patching each other. For every worm interaction type, there are two basic characters: predator: a worm that terminates or patches another worm, prey: a worm that is terminated or patched by another worm. To describe these interactions, we develop a novel Worm Interaction Model extending the epidemic model. Note that two-sided interaction model is built to explain the interaction between malicious worms (both worms are predator and prey simultaneously) while one-sided interaction model focuses on explaining benign worms (predator) terminating malicious worms (prey).

Our Worm Interaction Model is validated through extensive ns 2 simulations for investigating the effect of our proposed network-delay factor that is the function of packet size, link latency, queuing delay and bandwidth on the worm interaction. Our Worm Interaction Model can be easily extended to cover complex multiple worm interactions. In addition, we propose a new set of metrics to measure the effectiveness of one worm terminating another worm: total infected hosts and individual life span of terminated worm. The total infected host is the number of prey infected hosts including infected hosts that have been removed and the individual life span is the time between the start of infection and the end of infection i.e. infectious period for individual replication of prey caused by prey termination. We show the relationships of such metrics to the worm interaction. Our model can accurately approximate these metrics with properly chosen network-delay factors.

We also find that scan (attempt) rate ratio between predator and prey has much more impact on worm propagation pattern than initial infected host ratio between predator and prey for every type of interaction. With similar scan rate ratios, for every type of interaction, it always results in the same maximum prey infected hosts. While we focus on one-sided interaction, our model shows promising accuracy in estimating individual life span and total infectives for different scenarios.

References

1. Frauenthal, J.C.,. Mathematical Modeling in Epidemiology. Springer-Verlag,New York,1988
2. Ganesh, A., Massoulie , L., and Towsley, D., The Effect of Network Topology on the Spread of Epidemics, in IEEE INFOCOM 2005
3. Tanachaiwiwat, S., Helmy, A., "Analyzing the Interactions of Self-Propagating Codes in Multi-hop Networks", Tech Report CS 06-884, CS Department, USC
4. Trend Micro Annual Virus Report 2004 http://www.trendmicro.com

Brief Announcement: Towards Modular Verification of Stabilisation in Self-adaptive Embedded Systems*

Ina Schaefer and Arnd Poetzsch-Heffter

Software Technology Group, Technische Universität Kaiserslautern, Germany
{inschaef, poetzsch}@informatik.uni-kl.de

Abstract. We introduce a formal semantic-based modelling framework to model, specify and verify the functional and adaptive behaviour of synchronous adaptive systems.

1 Motivation

Self-adaptive embedded systems, e.g. in the automotive domain, autonomously adapt to changing environment conditions and increase their dependability by downgrading functionality in case of failures. However, adaptation in embedded systems significantly complicates system design, in particular, as adaptations trigger further adaptations in other modules potentially leading to inconsistent and unstable configurations. Hence, stabilisation of adaptation in self-adaptive systems is crucial. Formal verification as applied in safety-critical applications must therefore be able to consider not only temporal and functional properties, but also dynamic adaptation according to external and internal stimuli.

2 Modelling Synchronous Adaptive Systems

While most approaches formalizing self-adaptation [1] so far intertwine functionality and adaptation, the proposed modelling framework [3] decouples functional and adaptive behaviour providing a clear formal account of both aspects in separation. This reduces design complexity and enables explicit and uniform reasoning about functional, adaptive and combined properties. The modelling is based on state-transition systems. It describes adaptation of module behaviour in terms of an adaptation aspect on top of a set of possible predetermined configurations. Restricting adaptation to predetermined reconfiguration makes systems predictable and improves analysis results. Figure 1 depicts the intuitive notion of a module. The configurations specify local state transitions and computation of output. Before executing the actual functionality, the adaptation aspect evaluates the configuration guards and selects an applicable configuration. Furthermore, it computes adaptation signals for other system modules.

---

* Supported by the Rheinland-Pfalz Cluster of Excellence 'Dependable Adaptive Systems and Mathematical Modelling' (DASMOD).

A.K. Datta and M. Gradinariu (Eds.): SSS 2006, LNCS 4280, pp. 584–585, 2006.

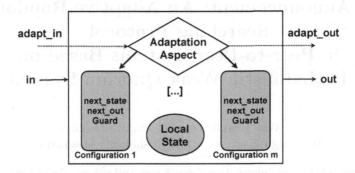

Fig. 1. Separating Functionality and Adaptation in a Module

Synchronous adaptive systems are composed from a set of modules connected via links between input and output variables where data and adaptation flow do not follow the same links. Adaptations in one module may trigger adaptations in other modules by propagation of adaptation signals. The systems are open systems with a non-deterministic environment and operate synchronously as simultaneously invoked actions are executed in true concurrency.

3   Verifying Stabilisation of Adaptation

For specification purposes, we adopt a variant of the linear time logic LTL by adding special basic predicates for functional and adaptive behaviour to standard first-order and temporal connectives. Stabilisation of adaptation with respect to a property φ is defined along the lines of [2]. It can be re-phrased in linear logic as $\mathbf{G}\ (\psi \rightarrow \mathbf{F}\,\mathbf{G}\,\varphi)$ where ψ is a formula which first becomes true in a state in which the adaptation occurs. The proposed framework enables modular reasoning exploiting the system's modular specification. A global system property can be decomposed into local properties of single modules entailing the global property. Furthermore, incorporating abstraction mechanisms, for instance to reduce unbounded data domains to finite discrete domains, facilitates the efficient integration of existing model checking techniques into the verification of self-adaptive systems for discharging certain sub-proof goals automatically.

References

1. J.S. Bradbury, J.R. Cordy, J. Dingel, and M. Wermelinger. A Survey of Self-Management in Dynamic Software Architecture Specifications. In *Proc. of Intl. Workshop on Self-Managed Systems (WOSS'04)*, 2004.
2. E.W. Dijkstra. Self-Stabilizing Systems in spite of Distributed Control. *Communications of the ACM 17(11)*, pages 643–644, 1974.
3. I. Schaefer and A. Poetzsch-Heffter. Using Abstraction in Modular Verification of Synchronous Adaptive Systems. In *Proc. of "Workshop on Trustworthy Software"*, Saarbrücken, Germany, May 18-19, 2006.

Brief Announcement: An Adaptive Randomised Searching Protocol in Peer-to-Peer Systems Based on Probabilistic Weak Quorum System

Yu Wu, Taisuke Izumi, Fukuhito Ooshita,
Hirotsugu Kakugawa, and Toshimitsu Masuzawa

Graduate School of Information Science and Technology, Osaka University
{wu-yu, t-izumi, f-oosita, kakugawa, masuzawa}@ist.osaka-u.ac.jp

1 Background

Searching problem, which is to identify the peer that has some target resource, is an important and unique problem in Peer-to-Peer (P2P) file sharing systems. Since P2P file sharing systems maintain large and dynamic set of peers, the searching protocol is desired to be scalable and adaptive. To achieve such requirements, many kinds of search protocols are proposed. As one of those protocols, the searching protocol based on Probabilistic Weak Quorum System (PWQS) is recently proposed [1]. The principle of this protocol is as follows: In advance, a number of indices (location informations of an object) of each object are disseminated to randomly selected peers. When searching, the searcher sends a number of queries to randomly selected peers. If a query reaches a peer holding the index of the target object, search succeeds. It is shown that the protocol has advantages in the point of scalability, load balance and fault-tolerance.

In this paper we present Adaptive Randomized Search Protocol (ARSP), which is an efficient extension of the PWQS-based search protocol. ARSP borrows the random search principle from the PWQS based search protocol. The objective of ARSP is to minimizes the system communication overhead, which consists of index maintenance overhead and search query overhead.

In the original protocol, for any object, a same constant number of indices are disseminated. Each index have time-to-live, and refreshed by periodical re-dissemination. Then, the number of disseminated indices strongly affects the system communication overhead. An object having more indices can be found with less number of query messages per search. However, its index maintenance consumes a large number of messages by periodical re-dissemination. Conversely, the small number of indices yields the low index maintenance overhead and high search query overhead. This implies that there is a trade-off between the two kinds of overheads. The main idea of ARSP is to adjust the number of indices according to objects' popularity. That is, the popular objects have large number of indices, and the unpopular ones have less indices. Interestingly, the protocol works in the self-adaptive manner: it can automatically adapt to the dynamics of network environments.

A.K. Datta and M. Gradinariu (Eds.): SSS 2006, LNCS 4280, pp. 586–587, 2006.

2   Our Contribution

In the followings, we briefly explain the ARSP protocol. In ARSP, the system message overhead is minimized when the message cost for each object is minimized because the search mechanism for each object is independent. The message cost for each object per time unit M consists of index maintenance overhead M_i and searching overhead M_s. Letting T be the length of TTL for indices, the index maintenance cost per time unit M_i for an object with q_i indices is q_i/T. Searchers repeatedly send queries until the target object is found. To find an object with q_i indices in n peers, the expected number of query messages q_s is n/q_i. Letting f be the search times of the object per time unit, we obtain $E[M_s] = fn/q_i$. Thus, the expectation of M is $E[M] = M_i + E[M_s] = q_i/T + fn/q_i$. Its minimum is $E[M]_{min} = 2\sqrt{fn/T}$ when q_i is $\sqrt{fnT}$.

The value of $\sqrt{fnT}$ can not be computed directly because n and f are unknown. However from the above equalities we obtain an interesting rule: No matter how much q_i is, $M_i \cdot E[M_s] = fn/T$ always holds. To the owner of the object, M_i is known and $E[M_s]$ can be estimated from the number of queries used per search, which can be easily collected from searchers. Thus the owner of the object can obtain $\sqrt{fnT}$ by computing $T\sqrt{M_i \cdot E[M_s]}$ without any knowledge of n and f. Because the above equalities holds regardless of the values of n and f, ARSP can self-adapt to the change of n and f.

In the full version of this paper, we also consider the decrease of indices by peer leave in one TTL period. We propose a more sophisticated mechanism of index dissemination. This mechanism does not use periodical dissemination of indices, but a continuous dissemination of indices. Under some assumption about the peer leaving behavior, it is proven to be more effective than one proposed above.

Acknowledgement

This work is supported in part by MEXT: "The 21st Century Center of Excellence Program", JSPS: Grant-in-Aid for Scientific Research ((B)15300017 and (B)17300020), MEXT: Grant-in-Aid for Scientific Research on Priority Areas (16092215), MEXT: Grand-in-Aid for Young Scientists ((B)18700059), MIC: Strategic Information, Communications R&D Promotion Programme (SCOPE), and Ookawa Foundation Research Grant.

References

1. K. Miura, T. Tagawa, and H. Kakugawa. A quorum-based protocol for searching objects in peer-to-peer networks. *IEEE Transactions on Parallel and Distributed Systems*, 17(1):25–37, January 2006.

Author Index

Lecture Notes in Computer Science

For information about Vols. 1–4208

please contact your bookseller or Springer

Vol. 4252: B. Gabrys, R.J. Howlett, L.C. Jain (Eds.), Knowledge-Based Intelligent Information and Engineering Systems, Part II. XXXIII, 1335 pages. 2006. (Sublibrary LNAI).

Vol. 4251: B. Gabrys, R.J. Howlett, L.C. Jain (Eds.), Knowledge-Based Intelligent Information and Engineering Systems, Part I. LXVI, 1297 pages. 2006. (Sublibrary LNAI).

Vol. 4249: L. Goubin, M. Matsui (Eds.), Cryptographic Hardware and Embedded Systems - CHES 2006. XII, 462 pages. 2006.

Vol. 4248: S. Staab, V. Svátek (Eds.), Managing Knowledge in a World of Networks. XIV, 400 pages. 2006. (Sublibrary LNAI).

Vol. 4247: T.-D. Wang, X. Li, S.-H. Chen, X. Wang, H. Abbass, H. Iba, G. Chen, X. Yao (Eds.), Simulated Evolution and Learning. XXI, 940 pages. 2006.

Vol. 4246: M. Hermann, A. Voronkov (Eds.), Logic for Programming, Artificial Intelligence, and Reasoning. XIII, 588 pages. 2006. (Sublibrary LNAI).

Vol. 4245: A. Kuba, L.G. Nyúl, K. Palágyi (Eds.), Discrete Geometry for Computer Imagery. XIII, 688 pages. 2006.

Vol. 4244: S. Spaccapietra (Ed.), Journal on Data Semantics VII. XI, 267 pages. 2006.

Vol. 4243: T. Yakhno, E.J. Neuhold (Eds.), Advances in Information Systems. XIII, 420 pages. 2006.

Vol. 4242: A. Rashid, M. Aksit (Eds.), Transactions on Aspect-Oriented Software Development II. IX, 289 pages. 2006.

Vol. 4241: R.R. Beichel, M. Sonka (Eds.), Computer Vision Approaches to Medical Image Analysis. XI, 262 pages. 2006.

Vol. 4239: H.Y. Youn, M. Kim, H. Morikawa (Eds.), Ubiquitous Computing Systems. XVI, 548 pages. 2006.

Vol. 4238: Y.-T. Kim, M. Takano (Eds.), Management of Convergence Networks and Services. XVIII, 605 pages. 2006.

Vol. 4237: H. Leitold, E. Markatos (Eds.), Communications and Multimedia Security. XII, 253 pages. 2006.

Vol. 4236: L. Breveglieri, I. Koren, D. Naccache, J.-P. Seifert (Eds.), Fault Diagnosis and Tolerance in Cryptography. XIII, 253 pages. 2006.

Vol. 4234: I. King, J. Wang, L. Chan, D. Wang (Eds.), Neural Information Processing, Part III. XXII, 1227 pages. 2006.

Vol. 4233: I. King, J. Wang, L. Chan, D. Wang (Eds.), Neural Information Processing, Part II. XXII, 1203 pages. 2006.

Vol. 4232: I. King, J. Wang, L. Chan, D. Wang (Eds.), Neural Information Processing, Part I. XLVI, 1153 pages. 2006.

Vol. 4231: J. F. Roddick, R. Benjamins, S. Si-Saïd Cherfi, R. Chiang, C. Claramunt, R. Elmasri, F. Grandi, H. Han, M. Hepp, M. Hepp, M. Lytras, V.B. Mišić, G. Poels, I.-Y. Song, J. Trujillo, C. Vangenot (Eds.), Advances in Conceptual Modeling - Theory and Practice. XXII, 456 pages. 2006.

Vol. 4230: C. Priami, A. Ingólfsdóttir, B. Mishra, H.R. Nielson (Eds.), Transactions on Computational Systems Biology VII. VII, 185 pages. 2006. (Sublibrary LNBI).

Vol. 4229: E. Najm, J.F. Pradat-Peyre, V.V. Donzeau-Gouge (Eds.), Formal Techniques for Networked and Distributed Systems - FORTE 2006. X, 486 pages. 2006.

Vol. 4228: D.E. Lightfoot, C.A. Szyperski (Eds.), Modular Programming Languages. X, 415 pages. 2006.

Vol. 4227: W. Nejdl, K. Tochtermann (Eds.), Innovative Approaches for Learning and Knowledge Sharing. XVII, 721 pages. 2006.

Vol. 4226: R.T. Mittermeir (Ed.), Informatics Education – The Bridge between Using and Understanding Computers. XVII, 319 pages. 2006.

Vol. 4225: J.F. Martínez-Trinidad, J.A. Carrasco Ochoa, J. Kittler (Eds.), Progress in Pattern Recognition, Image Analysis and Applications. XIX, 995 pages. 2006.

Vol. 4224: E. Corchado, H. Yin, V. Botti, C. Fyfe (Eds.), Intelligent Data Engineering and Automated Learning – IDEAL 2006. XXVII, 1447 pages. 2006.

Vol. 4223: L. Wang, L. Jiao, G. Shi, X. Li, J. Liu (Eds.), Fuzzy Systems and Knowledge Discovery. XXVIII, 1335 pages. 2006. (Sublibrary LNAI).

Vol. 4222: L. Jiao, L. Wang, X. Gao, J. Liu, F. Wu (Eds.), Advances in Natural Computation, Part II. XLII, 998 pages. 2006.

Vol. 4221: L. Jiao, L. Wang, X. Gao, J. Liu, F. Wu (Eds.), Advances in Natural Computation, Part I. XLI, 992 pages. 2006.

Vol. 4220: C. Priami, G. Plotkin (Eds.), Transactions on Computational Systems Biology VI. IX, 247 pages. 2006. (Sublibrary LNBI).

Vol. 4219: D. Zamboni, C. Kruegel (Eds.), Recent Advances in Intrusion Detection. XII, 331 pages. 2006.

Vol. 4218: S. Graf, W. Zhang (Eds.), Automated Technology for Verification and Analysis. XIV, 540 pages. 2006.

Vol. 4217: P. Cuenca, L. Orozco-Barbosa (Eds.), Personal Wireless Communications. XV, 532 pages. 2006.

Vol. 4216: M.R. Berthold, R. Glen, I. Fischer (Eds.), Computational Life Sciences II. XIII, 269 pages. 2006. (Sublibrary LNBI).

Vol. 4215: D.W. Embley, A. Olivé, S. Ram (Eds.), Conceptual Modeling - ER 2006. XVI, 590 pages. 2006.

Vol. 4213: J. Fürnkranz, T. Scheffer, M. Spiliopoulou (Eds.), Knowledge Discovery in Databases: PKDD 2006. XXII, 660 pages. 2006. (Sublibrary LNAI).

Vol. 4212: J. Fürnkranz, T. Scheffer, M. Spiliopoulou (Eds.), Machine Learning: ECML 2006. XXIII, 851 pages. 2006. (Sublibrary LNAI).

Vol. 4211: P. Vogt, Y. Sugita, E. Tuci, C. Nehaniv (Eds.), Symbol Grounding and Beyond. VIII, 237 pages. 2006. (Sublibrary LNAI).

Vol. 4210: C. Priami (Ed.), Computational Methods in Systems Biology. X, 323 pages. 2006. (Sublibrary LNBI).

Vol. 4209: F. Crestani, P. Ferragina, M. Sanderson (Eds.), String Processing and Information Retrieval. XIV, 367 pages. 2006.